Java™ for Engineers and Scientists

SECOND EDITION

Java™ for Engineers and Scientists

SECOND EDITION

Stephen J. Chapman
BAE SYSTEMS Australia

An Alan R. Apt Book

PEARSON
Prentice
Hall

Upper Saddle River, NJ 07458

Library of Congress Cataloging-in-Publication Data
CIP DATA AVAILABLE.

Vice President and Editorial Director, ECS: *Marcia J. Horton*
Publisher: *Alan R. Apt*
Associate Editor: *Toni Dianne Holm*
Editorial Assistant: *Patrick Lindner*
Vice President and Director of Production and Manufacturing, ESM: *David W. Riccardi*
Executive Managing Editor: *Vince O'Brien*
Managing Editor: *Camille Trentacoste*
Production Editor: *Irwin Zucker*
Director of Creative Services: *Paul Belfanti*
Creative Director: *Carole Anson*
Art Director and Cover Manager: *Jonathan Boylan*
Cover Designer: *Daniel Conte*
Cover Illustration: *NASA/EAC Images / Aurora Photos*
Managing Editor, AV Management and Production: *Patricia Burns*
Art Editor: *Gregory Dulles*
Manufacturing Manager: *Trudy Pisciotti*
Manufacturing Buyer: *Lisa McDowell*
Marketing Manager: *Pamela Shaffer*

© 2004 Pearson Education, Inc.
Pearson Prentice Hall
Pearson Education, Inc.
Upper Saddle River, NJ 07458

The author and publisher of this book have used their best efforts in preparing this book. These efforts include the development, research, and testing of the theories and programs to determine their effectiveness. The author and publisher make no warranty of any kind, expressed or implied, with regard to these programs or the documentation contained in this book. The author and publisher shall not be liable in any event for incidental or consequential damages in connection with, or arising out of, the furnishing, performance, or use of these programs.

Printed in the United States of America
10 9 8 7 6 5 4 3 2 1

ISBN 0-13-033520-7

Pearson Education Ltd., *London*
Pearson Education Australia Pty. Ltd., *Sydney*
Pearson Education Singapore, Pte. Ltd.
Pearson Education North Asia Ltd., *Hong Kong*
Pearson Education Canada, Inc., *Toronto*
Pearson Educación de Mexico, S.A. de C.V.
Pearson Education—Japan, *Tokyo*
Pearson Education Malaysia, Pte. Ltd.
Pearson Education, Inc., *Upper Saddle River, New Jersey*

DEDICATION

This book is dedicated to my son Avi and daughter-in-law Kath,
as they commence their lives' journey together.

Preface

The aim of this book is to simultaneously teach the Java programming language, structured programming techniques, and good programming practice to an audience of engineering and science students.

Java is a relatively new programming language that is taking the world by storm. It has enormous appeal for many reasons. One major advantage is that it is almost entirely *platform independent*, so that an application written for one computer is very likely to run unchanged on another computer. A single application can be written to execute across all of a company's computers, whether they be PCs, Macs, or Unix workstations. A second major advantage is that Java has a C-like syntax but drops many of the more obscure and messier features of C. The C-like syntax makes it already partially familiar to millions of people, aiding its acceptance. An example of Java's improvement over C is its treatment of character strings as objects, manipulated by a set of standard methods. In C, strings are manipulated with pointers, which is a much more error-prone process.

A third major advantage of Java is that it is object oriented, which should make code written in Java more reusable between applications. With a little forethought, classes and methods written for one application are usable in another application unchanged, because the way that the data and methods are encapsulated in the objects prevents undesirable interactions among them.

A fourth major advantage of Java is that it lends itself to *device-independent* graphics applications. Languages such as C and Fortran do not provide device-independent graphics, because the programmer must be concerned with the specific details of the hardware being used to display the graphics. The language definitions do not include standard APIs for working with graphics at a higher level. By contrast, Java's Swing Graphics classes provide a higher-level abstraction that is the same across all Java implementations, making device-independent graphics practical.

A final advantage of Java is that it is free. Sun provides a free Java Software Development Kit for download from its World Wide Web site (`http://java.sun.com`). This kit includes free Java compilers, development tools, and class libraries. Vendors such as Borland, IBM, and Sun all offer free personal editions of their Java Integrated Development Environments, which include graphic layout tools and excellent debuggers. This is the right price for many budgets. The Unix operating system and C language reached their current strong positions because AT&T made Unix available essentially free to universities in the 1970s and 1980s, where generations of students were trained to use them, going on to spread their use widely throughout the working world. Java is poised for a similar but more rapid spread.

Java also makes it easy to create applets that can be exchanged and executed freely across the Web. This adds enormous appeal in today's interconnected world.

The principal disadvantage of Java is that, since it is a new language, no large library of reusable classes is available to solve scientific and engineering problems. These libraries will appear over the next few years as more and more universities adopt Java. A secondary disadvantage is that the Java I/O system is very complex and confusing. This book avoids that problem by using a small subset of the Java I/O system's capabilities in the early chapters, leaving the full complexities until Chapter 16.

Another disadvantage of Java is its very complex Applications Programming Interface (API). This is the flip side of Java's flexibility and power. The standard API allows a programmer to do many things in a platform-independent manner, but a complex API takes a long time to learn. Some texts attempt to hide Java's complexities from novice programmers by using custom-written convenience classes in the early chapters, until the student develops enough programming sophistication to understand the raw Java API itself. There has been a lot of resistance to this approach among some instructors and students, and this book addresses their concerns. With a single exception, *every* class used in this book is a part of the standard Java SDK 1.2 or later. The sole exception is a plotting class introduced in Chapter 5 and used thereafter to display engineering data. This use is temporary, since in Chapter 12 students learn how to write their own plotting classes using only the standard Java SDK.

THE BOOK

This book grew out of my experience writing and maintaining large programs in both the defense and geophysical fields. I saw that the strategies and techniques required to write large, *maintainable* programs were quite different from what new engineers were learning in their programming classes at school. The incredible cost of maintaining and modifying large programs demands that they be easily understood and modified by people other than their original programmers. The Java programming language meets this requirement, because its platform independence allows a program to be easily transported from computer to computer as a company's needs grow, and its straightforward syntax (compared to C) and strict object orientation encourage a cleaner programming style. This book teaches simultaneously both the fundamentals of the Java language and a programming style that results in good, maintainable programs.

It is quite difficult to teach undergraduates the importance of investing extra effort during the early stages of the program design process in order to make their programs more maintainable. Class programming assignments must by their very nature be simple enough for one person to complete in a short period of time, and they do not have to be maintained for years. Because the projects are simple, a student can often "wing it" and still produce working code. A student can take a course, perform all of the programming assignments, pass all of the tests, and still not learn the habits that are really needed when working on large projects in industry.

From the very beginning, this book teaches Java in a style suitable for use on large projects. It emphasizes the importance of going through a detailed design process before any code is written, using a top-down design technique to break the program up into logical portions (classes and methods) that can be implemented separately.[1] The book demonstrates object reusability by building later examples on the classes and methods created in earlier examples. Finally, it emphasizes the importance of exhaustively testing the finished program with many different input data sets before releasing it for use.

The book attempts to make learning an interactive experience by providing all sources for all examples at the book's Web site, and encouraging the student to download, execute, and modify them. Some end-of-chapter exercises are built on the examples. The Web site also contains the plotting package used in some of the exercises.

This book also caters to the structure of the introductory programming course taken by most engineers. Often this course is a module within an "Introduction to Engineering Problem Solving" course, and the time available for learning the language is quite limited. Such courses usually teach simple procedural programming in some computer language such as Fortran, C, Basic, or Pascal, with advanced materials being presented in a separate course. Chapters 2 through 6 of this book provide a sound introduction to procedural programming

---

[1]While this book emphasizes the importance of breaking down problems into classes and methods, it does not introduce any of the formal object-oriented design methodologies. That is a topic for a separate text.

and can be used as the basis for such an introductory course. The students learn the structured programming techniques inherent in a language such as Pascal, but in a language that has more practical day-to-day use. In addition, in Chapter 5 novice programmers can begin creating plots, something that is not possible in standard Fortran, C, Basic, or Pascal.

TOPICS COVERED IN THIS BOOK

A quick glance at other Java books shows that most of them run to 1000+ pages, devoted mostly to examples of how to use the thousands of classes in the Java API. This book takes a different approach, concentrating on only the small subset of the Java API necessary to perform technical calculations and display the results. For example, it concentrates on such modern features as Java2D graphics and the Swing Graphical User Interface, completely ignoring older ways to display data. This choice allows more time to concentrate on programming techniques and the solution of technical problems, while still leaving the book about half the length of many competitors.

Chapter 1 introduces Java *applications* (as opposed to browser-based *applets*), which are used to illustrate all of the basic principles introduced in the book. Applications are better suited to teaching basic principles, because they can be very simple, and they don't obscure the point that the example is trying to illustrate. The book builds in a series of logical steps from the basics of the programming language (Chapters 2 through 4) to arrays (Chapter 5), methods (Chapter 6), classes (Chapter 7), strings (Chapter 8), and object-oriented programming features. Graphics and the device-independent display of data are introduced in Chapters 12 through 14, and Chapter 15 gives a brief explanation of applets. The book concludes with the Java I/O system in Chapter 16.

FEATURES OF THIS BOOK

Many features of this book are designed to emphasize the proper way to write reliable Java programs. These features should serve students well as they are learning Java and should also be useful to the practitioner on the job. They include:

1. **Emphasis on Problem Solving**

   From the beginning, the book develops and executes practical examples useful for solving problems in an engineering environment. It emphasizes solving problems in the language, introducing only the bare minimum of Java classes required to make a program execute. The book starts with standalone Java programs to solve a particular problem, rather than applets designed to run within a Web browser. Arrays, strings, graphics, and details of class libraries are introduced in a gradual fashion in later chapters.

2. **Emphasis on Interactive Learning**

   All examples in the book are available for download from the book's Web site. Students are encouraged to execute each example on their own computers. In addition, end-of-chapter exercises require the students to modify and enhance the on-line code. Students are encouraged to re-use these components in their own programs.

3. **Emphasis on Strong Typing and Data Dictionaries**

   Every variable and reference in Java classes and methods must be explicitly typed, so strong typing is an inherent feature of the language. In conjunction with the explicit declaration of every variable and reference in each method, the book emphasizes the importance of creating a data dictionary that describes the purpose of each variable to make the code more understandable.

4. **Emphasis on Top-Down Design Methodology**

Chapter 3 introduces a top-down design methodology, which is used consistently throughout the rest of the book. This methodology encourages a student to think about the proper design of a program *before* beginning to code. It emphasizes the importance of clearly defining the problem to be solved and the required inputs and outputs before any other work is begun. Once the problem is properly defined, the student learns to break it down into discrete classes representing the "things" within the program, and methods representing the behavior of those "things." Finally, the book teaches the importance of testing at all stages of the process, both unit testing of the component classes and methods and exhaustive testing of the final product. Examples are given of programs that work properly for some data sets and then fail for others.

Pseudocode and flowcharts are introduced as tools for use during the stepwise refinement process, and pseudocode is used consistently in all examples.

The formal design process taught by the book may be summarized as follows:

1. Determining the user requirements
2. Analysis and decomposition
3. Detailed design
4. Implementation: converting algorithms to Java statements
5. Testing

5. **Emphasis on Java Class Libraries**

A great advantage of Java is that it contains portable class libraries (packages) designed to perform many of the functions required to write working Java programs. Implementing a feature from scratch makes no sense when the compiler vendor has already provided working, tested, and portable classes and methods to implement the feature. The reusable nature of objects derived from Java classes makes programming more rapid, simple, and reliable. The book emphasizes the advantages of reuse inherent in the Java language.

6. **Good Programming Practice Boxes**

For the convenience of the student, these boxes highlight good programming practices when they are introduced. In addition, all good programming practices introduced in a chapter are summarized at the end of the chapter. An example Good Programming Practice Box is shown below.

GOOD PROGRAMMING PRACTICE

Always indent the body of any structure by three or more spaces to improve the readability of the code.

---

7. **Programming Pitfalls Boxes**

These boxes highlight common errors so that they can be avoided. An example Programming Pitfalls Box is shown below.

PROGRAMMING PITFALLS

Adding a semicolon after a `while` statement can produce a logical error. Java will compile and execute the program, but the program may go into an infinite loop.

PEDAGOGICAL FEATURES

The book includes several features designed to aid student comprehension. One or two quizzes appear in each chapter, with answers being provided in Appendix C. These quizzes can serve as a useful self-test of comprehension. There are also approximately 250 end-of-chapter exercises, with the answers to selected exercises appearing at the book's Web site. Good programming practices are highlighted in all chapters with special Good Programming Practice boxes, and common errors are highlighted in Programming Pitfalls boxes. End-of-chapter materials include summaries, lists of key terms, and summaries of good programming practices. Finally, a description of the special classes written for this book is available for download from the book's Web site.

SETTING THE **CLASSPATH** ENVIRONMENT VARIABLE

In order to use the special plotting class JPlot2D supplied with this book, a programmer must first set the CLASSPATH environment variable on his or her computer to tell the Java compiler where to look for the packages. This variable must contain the name of the *parent directory* of the class path structure. For example, if the extra packages appear as subdirectories of directory c:\packages, then the CLASSPATH variable must include the directory c:\packages.

The manner in which the environment variable is set will vary among different types of operating systems. In Windows NT 4.0/2000/XP, the environment variable is set through the *System* option in the *Control Panel*. See the Windows help system for details.

In Windows 95/98, the CLASSPATH environment variable is set by including the line

```
set CLASSPATH=.;c:\packages
```

in the autoexec.bat file. If a CLASSPATH already exists in the file, add a semicolon (;) followed by c:\packages to the end of the existing path.

For Linux and Unix systems running the C shell, the class path is set by opening the .login file with a text editor and adding the lines

```
setenv CLASSPATH .:$HOME/packages
```

If a CLASSPATH already exists in the file, add a colon (:) followed by $HOME/packages to the end of the existing path.

For Linux and Unix systems running the Bourne or Korn shells, the class path is set by opening the .profile file with a text editor and adding the lines

```
CLASSPATH=.:$HOME/packages
export CLASSPATH
```

If a CLASSPATH already exists in the file, add a colon (:) followed by $HOME/packages to the end of the existing path.

A FINAL NOTE TO THE USER

No matter how carefully I proofread a document like this book, some typographical errors inevitably slip through and appear in print. If you should spot any such errors, please drop me a note via the publisher, and I will do my best to get them eliminated from subsequent printings and editions. Thank you very much for your help in this matter.

You are free to use and modify the classes distributed in this book for any non-commercial use in accordance with the license agreement included with the software. I do make one specific request, though. If you find and fix bugs, or if you enhance the functionality of some class, please send me a copy of the bug fix or enhancement. My current email address should always be available through the book's Web site.

I will maintain a complete list of errata and corrections at the book's Web site, `http://www.prenhall.com/author_chapman/`. Please check that site for updates or corrections.

ACKNOWLEDGMENTS

I would also like to thank Alan Apt, Toni Holm, and the crew at Prentice Hall. They have been a pleasure to work with.

We would like to thank the reviewers who provided helpful feedback:

Chris Dovolis, University of Minnesota
Rubin Landau, Oregon State University
Chi Thai, University of Georgia
Tom Walker, Virginia Polytechnic Institute and State University
Lyle Long, Pennsylvania State University
Pete Petersen, Texas A & M University

Finally, I would like to thank my wife Rosa, and our children Avi, David, Rachel, Aaron, Sarah, Naomi, and Shira for being such delightful people, and the inspiration for my efforts.

STEPHEN J. CHAPMAN
Melbourne, Australia

Contents

Java™ for Engineers and Scientists

SECOND EDITION

1

Introduction to Computers and the Java™ Programming Language

The computer is probably the most important invention of the twentieth century. It affects our lives profoundly in very many ways. When we go to the grocery store, the scanners that check out our groceries are run by computers. Our bank balances are maintained by computers, and the automatic teller machines that allow us to make banking transactions at any time of the day or night are run by computers. Computers control our telephone and electric power systems, run our microwave ovens and other appliances, and even control the engines in our cars. Together with the Internet, computers make instant data access possible anywhere in the world. Almost any business in the developed world would collapse overnight if it were suddenly deprived of its computers. Considering their importance in our lives, it is almost impossible to believe that the first electronic computers were invented just about 60 years ago.

Just what is this device that has had such an impact on our lives? A **computer** is a special type of machine that stores information, and can perform mathematical calculations on that information at speeds much faster than human beings can think. A **program**, which is stored in the computer's memory, tells the computer what sequences of calculations are required, and which information to perform the calculations on. Most computers are very flexible. For example, the computer on which I write these words can also balance my checkbook, if I just load it with a different program.

Computers can store huge amounts of information, and with proper programming, they can make that information instantly available when it is needed. For example, a bank's computer can hold the complete list of all the checks and deposits made by every one of its customers. On a larger scale, credit companies use their computers to hold the

OBJECTIVES

- Identify the elements of the Java™ Programming Language (Java).
- Know the basic types of data stored in a computer.
- Know the difference between applets and applications.
- Compile and execute a Java program.

credit histories of every person in the United States—literally billions of pieces of information. When requested, they can search through those billions of pieces of information to recover the credit records of any single person and then present those records to the user in a matter of seconds.

It is important to realize that *computers do not think*. They merely follow the steps contained in their programs. When a computer appears to be doing something clever, it is because a clever person has written the program that it is executing. That is where we humans come into the act. It is our collective creativity that allows the computer to perform its seeming miracles. This book will help teach you how to write programs of your own in the Java language, so that the computer will do what *you* want it to do.

1.1 THE COMPUTER

A block diagram of a typical computer is shown in Figure 1.1. The major components of the computer are the **central processing unit (CPU)**, **main memory**, **secondary memory**, and **input** and **output devices**. These components are described in the paragraphs below.

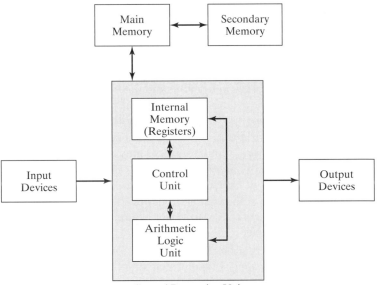

Figure 1.1. A block diagram of a typical computer.

1.1.1 The CPU

The central processing unit is the heart of any computer. It is divided into a *control unit*, an *arithmetic logic unit (ALU)*, and internal memory. The control unit within the CPU controls all the other parts of the computer, while the ALU performs the actual data manipulation. The internal memory within a CPU consists of a series of *memory registers* used for the temporary storage of intermediate results during calculations.

The control unit of the CPU interprets the instructions of the computer program. It also fetches data values from input devices or main memory and stores them in the memory registers, and sends data values from memory registers to output devices or main memory. For example, if a program says to multiply two numbers together and save the result, the control unit will fetch the two numbers from main memory and store them in registers. Then, it will present the numbers in the registers to the ALU along with directions to multiply them and store the results in another register. Finally, after the ALU multiplies the numbers, the control unit will take the result from the destination register and store it back into main memory.

1.1.2   Main and Secondary Memory

The memory of a computer is divided into two major types: *main* or *primary memory* and *secondary memory*. Main memory usually consists of semiconductor chips. It is very fast and relatively expensive. Data that is stored in main memory can be fetched for use in 75 nanoseconds or less (sometimes *much* less) on a modern computer. Because it is so fast, main memory is used to temporarily store the program currently being executed by the computer, as well as the data that the program requires.

Main memory is not used for the permanent storage of programs or data. Most main memory is *volatile*, meaning that it is erased whenever the computer's power is turned off. Besides, main memory is relatively expensive, so we buy only enough to hold the largest programs actually being executed at any given time.

Secondary memory consists of devices that are slower and cheaper than main memory. They can store much more information for much less money than main memory can. In addition, most secondary memory devices are *nonvolatile*, meaning that they retain the programs and data stored in them whenever the computer's power is turned off. Typical secondary memory devices are *hard disks, floppy disks*, CDs, DVDs, and tape drives. Secondary storage devices are normally used to store programs and data that are not needed at the moment, but which may be needed at some time in the future.

1.1.3   Input and Output Devices

Data is entered into a computer through an input device and is output through an output device. The most common input device on a modern computer is a keyboard. Using a keyboard, we can type programs or data into a computer. Other types of input devices found on some computers are mice, scanners, and microphones. Computers can also receive data from networks (Ethernet, modems, and so on).

Output devices permit us to use the data stored in a computer. The most common output devices on today's computers are video monitors and printers. Other types of output devices include plotters and speakers. Computers can also send data to networks (Ethernet, modems, and so on).

1.2   DATA REPRESENTATION IN A COMPUTER

Computer memories are composed of millions of individual switches, each of which can be ON or OFF but not at a state in between. Each switch represents one **binary digit** (also called a **bit**); the ON state is interpreted as a binary 1, and the OFF state is interpreted as a binary 0. Taken by itself, a single switch can represent only two values (for example, the numbers 0 and 1). For convenience, we usually represent the ON state of the switch with the number 1 and the OFF state with the number 0.

Groups of bits can be combined to represent more complex information. For example, a group of 2 bits can represent one of four (2^2) unique values: 00, 01, 10, and 11. Similarly, a group of 3 bits can represent one of eight (2^3) unique values: 000, 001, 010, 011, 100, 101, 110, 111. A group of 8 bits can represent one of 256 (2^8) unique values, while a group of 16 bits can represent one of 65,536 (2^{16}) unique values.

Computers store and manipulate information by assigning special meanings to each value in a group of bits. For example, a group of 8 bits can be used to encode one of 256 possible values. If each value is assigned to a character, then one bit pattern will represent the letter A, another will represent the letter B, and so forth. Other groups of bits are used to encode numbers instead of letters. As long as we understand the encoding applied to a particular group of bits, we can always recover the original information.

Groups of bits are often used to represent a number in the *binary* (base 2) *number system*.

The smallest common grouping of bits is called a **byte**. *A byte is a group of 8 bits that are used together to represent a binary number.* The byte is the fundamental unit used to measure the capacity of a computer's memory. For example, the personal computer on which I am writing these words has a main memory of 256 megabytes (256,000,000 bytes) and a secondary memory (disk drive) with a storage of 20 gigabytes (20,000,000,000 bytes).

The next larger grouping of bits in a computer is called a **word**. A word consists of 2, 4, or more consecutive bytes that are used to represent a single number in memory. The size of a word varies from computer to computer, so words are not a particularly good way to judge the size of computer memories.

1.2.1   The Binary Number System

In the familiar base 10 number system, the smallest (rightmost) digit of a number is the ones place (10^0). The next digit is in the tens place (10^1), the next is in the hundreds place (10^2), and so on. Thus, the number 122_{10} is really $(1 \times 10^2) + (2 \times 10^1) + (2 \times 10^0)$. Each digit is worth a power of 10 more than the digit to the right of it in the base 10 system [see Figure 1.2(a)].

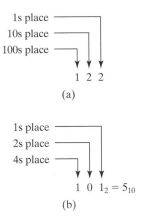

(a)

(b)

Figure 1.2.   (a) The base 10 number 122 is really $(1 \times 10^2) + (2 \times 10^1) + (2 \times 10^0)$. (b) Similarly, the base 2 number 101_2 is really $(1 \times 2^2) + (0 \times 2^1) + (1 \times 2^0)$.

Similarly, in the binary number system, the smallest (rightmost) digit is the ones place (2^0). The next digit is in the twos place (2^1), the next one is in the fours place (2^2), and so on. Each digit is worth a power of 2 more than the digit to the right of it in the base 2 system. For example, the binary number 101_2 is really $(1 \times 2^2) + (0 \times 2^1) + (1 \times 2^0) = 5$, and the binary number $111_2 = 7$ (see Figure 1.2(b)].

Note that three binary digits can be used to represent eight possible values: $0 (= 000_2)$ to $7 (= 111_2)$. In general, *if n bits are grouped together to form a binary number, then they can represent 2^n possible values.* Thus a group of 8 bits (1 byte) can represent 256 possible values; a group of 16 bits (2 bytes), can represent 65,536 possible values; and a group of 32 bits (4 bytes), can represent 4,294,967,296 possible values.

In a typical implementation, half of all possible bit patterns are reserved for representing negative numbers, and half are reserved for representing positive numbers. Thus, a group of 8 bits (1 byte) is usually used to represent numbers between -128 and $+127$, inclusive, and a group of 16 bits (2 bytes) is usually used to represent numbers between -32768 and $+32767$, inclusive.

1.2.2   Octal and Hexadecimal Representations of Binary Numbers

Computers work in the binary number system, but people think in the decimal number system. Fortunately, we can program the computer to accept inputs and give its outputs in the decimal system, converting them internally to binary form for processing. Most of the time, the fact that computers work with binary numbers is irrelevant to the programmer.

However, there are some cases in which an engineer or scientist has to work directly with the binary representations coded into the computer. For example, individual bits or groups of bits within a word might contain status information about the operation of some machine. If so, the programmer will have to consider the individual bits of the word, and work in the binary number system.

Binary numbers are unwieldy to work with. For example, the value 1100_{10} in the decimal system is the same as 010001001100_2 in the binary system. It is easy to get lost working with such a number! To avoid this problem, we customarily break binary numbers down into groups of 3 or 4 bits, and represent those bits by a single base 8 (octal) number or base 16 (hexadecimal) number.

To understand this idea, note that a group of 3 bits can represent any number between 0 ($=000_2$) and 7 ($=111_2$). These are the numbers found in an **octal** or base 8 arithmetic system. An octal number system has 7 digits: 0 through 7. We can break a binary number into groups of 3 bits and substitute the appropriate octal digit for each group. Let's use the number 010001001100_2 as an example. Breaking the number into groups of 3 digits yields $010|001|001|100_2$. If each group of 3 bits is replaced by the appropriate octal number, the value can be written as 2114_8. The octal number 2114_8 represents exactly the same pattern of bits as the binary number, but more compactly.

Similarly, a group of 4 bits can represent any number between 0 ($= 0000_2$) and 15 ($=1111_2$). These are the numbers found in a **hexadecimal** or base 16 arithmetic system. Since the hexadecimal system needs 16 digits, we use digits 0 through 9 for the first 10 of them, and then letters A through F for the remaining 6. Thus, $9_{16} = 9_{10}$, $A_{16} = 10_{10}$, $B_{16} = 11_{10}$, and so forth. We can break a binary number up into groups of 4 bits and substitute the appropriate hexadecimal digit for each group. Let's use the number 010001001100_2 again as an example. Breaking the number into groups of 4 digits yields $0100|0100|1100_2$. If each group of 4 bits is replaced by the appropriate hexadecimal number, the value can be written as $44C_{16}$. The hexadecimal number represents exactly the same pattern of bits as the binary number, but more compactly.

Some computer vendors prefer to use octal numbers to represent bit patterns, while others prefer hexadecimal numbers. Both representations are equivalent, in that they represent the pattern of bits in a compact form. A computer program can be designed to accept values or write output values in any of the four formats (decimal, binary, octal, or hexadecimal). (See Table 1.1.)

1.2.3   Types of Data Stored in Memory

Three common types of data are stored in a computer's memory by assigning different meanings to groups of bits: **character data** (characters and symbols), **integer data** (positive and negative integers plus zero), and **floating-point data** (numbers with a

TABLE 1.1   Decimal, Binary, Octal, and Hexadecimal Numbers

Decimal	Binary	Octal	Hexadecimal
0	0000	0	0
1	0001	1	1
2	0010	2	2
3	0011	3	3
4	0100	4	4
5	0101	5	5
6	0110	6	6
7	0111	7	7
8	1000	10	8
9	1001	11	9
10	1010	12	A
11	1011	13	B
12	1100	14	C
13	1101	15	D
14	1110	16	E
15	1111	17	F

decimal point). Each type of data has different characteristics and takes up a different amount of memory in the computer.

Character Data

For character data, each group of bits in memory is interpreted as a character. The **character data** type consists of characters, numbers, and symbols. A **character set** is the complete collection of characters, numbers, and symbols that can be represented on a given computer. Each character in the character set is represented by a unique bit pattern in memory.

Java uses the **Unicode character set**. Unicode is a special coding system in which each character is stored in 16 bits of memory. Since 16 bits are used to represent a character, there can be 65,536 possible characters in the set. Unicode assigns a unique number to each character in almost every alphabet used on Earth, including the ideograms used in oriental languages such as Chinese and Japanese. This support makes it possible to write Java programs that work with any language.

The first 128 characters in the Unicode character set are the same as the ASCII character set. These values are shown in Appendix A. ASCII stands for the American Standard Code for Information Interchange (ANSI X3.4 1977). The ASCII character set contains all of the characters actually used in writing Java programs.

Integer Data

The **integer data** type consists of all positive and negative whole numbers within a certain range, plus zero. For this data type, each bit pattern in memory is interpreted as a base 2 number. The amount of memory devoted to storing an integer will vary, depending on the type of integer declared. Java supports 1-, 2-, 4-, and 8-byte integers. Four-byte integers are the most common type in modern computers.

Since a finite number of bits are used to store each value, only integers that fall within a certain range can be represented on a computer. The smallest (most negative) number that can be stored in an n-bit integer is

$$\text{smallest integer value} = -2^{n-1}$$

(1.1)

and the largest (most positive) number that can be stored is

$$\text{largest integer value} = 2^{n-1} - 1 \tag{1.2}$$

For a 4-byte integer, the most negative and most positive possible values are $-2{,}147{,}483{,}648$ and $2{,}147{,}483{,}647$, respectively. Attempts to use an integer larger than the largest possible value or smaller than the smallest possible value result in an *overflow condition*.[1]

Floating-Point Data

The integer data type has two fundamental limitations:

1. It is not possible to represent numbers with fractional parts (0.25, 1.5, 3.14159, etc.) as integer data.

2. It is not possible to represent very large integers (either positive or negative), because there are not enough bits available to represent the value. The smallest negative integer and the largest positive integer that can be stored in a given memory location are given by Equations (1-1) and (1-2).

To get around these limitations, computers include a **floating-point** data type.

The floating-point data type stores numbers in a type of scientific notation. We all know that very large or very small numbers can be most conveniently written in scientific notation. For example, the speed of light in a vacuum is about 299,800,000 meters per second. This number is easier to work with in scientific notation: 2.998×10^8 m/s. The two parts of a number expressed in scientific notation are called the **mantissa** and the **exponent**. The mantissa of the number above is 2.998, and the exponent (in the base 10 system) is 8.

The floating-point numbers in a computer are similar to the scientific notation above, except that a computer works in the base 2 system. Java floating-point numbers occupy either 32 bits (4 bytes) or 64 bits (8 bytes) of computer memory. The 32-bit data type is called `float`, and the 64-bit data type is called `double`. A `float` number is divided into two components: a 24-bit mantissa and an 8-bit exponent, and a `double` number is divided into a 53-bit mantissa and an 11-bit exponent (see Figure 1.3). In either

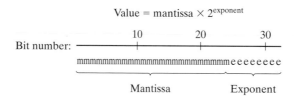

$$\text{Value} = \text{mantissa} \times 2^{\text{exponent}}$$

Figure 1.3. This floating-point number includes a 24-bit mantissa and an 8-bit exponent.

case, the mantissa contains a number between -1.0 and 1.0, and the exponent contains the power of 2 required to scale the number to its actual value.

Floating-point numbers are characterized by two quantities: **precision** and **range**. *Precision* is the number of significant digits that can be preserved in a number, and *range* is the difference between the largest and smallest numbers that can be represented. The precision of a floating-point number depends on the number of bits in its

---

[1]Java performs integer calculations that do not detect overflows. Instead, they return incorrect values, as described in Chapter 2.

mantissa, while the range of the number depends on the number of bits in its exponent. A 24-bit mantissa can represent approximately $\pm 2^{23}$ numbers, or about seven significant decimal digits, so the precision of 32-bit floating-point numbers is about seven significant digits. An 8-bit exponent can represent multipliers between 2^{-128} and 2^{127}, so the range of real numbers is from about 10^{-38} to 10^{38}. Note that the float data type can represent numbers much larger or much smaller than integers can, but with only seven significant digits of precision.

When a value with more than seven digits of precision is stored in a float variable, *only the most significant seven digits of the number will be preserved*. The remaining information will be lost forever. For example, if the value 12345678.9 is stored in a float variable, it will be rounded off to 12345680.0. This difference between the original value and the number stored in the computer is known as **roundoff error**.

Java floating-point numbers are based on the IEEE 754 Standard, and the calculations are *exactly the same* on any computer. Therefore, computations in a Java program will produce exactly the same result regardless of the computer it is executed on.

You will use the floating-point data types in many places throughout this book and in your programs after you finish this course. They are quite useful, but you must always remember the limitations associated with roundoff error, or your programs might give you an unpleasant surprise. For example, if your program must be able to distinguish between the numbers 1,000,000.0 and 1,000,000.1, then you cannot use the float data type.[2] It simply does not have enough precision to tell the difference between these two numbers!

PROGRAMMING PITFALLS

Always be aware of the precision and range of the data types with which you are working. Failure to do so can result in subtle programming errors that are very hard to find.

QUIZ 1-1

This quiz provides a quick check to see if you have understood the concepts introduced in Section 1.2. If you have trouble with the quiz, reread the section, ask your instructor, or discuss the material with a fellow student. The answers to this quiz are found in the back of the book.

1. Express the following decimal numbers as their binary equivalents:
   a. 27_{10}
   b. 11_{10}
   c. 35_{10}
   d. 127_{10}

2. Express the following binary numbers as their decimal equivalents:
   a. 1110_2
   b. 01010101_2
   c. 1001_2

---

[2]The double data type can represent 15 or 16 significant decimal digits, so we could use that type in a program that needs to distinguish between the numbers 1,000,000.0 and 1,000,000.1.

3. Express the following binary numbers as octal and hexadecimal numbers:
   a. 1110010110101101_2
   b. 1110111101_2
   c. 1001011100111111_2

4. Is the fourth bit of the number 131_{10} a 1 or a 0?

5. Find the maximum and minimum values that can be stored in a 2-byte integer variable.

6. Can a 4-byte variable of the `float` data type be used to store larger numbers than a 4-byte variable of an integer data type? Why or why not? If it can, what is given up by the floating-point variable to make this possible?

1.3 COMPUTER LANGUAGES

When a computer executes a program, it executes a string of very simple operations such as load, store, add, subtract, multiply, and so on. Each such operation has a unique binary pattern called an *operation code* (*op code*) to specify it. The program that a computer executes is just a string of op codes (and the data associated with the op codes[3]) in the order necessary to achieve a purpose. Op codes are collectively called **machine language**, since they are the actual language that a computer recognizes and executes.

Unfortunately, we humans find machine language very hard to work with. We prefer to work with Englishlike statements and algebraic equations that are expressed in forms familiar to us, instead of arbitrary patterns of zeros and ones. We like to program computers with **high-level languages**. We write out our instructions in a high-level language, and then use special programs called *compilers* and *linkers* to convert the instructions into the machine language that the computer understands.

There are many different high-level languages. Some of them are designed to work well for business problems, while others are designed for general scientific use. Still others are especially suited for applications like operating-systems programming. It is important to pick a proper language to match the problem that you are trying to solve.

Some common high-level computer languages today include Ada, Basic, C, C++, COBOL, Fortran, Java, and Pascal. Java is the newest language on this list, and it has benefited from lessons learned about problems in its predecessors, plus the latest in software engineering technology.

The earliest computer languages were called *procedural programming languages*, because their basic unit is a procedure. A procedure is also called a subroutine or a function, depending on the particular language. A procedure is a set of statements that describe how to solve some function, such as solving a quadratic equation. Ada 83, Basic, C, Fortran, and Pascal are all examples of procedural programming languages.

Beginning in the 1980s, *object-oriented programming languages* became popular. Objects are reusable software components that often model things in the real world. An object is a combination of *data* that define the characteristics of the object, plus *methods* that describe the behavior of the object. C++, Ada 95, and Java are examples of object-oriented programming languages.

---

[3]The data associated with op codes are called *operands*.

The first really widespread object-oriented programming language was C++, which was developed at Bell Laboratories from the C language during the early 1980s. This language was standardized in the 1990s, and it has been used to implement many large programs over the past decade. There are dozens of C++ compilers available from many different vendors, supporting many different types of computers and operating systems. One important example is the Gnu C++ compiler, which is a free compiler from the open-source community. This compiler has been implemented on most of the computers and operating systems in the world.

Unfortunately, the C++ language is a bit awkward to use, because it includes the ability to write both older C-style procedural programs and newer C++-style object-oriented programs. It preserves many difficult-to-use C language features (such as pointer arithmetic and multiple ways to allocate and deallocate memory).

Java is a purely object-oriented programming language that is based on C and C++ syntax, but with most of the more confusing features eliminated. It began as a research project within Sun Microsystems in the early 1990s. The language was developed just as the use of World Wide Web became popular, and Java was quickly adopted as a convenient way to execute programs through Web browsers. Since Java was designed so that the same code could execute on any computer, a Web site designer could produce a single application that would run in exactly the same way on any computer, whether it was a PC, a Mac, or a Unix workstation. The phenomenal interest in the World Wide Web spilled over onto Java, quickly making it a widely used standard for Web content.

1.4   THE JAVA PROGRAMMING LANGUAGE

Java is a relatively new but powerful programming language that has enormous appeal for many applications. One major reason is that it is largely *platform independent*, meaning that an application written for one computer is very likely to run unchanged on another computer. Thus, an engineer can write a single application that will execute across all of a company's computers, whether they are PCs, Macs, or Unix workstations. This "write once, run anywhere" philosophy means that an organization is not locked into a single type of computer hardware.

A second advantage of Java is that it is *object oriented*. As we will see, object-oriented programming languages make the design and maintenance of large programs easier by encapsulating data and the methods for modifying that data into discrete units, called **objects**. Because objects interact with each other only through well-defined interfaces, unintended side effects can be minimized, and the objects can be reused more easily in different programs.

Another advantage of Java is that the basic language is relatively simple. The Java language itself has a simpler syntax than C (upon which it was based), making it easier to master. Many of the trickiest and most error-prone portions of the C language (such as pointer manipulation) simply do not exist in Java, and other features are either greatly simplified or handled automatically. For example, memory allocation and deallocation, a major source of errors in C programs, happens automatically in Java.

In addition, the standard Java language includes *device-independent graphics*. While graphical output can be created in other languages such as C and Fortran, the code required is not standard, differing from computer to computer and even from device to device within the same computer. For example, the code to print graphics on a screen will be different from that to print the same graphics on a printer. In contrast, *Java has device-independent graphics built directly into the language*. A program that generates a graph on one computer will generate the same graph when executed on another computer, even if it is a different type and has a different operating system.

Finally, the Java language is *free*. The Java Development Kit may be downloaded for free from http://java.sun.com. This kit includes a Java compiler (javac), a Java run-time interpreter (java), a debugger (jdb), and all of the standard Java libraries. Fancier integrated development environments, such as the Forte™ for Java Community Edition, are also available for free from the same source. Other integrated development environments may be purchased from IBM, Symantec, Borland, and many other vendors.

Java does have some disadvantages. One is that it lacks certain important features of other languages. For example, languages such as Fortran, C, and C++ have simple output statements[4] that allow a programmer to display numeric data in specified formats, making it easy to specify the size and number of digits after the decimal point in the numbers being displayed and to produce tables of output data, which are very important in many engineering and scientific applications. For some reason, the ability to control the number of characters and the number of places after the decimal point was not made a part of done in a less flexible way in the standard Java language.

A second disadvantage of Java is that it is a new language, and it is evolving rapidly. While the basic language has been pretty much fixed, the Java Application Programming Interface (API) has changed rapidly between Java Software Development Kit (SDK) versions 1.0, 1.1, 1.2, 1.3, and 1.4. (SDK 1.2 and later are collectively known as Java 2.) Features of programs written with older versions of the SDK have sometimes been considered obsolescent only months after being created. Fortunately, the core portion of the Java API is beginning to mature and stabilize so that programmers can work with a consistent environment. This book teaches the Java API as it appears in the SDK for Java 2 (versions 1.2 and later).

A third disadvantage is that Java executes relatively slowly. Compiled Java programs (known as bytecode) are interpreted or compiled with a just-in-time (JIT) compiler each time they are used, and Java applications running under interpreters and JIT compilers execute more slowly than the same applications coded in a native language such as C++. (This disadvantage has been reduced in recent years, as computers have gotten faster and JIT compilers have gotten better.)

A fourth disadvantage of the language is its steep learning curve. The Java language includes an extremely large number of standard classes in libraries known as *packages*. These standard classes make it possible for programmers to create platform-independent programs with features such as graphics, audio, video, and Internet connectivity. However, the sheer number of classes means that a programmer has to know a great deal before he or she can write simple programs. Once one has climbed this steep learning curve, the language becomes much easier to use.

1.5   ELEMENTS OF JAVA

Java is composed of three distinct elements:

1.   **The Java Programming Language**
2.   **The Java Runtime Environment**
3.   **The Java Application Programming Interface (API)**

Java differs from other computer languages in that all Java programs are compiled to execute on a special type of computer known as the **Java Virtual Machine (Java VM)**.

---

[4]Formatted WRITE statements in Fortran, and fprintf statements in C and C++.

The Java VM is a computer having a special machine language known as **bytecode**. It is "virtual" because this computer does not really exist. Instead, it is *simulated* by a special program called the **Java Runtime Environment (JRE)**. A version of the JRE has been created for each computer and operating system combination that runs Java (Windows, Sun Solaris, Linux, Macintosh, etc.). All Java compilers produce bytecode, which can be directly executed on any Java VM, regardless of the type of computer that it is running on. This makes Java programs truly "write once, run anywhere."

The Java Runtime Environment contains all of the support necessary to execute Java on a given computer. When a Java program is executed, the JRE loads and verifies the bytecode to make sure that the program is valid. Then, it runs a special program known as a *Java interpreter* (or possibly a *just-in-time compiler*) that converts Java VM bytecode into the machine language of the particular computer on-the-fly as a Java program is executed. As long as a Java interpreter has been written for a given type of computer, that computer can run any Java program.

The process of compiling and executing a Java program is shown in Figure 1.4. A Java program may be created using any text editor and is stored in a file with the file extent `.java` (for example, `MyProgram.java`). The Java compiler compiles this program into bytecode for execution on the Java VM and stores the bytecode in a file with the file extent `.class` (in this example, `MyProgram.class`). This compilation occurs only once. When the program is executed on a computer, the Java interpreter translates the Java VM bytecode on-the-fly into instructions for the actual computer executing the program. This interpretation process happens every time that the Java program is executed. Note that the Java bytecode is independent of any particular computer hardware, so any computer with a Java interpreter can execute the compiled Java program, no matter what type of computer the program was compiled on.

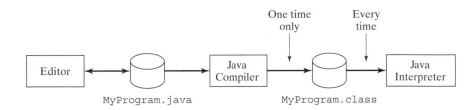

Figure 1.4.   A Java program is created using an editor and stored in a disk file with the file extent `.java`. Each program is compiled once using the Java compiler, producing a file of Java bytecodes with the file extent `.class`. This file is interpreted by the Java interpreter each time the program is executed.

The Java Application Programming Interface (API) is a large collection of ready-made software components that provide many useful capabilities. These components provide standard ways to read and write files, manipulate strings, display graphics, and perform many other essential functions. The components of the Java API are grouped into libraries (called *packages*) of related components. A programmer can save an enormous amount of time by using the objects in these standard packages to perform tasks instead of trying to "reinvent the wheel" each time he or she writes a program. The components in these packages are standard across all implementations of Java, so a program that uses them to implement some function will run properly on any computer system that implements Java. In addition, the components are already debugged, so using them reduces the total effort required to write and debug a program.

In the first seven chapters of this book we will concentrate on the features of the core Java language itself, with only a minimal discussion of classes from the Java API. The remainder of the book will concentrate on how to use selected contents from the Java API.

1.6   OBJECTS, METHODS, AND CLASSES

Java is an *object-oriented language*, and the fundamental building blocks of all Java programs are *objects*. An **object** is a reusable software component (containing both data and procedures) that models something in the real world.

The physical world is full of objects: cars, pencils, trees, and so on. Any real object can be characterized by two types of information: its *properties* and its *behavior*. The object's properties describe what it is, while its behaviors describe how it interacts with the rest of the world. For example, a car is a type of object. Each car has certain properties (color, type, speed, direction, fuel consumption) and certain behaviors (starting, stopping, turning, and so on). The properties describe the car itself, while the behaviors describe how the car functions when it is used.

In the software world, an **object** is a software component whose structure is like that of objects in the real world. Each software object consists of a combination of data (called **properties**) and behaviors (called **methods**). The properties are variables describing the object's essential characteristics, while the methods describe how the object behaves and how its properties can be modified. An object is a software bundle of variables, plus the related methods that modify or otherwise use these variables.

A **class** is a software construct that describes what an object will look like when it is created. It specifies the number and type of variables each object will contain, plus the methods that can be used to manipulate the data. Every Java program consists of one or more classes, and the principal class in the program must contain at least one method.

We will learn much more about objects, methods, and classes in Chapter 7, but we will begin using simple forms of them immediately.

1.7   APPLETS VERSUS APPLICATIONS

Java supports two different types of programs, *applications* and *applets*. Java applications are complete standalone programs that can be loaded and executed independently within your computer. They can have either command-line interfaces or graphical user interfaces, depending on the application's design. Applications are the sort of programs that are traditionally used for engineering calculations, so all of the examples in the first portion of this book are applications.

By contrast, an applet is a special type of Java program that runs within a World Wide Web browser when an HTML document containing the applet is loaded into the browser. Applets must follow strict rules to ensure proper integration with the browser. Applets tend to be small, so that they can be downloaded over the Internet in a small amount of time.

In Chapter 15 we will introduce applets and also show how to design a single program that can run either as an application or as an applet.

1.8   A FIRST JAVA APPLICATION

We will begin our study of Java with an old programming tradition: an application that does nothing more than print out "Hello, World!" A program of this sort is very simple, but it illustrates many important features that we will see in more complex programs. We will analyze the program, and show how to compile and execute it in the Java development environment.

A Java application consists of one or more classes defining data (variables) and methods (procedures containing calculations that modify the data). Every Java application must have *at least* one user-defined class, and that class must contain a method named `main`, which is where the program starts executing. The simplest possible Java application would consist of a single class containing the single method `main`, like the "Hello, World" application shown in Figure 1.5.

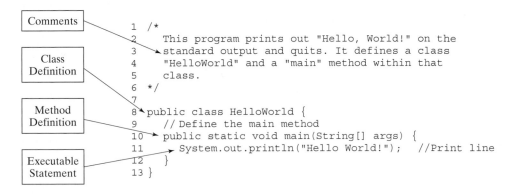

Figure 1.5. A simple application: the "Hello, World!" program.

The first six lines of this program are *comments*. A comment is a note the programmer writes to explain what a portion of a program is doing. Every program should begin with comments describing its purpose and should include further comments explaining how the various portions of the program function. The Java compiler completely ignores comments—they are for the benefit of humans looking at the code.

This program illustrates two of the three types of Java comments. Multiline comments may be created by beginning the comment with the symbol `/*` and ending the comment with the symbol `*/`. All of the text between the two symbols is a comment. Single-line comments begin with the symbol `//` and continue to the end of the line. Thus the entire block of text

```
/*
    This program prints out "Hello, World!" on the
    standard output and quits.  It defines a class
    "HelloWorld", and a "main" method within that
    class.
*/
```

is a comment, and the words `//  Define the main method` and `//Print line` are additional comments.

The third form of Java comment is a special marker used with the `Javadoc` documentation system. `Javadoc` is an automatic system for generating program documentation directly from comments embedded in Java programs. `Javadoc` comments start with the symbol `/**`, end with the symbol `*/`, and can stretch over multiple lines. These comments are automatically copied from Java source code into documentation when the `javadoc` program is executed. The `javadoc` program is described in the Java SDK documentation; it will not be covered in this text.

Line 7 of the program is completely blank. Blank lines, spaces, and tabs (which are collectively known as *white-space characters*) are used throughout Java programs to make them easier for humans to read. A single white-space character is required to separate adjacent keywords and variables (such as between `public` and `class` on Line 8). Extra white-space characters may be freely inserted to make the program easier to read; they are totally ignored by the Java compiler

Line 8 contains the characters

```
public class HelloWorld {
```

This line begins the *class definition* for class `HelloWorld`. A class declaration is introduced by the **class** keyword, which is immediately followed by a *class name*. The name of this class is `HelloWorld`. The **body** of the class definition includes all of the text between the open brace (`{`) at the end of this line and the close brace (`}`) on line 13. By convention, the left brace opening the class body is always included at the end of the line declaring the class's name, and the right brace is placed on a line by itself indented at the same level as the `class` statement. The possible components in the body of a class will be described in detail in Chapter 7.

This class definition begins with the **public** keyword. This modifier means that class `HelloWorld` can be accessed from any other class in a Java program. Every class in the first seven chapters of this book will have `public` access. We will discuss `public` and other types of access in detail in Chapter 7.

By convention, the first letter of each word in a Java class name is capitalized, with no spaces or underscores between the words. For example, `HelloWorld` and `MyFirstClass` would be typical class names.

As we mentioned previously, a class can contain data (variables) and methods. This particular class does not define any variables, but it does define a method named `main`. The execution of a Java application always begins with a method named `main` in the principal class of the program. The `main` method must always start with the rather cryptic definition `public static void main(String[] args)`. This line must appear *exactly* as shown in every Java application, or the program will not work.

What does this method definition mean? The keyword `public` in this line means that the method can be invoked by any caller. It must always be present in the `main` method, so that the method can be started by the JRE. The keyword `static` means that the method can be run without first creating an object from this class; it will be discussed in Chapter 7. The keyword `void` means that the method does not return a result when it finishes executing. The method's parameter list (`String[] args`) contains any command-line arguments passed to the program when it starts to execute. All of these features are discussed in detail in later chapters.

The body of the method begins with the left brace (`{`) at the end of line 10 and ends with the corresponding right brace (`}`) on line 12. As in class definitions, the left brace opening a method body is always included at the end of the line declaring the method's name, and the right brace is placed on a line by itself, indented at the same level as the `method`'s declaration.

The only executable statement in this method is on line 11. The statement `System.out.println("Hello World!")` invokes method `println` on object `out` in the `System` class. The object `System.out` represents the standard output device for the computer on which the program is executing, so invoking the `println` method prints the words `"Hello World!"` on the computer's standard output device.

Notice that the Java statement on line 11 ends in a semicolon. Every Java statement must end with a semicolon. A statement can occupy as many lines as desired, or several statements can fit on a single line. In either case, the compiler knows that the statement is complete when it sees the semicolon.

1.9 COMPILING AND EXECUTING A JAVA PROGRAM

To compile the `HelloWorld` application, it must be placed in a file called `HelloWorld.java`. Note that *the name of the class being defined must be the same as the name of the file containing the class*, with the file extension `.java` added. The name of the file must be *exactly* the same as the name of the class, including any capitalization, or the Java compiler will report an error.

PROGRAMMING PITFALLS

Be sure that the name of file containing a class is exactly the same as the name of the class being defined, with the addition of the file extension `.java`. It is an error for the name of the file not to agree with the name of the class.

This program can be compiled with the Java compiler `javac` by typing the command "`javac HelloWorld.java`" at the command prompt: [5]

```
D:\book\java\chap1>javac HelloWorld.java
```

Note that the command `javac` is followed by the name of the file, including the file extension. If there were an error in `HelloWorld`, the compiler would list the errors after this command is entered. If there are no errors, then the compiler will compile the class into bytecode and place the bytecode into a file called `HelloWorld.class`.

Once the program has been compiled, it may be executed using the Java interpreter or another Java Virtual Machine. This is done by invoking the Java interpreter together with the name of the class to execute:

```
D:\book\java\chap1>java HelloWorld
Hello World!
```

As you can see, the program prints out the words "Hello World!"

Note that the Java interpreter expects the name of the class to execute, *not* the name of the file containing that class. If the filename is used in the command, an error results.

```
D:\book\java\chap1>java HelloWorld.class
Can't find class HelloWorld/class
```

---

[5]The command prompt may vary from computer to computer. On my PC, the command prompt is the current directory: `D:\book\java\chap1>`; you may have something different.

Always specify the *file name* (not the class name) when using the Java compiler, and specify the *class name* (not the file name) when executing the compiled program.

When a program is executed, the Java run-time system first invokes a *class loader*, which loads the bytecode for all the required classes from disk. Once the bytecode is loaded, a *bytecode verifier* confirms that all of the bytecode is valid and that it does not violate Java's security restrictions. After the bytecode is verified, it is passed to the Java interpreter or just-in-time compiler for execution. All three of these steps occur when the user types the `java` command.

SUMMARY

- A computer is a special type of machine that stores information and can perform mathematical calculations on it at speeds much faster than human beings can think.
- A program, which is stored in the computer's memory, tells the computer what sequences of calculations are required, and which information to perform the calculations on.
- The major components of a computer are the central processing unit (CPU), main memory, secondary memory, and input and output devices. The CPU performs all of the computer's control and calculation functions. Main memory is fast, relatively expensive memory that is used to store the program being executed and its associated data. Main memory is volatile, meaning that its contents are lost whenever power is turned off. Secondary memory is slower and cheaper than main memory. It is nonvolatile. Hard disks are common secondary memory devices. Input and output devices are used to read data into and to output data from the computer. The most common input devices are the keyboard and mouse, and the most common output devices are the monitor and printer.
- Computer memories are composed of millions of individual switches, each of which can be ON or OFF, but not at a state in between. These individual switches are binary devices called *bits*. Eight bits are grouped together to form a *byte* of memory, and two or more bytes (depending on the computer) are grouped together to form a *word* of memory.
- Computer memories can be used to store *character*, *integer*, or *floating-point* data.
- Character variables store characters using the Unicode character set. Each character in this set occupies two bytes of memory. The 65,536 possible values in the two bytes allow for 65,536 possible character codes, including the characters of all of the world's major languages.
- Integer variables store positive and negative integers, plus zero.
- Floating-point variables store numbers in a kind of scientific notation. They occupy 4 or 8 bytes of memory. The bits are divided into a separate mantissa and exponent. The number's *precision* depends upon the number of bits in the mantissa and its *range* upon the number of bits in the exponent.
- Java is platform independent, meaning that programs written on one type of computer will run unchanged on another type of computer.
- A Java application is a complete standalone program that can be loaded and executed independently within a computer.

- A Java applet is a special type of program that runs within a World Wide Web browser when an HTML document containing the applet is loaded into the browser.
- Every Java application must contain a `main` method within its principal class. Program execution always starts in the `main` method.
- A comment that begins with `//` is a single-line comment.
- A comment that begins with `/*` and ends with `*/` may span multiple lines.
- The body of a class is enclosed in braces (`{}`).
- An application's class name is used as a part of its file name (with the file extension `.java`).
- A Java statement is always terminated by a semicolon. It may stretch over multiple lines if necessary.
- The principal Java class in a program must be defined in a file with the same name as the class, followed by the extent `.java`. For example, class `MyClass` would be defined in a file named `MyClass.java`.
- The Java compiler expects a file name including the file extent `.java` as an argument, not a class name. It complies Java classes and produces bytecode in a file with the extent `.class`. For example, class `MyClass` would be found in a file named `MyClass.java` and would be compiled into bytecode in a file named `MyClass.class`.
- The Java runtime expects a class name as an argument, not a file name. Do not use the file extent `".class"` when trying to execute the program.

TERMINOLOGY

applet	Java Runtime Environment (JRE)
application	Java Virtual Machine (Java VM)
binary digit	machine language
bit	main memory
byte	mantissa
bytecode	method
comments	package
computer	platform independent
CPU	precision
device-independent graphics	program
exponent	properties
fields	range
floating-point data	roundoff error
high-level language	secondary memory
information hiding	`System.out.println` method
integer data	Unicode character set
Java API	word

Exercises

1.   Express the following decimal numbers as their binary equivalents:

   a. 10_{10}

   b. 32_{10}

   c. 77_{10}

   d. 63_{10}

2.   Express the following binary numbers as their decimal equivalents:

    a. 01001000_2

    b. 10001001_2

    c. 11111111_2

    d. 0101_2

3.   Express the following numbers in both octal and hexadecimal forms:

    a. 1010111011110001_2

    b. 330_{10}

    c. 111_{10}

    d. 11111101101_2

4.   Express the following numbers in binary and decimal forms:

    a. 377_8

    b. $1A8_{16}$

    c. 111_8

    d. $1FF_{16}$

5.   The `double` floating-point data type occupies 8 bytes (64 bits), instead of the 4 bytes occupied by a `float` number. Fifty-three bits are used for the mantissa, and 11 bits for the exponent. How many significant digits does a `double` value have? What is the range of `double` numbers?

6.   Compile and execute the `HelloWorld` application on your computer. Are the results the same as shown in this chapter?

7.   Delete the final } in the file `HelloWorld.java` and attempt to compile the program. What happens?

2

Basic Elements of Java

The core of Java is relatively simple, but the Java API is extremely large and complex. In this and the next two chapters we will be concentrating on the fundamental core of the Java language, while postponing the complications of the Java API until later. By the end of Chapter 4, you will be able to write Java programs that perform complex calculations, including branches, loops, and disk input/output.

This chapter introduces the very basic elements of the Java language, such as Java names, the types of variables in the language, and some types of operations. By the end of the chapter, you will be able to write simple but functional Java programs.

2.1 JAVA NAMES

As we saw in the previous chapter, Java classes, methods, and variables all have names. A name in Java may consist of any combination of letters, numbers, the $ character, and the underscore character (_), but the first character of the name must not be a number. A Java name may be as short as one character or as long as desired—there is no maximum length. The following names are legal in Java:

```
ThisIsATest
Hello
ABC$
A1B2
a_12
_toUpper
```

and the following name is illegal:

```
1Day          // Begins with a number
```

By convention, Java class names always begin with a capital letter, and Java method names and variable names

OBJECTIVES

- Learn the rules for creating Java names.
- Learn how to create Java constants and variables.
- Understand how to use assignment statements.
- Learn the types of operations supported in Java, and their order of execution.
- Learn about type conversion, including promotion of operands and casting.
- Learn how to use standard Java mathematical methods.
- Learn how to read from the standard input stream and write to the standard output stream.

begin with a lowercase letter. For example, in Chapter 1 we capitalized the first letter of the class name `HelloWorld` and did not capitalize the first letter of method `main`. If a method or variable name consists of more than one word, such as `toUpper`, the words are joined together, and each word after the first begins with an uppercase letter.

Unfortunately, not all legal combinations of characters can be used as names. Some have special meanings to the Java compiler, such as `float`, `if`, `else`, `while`, and so forth. These special combinations of characters are known as **keywords**; they are used to declare elements of Java programs. Keywords are **reserved** for use by the compiler, and no Java name can be the same as a reserved keyword. A complete list of Java keywords is given in Table 2.1.

TABLE 2.1   List of Reserved Java Keywords

Reserved Keywords

abstract	assert	boolean	break	byte
case	catch	char	class	continue
default	do	double	else	extends
false	final	finally	float	for
if	implements	import	instanceof	int
interface	long	native	new	null
package	private	protected	public	return
short	static	super	switch	synchronized
this	throw	throws	transient	true
try	void	volatile	while	

Reserved But Not Used by Java

const	goto

GOOD PROGRAMMING PRACTICE

Always capitalize the first letter of a class name, and use a lowercase first letter for method and variable names.

GOOD PROGRAMMING PRACTICE

If a name consists of more than one word, the words are joined together, and each succeeding word should begin with an uppercase letter.

2.2   CONSTANTS AND VARIABLES

A **constant** is a data item whose value does not change during program execution, and a **variable** is a data item whose value can change during program execution. There are four basic types of data in Java (known as **primitive data types**): integer, floating-point, boolean, and character.

The integer data types store integer data. Java has four integer data types (`byte`, `short`, `int`, and `long`), which are 1, 2, 4, and 8 bytes long, respectively. The floating-point data types store real numbers (numbers with fractional parts) in a type of scientific notation, as described in Chapter 1. There are two floating-point data types in Java (float and double), with differing ranges and precisions. Booleans are logical values that are either true or false. Characters hold a single Unicode character.

The primitive data types are summarized in Table 2.2. Note that, unlike other languages, *the size and range of values supported by each data type is the same on any computer running Java*. This feature helps to guarantee that a Java program written on one computer will run properly on any other computer.

TABLE 2.2 Java Primitive Data Types

Type	Bits	Range	Comment
boolean	1	true or false	
char	16	'\u0000' to '\uFFFF'	ISO Unicode character set
byte	8	−128 to +127	8-bit integers
short	16	−32,768 to +32,767	16-bit integers
int	32	−2,147,483,648 to +2,147,483,648	32-bit integers
long	64	−9,223,372,036,854,775,808 to +9,223,372,036,854,775,807	64-bit integers
float	32	−3.40292347E + 38 to +3.40292347E + 38	IEEE 754 single-precision floating point. Numbers are represented with about 6 to 7 decimal digits of precision.
double	64	−1.79769313486231570E + 308 to +1.79769313486231570E + 308	IEEE 754 double-precision floating point. Numbers are represented with about 15 to 16 decimal digits of precision.

Java constants are written directly into a program. For example, in the line

```
x = y + 12;
```

the characters "12" represent an integer constant.

A variable is a data item of a primitive data type that can change value during the execution of a program. Java is a *strongly typed language*, meaning that every variable must be declared with an explicit type before it is used. (We will learn how to declare variables in the next few sections.) The type must be declared so that the compiler knows how much memory to reserve for the variable. When a Java compiler encounters a variable declaration, it reserves a known location in memory for the variable, and then references that memory location whenever the variable is used in the program.

It is a good idea to give your variables names that describe their contents. This mnemonic aid will help you or anyone else who may be working with your program to understand what it is doing. For example, if a variable in a program contains a currency exchange rate, it could be given the name exchangeRate.

GOOD PROGRAMMING PRACTICE

Use meaningful variable names whenever possible to make your programs clearer.

It is also important to include a **data dictionary** in the body of any classes or methods that you write. A data dictionary is a set of comments that define *each variable* used in a program. The definition should describe both the contents of the item and the units in which it is measured. A data dictionary may seem unnecessary while the program is being written, but it is invaluable when you or another person have to go back and modify the program at a later time.

GOOD PROGRAMMING PRACTICE

Create a data dictionary for each program to make program maintenance easier.

2.2.1   Integer Constants and Variables

Integer constants are integer values written directly into a Java program. They may be preceded by a + or − sign, but must not have embedded commas. By default, an integer constant is of type int, so it is restricted to be in the range −2,147,483,648 to +2,147,483,648. If a constant is to be of type long, it must be concluded with a letter L. The following examples show legal integer constants:

```
12
0
-123456
9999999999L                       // Type long
```

The following constants are illegal and will produce compile-time errors:

```
1,024                             // Embedded comma
9999999999                        // Value too large for int
```

When a Java compiler encounters a constant, it places its value in a known location in memory, and then references that memory location whenever the constant is used in the program. If more than one location in a program uses the same constant value, they all refer to the same location in memory. This optimization helps to reduce the size of Java programs.

An integer variable is declared in a **declaration statement**. The form of a declaration statement is the name of a primitive data type followed by one or more variable names. For example, the statements

```
int var1, var2;
short var3;
```

declare two integers of type int and one integer of type short. When a declaration statement is encountered, Java automatically creates a variable of the specified type and refers to it by the specified name.

When an integer is created, its value is undefined. An initial value can be assigned to the integer by including it in the declaration.

```
int var1 = 100; // Creates var1 and initializes it to 100
```

If addition or subtraction of two integers produces a value beyond the range of the data type, the calculation is said to "overflow". In this case, *the calculation will complete without error, but the resulting value will be incorrect.* For example, consider the simple program shown below. This program declares three int variables i1, i2, and i3. It assigns initial values to i1 and i2 and then adds them together, storing the result in i3.

```
1    /* Program to demonstrate integer overflows */
2    public class IntOverflow {
3        // Define the main method
4        public static void main(String[] args) {
5
6            // Declare variables
7            int i1 = 2147483647, i2 = 1, i3;
8
9            // Calculate and display i3
10           i3 = i1 + i2;
11           System.out.println(i3);
12
13       }
14   }
```

When this program is compiled and executed, the results are as shown below. Note that the contents of i3 "wrapped around" from positive to negative values without giving a warning that anything was wrong!

```
D:\book\java\chap2>java IntOverflow
-2147483648
```

It is your responsibility as a programmer to pick an integer type large enough to represent the largest integers that your program will ever need. If you choose an integer data type that is too small, your program may fail mysteriously on some occasions while it is being used.

PROGRAMMING PITFALLS

Always choose an integer data type large enough to handle the largest integers your program will ever have to work with. If you fail to do this, your program may sometimes calculate incorrect values without warning, producing a hard-to-find error.

2.2.2 Floating-Point Constants and Variables

Floating-point numbers are values stored in the computer in a kind of scientific notation. The bits used to store a floating-point number are divided into two separate portions, a **mantissa** and an **exponent**. A single-precision floating-point number (type float) occupies 32-bits of memory, divided into a 24-bit mantissa and an 8-bit exponent. A double-precision floating-point number (type double) occupies 64-bits of memory, divided into a 53-bit mantissa and an 11-bit exponent. In either case, the mantissa contains a number between −1.0 and 1.0, and the exponent contains the power of 2 required to scale the number to its actual value.

Floating-point numbers are characterized by two quantities: **precision** and **range**. Precision is the number of significant digits that can be preserved in a number, and range is the difference between the largest and smallest numbers that can be represented. The precision of a floating-point number depends on the number of bits in its mantissa, while the range of the number depends on the number of bits in its exponent.

A 24-bit mantissa can represent approximately $\pm 2^{23}$ numbers, or about seven significant decimal digits, so the precision of float numbers is about seven significant digits. An 8-bit exponent can represent multipliers between 2^{-128} and 2^{127}, so the range of single-precision floating-point numbers is from about 10^{-38} to 10^{38}.

Similarly, a 53-bit mantissa can represent approximately 15 to 16 decimal digits, so the precision of double-precision floating-point numbers is about 15 significant digits. An 11-bit exponent can represent multipliers between 2^{-1024} and 2^{1023}, so the range of double-precision floating-point numbers is from about 10^{-308} to 10^{308}.

When a value with more than seven digits of precision is stored in a single-precision variable, *only the most significant seven bits of the number will be preserved*. The remaining information will be lost forever. For example, if the value 12345678.9 is stored in a float variable, it will be rounded off to 12345680.0. This difference between the original value and the number stored in the computer is known as **roundoff error**. It is important to select a floating-point data type with enough precision to preserve the information needed to solve a particular problem.

A floating-point constant is a literal defining a floating-point value. It can be distinguished from an integer constant because it contains a decimal point and/or an exponent. If the constant is positive, it may be written either with or without a + sign. No commas may be embedded within a floating-point constant. By default, a floating-point constant is of type double, so it is restricted to be between $-1.79769313486231570E+308$ and $+1.79769313486231570E+308$.

A floating-point constant *must* have either a decimal point or an exponent and may have both. If used, the exponent consists of the letter E or e followed by a positive or negative integer that specifies the power of 10 used when the number is written in scientific notation.

The type of a floating-point constant may be specified by appending either the letter F for float or the letter D for double. If there is no appended letter, the constant is of type double. The following examples show legal floating-point constants:

```
12.            // Type double
12E2           // Type double
12.0e2         // Type double
3.14159F       // Type float
```

The following constants are not legal floating-point constants:

```
1.2e108F       // Too large for type float
1,234.0        // Embedded comma
1234           // An int constant, not floating-point
```

Floating-point variables are declared with a float or double declaration statement. For example, the statements

```
float pi = 3.14159F;
double x;
```

declare and initialize a single-precision floating-point variable pi, and declare a double-precision floating-point variable x. The value of variable x is undefined.

2.2.3 Boolean Constants and Variables

The boolean data type is a special one that contains one of only two possible values: true or false. These values are usually created as the result of logical comparisons, such as the expression "a > b". Boolean expressions are commonly used to control program execution, as we will see in Chapter 3.

The only valid logical constants are

```
true
false
```

Note that the words `true` and `false` are reserved—they can be used only as boolean constants. No variable, method, or class may use these names.

A boolean variable is a variable containing a value of the boolean data type. It is declared with a `boolean` declaration statement. For example, the statement

```
boolean test;
```

declares a boolean variable `test`. The value of variable `test` is undefined, because it was not initialized to either `true` or `false`.

2.2.4 Character Constants and Variables

All Java characters and strings use the **Unicode character set**. Unicode is a special coding system in which each character is stored in 16 bits of memory. Since 16 bits are used to represent a character, there can be 65,536 possible characters. Unicode assigns a unique number to each character in almost every alphabet used on Earth, including the ideograms used in oriental languages such as Chinese and Japanese. This support makes it possible to write Java programs that work with any language.

A character constant is a literal representing a *single* Unicode character. The literal is written between single quotes or apostrophes, such as `'a'` or `'0'`. Some important characters are not printable, but instead perform control functions. Examples include the carriage-return (CR) character, which moves the cursor back to the left-hand end of a line, the line-feed (LF) character, which moves the cursor down to the next line, and the tab character, which moves the cursor right by one tab stop. These characters can be represented by special **escape sequences** as shown in Table 2.3.

TABLE 2.3 Table of Common Escape Sequences

Sequence	Meaning
`'\n'`	Newline. Position the cursor at the beginning of the next line.
`'\t'`	Horizontal tab. Move cursor to next tab stop.
`'\r'`	Carriage return. Position the cursor at the beginning of the current line; do not advance to the next line.
`'\\'`	Backslash. Used to represent the backslash character.
`'\''`	Single quote. Used to represent the single quote.
`'\"'`	Double quote. Used to represent the double quote.
`'\u####'`	Unicode character specified by sequence number. Used to specify any Unicode character constant. The #### is the hexadecimal representation of the character's sequence number.

A character variable is a variable containing a value of the character data type. It is declared with a `char` declaration statement. For example, the statements

```
char ch1 = 'A';
char ch2;
```

declare and initialize character variable `ch1`, and declare character variable `ch2`. Variable `ch2` is undefined.

2.2.5 Keeping Constants Consistent in a Program

It is important to always keep your physical constants consistent throughout a program. For example, do not use the value 3.14 for π at one point in a program, and 3.141593 at another point in the program. Also, you should always write your constants with as much precision as the data type you are using will accept. For example, the `float` data type has seven significant digits of precision, so π in a `float` data type should be written as 3.141593, *not* as 3.14!

The best way to achieve consistency and precision throughout a program is to *assign a name to a constant and then use that name to refer to the constant throughout the program*. If we assign the name `PI` to the constant 3.141593, then we can refer to `PI` by name throughout the program and be certain that we are getting the same value everywhere. Furthermore, assigning meaningful names to constants improves the overall readability of our programs, because a programmer can tell at a glance just what the constant represents.

Named constants or **final variables** are created using the `final` keyword in a type declaration statement. This keyword means that the value assigned to a name is final and will never change. For example, the following program defines and uses a named constant `PI` containing the value of π to seven significant digits.

```
1   public class Constant {
2      public static void main(String[] args) {
3
4         // Declare constant
5         final float PI = 3.141593F;
6
7         // Print out 2*pi
8         System.out.println("2*pi = " + 2*PI);
9      }
10  }
```

When this program is executed, the results are

```
D:\book\java\chap2>java Constant
2*pi = 6.283186
```

Any attempt to modify a final value will produce a compile-time error. For example, the following program attempts to modify the final variable `PI`, producing a compile-time error.

```
1   pubic class BadConstant {
2      public static void main(String[] args) {
3
4         final float PI = 3.14159F;
5         PI = 3.0F;
6      }
7  }
```

```
D:\book\java\chap2>javac BadConstant.java
BadConstant.java:5: Can't assign a value to a final
variable: PI
      PI = 3.0F;
         ^
1 error
```

Keep your physical constants consistent and precise throughout a program. To improve the consistency and understandability of your code, assign a name to any important constants, and refer to them by name in the program.

By convention, named constants are written in all capital letters, with underscores separating the words. This style makes constants stand out from class names, method names, and instance variables. For example, a constant describing the maximum number of values that a program can process might be written as

```
final int MAX_VALUES = 1000;
```

2.3 STRINGS

Strings are groups of one or more characters linked together. Unlike the primitive data types described in Section 2.3, strings are Java *objects*. We will introduce String constants here so that they can be used in output statements in Java programs. A detailed discussion of String variables will be postponed until Chapter 8, after we learn more about objects in general.

A String constant is defined in Java by placing the desired characters between double quotes. For example, the following expressions are all valid strings:

```
"This is a string!"
"Line1\nLine2"
"A"
```

Note that escape sequences may be embedded into strings.

A double quote may not appear in the middle of a string, since the double-quote character will be interpreted as the end of the string, producing a compile-time error. If a double quote is needed in a string, use the escape sequence \" to represent it. For example, the statement

```
System.out.println("She said \"Hello\".");
```

will print out the string

```
She said "Hello".
```

A Java string is fundamentally different from a Java character. A Java character is a *primitive data type*, while a Java string is an *object*. We will learn much more about strings in Chapter 8, but meanwhile we will use String constants in many I/O statements.

The names of constants in your program should be in all capital letters, with underscores separating the words.

This quiz provides a quick check to see if you have understood the concepts introduced in Sections 2.1 through 2.4. If you have trouble with the quiz, reread the section, ask your instructor, or discuss the material with a fellow student. The answers to this quiz are found in the back of the book.

Questions 1 to 14 contain a list of valid and invalid constants. State whether or not each constant is valid. If the constant is valid, specify its type. If it is invalid, say why it is invalid.

1. `10.0`
2. `-100,000`
3. `123E-5`
4. `'T'`
5. `'''`
6. `3.14159`
7. `"Who are you?"`
8. `true`

Questions 9 to 11 contain two real constants each. Tell whether or not the two constants represent the same value within the computer:

9.   `4650.;  4.65E+3`
10. `-12.71;  -1.271E1`
11. `0.0001;  1.0e4`

Questions 12 and 16 contain a list of valid and invalid Java names. State whether or not each name is valid. If it is invalid, say why it is invalid. If it is valid, state what type of item the name represents (assuming that Java conventions are followed).

12. `isVector`
13. `MyNewApp`
14. `2ndChance`
15. `true`
16. `MIN_DISTANCE`

Are the following declarations correct or incorrect? If a statement is incorrect, state why it is invalid.

17. `int firstIndex = 20;`
18. `final short MAX_COUNT = 100000;`
19. `char test = "Y";`
20. Are the following statements legal or illegal? If they are legal, what is their result? If they are illegal, what is wrong with them?

```
int i, j;
final int k = 4;
i = k * k;
j = i / k;
k = i + j;
```

2.4 ASSIGNMENT STATEMENTS AND ARITHMETIC CALCULATIONS

Calculations are specified in Java with an **assignment statement**, whose general form is

```
variable_name = expression;
```

The assignment statement calculates the value of the expression to the right of the equal sign and *assigns* that value to the variable named on the left of the equal sign. Note that the equal sign does not mean equality in the mathematical sense of the word. Instead, it means: *store the value of* expression *into location* variable_name. For this reason, the equal sign is called the **assignment operator**. A statement like

```
i = i + 10;
```

is complete nonsense in ordinary algebra but makes perfect sense in Java. In Java, it means: take the current value stored in variable i, add ten to it, and store the result back into variable i.

The expression to the right of the assignment operator can be any valid combination of constants, variables, parentheses, and arithmetic or Boolean operators. The standard arithmetic operators included in Java are given in Table 2.4.

TABLE 2.4 Arithmetic Operators

Type	Symbol	Algebraic Expression	Java Expression
Addition	+	$a + b$	a + b
Subtraction	−	$a - b$	a − b
Multiplication	*	ab	a * b
Division	/	a / b or $\frac{a}{b}$ or $a \div b$	a / b
Modulus (remainder)	%	$a \bmod b$	a % b

Addition, subtraction, multiplication, and division will be familiar to all readers, but the **modulus** operation may be unfamiliar. The modulus operation calculates the *remainder* left after a whole-number division has been performed. For example, $23 \div 5$ is 4 with a remainder of 3, so

```
23 % 5 = 3
```

The five arithmetic operators described above are **binary operators**, which means that they should occur between and apply to two variables or constants (called **operands**), as shown in the right-hand column of the table. In addition, the + and − symbols can occur as **unary operators**, which means that they apply to one variable or constant, as shown:

```
+23
−a
```

Unary arithmetic operators are evaluated from right to left, so an expression like $--z$ will be evaluated as $-(-z)$.

2.4.1   Integer Arithmetic

Integer arithmetic is involves only integer data. Integer arithmetic always produces an integer result. This is especially important to remember when an expression involves division, since there can be no fractional part in the answer. If the division of two integers is not itself an integer, the computer automatically discards the fractional part of the answer. This behavior can lead to surprising and unexpected answers. For example, integer arithmetic produces the following results:

$$\frac{3}{4} = 0 \qquad \frac{4}{4} = 1 \qquad \frac{5}{4} = 1 \qquad \frac{6}{4} = 1$$

$$\frac{7}{4} = 1 \qquad \frac{8}{4} = 2 \qquad \frac{9}{4} = 2$$

Because of this behavior, integers should *never* be used to calculate real-world quantities that vary continuously, such as distance, speed, or time. They should be used only for things that are intrinsically integer in nature, such as the number of times an event occurs, the number of particles detected, and so on.

PROGRAMMING PITFALLS

Beware of integer arithmetic. Integer division often gives unexpected results.

2.4.2   Floating-Point Arithmetic

Floating-point arithmetic is arithmetic involving floating-point constants and variables. Floating-point arithmetic always produces a floating-point result that is essentially what we would expect. For example, floating-point arithmetic produces the following results:

$$\frac{3.}{4.} = 0.75 \qquad \frac{4.}{4.} = 1. \qquad \frac{5.}{4.} = 1.25 \qquad \frac{6.}{4.} = 1.50$$

$$\frac{7.}{4.} = 1.75 \qquad \frac{8.}{4.} = 2. \qquad \frac{9.}{4.} = 2.25 \qquad \frac{1.}{3.} = 0.3333333$$

However, floating-point numbers do have peculiarities of their own. Because of the finite number of bits used to store a floating-point number, some numbers cannot be represented exactly. For example, the number 1/3 is equal to 0.33333333333 ..., but since the numbers stored in the computer have limited precision, the representation of 1/3 in the computer might be 0.3333333. As a result of this limitation in precision, some quantities that are theoretically equal will not be equal when evaluated by the computer. For example, in some computer languages on some types of computers

$$3.*(1./3.) \neq 1.,$$

but

$$2.*(1./2.) = 1.$$

Tests for equality must be performed very cautiously when working with real numbers. We will learn how to perform such tests safely in Chapter 3.

PROGRAMMING PITFALLS

Beware of floating-point arithmetic. Owing to limited precision, two theoretically identical expressions often give slightly different results.

2.4.3 Hierarchy of Operations

Often, many arithmetic operations are combined into a single expression. For example, consider the equation for the distance traveled by an object subjected to a constant acceleration:

```
dist = d0 + v0 * time + 0.5 * acc * time * time;
```

There are four multiplications and two additions in this expression. In such an expression, it is important to know the order in which the operations are evaluated. If addition is evaluated before multiplication, this expression is equivalent to

```
dist = (d0 + v0) * (time + 0.5) * acc * time * time;
```

But if multiplication is evaluated before addition, this expression is equivalent to

```
dist = d0 + (v0 * time) + (0.5 * acc * time * time);
```

These two equations have different results, and we must be able to distinguish unambiguously between them.

To make the evaluation of expressions unambiguous, Java has established a series of rules governing the hierarchy or order in which operations are evaluated within an expression. The Java rules generally follow the normal rules of algebra. The order in which the arithmetic operations are evaluated is:

1. The contents of all parentheses are evaluated first, starting from the innermost parentheses and working outward.
2. Next, all multiplications, divisions, and modulus operations are evaluated, working from left to right.
3. Next, all additions and subtractions are evaluated, working from left to right.

Following these rules, we see that the second of our two possible interpretations is correct—the multiplications are performed before the additions.

Note that all of the above operations were applied in order from left to right across an expression. In Java, we say that the **associativity** of the operators is from left to right. Later we will see other operators whose associativity is from right to left.

EXAMPLE 2.1

Assume that the `double` variables a, b, c, d, e, f, and g have been initialized to the following values:

```
a = 3.    b = 2.    c = 5.    d = 4.
e = 10.   f = 2.    g = 3.
```

Evaluate the following Java assignment statements:

(a)   `output = a*b+c%d+e/f+g;`
(b)   `output = a*(b+c)%d+(e/f)+g;`
(c)   `output = a*(b+c)%(d+e)/f+g;`

SOLUTION

(a)   Expression to evaluate: `output = a*b+c%d+e/f+g;`
       Fill in numbers: `output = 3.*2.+5.%4.+10./2.+3.`

       First, evaluate multiplications,
       divisions, and modulus from
       left to right: `output = 6. +5. %4. + 10. / 2. + 3.`

                                         `output = 6. + 1. + 10. / 2. + 3.`

                                         `output = 6. + 1. + 5. + 3.`

       Now evaluate additions: `output = 15;`

(b)   Expression to evaluate: `output = a*(b+c)%d+(e/f)+g;`
       Fill in numbers: `output = 3.*(2.+5.)%4.+(10./2.)+3.;`
       First, evaluate parentheses: `output = 3. * 7. % 4. + 5. + 3.;`
       Evaluate mult / div / mod
       from left to right: `output = 21.     % 4. + 5. + 3.;`
                                         `output = 1.            + 5. + 3.;`
       Evaluate additions: `output = 9.;`

(c)   Expression to evaluate: `output = a*(b+c)%(d+e)/f+g;`
       Fill in numbers: `output = 3. * (2.+5.)%(4.+10.)/2.+3.;`
       First, evaluate parentheses: `output = 3. * 7.      %14.      /2.+3.;`
       Evaluate mult / div / mod from
       left to right: `output = 21.           %14.      /2.+3.;`
                                         `output = 7.                      /2.+3.;`
                                         `output = 3.5                       +3.;`
       Finally, evaluate addition: `output = 6.5;`   ■

As we saw above, the order in which operations are performed has a major effect on the final result of an algebraic expression.

It is important that every expression in a program be made as   clear as possible. Any good program will be used for a long period of time and must be maintained and modified when necessary. You should always ask yourself: "Will I easily understand this expression if I come back to it in six months? Can another programmer look at my code and easily understand what I am doing?" If there is any doubt in your mind, use extra parentheses in the expression to make it as clear as possible.

GOOD PROGRAMMING PRACTICE

Use parentheses as necessary to make your equations clear and easy to understand.

If parentheses are used within an expression, then they must be balanced. That is, there must be an equal number of open parentheses and close parentheses within the expression. It is an error to have more of one type than of the other. Errors of this sort are usually typographical, and the Java compiler catches them. For example, the expression

```
(2. + 4.) / 2.)
```

produces an error during compilation because of the mismatched parentheses.

2.4.4 Numeric Promotion of Operands

When an arithmetic operation is performed using two `double` numbers, its immediate result is of type `double`. Similarly, when an arithmetic operation is performed using two `int` numbers, the result is of type `int`. In general, arithmetic operations are only defined between numbers of the same type. For example, the addition of two `double` numbers is a valid operation, and the addition of two `int` numbers is a valid operation, but the addition of a `double` and an `int` is *not* a valid operation. This is true because floating-point numbers and integers are stored in completely different forms in the computer.

What happens if an operation is between a floating-point number and an integer? Expressions containing both floating-point numbers and integers are called *mixed-mode expressions*, and arithmetic involving both is called *mixed-mode arithmetic*. In the case of an operation between a `double` and an `int`, the value of the `int` is automatically converted by the computer into a `double` and stored in a temporary variable, and then floating-point arithmetic is used to perform the operation (see Figure 2.1). After the operation, the temporary `double` variable is discarded. This automatic conversion is known as **numeric promotion**.

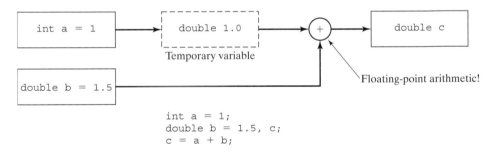

```
int a = 1;
double b = 1.5, c;
c = a + b;
```

Figure 2.1. An example of numeric promotion. When an `int` and a `double` value are added together, the `int` is converted to a `double` in a temporary variable, and the two `double`s are added together. Note that the original `int` variable is unchanged!

The rules of numeric promotion are designed to preserve as much precision as possible during each calculation. The following rules apply to numeric promotion during operations involving binary operators:

1. If either operand is of type `double`, the other operand is converted to `double`.

2. Otherwise, if either operand is of type `float`, the other operand is converted to `float`.

3. Otherwise, if either operand is of type `long`, the other operand is converted to `long`.

4. Otherwise, both operands are converted to type `int`.

The rules governing numeric promotion can be confusing to beginning programmers, and even experienced programmers may trip up on them from time to time. This is especially true when the expression involves division. Consider the following expressions:

Expression	Result
1. `1 + 1/4`	`1`
2. `1.0 + 1/4`	`1.0`
3. `1 + 1.0/4`	`1.25`

Expression 1 contains only `int`s, so it is evaluated by integer arithmetic. In integer arithmetic, `1 / 4 = 0`, and `1 + 0 = 1`, so the final result is 1 (an `int`). Expression 2 is a mixed-mode expression containing both `double`s and `int` variables. However, the first operation to be performed is a division, since division comes before addition in the hierarchy of operations. The division is between `int`s, so the result is `1 / 4 = 0`. Next comes an addition between a `double 1.0` and an `int 0`, so Java promotes the integer 0 into a `double` and then performs the addition. The resulting number is 1. (a `double`). Expression 3 is also a mixed-mode expression containing both `double`s and `int`s. The first operation to be performed is a division between a `double` and an `int`, so Java promotes the 4 into a `double 4.0` and then performs the division. The result is a `double` value `0.25`. The next operation to be performed is an addition between an `int 1` and a `double 0.25`, so the Java promotes integer 1 to a `double` and then performs the addition. The resulting number is `1.25` (a `double`).

The following Java program demonstrates these results:

```
1   // This program illustrates numeric promotion
2   public class TestPromotion {
3
4      // Define the main method
5      public static void main(String[] args) {
6
7         // Demonstrate numeric promotion.
8         System.out.println(1   + 1/4);
9         System.out.println(1.0 + 1/4);
10        System.out.println(1 + 1.0/4);
11     }
12  }
```

When this program is compiled and executed, the results are

```
D:\book\java\chap2>javac TestPromotion.java
D:\book\java\chap2>java TestPromotion
1
1.0
1.25
```

To summarize,

1. A binary operation between numbers of different types is called a mixed-mode operation.

2. When a mixed-mode operation is encountered, Java promotes one or both of the operands according to the rules specified above, and then performs the operation.

3. The numeric promotion does not occur until two values of different types both appear in the *same* operation. Therefore, it is possible for a portion of an expression to be evaluated in integer arithmetic, followed by another portion evaluated in real arithmetic.

Mixed-mode arithmetic can be avoided by using the *casting operator*, as we will explain in the next section.

PROGRAMMING PITFALLS

Mixed-mode expressions are dangerous because they are hard to understand and may produce misleading results. Avoid them whenever possible.

2.4.5 Assignment Conversion and Casting Conversion

Automatic type conversion can also occur when the variable to which the expression is assigned is of a different type than the result of the expression. Such conversion is called **assignment conversion**. There are two possible cases for assignment conversion:

1. The result of an integer expression is assigned to a floating-point variable. This is an example of a **widening conversion**, since any value that can be represented by an integer can also be represented by a floating-point variable (albeit possibly with some loss of precision). *Widening assignment conversions are legal and happen automatically*. For example, the following code is legal, and results in a value of 4.0 being stored in y.

```
int x = 4;
double y;
y = x;                    // Legal:  y = 4.0
```

2. The result of a floating-point expression is assigned to an integer variable. This is an example of a **narrowing conversion**, since there is a loss of precision in assigning a floating-point expression to an integer variable. (For example, the floating-point value 3.141592 would become a 3 when stored in an ingeter variable.) *Narrowing assignment conversions are illegal and produce a compile-time error.* For example, the following code is illegal, producing a compile-time error.

```
int x;
double y = 1.25;
x = y;                    // Illegal!
```

It is possible to explicitly convert or "cast" any numeric type into any other numeric type using a **cast operator**, regardless of whether the conversion involves widening or narrowing. A cast operator creates a new temporary variable of the specified data type, converts the original expression to that type, and then uses the temporary value in the remainder of the expression.

A cast operator is created by placing the desired data type in parentheses before the expression to be converted. For example, the statements

```
int x;
double y = 1.25;
x = (int) y + 1;                  // Legal: x = 2
```

convert the double value 1.25 to an integer and store that value in a temporary variable. When a floating-point number is converted to an integer, the fractional part of the number is discarded. Thus the number stored in the temporary variable is the integer 1. Finally, this temporary integer variable is added to an integer 1 (using integer arithmetic) to calculate the value of x (see Figure 2.2).

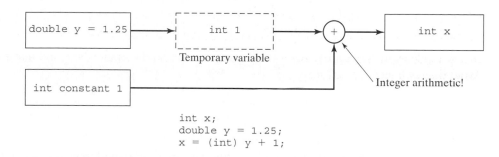

```
int x;
double y = 1.25;
x = (int) y + 1;
```

Figure 2.2. An example of casting. Here the double variable y is cast to an integer and used in a calculation. The computer creates a temporary integer variable and places the truncated value of y in that variable. It then uses integer arithmetic to calculate the value of x, and the temporary variable is discarded. Note that the original double variable is unchanged!

Note that we can assign a double value to an int variable (a narrowing conversion) if we use an explicit cast operator.

The cast operator can be used to make numeric conversions explicit and thus avoid possible confusion due to mixed-mode arithmetic. The following Java program demonstrates the use of the cast operator:

```
1    // This program illustrates the cast operator
2    public class TestCast {
3
4        // Define the main method
5        public static void main(String[] args) {
6
7            double x = 3.99, y = 1.1e38;
8            System.out.println("(int) x = " + (int) x);
9            System.out.println("(int) y = " + (int) y);
10           System.out.println("x       = " + x);
11           System.out.println("y       = " + y);
12       }
13   }
```

When this program is compiled and executed, the results are

```
D:\book\java\chap2>java TestCast
(int) x = 3
(int) y = 2147483647
x       = 3.99
y       = 1.1E38
```

Note that the value of y was too large to be represented as an int, so the cast operator converted it into the largest possible integer. In general, if the value being cast is out of range for the new data type, Java converts it value to the closest possible number in the new data type.

Also, note that the cast operator does not affect the actual values stored in x and y. These original values remained unchanged, since the cast operator stores its results in a temporary variable (see Figure 2.2).

GOOD PROGRAMMING PRACTICE

Use cast operators to avoid mixed-mode expressions and make your intentions clear.

QUIZ 2-2

This quiz provides a quick check to see if you have understood the concepts introduced in Section 2.3. If you have trouble with the quiz, reread the section, ask your instructor, or discuss the material with a fellow student. The answers are found in the back of the book.

1.   In what order are the arithmetic operations evaluated if they appear within an arithmetic expression? How do parentheses modify this order?

2.   Are the following expressions legal or illegal? If they are legal, what is their result? If they are illegal, what is wrong with them?
   a.   37 / 3
   b.   37 + 17 / 3
   c.   28 / 3 / 4
   d.   28 / 3 / (double) 4
   e.   (float) 28 / 3 / 4
   f.   (28 / 3) % 4

3.   Evaluate the following expressions:
   a.   2 + 5 * 2 - 5
   b.   (2 + 5) * (2 - 5)
   c.   2 + (5 * 2) - 5
   d.   (2 + 5) * 2 - 5

Are the following sets of statements legal or illegal? If they are legal, state the result of the calculations. If they are illegal, state why.

4.   int x = 16, y = 3;
     double result;
     result = x + y/2.0;

5.   int x = 16, y = 3;
     int result;
     result = x + y/2.0;

2.5   ASSIGNMENT OPERATORS

Java includes several special assignment operators that combine assignment and a binary operation in a single expression. These assignment operators are convenient shortcuts that reduce the typing required in a program. For example, the assignment statement

```
a = a + 5;
```

can be abbreviated using the addition assignment operator += as

```
a += 5;
```

The += operator adds the value of the variable on the left of the operator to the value to the expression on the right of the operator and stores the result in the variable to the left of the operator.

A similar abbreviation is possible for many other binary operators, including some we have not met yet. Table 2.5 contains a list of the arithmetic assignment operators corresponding to the operators we have seen so far.

TABLE 2.5   Arithmetic Assignment Operators

Assignment Operator	Sample Expression	Expanded Expression	Result
Assume: int a = 3,	b = 11;		
+=	a += 3;	a = a + 3;	6 stored in a
-=	a -= 2;	a = a - 2;	1 stored in a
*=	a *= 4;	a = a * 4;	12 stored in a
/=	a /= 2;	a = a / 2;	1 stored in a
%=	b %= 3;	b = b % 3;	2 stored in b

2.6   INCREMENT AND DECREMENT OPERATORS

Java also includes a unary **increment operator** ($++$) and a unary **decrement operator** ($--$). Increment and decrement operators *increase or decrease the value stored in an integer variable by 1*. For example, suppose that an integer variable c is to be increased by 1. Any of the following statements will perform this operation:

```
c = c + 1;
c += 1;
c++;
```

The increment and decrement operators can be confusing to novice programmers because they *change the value of a variable without an equal sign appearing in the expression*. However, they are commonly used because they are so much more compact than the alternative ways of performing the same function.

If the increment or decrement operator is placed *before* a variable, it is called a **preincrement** or **predecrement** operator. The preincrement and predecrement operators cause the variable to be incremented or decremented by 1, and then the new value is used in the expression in which it appears. For example, suppose that the variables i and j are defined as shown below. After these statements are executed, the value of i will be 4 and the value of k will be **8**, because the value of i will be incremented *before* the addition is performed.

```
int i = 3, j = 4, k;
k = ++i + j;                    // k = 8
```

If the increment or decrement operator is placed *after* a variable, it is called a **postincrement** or **postdecrement** operator. The postincrement and postdecrement operators cause the old value of the variable to be used in the expression in which it appears, and then the variable to be decremented or decremented by 1. For example, suppose that the variables i and j are defined as shown below. After these statements are executed, the value of i will be 4 and the value of k will be **7**, because the value of i will be incremented *after* the addition is performed.

```
int i = 3, j = 4, k;
k = i++ + j;                    // k = 7
```

The operation of these operators is summarized in Table 2.6.

TABLE 2.6 The Increment and Decrement Operators

Operator	Sample Expression	Expanded Expression Result
preincrement	++a	Increment a by 1 and then use the new value of a in the expression in which a is located.
postincrement	a++	Use the current value of a in the expression in which a is located, and then increment a by 1.
predecrement	− −a	Decrement a by 1 and then use the new value of a in the expression in which a is located.
postdecrement	a− −	Use the current value of a in the expression in which a is located, and then decrement a by 1.

Increment and decrement operators can get very confusing if they are combined in complex expressions, causing unexpected or hard-to-understand results. Never use more than one of these operators on a single variable in a single expression—if you do, the resulting expression will be very hard to understand. An example of the misuse of these operators is shown in the program below.

```
 1  // This program illustrates the mis-use of pre-
 2  // incrementing and decrementing
 3  public class TestIncrement {
 4      // Define the main method
 5      public static void main(String[] args) {
 6
 7          int i = 4, k = 0;
 8          k = i-- + 2 * i * ++i;
 9          System.out.println( "i = " + i );
10          System.out.println( "k = " + k );
11
```

```
12          k = --i + 2 * i * i++;
13          System.out.println( "i = " + i );
14          System.out.println( "k = " + k );
15      }

16  }
```

When this program executes, the results are

```
D:\book\java\chap2>java TestIncrement
i = 4
k = 28
i = 4
k = 21
```

In line 8, the value of k was 28, while in line 12, the value of k was 21. The value of i was 4 at the beginning and the end of each statement. Can you determine why the two expressions produced these values of k?

Never write programs containing statements like the ones shown above. The programs will be very error prone and difficult to understand!

GOOD PROGRAMMING PRACTICE

Always keep expressions containing increment and decrement operators simple and easy to understand.

2.7   MATHEMATICAL METHODS

In mathematics, a *function* is an expression that accepts one or more input values and calculates a single result from them. Scientific and technical calculations usually require functions that are more complex than the simple addition, subtraction, multiplication, division, and modulo operations that we have discussed so far. Some of these functions are very common and are used in many different technical disciplines. Others are rarer and specific to a single problem or a small number of problems. Examples of very common functions are the trigonometric functions, logarithms, and square roots. Examples of rarer functions include the hyperbolic functions, Bessel functions, and so forth.

The Java language has mechanisms to support both the very common functions and the less common ones. Many of the common mathematical functions are implemented as methods in the Math class in the java.lang package. These methods are automatically available to any Java program. Less common functions are not included in the Java language, but they may be implemented as user-defined methods. User-defined methods are discussed in more detail in Chapter 6.

A Java mathematical method takes one or more input values and calculates a single output value from them. The input values to the method are known as *arguments*; they appear in parentheses immediately after the method name. The output of a mathematical method is a single number, which can be used together with other methods, constants, and variables in Java expressions. When a method name appears in a Java statement, the arguments of the method are passed to the method. The method calculates a result, which is used in place of the method name in the original expression (see Figure 2.3).

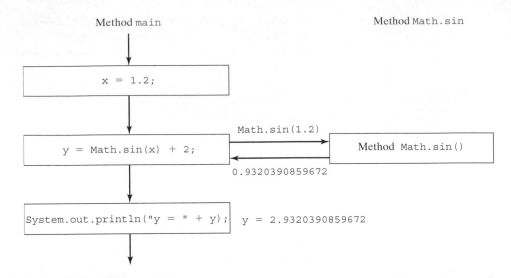

Figure 2.3. When a mathematical method appears in a Java expression, the compiler generates a call to that method, then uses the result returned by the method in the original expression. In this case, the compiler generates the call `Math.sin(1.2)` and uses the result `0.9320390859672` in the original expression.

A list of the mathematical methods in class `Math` is given in Table 2.7. In addition to the methods shown in the table, the class defines two important constants, `Math.PI` (π) and `Math.E` (e, the base of the natural logarithms).

Mathematical methods are used by including them in a Java expression. We must name both the class containing the method and the method name, with a period in between them. For example, the method `Math.sin()` can be used to calculate the sine of a number as follows:

```
y = Math.sin(theta);
```

where `theta` is the argument of the method `sin`. After this statement is executed, the variable `y` contains the sine of the value stored in variable `theta`. Note from Table 2.7 that the trigonometric methods expect their arguments to be in radians. If the variable `theta` is in degrees, then we must convert degrees to radians ($180° = \pi$ radians) before computing the sine. This conversion can be done in the same statement as the sine calculation:

```
y = Math.sin(theta*(3.141593/180.));
```

Alternately, we could create a named constant containing the conversion factor, and refer to that constant when the method is executed:

```
final double DEG_2_RAD = Math.PI / 180.;
...
y = Math.sin(theta * DEG_2_RAD);
```

PROGRAMMING PITFALLS

The arguments for all trigonometric functions must be in units of *radians*. It is very common for novice programmers to use degrees by mistake.

TABLE 2.7 Mathematical Methods

Method Name and Parameters	Method Value	Parameter Type	Result Type	Comments
`Math.abs(x)`	$\lvert x \rvert$	`float, double, int, or long`	Same as parameter	Absolute value of x
`Math.acos(x)`	$\cos^{-1} x$	`double`	`double`	Inverse cosine of x for $-1 \le x \le 1$ (results in *radians*)
`Math.asin(x)`	$\sin^{-1} x$	`double`	`double`	Inverse sine of x for $-1 \le x \le 1$ (results in *radians*)
`Math.atan(x)`	$\tan^{-1} x$	`double`	`double`	Inverse tangent of x (results in *radians* in the range $-\pi/2 \le x \le \pi/2$)
`Math.atan2(y,x)`	$\tan^{-1} \dfrac{y}{x}$	`double`	`double`	Inverse tangent of x (results in *radians* in the range $-\pi \le x \le \pi$)
`Math.ceil(x)`		`double`	`double`	Returns the smallest integer not less than x: `ceil(2.2) = 3` and `ceil(-2.2) = -2`
`Math.cos(x)`	$\cos x$	`double`	`double`	Cosine of x, where x is in radians
`Math.exp(x)`	e^x	`double`	`double`	
`Math.floor(x)`		`double`	`double`	Returns the largest integer not greater than x: `floor(2.2)` `= 2` and `floor(-2.2) = -3`
`Math.log(x)`	$\log x$	`double`	`double`	Natural logarithm of x, for $x > 0$
`Math.max(x,y)`		`float, double, int, or long`	Same as parameter	Returns the larger of x or y
`Math.min(x,y)`		`float, double, int, or long`	Same as parameter	Returns the smaller of x or y
`Math.random()`		`none`	`double`	Returns a uniformly distributed random value between 0 and 1
`Math.pow(x,y)`	x^y	`double`	`double`	`Math.pow(2,5) = 32` `Math.pow(9,.5) = 3`
`Math.rint(x)`		`double`	`double`	Rounds floating-point number to the nearest integer, and returns the result as a floating-point number.
`Math.round(x)`		`double or float`	`long or int`	Rounds floating-point number to the nearest integer, and returns the result as an integer: `round(2.2) = 2` and `round(-2.2) = -2`
`Math.sin(x)`	$\sin x$	`double`	`double`	Sine of x, where x is in radians
`Math.sqrt(x)`	$\sqrt{x}$	`double`	`double`	Square root of x, for $x \ge 0$
`Math.tan(x)`	$\tan x$	`double`	`double`	Tangent of x, where x is in radians

2.8 STANDARD INPUT AND OUTPUT

For a computer program to be useful, there must be some way to read in the data to be processed and to write out the results of the calculations. The process of reading in data and writing out results is known as *input/output (I/O)*. There are many different ways to read in and write out data in a Java program, and we will see many of them in the chapter on I/O (Chapter 16). However, the simplest way to read and write data from a program is through the *standard input* and *standard output* devices of a computer.

The standard input device is a special input source that is usually connected to the computer's keyboard, so that the program can accept values that a user types while the program is running. (This is not always true—the standard input device can be redirected to come from a file or from the output of another program.) The standard output device usually displays the data sent to it on the computer's monitor. (The standard output device may also be redirected.) In Java, the data from these devices is *encapsulated* (hidden) inside objects, which are called *data streams*.

Every Java program has three standard I/O objects: `System.in`, `System.out`, and `System.err`. These objects are ready to read data from or write data to when the program begins executing. `System.in` is an object representing the **standard input stream**, which is usually the keyboard. When the program reads input data from this object, the program actually reads values typed by the user at the keyboard. `System.out` is an object representing the **standard output stream**, which is usually the monitor of the computer. When the program writes data to this object, the values are displayed on the monitor. Finally, `System.err` is a special object representing the **standard error stream**. It is a special stream used for displaying severe program errors.

All three standard I/O objects share the characteristic that *they process input or output data one byte at a time*. Sending data to the standard output stream is relatively easy, since there are standard methods that convert the data to be printed into a stream of bytes, and send those bytes to the output stream. We have already seen the `println` method, which performs this function.

However, reading data from the standard input stream is much harder. The standard input stream presents data to the program one byte at a time, and *it is the programmer's responsibility to clump successive bytes together to form meaningful numbers or strings* before attempting to process them. For example, if a user were to type the value 123.4, the program would have to read the characters in one byte at a time and convert the entire string into the appropriate `double` value after all characters had been read. Java includes standard classes and methods to collect and buffer the input bytes until enough are available to translate into a meaningful number or string. We will introduce these classes in Section 2.8.2.

2.8.1 Using the Standard Output Stream

We have already used the `System.out` object, which represents the standard output stream, in a number of programs. There are two important methods that we will learn to use with this object: `print` and `println`. The `print` method accepts a single argument and prints out the value of its argument on the standard output device. It does *not* send a newline character at the end of the value, so any additional calls to `print` will be displayed on the same line. In contrast, the `println` method accepts a single argument and prints out the value of its argument *followed by a newline character*. Thus `println` terminates the output on a given line.

The behavior of theses two methods is illustrated in the program below. This program outputs two variables `i` and `j` and a string using both the `print` and `println` methods.

```
1   // This program illustrates the use of
2   // the print and println methods.
3   public class TestOutput {
```

```
4        // Define the main method
5        public static void main(String[] args) {
6
7            int i = 1; float j = 1.35F;
8            // Demonstrate output
9            System.out.print( i );
10           System.out.print( j );
11           System.out.print( "String\n" );
12
13           System.out.println( i );
14           System.out.println( j );
15           System.out.println( "String" );
16       }
17   }
```

Line 9 prints out the value "1", line 10 prints out the value "1.35", and line 11 prints out the string "String" followed by a newline character. Since these values were printed with the print method, they all appear in consecutive characters on a single line. Line 13 prints out the value "1", line 14 prints out the value "1.35", and line 15 prints out the string "String". Since these values were printed with the println method, they all appear as consecutive lines. When this program is executed, the results are:

```
D:\book\java\chap2>java TestOutput
11.35String
1
1.35
String
```

Note that there is no space between the values printed out by the print method. If you want space between the values, you must explicitly print the spaces. For example, the statements

```
System.out.print( i );
System.out.print( " " );
System.out.print( j );
System.out.print( " " );
System.out.print( "String\n" );
```

would produce the output

```
1 1.35 String
```

The + operator has a special meaning when used with strings. If the + operator appears between two strings, it **concatenates** them together into one long string. Furthermore, if data of any other type is combined with a string using the + operator, *that data will automatically be converted into a string and concatenated with the other string.* For example, suppose v1 is a variable of type double containing the value 1.25. Then the statement

```
System.out.println("value = " + v1);
```

converts the contents of variable v1 into a string and concatenates it with the string "value = ". The statement prints out the line

```
value = 1.25
```

The standard error stream works exactly the same way as the standard output stream, except that the object `System.err` is substituted for `System.out`. This data stream is only used for reporting critical errors, so it is rarely used.

2.8.2 Using the Standard Input Stream to Read Strings

The standard input stream is used to read data from the keyboard or some other specified source. The data in the standard input stream is presented to the program *one byte at a time*, and the program must combine the bytes after they are read in to create the numbers or strings that the program needs to process. Fortunately, Java provides standard API classes and methods to combine the bytes read from the standard input stream into a string of characters, and other API classes and methods that can convert the string into integer, floating-point, or boolean values.

The data in the standard input stream can be clumped together to form meaningful strings using an object of the `BufferedReader` class, which is a part of the `java.io` package. The `BufferedReader` object accepts the data from the standard input stream one byte at a time until an entire line of data has been accumulated. When the entire line is available, the `BufferedReader` method `readLine()` will return it to the program in a `String`.

The statement required to create a `BufferedReader` object on the standard input stream is

```
BufferedReader in1 = new BufferedReader(
                        new InputStreamReader
                           (System.in));
```

This statement creates an `InputStreamReader` object to read data from the standard input stream, and then a `BufferedReader` object to collect and store the characters output by the `InputStreamReader` object. These objects will be explained in detail in Chapter 16, when we discuss the Java I/O system. The phrase `BufferedReader in1` declares `in1` to be a **reference** to the `BufferedReader` object that we have created. This object (and thus the standard input stream) can be used in the program by including the reference `in1` in a statement.

A sample program that reads lines of text from the standard input stream is shown below, with the key features in boldface.

```
1    // This program tests reading lines from the standard
2    // input stream.
3    import java.io.*;
4    public class ReadString {
5
6        // Define the main method
7        public static void main(String[] args) throws IOException {
8
9            String str;
10
11           // Create a buffered reader
12           BufferedReader in1 = new BufferedReader(
13                   new InputStreamReader(System.in));
14
15           // Prompt for a String value
```

```
16        System.out.print("Enter a String value: ");
17        str = in1.readLine();
18        System.out.println("Value = " + str );
19
20    }
21 }
```

Note that line 3 *imports* the java.io package into the program, so that the BufferedReader and InputStreamReader classes will be defined and available for use. If the package is not imported, the Java compiler will not be able to find the definitions of these classes, and so will not know how to use them. The compiler will not be able to compile the program.

A programmer must import any package that contains classes used in a program, except for package java.lang. This package contains the very basics of the Java language, and it is automatically imported into every Java program without an import statement. (For example, class System is included in package java.lang, so the method System.out.println is always available in any program at any time.)

Also note that the class definition on line 7 includes the words "throws IOException". If the BufferedReader class encounters an error when it tries to read a line, the class will produce a special type of error called an *exception*. We will learn about exceptions in Chapter 8. For now, simply add the clause "throws IOException" to the definitions of classes that use BufferedReader.

Lines 12 and 13 of this program create a BufferedReader object and store a reference to that object in in1. This object collects and stores up characters from System.in. Line 17 calls the BufferedReader method readLine() on the object that we have created, and that method returns an entire line from the buffer in the String called str. Line 18 then writes the resulting string to the standard output stream.

When this program is executed, the results are as shown below (user inputs are in boldface):

```
D:\book\java\chap2>java ReadString
Enter a String value: This is a test!
Value = This is a test!
```

2.8.3 Using the Standard Input Stream to Read Numbers and Boolean Values

Now that we can read strings of characters from the standard input stream, we need to be able to convert the strings into the data type that they represent. For example, we must be able to convert the string "123.4" into the double value 123.4. Fortunately, the Java API includes a number of methods that will convert a string of characters into an int, double, or boolean data type. Three of these methods are summarized in Table 2.8. These methods can be used to convert any line into a value of an appropriate data type.

A sample program that reads lines of text from the standard input stream and converts them into double, int, and boolean data types is shown below, with the type conversions in boldface.

```
1 // This program tests reading values from the standard
2 // input stream.
3 import java.io.*;
4 public class ReadStdIn {
```

TABLE 2.8 Type Conversion Methods

Method Name and Parameters	Result Type	Comments
`Integer.parseInt(str)`	int	Converts contents of the string into an int value
`Double.parseDouble(str)`	double	Converts contents of the string into a double value
`Boolean.valueOf(str).booleanValue()`	boolean	Converts contents of the string into a boolean value

```
5
6       // Define the main method
7     public static void main(String[] args)throws IOException{
8
9         double v1; int i1; boolean test;
10        String str;
11
12        // Create a buffered reader
13      BufferedReader in1 = new BufferedReader(
14              new InputStreamReader(System.in));
15
16        // Prompt for a double value
17        System.out.print("Enter a double value: ");
18        str = in1.readLine();
19        v1 = Double.parseDouble(str);
20        System.out.println("Value = " + v1 );
21
22        // Prompt for an int value
23        System.out.print("Enter an int value: ");
24        str = in1.readLine();
25        i1 = Integer.parseInt(str);
26        System.out.println("Value = " + i1 );
27
28        // Prompt for a boolean value
29        System.out.print("Enter a boolean value: ");
30        str = in1.readLine();
31        test = Boolean.valueOf(str).booleanValue();
32        System.out.println("Value = " + test );
33    }
34 }
```

When this program is executed, the results are as shown below. User inputs are shown in boldface.

```
D:\book\java\chap2>java ReadStdIn
Enter a double value: 45.6
Value = 45.6
Enter an int value: -123
Value = -123
```

```
Enter a boolean value: true
Value = true
```

This program has converted the input strings into the appropriate values.

What happens in this program when the user makes an error typing an input value? For example, suppose that a user had typed $5.6 instead of 45.6 above. This error means that the method cannot covert the string into a `double` value, so it produces an exception called a `NumberFormatException`, and the program crashes.

```
D:\book\java\chap2>java ReadStdIn
Enter a double value: $5.6
Exception in thread "main"
java.lang.NumberFormatException: $5.6
    at java.lang.FloatingDecimal.readJavaFormatString (Unknown Source)
    at java.lang.Double.parseDouble(Unknown Source)
    at ReadStdIn.main(ReadStdIn.java:19)
```

In Chapter 8 we will learn how to recover from such exceptions and to continue program execution. Until then, if a user makes a mistake entering numeric values into a program, the program will crash.

EXAMPLE 2.2

Area of a Circle: Write a program to prompt a user for the radius of a circle, and then calculate and display its area.

SOLUTION

The area of a circle is given by the equation

$$A = \pi r^2 \qquad (2.1)$$

where r is the radius of the circle and A is the resulting area. This program must prompt the user for the radius of the circle, read the value supplied by the user, and calculate and display the resulting area.

We will use method `System.out.println` to prompt the user and to display the resulting area, class `BufferedReader` to read in the radius as a string from the standard input stream, and method `Double.parseDouble()` to convert the string to a `double` value. The resulting program is shown in Figure 2.4, with the input and output statement in boldface.

To test the completed program, we will run it with the known input values and compare the results. If the radius of the circle is 1.0, then from Equation (2.1) the area of the circle should be π. Similarly, if the radius of the circle is 2, the area of the circle should be 4π.

```
D:\book\java\chap2>java CalcArea
Enter the radius of the circle: 1
The area of the circle is 3.141592653589793

D:\book\java\chap2>java CalcArea
Enter the radius of the circle: 2
The area of the circle is 12.566370614359172
```

The results of the program match the expected values.

```
/*
    Purpose:
      To calculate the area of a circle.

    Record of revisions:
        Date          Programmer              Description of change
        ====          ==========              =====================
      05/02/2002    S. J. Chapman             Original code
*/
import java.io.*;
public class CalcArea {

    // Define the main method
    public static void main (String[] args) throws IOException {

        // Declare variables, and define each variable
        double area;          // Area of circle
        double radius;        // Radius of circle
        String str;           // Input line

        // Create a BufferedReader object
        BufferedReader in1 = new BufferedReader(
                        new InputStreamReader(System.in));

        // Prompt the user for the input temperature.
        System.out.print("Enter the radius of the circle: ");
        str = in1.readLine();
        radius = Double.parseDouble(str);

        // Calculate area
        area = Math.PI * radius * radius;

        // Write out the result.
        System.out.println("The area of the circle is " + area);
    }
}
```

Figure 2.4 Program to calculate and display the area of a circle.

QUIZ 2-3

This quiz provides a quick check to see if you have understood the concepts introduced in Sections 2.4 through 2.8. If you have trouble with the quiz, reread the sections, ask your instructor, or discuss the material with a fellow student. The answers are found in the back of the book.

Convert the following algebraic equations into Java assignment statements:

1. The equivalent resistance R_{eq} of four resistors R_1, R_2, R_3, and R_4 connected in series:

$$R_{eq} = R_1 + R_2 + R_3 + R_4$$

2. The equivalent resistance R_{eq} of four resistors R_1, R_2, R_3, and R_4 connected in parallel:

$$R_{eq} = \frac{1}{\dfrac{1}{R_1} + \dfrac{1}{R_2} + \dfrac{1}{R_3} + \dfrac{1}{R_4}}$$

3. The period T of an oscillating pendulum:

$$T = 2\pi\sqrt{\frac{L}{g}}$$

where L is the length of the pendulum, and g is the acceleration due to gravity.

4. The equation for damped sinusoidal oscillation:

$$v(t) = V_M e^{-\alpha t} \cos \omega t$$

where V_M is the maximum value of the oscillation, α is the exponential damping factor, and ω is the angular velocity of the oscillation.

Convert the following Java assignment statements into algebraic equations:

5. The motion of an object in a constant gravitational field:

```
distance = 0.5 * accel * Math.pow(t, 2) + vel0 * t + pos0;
```

6. The oscillating frequency of a damped *RLC* circuit:

```
freq = 1 / (2* Math.PI * Math.sqrt(l * c));
```

7. Energy storage in an inductor:

```
energy = 1. / 2. * inductance * Math.pow(current,2);
```

8. Given the definitions below, are the statements shown legal or illegal? If a statement is legal, what is the result? If illegal, tell why it is illegal.

```
double a = 2., b = 3., c;
int i = 3, j = 2, k;
```

(a) c = Math.sin(a * Math.PI));
(b) k = a / b;
(c) k = (int) a / b;
(d) b += a / i;
(e) c = a / (j / i);

9. After the following statements are executed, what is stored in each of the variables?

```
double a = 2., b = 3., c;
int i = 3, j = 2, k;
k = ++i - j--;
c = i++/j-- + a/b;
```

10. Write a Java program to calculate the hypotenuse of a triangle, given the lengths of its two sides. Read the lengths of the sides using the standard input stream, and write the output to the standard output stream.

2.9   PROGRAM EXAMPLES

In Chapter 2 we have presented the fundamental concepts required to write simple but functional Java programs. We will now present a few example problems in which these concepts are used.

EXAMPLE 2.3

Temperature Conversion: Design a Java program that reads an input temperature in degrees Fahrenheit, converts it to an absolute temperature in kelvins, and writes out the result.

SOLUTION

The relationship between temperature in degrees Fahrenheit (°F) and temperature in kelvins (K) can be found in any physics textbook. It is

$$T \text{ (in kelvins)} = \frac{5}{9} [T \text{ (in °F)} - 32.0] + 273.15 \tag{2.2}$$

The physics books also give us sample values on both temperature scales, which we can use to check the operation of our program. Two such values are:

The boiling point of water	212°F	373.15 K
The sublimation point of dry ice	− 110°F	194.26 K

Our program must perform the following steps:

1. Prompt the user to enter an input temperature in °F.
2. Read the input temperature.
3. Calculate the temperature in kelvins from Equation (2.2).
4. Write out the result, and stop.

The resulting program is shown in Figure 2.5.

To test the completed program, we will run it with the known input values given above. Note that user inputs appear in boldface below.

```
C:\book\java\chap2>java TempConversion
Enter the temperature in deg Fahrenheit: 212
212.0 deg F = 373.15 K

C:\book\java\chap2>java TempConversion
Enter the temperature in deg Fahrenheit: -110
-110.0 deg F = 194.2611111111111 K
```

The results of the program match the values from the physics book.

In the above program, we echoed the input values and printed the output values together with their units. The results of this program make sense only if the units (degrees Fahrenheit and kelvins) are included together with their values. As a general rule, the units associated with any input value should always be printed along with the prompt that requests the value, and the units associated with any output value should always be printed along with that value.

GOOD PROGRAMMING PRACTICE

Always include the appropriate units with any values that you read or write in a program.

```
/*
    Purpose:
      To convert an input temperature from degrees Fahrenheit to
      an output temperature in kelvins.

    Record of revisions:
        Date          Programmer              Description of change
        ====          ==========              =====================
      06/02/2002    S. J. Chapman             Original code
*/
import java.io.*;
public class TempConversion {

    // Define the main method
    public static void main(String[] args) throws IOException {

        // Declare variables, and define each variable
        String str;              // Input string
        double tempF;            // Temperature in degrees Fahrenheit
        double tempK;            // Temperature in kelvins

        // Create a buffered reader
        BufferedReader in1 = new BufferedReader(
                            new InputStreamReader(System.in));

        // Prompt the user for the input temperature.
        System.out.print("Enter the temperature in deg Fahrenheit: ");
        str = in1.readLine();
        tempF = Double.parseDouble(str);

        // Convert to kelvins
        tempK = (5. / 9.) * (tempF - 32.) + 273.15;

        // Write out the result.
        System.out.println(tempF + " deg F = " + tempK + " K");
    }
}
```

Figure 2.5. Program to convert degrees Fahrenheit into kelvins.

The above program exhibits many of the good programming practices that we have described in this chapter. It includes a data dictionary defining the meanings of all of the variables in the program. It also uses descriptive variable names. Appropriate units are attached to all printed values.

EXAMPLE 2.4

Electrical Engineering: Calculating Real, Reactive, and Apparent Power:
Figure 2.6 shows a sinusoidal ac voltage source with voltage V supplying a load of impedance $Z \angle \theta \, \Omega$, where Z is the magnitude of the impedance in ohms, and θ is the phase angle between the voltage drop across the load and the current flowing through the load. From simple circuit theory, the rms current I, the real power P, reactive

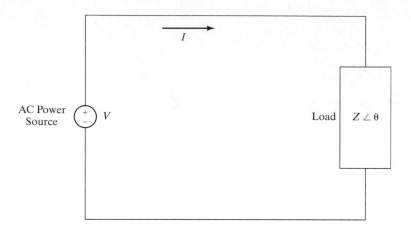

Figure 2.6. A sinusoidal ac voltage source with voltage V supplying a load of impedance $Z\angle\theta$ Ω.

power Q, apparent power S, and power factor PF supplied to the load are given by the equations

$$I = \frac{V}{Z} \tag{2.3}$$

$$P = VI \cos\theta \tag{2.4}$$

$$Q = VI \sin\theta \tag{2.5}$$

$$S = VI \tag{2.6}$$

$$PF = \cos\theta \tag{2.7}$$

where V is the rms voltage of the power source in units of volts (V). The units of current are amperes (A), of real power are watts (W), of reactive power are volt-amperes-reactive (VAR), and of apparent power are volt-amperes (VA). The power factor has no units associated with it.

Given the rms voltage of the power source and the magnitude and angle of the impedance Z, write a program that calculates the rms current I, the real power P, reactive power Q, apparent power S, and power factor PF of the load.

SOLUTION

In this program, we need to read in the rms voltage V of the voltage source and the magnitude Z and angle θ of the impedance. The input voltage source will be measured in volts, the magnitude of the impedance Z in ohms, and the angle of the impedance θ in degrees. Once the data is read, we must convert the angle θ into radians for use with the Java trigonometric functions. Next, the desired values must be calculated, and the results must be printed out.

The program will perform the following steps:

1. Prompt the user to enter the source voltage in volts.
2. Read the source voltage.
3. Prompt the user to enter the magnitude and angle of the impedance in ohms and degrees.
4. Read the magnitude and angle of the impedance.
5. Calculate the current I from Equation (2.3).

6.   Calculate the real power *P* from Equation (2.4).
7.   Calculate the reactive power *Q* from Equation (2.5).
8.   Calculate the apparent power *S* from Equation (2.6).
9.   Calculate the power factor PF from Equation (2.7).
10. Write out the results, and stop.

The final Java program is shown in Figure 2.7.

```
/*
  Purpose:
    To calculate the current, real, reactive, and apparent power,
    and the power factor supplied to a load.
  Record of revisions:
      Date         Programmer          Description of change
      ====         ==========          =====================
   06/02/2002   S. J. Chapman        Original code
*/
import java.io.*;
public class Power {
   // Define the main method
   public static void main(String[] args) throws IOException {

      // Declare constants
      final double CONV = Math.PI / 180;    // Degrees to radians

      // Declare variables, and define each variable
      double amps;        // Current in the load (A)
      double p;           // Real power of load (W)
      double pf;          // Power factor of load
      double q;           // Reactive power of the load (VA)
      double s;           // Apparent power of the load (VAR)
      String str;         // Input string
      double theta;       // Impedance angle of the load (deg)
      double volts;       // Rms voltage of the power source (V)
      double z;           // Magnitude of the load impedance (ohms)

      // Create a buffered reader
      BufferedReader in1 = new BufferedReader(
                        new InputStreamReader(System.in));

      // Prompt the user for the rms voltage.
      System.out.print("Enter the rms voltage of the source: ");
      str = in1.readLine();
      volts = Double.parseDouble(str);

      // Prompt the user for the magnitude of the impedance
      System.out.print("Enter the magnitude of the impedance (ohms): ");
      str = in1.readLine();
      z = Double.parseDouble(str);

      // Prompt the user for the angle of the impedance
      System.out.print("Enter the angle of the impedance (deg): ");
```

Figure 2.7.   Program to calculate the real power, reactive power, apparent power, and power factor supplied to a load.

```
        str = in1.readLine();
        theta = Double.parseDouble(str);

        // Perform calculations
        amps = volts / z;                           // Rms current
        p = volts * amps * Math.cos(theta * CONV); // Real power
        q = volts * amps * Math.sin(theta * CONV); // Reactive power
        s = volts * amps;                           // Apparent power
        pf = Math.cos(theta * CONV);                // Power factor

        // Write out the results.
        System.out.println("Voltage         = " + volts + " volts");
        System.out.println("Impedance       = " + z + " ohms at "
                        + theta + " degrees");
        System.out.println("Voltage         = " + volts + " volts");
        System.out.println("Current         = " + amps + " amps");
        System.out.println("Real Power      = " + p + " W");
        System.out.println("Reactive Power = " + q + " VAR");
        System.out.println("Apparent Power = " + s + " VA");
        System.out.println("Power Factor    = " + pf);
    }
}
```

Figure 2.7. (Continued).

To verify the operation of program Power, we will do a sample calculation by hand and compare the results with the output of the program. If the rms voltage V is 120 V, the magnitude of the impedance Z is 5 Ω, and the angle θ is 30°, then the values are

$$I = \frac{V}{Z} = \frac{120 \text{ V}}{5 \text{ }\Omega} = 24 \text{ A} \tag{2.3}$$

$$P = VI \cos \theta = (120 \text{ V})(24 \text{ A}) \cos 30° = 2494 \text{ W} \tag{2.4}$$

$$Q = VI \sin \theta = (120 \text{ V})(24 \text{ A}) \sin 30° = 1440 \text{ VAR} \tag{2.5}$$

$$S = VI = (120 \text{ V})(24 \text{ A}) = 2880 \text{ VA} \tag{2.6}$$

$$PF = \cos \theta = \cos 30° = 0.86603 \tag{2.7}$$

When we run program **Power** with the specified input data, the results are identical with our hand calculations:

```
C:\book\java\chap2>java Power
Enter the rms voltage of the source: 120
Enter the magnitude of the impedance (ohms): 5
Enter the angle of the impedance (deg): 30
Voltage       = 120.0 volts
Impedance     = 5.0 ohms at 30.0 degrees
Voltage       = 120.0 volts
Current       = 24.0 amps
```

```
Real Power      = 2494.1531628991834 W
Reactive Power  = 1439.9999999999998 VAR
Apparent Power  = 2880.0 VA
Power Factor    = 0.8660254037844387
```

EXAMPLE 2.5

Carbon 14 Dating: A radioactive isotope of an element is a form of the element that is not stable. Instead, it spontaneously decays into another element over a period of time. Radioactive decay is an exponential process. If Q_0 is the initial quantity of a radioactive substance at time $t = 0$, then the amount of that substance which will be present at any time t in the future is given by

$$Q(t) = Q_0 e^{-\lambda t} \tag{2.8}$$

where λ is the radioactive decay constant.

Because radioactive decay occurs at a known rate, it can be used as a clock to measure the time since the decay started. (See Figure 2.8.) If we know the initial amount of the radioactive material Q_0 present in a sample, and the amount of the material Q left at the current time, we can solve for t in Equation (2.8) to determine how long the decay has been going on. The resulting equation is

$$t_{\text{decay}} = -\frac{1}{\lambda} \log \frac{Q}{Q_0} \tag{2.9}$$

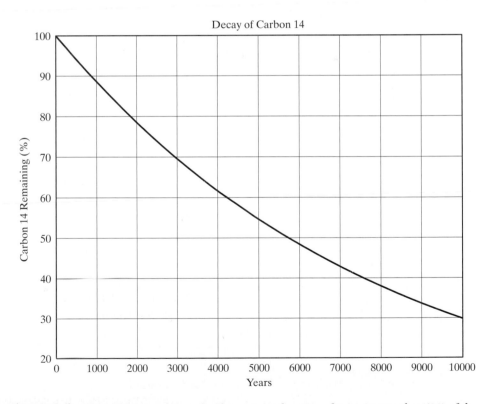

Figure 2.8. The radioactive decay of carbon 14 as a function of time. Notice that 50% of the original carbon 14 is left after about 5730 years have elapsed.

Equation (2.9) has practical applications in many areas of science. For example, archaeologists use a radioactive clock based on carbon 14 to determine the time that has passed since a once-living thing died. Carbon 14 is continually taken into the body while a plant or animal is living, so the amount of it present in the body at the time of death is assumed to be known. The decay constant λ of carbon 14 is well known to be 0.00012097/year, so if the amount of carbon 14 remaining now can be accurately measured, then Equation (2.9) can be used to determine how long ago the living thing died.

Write a program that reads the percentage of carbon 14 remaining in a sample, calculates the age of the sample from it, and prints out the result with proper units.

SOLUTION

Our program must perform the following steps:

1. Prompt the user to enter the percentage of carbon 14 remaining in the sample.
2. Read in the percentage.
3. Convert the percentage into the fraction Q/Q_0.
4. Calculate the age of the sample in years using Equation (2.9).
5. Write out the result, and stop.

The resulting code is shown in Figure 2.9.

```
/*
   Purpose:
     To calculate the age of an organic sample from the percentage
     of the original carbon 14 remaining in the sample.

   Record of revisions:
       Date          Programmer              Description of change
       ====          ==========              =====================
     06/02/2002    S. J. Chapman             Original code
*/
import java.io.*;
public class C14Date {

   // Define the main method
   public static void main(String[] args) throws IOException {

      // Declare constants
      final double LAMDA = 0.00012097;   // C14 decay constant (1/year)

      // Declare variables, and define each variable
      double age;        // Age of the sample (years)
      double percent;    // Percentage of carbon 14 remaining
      double ratio;      // Ratio of the C-14 remaining at the time
                         // of the measurement to the original amount
                         // of C-14.
      String str;        // Input string

      // Create a buffered reader
      BufferedReader in1 = new BufferedReader(
                         new InputStreamReader(System.in));
```

Figure 2.9.   Program to calculate the age of a sample from the percentage of carbon 14 remaining in it.

```
    // Prompt the user for the percentage of C-14 remaining.
    System.out.print("Enter the percentage of carbon 14 remaining: ");
    str = in1.readLine();
    percent = Double.parseDouble(str);

    // Perform calculations
    ratio = percent / 100;                    // Convert to ratio
    age = (-1.0 / LAMDA) * Math.log(ratio);   // Get age in years

    // Tell the user about the age of the sample.
    System.out.println ("The age of the sample is "
        + age + " years."");
  }
}
```

Figure 2.9 (Continued).

To test the completed program, we will calculate the time it takes for half of the carbon 14 to disappear. This time is known as the *half-life* of carbon 14. When this program is executed, the results are:

```
C:\book\java\chap2>java C14Date
Enter the percentage of carbon 14 remaining: 50
The age of the sample is 5729.90973431384 years.
```

The *CRC Handbook of Chemistry and Physics* states that the half-life of carbon 14 is 5730 years, so the output of the program agrees with the reference book. ∎

2.10 DEBUGGING JAVA PROGRAMS

There is an old saying that the only sure things in life are death and taxes. We can add one more certainty to that list: if you write a program of any significant size, it won't work the first time you try it! Errors in programs are known as *bugs*, and the process of locating and eliminating them is known as *debugging*. Given that we have written a program and it is not working, how do we debug it?

Three types of errors are found in Java programs. The first type is a *compile-time error* or *syntax error*. Compile-time errors are in the Java statement itself, such as spelling errors or punctuation errors. These errors are detected by the compiler during compilation. The second type is the *run-time error*. A run-time error occurs when an illegal mathematical operation is attempted during program execution (for example, attempting to divide by 0). These errors cause exceptions in Java programs. Unless the exception is caught by an exception handler, the program will abort (crash) when the execution occurs. The third type is a *logic error*. Logic errors occur when the program compiles and runs successfully but produces the wrong answer.

The most common mistakes made during programming are *typographical errors*, where a user simply types the wrong name, leaves out a parenthesis, or the like. Some typographical errors create invalid Java statements, which are caught by the Java compiler. Other typographical errors occur in variable names. For example, the letters in some variable names might have been transposed. Most of these errors will also be caught by the compiler. However, if one legal variable name is substituted for another, the compiler cannot detect the error. This sort of substitution might occur if you have two similar variable names. For example, if variables `vel1` and `vel2` are both used for velocities in the program, then at some point one of them might be inadvertently used instead of the other. This will produce a logic error. You must check for the source of this sort of error by manually inspecting the code, since the compiler cannot catch it.

Sometimes it is possible to successfully compile and link the program, but runtime or logic errors occur when the program is executed. In this case, there is something wrong with either the input data or the logical structure of the program. The first step in locating this sort of bug should be to *check the input data to the program*. Verify that the input values are what you expect them to be.

If the variable names seem to be correct and the input data are correct, then you are probably dealing with a logic error. You should check each of your assignment statements.

1.   If an assignment statement is very long, break it into several smaller ones. Smaller statements are easier to verify.
2.   Check the placement of parentheses in your assignment statements. It is a very common error to have the operations in an assignment statement evaluated in the wrong order. If you have any doubts as to the order in which the variables are being evaluated, add extra sets of parentheses to make your intentions clear.
3.   Make sure that you have initialized all of your variables properly.
4.   Be sure that any functions you use are in the correct units. For example, the input to trigonometric functions must be in units of radians, not degrees.
5.   Check for possible errors due to integer or mixed-mode arithmetic.

If you are still getting the wrong answer, place `println` statements at various points in your program to print out the results of intermediate calculations. If you can locate the point where the calculations go bad, then you know just where to look for the problem, which is 95% of the battle.

If you still cannot find the problem after all of the above steps, explain what you are doing to another student or to your instructor, and let them look at the code. It is very common for people to see just what they expect to see when they look at their own code. Another person can often quickly spot an error that you have overlooked time after time.

All modern compilers have special debugging tools called *symbolic debuggers*. A symbolic debugger allows you to walk through the execution of your program one statement at a time, and to examine the values of any variables at each step along the way. It allows you to see all of the intermediate results without having to insert a lot of debugging print statements into your code. Symbolic debuggers are powerful and flexible, but unfortunately they are different for every compiler vendor. If you will be using a symbolic debugger in your class, your instructor will introduce you to the one that is appropriate for your compiler and computer.

SUMMARY

- Java names may consist of any combination of letters, numbers, the $ character, and the underscore character (_), but must not begin with a number. They may be of any length.
- Java names may not be the same as any Java keyword. Java keywords are listed in Table 2.1.

- By convention, class names begin with a capital letter, and the first letter of each succeeding word is also capitalized.
- By convention, local variables and method names begin with a lowercase letter, and the first letter of each succeeding word is capitalized.
- By convention, named constants (final variables) are written in all capital letters, with underscores between the words.
- Java includes eight primitive data types: `float`, `double`, `char`, `byte`, `short`, `int`, `long`, and `boolean`. Each type is identical on every platform supported by Java.
- Java is a strongly typed language, which means that every variable must be explicitly declared before it is used.
- A Java named constant (also known as a final variable) may be created by prefixing the keyword `final` in front of the type in a declaration statement.
- An assignment statement assigns the value to the right of the equal sign to the variable on the left of the equal sign.
- The preincrement and predecrement operators are placed before a variable, and the postincrement and postdecrement operators are placed after a variable. The preincrement and predecrement operators cause the variable to be incremented or decremented by 1, and then the new value is used in the expression in which it appears. The postincrement and postdecrement operators cause the old value of the variable to be used in the expression in which it appears, and then the variable is decremented or decremented by 1.
- The cast operator explicitly converts a numeric value of one data type into a numeric value of another data type.
- Java's built-in mathematical methods are contained in the `Math` class of the `java.lang` package. Since this package is automatically imported into any Java program, these methods may be used by simply naming them in a statement. The methods are summarized in Table 2.7.
- Java automatically converts arguments of an incorrect type into arguments of the type required by the method, as long as the process involves a widening conversion. This process is known as the *coercion of arguments*.
- Every Java program has three standard I/O objects: `System.in`, `System.out`, and `System.err`. These objects either accept or supply data one byte at a time. *It is the programmer's responsibility to clump successive bytes together to form meaningful numbers or strings* before attempting to process them.
- The data from the standard input stream can be buffered into a `String` containing a complete line using the `BufferedReader` class from the `java.io` package. These strings can be converted into `int`, `double`, or `boolean` data using the methods given in Table 2.8.
- When the + operator is used between strings, it concatenates them together. If it is used between a string and another operand, it converts the other operand into a string and concatenates the two strings together.

SUMMARY OF GOOD PROGRAMMING PRACTICES

Every Java program should be designed so that another person who is familiar with Java can easily understand it. This is very important, since a good program may be used for a long period of time. Over that time, conditions will change, and the program will need to be modified to reflect the changes. The program modifications may be done by someone other than the original programmer. The programmer making the modifications must understand the original program well before attempting to change it.

It is much harder to design clear, understandable, and maintainable programs than it is to simply write programs. To do so, a programmer must develop the discipline to properly document his or her work. In addition, the programmer must be careful to avoid known pitfalls along the path to good programs. The following guidelines will help you to develop good programs:

1. Always capitalize the first letter of a class name, and use a lowercase first letter for method and variable names.
2. If a name consists of more than one word, the words should be joined together and each succeeding word should begin with an uppercase letter.
3. Use meaningful variable names whenever possible to make your programs clearer.
4. Create a data dictionary in each program that you write. The data dictionary should explicitly declare and define each variable in the program. Be sure to include the physical units associated with each variable, if applicable.
5. Keep your physical constants consistent and precise throughout a program. To improve the consistency and understandability of your code, assign a name to any important constants, and refer to them by name in the program.
6. The names of constants should be in all capital letters, with underscores separating the words.
7. Use parentheses as necessary to make your equations clear and easy to understand.
8. Use cast operators to avoid mixed-mode expressions and make your intentions clear.
9. Always keep expressions containing increment and decrement operators simple and easy to understand.

TERMINOLOGY

assignment conversion	named constant
assignment operator	narrowing conversion
assignment statement	numeric promotion
associativity	overloaded methods
binary operator	postdecrement
`Boolean.valueOf(str).booleanValue()`	postincrement
`BufferedReader` class	precision
cast operator	predecrement
coercion of arguments	preincrement
concatenate	primitive data type
constant	range
`Double.parseDouble(str)` method	reference
declaration statement	reserved
escape sequence	roundoff error
exception	standard error stream
exponent	standard input stream
final	standard output stream
final variable	`String`
hierarchy of operations	strongly typed language
increment operator	unary operator
`Integer.parseInt(str)` method	Unicode character set
keyword	variable
mantissa	widening conversion

Exercises

1. State whether or not each of the following Java constants is valid. If valid, state what type of constant it is. If not, state why it is invalid. (If you are not certain, try to compile the constant in a Java program to check your answer.)

   a. `3.141592`

   b. `true`

   c. `-123,456.789`

   d. `+1E-12`

   e. `"Who's coming for dinner?"`

   f. `'Hello'`

   g. `"Enter name:"`

   h. `17.0f`

2. State whether each of the Java names is valid or not. If not, state why the name is invalid. If a name is valid, state what a name of that sort should represent, using the Java conventions.

   a. `junk`

   b. `3rd`

   c. `executeAlgorithm`

   d. `timeToIntercept`

   e. `MyMath`

   f. `START_TIME`

3. Which of the following expressions are legal in Java? If an expression is legal, evaluate it.

   a. `5 + 10 % 3 + 2`

   b. `5 + 10 % (3 + 2)`

   c. `23 / (4 / 8)`

4. Which of the following expressions are legal in Java? If an expression is legal, evaluate it.

   a. `((58/4)*(4/58))`

   b. `((58/4)*(4/58.))`

   c. `((58./4)*(4/58.))`

   d. `((58./4*(4/58.))`

5. Assume that the variables a, b, c, i, and j are initialized as shown in the following code fragment. What is the value of each variable after these statements are executed?

```
int i = 5, j = 2;
double a = 6, b, c = 0;
b = ++i - j--
j = (int) b / 2;
a += b / j;
```

6. Figure 2.10 shows a right triangle with a hypotenuse of length c and angle θ. From elementary trigonometry, the lengths of sides a and b are given by

$$a = c \cos \theta$$
$$b = c \sin \theta$$

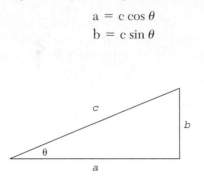

Figure 2.10. The right triangle of Exercise 2.6.

The following program is intended to calculate the lengths of sides a and b, given the hypotenuse c and angle θ. Will this program run? Will it produce the correct result? Why or why not?

```java
import java.io.*;
public class CalcTriangle {
    // Define the main method
    public static void main(String[] args) {

        double a, b, c, theta;
        String str;

        // Create a buffered reader
        BufferedReader in1 = new BufferedReader(
                            new InputStreamReader(System.in));

        // Prompt for the hypotenuse
        System.out.print("Enter the length of the hypotenuse c: ");
        str = in1.readLine();
        c = Double.parseDouble(str);

        // Prompt for the angle
        System.out.print("Enter the angle theta in degrees: ");
        str = in1.readLine();
        theta = Double.parseDouble(str);

        // Calculate sides
        a = c * Math.cos( theta );
        b = c * Math.sin( theta );

        // Write results
        System.out.println(" Adjacent side = " + a);
        System.out.println(" Opposite side = " + b);
    }

}
```

7. Write a Java program that calculates an hourly employee's weekly pay. The program should ask the user for the person's pay rate and the number of hours worked during the week. It should then calculate the total pay from the formula

    Total Pay = Hourly Pay Rate × Hours Worked

    Finally, it should display the total weekly pay. Check your program by computing the weekly pay for a person earning $7.50 per hour and working for 39 hours.

8. The potential energy of an object due to its height above the surface of the earth is given by the equation

    $$PE = mgh \qquad (2.10)$$

    where m is the mass of the object, g is the acceleration due to gravity, and h is the height above the surface of the earth. The kinetic energy of a moving object is given by the equation

    $$KE = \frac{1}{2}mv^2 \qquad (2.11)$$

    where m is the object's mass and v is its velocity. Write a Java statement for the total energy (potential plus kinetic) possessed by an object in the earth's gravitational field.

9. Write a Java program that calculates the percentage of carbon 14 that will be left after a given number of years. The program should read the number of years from the standard input stream.

10. If a stationary ball is released at a height h above the surface of the earth, the velocity of the ball v when it hits the earth is given by the equation

    $$v = \sqrt{2gh} \qquad (2.12)$$

    where g is the acceleration due to gravity, and h is the height above the surface of the earth (assuming no air friction). Write a Java statement for the velocity of the ball when it hits the earth.

11. **Period of a Pendulum**   The period of an oscillating pendulum T (in seconds) is given by the equation

    $$T = 2\pi\sqrt{\frac{L}{g}} \qquad (2.13)$$

    where L is the length of the pendulum in meters, and g is the acceleration due to gravity in meters per second squared. Write a Java program to calculate the period of a pendulum of length L. The length of the pendulum will be specified by the user when the program is run. Use good programming practices in your program. (The acceleration due to gravity at the Earth's surface is 9.81 m/sec^2. Treat it as a constant in your program.)

12. The area of a triangle is given by the equation

    $$A = \frac{1}{2}bh \qquad (2.14)$$

where b is the length of the triangle's base, h is the triangle's height, and A is the resulting area (see Figure 2.11). Write a program to calculate the area of a triangle, given the length of its base and its height. Use good programming practices in your program.

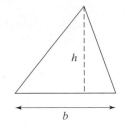

Figure 2.11. The triangle of Exercise 2.12.

13.   Figure 2.12 shows two points (x_1, y_1) and (x_2, y_2) on a Cartesian coordinate plane. The distance between these two points is given by the equation

$$d = \sqrt{(x_1 - x_2)^2 + (y_1 - y_2)^2} \qquad (2.15)$$

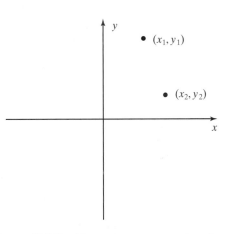

Figure 2.12. Two points on a cartesian plane.

Write a Java program to calculate the distance between any two points (x_1, y_1) and (x_2, y_2) specified by the user. Use good programming practices in your program. Use the program to calculate the distance between the points $(2, 3)$ and $(8, -5)$.

14.   **Decibels**   Engineers often measure the ratio of two power measurements in *decibels*, or dB. The equation for the ratio of two power measurements in dB is

$$dB = 10 \log_{10} \frac{P_2}{P_1} \qquad (2.16)$$

where P_2 is the power level being measured, and P_1 is some reference power level. Assume that the reference power level P_1 is 1 milliwatt, and write a program that accepts an input power P_2 and converts it into dB with respect to the 1 mW reference level.

15. **Hyperbolic Cosine**   The hyperbolic cosine function is defined by the equation

$$\cosh x = \frac{e^x + e^{-x}}{2} \tag{2.17}$$

Write a Java program to calculate the hyperbolic cosine of a user-supplied value x, using any form of I/O that you desire. Use the program to calculate the hyperbolic cosine of 3.0.

16. **Radio Receiver**   A simplified version of the front end of an AM radio receiver is shown in Figure 2.13. This receiver consists of an *RLC* tuned circuit containing a resistor, capacitor, and an inductor connected in series. The *RLC* circuit is connected to an external antenna and ground as shown in the picture.

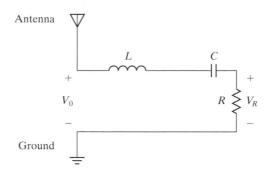

Figure 2.13   A simplified representation of an AM radio set.

The tuned circuit allows the radio to select a specific station out of all the stations transmitting on the AM band. At the resonant frequency of the circuit, essentially all of the signal V_0 appearing at the antenna appears across the resistor, which represents the rest of the radio. In other words, the radio receives its strongest signal at the resonant frequency. The resonant frequency of the *LC* circuit is given by the equation

$$f_0 = \frac{1}{2\pi\sqrt{LC}} \tag{2.18}$$

where L is inductance in henrys (H) and C is capacitance in farads (F). Write a program that calculates the resonant frequency of this radio set, given specific values of L and C. Test your program by calculating the frequency of the radio when $L = 0.1$ mH and $C = 0.25$ nF.

3

Branching Structures and Program Design

In the previous chapter, we developed several complete working Java programs. However, all of them were very simple, consisting of a single method containing a series of Java statements, executed one after another in a fixed order. These programs are called *sequential* programs. They read input data, process it to produce a desired answer, print out the answer, and quit. There is no way to execute selectively only certain portions of the program, depending on values of the input data, and there is no way to repeat sections of the program.

In this chapter and the next, we will introduce a number of Java statements that allow us to control the order in which statements are executed in a program. There are two broad categories of control statements: **selection** or **branching**, which select specific sections of the code to execute, and **repetition**, which cause specific sections of the code to be repeated. This chapter will deal with selection structures, while Chapter 4 will cover repetition structures

The operation of selection structures is controlled by boolean values (`true` or `false`). Before covering selection structures, we will introduce Java's relational and logical operations, which yield boolean results that are used to control the selection structures.

Also, with the introduction of selection statements and repetition statements, our programs will become more complex, and it will get easier to make mistakes. To help avoid programming errors, we will introduce a formal program design procedure based upon the technique known as top-down design. We will also introduce a common algorithm development tool, pseudocode.

SECTIONS

3.1 Introduction to Program Design Techniques
3.2 Use of Pseudocode and Flowcharts
3.3 Relational and Logical Operators
3.4 Selection Structures
3.5 GUI Input and Output

OBJECTIVES

- Learn about the program development process, pseudocode, and flowcharts.
- Understand relational and logical operators.
- Learn how to use `if` and `switch` structures.
- Learn how to read data with input dialog boxes, and write data with message dialog boxes.

3.1   INTRODUCTION TO PROGRAM DESIGN TECHNIQUES

Suppose that you are an engineer working in industry and you need to write a Java program to solve some problem. How do you begin?

When given a new problem, there is a natural tendency to sit down at a terminal and start programming without "wasting" a lot of time thinking about it first. It is often possible to get away with this "on-the-fly" approach to programming for very small problems, such as many of the examples in this book. In the real world, however, problems are larger, and a programmer attempting this approach will become hopelessly bogged down. For larger problems, it pays to completely think out the problem and the approach you are going to take to it before writing a single line of code.

We will introduce a formal program design process in this section and then apply it to major applications developed in the remainder of the book. For the simple examples that we will be doing, the design process will seem like overkill. However, as the problems that we solve get larger and larger, the process becomes more and more essential to successful programming.

When I was an undergraduate, one of my professors was fond of saying, "Programming is easy. It's knowing what to program that's hard." His point was forcefully driven home to me after I left university and began working in industry on larger-scale software projects. I found that the most difficult part of my job was to *understand the problem* I was trying to solve. Once I really understood the problem, it became easy to break the problem apart into smaller, more easily manageable pieces with well-defined functions, and then to tackle those pieces one at a time.

Top-down design is the process of starting with a large task and breaking it down into smaller, more easily understandable pieces (subtasks) that perform a portion of the desired task. Each subtask may in turn be subdivided into smaller subtasks if necessary. Once the program is divided into small pieces, each piece can be coded and tested independently. We do not attempt to combine the subtasks into a complete task until each has been verified to work properly by itself.

The concept of top-down design is an essential component of our formal program design process. We will now introduce the details of the process, which is illustrated in Figure 3.1.

Determining the User Requirements

Programs are usually written to fill some perceived need, but that need may not be articulated clearly by the person requesting the program. For example, a user may ask for a program to solve a system of simultaneous linear equations. This request is not clear enough to allow a programmer to design a program to meet the need; he or she must know much more about the problem to be solved. Is the system of equations to be solved real or complex? What is the maximum number of equations and unknowns that the program must handle? Are there any symmetries in the equations which might be exploited to make the task easier? The program designer will have to talk with the user requesting the program, and together they will have to come up with a clear statement of exactly what they are trying to accomplish. This clear statement will prevent misunderstandings and will help the program designer to properly organize his or her thoughts.

The program designer must also consider the inputs to the program and the outputs produced by the program. These inputs and outputs must be specified so that the new program will properly fit into the overall processing scheme. The coefficients of the linear equations mentioned above, for example, are probably in some preexisting order, and our new program needs to be able to read them in that order. Similarly, it

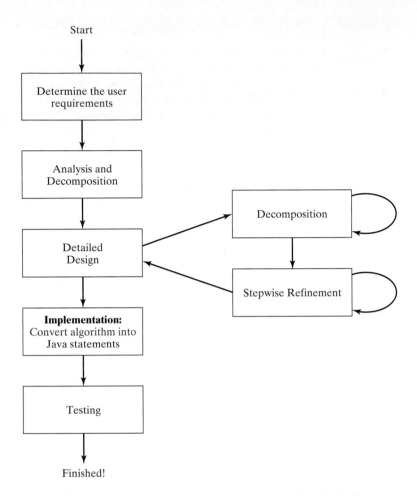

Figure 3.1. The program design process used in this book.

needs to produce the answers required by the programs which may follow it in the overall processing scheme, and to write out those answers in the format those programs require.

On large software projects, both the user requirements and the inputs and outputs are formalized in a System Requirements document, and this document is reviewed by the customer and the program designer in a meeting called a **Systems Requirements Review (SRR)**. The two parties agree to the requirements, which become the "contract" for the writing of the program.

On small projects such as the ones in this book, the process of determining and reviewing requirements is much more informal. However, it is still the essential first step in creating a good program. In the simple example we have been describing, a proper statement of the requirements might be:

> Create a program to solve a system of simultaneous linear equations having real coefficients and with up to 20 equations in 20 unknowns. Read the input data from a disk file with format (*specify input format here*), and write the output data to a disk file with format (*specify output format here*).

Analysis and Decomposition

In the analysis and decomposition phase, the program designer attempts to partition the program into subsections, where each subsection represents a logical portion of the program. In Java, each subsection is implemented as one or more classes. The designer also defines a set of methods for each class that implement its functionality.

In a large project, the analysis phase goes through three discrete steps. The first step is dividing the whole project up into major segments and describing their functions and how they relate to each other. This step results in a document called the **System/Subsystem Design Document (SSDD)**. Each subsystem will be composed of one or more classes (usually many).

The second step is to "flow down" the original user requirements to each subsystem, indicating which requirements will be satisfied by each subsystem. This process leads to **Software Requirement Specification (SRS)** and **Interface Requirement Specification (IRS)** for each subsystem, detailing exactly what that subsystem is required to do.

The third step is to trace the original user requirements down to the individual SRS where they are satisfied, and to trace the SRS requirements back up to the original user requirements. The purpose is to ensure that none of the user's requirements "slip through the cracks."

When the analysis is complete, a **Preliminary Design Review (PDR)** is held with the customer and outside peer reviewers to review and check the work to date.

On small projects, such as those in this book, the analysis process is much less formal. As with large projects, we will partition the user's requirements into segments, which will be implemented as separate classes. In addition, we will define the methods required for each class to satisfy the user's original requirements.

Detailed Design

At this stage, the program designer will do the detailed design of the algorithms to be implemented by each method in each class. An **algorithm** is a step-by-step procedure or recipe for performing some function. At this stage top-down design techniques come into play. The designer looks for logical divisions within a class and/or method and divides it up into subtasks along those lines. This process is called *decomposition*. If the subtasks are themselves large, the designer can break them up into even smaller sub-subtasks. This process continues until the problem has been divided into many small pieces, each of which does a simple, clearly understandable job. (As we shall see in later chapters, these separate pieces can become separate methods.)

After a method has been decomposed into small pieces, each piece is further refined through a process called *stepwise refinement*. Starting with a general description of what the piece of code should do, a designer defines the functions of the piece in greater and greater detail until they are specific enough to be turned into Java statements. Stepwise refinement is usually done with **pseudocode**, which will be described in the next section.

In large projects, a **Critical Design Review (CDR)** is held after the algorithms to be implemented in every class and method have been fully refined. The customer and outside peer reviewers examine the algorithms, seeking to catch errors before the program is actually implemented.

On small projects, such as those in this book, we will perform decomposition and stepwise refinement, but the results will be presented in an informal manner.

It is often helpful to solve a simple example of the problem by hand during the algorithm development process. If the designer understands the steps involved in solving the problem by hand, then he or she will be better able to apply decomposition and stepwise refinement to the problem.

Implementation: Converting algorithms into Java statements

If the decomposition and stepwise refinement process was carried out properly, this step will be very simple. The programmer need only replace pseudocode in each class and method with the corresponding Java statements on a one-for-one basis.

Testing

This step is the real killer. The components of the program must first be tested individually, if possible, and then the program as a whole must be tested. We must verify that it works correctly for *all legal input data sets*. It is very common for a program to be written, tested with some standard data set, and released for use, only to produce the wrong answers (or to crash) with a different input data set. If the algorithm implemented in a program includes different branches, we must test all of the possible branches to confirm that the program operates correctly under every possible circumstance.

Large programs typically go through a series of tests before they are released for general use (see Figure 3.2). The first stage of testing is sometimes called **unit testing**. Here, the individual components of the program are tested separately to confirm that they work correctly. Next, the program goes through a series of *builds*, during which the individual components are combined to produce the final program. The first build of the program typically includes only a few of the components. It is used to check the interactions

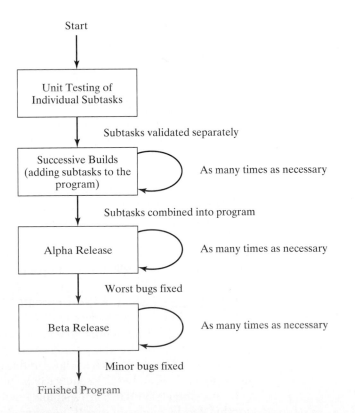

Figure 3.2. A typical testing process for a large program.

among those components and the functions performed by their associated methods. In successive builds, more and more components are added, until the entire program is complete. Testing is performed on each build, and any errors (bugs) which are detected are corrected before moving on to the next build.

Testing continues even after the program is complete. The first complete version of the program is usually called the **alpha release**. It is exercised by the programmers and others very close to them in as many different ways as possible, and the bugs discovered during the testing are corrected. When the most serious bugs have been removed from the program, a new version called the **beta release** is prepared. The beta release is normally given to "friendly" outside users who have a need for the program in their normal day-to-day jobs. These users put the program through its paces under many different conditions and with many different input data sets, and they report to the programmers any bugs that they find. When those bugs have been corrected, the program is ready to be released for general use.

In large formal software projects, final qualification testing is documented in a **Software Test Plan (STP)**. The STP defines a series of tests that collectively demonstrate that the program satisfies all of the user's original requirements. Each individual test is in turn described in a **Software Test Description (STD)**. The STD tells exactly how each test is to be performed, what the results should be, and which of the user's requirements are satisfied by the test. The STP and STDs are reviewed by the customer and outside peer reviewers, to ensure that they do test all of the original requirements. After the review, the tests are conducted and witnessed by a representative of the customer.

On small projects, such as those in this book, testing is much less formal but no less important. We will not go through the sort of extensive testing described above. However, we will follow the basic principles in testing all of our programs. Where possible, we will attempt to test each and every branch through our programs.

The program design process may be summarized as follows:

1. Determine the User Requirements.
2. Analysis and Decomposition.
3. Detailed Design.
4. Implementation: Convert algorithms to Java statements.
5. Testing.

GOOD PROGRAMMING PRACTICE

Follow the steps of the program design process to produce reliable, understandable Java programs.

In a large programming project, the time actually spent programming is surprisingly small. In his book *The Mythical Man-Month*,[1] Frederick P. Brooks, Jr., suggests that in a typical large software project, one-third of the time is spent planning what to do (steps 1 through 3), one-sixth of the time is spent actually writing the program (step 4), and fully one-half of the time is spent in testing and debugging the program! Clearly, anything that we can do to reduce the testing and debugging time will be very helpful. Especially, we can do a very careful job in the planning phase, and we can use good programming practices, which will reduce the number of bugs in the program and make the ones that do creep in easier to find.

---

[1]Frederick P. Brooks, Jr., *The Mythical Man-Month*, Anniversary Edition, Addison-Wesley, 1995.

Once a program has been created, it may be used over a lifetime of 20 years or more. Conditions will change during that time, and the program will have to be modified repeatedly over the course of its life. *The cost of the maintenance and modification of a program over its lifetime usually exceeds the cost of writing the program in the first place.* The modifications will usually be made by programmers other than the ones who originally wrote the code, and these programmers will be relatively unfamiliar with the program. It is during maintenance that good programming practices really pay off. If a program is well designed, well documented, and uses good programming practices, it will be easier (and cheaper) to modify without introducing new bugs.

Maintenance and through-life support are such an important part of the software life cycle that many people include it as a sixth step in the program development process. It is not included separately here, because the small programs that we create in this book don't have long lives, and therefore won't require maintenance over the course of years.

3.2   USE OF PSEUDOCODE AND FLOWCHARTS

As a part of the design process, it is necessary to describe the algorithm that you intend to implement. The description should be in a standard form which is easy for both you and other people to understand, and it should aid you in turning your concept into Java code. The standard forms that we use to describe algorithms are called **structures**.

The constructs used to build algorithms can be described in pseudocode or in flowcharts. **Pseudocode** is a hybrid mixture of Java and English. It is structured like Java, with a separate line for each distinct idea or segment of code, but the descriptions on each line are in English. Each line should describe its idea in plain, easily understandable English. Pseudocode is very useful for developing algorithms, since it is flexible and easy to modify. It is especially useful because it can be written and modified in the same editor used to write the Java program—no special graphical capabilities are required.

For example, the pseudocode for the algorithm in Example 2-3 is:

```
Prompt user to enter temperature in degrees Fahrenheit
Read temperature in degrees Fahrenheit (tempF)
tempK in kelvins ← (5./9.) * (tempF - 32) + 273.15
Write temperature in kelvins
```

Notice that a left arrow (←) is used instead of an equal sign (=) to indicate that a value is stored in a variable, since this avoids any confusion between assignment and equality. Pseudocode is intended to aid you in organizing your thoughts before converting them into Java code.

Flowcharts are a way to describe algorithms graphically. Different graphical symbols represent the different operations in the algorithm, and our standard structures are made up of collections of one or more of these symbols. Flowcharts used to be a very common way to describe the structure of a program, but they have declined in importance in recent years. Flowcharts can be very useful for describing the algorithm implemented in a program after it is completed. However, since they are graphical, flowcharts tend to be cumbersome to modify, and they are not very useful during the preliminary stages of algorithm definition, when rapid changes are occurring. The most common graphical symbols used in flowcharts are shown in Figure 3.3, and the flowchart for the algorithm in Example 2-3 is shown in Figure 3.4.

In this book, we will use flowcharts to illustrate the operation of basic program structures, but we will not be creating flowcharts of entire programs.

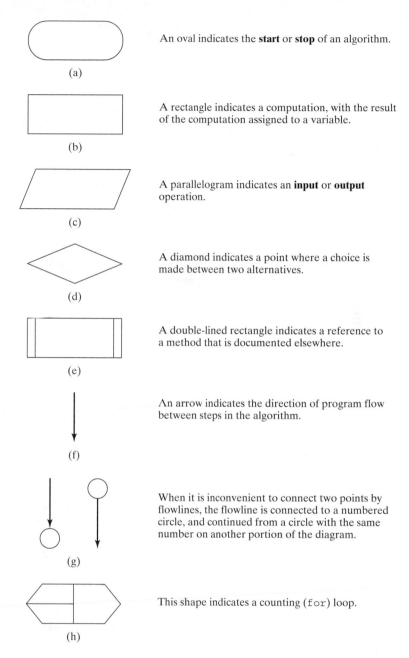

An oval indicates the **start** or **stop** of an algorithm.

(a)

A rectangle indicates a computation, with the result of the computation assigned to a variable.

(b)

A parallelogram indicates an **input** or **output** operation.

(c)

A diamond indicates a point where a choice is made between two alternatives.

(d)

A double-lined rectangle indicates a reference to a method that is documented elsewhere.

(e)

An arrow indicates the direction of program flow between steps in the algorithm.

(f)

When it is inconvenient to connect two points by flowlines, the flowline is connected to a numbered circle, and continued from a circle with the same number on another portion of the diagram.

(g)

This shape indicates a counting (`for`) loop.

(h)

Figure 3.3. Common symbols used in flowcharts.

3.3 RELATIONAL AND LOGICAL OPERATORS

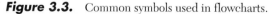

The results of **relational operators** and **logical operators** are boolean `true` or `false` values. They are used to control many selection and repetition structures in Java, as we shall see in this chapter and in Chapter 4.

3.3.1 Relational Operators

Relational operators have *two numerical operands* that yield a boolean (true/false) result. Because the result depends on the *relationship* between the two values being

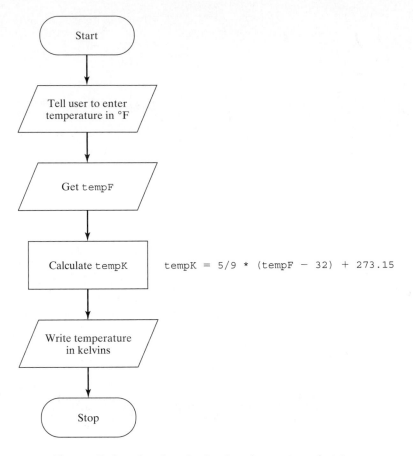

Figure 3.4. Flowchart for the algorithm in Example 2-3.

compared, these operators are called relational. If the relationship expressed by the operator is true, then the result of the operation is `true`; otherwise, the result is `false`. The six relational operators are summarized in Table 3.1.

All of these operators associate from left to right. The relational operators >, <, >=, and <= are of equal precedence, below that of the + and – operators. The equality operators == and != are also of equal precedence, just below the relational operators.

TABLE 3.1 Relational Operators

Operator	Sample Expression	Meaning
Relational operators:		
>	x > y	true if $x > y$
<	x < y	true if $x < y$
>=	x >= y	true if $x \geq y$
<=	x <= y	true if $x \leq y$
Equality operators:		
==	x == y	true if $x = y$
!=	x != y	true if $x \neq y$

Some relational operations and their results are given below:

Operation	Result
3 < 4	true
3 <= 4	true
3 == 4	false
3 > 4	false
4 <= 4	true
'A' < 'B'	true

The last logical expression is true because characters are compared according to their positions in the Unicode character set and 'A' (sequence number 65) is less than 'B' (sequence number 66).

The equivalence relational operator is written with two equal signs, while the assignment operator is written with a single equal sign. These are very different operators, which beginning programmers often confuse. The == symbol is a *comparison* operation which returns a boolean result, while the = symbol *assigns* the value of the expression to the right of the equal sign to the variable on the left of the equal sign. It is a very common mistake for beginning programmers to use a single equal sign when trying to do a comparison.

PROGRAMMING PITFALLS

Be careful not to confuse the equivalence relational operator (==) with the assignment operator (=).

The difference between the assignment operator and the equivalence relational operator is demonstrated in the following program. Note that there is an assignment operator in the println statement on line 12, and an equivalence relational operator in the println statement on line 17. The assignment operator on line 12 assigns the value of 1 to x and then prints out that value. The equivalence relational operator on line 17 compares the value of x to 2. Since they are not equal, the result of the comparison is false, and the println statement prints out false. Note that the value of x is unchanged by the comparison.

```
1    // Compare assignment with equivalence
2    public class AssignVsEquivalence {
3
4        // Define the main method
5        public static void main(String[] args) {
6
7            // Declare variables, and define each variable
8            int x = 0;              // Test variable
9
10           // Demonstrate assignment in a println statement
11           System.out.println("Before assignment:  x = " + x);
12           System.out.println( x = 1 );
13           System.out.println("After  assignment:  x = " + x);
```

```
14
15          // Demonstrate equivalence in a println statement
16          System.out.println("Before equivalence: x = " + x);
17          System.out.println( x == 2 );
18          System.out.println("After equivalence: x = " + x);
19
20      }
21  }
```

When this program is compiled and executed, the results are as shown below.

```
D:\book\java\chap3>java AssignVsEquivalence
Before assignment:  x = 0
1
After  assignment:  x = 1
Before equivalence: x = 1
false
After  equivalence: x = 1
```

In the hierarchy of operations, relational operators are evaluated after all arithmetic operators have been evaluated. Therefore, the following two expressions are equivalent (both are `true`):

$$7 + 3 < 2 + 11$$
$$(7 + 3) < (2 + 11)$$

If a comparison is between (for example) `double` and `int` values, then the `int` value is promoted to a `double` value before the comparison is performed. Comparisons between numerical data and character data are legal, the comparison being based on the order in which the characters appear within the character set (known as the *collating sequence*):

4 == 4.	true	(int is converted to double and comparison is made)
65 <= 'A'	true	(the sequence value of 'A' is 65, so 65 <= 65)

3.3.2   Logical Operators

Logical operators have *one or two boolean operands* that yield a boolean (true/false) result. There are six logical operators: && (logical AND), & (boolean logical AND), || (logical OR), | (boolean logical inclusive OR), ^ (boolean logical exclusive OR), and ! (logical NOT). These operators all accept boolean (true/false) operands and return a boolean result.

The general form of a binary logical operation is

$$l_1 \text{ op } l_2$$

where l_1 and l_2 are boolean expressions, variables, or constants, and `op` is one of the first five binary logical operators mentioned above.

The results of the operators are summarized in Tables 3.2 through 3.5, which are known as *truth tables*. These tables show the result of each operation for all possible combinations of l_1 and l_2.

TABLE 3.2 Truth Table & and && (AND) Operators

l_1	l_2	Result
false	false	false
false	true	false
true	false	false
true	true	true

Logical ANDs

The result of and AND operator is `true` if and only if both input operands are `true`. If either or both operands are `false`, the result is `false`, as shown in Table 3.2.

Note that there are two logical AND operators: `&&` and `&`. Why are there two, and what is the difference between them? The basic difference is that `&&` supports *short-circuit evaluations* (or *partial evaluations*), while `&` doesn't. That is, `&&` will evaluate expression l_1 and immediately return a `false` value if l_1 is `false`. If l_1 is `false`, the operator never evaluates l_2, because the result of the operator will be `false` regardless of the value of l_2. In contrast, the `&` operator always evaluates both l_1 and l_2 before returning an answer.

This difference is illustrated in the program shown below:

```
1    // This program illustrates the use of the AND operators
2    public class TestAnd {
3        // Define the main method
4        public static void main(String[] args) {
5
6            int i = 10, j = 9;
7            boolean test;
8
9            // Demonstrate &&
10           test = i > 10 && j++ > 10;
11           System.out.println(i);
12           System.out.println(j);
13           System.out.println(test);
14
15           // Demonstrate &
16           test = i > 10 & j++ > 10;
17           System.out.println(i);
18           System.out.println(j);
19           System.out.println(test);
20       }
21   }
```

When this program is executed, the results are:

```
D:\book\java\chap3>java TestAnd
10
9
false
10
10
false
```

Note that the `j++` on line 10 is never executed, since the first operand is already `false`. Therefore, the value of `j` remains 9. The `j++` on line 16 *is* executed, since the `&` operation always evaluates both operands before reaching a decision. Therefore, the value of `j` is increased to 10.

When should you use `&&` and when should you use `&` in a program? Most of the time, it doesn't matter which one is used. However, if you need to ensure that the second operand is evaluated every time a line is executed, you should use `&`. For example, the expression `j++` in line 16 above will always be executed, while the expression `j++` in line 10 will be evaluated only if `i > 10`.

Conversely, if it is not necessary to always evaluate l_2, then use the `&&` operator. In cases where the first operand is `false`, the partial evaluation will make the operation faster.

In addition, sometimes operand l_2 is valid only if the first operand l_1 is `true`. In such cases, evaluating l_2 while l_1 is `false` would cause an error. Using the `&&` operator will keep this from occurring.

GOOD PROGRAMMING PRACTICE

Use the `&` AND operator if you need to ensure that both operands are evaluated in an expression. Otherwise, use the `&&` AND operator, since the partial evaluation will make the operation faster in cases where the first operand is `false`.

Logical Inclusive ORs

The result of an inclusive OR operator is `true` if either of the input operands is `true`. If both are `false`, the result is `false`, as shown in Table 3.3.

TABLE 3.3 Truth Table for `|` and `||` (Inclusive OR) Operators

l_1	l_2	Result
false	false	false
false	true	true
true	false	true
true	true	true

Note that there are two inclusive OR operators: `||` and `|`. Why are there two, and what is the difference between them? The basic difference is that `||` supports partial evaluations, while `|` doesn't. That is, `||` will evaluate expression l_1 and immediately return a `true` value if l_1 is `true`. If l_1 is `true`, the operator never evaluates l_2, because the result of the operator will be `true` regardless of the value of l_2. In contrast, the `|` operator always evaluates both l_1 and l_2 before returning an answer.

This difference is illustrated in the program shown below:

```
1   // This program illustrates the use of the inclusive OR
2   public class TestOr {
3       // Define the main method
4       public static void main(String[] args) {
5
6           int i = 10, j = 9;
```

```
7          boolean test;
8
9          // Demonstrate ||
10         test = i > 9 || j++ > 10;
11         System.out.println(i);
12         System.out.println(j);
13         System.out.println(test);
14
15         // Demonstrate |
16         test = i > 9 | j++ > 10;
17         System.out.println(i);
18         System.out.println(j);
19         System.out.println(test);
20     }
21  }
```

When this program is executed, the results are

```
D:\book\java\chap3>java TestOr
10
9
true
10
10
true
```

Note that in the j++ on line 10 is never executed, since the first operand is already true. Therefore, the value of j remains 9. The j++ on line 16 *is* executed, since the | operation always evaluates both operands before reaching a decision. Therefore, the value of j is increased to 10.

When should you use || and when should you use | in a program? Most of the time, it doesn't matter which one is used. However, if you need the second operand to be evaluated every time a line is executed, you should use |. For example, the expression j++ in Line 16 above will always be executed, while the expression j++ in line 10 will be evaluated only if i > 10.

Conversely, if it is not necessary to always evaluate l_2, then use the || operator. In cases where the first operand is true, the partial evaluation will make the operation faster.

GOOD PROGRAMMING PRACTICE

Use the | inclusive OR operator if you need to ensure that both operands are evaluated in an expression. Otherwise, use the || operator, since the partial evaluation will make the operation faster in cases where the first operand is true.

Logical Exclusive OR

The result of an exclusive OR operator is true if and only if one operand is true and the other is false. If both operands are true or both are false, then the result is false, as shown in Table 3.4. Note that both operands must always be evaluated in order to calculate the result of an exclusive OR.

TABLE 3.4 Truth Table for ^ (Exclusive OR) Operator

I_1	I_2	Result
false	false	false
false	true	true
true	false	true
true	true	false

Logical NOT

The NOT operator is a unary operator, having only one operand. The result of a NOT operator is true if its operand is false, and false if its operand is true, as shown in Table 3.5.

TABLE 3.5 Truth Table for ! (NOT) Operator

I_1	Result
false	true
true	false

Using Logical Operators

To understand these operators, let's consider the following expressions and their results:

```
(7 > 6) && (2 < 1)        false
(7 > 6) || (2 < 1)        true
!(7 > 6)                  false
```

Remember that relational operators produce a boolean result. In the first case, `7 > 6` is true, and `2 < 1` is false. Thus the result of the logical AND `(7 > 6) && (2 < 1)` is false, while the result of the logical OR `(7 > 6) || (2 < 1)` is true. Similarly, since `7 > 6` is true, `!(7 > 6)` is false.

Logical operators are most commonly used to combine the results of two or more relational operators to create some test. For example, suppose that we are examining pairs of (x, y) points in a Cartesian plane, and we would like to determine if a point lies in the second quadrant. For a point to lie in the second quadrant, it must have an x value less than 0 and a y value greater than 0, as shown in Figure 3.5. A test to determine

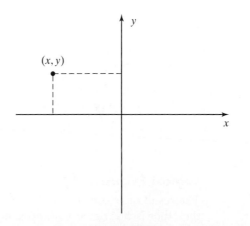

Figure 3.5. For a point (x, y) to lie in the second quadrant of a cartesian plane, its x-value must be less than zero and its y value greater than zero.

whether the point lies in the second quadrant would be:

```
boolean quadrant2;
...
quadrant2 = x < 0 && y > 0;
```

The result of the relational operator x < 0 is true or false, and the result of the relational operator y > 0 is also true or false. The logical operator then combines these two boolean values to calculate the result of the overall expression.

In the hierarchy of operations, logical operators are evaluated *after all arithmetic operations and all relational operators have been evaluated*. Therefore, the boolean results of the relational operators are calculated before the AND operator attempts to use them.

The hierarchy of all operations that we have seen so far is summarized in Table 3.6. In this table, all operators on the same line have equal precedence, and they are evaluated in the order indicated by the associativity property for that line.

TABLE 3.6   Hierarchy of Operations

Operators	Associativity	Type
( )	left to right	parentheses
++ −−	right to left	unary postfix
++ −− + − ! (type)	right to left	unary prefix
* / %	left to right	multiplicative
+ −	left to right	additive
< <= > >=	left to right	relational
== !-	left to right	equality
&	left to right	boolean logical AND
^	left to right	boolean logical exclusive OR
|	left to right	boolean logical inclusive OR
&&	left to right	logical AND
||	left to right	logical OR
?:	right to left	conditional (*described later in this chapter*)
= += −= *= /= %=	right to left	assignment

EXAMPLE 3.1

Logical Operators: Assume that the following variables are initialized with the values shown, and calculate the result of the specified expressions:

```
var1 = true;
var2 = true;
var3 = false;
```

	Expression	Result
(a)	var1 | var3	true
(b)	var1 && var3	false
(c)	var1 | var2	true
(d)	var1 ^ var2	false
(e)	var1 && var2 || var3	true
(f)	var1 | var2 & var3	true
(g)	(var1 | var2) & var3	false
(h)	! var1	false

The & operator is evaluated before the | operator in Java. Therefore, the parentheses in part (g) of the above example were required. If they had been absent, the expression in part (g) would have been evaluated in the order `var1 | (var2 & var3)`.

3.4   SELECTION STRUCTURES

Selection structures are Java statements that permit us to select and execute specific sections of code (called blocks) while skipping other sections of code. They are variations of the `if` structure and the `switch` structure.

3.4.1   The `if` Structure

The `if` structure specifies that a statement (or a block of code) will be executed *if and only if a certain boolean expression is true*. For example, suppose that we were writing a grading program, and we wanted to write out a statement that a student passed if and only if his or her grade was greater than 70. If the student's grade is less than or equal to 70, then the program will not write out anything. The plain-English pseudocode for such a structure would be

```
If the student's grade is greater than 70
    Print "Passed"
```

and the flowchart for this structure is shown in Figure 3.6.

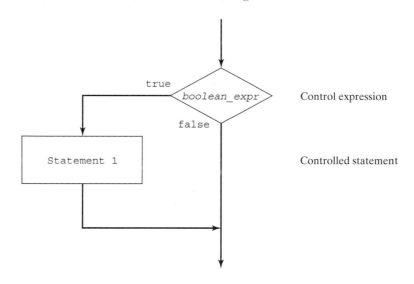

Figure 3.6. Flowchart for a simple `if` structure consisting of a control expression and a controlled statement. The controlled statement will be executed if and only if the control expression evaluates to `true`.

The Java `if` structure has the form

```
if ( boolean_expr )
    statement;
```

or

```
if ( boolean_expr ) statement;
```

If the boolean expression is true, the program executes the statement. If the boolean expression is false, then the program skips the statement and executes the next statement

To illustrate the use of the if/else structure, let's reconsider the quadratic equation once more. Suppose that we wanted to examine the discriminant of a quadratic equation and to tell a user whether the equation has real or complex roots. If the discriminant is greater than or equal to zero, there are real roots. Otherwise, the equation has complex roots. In pseudocode, this if/else structure would take the form

```
If (b*b - 4.*a*c) >= 0
    Write message that equation has real roots.
else
    Write message that equation has complex roots.
```

The Java statements to do this are

```
if ( (b*b - 4.*a*c) >= 0. )
    System.out.println("There are real roots.");
else
    System.out.println("There are two complex roots.");
```

Note that *the statement in the* if/else *clause of an* if/else *structure can be another* if/else *structure*. This cascading of structures allows us to make more complex selections. An example of cascaded if structures is shown below:

```
if (boolean_expr_1)
    statement 1;
else if (boolean_expr_2)
    statement 2;
else
    statement 3;
```

If *boolean_expr_1* is true, then the program executes statement 1 and skips to the statement following statement 3. Otherwise, the program tests the second boolean expression. If *boolean_expr_2* is true, then the program executes statement 2 and skips to the statement following statement 3. If both *boolean_expr_1* and *boolean_expr_2* are false, then the program executes statement 3. This structure might be more clearly represented as

```
if (boolean_expr_1)
    statement 1;
else
    if (boolean_expr_2)
        statement 2;
    else
        statement 3;
```

since this form emphasizes the fact that the later ifs are inside the else clauses of the previous ifs. Since Java ignores white space, both ways of writing this structure are equivalent. The flowchart corresponding to this cascaded if structure is shown in Figure 3.9.

Any number of if/else structures can be cascaded to produce arbitrarily complex selection structures.

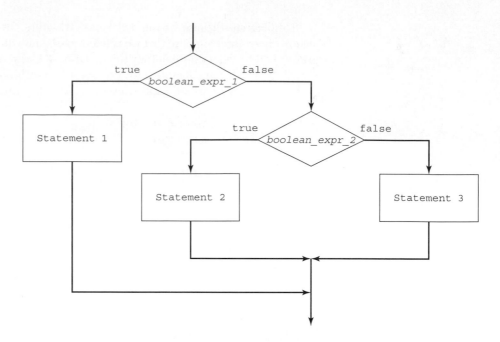

Figure 3.9. Flowchart of a pair of cascaded if/else structures.

To illustrate the use of cascaded if/else structures, let's reconsider the quadratic equation once more. Suppose that we wanted to examine the discriminant of a quadratic equation and tell a user whether the equation had two complex roots, two identical real roots, or two distinct real roots. In pseudocode, this construct would take the form

```
If (b*b - 4.*a*c) < 0
    Write message that equation has two complex roots.
else if (b*b - 4.*a*c) == 0.
    Write message that equation has two identical real roots.
else
    Write message that equation has two distinct real roots.
```

The Java statements to do this are

```
if ((b*b - 4.*a*c) < 0. )
    System.out.println("There are two complex roots.");
else if ( (b*b - 4.*a*c) == 0. )
    System.out.println("There are 2 identical real roots.");
else
    System.out.println("There are 2 distinct real roots.");
```

3.4.3 Executing Multiple Statements in an if Structure

The if and if/else structures are each designed to execute a *single statement* if a particular condition is true. What would happen if we needed to execute multiple statements in response to a condition? Java's answer to this problem is the **compound statement**.

A compound statement is a set of statements enclosed between a pair of braces ({ and }). A compound statement can be used anywhere in Java where an ordinary statement is expected. Thus, an if/else structure containing multiple lines looks like

```
if (logical_expr) {
    statement 1;
    statement 2;
    statement 3;
}
else {
    statement 4;
    statement 5;
    statement 6;
}
```

3.4.4   Examples Using if Structures

We will now look at two examples that illustrate the use of if structures.

EXAMPLE 3.2

SOLUTION

The Quadratic Equation: Design and write a program to solve for the roots of a quadratic equation, regardless of type.

We will follow the design steps outlined earlier in the chapter.

Determine the User Requirements

The user requirements for this program are trivial. We need to create a program that will solve for the roots of a quadratic equation, whether they are distinct real roots, repeated real roots, or complex roots. The required inputs are the coefficients a, b, and c of the quadratic equation

$$ax^2 + bx + c = 0 \tag{3.1}$$

They will be read from the standard input stream. The outputs from the program will be the roots of the quadratic equation, whether they are distinct real roots, repeated real roots, or complex roots. They will be written to the standard output stream.

Analysis and Decomposition

For the next few chapters this step will be trivial, because every program will have only one class and one method. In Chapter 6 we will begin learning how to decompose problems into separate methods, and in Chapter 7 we will begin learning how to decompose problems into separate classes. For now, there will be a single class, and only the main method within that class. We will call the class QuadraticEquation.

Detailed Design

There is only one method in this program. The main method can be broken down into three major sections, whose functions are input, processing, and output:

```
Read the input data
Calculate the roots
Write out the roots
```

We now break each of the above major sections into smaller, more detailed pieces. The first section reads the input data. This section can be refined and expanded into a series of prompts and reads for the required values. The expanded pseudocode for this section is:

```
Prompt the user for the coefficient a.
Read a
Prompt the user for the coefficient b.
Read b
Prompt the user for the coefficient c.
Read c
```

There are three possible ways to calculate the roots, depending on the value of the discriminant, so it is logical to implement this algorithm with an `if/else if/else` structure. Also, the output statements will vary depending on the types of roots, so the output statements should appear within the same structure. The resulting pseudocode is:

```
discriminant ← b*b - 4. * a * c
if discriminant > 0 {
    x1 ← ( -b + sqrt(discriminant) ) / ( 2. * a )
    x2 ← ( -b - sqrt(discriminant) ) / ( 2. * a )
    Write message that equation has two distinct real roots.
    Write out the two roots.
    }
else if discriminant equals 0 {
    x1 ← -b / ( 2. * a )
    Write message that equation has repeated real roots.
    Write out the repeated root.
    }
else {
    realPart ← -b / ( 2. * a )
    imagPart ← sqrt ( abs( discriminant ) ) / ( 2. * a )
    Write message that equation has two complex roots.
    Write out the two roots.
    }
```

Implementation: Convert Algorithms to Java Statements

The final Java code is shown in Figure 3.10. It is essentially a direct translation of the pseudocode. Note that the `if` structure is shown in boldface.

Testing

Next, we must test the program using real input data. Since there are three possible paths through the program, we must test all three before we can be certain that the program is working properly. From Equation (3.2), it is possible to verify the solutions to the equations given below:

$$x^2 + 5x + 6 = 0 \qquad x = -2, \text{ and } x = -3$$
$$x^2 + 4x + 4 = 0 \qquad x = -2$$
$$x^2 + 2x + 5 = 0 \qquad x = -1 \pm i2$$

```
/*
   Purpose:
     This program solves for the roots of a quadratic equation
     of the form a*x*x + b*x + c = 0.  It calculates the
     answers regardless of the type of roots that the equation
     possesses.

   Record of revisions:
       Date          Programmer           Description of change
       ====          ==========           =====================
     12/27/2001    S. J. Chapman          Original code
*/
import java.io.*;
public class QuadraticEquation {

   // Define the main method
   public static void main(String[] args) throws IOException {

      // Declare variables, and define each variable
      double a;              // Coefficient of x**2 term
      double b;              // Coefficient of x term
      double c;              // Constant term
      double discriminant;   // Discriminant of the equation
      double imag_part;      // Imag part of eqn (complex roots)
      double real_part;      // Real part of eqn (complex roots)
      double x1;             // 1st soln of eqn (real roots)
      double x2;             // 2nd soln of eqn (real roots)

      // Create a buffered reader
      BufferedReader in1 = new BufferedReader(
                        new InputStreamReader(System.in));//

      // Prompt the user for the coefficients of the equation
      System.out.println("This program solves for the roots of ");
      System.out.println("a quadratic equation of the form ");
      System.out.println("A * X**2 + B * X + C = 0.");
      System.out.print("Enter the coefficient A: ");
      a = Double.parseDouble( in1.readLine() );
      System.out.print("Enter the coefficient B: ");
      b = Double.parseDouble( in1.readLine() );
      System.out.print("Enter the coefficient C: ");
      c = Double.parseDouble( in1.readLine() );//

      // Calculate discriminant
      discriminant = b*b - 4. * a * c;//

      // Solve for the roots, depending on the discriminant
      if ( discriminant > 0. ) {

         // Two real roots...
         x1 = ( -b + Math.sqrt(discriminant) ) / ( 2. * a );
         x2 = ( -b - Math.sqrt(discriminant) ) / ( 2. * a );
         System.out.println("This equation has 2 real roots:");
         System.out.println("X1 = " + x1 + ", X2 = " + x2);
      }
```

Figure 3.10. Program to solve for the roots of a quadratic equation.

```
        else if ( discriminant == 0. ) {

            // One repeated root...
            x1 = ( -b ) / ( 2. * a );
            System.out.println("This equation has repeated real roots:");
            System.out.println("X1 = X2 = " + x1);
        }

        else {

            // Complex roots...
            real_part = ( -b ) / ( 2. * a );
            imag_part = Math.sqrt( Math.abs( discriminant ) ) / ( 2. * a );
            System.out.println("This equation has complex roots:");
            System.out.println("X1 = " + real_part + " +i " + imag_part);
            System.out.println("X2 = " + real_part + " -i " + imag_part);
        }
    }
}
```

Figure 3.10. (Continued).

If this program is compiled and then run three times with the above coefficients, the results are as shown below (user inputs are shown in boldface):

```
C:\book\java\chap3>java QuadraticEquation
This program solves for the roots of a quadratic
equation of the form A * X**2 + B * X + C = 0.
Enter the coefficient A: 1
Enter the coefficient B: 5
Enter the coefficient C: 6
This equation has two real roots:
X1 = -2.0, X2 = -3.0

C:\book\java\chap3>java QuadraticEquation
This program solves for the roots of a quadratic
equation of the form A * X**2 + B * X + C = 0.
Enter the coefficient A: 1
Enter the coefficient B: 4
Enter the coefficient C: 4
This equation has repeated real roots:
X1 = X2 = -2.0

C:\book\java\chap3>java QuadraticEquation
This program solves for the roots of a quadratic
equation of the form A * X**2 + B * X + C = 0.
Enter the coefficient A: 1
Enter the coefficient B: 2
Enter the coefficient C: 5
This equation has complex roots:
X1 = -1.0 +i 2.0
X2 = -1.0 -i 2.0
```

The program gives the correct answers for our test data in all three possible cases. ■

EXAMPLE 3.3

Evaluating a Function of Two Variables: Write a Java program to evaluate a function $f(x, y)$ for any two user-specified values x and y. The function $f(x, y)$ is defined as follows.

$$f(x, y) = \begin{cases} x + y & x \geq 0 \text{ and } y \geq 0 \\ x + y^2 & x \geq 0 \text{ and } y < 0 \\ x^2 + y & x < 0 \text{ and } y \geq 0 \\ x^2 + y^2 & x < 0 \text{ and } y < 0 \end{cases}$$

SOLUTION

The function $f(x, y)$ is evaluated differently, depending on the signs of the two independent variables x and y. To determine the proper equation to apply, we need to check for the signs of the x- and y-values supplied by the user.

Determine the User Requirements

The user requirements for this program are trivial. The program must evaluate the function $f(x, y)$ for any user-supplied values of x and y. The required inputs are the coefficients x and y. They will be read from the standard input stream. The outputs from the program will be the value of the function $f(x, y)$. It will be written to the standard output stream.

Analysis and Decomposition

Again, there will be a single class, and only the `main` method within that class. We will call the class `EvalFunction`.

Detailed Design

The `main` method can be broken down into three major sections, whose functions are input, processing, and output:

```
Read the input values x and y
Calculate f(x,y)
Write out f(x,y)
```

We will now decompose each of the above major sections into smaller, more detailed pieces. The first section reads the input data. This section can be refined and expanded into a series of prompts and reads for the required values. The expanded pseudocode for this section is

```
Prompt the user for the value x.
Read x
Prompt the user for the value x.
Read y
```

The second section performs the actual calculations. There are four possible ways to calculate the function $f(x, y)$, depending on the values of x and y, so it is logical to implement this algorithm with a four-branched `if/else` structure.

```
if x >= 0 and y >= 0
    fun ← x + y
else if x >= 0 and y < 0
    fun ← x + y**y
```

```
          else if x < 0 and y >= 0
              fun ← x*x + y
          else
              fun ← x*x + y**y
```

The third section displays the results. It does not need further elaboration.

```
          Write out f(x,y)
```

Implementation: Convert algorithms to Java statements

The final Java code is shown in Figure 3.11.

```
/*
   Purpose:
     This program solves the function f(x,y) for a
     user-specified x and y, where f(x,y) is defined as:

                         _
                        |
                        |    x + y               x >= 0 and y >= 0
                        |    x + y*y             x >= 0 and y < 0
         f(x,y) =       |    x*x + y             x < 0  and y >= 0
                        |    x*x + y*y           x < 0  and y < 0
                        |
                        |_

   Record of revisions:
       Date          Programmer            Description of change
       ====          ==========            =====================
     01/02/2002    S. J. Chapman           Original code
*/
import java.io.*;
public class EvalFunction {

   // Define the main method
   public static void main(String[] args) throws IOException {

      // Declare variables, and define each variable
      double x;            // First independent variable
      double y;            // Second independent variable
      double fun;          // Resulting function
      String str;          // Input string

      // Create a buffered reader
      BufferedReader in1 = new BufferedReader(
                          new InputStreamReader(System.in));

      // Prompt the user for the coefficients of the equation
      System.out.print("Enter x: ");
      str = in1.readLine();
      x = Double.parseDouble(str);
      System.out.print("Enter y: ");
      str = in1.readLine();
      y = Double.parseDouble(str);
```

Figure 3.11.   Program EvalFunction from Example 3.3.

```
        // Calculate the function f(x,y) based on the signs
        // of x and y
        if ( (x >= 0) && (y >= 0) )
            fun = x + y;
        else if ( (x >= 0) && (y < 0) )
            fun = x + y*y;
        else if ( (x < 0) && (y >= 0) )
            fun = x*x + y;
        else
            fun = x*x + y*y;

        // Write the value of the function.
        System.out.println("The value of the function is: " + fun);
    }
}
```

Figure 3.11. (Continued).

Testing

Next, we must test the program using real input data. Since there are four possible paths through the program, we must test all four paths before we can be certain that the program is working properly. We will execute the program with the four sets of input values $(x, y) = (2, 3)$, $(-2, 3)$, $(2, -3)$, and $(-2, -3)$. Calculating by hand, we see that

$$f(2, 3) = 2 + 3 = 5$$
$$f(2, -3) = 2 + (-3)^2 = 11$$
$$f(-2, 3) = (-2)^2 + 3 = 7$$
$$f(-2, -3) = (-2)^2 + (-3)^2 = 13$$

If this program is compiled and then run four times with the above values, the results are:

```
C:\book\java\chap3>java EvalFunction
Enter x: 2
Enter y: 3
The value of the function is: 5.0

C:\book\java\chap3>java EvalFunction
Enter x: 2
Enter y: -3
The value of the function is: 11.0

C:\book\java\chap3>java EvalFunction
Enter x: -2
Enter y: 3
The value of the function is: 7.0

C:\book\java\chap3>java EvalFunction
Enter x: -2
Enter y: -3
The value of the function is: 13.0
```

The program gives the correct answers for our test values in all four possible cases. ∎

3.4.5 Testing for Equality in `if` Structures

A common problem with `if` statements occurs when *floating-point* (`float` *and* `double`) *variables are tested for equality*. Because of small roundoff errors during floating-point arithmetic operations, two numbers that theoretically should be equal will differ by a tiny amount, and the test for equality will fail. This failure can cause a program to execute the wrong statement in an `if`/`else` structure, producing a subtle and hard-to-find bug. For example, consider the quadratic-equation program of Example 3.2. We concluded that a quadratic equation had two identical real roots if the discriminant $b^2 - 4ac == 0$. Depending on the coefficients of the equation, roundoff errors might cause the discriminant to be a very small nonzero number (say 10^{-14}) when it should theoretically be zero. If this happened, then the test for identical real roots would fail.

When working with floating-point variables, it is usually a good idea to replace a test for equality with a test for *near-equality*. For example, instead of testing to see if the `double` value x is equal to `10.0`, you should test to see if $|x - 10.0| < 1e{-}10$. Any value of x between 9.9999999999 and 10.0000000001 will satisfy the latter test, so roundoff error will not cause problems. In Java statements,

```
if ( x == 10.0 )
```

would be replaced by

```
if ( Math.abs(x - 10.0) <= 1E-10 )
```

The potential problem caused in testing for equality is illustrated in the program shown below. This program calculates the value of sin 2π, which theoretically should be exactly zero. It then tests to see if the result is zero using both the test for exact equality and the test for near-equality.

```
1    // This program illustrates problems in testing
2    // for exact equality
3    public class TestEquality {
4        // Define the main method
5        public static void main(String[] args) {
6
7            final double EPS = 1.0e-14;   // Error bound
8            double sinX;                   // sin(x)
9
10           // Calculate sin(2*PI)
11           sinX = Math.sin( Math.PI );
12
13           // Test for equality
14           System.out.print("Equality test:       ");
15           if (sinX == 0.0)
16              System.out.println("sin(2*PI) = 0");
17           else
18              System.out.println("sin(2*PI) != 0");
19
20           // Test for near equality
21           System.out.print("Near equality test: ");
22           if ( Math.abs(sinX - 0.0) < EPS )
23              System.out.println("sin(2*PI) = 0");
24           else
25              System.out.println("sin(2*PI) != 0");
26
```

```
27              // Print actual value of sin(x)
28              System.out.println("\nActual values:");
29              System.out.println("sin(2*PI) = " + sinX);
30          }
31      }
```

When this program is executed, the results are:

```
D:\book\java\chap3>java TestEquality
Equality test:       sin(2*PI) != 0
Near equality test: sin(2*PI) = 0

Actual values:
sin(2*PI) = 1.2246063538223773E-16
```

The test for *exact* equality failed because of the very slight roundoff error in the calculation of sin 2π, while the test for near-equality worked properly.

GOOD PROGRAMMING PRACTICE

When working with floating-point values, it is a good idea to replace the test for equality with tests for near-equality to avoid improper results due to cumulative roundoff errors.

3.4.6   Nested `if` Structures

The `if` structure is very flexible. Since any number of `if` structures can be cascaded in an if/else if/else if/else structure, where each succeeding `if` lies in the `else` clause of the preceding `if`, it is possible to implement any desired selection construct. When an `if` structure lies inside another `if` structure, they are said to be **nested**.

Note that if two `if` structures are nested, then the inner structure must lie *entirely* within either the `if` clause or the `else` clause of the outer one — it cannot stretch between them (see Figure 3.12).

Nested `if` structures are very useful and flexible, but they are also a very common source of bugs in Java programs. This happens because novice programmers often make mistakes in the use of `else` clauses. *The Java compiler always associates an `else` statement with the immediately preceding `if` statement*, unless told to do otherwise by the proper use of braces ({ }). Bugs can occur when using `else` clauses with nested `if` structures, because the Java compiler associates the `else` clause with a different `if` than the programmer expected it to.

Let's take a simple example to illustrate this problem. Suppose that we want to test two variables x and y to determine if they are both greater than zero. If they are, we will print out the string "x and y are > 0". If x is <= 0, we would like to print out the string "x <= 0" instead. A programmer might attempt to implement this behavior as follows:

```
if ( x > 0)
    if (y > 0)
        System.out.println("x and y are > 0");
else
    System.out.println("x <= 0");
```

At first glance, this code seems to be saying that if x > 0, then we will test to see if y > 0 and print the string if true, while if x <= 0, we will print out "x <= 0". In

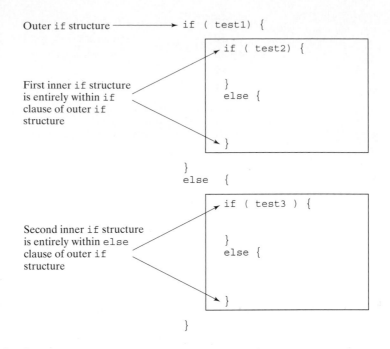

Outer `if` structure ──────────▶ `if ( test1) {`

First inner `if` structure is entirely within `if` clause of outer `if` structure

```
    if ( test2) {


    }
    else {



    }
}
else  {
```

Second inner `if` structure is entirely within `else` clause of outer `if` structure

```
    if ( test3 ) {


    }
    else {



    }
}
```

Figure 3.12. If two `if` structures are nested, the inner `if` structure must lie entirely within either the `if` or the `else` clause of the outer `if` structure—it cannot stretch across both of them.

other words, the `else` clause seems to be associated with the `if  (x > 0)` statement. However, *the Java compiler associates the `else` with the immediately preceding `if` statement*, so the compiler actually interprets the structure as

```
if ( x > 0)
    if (y > 0)
        System.out.println("x and y are > 0");
    else
        System.out.println("x <= 0");
```

The code will actually print out `"x <= 0"` when `x > 0` and `y <= 0`! This sort of error is known as the **dangling-else problem**.

The dangling-else problem can be avoided by using braces to force the `else` to be associated with the proper `if`.

```
if ( x > 0) {
    if (y > 0)
        System.out.println("x and y are > 0");
}
else
    System.out.println("x <= 0");
```

The braces indicate to the compiler that the inner `if` structure is inside the `if` clause of the outer `if`, and that the `else` is matched with the outer `if`. (If the `else` had been *inside* the braces, it would have been matched with the inner `if`.)

GOOD PROGRAMMING PRACTICE

Use braces in nested `if` structures to make your intentions clear and avoid dangling `else` clauses.

Another common error with cascaded `if`/`else` structures occurs when a programmer fails to carefully consider the order of tests that he or she is performing. For example, suppose that we want to write out messages depending on the current temperature in degrees Fahrenheit:

$$\begin{array}{ll}
\texttt{temp} < 60 & \text{``cold''} \\
\texttt{temp} > 70 & \text{``warm''} \\
\texttt{temp} > 90 & \text{``hot''}
\end{array}$$

One possible structure might be

```
if (temp < 60)
    System.out.println("cold");
else if (temp > 70)
    System.out.println("warm");
else if (temp > 90)
    System.out.println("hot");
```

This structure will compile and execute, but *it will not work properly*. If the temperature is greater than 90, we would like to print out "hot". However, the statement `if (temp > 70)` will be executed first, and since it is true, the message "warm" will be printed out. *The test `if (temp > 90)` will never be executed*. This is an example of a logical error in a program.

If the statements were restructured as shown below, they would work correctly.

```
if (temp > 90)
    System.out.println("hot");
else if (temp > 70)
    System.out.println("warm");
else if (temp < 60)
    System.out.println("cold");
```

PROGRAMMING PITFALLS

Carefully consider the order in which you perform tests in you `if` structures to avoid creating incorrect branches.

3.4.7 The Conditional Operator

The **conditional operator** (`?:`) is essentially a compact `if`/`else` structure. It is a **ternary operator**, which means that it takes three arguments that together form a conditional expression. The first operand is a `boolean` expression, whose result must be either `true` or `false`. The second operand is the value of the expression if the condition is true, while the third is the value of the expression if the condition is false. For example, the `if`/`else` structure

```
if ( grade > 70 )
    System.out.println( "Passed");
else
    System.out.println( "Failed");
```

could also be written with the conditional operator as

```
System.out.println( grade > 70 ? "Passed" : "Failed");
```

The precedence of the conditional operator is very low, ranking after all relational and logical operators and before assignment operators, so the expression `grade > 70` is evaluated to a `boolean` result before the conditional operator is evaluated.

3.4.8 The `switch` Structure

The `switch` structure is another form of selection. It allows a program to select one of many *mutually exclusive* possibilities, depending on the value of the *switch_expr*, which must be an integer or character value. The general form of a `switch` structure is:

```
switch (switch_expr) {
   case case_selector_1:
      Statement 1;        //
      Statement 2;        // Block 1
                          //

      ...
      break;
   case case_selector_2:
      Statement 1;        //
      Statement 2;        // Block 2
      ...                 //
      break;
   ...
   ...
   default:
      Statement 1;        //
      Statement 2;        // Block n
      ...                 //
}
```

where *switch_expr* is an integer or character expression, and *case_selector_1*, *case_selector_2*, and so on, are unique integer or character constants. (No two case selectors can be the same.) The flowchart for a switch structure is shown in Figure 3.13.

When a `switch` structure is encountered, Java evaluates *switch_expr*, and execution jumps to the case whose selector matches the value of the expression. For example, if *switch_expr* evaluates to 1, then the code will jump to `case 1`, etc. The program executes statements in order from that point on until a `break` statement is encountered, skipping then to the first statement after the end of the `switch` structure.

If *switch_expr* does not match any case selector, execution will jump to the `default` case if it is present. If it is not present, execution continues with the first statement after the end of the switch.

A program containing a simple `switch` structure is shown below. The switch expression a is read from the standard input stream, and cases 1, 2, and `default` are defined. Note that the `switch` structure is shown in boldface.

```
1   // This program tests the switch structure
2   import chapman.io.*;
3   public class TestSwitch {
4
5      // Define the main method
6      public static void main(String[] args) {
7
8         int a;
9
10        // Create a StdIn object
```

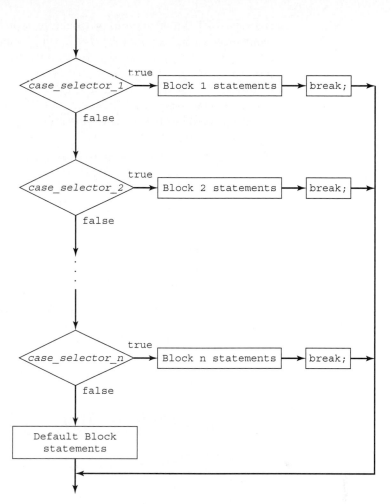

Figure 3.13.   Flowchart of a switch structure.

```
11              StdIn in = new StdIn();
12
13              // Prompt for an integer
14              System.out.print("Enter an integer: ");
15              a = in.readInt();
16
17              // Switch
18              switch (a) {
19                case 1:
20                  System.out.println("Value is 1");
21                  break;
22                case 2:
23                  System.out.println("Value is 2");
24                  break;
25                default:
26                  System.out.println("Other than 1 or 2");
27              } // End switch
28              System.out.println("After switch");
29          }
30    }
```

If a value of 1 is read into this program, the switch expression a will be 1, so the statements from case 1 until the break will be executed, followed by the first statement after the end of the switch structure. Similarly, if a value of 2 is read into this program, the switch expression a will be 2, so the statements from case 2 until the break will be executed, followed by the first statement after the end of the switch structure. If any value other than 1 or 2 is read in, then the statements after default will be executed, followed by the first statement after the switch.

```
C:\book\java\chap3>java TestSwitch
Enter an integer: 1
Value is 1
After switch

C:\book\java\chap3>java TestSwitch
Enter an integer: 2
Value is 2
After switch

C:\book\java\chap3>java TestSwitch
Enter an integer: 17
Other than 1 or 2
After switch
```

GOOD PROGRAMMING PRACTICE

The switch structure may be used to select among *mutually exclusive* options based on the results of a single integer or character expression.

Note that the break statements are essential for the proper operation of a switch structure. If they are missing, then execution will "fall through" from the selected case into the cases following it. For example, suppose that the switch structure in the previous program did not have break statements:

```java
switch (a) {
   case 1:
      System.out.println("Value is 1");
   case 2:
      System.out.println("Value is 2");
   default:
      System.out.println("Other than 1 or 2");
}
```

then the results would have been as shown:

```
C:\book\java\chap3>java TestSwitchBad
Enter an integer: 1
Value is 1
```

```
Value is 2
Other than 1 or 2
After switch

C:\book\java\chap3>java TestSwitchBad
Enter an integer: 2
Value is 2
Other than 1 or 2
After switch

C:\book\java\chap3>java TestSwitchBad
Enter an integer: 17
Other than 1 or 2
After switch
```

As you can see, the program will still compile properly and execute, but the results will be incorrect! Be careful—this error can produce subtle and hard-to-find bugs in your programs.

PROGRAMMING PITFALLS

Be sure to include `break` statements in each case of a `switch` structure, so that only the statements in that case are executed when the case is selected.

The `switch` structure is never really necessary, since any selection that can be represented by a `switch` can also be represented by a cascaded `if/else` structure. For example, the switch in the above program could be rewritten as

```
if (a == 1)
    System.out.println("Value is 1");
else if (a == 2)
    System.out.println("Value is 2");
else
    System.out.println("Other than 1 or 2");
```

The `switch` structure is just a limited form of the cascaded `if/else` structure. However, some programmers prefer it for stylistic reasons.

3.5   GUI INPUT AND OUTPUT

The vast majority of Java programs use a Graphical User Interface (GUI) to communicate with the user. A GUI-based program will have one or more graphical windows, with input (push buttons, menu selections, text values) and output (data, plots, and so on) being displayed in the windows. Users supply data to GUI-based programs in windows, instead of using the standard input and output streams. We will learn how to write GUI-based programs beginning in Chapter 13. These programs are generally too complicated for us to write until we have learned much more about the Java language.

However, the Java API includes a special class called `JOptionPane` that allows a user to create GUI dialog boxes with a single statement. Some of the methods in this class display information, or prompt a user to enter input data as a character string. This class is a part of the `javax.swing` package, which must be imported into any program using class `JOptionPane`.

Two important methods in class JOptionPane are showMessageDialog and showInputDialog. Method showMessageDialog displays a user-defined message in a dialog box, and method showInputDialog prompts a user for an input string. The simplest forms of these two methods are described in Table 3.7.

TABLE 3.7 JOptionPane Methods

Method Name and Parameters	Comments
JOptionPane.showMessageDialog(null, str)	Displays the contents of String str in a dialog box.
str2 = JOptionPane.showInputDialog(null, str1)	Displays the contents of String str1 in a dialog box, and returns user input in String str2.

A sample program using these two methods is shown in Figure 3.14(a). This program uses method showInputDialog to prompt the user to enter a character string and uses method showMessageDialog to display the resulting string. The input dialog and message dialog boxes produced by this program are also shown in Figure 3.14. Note that this program imports the javax.swing package, so that the JOptionPane class will be available in the program.

Also, the method System.exit(0) is used to terminate the program. This call is always necessary to end GUI-based programs—we will use it regularly in all such programs that we create. The argument 0 here indicates that the program terminated successfully; a nonzero number would indicate that some sort of error had occurred. Under Windows-, Linux-, or Unix-based computer systems, this value is passed back to the command window that started the Java program. The batch files (on Windows-based computers) or shell scripts (on Linux- and Unix-based computers) can use this return value to determine how to respond when a program error occurs. Since the System class is in the java.lang package, it does not have to be explicitly imported into the program.

```
1   // This program tests input & message dialog boxes.
2   import javax.swing.*;
3   public class TestDialog {
4
5      // Define the main method
6      public static void main(String[] args) {
7
8         // Create an input dialog
9         str = JOptionPane.showInputDialog( null,
10           "Enter a character string:" );
11
12        // Display result
13        JOptionPane.showMessageDialog( null,
14           "String = " + str );
15
16        // Stop program
17        System.exit(0);
18     }
19  }
```

(a)

Figure 3.14. (a) Program that displays input and message dialog boxes. (b) The resulting input dialog box. (c) The resulting message dialog box.

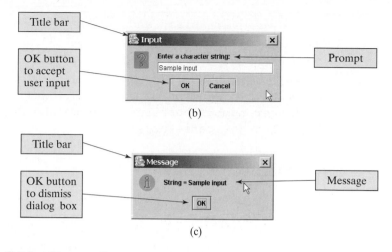

Figure 3.14. (Continued).

Once a `String` has been read in using the input dialog box, it can be converted to an `int`, `double`, or `boolean` value using the methods in Table 3.7.

EXAMPLE 3.4

Selecting the Day of the Week with a switch Structure: Write a program that reads an integer from the standard input stream and displays the day of the week corresponding to that integer. Use GUI dialog boxes in your program to read the input data and display the resulting day of week. Also, be sure to handle the case of an illegal input value.

SOLUTION

In this example, we prompt the user to enter an integer between 1 and 7. We use a `switch` structure to select the day of the week corresponding to that number, using the convention that Sunday is the first day of the week. The switch structure will also include a default case to handle illegal days of the week. The resulting program is shown in Figure 3.15.

```
/*
   Purpose:
     This program reads an input integer, and prints the
     day of the week corresponding to that integer.

   Record of revisions:
       Date          Programmer              Description of change
       ====          ==========              =====================
    12/29/2001   S. J. Chapman             Original code
*/
import javax.swing.*;
public class DayOfWeek {

   // Define the main method
   public static void main(String[] args) {
```

Figure 3.15. Program DayOfWeek from Example 3.4.

```java
// Declare variables, and define each variable
int day;              // Number of day
String str;           // String

// Prompt the user for the day of the week.
str = JOptionPane.showInputDialog( null,
    "Enter number corresponding to the day of the week:" );
day = Integer.parseInt(str);

// Get string with day of week
switch ( day ) {
    case 1:
        str = "Day " + day + " is Sunday";
        break;
    case 2:
        str = "Day " + day + " is Monday";
        break;
    case 3:
        str = "Day " + day + " is Tuesday";
        break;
    case 4:
        str = "Day " + day + " is Wednesday";
        break;
    case 5:
        str = "Day " + day + " is Thursday";
        break;
    case 6:
        str = "Day " + day + " is Friday";
        break;
    case 7:
        str = "Day " + day + " is Saturday";
        break;
    default:
        str = "Day " + day + " is Illegal";
        break;
}

// Display day of week
JOptionPane.showMessageDialog( null, str );

// Stop program
System.exit(0);
    }
}
```

Figure 3.15. (Continued).

When this program is executed, the results are as shown in Figure 3.16. As you can see, this program produces the right day of week for legal input values, and a statement of illegality for illegal input values. The program appears to be working correctly.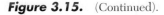

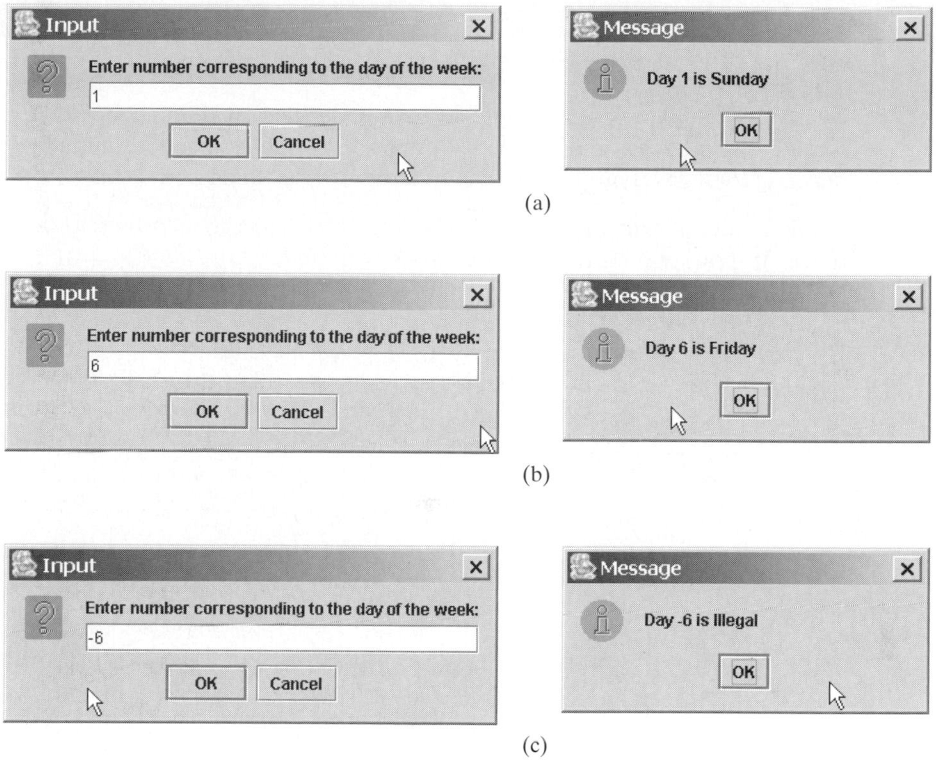

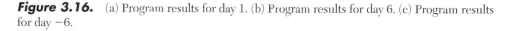

Figure 3.16. (a) Program results for day 1. (b) Program results for day 6. (c) Program results for day −6.

QUIZ 3-1

This quiz provides a quick check to see if you have understood the concepts introduced in Sections 3.1 through 3.5. If you have trouble with the quiz, reread the section, ask your instructor, or discuss the material with a fellow student. The answers are found in the back of the book.

1. Suppose that the `double` variables a, b, and c contain the values −10., 0.1, and 2.1, respectively, and that the `boolean` variables b1, b2, and b3 contain the values `true`, `false`, and `false`, respectively. Is each of the following expressions legal or illegal? If an expression is legal, what will its result be?

    (a) `a > b || b > c`

    (b) `(! a) || b1`

    (c) `b1 & ! b2`

    (d) `a < b == b < c`

    (e) `b1 || b2 && b3`

    (f) `b1 | b2 && b3`

    Write Java statements that perform the functions described below.

2. If x is greater than or equal to zero, then assign the square root of x to variable `sqrtX` and print out the result. Otherwise, print out an error message about the argument of the square-root function, and set `sqrtX` to zero.

3. A variable `fun` is calculated as `numerator / denominator`. If the absolute value of `denominator` is less than 1.0E-30, write "Divide by 0 error." Otherwise, calculate and print out `fun`.

4. The cost per mile for a rented vehicle is $0.50 for the first 100 miles, $0.30 for the next 200 miles, and $0.20 for all miles in excess of 300 miles. Write Java statements that determine the total cost and the average cost per mile for a given number of miles (stored in variable `distance`).

   Examine the following Java statements. Are they correct or incorrect? If they are correct, what is output by them? If they are incorrect, what is wrong with them?

5.
```java
if (volts > 125)
    System.out.println("WARNING: High voltage on line.");
if (volts < 105)
    System.out.println("WARNING: Low voltage on line.");
else
    System.out.println("Line voltage is within tolerances.");
```

6.
```java
double i = 3., j = 5., k;
k = i > j ? i / j : j / i;
System.out.println("k = " + k);
```

7.
```java
double a = 2 * Math.PI;
double b;
switch( a ) {
    case 1:
        b = Math.sqrt(a);
        break;
    case 2:
        b = Math.pow(a,3);
        break;
    default:
        b = a;
}
```

8.
```java
int a;
double b;
a = 5/2;
switch( a ) {
    case 1:
        b = 10;
    case 2:
        b = 0;
        break;
    default
        b = a;
}
```

9.
```java
if (temperature > 37.)
    System.out.println("Human body temperature exceeded.");
Else if (temperature > 100.)
    System.out.println("Boiling point of water exceeded.");
```

SUMMARY

- Pseudocode is a hybrid mixture of Java and English used to express programming thoughts without worrying about the details of Java syntax.
- The relational operators (>, >=, <, <=, ==, !=) compare two numerical operands, and produce a boolean result based on that comparison.
- The logical operators (&&, &, ||, |, ^, !) accept two boolean operands and produce a boolean result based on the values of the operands. The results of the operations are given in Tables 3.2 through 3.5.
- The hierarchy of Java operations is summarized in Table 3.6.
- Selection structures are Java statements that permit a program to select and execute specific sections of code (statements or compound statements) while skipping other sections of code.
- The `if` selection structure executes a code block if its condition is `true` and skips the code block if its condition is `false`.
- The `if/else` selection structure executes one code block if its condition is `true` and another code block if its condition is `false`.
- The Java compiler always associates an `else` clause with the most recent `if`, unless braces are used to force it to associate the `else` clause with a specific `if` statement.
- The conditional operator (`?:`) is essentially a compact `if/else` structure that selects the value of one of two possible expressions depending on the result of a boolean control expression.
- The `switch` selection structure allows a program to select one of many sets of statements to execute based on the value of an integer control expression. The cases in the `switch` structure must be mutually exclusive.
- Data can also be read and results displayed using GUI-based dialog boxes. These boxes are created using the `JOptionPane` class in the `javax.swing` package.

SUMMARY OF GOOD PROGRAMMING PRACTICES

The following guidelines introduced in this chapter will help you to develop good programs:

1. Follow the steps of the program design process to produce reliable, understandable Java programs.
2. Always indent the body of any structure by three or more spaces to improve the readability of the code.
3. When working with floating-point values, it is a good idea to replace the test for equality with tests for near equality to avoid improper results due to cumulative roundoff errors.
4. Use braces in nested `if` structures to make your intentions clear and avoid dangling `else` clauses.
5. The `switch` structure may be used to select among *mutually exclusive* options based on the results of a single integer or character expression.
6. Be sure to include `break` statements in each case of a `switch` structure, so that only the statements in that case are executed when the case is selected.

TERMINOLOGY

algorithm	compound statement
alpha release	conditional operator
beta release	Critical Design Review (CDR)
break statement	dangling-else problem

flowchart	selection
if structure	Software Requirement Specification (SRS)
if/else structure	Software Test Description (STD)
JOptionPane class	Software Test Plan (STP)
Interface Requirement Specification (IRS)	structure
logical operator	structured program
nested if structures	switch structure
null statement	System Requirements Review (SRR)
Preliminary Design Review (PDR)	System/Subsystem Design Document (SSDD)
pseudocode	ternary operator
relational operator	top-down design
repetition	unit testing

Exercises

1. The tangent function is defined as $\tan \theta = \sin \theta / \cos \theta$. This expression can be evaluated to solve for the tangent as long as the magnitude of $\cos \theta$ is not too near to 0. (If $\cos \theta$ is 0, evaluating the equation for $\tan \theta$ will produce the non-numerical value Inf.) Assume that θ is given in degrees, and write Java statements to evaluate $\tan \theta$ as long as the magnitude of $\cos \theta$ is greater than or equal to 10^{-20}. If the magnitude of $\cos \theta$ is less than 10^{-20}, write out an error message instead.

2. Which of the following expressions are legal in Java? If an expression is legal, evaluate it.

   (a) `5.5 >= 5`

   (b) `20 > 20`

   (c) `!(6 > 5)`

   (d) `15 <= 'A'`

   (e) `true > false`

   (f) `35 / 17. > 35 / 17`

   (g) `17.5 && (3.3 > 2)`

3. The following Java statements are intended to alert a user to dangerously high oral thermometer readings (values are in degrees Fahrenheit). Are they correct or incorrect? If they are incorrect, explain why and correct them.

   ```
   if ( temp < 97.5 )
      System.out.println("Temperature below normal");
   else if ( temp > 97.5 )
      System.out.println("Temperature normal");
   else if ( temp > 99.5 )
      System.out.println("Temperature slightly high");
   else if ( temp > 103.0 )
      System.out.println("Temperature dangerously high");
   ```

4. The cost of sending a package by an express delivery service is $10.00 for the first two pounds, and $3.75 for each pound or fraction thereof over 2 pounds. If the package weighs more than 70 pounds, a $10.00 excess-weight surcharge is added to the cost. No package over 100 pounds will be accepted. Write a program

that accepts the weight of a package in pounds and computes the cost of mailing the package. Be sure to handle the case of overweight packages. Use GUI-based I/O in your program.

5. Modify program `QuadraticEquation` to treat test for near-equality instead of equality. The discriminant should be considered to be equal to zero if $|b^2 - 4ac| < 10^{-14}$.

6. The inverse sine method `Math.asin(x)` is defined only for the range $-1.0 \le x \le 1.0$. If x is outside this range, an error will occur when the function is evaluated. The following Java statements calculate the inverse sine of a number if it is in the proper range, and print an error message if it is not. Assume that x and `inverseSine` are both type `double`. Is this code correct or incorrect? If it is incorrect, explain why and correct it.

```
if ( Math.abs(x) <= 1.0 )
    inverseSine = Math.asin(x);
else
    System.out.println(x + " is out of range!");
```

7. What is wrong with the following code segment?

```
switch (n) {
case 1:
    System.out.println("Number is 1");
case 2:
    System.out.println("Number is 2");
    break;
default:
    System.out.println("Number is not 1 or 2");
    break;
}
```

8. Write a Java program that reads an integer value between 1 and 12 and prints out the corresponding month of the year. Use a `switch` structure to select the month to print out, and use dialog boxes for all input and output. Also, be sure to handle the case of an illegal input value.

9. Write a Java program to evaluate the function

$$y(x) = \ln \frac{1}{1 - x} \tag{3.3}$$

for any user-specified value of x, where ln is the natural logarithm (logarithm to the base e). Note that the natural logarithm is defined only for positive values; when an illegal value of x is entered, tell the user and terminate the program. Use the standard input and standard output streams in your program.

10. The power supplied to a dc electric motor can be calculated from the equation

$$P = VI \tag{3.4}$$

where P is the power supplied to the motor in watts, V is the rms voltage supplied to the terminals of the motor in volts, and I is the current flowing into the motor in amps. Therefore, if the power and voltage of the motor are known, the current supplied to the motor can be calculated by solving Equation (3.4) for I:

$$I = \frac{P}{V} \tag{3.5}$$

Assume that an electrical supply store sells 10-amp, 20-amp, and 30-amp cables. Write a program that accepts the power and voltage supplied to a motor and recommends one of the available cable sizes for use with the motor. The program should also handle the case where no available cable size is acceptable. You may use any form of I/O that you desire.

11. **Refraction** When a ray of light passes from a region with an index of refraction n_1 into a region with a different index of refraction n_2, the light ray is bent (see Figure 3.17). The angle of bending is given by *Snell's law*

$$n_1 \sin \theta_1 = n_2 \sin \theta_2 \tag{3.6}$$

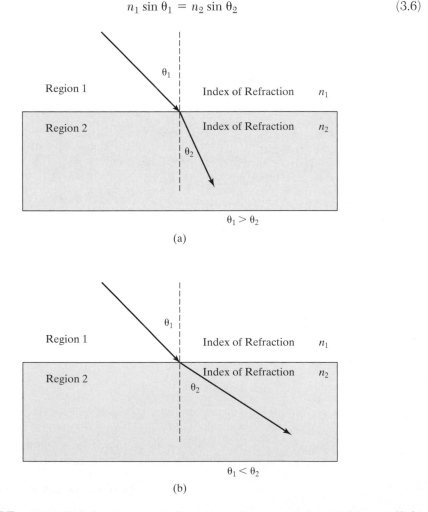

Figure 3.17. A ray of light bends as it passes from one medium into another. (a) If the ray of light passes from a region with a low index of refraction into one with a higher index of refraction, the ray of light bends more toward the vertical. (b) If the ray of light passes from a region with a high index of refraction into one with a lower index of refraction, the ray of light bends away from the vertical.

where θ_1 is the angle of incidence of the light in the first region, and θ_2 is the angle of incidence of the light in the second region. Using Snell's law, it is possible to predict the angle of incidence of a light ray in Region 2 if the angle of incidence θ_1 in Region 1 and the indices of refraction n_1 and n_2 are known. The equation to perform this calculation is

$$\theta_2 = \sin^{-1}\left(\frac{n_1}{n_2}\sin\theta_1\right) \tag{3.7}$$

Write a Java program to calculate the angle of incidence (in degrees) of a light ray in Region 2, given the angle of incidence θ_1 (in degrees) in Region 1 and the indices of refraction n_1 and n_2. (*Note:* If $n_1 > n_2$, then for some angles θ_1, Equation (3.7) will have no real solution, because the absolute value of the quantity $\left(\frac{n_1}{n_2}\sin\theta_1\right)$ will be greater than 1.0. When this occurs, all light is reflected back into Region 1, and no light passes into Region 2 at all. Your program must be able to recognize and properly handle this condition.) Test your program by running it for the following two cases: (a) $n_1 = 1.0$, $n_2 = 1.7$, and $\theta_1 = 45°$ (b) $n_1 = 1.7$, $n_2 = 1.0$, and $\theta_1 = 45°$.

4

Repetition Structures

This chapter focuses on a different type of structure that allows us to control the order in which Java statements are executed: repetition structures or loops. Repetition structures are Java structures that permit us to execute a sequence of statements more than once. There are three basic types of repetition structures: **while** loops, **do/while** loops, and **for** loops. The first two repeat a sequence of statements an indefinite number of times until some specified control condition becomes `false`. In contrast, the `for` loop repeats a sequence of statements a specified number of times, the number of repetitions being known before the loop starts.

4.1 THE `while` LOOP

A **while loop** is a statement or block of statements that is repeated indefinitely as long as some condition is satisfied. The general form of a `while` loop in Java is

```
while ( boolean_expr )
    statement;
```

or, with a compound statement,

```
while ( boolean_expr ) {
    statement 1;
    statement 2;
    ...
}
```

When a `while` loop is encountered, Java first evaluates the boolean expression. If *boolean_expr* is `true`, Java executes the statement(s) in the loop body. It then evaluates *boolean_expr* again. If it is still `true`, the statement is executed again. This process is repeated until the expression becomes `false`. The execution then skips to the first statement after the loop. The flowchart of a `while` loop is shown in Figure 4.1.

OBJECTIVES

- Learn how to use `while` and `do/while` loops.
- Learn how to use `for` loops.
- Learn how to use `break` and `continue` statements.
- Learn how to write out nicely formatted numbers using the `DecimalFormat` class.

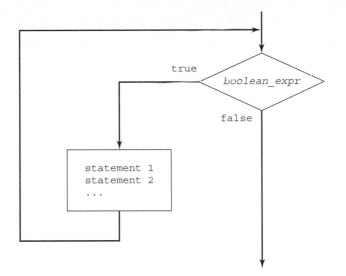

Figure 4.1. Flowchart for a `while` loop. Note that the boolean expression is evaluated *first*, and the statement(s) are executed only if the expression is `true`.

Note that the boolean expression is evaluated *before the loop is executed* on each pass through the loop. In computer science parlance, this is known as a *pretest*, because the test occurs before the loop is executed.

For example, consider the loop shown below:

```
k = 3;
while ( k < 5 ) {
    System.out.print(" " + k);
    k++;
}
```

When this loop is first executed, k is equal to 3. The boolean expression k < 5 is `true`, so the statements in the block are executed, writing out k and incrementing its value to 4. Then the boolean expression is evaluated again. Since k < 5 is still `true`, the statements in the block are executed again, writing out k and incrementing its value to 5. Then the boolean expression is evaluated again. This time k < 5 is `false`, so execution skips to the first statement following the loop. The resulting output is

```
3 4
```

If the *boolean_expr* controlling a `while` loop is `false` the first time that the expression is evaluated, the statement(s) in the loop will never be executed at all! For example, the following loop is never executed, because the boolean expression is `false` when the loop is first reached.

```
k = 5;
while ( k < 5 ) {
    System.out.print(" " + k);
    k++;
}
```

4.1.1 Controlling a `while` Loop

The execution of a `while` loop is controlled by a boolean expression, which is tested before the loop is executed. *It is important that the variables in the boolean expression controlling a `while` loop be modified by some action within the loop.* If the variables are *not* modified within the loop, then the value of the boolean expression will never change. If the value is `true` and is never modified, then the loop will be executed over and over forever, producing an **infinite loop**.

An example of a correct `while` loop is shown below. This loop is controlled by the value of variable `k`, and that value is modified within the loop.

```
k = 1;
while ( k < 5 ) {
    System.out.print(" " + k);
    k++;
}
```

The value of `k` is incremented each time that the loop is executed, so the loop will be executed four times, and then execution will transfer to the next statement after the end of the loop because the condition `k < 5` will be `false`.

In contrast, consider the following incorrect `while` loop. This loop is controlled by the value of `k`, but `k` is never changed within the loop. Since the expression `k < 5` will always be `true`, this loop will be repeated forever until the program containing it is killed. This code has produced an infinite loop.

```
k = 1;
while ( k < 5 ) {
    System.out.print(" " + k);
}
```

GOOD PROGRAMMING PRACTICE

Always include a statement within the body of a `while` loop that modifies the condition controlling the loop. This modification allows the loop to eventually terminate.

It is important to ensure that the modifications of the control variable within the `while` loop will eventually cause the loop to terminate. If the variations never make the boolean expression `false`, then the loop will never terminate. For example, consider the following `while` loop:

```
int k = 1;
while ( k < 5 ) {
    System.out.print(" " + k);
    k--;
}
```

In this case, the value of `k` starts at 1 and decreases with each iteration of the loop. This value will always be less than 5, until the variable `k` finally overflows in the negative direction. The result is the most positive integer, which will finally terminate the loop. However, this loop will execute more than two billion times before it terminates!

PROGRAMMING PITFALLS

Make sure that the variations in the values controlling the `while` loop will eventually cause the loop to terminate.

The way that `while` loops are defined in Java produces a nasty trap for programmers, one that you will probably stumble into several times as you learn the language. A typical Java `while` loop might be written as

```
x = 4;
while ( x < 10 )
    x += 4;
```

Note that *there is no semicolon after the* `while`—the `while` structure is not terminated until after the loop body. If we make a mistake and place a semicolon after the `while`, the statements will be:

```
x = 4;
while ( x < 10 );
    x += 4;
```

Unfortunately, this error creates a disaster. A semicolon by itself represents an **empty statement**, which is a statement that does nothing. Recall that Java will happily accept multiple statements on a single line. In this case, the semicolon will create a null statement that is the body of the loop, and the original loop body `x += 4;` will be *outside* of the loop. In other words, it is as though we wrote

```
x = 4;
while ( x < 10 )
    ;
x += 4;
```

The Java compiler will compile this program with no warnings, and when the program executes, it will go into an infinite loop! Since the null statement never changes `x`, `x` will always be less than 10, and the loop will execute forever.

What makes this bug particularly deadly is that the compiler gives no warning that anything is wrong. The program executes and runs, but produces an infinite loop. The error is very hard to spot unless you are specifically looking for it.

PROGRAMMING PITFALLS

Adding a semicolon after a `while` statement can produce a logic error. Java will compile and execute the program, but the program may go into an infinite loop.

4.1.2   Example Using a `while` Loop

We will now show an example statistical analysis program that is implemented using a `while` loop.

EXAMPLE 4.1

Statistical Analysis: It is very common in science and engineering to work with large sets of numbers, each of which is a measurement of some particular property that we are interested in. A simple example would be the grades on an exam. Each grade would be a measurement of how much a particular student has learned.

Much of the time, we are not interested in looking closely at every single measurement that we make. Instead, we want to summarize the results of a set of measurements with a few numbers that tell us a lot about the overall data set. Two such numbers are the *average* (or *arithmetic mean*) and the *standard deviation* of the set of measurements. The average or arithmetic mean of a set of numbers is defined as

$$\bar{x} = \frac{1}{N}\sum_{i=1}^{N} x_i \tag{4.1}$$

where x_i is sample i out of N samples. The standard deviation of a set of numbers is defined as

$$\sigma = \sqrt{\frac{N\sum_{i=1}^{N} x_i^2 - \left(\sum_{i=1}^{N} x_i\right)^2}{N(N-1)}} \tag{4.2}$$

Standard deviation is a measure of the amount of scatter on the measurements; the greater the standard deviation, the more scattered the points in the data set are.

Implement an algorithm that reads in a set of measurements from the standard input stream and calculates the mean and the standard deviation of the input data set.

SOLUTION

This program must be able to read in an arbitrary number of measurements and then calculate their mean and standard deviation. We will use a `while` loop to accumulate the input measurements before performing the calculations.

When all of the measurements have been read, we must have some way of telling the program that there is no more data to enter. For now, we will assume that all the input measurements are either positive or zero, and we will use a negative input value as a *flag* to indicate that there is no more data to read. If a negative value is entered, then the program will stop reading input values and will calculate the mean and standard deviation of the data set.

1. **Determine the User Requirements**

    Since we assume that the input numbers must be positive or zero, a proper statement of the user's requirements would be: *calculate the average and the standard deviation of a set of measurements, assuming that all of the measurements are either positive or zero, and assuming that we do not know in advance how many measurements are included in the data set. A negative input value will mark the end of the set of measurements. Read the input values as* `doubles` *from the standard input stream, and write the mean and standard deviation to the standard output stream.* In addition, we will print out the number of data points input to the program, since this is a useful check that the input data was read correctly.

2. **Analysis and Decomposition**

    Again, there will be a single class, and only the `main` method within that class. We will call the class `Stats`.

3. **Detailed Design**

    The `main` method can be broken down into three major sections, whose functions are accumulating input data, processing, and output:

```
Accumulate the input data
Calculate the mean and standard deviation
Write out the mean, standard deviation, and num-
    ber of points
```

The first major step of the program is to accumulate the input data. To do this, we will prompt the user to enter the desired numbers. We will have to keep track of the number of values entered, plus the sum and the sum of the squares of those values. The pseudocode for these steps is:

```
Initialize n, sumX, and sumX2 to 0
Prompt user for first number
Read in x
while (x >= 0)
    ++n;
    sumX ← sumX + x;
    sumX2 ← sumX2 + x*x;
    Prompt user for next number
    Read in next x
End of while
```

Note that we have to read in the first value before the `while` loop starts, so that the `while` loop can have a value to test the first time it executes.

Next, we must calculate the mean and standard deviation. The pseudocode for this step is just the Java versions of Equations (4.1) and (4.2).

```
xBar ← sumX / n
stdDev ← Math.sqrt((n*sumX2 - sumX*sumX) / (n*(n-1)))
```

Finally, we must write out the results.

```
Write out the mean value xBar
Write out the standard deviation stdDev
Write out the number of input data points n
```

4. **Implementation: Convert Algorithms to Java Statements**

The final Java program is shown in Figure 4.2, with the `while` loop shown in boldface.

```
/*
   Purpose:
     To calculate mean and the standard deviation of an input
     data set containing an arbitrary number of input values.

   Record of revisions:
      Date          Programmer              Description of change
      ====          ==========              =====================
   02/26/2002    S. J. Chapman              Original code
*/
import java.io.*;
public class Stats {

   // Define the main method
   public static void main(String[] args) throws IOException {
```

Figure 4.2. Program to calculate the mean and standard deviation of a set of nonnegative real numbers.

```
// Declare variables, and define each variable
int n = 0;                // The number of input samples.
double stdDev = 0.;       // The std dev of the input samples.
String str;               // Input string
double sumX = 0.;         // The sum of the input values.
double sumX2 = 0.;        // The sum of the squares of input values.
double x = 0.;            // An input data value.
double xBar = 0.;         // The average of the input samples.

// Create a buffered reader
BufferedReader in1 = new BufferedReader(
                      new InputStreamReader(System.in));

// Get first input value
System.out.print("Enter first value: ");
str = in1.readLine();
x = Double.parseDouble(str);

// While loop to accumulate input values.
while ( x >= 0 ) {

    // Accumulate sums.
    ++n;
    sumX += x;
    sumX2 += x*x;

    // Read next value
    System.out.print("Enter next value: ");
    str = in1.readLine();
    x = Double.parseDouble(str);
}

// Calculate the mean and standard deviation
xBar = sumX / n;
stdDev = Math.sqrt( (n * sumX2 - sumX*sumX ) / (n * (n-1)) );

// Tell user.
System.out.println("The mean of this data set is:  " + xBar);
System.out.println("The standard deviation is:     " + stdDev);
System.out.println("The number of data points is:  " + n);
    }
}
```

Figure 4.2.   (Continued).

5.   **Testing**

To test this program, we will calculate the answers by hand for a simple data set, then compare the answers to the results of the program. If we used three input values: 3, 4, and 5, then the mean and standard deviation would be

$$\bar{x} = \frac{1}{N}\sum_{i=1}^{N} x_i = \frac{1}{3}(12) = 4$$

$$\sigma = \sqrt{\frac{N\sum_{i=1}^{N} x_i^{\,2} - \left(\sum_{i=1}^{N} x_i\right)^2}{N(N-1)}} = 1$$

When the above values are fed into the program, the results are

```
C:\book\java\chap4>java Stats
Enter first value: 3
Enter next value:  4
Enter next value:  5
Enter next value:  -1
The mean of this data set is: 4.0
The standard deviation is:    1.0
The number of data points is: 3
```

The program gives the correct answers for our test data set.

4.2   THE do/while LOOP

There is another form of the while loop in Java, called the **do/while loop**. The do/while structure has the form

```
do {
    Statement 1;
    ...
    Statement n;
} while ( boolean_expr )
```

In this loop, statements 1 through *n* will be executed, and then the boolean expression will be tested. If the boolean expression is true, then statements 1 through *n* will be executed again. This process will be repeated until the boolean expression becomes false. When the bottom of the loop is reached with the boolean expression false, the program will execute the first statement after the end of the loop. The operation of a do/while loop is illustrated in Figure 4.3.

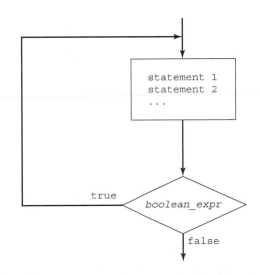

Figure 4.3.   Flowchart for a do/while loop. Note that the statement(s) are executed first, and then the boolean expression is evaluated. The statement(s) in this loop will be executed *at least once* even if the boolean expression is false before the loop starts.

The major difference between the while loop and the do/while loop is that *the test for the* while *loop is executed at the* **top** *of the loop, while the test for the* do/while *loop is executed at the* **bottom** *of the loop.* Because of this difference, the statements in a do/while loop will always be executed at least once.

> GOOD PROGRAMMING PRACTICE
>
> Use a while or do/while loop to repeat a set of statements indefinitely until a condition becomes false. Use the do/while loop in cases where the loop must be executed at least once. Otherwise, the while loop is preferred.

Program Stats in Example 4.1 is an excellent candidate for a do/while loop. In that example, the program had to read the first input value *before the beginning of the* while *loop* so that there would be an input value to test in the while statement. If this loop is replaced by a do/while loop, then we can use a single readline() statement within the body of the loop. The modified Java program is shown in Figure 4.4, with the do/while loop shown in boldface.

```
/*
    Purpose:
      To calculate the mean and standard deviation of an input
      data set containing an arbitrary number of input values.

    Record of revisions:
        Date         Programmer          Description of change
        ====         ==========          =====================
      02/26/2002  S. J. Chapman          Original code
  1   02/27/2002  S. J. Chapman          Modified for do/while loop
*/
import java.io.*;
public class Stats2 {

   // Define the main method
   public static void main(String[] args) throws IOException {

      // Declare variables, and define each variable
      int n = 0;             // The number of input samples.
      double stdDev = 0;     // The std dev of the input samples.
      String str;            // Input string
      double sumX = 0;       // The sum of the input values.
      double sumX2 = 0;      // The sum of the squares of input values.
      double x = 0;          // An input data value.
      double xBar = 0;       // The average of the input samples.

      // Create a buffered reader
      BufferedReader in1 = new BufferedReader(
                          new InputStreamReader(System.in));

      // Do/while loop to accumulate input values.
      do {
```

Figure 4.4.   Program to calculate the mean and standard deviation of a set of nonnegative real numbers using a do/while loop.

```
        // Read input value
        System.out.print("Enter value: ");
        str = in1.readLine();
        x = Double.parseDouble(str);

        // Accumulate sums.
        if (x >= 0) {
            ++n;
            sumX += x;
            sumX2 += x*x;
        }

    } while ( x >= 0 );

    // Calculate the mean and standard deviation
    xBar = sumX / n;
    stdDev = Math.sqrt( (n * sumX2 - sumX*sumX ) / (n * (n-1)) );
    // Tell user.
    System.out.println("The mean of this data set is:  " + xBar);
    System.out.println("The standard deviation is:     " + stdDev);
    System.out.println("The number of data points is:  " + n);
    }
}
```

Figure 4.4. (Continued).

4.3 THE **for** LOOP

In the Java language, a loop that executes a block of statements a specified number of times is called a **for loop**. The for loop structure has the form

```
for ( index = initExpr; continueExpr; incrementExpr )
    Statement;
```

or

```
for ( index = initExpr; continueExpr; incrementExpr ) {
    Statement 1;
    . . .
    Statement n;
}
```

where the expressions within the parentheses control the operation of the loop. The *index* is an integer whose value varies each time the loop is executed. This value is initialized to the value of *initExpr* when the loop first starts to execute. The *continueExpr* is then evaluated. If this expression is true, then the statement is executed. After the statement is executed, the *incrementExpr* is executed to increment the value of the loop index, and *continueExpr* is re-evaluated. If the expression is still true, then the statement is executed again. This process is repeated until the *continueExpr* is false, at which time execution continues with the first statement following the loop. The operation of a for loop is illustrated in Figure 4.5.

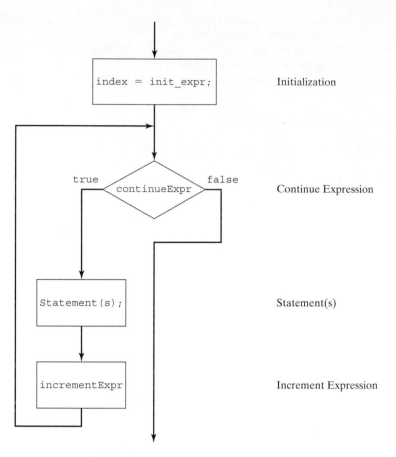

Figure 4.5. The structure of a for loop.

A simple example of the for loop is shown below.

```
for ( int i = 1; i <= 2; i++)
    System.out.println("i = " + i);
```

The index variable in this loop is i. When the loop first starts, i is initialized to 1, and the expression i <= 2 is evaluated. Since this expression is true, the print statement is executed. After the statement is executed, i++ is evaluated, increasing i to 2, and the expression i <= 2 is evaluated again. Since this expression is still true, the print statement is executed again. After the statement is executed, i++ is evaluated, increasing i to 3, and the expression i <= 2 is evaluated a third time. The expression is false this time, so execution transfers to the first statement after the loop. The output of this loop is

```
i = 1
i = 2
```

Let's look at a number of specific examples to make the operation of the for loop clearer. First, consider the following example:

```
for ( int count = 1; count <= 10; count++ ) {
    Statement 1;
    . . .
    Statement n;
}
```

In this case, statements 1 through *n* will be executed 10 times. The index variable count will be 1 on the first time, 2 on the second time, and so on. The index variable will be 10 on the last pass through the statements. At the end of the tenth pass, the index variable count will be increased to 11. Since the expression count <= 10 is false, control will transfer to the first statement after the loop.

Second, consider the following example:

```
for ( int count = 1; count <= 10; count += 2 ) {
    Statement 1;
    ...
    Statement n;
}
```

In this case, statements 1 through *n* will be executed five times. The index variable count will be 1 on the first time, 3 on the second time, and so on. The index variable will be 9 on the fifth and last pass through the statements. At the end of the fifth pass, the index variable count will be increased to 11. Since the expression count <= 10 is false, control will transfer to the first statement after the loop.

Third, consider the following example:

```
for ( int count = 10; count <= 1; count++ ) {
    Statement 1;
    ...
    Statement n;
}
```

Here, *statements 1 through n will never be executed*, since the expression count <= 1 is false when the continue expression is first evaluated. Instead, control will transfer to the first statement after the loop.

Finally, consider the example:

```
for ( int count = 3; count >= -3; count -= 2 ) {
    Statement 1;
    ...
    Statement n;
}
```

In this case, statements 1 through *n* will be executed four times. The index variable count will be 3 the first time, 1 the second time, −1 the third time, and −3 the fourth time. At the end of the fourth pass, the index variable count will be decreased to −5. Since the expression count >= −3 is false, control will transfer to the first statement after the loop.

EXAMPLE 4.2

The Factorial Function: We will illustrate the operation of a for loop by creating one to calculate the value of a factorial function. The factorial function is defined as

$$n! = \begin{cases} 1 & n = 0 \\ n \times (n-1) \times (n-2) \times \cdots \times 3 \times 2 \times 1 & n > 0 \end{cases} \quad (4.3)$$

The Java code to calculate n factorial for positive value of n would be

```
n_factorial = 1;
for (int count = 1; count <= n; count++)
    n_factorial *= count;
```

Suppose that we wish to calculate the value of 5!. If n is 5, this loop will be executed 5 times, with the variable count taking on values of 1, 2, 3, 4, and 5 in the successive loops. The resulting value of n_factorial will be 1 × 2 × 3 × 4 × 5 = 120. ∎

EXAMPLE 4.3

Calculating the Day of Year: The *day of year* is the number of days (including the current day) that have elapsed since the beginning of a given year. It is a number in the range 1 to 365 for ordinary years, and 1 to 366 for leap years. Write a Java program that accepts a day, month, and year and calculates the day of year corresponding to that date.

SOLUTION

To determine the day of year, this program will need to sum up the number of days in each month preceding the current month, plus the number of elapsed days in the current month. A `for` loop will be used to perform this sum. Since the number of days in each month varies, it is necessary to determine the correct number of days to add for each month. A `switch` structure will be used to determine the proper number of days to add for each month.

During a leap year, an extra day must be added to the day of year for any month after February. This extra day accounts for the presence of February 29 in the leap year. Therefore, to perform the day-of-year calculation correctly, we must determine which years are leap years. In the Gregorian calendar, leap years are determined by the following rules:

1. Years evenly divisible by 400 are leap years.
2. Years evenly divisible by 100 but *not* by 400 are not leap years.
3. All years divisible by 4 but *not* by 100 are leap years.
4. All other years are not leap years.

We will use the modulus operator (`%`) to determine whether or not a year is evenly divisible by a given number. If the result is zero, then the year was evenly divisible.

1. **Determine the User Requirements**

   The user requirement for this program is to accept three numeric values representing a day, month, and year and to calculate the day of year corresponding to that date. The program should take leap years into account.

2. **Analysis and Decomposition**

   Again, there will be a single class, and only the `main` method within that class. We will call the class `DayOfYear`.

   The inputs required by this program are three integers representing the month, day, and year to be translated. The output from this program is an integer representing the day of year corresponding to that date.

3. **Detailed Design**

   The `main` method can be broken down into four major sections, as follows:

   ```
   Read the month, day, and year
   Check to see if this is a leap year
   Add up the days until now in current year
   Write out the day of year
   ```

   The first major step of the program is to read the month, day, and year. To do this, we will have to prompt the user to enter the desired numbers. The pseudocode for this step is:

   ```
   Prompt user for the month
   Read in month
   Prompt user for the day
   Read in day
   Prompt user for the year
   Read in year
   ```

Next, we must determine if this is a leap year, using the algorithm described above. The pseudocode for this step is:

```
if year is divisible by 400
    leap_day ← 1;
else if year is divisible by 100
    leap_day ← 0;
else if year is divisible by 4
    leap_day ← 1;
else
    leap_day ← 0;
```

Then, we must add up the days in the month so far plus all the days in all months before the current one. The pseudocode for this step is:

```
day_of_year ← day;
for ( int i = 1; i <= month-1; i++ ) {
    switch (i) {
        case 1: case 3: case 5: case 7: case 8:
        case 10: case 12:
            day_of_year ← day_of_year + 31;
            break;
        case 4: case 6: case 9: case 11:
            day_of_year ← day_of_year + 30;
            break;
        case 2:
            day_of_year ← day_of_year + 28 + leap_day;
    }
}
```

Finally, we must write out the results.

```
Write out the current day of year
```

4. **Implementation: Convert Algorithms to Java Statements**

The final Java program is shown in Figure 4.6.

```
/*
   Purpose:
     This program calculates the day of year corresponding to a
     specified date. It illustrates the use for loops and the
     switch structure.

   Record of revisions:
      Date          Programmer          Description of change
      ====          ==========          =====================
    03/02/2002   S. J. Chapman          Original code
*/
import java.io.*;
public class DayOfYear {

   // Define the main method
   public static void main(String[] args) throws IOException {

      // Declare variables, and define each variable
```

Figure 4.6.   A program to calculate the equivalent day of year from a given day, month, and year.

```
    int day;                // Day (dd)
    int day_of_year;        // Day of year
    int leap_day;           // Extra day for leap year
    int month;              // Month (mm)
    int year;               // Year (yyyy)

  // Create a buffered reader
  BufferedReader in1 = new BufferedReader(
                      new InputStreamReader(System.in));

  // Get day, month, and year to convert
  System.out.println("This program calculates the day of year");
  System.out.print("given the current date. ");
  System.out.print("Enter current month (1-12): ");
  month = Integer.parseInt( in1.readLine() );
  System.out.print("Enter current day(1-31): ");
  day = Integer.parseInt( in1.readLine() );
  System.out.print("Enter current year (yyyy): ");
  year = Integer.parseInt( in1.readLine() );

// Check for leap year, and add extra day if necessary
if ( year % 400 == 0 )
   leap_day = 1;          // Years divisible by 400 are leap years
else if ( year % 100 == 0 )
   leap_day = 0;          // Other centuries are not leap years
else if ( year % 4 == 0 )
   leap_day = 1;          // Otherwise every 4th year is a leap year
else
   leap_day = 0;          // Other years are not leap years

// Calculate day of year
day_of_year = day;
for ( int i = 1; i <= month-1; i++ ) {

   // Add days in months from January to last month
   switch (i) {
      case 1: case 3: case 5: case 7: case 8:
      case 10: case 12:
         day_of_year = day_of_year + 31;
         break;
      case 4: case 6: case 9: case 11:
         day_of_year = day_of_year + 30;
         break;
      case 2:
         day_of_year = day_of_year + 28 + leap_day;
      }
   }

// Tell user
System.out.println("Day        = " + day);
System.out.println("Month      = " + month);
System.out.println("Year       = " + year);
System.out.println("day of year = " + day_of_year);
   }
}
```

Figure 4.6. (Continued).

5.   **Testing**

To test this program, we must test the program with both dates that are in leap years and dates that are not in leap years. We will use the following known results to test the program:

1.   Year 1999 is not a leap year. January 1 must be day of year 1, and December 31 must be day of year 365.

2.   Year 2000 is a leap year. January 1 must be day of year 1, and December 31 must be day of year 366.

3.   Year 2001 is not a leap year. March 1 must be day of year 60, since January has 31 days, February has 28 days, and this is the first day of March.

```
C:\book\java\chap4>java DayOfYear
This program calculates the day of year,
given the current date. Enter current month (1-12): 1
Enter current day (1-31): 1
Enter current year (yyyy): 1999
Day =               1
Month =             1
Year =              1999
day of year = 1

C:\book\java\chap4>java DayOfYear
This program calculates the day of year,
given the current date. Enter current month (1-12): 12
Enter current day (1-31): 31
Enter current year (yyyy): 1999
Day =               31
Month =             12
Year =              1999
day of year = 365

C:\book\java\chap4>java DayOfYear
This program calculates the day of year
given the current date. Enter current month (1-12): 1
Enter current day (1-31): 1
Enter current year (yyyy): 2000
Day =               1
Month =             1
Year =              2000
day of year = 1

C:\book\java\chap4>java DayOfYear

This program calculates the day of year
given the current date. Enter current month (1-12): 12
Enter current day (1-31): 31
Enter current year (yyyy): 2000
Day =               31
Month =             12
Year =              2000
day of year = 366
```

```
C:\book\java\chap4>java DayOfYear
This program calculates the day of year
given the current date. Enter current month (1-12): 3
Enter current day (1-31): 1
Enter current year (yyyy): 2001
Day =              1
Month =            3
Year =             2001
day of year = 60
```

The program gives the correct answers for our test dates in all five test cases. ∎

EXAMPLE 4.4

Statistical Analysis: Implement an algorithm that reads in a set of measurements and calculates the mean and the standard deviation of the input data set, when any value in the data set can be positive, negative, or zero.

SOLUTION

This program must be able to read in an arbitrary number of measurements and then calculate their mean and standard deviation. Each measurement can be positive, negative, or zero.

Since we cannot use a data value as a flag this time, we will ask the user for the number of input values and then use a for loop to read them in. This program is shown in Figure 4.7. Note that the while loop has been replaced by a for loop. Verify its operation for yourself by finding the mean and standard deviation of the following five input values: 3., −1., 0., 1., and −2.

```
/*
   Purpose:
     To calculate mean and the standard deviation of an input
     data set, where each input value can be positive, negative,
     or zero.

   Record of revisions:
       Date          Programmer           Description of change
       ====          ==========           =====================
     03/05/2002    S. J. Chapman          Original code
*/
import java.io.*;
public class Stats3 {

   // Define the main method
   public static void main(String[] args) throws IOException {

      // Declare variables, and define each variable
      int i;                   // Loop index
      int n = 0;               // The number of input samples.
      double stdDev = 0;       // The standard deviation of the input samples
      String str;              // String
      double sumX = 0;         // The sum of the input values.
      double sumX2 = 0;        // The sum of the squares of the input values
      double x = 0;            // An input data value.
      double xBar = 0;         // The average of the input samples
```

Figure 4.7. Modified statistical analysis program that works with both positive and input values.

```
      // Create a buffered reader
      BufferedReader in1 = new BufferedReader(
                            new InputStreamReader(System.in));

      // Get the number of points to input
      System.out.print("Enter number of points: ");
      str = in1.readLine();
      n = Integer.parseInt(str);

      // Check to see if we have enough input data.
      if ( n < 2 )
         System.out.println("At least 2 values must be entered!");
      else {

         // Loop to read input values
         for ( i = 1; i <= n; i++) {

            // Read values
            System.out.print("Enter number: ");
            str = in1.readLine();
            x = Double.parseDouble(str);

            // Accumulate sums
            sumX += x;
            sumX2 += x*x;
         }

         // Calculate the mean and standard deviation
         xBar = sumX / n;
         stdDev = Math.sqrt( (n * sumX2 - sumX*sumX ) / (n * (n-1)) );

         // Tell user
         System.out.println("The mean of this data set is:   " + xBar);
         System.out.println("The standard deviation is:      " + stdDev);
         System.out.println("The number of data points is:  " + n);
      }
   }
}
```

Figure 4.7.   (Continued). ■

4.3.1   Details of Operation

Now that we have seen examples of a `for` loop in operation, we will examine some of the important details required to use `for` loops properly.

1.   It is not necessary to indent the body of the `for` loop as we have shown above. The Java compiler will recognize the loop even if every statement in it starts in column 1. However, the code is much more readable if the body of the `for` loop is indented, so you should always indent the bodies of your loops.

GOOD PROGRAMMING PRACTICE

Always indent the body of a `for` loop by three or more spaces to improve the readability of the code.

2. The index variable of a `for` loop *must not be modified anywhere within the* `for` *loop*. Since the index variable is used to control the repetitions in the loop, changing it could produce unexpected results. In the worst case, modifying the index variable could produce an *infinite loop* that never completes. Consider the following example:

```
int i;
for ( i = 1; i <= 10; i++) {
    System.out.println("i = " + i);
    i = 5;
}
```

If `i` is reset to 5 every time through the loop, the loop will never end, because the index variable can never be greater than 10! This loop will run forever unless the program containing it is killed. You should *never* modify the loop index within the body of a `for` loop.

PROGRAMMING PITFALLS

Never modify the value of a `for` loop index variable while inside the loop.

3. Never use `float` or `double` variables as the index variable in a `for` loop. If you do, roundoff errors can sometimes cause unexpected results. For example, consider the following loop.

```
// This program tests a double index in a for loop
public class TestDoubleIndex {
    // Define the main method
    public static void main(String[] args) {
        // Set up for loop
        for ( double i = 0.1; i < 1.0; i += 0.1) {
            System.out.println("i = " + i);
        }
    }
}
```

This loop *should* execute nine times, with the results being $i = 0.1$, $0.2, \ldots, 0.9$. The next pass through the loop, `i` would be 1.0, so the condition `i < 1.0` should be false, and the loop would terminate. When we execute this program, however, the results are

```
C:\book\java\chap4>java TestDoubleIndex
i = 0.1
i = 0.2
i = 0.30000000000000004
i = 0.4
i = 0.5
i = 0.6
i = 0.7
i = 0.7999999999999999
i = 0.8999999999999999
i = 0.9999999999999999
```

The loop really executed *ten times*, because roundoff errors prevented i from being exactly equal to 1.0 on the tenth pass. This sort of problem can never happen with integer loop indexes.

Always use integer variables as `for` loop indexes.

4. It is a very common error to use a comma instead of a semicolon to separate the control statements in a `for` structure. This is a syntax error that will be caught by the compiler. For example, the incorrect loop shown below

```
for ( j = 1; j <= 3, j++) {
    ...
}
```

will produce the following compiler error:

```
TestFor.java:10: ';' expected.
        for ( j = 1; j <= 3, j++) {
                            ^
1 error
```

Be sure to separate the control statements in a `for` structure with a semicolon.

5. Placing a semicolon after the `for` in a `for` loop produces a logic error. A typical Java `for` loop may be written as

```
for (j = 1; j <= 10; j++)
    statement;
```

Note that *there is no semicolon after the* `for`—the `for` structure is not terminated until after the loop body. If we make a mistake and place a semicolon after the `for`, the statements will be:

```
for (j = 1; j <= 10; j++);
    statement;
```

Unfortunately, this creates a serious error *that is not detected by the compiler.* A semicolon by itself represents an **empty statement**—a statement that does nothing. As with the `while` loop, the semicolon will create a null statement that is the body of the loop, and the original `statement` will be outside of the loop. In other words, it is as though we wrote

```
for (j = 1; j <= 10; j++)
    ;
    statement;
```

The Java compiler will compile this program with no warnings, and when the program executes, it will increment j from 1 to 10 while doing nothing, and afterward execute the statement one time only! This is an type of bug example of a logic error.

What makes this bug particularly deadly is that the compiler gives no warning that anything is wrong. The program executes and runs, but produces the wrong answer. The error is very hard to spot unless you are specifically looking for it.

PROGRAMMING PITFALLS

Adding a semicolon after a `for` statement can produce a logic error. Java will compile and execute the program, but the program will produce incorrect results.

---

6. It is possible to design `for` loops that count down as well as up. The following `for` loop executes three times, with `j` being 3, 2, and 1 in the successive loops.

```
for ( j = 3; j >= 1; j--) {
    ...
}
```

4.3.2 The `continue` and `break` Statements

Two additional statements can be used to control the operation of loops: **continue** and **break**.

If the `continue` statement is executed in the body of a `for` loop, the execution of the body will stop, and control will be returned to the top of the loop. The loop index will be incremented, and execution will resume again if the continuation condition is still true. An example of the `continue` statement in a `for` loop is shown below.

```
// This program tests the continue statement
public class TestContinue {

    // Define the main method
    public static void main(String[] args) {

        int i;

        // Set up for loop
        for ( i = 1; i <= 5; i++) {
            if ( i == 3 ) continue;
            System.out.println("i = " + i);
        }
        System.out.println("End of loop!");
    }
}
```

When this program is executed, the output is:

```
C:\book\java\chap4>java TestContinue
i = 1
i = 2
i = 4
i = 5
End of loop!
```

Note that the `continue` statement was executed on the iteration when `i` was 3, and control returned to the top of the loop without executing the output statement.

The continue statement also works with while and do/while loops. When a continue statement is executed within a while loop, execution returns to the *top* of the loop, and execution will continue if the boolean expression is still true. When a continue statement is executed within a do/while loop, execution returns to the *bottom* of the loop, and execution will continue if the boolean expression is still true.

If the break statement is executed in the body of a while, do/while, or for loop, the execution of the body will stop, and control will be transferred to the first executable statement after the loop. An example of the break statement in a for loop is shown below.

```java
// This program tests the break statement
public class TestBreak {

    // Define the main method
    public static void main(String[] args) {

        int i;

        // Set up for loop
        for ( i = 1; i <= 5; i++) {
            if ( i == 3 ) break;
            System.out.println("i = " + i);
        }
        System.out.println("End of loop!");
    }
}
```

When this program is executed, the output is:

```
C:\book\java\chap4>java TestBreak
i = 1
i = 2
End of loop!
```

Note that the break statement was executed on the iteration when i was 3, and control transferred to the first executable statement after the loop without executing the output statement.

4.3.3   Nesting Loops

It is possible for one loop to be completely inside another loop. The two loops are called **nested loops**. The following example shows two nested for loops used to calculate and write out the product of two integers.

```java
// This program tests nested for loops
public class NestedFor {

    // Define the main method
    public static void main(String[] args) {

        int i, j, product;

        for ( i = 1; i <= 3; i++) {
            for ( j = 1; j <= 3; j++) {
                product = i * j;
                System.out.println(i + " * " + j + " = " + product);
            }
        }
    }
}
```

In this example, the outer for loop will assign a value of 1 to index variable i, and then the inner for loop will be executed. The inner for loop will be executed three times, with index variable j having values 1, 2, and 3. When the entire inner for loop has been completed, the outer for loop will assign a value of 2 to index variable i, and the inner for loop will be executed again. This process repeats until the outer for loop has executed three times, and the resulting output is

```
1 * 1 = 1
1 * 2 = 2
1 * 3 = 3
2 * 1 = 2
2 * 2 = 4
2 * 3 = 6
3 * 1 = 3
3 * 2 = 6
3 * 3 = 9
```

Note that the inner for loop executes completely before the index variable of the outer for loop is incremented.

If for loops are nested, they must have independent index variables. Otherwise, the inner loop would be modifying the loop variable of the outer loop, causing the outer loop to behave improperly.

4.3.4   Labeled break and continue Statements

If a break statement appears in a nested loop structure, it breaks out of the *innermost loop* only. The outer loops will continue to execute. For example, consider the following program:

```java
public class TestBreak2 {

   // Define the main method
   public static void main(String[] args) {

      int i, j, product;

      for ( i = 1; i <= 3; i++) {
         for ( j = 1; j <= 3; j++) {
            product = i * j;
            if ( j == 3 ) break;
            System.out.println(i + " * " + j + " = " + product);
         }
      }
   }
}
```

This break statement is executed when j is 3. When the break statement is executed, only the *innermost* loop will be terminated. The outer loop continues to execute, producing the following results:

```
1 * 1 = 1
1 * 2 = 2
2 * 1 = 2
2 * 2 = 4
3 * 1 = 3
3 * 2 = 6
```

To break out of more than one level of a nested structure, we must use a **labeled break statement**. We must place a **label** on the loop that we wish to break out of, and then specify that label in the break statement.

For example, suppose that we wish to modify the previous program to break out of both loops when the break statement is executed. We place a label on the outer loop and then refer to that label in the break statement:

```java
public class TestBreak3 {

    // Define the main method
    public static void main(String[] args) {

        int i, j, product;

        outer: for ( i = 1; i <= 3; i++) {
            for ( j = 1; j <= 3; j++) {
                product = i * j;
                if ( j == 3 ) break outer;
                System.out.println(i + " * " + j + " = " + product);
            }
        }
        System.out.println("Outside outer loop.");
    }
}
```

When this program is executed, the results are:

```
C:\book\java\chap4>java TestBreak3
1 * 1 = 1
1 * 2 = 2
Outside outer loop.
```

The break statement executed when j was equal to 3, and the program broke out of both loops at that time.

Similarly, if a continue statement appears in a nested loop structure, it breaks out of the *innermost* loop only. The outer loops will continue to execute. For example, consider the following program:

```java
public class TestContinue2 {

    // Define the main method
    public static void main(String[] args) {

        int i, j, product;

        for ( i = 1; i <= 3; i++) {
            for ( j = 1; j <= 3; j++) {
                product = i * j;
                if ( j == 2 ) continue;
                System.out.println(i + " * " + j + " = " + product);
            }
        }
    }
}
```

This `continue` statement is executed when j is 2. The remaining statements in the *innermost* loop are skipped, and execution continues at the top of the inner loop. The outer loop remains totally unaffected. The results of this program are:

```
1 * 1 = 1
1 * 3 = 3
2 * 1 = 2
2 * 3 = 6
3 * 1 = 3
3 * 3 = 9
```

To cause a higher-level loop to continue, we must use a **labeled continue statement**. We place a label on the loop that we wish to continue, and then specify that label in the `continue` statement. For example, the following program causes the *outer* loop to continue each time that j reaches 2 in the inner loop.

```java
public class TestContinue3 {

    // Define the main method
    public static void main(String[] args) {
        int i, j, product;
        outer: for ( i = 1; i <= 3; i++) {
            inner: for ( j = 1; j <= 3; j++) {
                product = i * j;
                if ( j == 2 ) continue outer;
                System.out.println(i + " * " + j + " = " + product);
            }
        }
    }
}
```

When this program is executed, the results are:

```
1 * 1 = 1
2 * 1 = 2
3 * 1 = 3
```

Compare this result to that of the previous example, where the innermost loop was affected by the `continue` statement.

GOOD PROGRAMMING PRACTICE

Use labeled `break` or `continue` statements to break out of or continue outer loops in a nested loop structure.

When a program contains many large nested loops, it can become difficult to determine which close brace (}) goes with which loop. In that case, it is good practice to label each loop whether we use `break` and `continue` statements or not. It is also good practice to place a comment with the loop label after the close brace (}) associated with that loop, to make it clear to programmers where the loop ends.

For example, suppose that a program contains three nested `for` loops. These loops could be labeled as follows:

```
outer: for ( i = 1; i <= 5; i++) {
    middle: for ( j = 1; j <= 5; j++) {
        inner: for ( k = 1; k <= 10; k++) {
            . . .
            . . .
            . . .
        } // inner
    } // middle
} // outer
```

GOOD PROGRAMMING PRACTICE

Use labels on the beginnings and ends of each loop in a complex set of nested loops to to make clear which loops go with which close braces.

QUIZ 4-1

This quiz provides a quick check to see if you have understood the concepts introduced in Sections 4.1 through 4.3. If you have trouble with the quiz, reread the section, ask your instructor, or discuss the material with a fellow student. The answers are found in the back of the book.

Examine the control parameters of the following `for` loops and determine how many times each loop will be executed.

1. `for (index = 7; index <= 10; index++)`
2. `for (j = 7; j <= 10; j--)`
3. `for (index = 1; index <= 10; index += 10)`
4. `for (k = 1; k < 10; k++)`
5. `for (counter = -2; counter <= 10; counter += 2)`
6. `for (time = -2; time >= -10; time--)`
7. `for (i = -10; i <= 27; i -= 3)`

Examine the following loops and determine the value in `ires` at the end of each of the loops. Assume that `ires`, `index`, and all loop variables are integers. How many times does each loop execute?

8.
```
ires = 0;
for (index = 1; index <= 10; index++)
    ires++;
```

9.
```
ires = 0;
for (index = 1; index <= 10; index++)
    ires += index;
```

10.
```
ires = 0; index = 0;
while ( ires < 12 )
    ires += ++index;
```

11.
```
ires = 0; index = 0;
while ( index < 5 )
    ires += ++index;
```

12.
```
ires = 0; index = 0;
do {
    ires += ++index;
} while ( index < 5 );
```

13.
```
ires = 0;
for (index = 1; index <= 6; index++) {
    if ( index == 3 )
        continue;
    ires += index;
}
```

14.
```
ires = 0;
for (index = 1; index <= 6; index++) {
    if ( index == 3 )
        break;
    ires += index;
}
```

15.
```
ires = 0;
for (index1 = 1; index1 <= 5; index1++) {
    for (index2 = 1; index2 <= 5; index2++) {
        ires++;
    }
}
```

16.
```
ires = 0;
for (index1 = 1; index1 <= 5; index1++) {
    for (index2 = index1; index2 <= 5; index2++) {
        ires++;
    }
}
```

17.
```
ires = 0;
loop1: for (index1 = 1; index1 <= 5; index1++) {
    loop2: for (index2 = 1; index2 <= 5; index2++) {
        if ( index2 == 3)
            break loop1;
        ires++;
    }
}
```

18.
```
ires = 0;
loop1: for (index1 = 1; index1 <= 5; index1++) {
    loop2: for (index2 = 1; index2 <= 5; index2++) {
        if ( index2 == 3)
            break loop2;
        ires++;
    }
}
```

Examine the following Java statements and tell whether or not they are valid. If they are invalid, indicate why.

```
19.  loop1: for (i = 1; i <= 10; i++ ) {
         loop2: for (i = 1; i <= 10; i++ ) {
             ...
         }
     }

20.  x = 10;
     while ( x > 0);
         x -= 3;

21.  ires = 0;
     for (i = 1; i <= 10; i++) {
         ires += i--;
     }
```

4.4 FORMATTING OUTPUT DATA

One serious limitation of the standard Java API is that there is no convenient way to format numbers for display. When Java prints out a number, it displays *all nonzero significant digits* of the number. While this is suitable under some circumstances, it is not particularly useful under others.

For example, suppose that we were interested in creating a program that reads in the prices of a series of purchases and calculates the average price. If the average price is written out with a statement like

```
System.out.println("Average price = " + ave);
```

the result might be

```
Average price = $3.766666666666667
```

This output is not very useful, since monetary amounts are significant only to the nearest cent.

A similar problem happens if we are trying to create tables of information. If the values in the table contain different numbers of significant digits, then the columns of data in the table will not line up. For example, the program shown below calculates a table of the square roots and cube roots of all integers from 0 to 10.

```java
public class SquareCubeRoot {
    public static void main(String[] args) {

        // Declare variables, and define each variable
        int i;                  // Loop index
        double cubeRoot;        // Cube root of index
        double squareRoot;      // Square root of index

        // Print title
        System.out.println("Table of Square and Cube Roots:");
```

```
        // Calculate and print values
        for ( i = 0; i <= 10; i++ ) {
            squareRoot = Math.sqrt(i);
            cubeRoot = Math.pow(i,1./3.);
            System.out.println(i + " " + squareRoot + " " + cubeRoot);
        }
    }
}
```

When this program is executed, the results are:

```
        Table of Square and Cube Roots:
        0 0.0 0.0
        1 1.0 1.0
        2 1.4142135623730951 1.2599210498948732
        3 1.7320508075688772 1.4422495703074083
        4 2.0 1.5874010519681994
        5 2.23606797749979 1.7099759466766968
        6 2.449489742783178 1.8171205928321397
        7 2.6457513110645907 1.912931182772389
        8 2.8284271247461903 2.0
        9 3.0  2.080083823051904
        10 3.1622776601683795 2.154434690031884
```

This output looks terrible! It would be completely unacceptable for any real task.

Fortunately, the Java API includes a class called DecimalFormat that makes it possible to conveniently create strings containing formatted numbers. This class is a part of the java.text package. It allows a programmer to specify the way that a number will be displayed, including the number of digits before and after the decimal point, whether or not thousands separators are used, whether or not a currency symbol ($, €, etc.) is used, and whether or not the number should be displayed in exponential format.

An object of class DecimalFormat is created by the following statement:

```
        DecimalFormat df = new DecimalFormat(formatString);
```

where formatString is a string describing the format to be applied to a number. The DecimalFormat class includes a method called format, which applies the specified formatString to a particular number.

For example, the following program will print out a number formatted with five places before the decimal point, one place after the decimal point, and a thousands separator.

```
import java.text.*;
public class DecimalFormat1 {
    public static void main(String args[]) {
        DecimalFormat df = new DecimalFormat("00,000.0");
        System.out.println("value = " + df.format(12345.678));
    }
}
```

When this program is executed, the results are as follows.

```
        D:\book\java\chap4>java DecimalFormat1
        value = 12,345.7
```

The characters that can be used in a formatString are shown in Table 4.1. Table 4.2 shows the way that the number 12345.6 would be displayed with various format strings.

TABLE 4.1   Characters in a Format String

Character	Meaning
.	A period. This symbol indicates the location of a decimal point.
,	A comma. This symbol indicates the location of a group separator, which is used to divide numbers up into thousands (for example, 1,000,000)
#	This symbol indicates the location of an optional digit. If there is no character corresponding to this location, no value is included in the output string.
0	This symbol indicates the location of a nonoptional digit. If there is no character corresponding to this location, a zero is included in the output string.
E	This symbol indicates the location of the "E" symbol in a number in scientific format. The symbols before the "E" represent the format of the mantissa, and those after the "E" represent the format of the exponent.
space	This symbol indicates the location of a nonoptional digit. If there is no character corresponding to this location, a blank is included in the output string.
$, £, €, etc.	This symbol indicates the location of a currency symbol.

TABLE 4.2   Sample Format Strings and Outputs

Format String	Result	Comment
"########"	12346	Format string with eight optional decimal values and no fractional part. The number is rounded to the nearest integer, and only five characters are displayed.
"00000000"	00012346	Format string with eight nonoptional decimal values and no fractional part. The number is rounded to the nearest integer, and eight characters are displayed, with the missing ones being zero.
" "	ƀƀƀ12346	Format string with eight nonoptional decimal values and no fractional part. The number is rounded to the nearest integer, and eight characters are displayed, with the missing ones being blanks (ƀ).
"######.##"	12345.6	Format string with six optional decimal values and two optional fractional values. The number is displayed with five digits before the decimal point and one digit after the decimal point.
"######.00"	12345.60	Format string with six optional decimal values and two nonoptional fractional values. The number is displayed with five digits before the decimal point and two digits after the decimal point.
"###,###.00"	12,345.60	Format string with a group separator.
"$###,###,###.00"	$12,345.60	Format string with currency symbol and a group separator.
"#.###E00"	1.235E04	Format string for scientific notation.

EXAMPLE 4.5

If i, pi, and e are initialized as shown, then the following statements will produce the indicated results. Can you explain why each result is produced?

```
int i = 12345;
double pi = 3.14159265358979;
double e = -1.602e-19;
DecimalFormat df;
```

Expression	Result

a. df = new DecimalFormat("######");   i = 12345
   System.out.println("i = " + df.format(i));

b. df = new DecimalFormat("000000");   i = 012345
   System.out.println("i = " + df.format(i));

c. df = new DecimalFormat("######.000");   i = 12345.000
   System.out.println("i = " + df.format(i));

d. df = new DecimalFormat("######.###");   i = 12345
   System.out.println("pi = " + df.format(pi));

e. df = new DecimalFormat("######.000");   i = 3.142
   System.out.println("i = " + df.format(i));

f. df = new DecimalFormat("#.####E00");   e = -1.602E-19
   System.out.println("e = " + df.format(e));

EXAMPLE 4.6

Generating a Table of Information: Write a program to generate a table containing the square roots and cube roots of all integers between 0 and 10. Use formatted output to generate a neat table with five places after the decimal point.

SOLUTION

This program will be similar to class SquareCubeRoot above, except that the output will use the DecimalFormat class to format the data. The resulting program is

```
import java.text.*;
public class SquareCubeRoot1 {
   public static void main(String[] args) {

      // Declare variables, and define each variable
      int i;                  // Loop index
      double cubeRoot;        // Cube root of index
      double squareRoot;      // Square root of index

      //
      DecimalFormat df1 = new DecimalFormat("00");
      DecimalFormat df2 = new DecimalFormat("0.00000");

      // Print title
      System.out.println("Table of Square and Cube Roots:");

      // Calculate and print values
      for ( i = 0; i <= 10; i++ ) {
         squareRoot = Math.sqrt(i);
         cubeRoot = Math.pow(i,1./3.);
```

```
        System.out.print( df1.format(i) + " ");
        System.out.print( df2.format(squareRoot) + " ");
        System.out.println( df2.format(cubeRoot) );
      }
   }
}
```

When this program is executed, the results are much nicer than before:

```
D:\book\java\chap4>java SquareCubeRoot1
Table of Square and Cube Roots:
00     0.00000     0.00000
01     1.00000     1.00000
02     1.41421     1.25992
03     1.73205     1.44225
04     2.00000     1.58740
05     2.23607     1.70998
06     2.44949     1.81712
07     2.64575     1.91293
08     2.82843     2.00000
09     3.00000     2.08008
10     3.16228     2.15443
```

Note that the integers in the first column have leading zeros. There is no way to suppress these leading zeros and still keep a fixed width on column 1 if we use only the DecimalFormat class. In a later chapter, we will learn how to create nicely formatted columns without the leading zeros. ■

4.5 EXAMPLE PROBLEM

EXAMPLE 4.7

Physics—The Flight of a Ball: If we assume negligible air friction and ignore the curvature of the earth, a ball that is thrown into the air from any point on the earth's surface will follow a parabolic flight path [see Figure 4.8(a)]. The height of the ball at any time t after it is thrown is given by

$$y(t) = y_0 + v_{y0}t + \frac{1}{2}gt^2 \qquad (4.4)$$

where y_0 is the initial height of the object above the ground, v_{y0} is the initial vertical velocity of the object, and g is the acceleration due to the earth's gravity. The horizontal distance (range) traveled by the ball as a function of time after it is thrown is given by

$$x(t) = x_0 + v_{x0}t \qquad (4.5)$$

where x_0 is the initial horizontal position of the ball on the ground, and v_{x0} is the initial horizontal velocity of the ball.

If the ball is thrown with some initial velocity v_0 at an angle of θ degrees with respect to the earth's surface, then the initial horizontal and vertical components of velocity will be

$$v_{x0} = v_0 \cos \theta \qquad (4.6)$$

$$v_{y0} = v_0 \sin \theta \qquad (4.7)$$

Assume that the ball is initially thrown from position $(x_0, y_0) = (0, 0)$ with an initial velocity v of 20 meters per second at an initial angle of θ degrees. Write and test a program

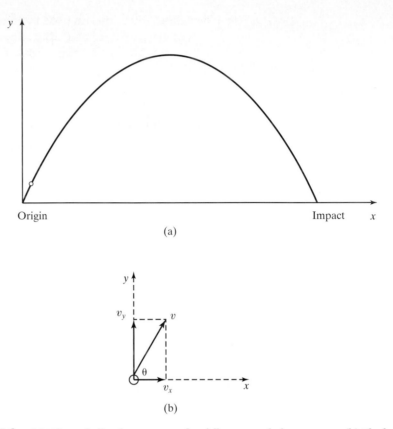

Figure 4.8. (a) When a ball is thrown upward, it follows a parabolic trajectory. (b) The horizontal and vertical components of a velocity vector v at an angle θ with respect to the horizontal.

that will determine the horizontal distance traveled by the ball from the time it was thrown until it touches the ground again. The program should do this for all angles θ from 0 to 90 degrees in 1-degree steps. Determine the angle θ that maximizes the range of the ball.

SOLUTION

In order to solve this problem, we must determine an equation for the range of the thrown ball. We can do this by first finding the time that the ball remains in the air, then finding the horizontal distance that the ball can travel during that time.

The time that the ball will remain in the air after it is thrown may be calculated from Equation (4.4). The ball will touch the ground at the time t for which $y(t) = 0$. Remembering that the ball will start from ground level ($y(0) = 0$), and solving for t, we get:

$$y(t) = y_0 + v_{y0}t + \frac{1}{2}gt^2$$

$$0 = 0 + v_{y0}t + \frac{1}{2}gt^2$$

$$0 = \left(v_{y0} + \frac{1}{2}gt\right)t \tag{4.4}$$

so the ball will be at ground level at time $t_1 = 0$ (when we threw it), and at time

$$t_2 = -\frac{2v_{y0}}{g}$$

The horizontal distance that the ball will travel in time t_2 is found using Equation (4.5):

$$\text{range} = x(t_2) = x_0 + v_{x0}t_2$$

$$\text{range} = 0 + v_{x0}\left(-\frac{2v_{y0}}{g}\right)$$

$$\text{range} = -\frac{2\,v_{x0}\,v_{y0}}{g} \tag{4.5}$$

We can substitute Equations (4.6) and (4.7) for v_{x0} and v_{y0} to get an equation expressed in terms of the initial velocity v and initial angle θ:

$$\text{range} = -\frac{2(v_0 \cos\theta)(v_0 \sin\theta)}{g}$$

$$\text{range} = -\frac{2\,v_0^2 g}{\cos\theta \sin\theta} \tag{4.8}$$

From the problem statement, we know that the initial velocity v_0 is 20 meters per second and that the ball will be thrown at all angles from 0 to 90 degrees in 1-degree steps. Finally, any elementary physics textbook will tell us that the acceleration due to the earth's gravity is −9.81 meters per second squared.

Now let's apply our design technique to this problem.

1. **Determine the User Requirements**

   This program must calculate the horizontal distance that a ball will travel if it is thrown into the air with an initial speed of 20 meters per second at an angle θ, where θ varies in 1-degree steps between 0 and 90 degrees. It should print the angle θ and the corresponding range for each angle. Finally, the program must determine the angle θ that results in the maximum range, and print out that angle.

2. **Analysis and Decomposition**

   Again, there will be a single class, and only the `main` method within that class. We will call the class `Ball`.

   As the problem is defined above, no inputs are required. We know from the problem statement what the values of v_0 and θ will be, so there is no need to read them in. The outputs from this program will be a table showing the range of the ball for each angle θ, and the angle θ for which the range is maximum.

3. **Detailed Design**

   There is only one method in this program. The `main` method can be broken down into the following major steps

```
for theta = 0 to 90 degrees in 1 degree steps {
   Calculate the range of the ball for each angle theta
   Determine if this theta yields the maximum range so far
   Write out the range as a function of theta
}
WRITE out the theta yielding maximum range
```

   A `for` loop is appropriate for this algorithm, since we are calculating the range of the ball for a specified number of angles. We will calculate the range for each value of θ and compare each range with the maximum range found so far to determine which angle yields the maximum range. Note that the trigonometric functions work in radians, so the angles in degrees must be converted to radians before the range is calculated. The detailed pseudocode for this algorithm is

```
Declare variables
Initialize v0 to 20 meters/second
for theta = 0 to 90 degrees in 1 degree steps {
    rad ← theta * degrees_2_rad;        (Convert degrees to radians)
    angle ← (-2. * v0**2 / gravity ) * sin(rad) * cos(rad);
    Write out theta and range
    if range > max_range then
        max_range ← range;
        max_degrees ← theta;
    }
}
Write out max_degrees, max_range
```

4. **Implementation: Convert Algorithms to Java Statements**

The final Java program is shown in Figure 4.9.

```
/*
 Purpose:
   To calculate distance traveled by a ball thrown at a specified
   angle theta and at a specified velocity V0 from a point on the
   surface of the earth, ignoring the effects of air friction and
   the earth's curvature.

 Record of revisions:
     Date        Programmer          Description of change
     ====        ==========          =====================
   03/12/2002   S. J. Chapman        Original code
*/
import java.text.*;
public class Ball  {

    // Define the main method
    public static void main(String[] args) {

        // Declare variables, and define each variable
        double gravity = -9.81; // Accel. due to gravity (m/s/s)
        final double DEG2RAD = Math.PI / 180.; // Deg ==> rad conv. factor
        int max_degrees = 0;      // Angle at which the max range occurs (deg)
        double max_range = 0.;    // Max range for the ball at vel v0 (m)
        double range;             // Range of the ball at a given angle (m)
        double rad;               // Angle of throw (radians)
        String str;               // Input string
        int theta;                // Angle of throw (deg)
        double v0 = 20.;          // Velocity of the ball (m/s)
```

Figure 4.9. Program Ball to determine the angle which maximizes the range of a thrown ball.

```
    // Declare the output format for the data
    DecimalFormat df = new DecimalFormat("####0.00");

    // Calculate the range for every angle theta
    for ( theta = 0; theta <= 90; theta++ ) {

        // Get angle in radians
        rad = theta * DEG2RAD;

        // Calculate range in meters.
        range = (-2.*v0*v0/gravity) * Math.sin(rad) * Math.cos(rad);

        // Write out the range for this angle.
        System.out.print("Theta = " + theta + " degrees ");
        System.out.println("Range = " + df.format(range) + " meters");

        // Compare the range to the previous maximum range. If this
        // range is larger, save it and the angle at which it occurred.
        if ( range > max_range ) {
            max_range = range;
            max_degrees = theta;
        }
    }

    // Skip a line, and then write out the maximum range and
    // the angle at which it occurred.
    System.out.println("\nMax range = " + df.format(max_range) +
                       " at " + max_degrees + " degrees.");

    }
}
```

Figure 4.9. (Continued).

The degrees-to-radians conversion factor is always a constant, so in the program it is declared as a named constant, and all references to the constant within the program use that name. The acceleration due to gravity at sea level can be found in any physics text. It is about 9.81 m/sec^2, directed downward.

5. **Testing**

To test this program, we will calculate the answers by hand for a few of the angles and compare the results with the output of the program.

$$\theta = 0°: \quad \text{range} = -\frac{2(20^2)}{-9.81} \cos 0 \sin 0 = 0 \text{ meters}$$

$$\theta = 5°: \quad \text{range} = -\frac{2(20^2)}{-9.81} \cos\left(\frac{5\pi}{180}\right) \sin\left(\frac{5\pi}{180}\right) = 7.080 \text{ meters}$$

$$\theta = 40°: \quad \text{range} = -\frac{2(20^2)}{-9.81} \cos\left(\frac{40\pi}{180}\right) \sin\left(\frac{40\pi}{180}\right) = 40.16 \text{ meters}$$

$$\theta = 45°: \quad \text{range} = -\frac{2(20^2)}{-9.81} \cos\left(\frac{45\pi}{180}\right) \sin\left(\frac{45\pi}{180}\right) = 40.77 \text{ meters}$$

When program `Ball` is executed, a 90-line table of angles and ranges is produced. To save space, only a portion of the table is reproduced below.

```
D:\book\java\chap4>java Ball
Theta = 0 degrees   Range = 0.00 meters
Theta = 1 degrees   Range = 1.42 meters
Theta = 2 degrees   Range = 2.84 meters
Theta = 3 degrees   Range = 4.26 meters
Theta = 4 degrees   Range = 5.67 meters
Theta = 5 degrees   Range = 7.08 meters
Theta = 6 degrees   Range = 8.48 meters
Theta = 7 degrees   Range = 9.86 meters
Theta = 8 degrees   Range = 11.24 meters
Theta = 9 degrees   Range = 12.60 meters
Theta = 10 degrees   Range = 13.95 meters
. . .
Theta = 40 degrees   Range = 40.16 meters
Theta = 41 degrees   Range = 40.38 meters
Theta = 42 degrees   Range = 40.55 meters
Theta = 43 degrees   Range = 40.68 meters
Theta = 44 degrees   Range = 40.75 meters
Theta = 45 degrees   Range = 40.77 meters
Theta = 46 degrees   Range = 40.75 meters
Theta = 47 degrees   Range = 40.68 meters
Theta = 48 degrees   Range = 40.55 meters
Theta = 49 degrees   Range = 40.38 meters
Theta = 50 degrees   Range = 40.16 meters
. . .
Theta = 80 degrees   Range = 13.95 meters
Theta = 81 degrees   Range = 12.60 meters
Theta = 82 degrees   Range = 11.24 meters
Theta = 83 degrees   Range = 9.86 meters
Theta = 84 degrees   Range = 8.48 meters
Theta = 85 degrees   Range = 7.08 meters
Theta = 86 degrees   Range = 5.67 meters
Theta = 87 degrees   Range = 4.26 meters
Theta = 88 degrees   Range = 2.84 meters
Theta = 89 degrees   Range = 1.42 meters
Theta = 90 degrees   Range = 0.00 meters

Max range = 40.77 at 45 degrees.
```

The program output matches our hand calculation for the angles calculated above to the 4-digit accuracy of the hand calculation. Note that the maximum range occurred at an angle of 45 degrees. ■

4.6   MORE ON DEBUGGING JAVA PROGRAMS

It is much easier to make a mistake when writing a program containing selection structures and loops than it is when writing simple sequential programs. Even after going through the full design process, a program of any size is almost guaranteed not to be completely correct the first time it is used.

Programs with many levels of `if` structures, `for` loops, and so on will contain many nested layers of braces (`{}`). One of the most common problems is to have *mismatched braces* within a program. A Java compiler will always catch this error, but the error message may not be very informative. For example, consider a portion of the program Ball from Figure 4.9. Suppose that by accident we leave out the opening brace of the `for` loop:

```
for ( theta = 0; theta <= 90; theta++ ) // { missing

   // Get angle in radians
   rad = theta * DEG2RAD;

   // Calculate range in meters.
   range = (-2*v0*v0/gravity) * Math.sin(rad) * Math.cos(rad);

   // Write out the range for this angle.
   System.out.print("Theta = " + theta + " degrees    ");
   System.out.println("Range = " + df.format(range)    + " meters");

   // Compare the range to the previous maximum range. If this
   // range is larger, save it and the angle at which it occurred.
   if ( range > max_range ) {
      max_range = range;
      max_degrees = theta;
   }
 }
// Skip a line, and then write out the maximum range and
// the angle at which it occurred.
System.out.println("\nMax range = " + df.format(max_range) +
                " at " + max_degrees + " degrees.");
```

If we compile this modified program with the Java compiler, the result is:

```
C:\book\java\chap4>javac Ball.java
Ball.java:56: <identifier> expected
      System.out.println("\nMax range = " + df.format(max_range) +
                      ^
Ball.java:59: 'class' or 'interface' expected
 }
 ^
```

The compiler knows that something is wrong, but the resulting error message seems to be complete nonsense. In fact, the compiler has interpreted the closing brace of the `for` loop as the closing brace of the `main` method, so it thinks that the next statement is a new method definition, and it says that the definition has the wrong syntax. The true error was many lines away from the point at which the compiler reported an error, and it had a very different cause. If you get a problem like this, you must inspect your program *very* carefully for syntax problems such as missing braces.

Suppose that we have built and compiled a program, and that the program executes, only to find that the output values are in error when it is tested. How do we go about finding the bugs and fixing them?

The *best* approach to locating the error is to use a symbolic debugger, if one is supplied with your compiler. A symbolic debugger will display the program that you are debugging and allow you to single-step from line to line, checking the values of all variables before and after each line is executed. Alternately, the program can be allowed to run until a *breakpoint* is reached. At the breakpoint, execution will stop and the debugger will allow the user to examine the values of all variables at that point. By locating the point where the values of the variables "go wrong", you can locate the invalid code within your program.

Figure 4.10 illustrates the Borland JBuilder 6.0 debugger running program Stats2. At the time shown, the program has executed to the breakpoint shown by the red line within the `if` structure. The bottom window shows the types and values of all local variables at this time. By stepping through the program a line at a time and watching the values change, a programmer can see if the program is doing what is expected.

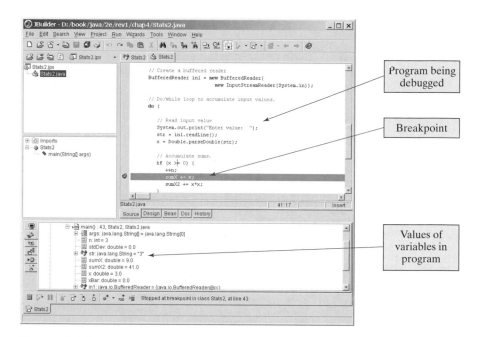

Figure 4.10. A program being debugged in the Borland JBuilder symbolic debugger.

Unfortunately, symbolic debuggers are not a standard part of Java. Each tools vendor creates his or her own symbolic debugger, which will have a different appearance and will use different commands. Since we do not know in advance which type of debugger you might have available, you must ask your instructor or else check with your system's manuals to determine how to use the symbolic debugger supplied with your particular compiler and computer.

If you do not have access to a symbolic debugger, an alternate approach to locating the error is to insert output statements into the code to print out important variables at key points in the program. When the program is run, the output statements will print out the values of the key variables. These values can be compared to the ones you expect, and the places where the actual and expected values differ will serve as clues to help you locate the problem. For example, to verify the operation of a `for` loop, the following output statements could be added to the program.

```
System.out.println("At loop1: ist, ien = " + ist + ", " + ien);
loop1: for (i = ist; i <= ien; i++) {
   System.out.println("In loop1: i = ", + i);
   ...
}
System.out.println("loop1 completed");
```

When the program is executed, its output listing will contain detailed information about the variables controlling the `for` loop and just how many times the loop was executed. Similar output statements could be used to debug the operation of an `if` structure.

Once you have located the portion of the code in which the error occurs, you can take a look at the specific statements in that area to locate the problem. A list of some common errors is given below. Be sure to check for them in your code.

1. *If the problem is in an `if` structure, check to see if you used the proper relational operator in your logical expressions.* Did you use $>$ when you really intended $>=$, and so on? Logic errors of this sort can be very hard to spot, since the compiler will not give an error message for them.

2. *Another common problem with `if` statements occurs when floating-point (`float` and `double`) variables are tested for equality.* Because of small roundoff errors during floating-point arithmetic operations, two numbers which theoretically should be equal will differ by a tiny amount, and the test for equality will fail. Instead of testing for equality, you should test for *near-equality*, as described in Chapter 3.

3. *Most errors in `for` loops involve mistakes with the loop parameters.* If you add output statements to the `for` loop as shown above, the problem should be fairly clear. Did the `for` loop start with the correct value? Did it end with the correct value? Did it increment at the proper step? If not, check the parameters of the `for` loop closely. You will probably spot an error in the control parameters.

4. Errors in `while` and `do/while` loops are usually related to errors in the logical expression used to control their function. These errors may be detected by examining the test expression of the loop with output statements. Errors can also be caused by using a `while` where a `do/while` is required, and vice versa. In other words, confirm whether you want to test for the loop condition at the beginning or at the end of each loop.

SUMMARY

- A `while` loop executes a block of statements repeatedly until its boolean control expression becomes false. The control-expression test occurs before the loop executes.
- A `do/while` loop executes a block of statements repeatedly until its boolean control expression becomes false. The control-expression test occurs after the loop executes.
- A `for` loop executes a block of statements a specified number of times.
- The `continue` statement causes execution of the remaining statements within the body of a loop to be skipped, and execution resumes at the top of the loop. If the loop is a `for` loop, the loop-increment expression is executed.
- The `break` statement causes execution of the remaining statements within the body of a loop to be skipped, and execution resumes at the next statement following the end of the loop.

- If `if`, `while`, `do/while`, or `switch` structures are nested, a `break` or `continue` statement applies to the *innermost* structure containing the statement.
- A labeled `break` or `continue` statement applies to the particular structure with that label, even if it is not the innermost one.
- The `DecimalFormat` class can be used to write out numbers with a user-defined format, including the number of decimal places, currency symbols, and thousands separators.

SUMMARY OF GOOD PROGRAMMING PRACTICES

The following guidelines introduced in this chapter will help you to develop good programs:

1. Always indent the body of any structure by three or more spaces to improve the readability of the code.

2. Use a `while` or `do/while` loop to repeat a set of statements indefinitely until a condition becomes false. Use the `do/while` loop in cases where the loop must be executed at least once. Otherwise, the `while` loop is preferred.

3. Use labeled `break` or `continue` statements to break out of or continue outer loops in a nested loop structure.

4. Use labels on the beginnings and ends of each loop in a complex set of nested loops to make clear which loops go with which close braces.

5. Always use integer variables as `for` loop indexes.

TERMINOLOGY

`break` statement	infinite loop
`continue` statement	label
`DecimalFormat` class	labeled `break` statement
`do/while` loop	labeled `continue` statement
empty statement	nested loops
`for` loop	`while` loop

Exercises

1. Write the Java statements required to calculate and print out the squares of all the even integers between 0 and 50. Create a neat table of your results.

2. Write a Java program to evaluate the equation $y(x) = x^2 - 3x + 2$ for all values of x between -1 and 3, in steps of 0.1.

3. Write a Java program to calculate the factorial function, as defined in Example 4.2. Be sure to handle the special cases of 0! and of illegal input values. Use GUI-based I/O in your program.

4. What is the difference in behavior between a `continue` statement and a `break` statement?

5. Modify program `Stats` to use class `DecimalFormat` for output. Display the average and standard deviation with four digits after the decimal place.

6. What is wrong with each of the following code segments?

    a.
    ```
    x = 5;
    while ( x >= 0 )
        x++;
    ```

    b.
    ```
    x = 1;
    while ( x <= 5 );
        x++;
    ```

    c.
    ```
    for ( x = 0.1; x < 1.0; x += 0.1)
        System.out.println("x = " + x);
    ```

    d.
    ```
    switch (n) {
    case 1:
        System.out.println("Number is 1");
    case 2:
        System.out.println("Number is 2");
        break;
    default:
        System.out.println("Number is not 1 or 2");
        break;
    }
    ```

7. What does the following program do?

    ```
    public class Print {

        // Define the main method
        public static void main(String[] args) {

            for ( int i = 1; i <= 10; i++ ) {
                for ( int j = i; j <= 10; j++ ) {
                    System.out.print("*");

                }
                System.out.println();
            }
        }
    }
    ```

8. Examine the following `for` statements and determine how many times each loop will be executed. (Assume that all loop index variables are integers.)

    a. `for ( range = -32768; range <= 32767; range++ )`
    b. `for ( j = 100; j >= 1; j -= 10 )`
    c. `for ( k = 2; k <= 3; k += 4 )`
    d. `for ( i = -4; i <= -7; i++ )`
    e. `for ( x = -10; x <= 10; x -= 10 )`

9. Examine the following `for` loops and determine the value of `ires` at the end of each of the loops, and also the number of times each loop executes. Assume that all variables are integers.

a.
```
ires = 0;
for ( index = -10; index <= 10; index++ )
    ires++;
}
```

b.
```
ires = 0;
loop1: for ( idx1 = 1; idx1 <= 20; idx1 += 5 ) {
    if ( idx1 <= 10 ) continue;
    loop2: for (idx2=idx1; idx2 <= 20; idx2 += 5) {
        ires = ires + idx2;
    }
}
```

c.
```
ires = 0;
loop1: for ( idx1 = 10; idx1 >= 4; idx1 -= 2) {
    loop2: for ( idx2 = 2; idx2 <= idx1; idx2 += 2 ) {
        if ( idx2 > 6 ) break loop2;
        ires = ires + idx2;
    }
}
```

10. Examine the following `while` loops and determine the value of `ires` at the end of each, and the number of times each loop executes. Assume that all variables are integers.

a.
```
ires = 1;
loop1: do {
    ires = 2 * ires;
} while ( ires / 10 == 0);
```

b.
```
ires = 2
loop2: while (ires <= 512) {
    ires = ires * ires;
    if ( ires == 128 ) break loop2;
}
```

11. Modify program `Ball` from Example 4.7 to read in the acceleration due to gravity at a particular location, and to calculate the maximum range of the ball for that acceleration. After modifying the program, run it with accelerations of -9.8 m/s^2, -9.7 m/s^2, and -9.6 m/s^2. What effect does the reduction in gravitational attraction have on the range of the ball? What effect does the reduction in gravitational attraction have on the best angle θ at which to throw the ball?

12. Write a program to calculate π from the infinite series:

$$\pi = 4 - \frac{4}{3} + \frac{4}{5} - \frac{4}{7} + \frac{4}{9} - \cdots$$

Print a table showing the value of π approximated by one term, two terms, and so on, from this series. The table should have three columns, showing the number of terms used, the approximate value of π, and the difference between the approximate value and the actual value. How many terms of this series are needed to get three significant digits of accuracy (3.14)?

13. Program `DayOfYear` in Example 4.3 calculates the day of year associated with any given month, day, and year. As written, this program does not check to see if the data entered by the user is valid. It will accept nonsense values for months and days and do calculations with them to produce meaningless results. Modify the program so that it checks the input values for validity before using them. If the inputs are invalid, the program should tell the user what is wrong, and quit. The year should be a number greater than zero, the month a number between 1 and 12, and the day a number between 1 and a maximum that depends on the month. Use a `switch` structure to implement the bounds checking performed on the day.

14. **Current Through a Diode**   The current flowing through the semiconductor diode shown in Figure 4.11 is given by the equation

$$i_D = I_0\left(\frac{q^{v_D}}{e^{KT}} - 1\right) \tag{4.8}$$

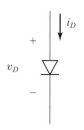

Figure 4.11.   A semiconductor diode.

where i_D = the voltage across the diode, in volts

v_D = the current flow through the diode, in amps

I_0 = the leakage current of the diode, in amps

q = the charge on an electron, 1.602×10^{-19} coulombs

k = Boltzmann's constant, 1.38×10^{-23} joule/K

T = temperature, in kelvins (K)

The leakage current I_0 of the diode is 2.0 μA. Write a computer program to calculate the current flowing through this diode for all voltages from −1.0 V to +0.7 V, in 0.1-V steps. Repeat this process for the following temperatures: 75° F and 100° F, and 125° F. Use the program of Example 2.2 to convert the temperatures from degrees Fahrenheit to kelvins.

15. **Tension on a Cable**   A 200-pound object is to be hung from the end of a rigid 8-foot horizontal pole of negligible weight, as shown in Figure 4.12. The pole is attached to a wall by a pivot and is supported by an 8-foot cable, which is attached to the wall at a higher point. The tension on this cable is given by the equation

$$T = \frac{W \cdot l_c \cdot l_p}{d\sqrt{l_p^2 - d^2}} \tag{4.10}$$

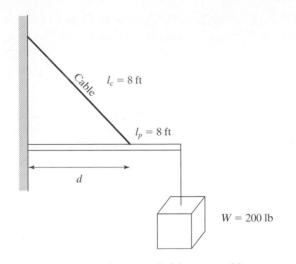

Figure 4.12. A 200-pound weight suspended from a rigid bar supported by a cable.

where T is the tension on the cable, W is the weight of the object, l_c is the length of the cable, l_p is the length of the pole, and d is the distance along the pole at which the cable is attached. Write a program to determine the distance d at which to attach the cable to the pole in order to minimize the tension on the cable. To do this, the program should calculate the tension on the cable at 0.1-foot intervals from $d = 1$ foot to $d = 7$ feet, and should locate the position d that produces the minimum tension.

16.   **Bacterial Growth**   Suppose that a biologist performs an experiment, in which he or she measures the rate at which a specific type of bacterium reproduces asexually in different culture media. The experiment shows that in Medium A the bacteria reproduce once every 60 minutes, and in Medium B they reproduce once every 90 minutes. Assume that a single bacterium is placed on each culture medium at the beginning of the experiment. Write a Java program that calculates and writes out the number of bacteria present in each culture at intervals of three hours from the beginning of the experiment until 24 hours have elapsed. How do the numbers of bacteria compare on the two media after 24 hours?

17.   **Decibels**   Engineers often measure the ratio of two power measurements in *decibels*, or dB. The equation for the ratio of two power measurements in decibels is

$$dB = 10 \log_{10} \frac{P_2}{P_1} \tag{4.11}$$

where P_2 is the power level being measured, and P_1 is some reference power level. Assume that the reference power level P_1 is 1 watt, and write a program that calculates the decibel level corresponding to power levels between 1 and 20 watts, in 0.5-W steps. Format your output neatly using the `Decimal-Format` class.

18.   **Infinite Series**   Trigonometric functions are usually calculated on computers by using a *truncated infinite series*. An *infinite series* is an infinite set of terms

that together add up to the value of a particular function or expression. For example, one infinite series used to evaluate the sine of a number is

$$\sin x = x - \frac{x^3}{3!} + \frac{x^5}{5!} - \frac{x^7}{7!} + \frac{x^9}{9!} + \cdots \tag{4.12a}$$

or

$$\sin x = \sum_{n=1}^{\infty} (-1)^{n-1} \frac{x^{2n-1}}{(2n-1)!} \tag{4.12b}$$

where x is in units of radians.

Since a computer does not have enough time to add an infinite number of terms for every sine that is calculated, the infinite series is *truncated* after a finite number of terms. The number of terms that should be kept in the series is just enough to calculate the function to the precision of the floating-point numbers on the computer on which the function is being evaluated. The truncated infinite series for $\sin x$ is

$$\sin x = \sum_{n=1}^{N} (-1)^{n-1} \frac{x^{2n-1}}{(2n-1)!} \tag{4.13}$$

where N is the number of terms to retain in the series.

Write a Java program that reads in a value for x in degrees, then calculates the sine of x using the sine intrinsic function. Next, calculate the sine of x using Equation (3-13), with $N = 1, 2, 3, \ldots, 10$. Compare the true value of $\sin x$ with the values calculated using the truncated infinite series. How many terms are required to calculate $\sin x$ to the full accuracy of your computer?

19. **Geometric Mean** The *geometric mean* of a set of numbers x_1 through x_n is defined as the nth root of the product of the numbers:

$$\text{geometric mean} = \sqrt[n]{x_1 \, x_2 \, x_3 \, \ldots \, x_n} \tag{4.14}$$

Write a Java program that will accept an arbitrary number of positive input values and calculate both the arithmetic mean (i.e., the average) and the geometric mean of the numbers. Use a `while` loop to get the input values, and terminate the inputs when a user enters a negative number. Test your program by calculating the average and geometric mean of the four numbers 10, 5, 2, and 5.

20. **RMS Average** The *root-mean-square (rms) average* is another way of calculating a mean for a set of numbers. The rms average of a series of numbers is the square root of the arithmetic mean of the squares of the numbers:

$$\text{rms average} = \sqrt{\frac{1}{N} \sum_{i=1}^{N} x_i^2} \tag{4.15}$$

Write a Java program that will accept an arbitrary number of positive input values and calculate the rms average of the numbers. Prompt the user for the number of values to be entered, and use a `for` loop to read in the numbers. Test your program by calculating the rms average of the four numbers 10, 5, 2, and 5.

21.   **Harmonic Mean** The *harmonic mean* is yet another way of calculating a mean for a set of numbers. The harmonic mean of a set of numbers is given by the equation:

$$\text{harmonic mean} = \frac{N}{\dfrac{1}{x_1} + \dfrac{1}{x_2} + \cdots + \dfrac{1}{x_N}} \tag{4.16}$$

Write a Java program that will read in an arbitrary number of positive input values and calculate the harmonic mean of the numbers. Use any method that you desire to read in the input values. Test your program by calculating the harmonic mean of the four numbers 10, 5, 2, and 5.

22.   Write a single Java program that calculates the arithmetic mean (average), rms average, geometric mean, and harmonic mean for a set of positive numbers. Use any method that you desire to read in the input values. Compare these values for each of the following sets of numbers:

a.   4, 4, 4, 4, 4, 4, 4

b.   4, 3, 4, 5, 4, 3, 5

c.   4, 1, 4, 7, 4, 1, 7

d.   1, 2, 3, 4, 5, 6, 7

23.   **Mean-Time-Between-Failure Calculations** The reliability of a piece of electronic equipment is usually measured in terms of *mean time between failures (MTBF)*, where MTBF is the average time that the piece of equipment can operate before a failure occurs in it. For large systems containing many pieces of electronic equipment, it is customary to determine the MTBFs of each component, and from these to calculate the overall MTBF of the system. If the system is structured like the one shown in Figure 4.13, every component must work in order for the whole system to work, and the overall system MTBF can be calculated as

$$\text{MTBF}_{sys} = \frac{1}{\dfrac{1}{\text{MTBF}_1} + \dfrac{1}{\text{MTBF}_2} + \cdots + \dfrac{1}{\text{MTBF}_n}} \tag{4.17}$$

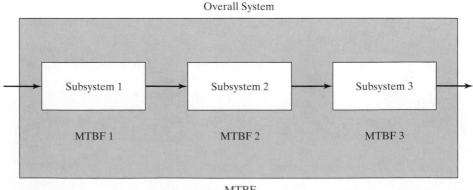

Figure 4.13. An electronic system containing three subsystems connected in series, with known MTBFs for each subsystem.

Write a program that reads in the number of series components in a system and the MTBFs for each component, then calculates the overall MTBF for the system. To test your program, determine the MTBF for a radar system consisting of an antenna subsystem with an MTBF of 2000 hours, a transmitter with an MTBF of 800 hours, a receiver with an MTBF of 3000 hours, and a computer with an MTBF of 5000 hours. Use GUI-based I/O for this program.

5

One-Dimensional Arrays, File Access, and Plotting

This chapter serves as an introduction to an important data structure: the array. An **array** is a group of contiguous memory locations that all have the same name and same type. Individual memory locations within the array are selected by adding a subscript to the array name. This data structure is implemented as an object in Java. We will learn about one-dimensional arrays of primitive data types (`int`, `double`, `float`, and so on) in this chapter. It is also possible to create arrays of objects, but that discussion will be postponed until Chapter 8, after we have formally introduced objects in Chapter 7. Finally, it is possible to create arrays with two or more dimensions. These arrays will be covered in Chapter 11.

An array is a convenient way to store and manipulate large quantities of data, but where does that data come from? It would not be reasonable to expect the user to manually type in hundreds or thousands of values in order to use your program! Instead, we typically save data in files on disk. The data is read from the file when a program needs it, and the results of the program are written back to a file. In this chapter, we will learn a simple (but limited) way to read data from a file into an array and to write it back out again. This limited file I/O will be further enhanced and improved in Chapter 10, after we learn about exceptions.

Finally, what does a typical scientist or engineer do with a data set once it has been collected? He or she plots it to look for patterns, trends, and so forth. This chapter will introduce a convenience class to allow us to begin plotting arrays of data. This class will be used until we learn about graphics and GUIs. After that, you will write your own plotting classes!

SECTIONS

OBJECTIVES

- Understand how to create, initialize, and use arrays of primitive data types (`int`, `double`, and so on).
- Know the difference between an array reference, an array object, and an array element.
- Be able to read numeric data from and write numeric data to disk files.
- Be able to sort numeric data stored in an array.
- Be able plot arrays of data using the `chapman.graphics.JPlot2D` class.

5.1   INTRODUCTION TO ARRAYS

An **array** is a special object containing (1) a group of memory locations that all have the same name and same type, and (2) a separate instance variable containing an integer constant equal to the number of elements in the array (see Figure 5.1). An individual

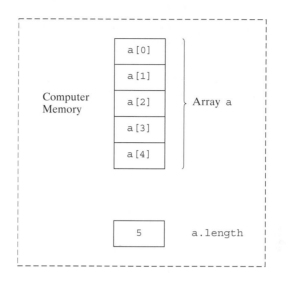

Figure 5.1.   An array object contains a set of elements, all of the same type, occupying successive locations in a computer's memory. It also contains an integer constant set equal to the number of elements in the array.

value within the array is called an **array element**; it is identified by the name of the array together with a **subscript** in square brackets. The subscript identifies the particular location within the array. Note that *the elements of Java arrays are numbered starting with 0 and working upward*. For example, the first element of the array shown in Figure 5.1 is referred to as a[0], and the fifth element is referred to as a[4]. The subscript of an array must be an integer. Either constants or variables may be used for array subscripts.

The length of any Java array is included as a separate memory location within the array object itself, and that length can be accessed by appending the string .length to the name of the array. Thus, the length of array a in Figure 5.1 can be accessed as a.length. The length of a Java array is specified when it is created, and it remains fixed for as long as the array exists.

PROGRAMMING PITFALLS

The elements of an n-element Java array arr have subscripts numbered 0, 1, 2, ..., n −1. Note that there is no element arr[n]! Novice programmers often make the mistake of trying to use this nonexistent element.

As we shall see, arrays can be extremely powerful tools. They permit us to apply the same algorithm over and over to many different data items with a simple loop. For example, suppose that we need to take the square root of 100 different floating-point numbers. If the numbers are stored as elements of an array a consisting of 100 `double` values, then the code

```
for ( i = 0; i < 100; i++ )
    a[i] = Math.sqrt(a[i]);
```

will take the square root of each number and store it back into the memory location that it came from. If we wanted to take the square root of 100 numbers without using arrays, we would have to write out a separate statement for each variable:

```
a0  = Math.sqrt(a0);
a1  = Math.sqrt(a1);
a2  = Math.sqrt(a2);
a3  = Math.sqrt(a3);
a1  = Math.sqrt(a4);
   . . .
       . . .
a99 = Math.sqrt(a99);
```

—100 separate statements! Arrays are obviously a *much* cleaner and shorter way to handle repeated similar operations.

As we shall see, it is possible to manipulate and perform calculations with individual elements of arrays one by one. We will first learn how to declare arrays in Java programs. Then we will learn how to use arrays in Java statements.

5.2 DECLARING ARRAYS

An array must be created before it can be used. This is a two-step process. First, we must declare a **reference** to an array, and then we actually create the array. A *reference* is a "handle" or "pointer" to an object that permits Java to locate the object in memory when it is needed. It serves as the name of the object when we want to use it.

A reference to an array is created by naming the object type followed by the reference name. It looks just like the declaration of an `int`, `double`, or any other primitive data type, except that the type is followed by square brackets (`[]`). For example, a reference to `double` array is created by the statement[1]

```
double[] x;              // Create an array reference
```

When this statement is executed, the array reference x is created. However, the value of the reference is initially **null**, since it doesn't "point to" an array object yet [see Figure 5.2(a)]. Attempting to use a null reference in a program will produce a run-time exception.

Once a reference has been created, we can create an array object to assign to the reference using the **new** operator. This operator **instantiates** (the Java word for "creates") an array object of the specified size. For example, the following statement creates a new five-element array and sets the reference x to refer to that array [see Figure 5.2(b)]:

```
x = new double[5];       // Create array object
```

---

[1]A reference to an array can also be declared with the [] attached to the reference instead of the data type:

```
double x[];              // Create an array reference
```

This form of reference declaration is the same as in C and C++. It may be freely used in Java if desired.

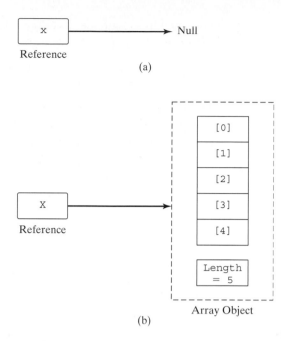

Figure 5.2.   An array reference is a "pointer" to an array object. (a) When a reference is first declared and not initialized, it does not point to an object. Using this null reference in a program will cause a run-time exception. (b) The statement "x = new double[5]" creates an array object containing five double elements, and sets reference x to refer to that object.

The new operator is followed by the data type of the array object to be created and square brackets containing the number of array elements to be allocated. When the elements are allocated, they are automatically initialized to zero.

Note that each array reference has a type, and *the reference can refer only to array objects of that type*. Thus, the statements below are illegal, since they attempt to assign a double array to an int reference:

```
int[] x;              // Create array reference
x = new double[5];    // Create array object (illegal)
```

The creation of an array reference and an array object may be written together on a single line as follows:

```
double[] x = new double[5];
```

It is also possible to create multiple reference and array objects in a single declaration. For example, the following declaration creates two double arrays a and b, having 5 and 10 elements, respectively.

```
double[] a = new double[5], b = new double[10];
```

5.3   USING ARRAY ELEMENTS IN JAVA STATEMENTS

Each element of an array is a variable just like any other variable, and *an array element may be used anywhere an ordinary variable of the same type may be used*. Array elements may be included in arithmetic and logical expressions, and the results of an expression may be assigned to an array element. For example, assume that arrays index and temp are declared as

```
int[] index = new int[5];
double[] temp = new double[4];
```

The five elements of array index would be addressed as index[0], index[1], index[2], index[3], and index[4], while the four elements of array temp would be addressed as temp[0], temp[1], temp[2], and temp[3]. With this definition, the following Java statements are perfectly valid:

```
index[0] = 1;
temp[3] = index[0] / 4.;
System.out.println("index[0] = ", index[0]);
```

Arrays are commonly used in loops to allow the same calculation to be applied to many different values stored in the array elements. For example, the simple program shown in Figure 5.3 calculates the squares of the numbers in array number, and then

```
// Calculates the squares of the numbers from 1 to 10
public class Squares {

   // Define the main method
   public static void main(String[] args) {

      double[] number = new double[10];   // Array of numbers
      double[] square = new double[10];   // Array of squares

      // Calculate squares
      for ( int i = 0; i < number.length; i++ ) {
         number[i] = i + 1;
         square[i] = number[i] * number[i];
      }

      // Write number and square
      for ( int i = 0; i < number.length; i++ ) {
         System.out.print("number = " + number[i]);
         System.out.println("  square = " + square[i]);
      }
   }
}
```

Figure 5.3. A program to calculate the squares of the integers from 1 to 10.

prints out the numbers and their squares. The for loop applies the same calculations to every element of arrays number and square.

Note that the for loops performing calculations on array number use the size of the array number.length as their continuation condition. This practice makes the program more flexible, since we can change the sizes of the arrays created in the program, and the number of passes through the body of the for loops will be updated automatically. Because the elements of the array are labeled 0, 1, 2, ..., number.length−1, the proper continuation test for the loop is i < number.length.

When this program is executed, the results are:

```
D:\book\java\chap5>java Squares
number = 1.0   square = 1.0
number = 2.0   square = 4.0
number = 3.0   square = 9.0
number = 4.0   square = 16.0
number = 5.0   square = 25.0
number = 6.0   square = 36.0
number = 7.0   square = 49.0
number = 8.0   square = 64.0
number = 9.0   square = 81.0
number = 10.0  square = 100.0
```

GOOD PROGRAMMING PRACTICE

When creating `for` loops to process the elements of an array, use the array object's `length` field in the continuation condition for the loop. This will allow the loop to adjust automatically for different-sized arrays.

GOOD PROGRAMMING PRACTICE

When processing an array `arr` in a `for` loop, use a continuation condition of the form

```
for ( j = 0; j < arr.length;+ j++ )
```

The "less than" relational operator is the correct one to use, because the elements of the array are numbered `0, 1, ..., arr.length-1`.

Although *array elements* may be used freely in Java expressions and statements wherever an ordinary variable would be used, *array references* may not. For a five-element integer array with a reference `arr`, the following statements are legal:

```
for (int i = 0; i < 5; i++)
    arr[i] += 2;
```

This statement adds 2 to the value of each element in the array, one element at a time. However, the statement

```
arr += 2;
```

is illegal and will produce a compilation error. This statement tried to add 2 to the value of the *array reference*, which is not a legal operation.

PROGRAMMING PITFALLS

It is illegal to use an array reference in a place where an ordinary variable would be used in a Java expression. Only individual array elements may be used in this manner.

5.3.1 Initializing Array Values

An array object may be created and initialized using an **array initializer** when its reference is declared. An array initializer is a comma-separated list of values enclosed in braces. It may only appear in an array reference declaration. For example, the following statement declares an array reference a, creates and assigns a five-element array object to the reference, and initializes the array elements to 1, 2, 3, 4, and 5.

```
int[] a = {1, 2, 3, 4, 5};
```

Array initializers work only in reference declaration statements. They may *not* be used to create an array object after its reference has been declared. For example, the following statements are illegal and will produce a compile-time error.

```
int[] a;
a[] = {1, 2, 3, 4, 5};  // This statement is illegal
```

The simple program shown in Figure 5.4 illustrates the use of an initializer to initialize the elements of array number. When this program is executed, the output is identical to the result of the previous program.

```
// Calculates the squares of the numbers from 1 to 10
public class Square2 {

   // Define the main method
   public static void main(String[] args) {

      double[] number = {1, 2, 3, 4, 5, 6, 7, 8, 9, 10};
      double[] square = new double[10];  // Array of squares

      // Calculate squares
      for ( int i = 0; i < number.length; i++ )
         square[i] = number[i] * number[i];

      // Write number and square
      for ( int i = 0; i < number.length; i++ ) {
         System.out.print("number = " + number[i]);
         System.out.println("  square = " + square[i]);
      }
   }
}
```

Figure 5.4. A program illustrating the use of array initializers.

5.3.2 Out-of-Bounds Array Subscripts

Each element of an array is addressed using an integer subscript. The range of integers that can be used to address array elements depends on the declared extent of the array. For a double array declared as

```
double[] a = new double[5];
```

the integer subscripts 0 through 4 address elements in the array. *Any other integers* (less than 0 or greater than 4) *could not be used as subscripts, since they do not correspond to allocated memory locations.* Such integers subscripts are said to be **out of bounds** for the array. But what happens if we make a mistake and try to access the out-of-bounds element a[5] in a program?

Every Java array "knows" its own length, and Java has automatic **bounds checking** built into the language. If an attempt is made to access an out-of-bounds array element, a run-time error occurs. Java calls such errors **run-time exceptions**, and the method in which the error occurs is said to **throw an exception**. We will see in Chapter 10 that Java has a special way of handling such exceptions when they occur. If an exception occurs and it is *not* handled, the program containing the exception will abort. The special exception produced by accessing an out-of-bounds array element is called an **ArrayIndexOutOf-BoundsException**.

The program shown in Figure 5.5 illustrates the behavior of a Java program containing incorrect array references. This simple program declares a five-element int array a. The array a is initialized with the values 1, 2, 3, 4, and 5, and then the program attempts to print out six array elements.

```java
// Test array bounds checking
public class TestBounds {

    // Define the main method
    public static void main(String[] args) {

        // Declare and initialize array
        int[] a = {1,2,3,4,5};

        // Write array (with an error!)
        for ( int i = 0; i <= 5; i++ )
            System.out.println("a[" + i + "] = " + a[i]);
    }
}
```

Figure 5.5. A simple program to illustrate the effect of out-of-bounds array references.

When this program is compiled and executed, the results are

```
C:\book\java\chap5>java TestBounds
a[0] = 1
a[1] = 2
a[2] = 3
a[3] = 4
a[4] = 5
Exception in thread "main"
    java.lang.ArrayIndexOutOfBoundsException: 5
        at TestBounds.main(TestBounds.java:12)
```

The program checked each array reference and aborted when an out-of-bounds expression was encountered. Note that the error message tells us what is wrong, and even the line number at which it occurred.

5.3.3   The Use of Named Constants with Array Declarations

In many Java programs, arrays are used to store large amounts of information. The amount of information that a program can process depends on the size of the arrays it contains. If the arrays are relatively small, the program will be small and will not require much memory to run, but it will be able to handle only a small amount of data. On the other hand, if the arrays are large, the program will be able to handle a lot of information, but it will require a lot of memory to run. The array sizes in such a program are frequently changed to make it run better for different problems or on different processors.

It is good practice to always declare the array sizes using named constants (also called final variables). Named constants make it easy to resize the arrays in a Java program. In the following code, the sizes of all arrays can be changed by simply changing the single named constant ARRAY_SIZE.

```
final int ARRAY_SIZE = 1000;
double[] array1 = new double [ARRAY_SIZE];
double[] array2 = new double [ARRAY_SIZE];
double[] array2 = new double [2*ARRAY_SIZE];
```

Note that, by convention, named constants are written in all capital letters, with underscores separating words.

This may seem like a small point, but it is *very* important to the proper maintenance of large programs. If all related array sizes in a program are declared using named constants, and if the built-in lengths of the arrays are used in any size tests in the program, then it will be much simpler to modify the program later. Imagine what it would be like if you had to locate and change every reference to array sizes within a 50,000-line program! The process could take weeks to complete and debug. By contrast, the size of a well-designed program could be modified in five minutes by changing only one statement.

GOOD PROGRAMMING PRACTICE

Declare the sizes of arrays in a Java program using named constants to make them easy to change.

EXAMPLE 5.1

Finding the Largest and Smallest Values in a Data Set: To illustrate the use of arrays, we will write a simple program that reads in data values and finds the largest and smallest numbers in the data set. The program will then write out the values, with the word LARGEST printed by the largest value and the word SMALLEST printed by the smallest value in the data set.

SOLUTION

This program must ask the user for the number of values to read, create an array large enough to hold those values, and then read the input values into the array. Once the values are all read, it must go through the data to find the largest and smallest values. Finally, it must print out the values, with the appropriate annotations beside the largest and smallest values.

1. **Determine the User Requirements**

   The basic requirement for this program is that it must read a set of numbers from the standard input stream, then write the values back to the standard output stream with the words LARGEST and SMALLEST printed by the largest and smallest values in the data set. However, a bit of information is missing here: What sort of numbers does the program need to read and write? To define the user requirement properly, we must go back and find out whether the person requesting the program wants to process integers or floating-point numbers. For this exercise, we will assume that the user wanted to process integers.

2. **Analysis and Decomposition**

   There are two types of inputs to this program:

   a. An integer containing the number of integer values to read. This value will come from the standard input device.

b.   The integer values in the data set. These values will also come from the standard input device.

The outputs from this program are the values in the data set, with the word LARGEST printed by the largest value, and the word SMALLEST printed by the smallest value.

This program will consist of a single class, containing the single method main. We will call the class Extremes.

3.   **Detailed Design**

The main method can be broken down into four major steps

```
Get the number of values to read
Read the input values into an array
Find the largest and smallest values in the array
Write out the data with the words "LARGEST" and
   "SMALLEST" at the appropriate places
```

The first two major steps of the program are to get the number of values to read in and to read the values into an input array. We must prompt the user for the number of values to read, and then create an array of that size. Then we should read in the data values. The detailed pseudocode for these steps is:

```
Prompt user for the number of input values nvals
Read in nvals
Create an integer array of size nvals
for (j = 0; j < nvals; j++) {
   Read in input value
}
...
...(Further processing here)
...
```

Next we must locate the largest and smallest values in the data set. We will use variables large and small as pointers to the array elements having the largest and smallest values. The pseudocode to find the largest and smallest values is:

```
// Find largest value
temp ← input[0];
large ← 0;
for ( j = 1; j < nvals; j++ ) {
   if (input[j] > temp) {
      temp ← input[j]
      large ← j
   }
}

// Find smallest value
temp ← input[0];
small ← 0;
```

```
for ( j = 1; j < nvals; j++ ) {
    if (input[j] < temp) {
        temp ← input[j]
        small ← j
    }
}
```

The final step is writing out the values with the largest and smallest numbers labeled:

```
for ( j = 0; j < nvals; j++ ) {
    if (small == j)
        Write "SMALLEST" and input[j]
    else if (large == j)
        Write "LARGEST" and input[j]
    else
        Write input[j]
}
```

4.   **Implementation: Convert Algorithms to Java statements**

The resulting Java program is shown in Figure 5.6.

```
/*
   Purpose:
     To find the largest and smallest values in a data set,
     and to print out the data set with the largest and smallest
     values labeled.

   Record of revisions:
       Date           Programmer            Description of change
       ====           ==========            =====================
     04/02/2002     S. J. Chapman            Original code
*/
import java.io.*;
public class Extremes {

   // Define the main method
   public static void main(String[] args) throws IOException {

      // Declare variables, and define each variable
      int j;                 // Loop index
      int large;             // Index of largest value
      int nvals;             // Number of vals in data set
      int small;             // Index of smallest value
      String str;            // String
      int temp;              // Temporary variable

      // Create a buffered reader
      BufferedReader in1 = new BufferedReader(
                        new InputStreamReader(System.in));

      // Get the number of points to input
      System.out.print("Enter number of elements in array: ");
```

Figure 5.6.   A program to read in a data set from the standard input device, find the largest and smallest values, and print the values with the largest and smallest values labeled.

```java
        str = in1.readLine();
        nvals = Integer.parseInt(str);

        // Create array of proper size
        int[] input = new int[nvals];

        // Get values
        for (j = 0; j < nvals; j++) {
            System.out.print("Enter value " + (j+1) + ": ");
            str = in1.readLine();
            input[j] = Integer.parseInt(str);
        }

        // Find largest value
        temp = input[0];
        large = 0;
        for ( j = 1; j < nvals; j++ ) {
            if (input[j] > temp) {
                temp = input[j];
                large = j;
            }
        }

        // Find smallest value
        temp = input[0];
        small = 0;
        for ( j = 1; j < nvals; j++ ) {
            if (input[j] < temp) {
                temp = input[j];
                small = j;
            }
        }

        // Write out results
        System.out.print("\nThe values are:\n");
        for ( j = 0; j < nvals; j++ ) {
            if (small == j)
                System.out.println(" SMALLEST: " + input[j]);
            else if (large == j)
                System.out.println(" LARGEST:  " + input[j]);
            else
                System.out.println("           " + input[j]);
        }
    }
}
```

Figure 5.6. (Continued).

5. **Testing**

To test this program, we will create a data set with six values: −6, 5, −11, 16, 9, and 0.

```
D:\book\java\chap5>java Extremes
Enter number of elements in array: 6
Enter value 1: -6
Enter value 2: 5
```

```
Enter value 3: -11
Enter value 4: 16
Enter value 5: 9
Enter value 6: 0

The values are:
                   -6
                    5
      SMALLEST:   -11
      LARGEST:     16
                    9
                    0
```

The program correctly labeled the largest and smallest values in the data set. Thus, the program gives the correct answer for our test data set. ∎

5.4 ARRAY REFERENCE ASSIGNMENTS AND DATA LEAKS

In Section 5.3 we mentioned that *array references* cannot be used like ordinary variables in Java expressions and statements. If the reference a is declared as

```
int[] a;
```

then an assignment statement such as

```
a = 2;
```

is illegal, and will produce a compile-time error. In general, array references cannot be used in Java expressions or assignment statements where ordinary variables would be used.

However, one array reference *can* be assigned to another array reference, as long as both references are of the same type. Suppose that two integer array references x and y are defined as follows:

```
int[] x = {1, 2, 3, 4, 5};
int[] y;
```

Reference x points to a five-element integer array, while reference y does not point to any array (that is, the reference is currently null, as shown in Figure 5.7(a)]. In this case, the statement

```
y = x;
```

is legal. It assigns the reference y to point to the *same array object* as reference x [see Figure 5.7(b)].

The program shown in Figure 5.8 illustrates this assignment. In this program, references x and y are both assigned to the same array object. When the value of x[2] is modified, the value of y[2] is also changed.

When this program is compiled and executed, the results are

```
C:\book\java\chap5>java ReferenceAssignment
 x = 1 2 3 4 5
 y = 1 2 3 4 5
 x = 1 2 -100 4 5
 y = 1 2 -100 4 5
```

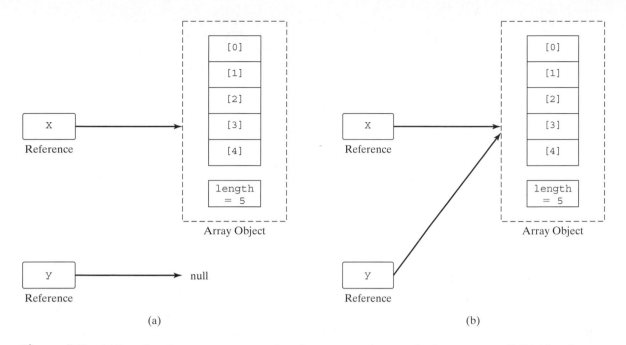

Figure 5.7. (a) Initially reference x points to a five-element array object, and reference y is null. (b) After the statement "y = x" is executed, both references x and y point to the *same* array object.

```
public class ReferenceAssignment {
    // Define the main method
    public static void main(String[] args) {
        // Declare variables
        int i;
        int[] x = {1, 2, 3, 4, 5};
        int[] y;

        // Assign reference
        y = x;

        // Display arrays
        System.out.print(" x = ");
        for (i = 0; i < x.length; i++) {
            System.out.print(x[i] + " ");
        }
        System.out.println(" ");

        System.out.print(" y = ");
        for (i = 0; i < y.length; i++) {
            System.out.print(y[i] + " ");
        }
        System.out.println(" ");

        // Change an element of array x
        x[2] = -100;
```

Figure 5.8. Program illustrating how two references can point to the same array.

```
                // Display arrays again
                System.out.print(" x = ");
                for (i = 0; i < x.length; i++) {
                    System.out.print(x[i] + " ");
                }
                System.out.println(" ");

                System.out.print(" y = ");
                for (i = 0; i < y.length; i++) {
                    System.out.print(y[i] + " ");
                }
                System.out.println(" ");
            }
        }
```

Figure 5.8. (Continued).

Array reference assignments can produce a serious problem in a Java program. Suppose that two array references x and y point to two different arrays [see Figure 5.9(a)]. If the statement "y = x" is executed, then *both* x and y point to the array that x originally pointed to. That array can be accessed by using either x or y. On the other hand, *the array that y originally pointed to is no longer accessible*. The contents of that array still exist, but they are forever lost to the program, since there is no longer a reference pointing to it [see Figure 5.9(b)].

This situation is called a **data leak**, since some of the data allocated by the program is no longer accessible. The memory itself is not lost, because Java has an independent

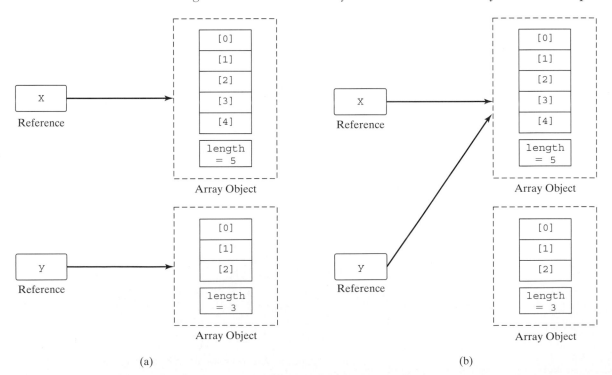

(a)   (b)

Figure 5.9. (a) Initially reference x points to a five-element array object, and reference y points to a three-element array object. (b) After the statement "y = x" is executed, both references x and y point to the five-element array object, and the three-element array object is "lost" to the program.

way to recover memory allocated to objects without references (called *garbage collection*), which we will study in Chapter 7. However, the program can never recover the data in the "lost" memory.

The program shown in Figure 5.10 illustrates data leaks. In this program, references x and y are initially assigned to two different objects. When the reference y is made the same as x, both references point to the five-element array, and the three-element array is lost to the program.

```
// Program illustrating a memory leak
public class ShowLeak {
    // Define the main method
    public static void main(String[] args) {
        // Declare variables
        int i;
        double[] x = {1., 2., 3., 4., 5.};
        double[] y = {-1., -2., -3.};
        // Output statements
        System.out.println("Before assignment:");
        for (i = 0; i < x.length; i++) {
            System.out.println("x[" + i + "] = " + x[i]);
        }
        System.out.println(" ");
        for (i = 0; i < y.length; i++) {
            System.out.println("y[" + i + "] = " + y[i]);
        }
        // Reference assignment causing memory leak
        y = x;
        // Output statements
        System.out.println("\nAfter assignment:");
        for (i = 0; i < x.length; i++) {
            System.out.println("x[" + i + "] = " + x[i]);
        }
        System.out.println(" ");
        for (i = 0; i < y.length; i++) {
            System.out.println("y[" + i + "] = " + y[i]);
        }
    }
}
```

Figure 5.10.   Program illustrating a data leak.

When this program is compiled and executed, the results are

```
C:\book\java\chap5>java ShowLeak
Before assignment:
x[0] = 1.0
x[1] = 2.0
x[2] = 3.0
x[3] = 4.0
x[4] = 5.0
```

```
y[0] = -1.0
y[1] = -2.0
y[2] = -3.0

After assignment:

x[0] = 1.0
x[1] = 2.0
x[2] = 3.0
x[3] = 4.0
x[4] = 5.0

y[0] = 1.0
y[1] = 2.0
y[2] = 3.0
y[3] = 4.0
y[4] = 5.0
```

Quiz 5-1

This quiz provides a quick check to see if you have understood the concepts introduced in Sections 5.1 through 5.4. If you have trouble with the quiz, reread the sections, ask your instructor, or discuss the material with a fellow student. The answers are found in the back of the book.

1. What is an array? What components are found with a Java array?
2. What is a reference? How do you declare a reference to an array?
3. How is an array object created?
4. How may an array be initialized?
5. Suppose you have created an 100-element array. What range of subscripts may be used to address the elements of this array?
6. How can arrays be "lost" in a Java program?

Determine which of the following Java statements are valid. For each valid statement, specify what will happen in the program.

7.
```
double[] arr;
arr = new double[10];
```

8.
```
double[] aaa;
aaa = new int[100];
```

9.
```
double[] bbb;
bbb[] = {1., 2., 3., 4., 5., 6.};
```

10.
```
double[] aaa, bbb= {1., 2., 3., 4., 5., 6.};
aaa = bbb[];
```

11.
```
double[] aaa, bbb= {1., 2., 3., 4., 5., 6.};
aaa = bbb;
```

12.
```
double aaa[] = {1., 2., 3., 4., 5.};
for ( i = 1; i < aaa.length; i++ )
   System.out.println("i = " + aaa[i]);
```

13.
```
double aaa[] = {1., 2., 3., 4., 5.};
for ( i = aaa.length-1; i >= 0; i-- )
   System.out.println("i = " + aaa[i]);
```

5.5 READING AND WRITING ARRAYS OF DATA TO FILES

Arrays are designed to hold and manipulate large amounts of data, so that we can apply the same basic calculations to many different values in just a few statements. Unfortunately, it is not quite so easy to read in and write out the large quantities of data. For example, suppose that we were working with a 10,000-element input array. Can you imagine entering all 10,000 elements by typing them one-by-one at the standard input stream?

What we really need is a convenient way to read and write data to disk files. There are two ways to accomplish this. One approach is to read data from the standard input stream and to write data to the standard output stream, but to *redirect* the standard input stream and standard output stream to disk files using **command-line redirection**. The standard input stream is redirected by typing a **<** followed by the file name on the command line, and the standard output stream is redirected by typing a **>** followed by the file name on the command line. If all of the inputs needed for a program are placed in the input file in the proper order, the program will be able to execute without further operator input. For example, the following command line starts program `Example`, which reads data from file `infile` and writes data to file `outfile`.

`D:\book\java\chap5>`**`java Example < infile > outfile`**

The other, more flexible approach is to open files and to read from or write to them directly from inside a Java program. Unfortunately, the Java I/O system is very complex, and it is not easy to simply open a file, read the data you want, and close it again. We will study the details of of the Java I/O system in Chapter 16.

Meanwhile we will introduce a few classes that allow us to read and write formatted files with a few restrictions. We can read formatted files using classes `FileReader` and `BufferedReader`. We can write formatted files using classes `FileWriter`, `BufferedWriter`, and `PrintWriter`. All of these classes are found in the `java.io` package. By combining them with what we already know about reading data from the standard input stream and writing data to the standard output stream, we will be able to perform simple file I/O.

5.5.1 Reading Files

Class `FileReader` is a class that opens a file so that a user can read data from it one character at a time. Since the standard input stream also presents characters to a Java program one at a time, everything that we have learned about reading from the standard input stream will also apply to reading from a file using this class.

Just as with the standard input stream, we will wrap a `BufferedReader` around the `FileReader` and use the `readLine()` method to read data one line at a time. Once a line has been read in, it can be converted into numeric data using the `Double.parseDouble(str)` or `Integer.parseInt(str)` methods.

A file is opened for reading with the following statement

```
BufferedReader in1 = new BufferedReader(
                        new FileReader(filename));
```

where `filename` is a string containing the name of the file to open. The reference to the resulting object is `in1`, and the file can now be manipulated by applying various methods to this reference.

Once the file is open, we can read data a line at a time using the `readLine()` method applied to reference `in1`.

```
str = in1.readLine();
```

If the end of the file has been reached, a **null string** will be returned. We can test for this condition by comparing the returned value to the **null keyword**—if they are equal, then we have reached the end of the file.

After the end of a file is reached, the file should be closed so that it is available for use by other programs. A file is closed using the `close()` method on the file's reference.

```
in1.close();
```

The program in Figure 5.11 uses the `FileReader` class to read a series of `double` values from a file. This program opens a file called `infile` and reads its contents one line at a time, using the `in1.readLine()` method in a `while` loop. After each line is read, this program tests to see that the string is not null. If it is not, it converts the line into a `double` value and saves the value in array a. Note that we are using the postincrement operator on the array index `nvals`, so that we save the new value into the current location in array a, and then increment `nvals` by 1 after saving the value. Since array indices start at 0, `nvals` will always contain the number of values that have been read.

When the string read from the file is null, the `while` loop terminates, and we close the file. The input values in the array are then displayed one at a time.

```java
// Test FileFileReader for double values
import java.io.*;
public class TestFileReader {

   // Define the main method
   public static void main(String arg[]) throws IOException {

      // Declare variables and arrays
      double a[] = new double[100];      // Input array
      int i = 0;                         // Loop index
      int nvals = 0;                     // Index
      String str;                        // Input string

        // Create a buffered reader
      BufferedReader in1 = new BufferedReader(
                              new FileReader("infile"));

      // Read the data
      str = in1.readLine();
      while ( str != null ) {
         a[nvals++] = Double.parseDouble(str);
         str = in1.readLine();
      }

      // We have finished reading, so close the file
      in1.close();

      // Display results
      for ( i = 0; i < nvals; i++ ) {
         System.out.println("a[" + i + "] = " + a[i]);
      }
   }
}
```

Figure 5.11. A program to read a data set from a file into an array and then display the data.

To test this program, we will create a file `infile` containing the following data:

```
1.0
-4.3
0.0
0.6
3.33333
```

When this program is executed, the results are:

```
D:\book\java\chap5>java TestFileReader
a[0] = 1.0
a[1] = -4.3
a[2] = 0.0
a[3] = 0.6
a[4] = 3.33333
```

As you can see, the program read the input file successfully.

The technique that we are using to read files has two very significant limitations. There can be only *one value per line* in the file to be read, and there can be *no blank lines* within the file. We will learn how to relax these restrictions and produce a more flexible file reader in Chapters 8 and 10. For now, please just live within these restrictions.

PROGRAMMING PITFALLS

The file-reading technique developed in this chapter works only for files with *one value per line* and with *no blank lines*. We will develop more general file-reading techniques beginning in Chapters 8 and 10.

5.5.2   Writing Files

Class `FileWriter` opens a file so that a user can write data to it one character at a time. Since the standard output stream also writes characters one at a time, everything that we have learned about writing to the standard output stream will also apply to reading from a file using this class.

A file is opened for writing with the following statement

```
PrintWriter out = new PrintWriter(
              new BufferedWriter(
                 new FileWriter(filename)));
```

where `filename` is a string containing the name of the file to open. The reference to the resulting object is `out`, and the file can now be manipulated by applying various methods to this reference.

In this statement, the `FileWriter` object opens the specified file for writing, while the `BufferedWriter` saves up output characters so that they can be sent to the file in large groups. Finally, the `PrintWriter` class allows us to use the `print` and `println` methods on this file.

After all of the data has been written to it, the file should be closed so that it is available for use by other programs. A file is closed using the `close()` method on the file's reference.

```
out.close();
```

The program in Figure 5.12 shows how to use class `FileWriter` to write data to a file.

```
// Declare variables
int i;                              // Loop index
double[] a = {-1., 6.2, 0., 3.2, 5.}; // double array

// Test open without append
PrintWriter out = new PrintWriter(
                new BufferedWriter(
                  new FileWriter("outfile")));

// Write data
for ( i = 0; i < a.length; i++ ) {
    out.println ("a[" + i + "] = " + a[i]);
}

// Close file
out.close();
    }
}
```

Figure 5.12.   A program to write data to an output file.

When this program is executed, the results are:

```
D:\book\java\chap5>java TestFileWriter
D:\book\java\chap5>type outfile
This is a line!
a[0] = -1.0
a[1] = 6.2
a[2] = 0.0
a[3] = 3.2
a[4] = 5.0
```

5.6   EXAMPLE PROBLEMS

Now we will examine two example problems that illustrate the use of arrays.

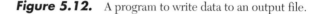

EXAMPLE 5.2

Sorting Data: In many scientific and engineering applications, it is necessary to take a random input data set and to sort it so that the numbers are either all in *ascending order* (lowest-to-highest) or all in *descending order* (highest-to-lowest). For example, suppose that you were a zoologist studying a large population of animals, and that you wanted to identify the largest 5% of the animals in the population. The most straightforward approach would be to sort the sizes of all of the animals in the population into ascending order and take the top 5% of the values.

Sorting data into ascending or descending order seems to be an easy job. After all, we do it all the time. It is simple matter for us to sort the data (10, 3, 6, 4, 9) into the order (3, 4, 6, 9, 10). How do we do it? We first scan the input data list (10, 3, 6, 4, 9) to find the smallest value in the list (3), then scan the remaining input data (10, 6, 4, 9) to find the next smallest value (4), and so on, until the complete list is sorted.

In fact, sorting can be a very difficult job. As the number of values to be sorted increases, the time required to perform the simple sort described above increases rapidly, since we must scan the input data set once for each value sorted. For very large data sets, this technique just takes too long to be practical. Even worse, how would we sort the data if there were too many numbers to fit into the main memory of the computer? The development of efficient sorting techniques for large data sets is an active area of research and is the subject of whole courses all by itself.

In this example, we will confine ourselves to the simplest possible algorithm to illustrate the concept of sorting. This is the **selection sort**. It is just a computer implementation of the mental math described above. The basic algorithm for the selection sort is:

1. Scan the list of numbers to be sorted to locate the smallest value in the list. Place that value at the front of the list by swapping it with the value currently at the front. If the value at the front is already the smallest value, then do nothing.

2. Scan the list of numbers from position 2 to the end to locate the next smallest value in the list. Place that value in position 2 of the list by swapping it with the value currently at that position. If the value in position 2 is already the next smallest value, then do nothing.

3. Scan the list of numbers from position 3 to the end to locate the third smallest value in the list. Place that value in position 3 of the list by swapping it with the value currently at that position. If the value in position 3 is already the third smallest value, then do nothing.

4. Repeat this process until the next-to-last position in the list is reached. After the next-to-last position in the list has been processed, the sort is complete.

Note that if we are sorting n values, this sorting algorithm requires $n-1$ scans through the data to accomplish the sort.

This process is illustrated in Figure 5.13. Since there are five values in the data set to be sorted, we will make four scans. During the first pass through the entire data set, the minimum value is 3, so the 3 is swapped with the 10 that was in position 1. Pass 2 searches for the minimum value in positions 2 through 5. That minimum is 4,

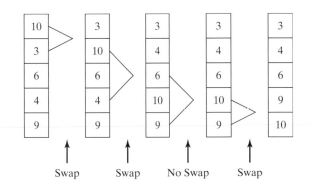

Figure 5.13.   An example problem demonstrating the selection sort algorithm.

so the 4 is swapped with the 10 in position 2. Pass 3 searches for the minimum value in positions 3 through 5. That minimum is 6, which is already in position 3, so no swapping is required. Finally, pass 4 searches for the minimum value in positions 4 through 5. That minimum is 9, so the 9 is swapped with the 10 in position 4, and the sort is completed.

We will now develop a program to read a data set from the standard input stream into an array, sort it into ascending order, and display the sorted data set.

The selection-sort algorithm is the easiest to understand, but it is computationally inefficient. *It should never be applied to sort really large data sets* (say, with more than 1000 elements). Over the years, computer scientists have developed much more efficient sorting algorithms. We will encounter one such algorithm in Chapter 6.

SOLUTION

This program must be able to read input data from the standard input stream, sort it, and write out the sorted data. The first value in the standard input stream will be the number of values to be read, and the remaining numbers will be the values to sort. The design process for this problem is given below.

1. **Determine the User Requirements**

    So far, we do not know the kind of data that must be sorted. Assume that the user tells us that he or she wishes to sort floating-point numbers. In that case, the program must be written to work with `double` data. A proper statement of the user's requirements would be: *Develop a program to read an arbitrary number of* `double` *input data values from an input file, sort the data into ascending order, and write the sorted data to the standard output device.*

2. **Analysis and Decomposition**

    There will be a single class, and only the `main` method within that class. We will call the class `SelectionSort`.

    There are two types of inputs to this program:

    a. The name of the file to open. This string must be read from the standard input stream.
    b. The values in the file, which will be the `double` values to sort.

    The outputs from this program are the sorted data values written to the standard output device.

3. **Detailed Design**

    The `main` method can be broken down into four major steps:

    ```
    Get file name and open input file
    Read the input data into the array
    Sort the data in ascending order
    Write the sorted data
    ```

    An expanded form of the pseudocode to open the file and read the input data is shown below.

    ```
    Prompt for name of file to read
    Read fileName from standard input stream
    Open input file
    Read the first line
    while ( str != null ) {
       Convert String to double
       arr[nvals++] ← Double.parseDouble(str);
       Read the next line
    }
    ```

    Next we have to sort the data. We will need to make `nvals` −1 passes through the data, finding the smallest remaining value each time. We will use a pointer to locate the smallest value in each pass. This value will be swapped to the top of the list, if it is not already there. (Note that in order to make nvals −1 passes, the for loop must run from 0 to nvals −2.)

```
for ( i = 0; i <= nvals-2; i++ ) {
    // Find the minimum value in arr[i] through arr[nvals-1]
    iptr ← i;
    for ( j = i+1; j <= nvals-1; j++ ) {
        if (arr[j] < arr[iptr])
            iptr ← j;
    }

    // iptr now points to the min value, so swap arr[iptr] with
    // arr[i] if iptr != i.
    if (i != iptr) {
        temp ← arr[i];
        arr[i] ← arr[iptr];
        arr[iptr] ← temp;
    }
}
```

The final step is writing out the sorted values. No refinement of the pseudocode is required for that step. The final pseudocode is the combination of the reading, sorting, and writing steps.

4. **Implementation: Convert Algorithms to Java Statements**

The resulting Java program is shown in Figure 5.14.

```
/*
   Purpose:
     To read in a set of double values from an input file,
     sort it into ascending order using the selection
     sort algorithm, and write the sorted data to the
     standard output stream.

   Record of revisions:
       Date          Programmer           Description of change
       ====          ==========           =====================
     04/01/2002    S. J. Chapman          Original code
*/
import java.io.*;
public class SelectionSort {

   // Define the main method
   public static void main(String[] args) throws IOException {

      // Define maximum array size
      final int MAXVAL = 1000;

      // Declare variables, and define each variable
      double[] arr = new double[MAXVAL];
                          // Array of input measurements
```

Figure 5.14. A program to read values from an input file and to sort them into ascending order.

```
      String fileName;        // Input file name
      int i = 0, j;           // Loop index
      int iptr;               // Pointer to smallest value
      int nvals;              // Number of data values to sort
      String str;             // Input string
      double temp;            // Temporary variable for swapping

      // Create a buffered reader on the standard input stream
      BufferedReader in = new BufferedReader(
                         new InputStreamReader(System.in));
      // Get input file name
      System.out.print("Enter file name: ");
      fileName = in.readLine();

      // Open the specified file
      BufferedReader in1 = new BufferedReader(
                         new FileReader(fileName));

      // Read the data
      nvals = 0;
      str = in1.readLine();
      while ( str != null ) {
         arr[nvals++] = Double.parseDouble(str);
         str = in1.readLine();
      }

      // Close file
      in1.close();

      // Sort values
      for ( i = 0; i <= nvals-2; i++ ) {

         // Find the minimum value in arr[i] through arr[nvals-1]
         iptr = i;
         for ( j = i+1; j <= nvals-1; j++ ) {
            if (arr[j] < arr[iptr])
               iptr = j;
         }

         // iptr now points to the min value, so swap
         // arr[iptr] with arr[i] if iptr != i.
         if (i != iptr) {
            temp = arr[i];
            arr[i] = arr[iptr];
            arr[iptr] = temp;
         }
      }

      // Write out sorted values
      for ( i = 0; i < nvals; i++ ) {
         System.out.println(arr[i]);
      }
   }
}
```

Figure 5.14.   (Continued).

5. **Testing**

To test this program, we will create an input data file containing the data to sort. The data set will contain a mixture of positive and negative numbers as well as at least one duplicated value to see if the program works properly under those conditions. The following data set will be placed in file `input1`:

```
13.3
12.
-3.0
 0.
 4.0
 6.6
 4.
-6.
```

The first value in the file is the number of values to read, and the remaining values are the data set to sort. Running these file values through the program yields the following result:

```
D:\book\java\chap5>java SelectionSort
Enter file name: input1
-6.0
-3.0
 0.0
 4.0
 4.0
 6.6
12.0
13.3
```

The program gives the correct answers for our test data set. Note that it works for both positive and negative numbers as well as for repeated numbers. ■

EXAMPLE 5.3

The Median: In Chapter 4 we examined two common statistical measures of data: averages (or means) and standard deviations. Another common statistical measure of data is the median. The median of a data set is the value such that half of the numbers in the data set are larger than the value and half of the numbers in the data set are smaller than the value. If there are an even number of values in the data set, then there cannot be a value exactly in the middle. In that case, the median is usually defined as the average of the two elements in the middle. The median value of a data set is often close to the average value, but not always. For example, consider the following data set:

```
  1
  2
  3
  4
100
```

The average or mean of this data set is 22, while the median is 3.

An easy way to compute the median of a data set is to sort it into ascending order, then to select the value in the middle as the median. If there are an even number of values in the data set, then average the two middle values to get the median.

In a language such as Java, where the array subscripts run from 0 to nvals-1, the median of a sorted data set is defined as:

$$\text{median} = \begin{cases} \texttt{a[nvals/2]} & \texttt{nvals odd} \\ \texttt{(a[nvals/2-1]+a[nvals/2])/2} & \texttt{nvals even} \end{cases} \qquad (5.1)$$

For example, in the sorted five-element array shown below, the middle element is a[nvals/2], which is a[2], or 3.

a[0]	1
a[1]	2
a[2]	3
a[3]	4
a[4]	100

Similarly, in the sorted four-element array shown below, the median is (a[nvals/2-1] + a[nvals/2])/2, which is (a[1] + a[2])/2, or 2.5.

a[0]	1
a[1]	2
a[2]	3
a[3]	4

Write a program to calculate the mean, median, and standard deviation of an input data set that is read from a standard input stream. Use GUI-based I/O for this program.

SOLUTION

This program must be able to read input measurements from the standard input stream and calculate the mean, median, and standard deviation of the data set. Note that the data will have to be sorted in order to calculate the median. The first value in the standard input stream will be the *number* of measurements in the data set, and the remaining numbers will be the actual measurements. The design process for this problem is given below.

1. **Determine the User Requirements**

   So far, we do not yet know the sort of data that must be processed. Assume that the user has told us that he or she wishes to find the median of an array of real numbers. In that case, the program must be written to work with double data. A proper statement of the user's requirements would be: *Calculate the average, median, and standard deviation of a set of read measurements which are read from an input file, and write those values out on the standard output device. Use GUI windows to get the name of the input file and to display the median of the data set.*

2. **Analysis and Decomposition**

   There will be a single class, and only the main method within that class. We will call the class Stats4.

   There are two types of inputs to this program:

   a. The name of the file to open. This string must be read from an input dialog box.
   b. The values in the file, which will be the double values to process.

   The output from this program is the average, median, and standard deviation of the data set. It must be displayed in a message dialog box.

3.   **Detailed Design**

The `main` method can be broken down into five major steps:

```
Get the file name and open the input file
Read the input data into the array
Sort the measurements in ascending order
Calculate the average, mean, and standard deviation
Write the average, median, and standard deviation
```

The detailed pseudocode for the first three steps is similar to that of the previous example:

```
Read the first line
while ( str != null ) {
   Convert String to double
   arr[nvals++] ← Double.parseDouble(str);
   Read the next line
}

for ( i = 0; i <= nvals-2; i++ ) {
   // Find the minimum value in arr[i] through arr[nvals-1]
   iptr ← i
   for ( j = i+1; j <= nvals-1; j++ ) {
      if (arr[j] < arr[iptr])
         iptr ← j
   }
   // iptr now points to the min value, so swap
   // arr[iptr] with arr[i] if iptr != i.
   if (i != iptr) {
      temp ← arr[i]
      arr[i] ← arr[iptr]
      arr[iptr] ← temp
   }
}
```

The fourth step is to calculate the required average, median, and standard deviation. To do this, we must first accumulate some statistics on the data ($\sum x$ and $\sum x^2$) and then apply the definitions of average, median, and standard deviation given previously. The pseudocode for this step is

```
for ( i = 0; i < nvals; i++ ) {
   sumX ← sumX + arr[i]
   sumX2 ← sumX2 + arr[i]*arr[i]
}
if (nvals >= 2) {
   xBar ← sumX / nvals
   stdDev ← Math.sqrt((nvals*sumX2 - sumX*sumX)/(nvals*(nvals-1)))
   if nvals is an even number
      median ← (arr[nvals/2-1] + arr[nvals/2]) / 2.
   else
      median ← arr[nvals/2]
}
else {
   Tell user about insufficient data.
}
```

We will decide whether `nvals` is an even number by using the modulo operator `nvals%2`. If `nvals` is even, this operation will return a 0; if `nvals` is odd, it will return a 1. Finally, we must write out the results.

```
Write out average, median, standard deviation,
and no. of points to a message dialog box
```

4.   **Implementation: Convert Algorithms to Java Statements**

The resulting Java program is shown in Figure 5.15(a).

```
/*
   Purpose:
      To read in a set of double values from an input file
      and calculate the mean, median, and standard deviation
      of the input data.  The mean, median, and standard
      deviation are written to a message dialog box.

   Record of revisions:
         Date          Programmer            Description of change
         ====          ==========            =====================
      04/04/2002    S. J. Chapman            Original code
*/
import java.io.*;
import javax.swing.*;
public class Stats4 {

   // Define the main method
   public static void main(String[] args) throws IOException {

      // Define maximum array size
      final int MAXVAL = 1000;

      // Declare variables, and define each variable
      double[] arr = new double[MAXVAL];
                              // Array of input measurements
      String fileName;        // Input file name
      int i = 0, j;           // Loop index
      int iptr;               // Pointer to smallest value
      double median;          // Median of the input measurements
      int nvals;              // Number of data values to sort
      double stdDev = 0;      // Standard dev. of the input samples
      String str;             // Input string
      double sumX = 0;        // The sum of the input values
      double sumX2 = 0;       // The sum of the squares of values
      double x = 0;           // An input data value
      double xBar = 0;        // Average of the input measurements
      double temp;            // Temporary variable for swapping

      // Get input file name
      fileName = JOptionPane.showInputDialog( null,
         "Enter file name containing data set:" );
```

Figure 5.15.   (a) A program to read values from an input file and to calculate their mean, median, and standard deviation. (b) The results when the program is executed with the sample data in file `input2`.

```
    // Open the specified file
    BufferedReader in1 = new BufferedReader(
                           new FileReader(fileName));

    // Read the data
    nvals = 0;
    str = in1.readLine();
    while ( str != null ) {
       arr[nvals++] = Double.parseDouble(str);
       str = in1.readLine();
    }

    // Close file
    in1.close();

    // Sort values
    for ( i = 0; i <= nvals-2; i++ ) {

       // Find the minimum value in arr[i] through arr[nvals-1]
       iptr = i;
       for ( j = i+1; j <= nvals-1; j++ ) {
          if (arr[j] < arr[iptr])
             iptr = j;
       }

       // iptr now points to the min value, so swap a[iptr]
       // with a[i] if iptr != i.
       if (i != iptr) {
          temp = arr[i];
          arr[i] = arr[iptr];
          arr[iptr] = temp;
       }
    }

    // Calculate sums
    for ( i = 0; i < nvals; i++ ) {
       sumX = sumX + arr[i];
       sumX2 = sumX2 + arr[i]*arr[i];
    }

    // Check to see if we have enough input data.
    if ( nvals >= 2 ) {

       // There is enough information, so calculate the
       // mean, median, and standard deviation
       xBar = sumX / nvals;
       stdDev = Math.sqrt( (nvals * sumX2 - sumX*sumX )
               / (nvals * (nvals-1)) );
       if (nvals%2 == 0)
          median = (arr[nvals/2-1] + arr[nvals/2]) / 2.;
```

Figure 5.15.   (Continued).

```
            else
                median = arr[nvals/2];

            // Tell user.
            JOptionPane.showMessageDialog( null,
                "Mean = " + xBar + "\n" +
                "Median = " + median + "\n" +
                "Std Dev = " + stdDev + "\n" +
                "Number of points = " + nvals);
        }

        else {
            // Error
            JOptionPane.showMessageDialog( null, "Insufficient data. " +
                "At least 2 values must be entered!");
        }

        // Stop program
        System.exit(0);
    }
}
```

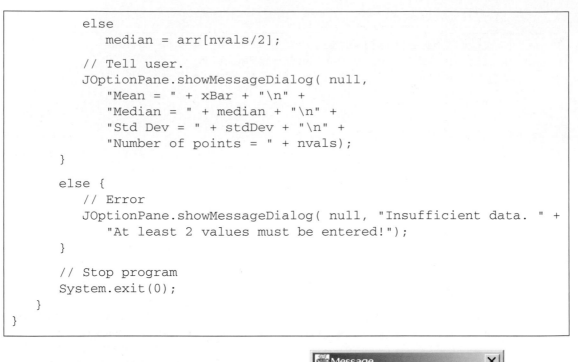

(b)

Figure 5.15.   (Continued).

5.   **Testing**

To test this program, we will calculate the answers by hand for a simple data set and then compare the answers to the results of the program. If we use five input values: 5, 3, 4, 1, and 9, then the mean and standard deviation will be

$$\bar{x} = \frac{1}{N}\sum_{i=1}^{N} x_i = \frac{1}{5}22 = 4.4$$

$$s = \sqrt{\frac{N\sum_{i=1}^{N} x_i^2 - \left(\sum_{i=1}^{N} x_i\right)^2}{N(N-1)}} = 2.966$$

$$\text{median} = 4$$

If these values are placed in the file input2 and the program is run with that file as an input, the results are as shown in Figure 5.15(b). The program gives the correct answers for our test data set.

5.7   INTRODUCTION TO PLOTTING

One great advantage of Java over other languages such as C and Fortran is that *device- and platform-independent graphics is built directly into the standard language*. While we will not learn the details of Java graphics until a later chapter, we will begin using Java's graphics capabilities here. The `chapman.graphics` package, which is supplied with this book, includes classes suitable for plotting arrays of data. For the time being, we will use these classes to examine and plot data contained in arrays. The ability to visualize data is essential for any scientist or engineer, and we will begin doing so in exercises now. Don't worry, though—the use of this convenience class is only temporary. Beginning in Chapter 12, you will be creating your own plotting programs from scratch.

We will now learn how to use a class from the `chapman.graphics` package called **JPlot2D** to create two-dimensional plots of data stored in arrays. Note that we must import the `chapman.graphics` package into our program in order to use this class.[2]

Java graphics are displayed in windows known as **frames**. A frame is a rectangular portion of a graphics display device that can be used to display Java graphics, including buttons, text boxes, plots, and so on. A Java program can open as many frames as desired, and each frame can display different types of graphical information. The support for frames is included in Java's Abstract Windowing Toolkit and in the Swing package. Any program that uses graphics must import packages `java.awt.*`, `javax.swing.*`, and `java.awt.event.*` from the Java SDK.

For now, we will introduce a template that creates a frame without explaining the full details of its operation, and we will use that template to display our plots. The detailed meaning of the statements in the template will be explained in Chapters 12 and 13.

Figure 5.16 displays a sample program that creates and displays a plot. This program creates arrays generated from the equations $y(x) = \sin x$ and $y(x) = 1.2 \cos x$ over the range $0 \le x \le 2\pi$, and plots the contents of those arrays. A new plot is created by instantiating a `JPlot2D` object, as shown

```
JPlot2D pl = new JPlot2D( x, y );
```

This plot object will now automatically plot *x* versus *y* in any frame to which the object is added. The following statements (beginning "`pl.`") modify the line color, line style,

```
import java.awt.*;
import java.awt.event.*;
import javax.swing.*;
import chapman.graphics.JPlot2D;
public class TestPlot2D {
    /**
     * This method is an example of how to use Class JPlot2D.
     * The method creates a frame, and then places a new
     * JPlot2D object within the frame. It draws two curves on
     * the object, and also illustrates the use of line styles,
     * titles, labels, and grids.
     */
    public static void main(String s[]) {
```

Figure 5.16.   Program to create and plot a data set. The portions of the program in boldface must be modified to create different types of plots; the remainder of the program is Java "boilerplate."

---

[2]It is also necessary to set the CLASSPATH variable as described in the Preface to this book.

```
//************************************************************
//
//   Create data to plot
//
//************************************************************

// Define arrays to hold the two curves to plot
double[] x = new double[81];
double[] y = new double[81];
double[] z = new double[81];

// Calculate a sine and a cosine wave
for ( int i = 0; i < x.length; i++ ) {
   x[i] = (i+1) * 2 * Math.PI / 40;
   y[i] = Math.sin(x[i]);
   z[i] = 1.2 * Math.cos(x[i]);
}

//************************************************************
//
// Create plot object and set plot information.
//
//************************************************************
JPlot2D pl = new JPlot2D( x, y );
pl.setPlotType ( JPlot2D.LINEAR );
pl.setLineColor( Color.blue );
pl.setLineWidth( 2.0f );
pl.setLineStyle( JPlot2D.LINESTYLE_SOLID );
pl.setMarkerState( JPlot2D.MARKER_ON );
pl.setTitle( "Plot of sin(x) and 1.2*cos(x) vs. x" );
pl.setXLabel( "x" );
pl.setYLabel( "sin(x) and 1.2 cos(x)" );
pl.setGridState( JPlot2D.GRID_ON );

// Add a second curve to the plot.
pl.addCurve( x, z );
pl.setLineWidth( 3.0f );
//************************************************************
//
// Create a frame and place the plot in the center of the
// frame.  Note that the plot will occupy all of the
// available space.
//
//************************************************************

JFrame fr = new JFrame("Plot2D ...");
// Create a Window Listener to handle "close" events
WindowHandler l = new WindowHandler();
fr.addWindowListener(l);

fr.getContentPane().add(pl, BorderLayout.CENTER);
fr.setSize(500,500);
```

Figure 5.16. (Continued).

```
      fr.setVisible( true );
   }
}
//*************************************************************
//
// Create a window listener to close the program.
//
//*************************************************************
class WindowHandler extends WindowAdapter {
   // This method implements a simple listener that detects
   // the "window closing event" and stops the program.
   public void windowClosing(WindowEvent e) {
      System.exit(0);
   };
}
```

Figure 5.16. (Continued).

title, axis labels, and so on, that will be plotted. The statement

```
        JFrame fr = new JFrame("Plot2D ...");
```

creates a new frame (a window) to display the plot in, and the statement

```
        fr.getContentPane().add(pl, BorderLayout.CENTER);
```

puts the plot into the frame.

When this program is executed, the results are shown in Figure 5.17.

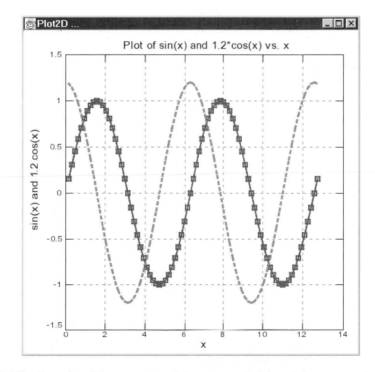

Figure 5.17.   Java plot of the equations $y(x) = \sin x$ and $y(x) = 1.2 \cos x$ over the range $0 \le x \le 2\pi$.

Once a plot object has been created, a large number of methods may be called to modify and enhance the basic plot. Some of them are summarized in Table 5.2, and all of them are included in the online Java documentation for class `JPlot2D`.

TABLE 5.2 Common Methods in Class JPlot2D

Method	Description
`addCurve(double[] x,` `         double[] y)`	Add an additional curve to the plot.
`setGridState(int gs)`	Set the grid state. Legal values are `JPlot2D.GRID_OFF` (default), `JPlot2D.GRID_ON`
`setLineColor(Color c)`	Set the line color. Legal values are any color defined in class `java.awt.Color`.
`setLineState(boolean b)`	Determine whether or not lines are to be plotted between data points on a curve. By default, lines *are* plotted. Legal values are: `JPlot2D.LINE_ON`, and `JPlot2D.LINE_OFF`.
`setLineStyle(int ls)`	Set the line style. Legal values are: `JPlot2D.LINESTYLE_SOLID`, `JPlot2D.LINESTYLE_DOT`, `JPlot2D.LINESTYLE_LONGDASH`, and `JPlot2D.LINESTYLE_SHORTDASH`.
`setLineWidth(float w)`	Set the line width, in pixels.
`setMarkerColor(Color c)`	Set the marker type. Legal values are any color defined in class `java.awt.Color`.
`setMarkerState(boolean b)`	Determine whether or not markers are to be plotted at data points on a curve. By default, markers are *not* plotted. Legal values are: `Plot2D.MARKER_ON`, and `JPlot2D.MARKER_OFF`.
`setMarkerStyle(int ms)`	Set the marker style. Legal values are: `JPlot2D.MARKER_CIRCLE`, and `JPlot2D.MARKER_SQUARE`.
`setPlotType(int t)`	Set the plot type. Legal values are: `JPlot2D.LINEAR` (default), `JPlot2D.SEMILOGX`, `JPlot2D.SEMILOGY`, `JPlot2D.LOGLOG`, `JPlot2D.BAR`, and `JPlot2D.POLAR`.
`setTitle(String s)`	Add a plot title.
`setXLabel(String s)`	Set the x-axis label.
`setYLabel(String s)`	Set the y-axis label.

SUMMARY

- An **array** is a special object containing (1) a group of memory locations that all have the same name and same type, and (2) a separate instance variable containing an integer constant equal to the number of elements in the array.

- The length of a Java array is specified when it is created, and it remains fixed for as long as the array exists.

- A *reference* is a "handle" or "pointer" to an object that permits Java to locate the object in memory when it is needed. A reference is declared by naming the object type followed by the reference name.

- Once an array reference exists, an array object can be created on that reference using the new operator.

- Arrays may be initialized with an array initializer, which is just a comma-separated list of values enclosed in braces.

- Java programs always include automatic bounds checking, and any attempt to address an out-of-bounds array element will produce an exception.

- Array elements may be used in Java expressions just like any other variable of the same type as the array.

- Array references can not be used in algebraic Java expressions.

- The value of one array reference may be assigned to another array reference.

- If only one array reference points to a Java array, and another array is assigned to that reference, the first array is no longer accessible to the Java program. The array still exists, but without a reference, it cannot be used. This situation is known as a data leak.

- Lines of character data can be read from a file using the `FileReader` and `BufferedReader` classes. These lines of data can be further converted into `int` or `double` values using the `Integer.parseInt(str)` or `Double.parseDouble(str)` methods. (Note that the technique we used to read data in this chapter fails if there is more than one number on a line, or if there are blank lines in the file.)

- Character data can be written to a file using the `FileWriter`, `Buffered-Writer`, and `PrintWriter` classes. Data can be written to the file using the `print` and `println` methods.

SUMMARY OF GOOD PROGRAMMING PRACTICES

The following guidelines introduced in this chapter will help you to develop good programs:

1. When creating `for` loops to process the elements of an array, use the array object's `length` field in the continuation condition for the loop. This will allow the loop to adjust automatically for different-sized arrays.

2. When processing an array `arr` in a `for` loop, use a continuation condition of the form

   ```
   for ( j = 0; j < arr.length; j++ ).
   ```

   The "less than" relational operator is the correct one to use, because the elements of the array are numbered `0, 1, ..., arr.length-1`.

3. Declare the sizes of arrays in a Java program using named constants to make them easy to change.

TERMINOLOGY

Abstract Windowing Toolkit	`FileReader` class
array	`FileWriter` class
array element	frame
`ArrayIndexOutOfBoundsException`	instantiate
array initializer	null
bounds checking	out of bounds
`BufferedReader` class	`PrintWriter` class
`BufferedWriter` class	reference
command-line redirection	subscript

Exercises

1. How are arrays declared?

2. What is the difference between an array reference, an array object, and an array element?

3. Determine whether or not the following Java program fragment is valid. If it is, specify what will happen in the program. If not, explain why not.

```
int b[] = new int[6][4];
int temp;

...

for ( i = 0; i < 6; i++ ) {
    for ( j = 0; j < 4; j++ ) {
        temp    = b(i,j);
        b(i,j) = b(j,i);
        b(j,i) = temp;
    }
}
```

4. **Polar-to-Rectangular Conversion**   A *scalar quantity* can be represented by a single number. For example, the temperature at a given location is a scalar. In contrast, a *vector* quantity has both a magnitude and a direction associated with it. For example, the velocity of an automobile is a vector, since it has both a magnitude and a direction.

   Vectors can be defined either by a magnitude and a direction, or by the components of the vector projected along the axes of a rectangular coordinate system. The two representations are equivalent. For two-dimensional vectors, we can convert back and forth between the representations using the following equations.

$$\mathbf{V} = V\angle\theta = V_x\mathbf{i} + V_y\mathbf{j}$$

$$V_x = V\cos\theta$$

$$V_y = V\sin\theta$$

$$V = \sqrt{V_x^{\,2} + V_y^{\,2}}$$

$$\theta = \tan^{-1}\frac{V_y}{V_x}$$

where **i** and **j** are the unit vectors in the x and y directions, respectively. The representation of the vector in terms of magnitude and angle is known as *polar coordinates*, and the representation of the vector in terms of components along the axes is known as *rectangular coordinates*.

   Write a program that reads the polar coordinates (magnitude and angle) of a two-dimensional vector into a two-element array polar (polar[0] will contain the magnitude V and polar[1] will contain the angle θ in degrees) and converts the vector from polar to rectangular form, storing the result in a two-element array rect. The first element of rect should contain the x-component of the vector, and the second element the y-component. After the

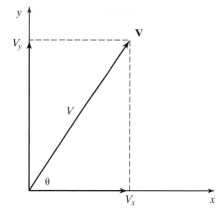

Figure 5.18. Representations of a vector.

conversion, display the contents of array `rect`. Test your program by converting the following polar vectors to rectangular form:

a. $5\angle-36.87°$

b. $10\angle45°$

c. $25\angle233.13°$

5. **Rectangular-to-Polar Conversion**   Write a program that reads the rectangular components of a two-dimensional vector into a two-element array `rect` (`rect[0]` will contain the component V_x and `rect[1]` will contain the component V_y) and converts the vector from rectangular to polar form, storing the result in a two-element array `polar`. The first element of `polar` should contain the magnitude of the vector, and the second should contain the angle of the vector in degrees. After the conversion, display the contents of array `polar`. (*Hint:* Look up function `Math.atan2`.) Test your program by converting the following rectangular vectors to polar form:

a. $3\mathbf{i} - 4\mathbf{j}$

b. $5\mathbf{i} + 5\mathbf{j}$

c. $-5\mathbf{i} + 12\mathbf{j}$

6. Assume that `values` is a 101-element array containing a list of measurements from a scientific experiment, which has been declared by the statement

```
double values[] = new double[101];
```

Write the Java statements that would count the number of positive values, negative values, and zero values in the array, and write out a message summarizing how many values of each type were found.

7. Write Java statements that would print out every fifth value in the array `values` described in Exercise 6. The output should take the form

```
values[0] = x.xx
values[5] = x.xx
...
values[100] = x.xx
```

8. Modify the selection sort program in Example 5.2 so that it writes the sorted data set to a user-specified file.

9. **Dot Product** A three-dimensional vector can be represented in rectangular coordinates as

$$\mathbf{V} = V_x\mathbf{i} + V_y\mathbf{j} + V_z\mathbf{k}$$

where V_x is the component of vector $\mathbf{V}$ in the x direction, V_y is the component of vector $\mathbf{V}$ in the y direction, and V_z is the component of vector $\mathbf{V}$ in the z direction. Such a vector can be stored in a three-element array, since there are three dimensions in the coordinate system. The same idea applies to an n-dimensional vector. An n-dimensional vector can be stored in a rank-1 array containing n elements.

A common mathematical operation between two vectors is the *dot product*. The dot product of two vectors $\mathbf{V}_1 = V_{x1}\mathbf{i} + V_{y1}\mathbf{j} + V_{z1}\mathbf{k}$ and $\mathbf{V}_2 = V_{x2}\mathbf{i} + V_{y2}\mathbf{j} + V_{z2}\mathbf{k}$ is a scalar quantity defined by the equation

$$\mathbf{V}_1 \cdot \mathbf{V}_2 = V_{x1}V_{x2} + V_{y1}V_{y2} + V_{z1}V_{z2}$$

Write a Java program that will read two vectors $\mathbf{V}_1$ and $\mathbf{V}_2$ into two one-dimensional arrays in computer memory, then calculate their dot product according to the equation given above. Test your program by calculating the dot product of vectors $\mathbf{V}_1 = 5\mathbf{i} - 3\mathbf{j} + 2\mathbf{k}$ and $\mathbf{V}_2 = 2\mathbf{i} + 3\mathbf{j} + 4\mathbf{k}$.

10. **Power Supplied to an Object** If an object is being pushed by a force $\mathbf{F}$ at a velocity $\mathbf{v}$, then the power supplied to the object by the force is given by the equation

$$P = \mathbf{F} \cdot \mathbf{v}$$

where the force $\mathbf{F}$ is measured in newtons, the velocity $\mathbf{v}$ in meters per second, and the power P in watts. Use the Java program written in Exercise 5.12 to calculate the power supplied by a force of $\mathbf{F} = 4\mathbf{i} + 3\mathbf{j} - 2\mathbf{k}$ newtons to an object moving with a velocity of $\mathbf{v} = 4\mathbf{i} - 2\mathbf{j} + 1\mathbf{k}$ meters per second. (See Figure 5.19.)

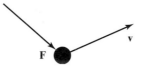

Figure 5.19. A force $\mathbf{F}$ applied to an object moving with velocity $\mathbf{v}$.

11. **Cross Product** Another common mathematical operation between two vectors is the *cross product*. The cross product of two vectors $\mathbf{V}_1 = V_{x1}\mathbf{i} + V_{y1}\mathbf{j} + V_{z1}\mathbf{k}$ and $\mathbf{V}_2 = V_{x2}\mathbf{i} + V_{y2}\mathbf{j} + V_{z2}\mathbf{k}$ is a vector quantity defined by the equation

$$\begin{aligned}
\mathbf{V}_1 \times \mathbf{V}_2 = {} & (V_{y1}V_{z2} - V_{y2}V_{z1})\mathbf{i} \\
& + (V_{z1}V_{x2} - V_{z2}V_{x1})\mathbf{j} \\
& + (V_{x1}V_{y2} - V_{x2}V_{y1})\mathbf{k}
\end{aligned}$$

Write a Java program that will read two vectors $\mathbf{V}_1$ and $\mathbf{V}_2$ into arrays in computer memory, then calculate their cross product according to the equation given above. Test your program by calculating the cross product of vectors $\mathbf{V}_1 = 5\mathbf{i} - 3\mathbf{j} + 2\mathbf{k}$ and $\mathbf{V}_2 = 2\mathbf{i} + 3\mathbf{j} + 4\mathbf{k}$.

12. **Velocity of an Orbiting Object** The vector angular velocity ω of an object moving with a velocity **v** at a distance **r** from the origin of the coordinate system is given by the equation

$$\mathbf{v} = \mathbf{r} \times \omega$$

where **r** is the distance in meters, ω is the angular velocity in radians per second, and **v** is the velocity in meters per second. If the distance from the center of the earth to an orbiting satellite is $\mathbf{r} = 300,000\mathbf{i} + 400,000\mathbf{j} + 50,000\mathbf{k}$ meters, and the angular velocity of the satellite is $\omega = -6 \times 10^{-3}\mathbf{i} + 2 \times 10^{-3}\mathbf{j} - 9 \times 10^{-4}\mathbf{k}$ radians per second, what is the velocity of the satellite in meters per second? (See Figure 5.20.) Use the program written in the previous exercise to calculate the answer.

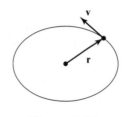

Figure 5.20.

13. Plot the function $y(t) = e^{-0.8t} \cos 4\pi t$ from $t = 0$ to $t = 3$. For what fraction of the interval is $y(t) > 0.5$?

14. Plot the function $y(x) = 2e^{-0.2x}$ from $x = 0$ to $x = 10$ on both a linear and a semilog scale. What does this function look like on each scale?

15. Figure 5.21 shows an electrical load with a voltage applied to it and a current flowing into it. Assume that the voltage applied to this load is given by the equation

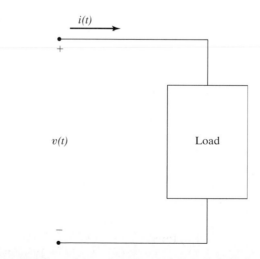

Figure 5.21. AC voltage and current supplied to an electrical load.

$v(t) = 17 \sin 377t$ V and the current flowing into the load is given by the equation $i(t) = 1.414 \sin(377t - \pi/6)$ A. Write a Java program the performs the following actions:

a. Create two arrays storing the voltage and current applied to the load as a function of time. There should be 1000 samples in each array, spaced at intervals of 0.1 ms.

b. Calculate the instantaneous power supplied to the load at each time from the equation $P(t) = v(t)i(t)$, and store the power in an array.

c. Plot the voltage, current, and power as a function of time from $t = 0$ s to $t = 0.1$ s.

d. Calculate the average power supplied to the load over this interval.

16. The location of any point P in a three-dimensional space can be represented by a set of three values (x, y, z), where x is the distance along the x-axis to the point, y is the distance along the y-axis to the point, and z is the distance along the z-axis to the point. If two points P_1 and P_2 are represented by the values (x_1, y_1, z_1) and (x_2, y_2, z_2), then the distance between the points P_1 and P_2 can be calculated from the equation

$$\text{distance} = \sqrt{(x_1 - x_2)^2 + (y_1 - y_2)^2 + (z_1 - z_2)^2}$$

Write a Java program to read in two points (x_1, y_1, z_1) and (x_2, y_2, z_2), and to calculate the distance between them. Test your program by calculating the distance between the points $(-1, 4, 6)$ and $(1, 5, -2)$.

6

Methods

A **method** is a separate piece of code that can be called by a main program or another method to perform some specific function. A method takes one or more input values and from them calculates an output result. Each method must be defined within the body of some class, and many methods can be defined within a single class.

A method may be **called** or **invoked** by a main program or another method. The values passed to the method are known as **arguments**; they appear in parentheses immediately after the method name. The output of a method is a single value or object. When a method name appears in a Java statement, the arguments of the method are passed to the method. The method calculates a result, which is used in place of the method name in the original expression.

There are two types of methods in Java: **static methods** and **instance methods**. Static methods can be used without first creating an object of their class. They are invoked using the class name followed by a period and the method name [for example, Math.sqrt()]. Every method that we have seen so far in this book has been a static method, and all of those in this chapter will also be static. We will learn about instance methods in Chapter 7.

Figure 6.1 shows a simple program consisting of a single class containing two methods. One is the main method that we have seen before, and the other is the static method square. Method square is defined on lines 15–18 of the program. This method accepts a single integer parameter and calculates and returns the square of that parameter to the calling program.

Method square is actually called in line 10 with the expression SquareInt.square(i). Note that the program names the class containing the method, followed by a period and the method name, followed by the calling arguments in parentheses. The value of integer i is passed to the method and stored in parameter x, and the method

OBJECTIVES

- Learn how to create and use methods
- Learn about the pass-by-value scheme used to pass arguments to methods
- Learn about variable duration
- Learn about recursive methods
- Learn how to use sort method in the java.util.Arrays class

calculates and returns x^2. The main program then uses the returned value in the `System.out.println` function on line 10 (see Figure 6.2).

```
1    // Calculates the squares of the numbers from 1 to 10
2    public class SquareInt {
3
4        // Define the main method
5        public static void main(String[] args) {
6
7            // Write number and square
8            for ( int i = 1; i <= 10; i++ ) {
9                System.out.print("number = " + i);
10               System.out.println("  square = " + SquareInt.square(i));
11           }
12       }
13
14       // Definition of square method
15       public static int square (int x) {
16
17           return x * x;
18       }
19   }
```

Figure 6.1. A program to calculate the squares of integers from 1 to 10. This program uses method `square` to calculate the squares of the integers.

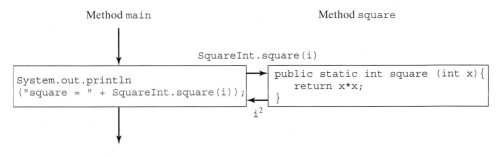

Figure 6.2. When the method name `square` appears in an expression, the method is called with the specified parameter `i`. The method then calculates i^2 and returns the result to the calling method. The calling method uses that result in its `println` statement.

When this program is executed, the results are

```
D:\book\java\chap6>java SquareInt
number = 0    square = 0
number = 1    square = 1
number = 2    square = 4
number = 3    square = 9
number = 4    square = 16
number = 5    square = 25
number = 6    square = 36
number = 7    square = 49
number = 8    square = 64
number = 9    square = 81
```

Note that method `square` was used 10 times to calculate 10 different squares. This same method could also have been used anywhere else within the program that we wanted to calculate the square of an integer.

6.1   WHY USE METHODS?

In Chapter 3 we learned the importance of good program design. The basic technique we used was top-down design. We started with a large task and broke it down into smaller, more easily understandable pieces (subtasks) that performed a portion of the desired task. Then, we broke down each subtask until we wound up with many small pieces, each of which did a simple, clearly understandable job. Finally, the individual pieces were turned into Java code.

Although we have followed this design process in our examples, the results have been somewhat restricted, because we have had to combine the final Java code generated for each subtask into a single large program. There has been no way to code, verify, and test each subtask independently before combining them into the final program.

Fortunately, Java has two special features designed to make subtasks easy to develop and debug independently before building the final program: **classes** and **methods**. Classes are separately compiled units containing data, together with the methods to manipulate that data. Methods are procedures that describe how to modify or manipulate the data contained in the class. Both classes and methods allow us to chop large programs up into smaller pieces that can be independently coded, tested, and verified. They also allow us to create *reusable* software, since a class created for one program can often be used intact in another program that needs the same features. We are studying methods in this chapter, to be followed by classes in Chapter 7.

Well-designed classes and methods enormously reduce the effort required on a large programming project. Their benefits include:

1. **Independent testing of subtasks.**   Each subtask can be coded and compiled as an independent unit. We can test the subtask separately to ensure that it performs properly by itself before combining it into the larger program. This step is known as **unit testing**. It eliminates a major source of problems before the final program is even built.

2. **Reusable code.**   In many cases, the same basic subtask is needed in many parts of a program. For example, it may be necessary to sort a list of values into ascending order many different times within a program, or even in other programs. It is possible to design, code, test, and debug a *single* method to do the sorting, and then to reuse that method whenever sorting is required. This reusable code has two major advantages: it reduces the total programming effort required, and it simplifies debugging, since the sorting method needs to be debugged only once.

3. **Isolation from unintended side effects.**   A caller communicates with the methods that it invokes through a list of values called an **argument list**. *The only values in the caller that are visible to the method are those in the argument list*. This is very important, since accidental programming mistakes can affect only the variables in the method in which the mistake occurred.

Once a large program is written and released, it has to be *maintained*. Program maintenance involves fixing bugs and modifying the program to handle new and unforeseen circumstances. The programmer who modifies a program during maintenance is often not the person who originally wrote it. In poorly written programs, often when a programmer modifies the program to make a change in one region of the code, that change causes unintended side effects in a totally different part of the program. This happens because variable names are reused in different portions of the program. When the programmer changes the values left behind in some of the variables, those values are accidentally picked up and used in other portions of the code.

The use of well-designed methods and classes minimizes this problem by **information hiding**. Except for the values in its argument list, *all of the variables within a called method are completely invisible from its calling method*, and *all of the variables in the calling method are completely invisible from the called method*. Since the variables in one method are invisible to the other method, one method cannot accidentally change the other method's variables. Thus, modifications in one of the methods will not cause unintended side effects in the other method.

GOOD PROGRAMMING PRACTICE

Whenever practical, break large program tasks into classes and methods to achieve the important benefits of independent component testing, reusability, and isolation from undesired side effects.

6.2   METHOD DEFINITIONS

The general form of a method definition is

```
[keywords] return-value-type method-name( parameter-list ) {
    declarations and statements
    (return statement)
}
```

The *method-name* is any valid Java identifier. The *return-value-type* is the data type of the result returned from the method to the caller. If no value is returned from the method, then the *return-value-type* is **void**. A *return-value-type* must be specified for every method. If the *return-value-type* is not **void**, then a **return** statement must appear in the body of the method to specify the value to be passed back to the calling program. The *keywords* are optional. They are modifiers such as public and static, which control certain details of the method's behavior. We will meet other keywords later in the book.

The *parameter-list* is a comma-separated list containing the declarations of the parameters received by the method whenever it is called. If the method does not receive any parameters, then the *parameter-list* is empty, but the parentheses are still required. A type must be declared for every parameter in the list.

The *declarations and statements* within the braces form the **method body**. The method body is a compound statement defining the local variables and actions performed by the method.

When a method is called, execution begins at the first statement in the method body and continues until either a return statement is executed or the end of the body is reached. There are two forms of the return statement. The simple statement

```
return;
```

stops execution of the method and returns control to the point at which the method was invoked *without returning a value to the calling method*. The statement

```
return expression;
```

stops execution of the method and returns control to the point at which the method was invoked, *returning the value of* expression to *the calling method*. The first form of return is used with void methods, and the second form is used with methods that return a value to the caller.

Another example method is shown in boldface in Figure 6.3. This method calculates the hypotenuse of a right triangle from the lengths of the other two sides.

```java
// Calculates the hypotenuse of a right triangle
import java.io.*;
public class Triangle {

   // Define the main method
   public static void main(String[] args) throws IOException {

      // Declare variables
      double side1;        // Side 1 of right triangle
      double side2;        // Side 2 of right triangle

      // Create a buffered reader
      BufferedReader in1 = new BufferedReader(
                 new InputStreamReader(System.in));

      // Get the two sides
      System.out.print("Enter side 1: ");
      side1 = Double.parseDouble( in1.readLine() );
      System.out.print("Enter side 2: ");
      side2 = Double.parseDouble( in1.readLine() );

      // Calculate hypotenuse and display result
      System.out.println("Hypotenuse = " +
         Triangle.hypotenuse(side1,side2) );
   }

   // Definition of method hypotenuse
   public static double hypotenuse (double side1, double side2) {

      // Declare local variable
      double hypot;        // Hypotenuse of triangle

      // Calculate and return hypotenuse
      hypot = Math.sqrt( side1*side1 + side2*side2 );
      return hypot;
   }
}
```

Figure 6.3. A method to calculate the hypotenuse of a right triangle.

This method has two arguments in its parameter list. These arguments are placeholders for the values that will be passed to the method when it is executed. The variable hypot is actually defined within the method. It is used in the method, but it is not accessible to any calling program. Variables that are used within a method and that are not accessible by calling methods are called **local variables**.

After `hypot` is declared, the method calculates the hypotenuse of the right triangle from the information about the two sides. Finally, the `return` statement returns the value of `hypot` to the calling method.

To test a method, it is necessary to write a program called a **test driver**. The test driver is a small method that invokes the new method with a sample data set for the specific purpose of testing it. The test driver for method `hypotenuse` is the `main` method of the class. When this program is executed, the results are:

```
D:\book\java\chap6>java Triangle
Enter side 1: 3
Enter side 2: 4
Hypotenuse = 5.0
```

6.3 VARIABLE PASSING IN JAVA: THE PASS-BY-VALUE SCHEME

Java programs communicate with their methods using a **pass-by-value** scheme. When a method call occurs, Java *makes a copy* of each calling argument and places that copy in the corresponding parameter of the method. This scheme is called pass-by-value, because the *value* of the calling argument is placed in the corresponding parameter. Similarly, the result produced by a method is returned by value.

Note that the method has a *copy* of the value of the original argument, not the argument itself. The method cannot accidentally modify the original argument, even if it modifies the parameter during its calculations. Thus the program is protected against an error caused by the called method accidentally modifying data in the method that called it.

A program illustrating the pass-by-value scheme is shown in Figure 6.4. The `main` method of this program declares a variable `i`, initializes it to 5, and prints out the 5. It

```java
// Tests the pass-by-value scheme
public class TestPassByValue {

    // Define the main method
    public static void main(String[] args) {

        // Initialize a value and print it out
        int i = 5;
        System.out.println("Before test: i = " + i);

        // Now call method test()
        int j = TestPassByValue.test(i);

        // Print out value after call
        System.out.println("After test:  i = " + i);

    }

    // Definition of test()
    public static int test (int i) {

        int j = ++i;
        System.out.println("In test:     i = " + i);
        return j;
    }
}
```

Figure 6.4. A program illustrating the pass-by-value scheme.

then calls method test(i), passing the *value* of i to the method. Method test increments the value of the parameter i that it receives, and prints out a 6. However, it does not affect the original value in the main method. After execution returns from method test, the main method prints i again, and its value is still 5.

When this program is executed, the results are:

```
D:\book\java\chap6>java TestPassByValue
Before test: i = 5
In test:     i = 6
After test:  i = 5
```

GOOD PROGRAMMING PRACTICE

The pass-by-value scheme prevents a method from accidentally modifying its calling arguments.

The pass-by-value scheme also applies to objects as well, but the results are different for that case. If an object such as an array is passed as a calling argument, the program *makes a copy of the reference* to the array and places the copy of the reference in the method parameter. Because the reference was copied, the called method cannot modify the original reference in the calling method. However, it *can* use the reference that was passed to it to read or modify the actual array or other object being referred to.

A program illustrating this effect is shown in Figure 6.5. The main method of this program declares an array a, initializes it, and prints out the values. It then calls method test(a), passing the *value of the reference to* a. Method test uses that reference to modify x[3], prints out the results, and returns to the calling method. After execution returns from method test, the main method prints a again, and we can see that its value has been modified (see Figure 6.6).

```java
// Tests the pass-by-value scheme
public class TestPassByValue2 {

    // Define the main method
    public static void main(String[] args) {

        // Initialize values and print them out.
        int[] a = {1, 2, 3, 4, 5};
        System.out.print("Before test: a = ");
        for ( int i = 0; i < a.length; i++ )
            System.out.print(a[i] + "   ");
        System.out.println();

        // Now call method test()
        TestPassByValue2.test(a);

        // Print out values after call
        System.out.print("After test:  a = ");
        for ( int i = 0; i < a.length; i++ )
            System.out.print(a[i] + "   ");
```

Figure 6.5. A program showing that a method can modify an array or other object whose reference is passed to it by value.

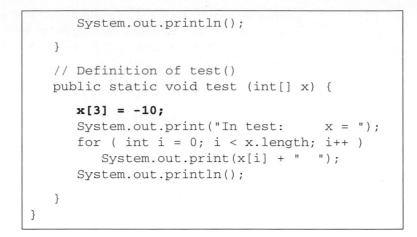

```
            System.out.println();

        }

        // Definition of test()
        public static void test (int[] x) {

            x[3] = -10;
            System.out.print("In test:      x = ");
            for ( int i = 0; i < x.length; i++ )
                System.out.print(x[i] + "   ");
            System.out.println();

        }
    }
```

Figure 6.5. (Continued).

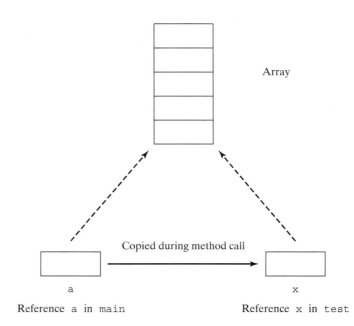

Reference a in main   Reference x in test

Figure 6.6. Reference a in main refers to a five-element array. When method test is called, reference a is copied into parameter x, so now method test can use and modify the same five-element array. Note that method test cannot modify reference a in the main program, but it *can* modify the object that a refers to.

When this program is executed, the results are:

```
D:\book\java\chap6>java TestPassByValue2
Before test: a = 1   2   3   4   5
In test:     a = 1   2   3   -10   5
After test:  a = 1   2   3   -10   5
```

There are advantages and disadvantages to passing arrays and objects by reference instead of copying the objects themselves. On the one hand, passing by reference weakens the security of the program, because the method can modify the calling method's data. On the other hand, the program is *much* more efficient. Imagine how much work would be involved if we attempted to pass a 10,000-element array by value! Every time that the array occurred in a method call, the program would have to make a new copy of all 10,000 elements.

A programmer must always be careful when working with arrays or other objects that are passed to methods. He or she must be certain that the method's calculations do not cause unintended modifications to the data in the arrays passed to the method. Such unintentional modifications are called **unintended side effects**, and they can create quite subtle and hard-to-find bugs.

PROGRAMMING PITFALLS

Beware of unintended side effects caused by accidentally modifying a calling method's data with references passed as parameters.

QUIZ 6-1

This quiz provides a quick check to see if you have understood the concepts introduced in Sections 6.1 to 6.3. If you have trouble with the quiz, reread the section, ask your instructor, or discuss the material with a fellow student. The answers are found in the back of the book.

For Questions 1 through 3, determine whether the method invocations are correct or not. If they are in error, specify what is wrong with them. If they are correct, explain what the methods do.

1.
```java
public class Test1 {

    public static void main(String[] args) {

        int i = 5; int[] j = {1, -2, 3, -4, 5};
        Test1.method1(i,j);
    }

    public static int method1(int[] i, int j) {
        for ( int k = 0; k < j; k++)
            System.out.println(i[k]);
    }
}
```

2.
```java
public class Test2 {

    public static void main(String[] args) {

        double i = 5; int j = 5;
        System.out.println("Result = " + Test2.method2(i,j));
    }

    public static void method2(double x, int y) {
        return (x / y);
    }
}
```

```
3.     public class Test3 {
           public static void main(String[] args) {
               int[] x = {1, -2, 3, -4, 5, -6};
               System.out.println( Test3.method3(x) );
           }

           public static double method3(int i[]) {
               int sum = 0;
               for ( int j = 0; j < i.length; j++)
                   sum += i[j];
               return ( (double) sum / i.length );
           }
       }
```

6.4   EXAMPLE PROBLEM

Let us now re-examine the sorting problem of Example 5.2, using methods where appropriate.

EXAMPLE 6.1

Sorting Data: Develop a program to read in a data set from a file, sort it into ascending order, and write the sorted data to an output file. Use methods where appropriate.

SOLUTION

The program in Example 5.2 read an arbitrary number of floating-point input data values from an input file, sorted the data into ascending order, and wrote the sorted data to the standard output stream. The sorting process would make a good candidate for a separate method, since only the array `arr` and its length `nvals` are in common between the sorting process and the rest of the program. The other change from Example 5.2 is that we must write the sorted output to a file instead of the standard output stream. Therefore, we must create a `FileWriter` object to open the output file, and write the data to that object.

The rewritten program using a sorting method and an output file is shown in Figure 6.7.

```
/*
   Purpose:
     To read in a set of double values from an input file,
     sort it into ascending order using the selection
     sort algorithm, and to write the sorted data to the
     standard output stream.

   Record of revisions:
       Date          Programmer              Description of change
       ====          ==========              =====================
     04/21/2002    S. J. Chapman            Original code
*/
import java.io.*;
public class SelectionSort2 {
```

Figure 6.7.   Program to sort real data values into ascending order using a `sort` method.

```
// Define the main method
public static void main(String[] args) throws IOException {

    // Define maximum array size
    final int MAXVAL = 1000;

    // Declare variables, and define each variable
    double[] arr = new double[MAXVAL];
                            // Array of input measurements
    String inFileName;    // Input file name
    int i;                // Loop index
    int nvals;            // Number of data values to sort
    String outFileName;   // Output file name
    String str;           // Input string

    // Create a buffered reader on the standard input stream
    BufferedReader in = new BufferedReader(
                        new InputStreamReader(System.in));

    // Get input file name
    System.out.print("Enter input file name: ");
    inFileName = in.readLine();

    // Get output file name
    System.out.print("Enter output file name: ");
    outFileName = in.readLine();

    // Open the specified input file
    BufferedReader in1 = new BufferedReader(
                        new FileReader(inFileName));

    // Open the specified output file
    PrintWriter out = new PrintWriter(
                        new BufferedWriter(
                        new FileWriter(outFileName)));

    // Read the data
    nvals = 0;
    str = in1.readLine();
    while ( str != null ) {
       arr[nvals++] = Double.parseDouble(str);
       str = in1.readLine();
    }

    // Close input file
    in1.close();

    // Sort values
    SelectionSort2.sort( arr, nvals );

    // Write out sorted values
    for ( i = 0; i < nvals; i++ ) {
       out.println(arr[i]);
    }
```

Figure 6.7. (Continued).

```
      // Close output file
      out.close();
}

// Define the sort method
public static void sort(double[] arr, int nvals) {

   // Declare variables, and define each variable
   int i, j;              // Loop index
   int iptr;              // Pointer to smallest value
   double temp;           // Temporary variable for swapping

   // Sort values
   for ( i = 0; i <= nvals-2; i++ ) {

      // Find the minimum value in arr[i] through arr[nvals-1]
      iptr = i;
      for ( j = i+1; j <= nvals-1; j++ ) {
         if (arr[j] < arr[iptr])
            iptr = j;
      }
      // iptr now points to the min value, so swap a[iptr]
      // with a[i] if iptr != i.
      if (i != iptr) {
         temp = arr[i];
         arr[i] = arr[iptr];
         arr[iptr] = temp;
      }
   }
}
}
```

Figure 6.7. (Continued).

Note that the sort method is declared to be void, meaning that it does not return a value to the calling method. Instead, it uses the reference to array arr passed by the calling method to directly manipulate the values in the array.

This new program can be tested just as the original program was, with identical results. The following data set will be placed in file input1:

```
13.3
12.
-3.0
 0.
 4.0
 6.6
 4.
-6.
```

Running these values through the program yields the following result:

```
D:\book\java\chap6>java SelectionSort2
Enter input file name: input1
Enter output file name: output1
```

```
D:\book\java\chap6>type output1
  -6.0000
  -3.0000
   0.0000
   4.0000
   4.0000
   6.6000
  12.0000
  13.3000
```

The program gives the correct answers for our test data set, as before.

Method `sort` performs the same function as the sorting code in the original example, but now `sort` is an independent method that we can re-use unchanged whenever we need to sort any array of `double` numbers.

Note that the array was declared in the `sort` method as

```
public static void sort(double[] arr, int nvals)
```

The statement tells the Java compiler that parameter `arr` is an array of `double` values. It does *not* specify the length of the array, since that will not be known until the program is actually executed.

6.5   VARIABLE DURATION AND SCOPE

Every variable in Java is characterized by a **duration** and a **scope**. A variable's *duration* is the time during which it exists, and its *scope* is the portion of the program from which the variable can be addressed.

Variables defined with the body of a method are sometimes called **local variables**. They may be defined anywhere within the method, and they are automatically created and initialized when program execution reaches that point in the method. Once created, such local variables continue to exist until the program exits the block in which they were defined. When that happens, the variables are automatically destroyed.

Such variables are said to have **automatic duration**, because they are automatically created when they are needed and automatically destroyed when they are no longer needed. Variables with automatic duration are known as **automatic variables**.

For example, consider the example method shown in Figure 6.8.

```
public static int sum ( int[] array ) {

    int i, total = 0;
    for ( i = 0; i < array.length; i++ ) {
        total += array[i];
    }
    return (total);
}
```

Figure 6.8.   An example method declaring two automatic variables.

In this method, integer variables `i` and `total` are automatic variables. They are automatically created when the method starts executing. When they are created, `total` will be automatically initialized to zero, as specified in the declaration statement.[1] The for loop sums up all of the elements in the input array, and the total is returned to the calling method. When the method stops executing, variables i and total are automatically destroyed. If the method is called again, new variables will be created and initialized as specified, and the process will start over again.

Automatic variables are very useful, because they conserve memory in a program. If they remained in memory, the local variables of all methods not currently being executed would just be taking up space without serving a useful purpose.

GOOD PROGRAMMING PRACTICE

Automatic variables conserve memory in a program by automatically removing unused variables when they are no longer needed in memory.

A **block** of code is a set of statements enclosed by braces { }. The body of a method is an example of a code block, and so are the bodies of for loops, if statements, and so on. Automatic variables are said to have **block scope**, *because they can only be used within the code block in which they are defined*, or within another block wholly contained within that block. We will learn about another type of scope in Chapter 7.

Figure 6.9 illustrates the concepts of duration and block scope. The program in that figure contains two instance variables, i1 and i2, that are defined in the body of

```
1    // Illustrates block scope
2    public class BlockScope {
3
4        // Define the main method
5        public static void main(String[] args) {
6
7            // Declare variables
8            int i1 = 1, i2 = 2;
9
10           // for loop
11           for (int i = 0; i < 3; i++) {          j is defined
12               int j;                              within the block
13               j = i1++ - i2;                      of the for loop.
14               System.out.println("j = " + j);
15           }
16
17           // This statement is illegal because j is undefined!
18           System.out.println("j = " + j);
19       }                                           j is illegal here,
20   }                                               because this is
                                                     outside the block.
```

Figure 6.9. A simple program illustrating block scope. Variable j is defined within the for loop, so it exists only while that block is executing, and can be accessed only from within that block.

---

[1]Note that i will be created but *not* initialized, since there is no initialization value in its declaration.

the `main` method, plus a variable `j` that is defined within the body of a `for` loop within the method. Variables `i1` and `i2` will exist as long as the `main` method is executing, but variable `j` will exist only as long as the `for` loop is executing. Thus the *duration* of variables `i1` and `i2` is the time that the `main` method is executing, and the duration of variable `j` is the time that the `for` loop is executing.

Variables `i1` and `i2` can be accessed anywhere within the body of the method, including within the `for` loop. In contrast, variable `j` can be accessed only within the body of the `for` loop. The attempt to access `j` at Line 18 will produce a compilation error, because the variable doesn't exist there! The *scope* of variables `i1` and `i2` is the body of the main method, and the scope of variable `j` is the body of the `for` loop.

It is also possible to declare variables that persist from the moment that the class defining them is first loaded into memory until the program stops executing. These variables are said to have **static duration**, and they are known as **static variables**. They can be used to preserve information between invocations of a method, or to share data between methods, as we will see in Chapter 7. We will learn how to declare static variables in Chapter 7.

6.6   RECURSIVE METHODS

For some classes of problems, it is convenient for a Java method to invoke itself. A **recursive method** invokes itself either directly or indirectly through another method. Java makes recursion easy, since all local variables are automatic, and new copies of each variable are created each time the method is invoked.

Certain classes of problems are easily solved recursively. For example, the factorial function can be defined as

$$N! = \begin{cases} N(N-1)! & N \geq 1 \\ 1 & N = 0 \end{cases} \tag{6.1}$$

This definition can easily be implemented recursively, with the procedure that calculates $N!$ calling itself to calculate $(N-1)!$, and that procedure calling itself to calculate $(N-2)!$, and so on, until finally the procedure is called to calculate $0!$.

A recursive method to calculate the factorial function is shown in Figure 6.10. Note that if $n > 1$, method `fact` calls itself with the argument $n - 1$. Method `fact` in this class includes two `println` statements, so that we can see happens as the method calls itself recursively.

When this program used to calculate the value of 5!, the results are:

```
D:\book\java\chap6>java Factorial
Enter integer to calculate factorial of: 5
In fact: n = 5
In fact: n = 4
In fact: n = 3
In fact: n = 2
In fact: n = 1
In fact: n = 0
In fact: n = 0 answer = 1
In fact: n = 1 answer = 1
In fact: n = 2 answer = 2
In fact: n = 3 answer = 6
In fact: n = 4 answer = 24
In fact: n = 5 answer = 120
5! = 120
```

```
/*
    Purpose:
      To calculate the factorial function N! through a
        recursive method.
    Record of revisions:
        Date          Programmer            Description of change
        ====          ==========            =====================
      04/23/2002    S. J. Chapman           Original code
*/
import java.io.*;
public class Factorial {

   // Define the main method
   public static void main(String[] args) throws IOException {
      int n;       // Integer to calculate factorial of

      // Create a buffered reader
      BufferedReader in1 = new BufferedReader(
                            new InputStreamReader(System.in));

      // Get number to calculate factorial of
      System.out.print("Enter integer to calculate factorial of: ");
      n = Integer.parseInt( in1.readLine() );

      // Output factorial
      System.out.print(n + "! = " + Factorial.fact(n));
   }

   // Define method factorial
   public static int fact ( int n ) {

      // Declare variables
      int answer;       // Result of calculation

      System.out.println("In fact: n = " + n);
      if ( n >= 1 )
         answer = n * fact(n-1);
      else
         answer = 1;
      System.out.println("In fact: n = "
                  + n + " answer = " + answer);
      return answer;
   }
}
```

Figure 6.10. A method to recursively implement the factorial function.

Note that the method was called by the main program with $n = 5$, and then the method called itself with $n = 4$, and so on, as shown in Figure 6.11. It is easy to verify by hand calculation that this method produced the correct answer.

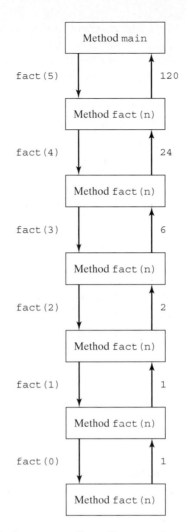

Figure 6.11. Method fact(n) calls itself recursively to calculate the value of 5!.

6.7 COERCION OF ARGUMENTS

What happens if the arguments passed to a method have a different type than the parameters of the method? For example, suppose that a function was declared with the statement

```
public static int fun1( double x1, double x2 ) {
```

and it is called from another method in the statement

```
x = fun1( 1, 2 );
```

In this case, the parameters of the function are of type `double`, but the calling arguments are of type `int`.

The answer is that *Java automatically converts arguments of an incorrect type into arguments of the type required by the method*. This process is known as the **coercion of arguments**. It applies only to widening conversions. A widening conversion occurs when the type of the method parameter can include any possible value of the calling argument, albeit possibly with some loss of precision. Since the range of possible `double` values exceeds the range of possible `int` values, conversions from `int` to `double` are widening conversions.

The program shown in Figure 6.12 illustrates coercion of arguments. This program includes a method that calculates and returns the square of a `double` value, and that method is being called repeatedly with `int` values. This program will compile and execute successfully, with each `int` value i being automatically converted into a `double` value when the method is called.

```
// Calculates the squares of the numbers from 1 to 10
public class SquareInt2 {

   // Define the main method
   public static void main(String[] args) {

      // Write number and square
      for ( int i = 1; i <= 10; i++ ) {
         System.out.print("number = " + i);
         System.out.println("  square = " + SquareInt2.square(i));
      }
   }

   // Definition of square method
   public static double square (double x) {
      return x * x;
   }
}
```

Figure 6.12. A program illustrating coercion of arguments. Each time method square is called, the int arguments are automatically converted into double values.

In contrast, the program shown in Figure 6.13 will fail to compile. This program includes a method that calculates and returns the square of an `int` value, and that

```
// Calculates the squares of the numbers from 1 to 10
public class SquareDouble {

   // Define the main method
   public static void main(String[] args) {

      // Write number and square
      for ( int i = 1; i <= 10; i++ ) {
         double a = (double) i;
         System.out.print("number = " + a);
         System.out.println("  square = " + SquareDouble.square(a));
      }
   }

   // Definition of square method
   public static int square (int x) {

      return x * x;
   }
}
```

Figure 6.13. A program showing a method with int parameters being called with double arguments. This program will *not* compile successfully.

method is being called repeatedly with `double` values. This program will *not* compile and execute successfully, because the conversion is a narrowing conversion (since `double`s can represent numbers larger than `int`s).

If it is necessary to call an `int` method with `double` arguments, then the arguments must be explicitly cast into type `int` in the method call. For example, the program in Figure 6.11 would compile and execute if the method call were changed to `SquareDouble.square ( (int) a)`.

6.8   METHOD OVERLOADING

Java allows several methods to be defined with the same name, as long as the methods have different sets of parameters (based on the number, types, and order of the parameters). This is called **method overloading**. When an overloaded method is called, the Java compiler selects the proper method by examining the number, type, and order of the calling arguments. Method overloading is commonly used to create several methods that perform the same function, but with different data types. For example, the program in Figure 6.14 includes two methods to calculate the square of a number, one for `int`s

```
// This program illustrates method overloading
public class Overload1 {

   // Define the main method
   public static void main(String[] args) {

      int i; double x;

      // Write number and square using integers
      System.out.println("Using integers:");
      for ( i = 1; i <= 5; i++ ) {
         System.out.print("number = " + i);
         System.out.println("  square = " + Overload1.square(i));
      }

      // Write number and square using doubles
      System.out.println("Using doubles:");
      for ( i = 1; i <= 5; i++ ) {
         x = i;
         System.out.print("number - " + x);
         System.out.println("  square = " + Overload1.square(x));
      }
   }

   // Definition of square method 1
   public static int square (int x) {
      return x * x;
   }

   // Definition of square method 2
   public static double square (double x) {
      return x * x;
   }
}
```

Figure 6.14.   A Java program illustrating method overloading.

and the other for doubles. Java determines which of the two methods to call based on the argument of a particular method call.

When this program is executed, the results are:

```
D:\book\java\chap6>java Overload1
Using integers:
number = 1   square = 1
number = 2   square = 4
number = 3   square = 9
number = 4   square = 16
number = 5   square = 25
Using doubles:
number = 1.0   square = 1.0
number = 2.0   square = 4.0
number = 3.0   square = 9.0
number = 4.0   square = 16.0
number = 5.0   square = 25.0
```

Note that Java used the first method when the method was invoked with an int argument, and the second method when the method was invoked with a double argument.

Overload methods are distinguished by their **signature**, which is a combination of the method name and the number, type, and order of parameters. If two methods have the same signature, then the Java compiler cannot distinguish between them. Defining two methods with the same signature produces a compile-time error. This is true *even if the two methods return different data types*. For example, the program shown in Figure 6.15 contains two methods with an identical signature but different return data types.

```
// This program contains two methods with identical
// signatures, which is an error.
public class Overload2 {

   // Define the main method
   public static void main(String[] args) {

      int i; double x;

      // Write number and square using integers
      for ( i = 1; i <= 5; i++ ) {
         System.out.print("number = " + i);
         System.out.println("  square = " + Overload1.square(i));
      }
   }

   // Definition of square method 1
   public int square (int x) {
      return x * x;
   }

   // Definition of square method 2
   public double square (int x) {
      return (double) x * x;
   }
}
```

Figure 6.15. A Java program containing two different methods with the same signature in the same class.

When this program is compiled, the results are:

```
D:\book\java\chap6>javac Overload2.java
Overload2.java:24: square(int) is already defined in
Overload2
   public double square (int x) {
                 ^
1 error
```

It is an error to define two different methods with the same signature in a single class.

EXAMPLE 6.2

Statistics Methods: Develop a set of reusable methods capable of determining the average and standard deviation of a data set consisting of numbers in an array. The method should work for data input arrays of int, float, and double types.

SOLUTION

To solve this problem, we will need to create six different methods, one each to determine the average and the standard deviation of int, float, and double arrays. Note that we will be using method overloading, so that the same method name may be called to get the average of a data set, whether it is int, float, on double. In addition, we will need to define a main method to test our six other methods.

1. **Determine the User Requirements**

   In this case, the user needs methods that will calculate the average and the standard deviation of an array of data, whether that array is of type int, float, or double. We will write six different methods: three forms of average to calculate the average of the three types of data sets, and three forms of stdDev to calculate the standard deviation of the three types of data sets.

   The input to each method will be an array of int, float, or double values. The output will be a double value containing either the average or the standard deviation of the data in the array. Note that we are using a double value in all cases, because the average and standard deviations of even the integer arrays will not in general be integer values.

2. **Analysis and Decomposition**

   We have not yet studied classes in detail, so for now there will be only one class. The class will contain six static methods to calculate the average and standard deviations, plus the main method to contain test driver code. We will call the class Stats4.

3. **Detailed Design**

   The pseudocode for the average methods is:
   ```
   Initialize sumX to zero
   if (arr.length >= 1) {
       for ( int i = 0; i < arr.length; i++ ) {
           sumX ← sumX + arr[i]
       }
       xBar ← sumX / arr.length
   ```

```
      else {
          Insufficient data: set xBar to 0.
      }
      return xBar;
```

The pseudocode for the `stdDev` methods is:

```
      Initialize sumX and sumX2 to zero
      if (arr.length >= 2) {
          for ( int i = 0; i < arr.length; i++ ) {
              sumX ← sumX + arr[i]
              sumX2 ← sumX2 + arr[i]*arr[i]
          }
          stdDev ← Math.sqrt((nvals*sumX2 - sumX*sumX)
                  / (arr.length*(arr.length-1)))
      else {
          Insufficient data: set stdDev to 0.
      }
      return stdDev;
```

The `main` method will have to test all six calculational methods, so it must define three arrays containing `int`, `float`, or `double` values and call both `average` and `stdDev` with each array. The pseudocode for the `main` method is:

```
int arr1 = { 8, 9, 10, 11, 12 };
float arr2 = { 8.F, 9.F, 10.F, 11.F, 12.F };
double arr3 = { 8., 9., 10., 11., 12. };
System.out.println("Integer array:");
System.out.println("Average            = " + average(arr1));
System.out.println("Standard Deviation = " + stdDev(arr1));
System.out.println("Float array:");
System.out.println("Average            = " + average(arr2));
System.out.println("Standard Deviation = " + stdDev(arr2));
System.out.println("Double array:");
System.out.println("Average            = " + average(arr3));
System.out.println("Standard Deviation = " + stdDev(arr3));
```

4. **Implementation: Convert Algorithms to Java Statements**

The resulting Java program is shown in Figure 6.16.

5. **Testing**

To test this program, we can calculate the average and standard deviation of the values 8, 9, 10, 11, 12 from the definitions of average and standard deviation:

$$\bar{x} = \frac{1}{N}\sum_{i=1}^{N} x_i = \frac{1}{5}(50) = 10.0 \tag{6.1}$$

$$s = \sqrt{\frac{N\sum_{i=1}^{N} x_i^2 - \left(\sum_{i=1}^{N} x_i\right)^2}{N(N-1)}} = 1.5811 \tag{6.2}$$

```
/*
   Purpose:
     To calculate the average and standard deviation of
     integer, float, or double arrays.  This class
     illustrates method overloading.

   Record of revisions:
       Date           Programmer                Description of change
       ====           ==========                =====================
     04/25/2002    S. J. Chapman           Original code
*/
public class Stats4 {

   // Define the average method for integer arrays
   public static double average( int[] arr ) {

      // Declare variables, and define each variable
      double sumX = 0;          // Sum of the input samples
      double xBar = 0;          // Average of input samples

      if (arr.length >= 1) {
         for ( int i = 0; i < arr.length; i++ ) {
            sumX += arr[i];
         }
         xBar = sumX / arr.length;
      }
      else {
         // Insufficient data
         xBar = 0;
      }
      return xBar;
   }

   // Define the average method for float arrays
   public static double average( float[] arr ) {

      // Declare variables, and define each variable
      double sumX = 0;          // Sum of the input samples
      double xBar = 0;          // Average of input samples

      if (arr.length >= 1) {
         for ( int i = 0; i < arr.length; i++ ) {
            sumX += arr[i];
         }
         xBar = sumX / arr.length;
      }
      else {
         // Insufficient data
         xBar = 0;
      }
      return xBar;
   }
```

Figure 6.16. Program to calculate the average and standard deviation of int, float, or double arrays. This program illustrates method overloading.

```
// Define the average method for double arrays
public static double average( double[] arr ) {

   // Declare variables, and define each variable
   double sumX = 0;         // Sum of the input samples
   double xBar = 0;         // Average of input samples

   if (arr.length >= 1) {
     for ( int i = 0; i < arr.length; i++ ) {
        sumX += arr[i];
     }
     xBar = sumX / arr.length;
   }
   else {
      // Insufficient data
      xBar = 0;
   }
   return xBar;
}

// Define the stdDev method for integer arrays
public static double stdDev( int[] arr ) {

   // Declare variables, and define each variable
   double stdDev = 0;       // Std deviation of input samples
   double sumX = 0;         // Sum of the input samples
   double sumX2 = 0;        // Sum of squares of input samples
   double xBar = 0;         // Average of input samples

   if (arr.length >= 2) {
     for ( int i = 0; i < arr.length; i++ ) {
        sumX += arr[i];
        sumX2 += arr[i] * arr[i];
     }
     stdDev = Math.sqrt((arr.length*sumX2 - sumX*sumX)
           / (arr.length*(arr.length-1)));
   }
   else {
      // Insufficient data
      stdDev = 0;
   }
   return stdDev;
}

// Define the stdDev method for float arrays
public static double stdDev( float[] arr ) {

   // Declare variables, and define each variable
   double stdDev = 0;       // Std deviation of input samples
   double sumX = 0;         // Sum of the input samples
   double sumX2 = 0;        // Sum of squares of input samples
   double xBar = 0;         // Average of input samples
```

Figure 6.16. (Continued).

```
      if (arr.length >= 2) {
        for ( int i = 0; i < arr.length; i++ ) {
           sumX += arr[i];
           sumX2 += arr[i] * arr[i];
        }
        stdDev = Math.sqrt((arr.length*sumX2 - sumX*sumX)
              / (arr.length*(arr.length-1)));
      }
      else {
         // Insufficient data
         stdDev = 0;
      }
      return stdDev;
   }

   // Define the stdDev method for double arrays
   public static double stdDev( double[] arr ) {

      // Declare variables, and define each variable
      double stdDev = 0;      // Std deviation of input samples
      double sumX = 0;        // Sum of the input samples
      double sumX2 = 0;       // Sum of squares of input samples
      double xBar = 0;        // Average of input samples

      if (arr.length >= 2) {
        for ( int i = 0; i < arr.length; i++ ) {
           sumX += arr[i];
           sumX2 += arr[i] * arr[i];
        }
        stdDev = Math.sqrt((arr.length*sumX2 - sumX*sumX)
              / (arr.length*(arr.length-1)));
      }
      else {
         // Insufficient data
         stdDev = 0;
      }
      return stdDev;
   }

   // Define the main method
   public static void main(String[] args) {

      // Declare test arrays
      int[] arr1 = { 8, 9, 10, 11, 12 };
      float[] arr2 = { 8.F, 9.F, 10.F, 11.F, 12.F };
      double[] arr3 = { 8., 9., 10., 11., 12. };

      // Calculate average and standard dev of each array
      System.out.println("Integer array:");
```

Figure 6.16. (Continued).

```
      System.out.println("Average        = " + Stats4.average(arr1));
      System.out.println("Std Deviation = " + Stats4.stdDev(arr1));
      System.out.println("Float array:");
      System.out.println("Average        = " + Stats4.average(arr2));
      System.out.println("Std Deviation = " + Stats4.stdDev(arr2));
      System.out.println("Double array:");
      System.out.println("Average        = " + Stats4.average(arr3));
      System.out.println("Std Deviation = " + Stats4.stdDev(arr3));
   }
}
```

Figure 6.16. (Continued).

When the program is executed, the results are:

```
D:\book\java\chap6>java Stats
Integer array:
Average            = 10.0
Standard Deviation = 1.5811388300841898
Float array:
Average            = 10.0
Standard Deviation = 1.5811388300841898
Double array:
Average            = 10.0
Standard Deviation = 1.5811388300841898
```

The results of the program agree with our hand calculations to the number of significant digits to which we performed the calculation. ■

6.9 SORTING USING CLASS `java.util.Arrays`

Beginning with the Java SDK version 1.2, Java includes a special class that contains some methods designed to make manipulating arrays easier. This class is named `Arrays`, and it is located in the `java.util` package. This class contains a very efficient overloaded sort method, based on the quicksort algorithm. The calling arguments for these methods are described in Table 6.1.

TABLE 6.1 Sort Methods in `java.util.Arrays`

Method Name	Description
`void sort(long[] a)`	These overloaded methods sort
`void sort(int[] a)`	the array a into ascending
`void sort(short[] a)`	numerical order. The sorting algorithm
`void sort(char[] a)`	is a tuned quicksort.
`void sort(byte[] a)`	Note that is possible to sort arrays of
`void sort(double[] a)`	`Objects` as well as primitive data types,
`void sort(float[] a)`	provided that the objects are
`void sort(Object[] a)`	mutually comparable.

The quicksort method implemented in this class is much more efficient than the selection sort method that we developed in Example 6.1. You will be asked to compare the sorting speeds of these two methods in Exercise 14 at the end of this chapter.

The Arrays class must be imported into a Java program before it can be used. The easiest way to do this is to include the statement

```
import java.util.*;         // Import Java utils package
```

before the class definition in which the methods will be used. Once the Arrays class has been imported, the methods can be invoked as Arrays.sort(array).

GOOD PROGRAMMING PRACTICE

Use the sort() method in the java.util.Arrays class to sort arrays in practical programs. This method is very efficient, already debugged, and built right into the basic Java environment.

QUIZ 6-2

This quiz provides a quick check to see if you have understood the concepts introduced in Sections 6.4 through 6.9. If you have trouble with the quiz, reread the sections, ask your instructor, or discuss the material with a fellow student. The answers are found in the back of the book.

1.   What is the duration of a variable? What types of duration exist in Java?
2.   What is the duration of local variables defined within a Java method?
3.   What is a recursive method?
4.   What happens when a method containing double parameters is called with int arguments? What happens when a method containing int parameters is called with double arguments?
5.   What is method overloading?

For Questions 6 and 7, determine whether there are any errors in these programs. If so, tell what the errors are. If not, tell what the output from each program will be.

6.
```java
public class Test {

    public static void main(String[] args) {

        int i = 2; int j = 3;

        while ( j > 0 ) {
            int i = j;
            System.out.println(i*j);
            j--;
        }
    }
}
```

```
7.      public class Test {
          public static void main(String[] args) {

            int a = 5, b = 10;
            System.out.println(Test.m1(a,b));
          }

          public static double m1 ( int i, int j) {
            return ( i + 2*j);
          }

          public static double m1 ( int x, int y) {
            return ( x - 2*y);
          }
        }
```

SUMMARY

- A **method** performs a specific function and returns (at most) a *single* value to the calling method. All methods must be defined within a Java class definition.

- A method definition includes four components: (1) optional keywords, (2) the data type of the returned value, (3) the method name, and (4) the list of parameters that the method expects to receive. This definition is followed by the body of the method within braces { }.

- A method calls or invokes another method by including its name, together with appropriate calling arguments in parentheses, in an expression.

- A method executes until the end of the body is reached, or until a `return` statement is executed. The value returned by the method is the value of the expression in the `return` statement.

- It is possible for a method to return no value to a calling method. In that case, the method is declared with a `void` data type.

- Local variables are variables defined within a method and not accessible to calling methods. These variables are automatic variables, meaning that they are automatically created when the methods starts executing, and automatically destroyed when the method stops executing.

- Java uses a *pass-by-value* scheme to pass the value of calling arguments to method parameters. A *copy* of the value of each calling argument is placed in the corresponding parameters. As a result, any modifications of the parameters within the method have no effect on the calling arguments.

- When an array or object is passed to a method, Java copies the value of the *reference* to the array or object and places it in the corresponding parameter. The method can then use that reference to modify the original array or object.

- Automatic variables are created when a body is executed, and destroyed when the execution of the body is completed.

- A recursive method is a method that calls itself, either directly or indirectly.

- Java supports automatic coercion or calling arguments, as long as the conversion is a widening conversion.

- Method overloading is the definition of two or more methods with the same name, distinguishable by the type, number, and order of their calling parameters.

- Overload methods are distinguished by their **signature**, which is a combination of the method name and the number, type, and order of parameters. No two methods in a single class may have the same signature.

SUMMARY OF GOOD PROGRAMMING PRACTICES

The following guidelines introduced in this chapter will help you to develop good programs:

1. Break large program tasks into classes and methods whenever practical to achieve the important benefits of independent component testing, reusability, and isolation from undesired side effects.
2. The pass-by-value scheme prevents a method from accidentally modifying its calling arguments.
3. Automatic variables conserve memory in a program by automatically removing unused variables when they are no longer needed in memory.
4. Use the sort() method in the java.util.Arrays class to sort arrays in practical programs. This method is very efficient, already debugged, and built right into the basic Java environment.

TERMINOLOGY

argument list	method overloading
automatic duration	parameters
automatic variables	pass-by-value
duration	recursive method
information hiding	return statement
java.util.Arrays class	signature
local variables	static duration
method	static variables
method body	test driver
method call	unit testing
method invocation	void

Exercises

1. When a method is called, how is data passed from the calling method to the called method, and how are the results of the method returned to the calling program?
2. What are the advantages and disadvantages of the pass-by-value scheme used in Java?
3. Suppose that a 15-element array a is passed to a method as a calling argument. What will happen if the method attempts to access element a[15]?
4. Determine whether the following method calls are correct or not. If they are in error, specify what is wrong with them. If they are correct, describe what the program does.

   a.
   ```java
   public class Test {
       public static void main(String[] args) {
           int[] arr = { 1, 2, 3, 4, 5};
           System.out.println(t.sum(arr));
       }
       public static int sum ( int a ) {
           int sum = 0;
           for ( int i = 0; i < a.length; i++ )
               sum += a[i];
           return (sum);
       }
   }
   ```

b.
```
public class Test {
    public static void main(String[] args) {
        int[] arr = {1, 2, 3, 4, 5};
        int i;

        // Print array
        System.out.print("Before: ");
        for ( i = 0; i < arr.length; i++ )
            System.out.print(arr[i] + " ");
        System.out.println();

        Test.calc(arr,6);

        System.out.print("After:  ");
        for ( i = 0; i < arr.length; i++ )
            System.out.print(arr[i] + " ");
        System.out.println();
    }
    public static void calc ( int[] a, int b ) {
        int sum = 0;
        for ( int i = 0; i < a.length; i++ )
            a[i] *= b;
            sum += a[i];
        return (sum);
    }
}
```

5. Modify the selection sort method developed in this chapter so that it sorts `double` values in *descending* order.

6. The mathematical method `Math.random()` returns a sample value from a uniform distribution in the range $[0, 1)$. Each time that the method is called, a random value in the range $0 \le value < 1$ is returned, with every possible value having an equal probability of occurrence. A method like `Math.random()` can be used to introduce an element of chance into a program.

   Every possible number between 0 and 1 should have an equal probability of being returned as a result from this method. Test the distribution of values returned from this method by calling it 10,000 times and calculating the number of values falling between 0 and 0.1, 0.1 and 0.2, and so on. Are the values evenly distributed between 0 and 1? Plot the number of values falling in each interval using the plotting classes provided in package `chapman.graphics`.

7. Use method `Math.random()` to generate arrays containing 1000, 10,000, and 100,000 random values between 0.0 and 1.0. Then, use the statistical methods developed in this chapter to calculate the average and standard deviation of values in the arrays. The theoretical average of a uniform random distribution in the range $[0, 1)$ is 0.5, and the theoretical standard deviation of the uniform random distribution is $1/\sqrt{12}$. How close do the random arrays generated by `Math.random()` come to behaving like the theoretical distribution?

8. Write a method that uses method `Math.random()` to generate a random value in the range $[-1.0, 1.0)$.

9. **Dice Simulation** It is often useful to be able to simulate the throw of a fair die. Write a Java method `dice()` that simulates the throw of a fair die by returning some random integer between 1 and 6 every time that it is called. [*Hint:* Call `Math.random()` to generate a random number. Divide the possible values out of `Math.random()` into six equal intervals, and return the number of the interval that a given random number falls into.]

10. **Road Traffic Density** Method `Math.random()` produces a number with a *uniform* probability distribution in the range [0.0, 1.0). This method is suitable for simulating random events if each outcome has an equal probability of occurring. However, in many events, the probability of occurrence is *not* equal for every event, and a uniform probability distribution is not suitable for simulating such events.

    For example, when traffic engineers studied the number of cars passing a given location in a time interval of length t, they discovered that the probability of k cars passing during the interval was given by the equation

$$P(k, t) = e^{-\lambda t}\frac{(\lambda t)^k}{k!} \qquad \text{for } t \geq 0, \lambda > 0, \text{ and } k = 0, 1, 2, \ldots \qquad (6.2)$$

This probability distribution is known as the *Poisson distribution*; it occurs in many applications in science and engineering. For example, the number of calls k to a telephone switchboard in time interval t, the number of bacteria k in a specified volume t of liquid, and the number of failures k of a complicated system in time interval t all have Poisson distributions.

    Write a method to evaluate the Poisson distribution for any k, t, and λ. Test your method by calculating the probability of 0, 1, 2, $\ldots$, 5 cars passing a particular point on a highway in 1 minute, given that λ is 1.6 per minute for that highway.

11. Write three Java methods to calculate the hyperbolic sine, cosine, and tangent functions:

$$\sinh(x) = \frac{e^x - e^{-x}}{2} \qquad \cosh(x) = \frac{e^x + e^{-x}}{2} \qquad \tanh(x) = \frac{e^x - e^{-x}}{e^x + e^{-x}}$$

Use your methods to calculate the hyperbolic sines, cosines, and tangents of the following values: -2, -1.5, -1.0, -0.5, -0.25, 0.0, 0.25, 0.5, 1.0, 1.5, and 2.0. Use the `chapman.graphics.JPlot2D` class to create plots of the shapes of the hyperbolic sine, cosine, and tangent functions.

12. **Cross Product** Write a method to calculate the cross product of two `double` vectors $\mathbf{V}_1$ and $\mathbf{V}_2$:

$$\mathbf{V}_1 \times \mathbf{V}_2 = (V_{y1}V_{z2} - V_{y2}V_{z1})\mathbf{i} + (V_{z1}V_{x2} - V_{z2}V_{x1})\mathbf{j} + (V_{x1}V_{y2} - V_{x2}V_{y1})\mathbf{k}$$

where $\mathbf{V}_1 = V_{x1}\mathbf{i} + V_{y1}\mathbf{j} + V_{z1}\mathbf{k}$ and $\mathbf{V}_2 = V_{x2}\mathbf{i} + V_{y2}\mathbf{j} + V_{z2}\mathbf{k}$. Note that this method will return a `double` array as its result. Use the method to calculate the cross product of the two vectors $\mathbf{V}_1 = [-2, 4, 0.5]$ and $\mathbf{V}_2 = [0.5, 3, 2]$.

13. **Sort with Carry** It is often useful to sort an array `arr1` into ascending order, while simultaneously carrying along a second array `arr2`. In such a sort, each time an element of array `arr1` is exchanged with another element of `arr1`, the corresponding elements of array `arr2` are also swapped. When the sort is over, the elements of array `arr1` are in ascending order, while the elements of array

arr2 that were associated with particular elements of array arr1 are still associated with them. For example, suppose we have the following two arrays:

Element	arr1	arr2
1.	6.	1.
2.	1.	0.
3.	2.	10.

After sorting array arr1 while carrying along array arr2, the contents of the two arrays will be:

Element	arr1	arr2
1.	1.	0.
2.	2.	10.
3.	6.	1.

Write a method to sort one double array into ascending order while carrying along a second one. Test the method with the following two nine-element arrays:

```
double a = { 1.,   11.,  -6.,  17., -23.,   0.,  5.,  1., -1. };
double b = {31.,  101.,  36., -17.,   0., 10., -8., -1., -1. };
```

14. **Comparing Sort Algorithms**   Write a program to compare the sorting speed of the selection-sort method developed in Example 6.1 with the quicksort sorting method included in the `java.util.Arrays` class. Use method `Math.random()` to generate two arrays containing 1000 and 10,000 random values between 0.0 and 1.0. Then, use both sorting methods to sort copies of these arrays. How does the sorting time compare for these two methods? [*Note:* The method `System.currentTimeMillis()` returns the current system time in milliseconds as a double value. You can determine the elapsed time required by a sorting algorithm by calling this method before and after the call to each sorting algorithm.]

15. **Linear Least-Squares Fit**   Develop a method that will calculate slope m and intercept b of the least-squares line that "best fits" an input data set. The input data points (x, y) will be passed to the method in two input arrays, x and y. The equations describing the slope and intercept of the least-squares line are

$$y = mx + b \qquad (6.3)$$

$$m = \frac{(\Sigma xy) - (\Sigma x)\bar{y}}{(\Sigma x^2) - (\Sigma x)\bar{x}} \qquad (6.4)$$

and

$$b = \bar{y} - m\bar{x} \qquad (6.5)$$

where

Σx is the sum of the x-values
Σx^2 is the sum of the squares of the x-values
Σxy is the sum of the products of the corresponding x- and y-values
$\bar{x}$ is the mean (average) of the x-values
$\bar{y}$ is the mean (average) of the y-values

Test your method using a test driver program that calculates the least-squares fit to the following 20-point input data set, and plots both the original input data and the resulting least-squares fit line:

No.	x	y	No.	x	y
\multicolumn{6}{c}{**Sample Data to Test Least-Squares Fit Method**}
1	−4.91	−8.18	11	−0.94	0.21
2	−3.84	−7.49	12	0.59	1.73
3	−2.41	−7.11	13	0.69	3.96
4	−2.62	−6.15	14	3.04	4.26
5	−3.78	−5.62	15	1.01	5.75
6	−0.52	−3.30	16	3.60	6.67
7	−1.83	−2.05	17	4.53	7.70
8	−2.01	−2.83	18	5.13	7.31
9	0.28	−1.16	19	4.43	9.05
10	1.08	0.52	20	4.12	10.95

16.   **Correlation Coefficient of Least-Squares Fit**   Develop a method that will calculate both the slope m and intercept b of the least-squares line that best fits an input data set, and also the correlation coefficient of the fit. The input data points (x, y) will be passed to the method in two input arrays, x and y. The equations describing the slope and intercept of the least-squares line are given in the previous problem, and the equation for the correlation coefficient is

$$r = \frac{n(\Sigma xy) - (\Sigma x)(\Sigma y)}{\sqrt{[(n\Sigma x^2) - (\Sigma x)^2][(n\Sigma y^2) - (\Sigma y)^2]}} \tag{6.6}$$

where

Σx is the sum of the x-values

Σy is the sum of the y-values

Σx^2 is the sum of the squares of the x-values

Σy^2 is the sum of the squares of the y-values

Σxy is the sum of the products of the corresponding x- and y-values

n is the number of points included in the fit

Test your method using a test driver program and the 20-point input data set given in the previous problem.

17.   **The Birthday Problem**   If there are a group of n people in a room, what is the probability that two or more of them have the same birthday? It is possible to answer this question by simulation. Write a method that calculates the probability that two or more of n people will have the same birthday, where n is a calling argument. (*Hint:* To do this, the method should create an array of size n and generate n birthdays in the range 1 to 365 randomly. It should then check to see if any of the n birthdays are identical. The method should perform this experiment at least 5000 times and calculate the fraction of those times in which two or more people had the same birthday.) Write a program that calculates and prints out the probability that 2 or more of n people will have the same birthday for $n = 2, 3, \ldots, 40$. Then, plot the probability as a function of

the number of people in the room. At what size group does the probability of having two people with the same birthday exceed 90%?

18. **Evaluating Infinite Series** The value of the exponential function e^x can be calculated by evaluating the following infinite series:

$$e^x = \sum_{n=0}^{\infty} \frac{x^n}{n!}$$

Write a Java method that calculates e^x using the first 12 terms of the infinite series. Compare the result of your method with the result of the intrinsic method `Math.exp(x)` for $x = -10., -5., -1., 0., 1., 5., 10.,$ and $15.$

19. **Gaussian (Normal) Distribution** Method `Math.random()` returns a uniformly distributed random variable in the range $[0,1)$, which means that there is an equal probability of any given number in the range occurring on a given call to the method. Another type of random distribution is the Gaussian distribution, in which the random value takes on the classic bell-shaped curve shown in Figure 6.17. A Gaussian distribution with an average of 0.0 and a standard deviation of 1.0 is called a *standardized normal distribution*, and the probability of any given value occurring in the standardized normal distribution is given by the equation

$$p(x) = \frac{1}{\sqrt{2\pi}} e^{-x^2/2} \tag{6.7}$$

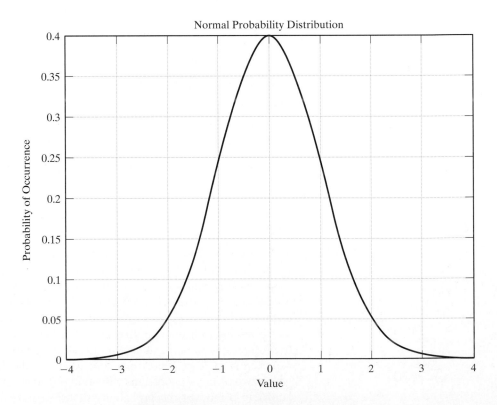

Figure 6.17. A normal probability distribution.

It is possible to generate a random variable with a standardized normal distribution starting from a random variable with a uniform distribution in the range $[-1, 1)$ as follows:

1. Select two uniform random variables x_1 and x_2 from the range $[-1, 1)$ such that $x_1^2 + x_2^2 < 1$. To do this, generate two uniform random variables in the range $[-1, 1)$, and see if the sum of their squares happens to be less than 1. If so, use them. If not, try again.

2. Then each of the values y_1 and y_2 in the equations below will be a normally distributed random variable.

$$y_1 = \sqrt{\frac{-2 \ln r}{r}} x_1 \tag{6.8}$$

$$y_2 = \sqrt{\frac{-2 \ln r}{r}} x_2 \tag{6.9}$$

where $$r = x_1^2 + x_2^2 \tag{6.10}$$

Write a method that returns a normally distributed random value each time that it is called. Test your method by getting 1000 random values and calculating the standard deviation. How close to 1.0 was the result?

20. Use the method developed in the previous problem to generate an array of 50,000 random samples. Test the distribution of the values returned from this method by calculating the number of values falling within the ranges -4.0 to -3.9, -3.9 to -3.8, and so on, up to 3.9 to 4.0. Divide the number of values in each bin by the total number of samples (50,000), and plot the resulting distribution. Also, plot Equation (6.7) on the same axes. How close does the distribution of samples from your method come to the theoretical normal distribution?

21. **Gravitational Force**   The gravitational force F between two bodies of masses m_1 and m_2 is given by the equation

$$F = \frac{Gm_1m_2}{r^2} \tag{6.11}$$

where G is the gravitation constant (6.672×10^{-11} N m^2/kg^2), m_1 and m_2 are the masses of the bodies in kilograms, and r is the distance between the two bodies. Write a method to calculate the gravitational force between two bodies, given their masses and the distance between them. Test your method by determining the force on an 800-kg satellite in orbit 38,000 km above the earth. (The mass of the earth is 5.98×10^{24} kg.)

7

Classes and Object-Oriented Programming

This chapter introduces the basic concepts of objects and object-oriented programming. It also teaches the basic components of a class, and how to instantiate objects from a class.

7.1 AN INTRODUCTION TO OBJECT-ORIENTED PROGRAMMING

Object-oriented programming (OOP) is the process of programming by modeling objects in software. Its principal features are described in the following sections.

7.1.1 Objects

The physical world is full of objects: cars, pencils, trees, and so on. Any real object can be characterized by two different aspects: its *properties* and its *behavior*. For example, a car can be modeled as an object. A car has certain properties (color, speed, direction, fuel consumption) and certain behaviors (starting, stopping, turning, and so on).

In the software world, an **object** is a software component whose structure is like that of objects in the real world. Each object consists of a combination of data (called **properties**) and behaviors (called **methods**). The properties are variables describing the essential characteristics of the object, while the methods describe how the object behaves and how the properties of the object can be modified. Thus, an object is a software bundle of variables and related methods.

A software object is often represented as shown in Figure 7.1. The object can be thought of as a cell, with a central nucleus of variables and an outer layer of methods that form an interface between the object's variables and the outside world. The nucleus of data is hidden from the outside world by the outer layer of methods. The object's variables are said

OBJECTIVES

- Understand the basics of objects and object-oriented programming
- Understand the structure of a class
- Understand instance variables and methods
- Understand class scope and the use of references to access instance variables and methods
- Understand the this reference
- Learn how to create and use packages
- Understand how and why to use member access modifiers
- Understand finalizers and the garbage-collection process
- Understand static variables and methods

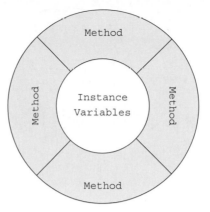

Figure 7.1. An object may be represented as a nucleus of data (instance variables) surrounded and protected by methods, which implement the object's behavior and form an interface between the variables and the outside world.

to be *encapsulated* within the object, meaning that no code outside of the object can see or directly manipulate them. Any access to the object's data must be through calls to the object's methods.

The variables and methods in a Java object are formally known as **instance variables** and **instance methods** to distinguish them from class variables and class methods (described later in Section 7.1.4).

Typically, encapsulation is used to hide the implementation details of an object from other objects in the program. If the other objects in the program cannot see the internal state of an object, they cannot introduce bugs by accidentally modifying the object's state. In addition, changes to the internal operation of the object will not affect the operation of the other objects in a program. As long as the interface to the outer world is unchanged, the implementation details of an object can change at any time without affecting other parts of the program.

Encapsulation provides two primary benefits to software developers:

- **Modularity**—An object can be written and maintained independently of the source code for other objects. Therefore, the object can be easily re-used in other programs.

- **Information Hiding**—An object has a public interface (the calling sequence of its methods) that other objects can use to communicate with it. However, the object's instance variables are not directly accessible to other objects. Therefore, if the public interface is not changed, an object's variables and methods can be changed at any time without introducing side effects in the other objects that depend on it.

7.1.2 Messages

Objects communicate by passing messages back and forth among themselves. These messages are method calls. For example, if Object A wants Object B to perform some action for it, it sends a message to Object B requesting the object to execute one of its methods (see Figure 7.2). The message causes Object B to execute the specified method.

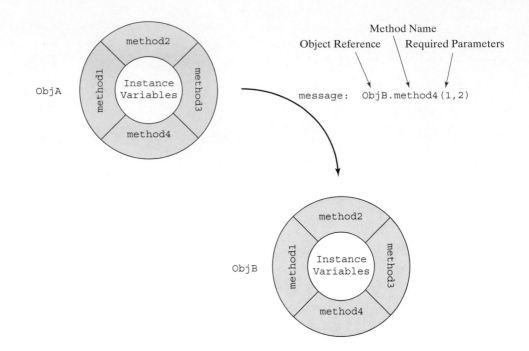

Figure 7.2. If object ObjA wants object ObjB to do some work for it, it sends a message to that object. The message contains three parts: a reference to the object to which it is addressed, the name of the method within the object which will do the work, and the required parameters. Note that the names of the object and method are separated by a period.

Each message has three components, which provide all the information necessary for the receiving object to perform the desired action:

1. A reference pointing to the object to which the message is addressed
2. The name of the method to perform on that object
3. Any parameters needed by the method

An object's behavior is expressed through its methods, so message passing supports all possible interactions between objects.

Note that objects don't need to be in the same process or even on the same computer to send and receive messages to each other. As long as a path to transmit messages exists, the object can interact. This characteristic makes object-oriented programs highly suited to client-server applications, in which the object sending the message resides on a different computer than the object performing the action.

7.1.3   Classes

Classes are the software blueprints from which objects are made. A class is a software construct that specifies the number and type of instance variables to be included in an object, and the instance methods that will be applied to the object. Each component of a class is known as a **member**. The two types of members are **fields**, which specify the data types defined by the class, and **methods**, which specify the operations on those fields. For example, suppose that we wished to create an object to represent a complex number. Such an object would have two instance variables, one for the real part of the number (`re`) and one for the imaginary part (`im`). In addition, it would have methods describing how to add, subtract, multiply, divide, and so on, with complex numbers. To create such objects, we would write a class `Complex` that defined the required fields `re` and `im`, together with their associated methods.

Note that a class is a *blueprint* for an object, not an object itself. The class describes what an object will look and behave like, once it is created. Each object is created or *instantiated* in memory from the blueprint provided by a class, and many different objects can be instantiated from the same class. For example, Figure 7.3 shows a class `Complex`, together with three objects a, b, and c created from that class. Each object has its own copies of the instance variables `re` and `im`, while sharing a single set of methods to modify them.

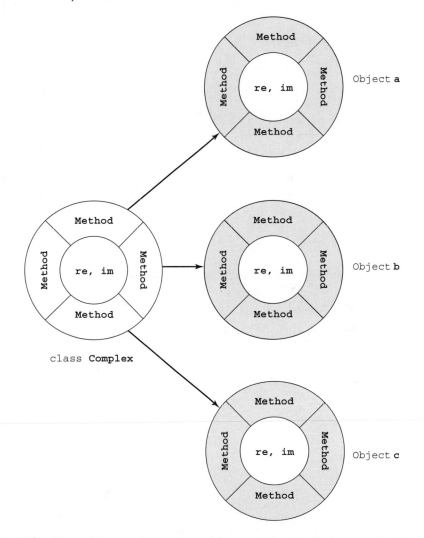

Figure 7.3.   Many objects can be instantiated from a single class. In this example, three objects a, b, and c have been instantiated from class `Complex`.

7.1.4 Class Variables and Methods

As we described above, each object created from a class receives its own copies of all the instance variables defined in the class. The instance variables in each object are independent of the instance variables in all other objects.

In addition to instance variables, it is possible to define **class variables**. Class variables differ from instance variables in that *there is only one variable for all objects created from the class, and every object has access to it*. Class variables are effectively "common" to all of the objects created from the class in which they are defined. They are created when an object is first instantiated from a class, and they remain in existence until all objects instantiated from that class have been destroyed. This idea is illustrated in Figure 7.4, which shows a new version of the Complex class containing two instance variables (re, im) and one class variable (count). The instance variables

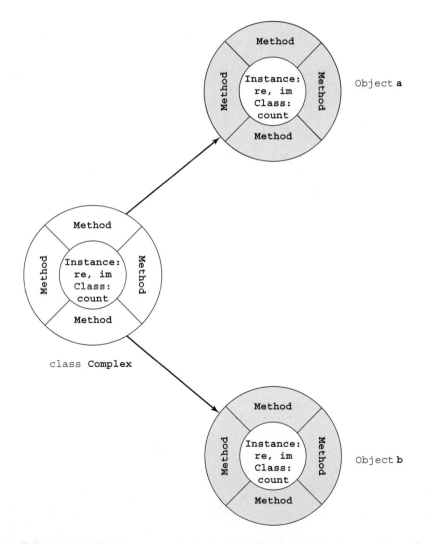

Figure 7.4. An example class containing both instance variables and class variables. The instance variables re and im are different in objects a and b, while the class variable count is common to both objects.

re and im will contain the real and imaginary part of the complex number stored in the object, while the class variable count might contain the number of objects instantiated from this class. Every object instantiated from this class will contain a unique copy of the variables re and im, but all the objects will use a single copy of the variable count.

Class variables are typically used to keep track of data that is common across all instances of a class. For example, count could be used to count the number of objects created using class Complex. Each time that a new Complex object is created, the value stored in count will be increased by one, and that new value will be available to every Complex object.

It is also possible to define **class methods** or **static methods**. Class methods are methods that exist independently of any objects defined from the class. These methods can access and modify class variables, but they cannot access instance variables or invoke instance methods.

Class methods are declared using the keyword static in the method definition. Class methods can be used without ever instantiating (creating) an object from the class in which they are defined. They are used by typing the class name followed by a period and by the method name. *Every method that we have created so far in this book has been a class or static method.*

7.1.5 Class Hierarchy and Inheritance

All classes in an object-oriented language are organized in a **class hierarchy**, with the highest-level classes being very general in behavior and lower-level ones becoming more specific. Each lower-level class is based on and derived from a higher-level class, and it *inherits both the instance variables and the instance methods* of the class from which it is derived. A new class starts with all of the nonprivate instance variables and methods of the class on which it is based, and the programmer then adds the additional variables and methods necessary for the new class to perform its function.

The class on which a new class is based is referred to as a **superclass**, and the new class is referred to as a **subclass**. The new subclass can itself become the superclass for another new subclass. A subclass normally adds instance variables and instance methods of its own, so a subclass is generally larger than its superclass. In addition, it can **override** some methods of its superclass, changing its behavior from that of its superclass. Because a subclass is more specific than its superclass, it represents a smaller group of objects.

For example, suppose that we define a class called Vector2D to contain two-dimensional vectors. Such a class would have two instance variables, x and y, to contain the x- and y-components of the 2D vectors, and it would need methods to manipulate the vectors, such as adding two vectors, subtracting two vectors, and calculating the length of a vector. Now suppose that we need to create a class called Vector3D to contain three-dimensional vectors. If this class is based on Vector2D, then it will automatically inherit instance variables x and y from its superclass, so the new class will only need to define a variable z. The new class will also override the methods used to manipulate 2D vectors to allow them to work properly with 3D vectors.

The concepts of class hierarchy and inheritance are extremely important, since inheritance allows a programmer to define certain behaviors only once in a superclass and

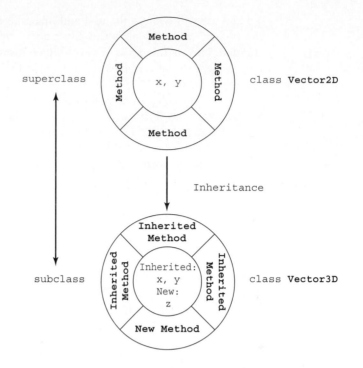

Figure 7.5. An example of inheritance. Class Vector2D has been defined to handle two-dimensional vectors. When class Vector3D is defined as a subclass of Vector2D, it inherits the instance variables x and y, as well as many methods. The programmer then adds a new instance variable z and new methods to the ones inherited from the superclass.

to re-use those behaviors over and over in many different subclasses. This reusability makes programming more efficient.

All classes in the Java language are ultimately derived from a superclass called Object. For example, a partial class hierarchy for the java.util package is shown in Figure 7.6.

7.1.6 Object-Oriented Programming

Object-oriented programming (OOP) is the process of programming by modeling objects in software. In OOP, a programmer examines the problem to be solved and tries to break it down into identifiable objects, each containing certain data and specific methods by which that data is manipulated. Sometimes these objects will correspond to physical objects in nature, and sometimes they will be purely abstract software constructs.

Once the objects making up the problem have been identified, the programmer identifies the type of data to be stored as instance variables in each object, and the exact calling sequence of each method needed to manipulate the data.

The programmer can then develop and test the classes in the model one at a time. As long as the *interfaces* between the classes (the calling sequence of the methods) are unchanged, each class can be developed and tested without the need to change any other part of the program.

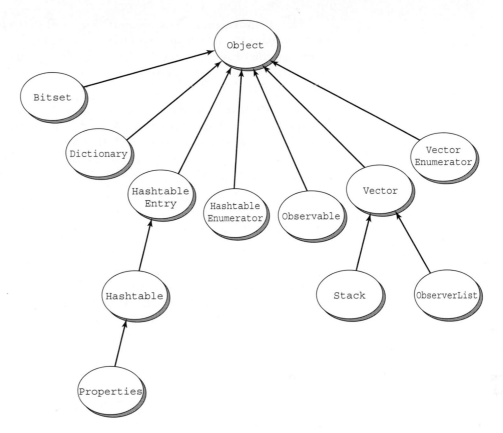

Figure 7.6.   A partial class hierarchy of the `java.util` package. Note that all classes ultimately derive from the `Object` class.

7.2   THE STRUCTURE OF A CLASS

The major components (class members) of a Java class are as follows (see Figure 7.7):

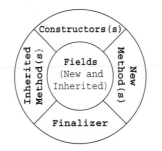

Figure 7.7.   A class consists of fields (data), one or more constructors to initialize the data, one or more methods to modify and manipulate the data, and up to one finalizer to clean up before the object is destroyed. Note that both fields and methods may be inherited from a superclass.

1.   **Fields.**   Fields define the instance variables that will be created when an object is instantiated from a class. Instance variables are the data encapsulated inside an object. A new set of instance variables is created each time an object is instantiated from the class.

2. **Constructors.** Constructors are special methods that specify how to initialize the instance variables in an object when it is created. Constructors are easy to identify, because they have the same name as the class that they are initializing, and they do not have a return data type. Constructors can be overloaded as long as the different constructors can be distinguished by their signatures.

3. **Methods.** Methods implement the behaviors of a class. Some methods may be explicitly defined in a class, while others may be inherited from superclasses of the class. As we learned in Chapter 6, methods may be overloaded as long as the different methods with the same name can be distinguished by their signatures.

4. **Finalizer.** Just before an object is destroyed, it makes a call to a special method called a finalizer. The method performs any necessary clean-up (releasing resources, and so on) before the object is destroyed. This special method is always named `finalize`. There can be at most one finalizer in a class, and many classes do not need a finalizer at all.

The members of a class, whether variables or methods, are accessed by referring to an object created from the class using the **member access operator**, also known as the **dot operator**. For example, suppose that a class `MyClass` contains an instance variable a and a method `processA`. If a reference to an object of this class were named `obj`, then the instance variable in `obj` would be accessed as `obj.a`, and the method would be accessed as `obj.processA()`.

7.3 FIRST EXAMPLE: A `Timer` CLASS

When developing software, it is often useful to be able to determine how long a particular part of a program takes to execute. This measurement can help us locate the "hot spots" in the code, the places where the program is spending most of its time, so that we can try to optimize them. This is usually done with an *elapsed-time calculator*.

An elapsed-time calculator makes a great first object, because it is so simple. It is analogous to a physical stopwatch. A stopwatch is an object that measures the elapsed time between a push on a start button and a push on a stop button (often they are the same physical button). The basic actions (methods) performed on a physical stopwatch are:

1. A button push to reset and start the timer.
2. A button push to stop the timer and display the elapsed time.

Internally, the stopwatch must remember the time of the first button push in order to calculate the elapsed time.

Similarly, an elapsed-time class needs to contain the following components (members):

1. A method to store the start time of the timer (`startTimer`). This method will not require any input parameters from the calling program and will not return any results to the calling program.
2. A method to return the elapsed time since the last start (`elapsedTime`). This method will not require any input parameters from the calling program, but it will return the elapsed time in seconds to the calling program.
3. A field (instance variable) to store the time that the timer started running, for use by the elapsed-time method.

In addition, the class must have a constructor to initialize the instance variable when an object is created. This class will not need a finalizer.

The timer class must be able to determine the current time whenever one of its methods is called. Fortunately, the `System` class (in the `java.lang` package) of the standard Java API includes a method to read the current time in milliseconds from the computer's system clock: **System.currentTimeMillis()**. This method will provide the current time information needed by the class.

7.3.1   Implementing The Timer Class

We will implement the timer class in a series of steps, defining the instance variables, constructor, and methods in succession.

Define Instance Variables.

The timer class must contain a single instance variable called savedTime, which contains the time at which the object was created or the last time at which startTimer method was called. It must be of type double, so that it can hold fractional parts of seconds.

Instance variables are declared after the class definition and before the constructors and methods. Therefore, class Timer will begin as follows:

```java
public class Timer {

    // Define instance variables
    private double savedTime; // Saved start time in ms

    ... (constructors and methods follow)
```

Create the Constructor.

The constructor for a class is automatically called by Java when an object is created from the class. The constructor must initialize the instance variables of the class and may perform other functions as well (such as opening files). In this class, the constructor will initialize the savedTime value to the time at which the Timer object is created.

A constructor looks just like a method, except that it has *exactly* the same name (including capitalization) as the class that it is defined in, and it does not have a return value. The constructor for the Timer class is shown below:

```java
    // Define class constructor
    public Timer() {
        savedTime = System.currentTimeMillis();
    }
```

Create the Methods.

The class must also include two methods to start the timer and to read the elapsed time. Method startTimer() simply resets the start time in the instance variable.

```java
    public void startTimer() {
        savedTime = System.currentTimeMillis();
    }
```

Method elapsedTime() returns the elapsed time since the start of the timer in seconds.

```java
public double elapsedTime() {
   double eTime;
   eTime = (System.currentTimeMillis() -   savedTime) / 1000.;
   return eTime;
}
```

The resulting Timer class is shown in Figure 7.8, and the source code for this class is shown in Figure 7.9.

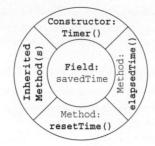

Figure 7.8. The Timer class.

```
1   /*
2      Purpose:
3        Object to measure the elapsed time between the most
4        recent call to method startTimer() and the call to
5        method elapsedTime().  This class creates and starts
6        a timer when a Timer object is instantiated, and
7        returns the elapsed time in seconds whenever
8        elapsedTime() is called.
9
10     Record of revisions:
11        Date          Programmer           Description of change
12        ====          ==========           =====================
13     04/28/2002    S. J. Chapman          Original code
14   */
15   public class Timer {
16
17      // Define instance variables
18      private double savedTime;    // Saved start time in ms
19
20      // Define class constructor
21      public Timer() {
22         savedTime = System.currentTimeMillis();
23      }
24
25      // startTimer() method
26      public void startTimer() {
27         savedTime = System.currentTimeMillis();
28      }
29
30      // elapsedTime() method returns elapsed time in seconds
31      public double elapsedTime() {
32         double eTime;
33         eTime = (System.currentTimeMillis() − savedTime) / 1000.;
34         return eTime;
35      }
36   }
```

Figure 7.9. The source code for the Timer class.

7.3.2 Using The Timer Class

To use this class in a program, the programmer must first instantiate a Timer object with a statement like

```
Timer t = new Timer();
```

This statement defines a reference t that refers to a Timer object. Also it uses the new keyword to create (instantiate) a new Timer object (see Figure 7.10). When the Timer object is instantiated, Java automatically calls the class constructor Timer to initialize the object. The constructor for this class begins on line 21; it resets the elapsed-time counter so that by default the object measures the elapsed time since the creation of the Timer object. After this line has been executed, the reference t points to the timer object, and the methods in the class can be called using that reference: t.startTimer() and t.elapsedTime().

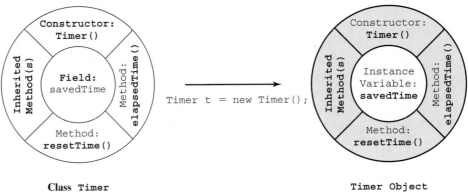

Class Timer   **Timer Object**

Figure 7.10. The statement "Timer t = new Timer();" creates (instantiates) a new Timer() object from the template provided by the class definition and makes reference t point to that object. This object has its own unique copy of the instance variable savedTime.

A program can reset the elapsed timer to zero at any time by calling method startTimer(), and it can get the elapsed time by calling method elapsedTime(). An example program that uses the Timer object is shown in Figure 7.11. The program tests this class by measuring the time required to perform 100,000,000 iterations of a pair of nested for loops.

```
/*
   Purpose:
     Class to test the operation of Timer.

   Record of revisions:
      Date          Programmer              Description of change
      ====          ==========              =====================
    04/28/2002   S. J. Chapman              Original code
*/
public class TestTimer {

   // Define the main method to test this object
   public static void main(String[] args) {

      // Declare variables, and define each variable
      double arr[];        // Data array to sort
      int i, j, k;         // Loop index
```

Figure 7.11. A program to test the Timer class.

```
       // Instantiate a Timer object
       Timer t = new Timer();

       // Start the timer running
       t.startTimer();

       // Waste some time
       for ( i = 1; i <= 10000; i++ ) {
          for ( j = 1; j <= 10000; j++ ) {
             k = i + j;
          }
       }

       // Read and display elapsed time
       System.out.println( "Time = " + t.elapsedTime() + " s" );
    }
}
```

Figure 7.11. (Continued).

When this program is executed on my Pentium III 733 MHz PC, the results are:

```
D:\book\java\chap7>java TestTimer
Time = 0.761 s
```

The measured time will, of course, differ on computers of different speeds.

7.3.3   Comments on The Timer Class

This section contains a few notes about the operation of our Timer class and of classes in general.

First, note that the Timer class saves its start time in the instance variable savedTime. Each time an object is instantiated from a class, it receives its *own copy* of all instance variables defined in the class. Therefore, many Timer objects can be instantiated and used simultaneously in a program, and *they will not interfere with each other*, because each timer has its own private copy of the instance variable savedTime.

Also, notice that each class member in Figure 7.9 is declared with either a public or private keyword. These keywords are examples of **member access modifiers**, which we will cover in detail later in this chapter. Any instance variable or method definition declared with the public member access modifier can be accessed from other classes in the program. Any instance variable or method declared with the private member access modifier is accessible only to methods of the object in which it is defined.

In this case, the instance variable savedTime is declared private, so it cannot be seen or modified by any method outside of the object in which it is defined. Since no method outside of Timer can see savedTime, it is not possible for some other method to accidentally modify the value stored there and so mess up the elapsed-time measurement. The only way that a program can utilize the elapsed-time measurement is through the public methods startTimer() and elapsedTime(). You should always declare all instance variables within your classes to be private.

GOOD PROGRAMMING PRACTICE

Always make instance variables private, so that they are hidden within an object. Such encapsulation makes your programs more modular and easier to modify.

7.4   SCOPE

The **scope** of a variable is the portion of the program from which it can be accessed. There are two possible scopes for Java variables: **class scope** and **block scope**.

The methods and the instance variables of a class have *class scope*. Class scope begins at the opening left brace (`{`) of a class definition and ends at the closing right brace (`}`). Class scope allows any method in the class to directly invoke any other method of the class (or any method inherited from a superclass) and to directly access any instance variable of the class. For example, any method in class `Timer` can access the instance variable `savedTime` just by using its name. Similarly, any method in a class can call any other method in the same class simply by using its name.[1]

Instance variables are effectively *global* with a class, since they can be seen from within any method in the class. Thus, instance variables can be used to communicate between methods in a class, or to retain information between invocations of a given method in the class.

Outside of a class's scope, those instance variables and methods that have been declared `public` can still be accessed, but *not* directly. Instead, they have to be accessed by reference to the object in which they are defined. Primitive data type instance variables would be accessed as `Reference.variableName`, and object instance variables and methods would be accessed as `Reference.objectName` or `Reference.methodName`. For example, the program in Figure 7.11 created a `Timer` object using a reference `t`, and then invoked method `elapsedTime()` using that reference: `t.elapsedTime()`.

By contrast, variables defined inside a block have *block scope*. A **block** is defined as a *compound statement*, which consists of all the statements between an open brace (`{`) and the corresponding close brace (`}`). For example, every method is a block, because it starts with an open brace and ends with a close brace.

Variables defined within a block are automatic variables, and they exist only as long as the block is executing. They are visible within the block and within any blocks contained within the block, but they are not visible (and in fact do not exist) after the block finishes executing. For example, the local variables defined at the beginning of a method have block scope. They are visible between the open brace (`{`) and the corresponding closing brace (`}`) of the method. They are also visible within any blocks contained within the block, such as `while` or `for` loops.

Any block may contain variable declarations that will be valid only for the duration of the block. For example, both variables `a` and `j` are declared in the following `for` loop and are accessible only from within that loop. Also, both will exist only as long as the `for` loop is executing:

```
for (int j = 0; j < n; j++ ) {
    double a = ...
    . . .
    . . .
}
```

It is illegal to declare a variable in an inner block that has the same name as a variable in an outer block. For example, the following code has two variables named `i`, one defined in the method body and one defined in a `for` loop within the method body. This code would produce a compile-time error:

---

[1] This statement is not quite true for `static` methods, as we shall see later in the chapter.

```
public int sum ( int array[] ) {
   int i = 0, total = 0;
   i += array[0];
   for ( int i = 0; i < array.length; i++ ) {
      total += array[i];
   return (total);
}
```

PROGRAMMING PITFALLS

It is illegal to declare a variable in an inner block that has the same name as a variable in an outer block.

It *is* legal to declare a variable within a block to have the same name as an instance variable or method in the class in which the block is defined. If this happens, then the instance variable is *hidden* from the method by the local variable, and the method cannot access it directly, even though the instance variable has class scope.

7.5   THE **this** REFERENCE

Java includes a special reference called this. The reference this always refers to the *current object*—the object within which the reference appears. It is very useful for accessing instance variables and methods within the class, even if their names have been hidden by local variable declarations.

For example, Figure 7.12 shows a portion of a Java class defining a point in two-dimensional space. This portion of the class contains two instance variables x and y, two constructors, and a method to set the value of the point.

```
public class Point {
   // Define instance variables
   private double x;      // x position of point
   private double y;      // y position of point

   // Define constructors
   public void Point() {
      x = 0;
      y = 0;
   }
   public void Point(double x, double y) {
      this.x = x;
      this.y = y;
   }
   public void setPoint(double x, double y) {
      this.x = x;
      this.y = y;
   }
   . . .
   . . .
}
```

Figure 7.12. Partial definition of a class, illustrating access to class instance variables having the same name as method variables.

Notice that method setPoint() includes two local variables x and y, which have the same names as the class instance variables x and y. The instance variables have *class scope*, so they are accessible in any method within the class. However, the local variables in setPoint() have the same names as the instance variables, and this prevents the method from just using the names x and y to access the instance variables. Instead, *the instance variables are referred to as* this.x *and* this.y. The reference this always refers to the *current object*, which is the object within which the reference appears. Therefore, this.x refers to the instance variable x defined in the current object, and this.y refers to the instance variable y defined in the current object.

GOOD PROGRAMMING PRACTICE

If the name of a class member is hidden by a local variable name in a method within the same class, use the this reference to refer to the class member.

7.6 CATEGORIES OF METHODS

Since instance variables are usually hidden within a class, the only way to work with them is through the interface formed by the class's methods. The methods are the public face of the class, providing a standard way to work with the information while hiding the unnecessary details of the implementation from the user.

A class's methods must perform certain common "housekeeping" functions, as well as the specific actions required by the class. These housekeeping functions fall into a few broad categories, and they are common to most classes regardless of their specific purpose. A class must usually provide a way to store data into its instance variables, read data from its instance variables, test the status of its instance variables, and display the contents of its instance variables in a human-readable form.

Since the instance variables in a class cannot be used directly, classes must define methods to store data into the instance variables and to read data from them. By Java convention, the names of methods that store data begin with "set" and are called **set methods**, while the names of methods that read data begin with "get" and are called **get methods**.

Set methods take information from the outside world and store the data into the class's instance variables. In the process, they *should also check the data for validity and consistency*. This checking prevents the instance variables of the class from being set into an illegal state.

For example, suppose that we have created a class Date containing instance variables day (with a range of 1–31), month (with a range of 1–12), and year (with a range of 1900–2100). If these instance variables were declared public, then any method in the program could modify them directly. For example, assume that a Date object was declared as

```
Date d1 = new Date();
```

With this declaration, any method in the program could directly set the day to an illegal value:

```
d1.day = 32;
```

Set methods and private instance variables prevent this sort of illegal behavior by testing the input parameters. If the parameters are valid, the method stores them in the appropriate instance variables. If the parameters are invalid, the method either modifies the inputs to be legal, or if that is not possible, raises an exception. (We will learn about exceptions in Chapter 10.)

Use set methods to check the validity and consistency of input data before it is stored in an object's instance variables.

Get methods are used to retrieve information from the instance variables and to format it properly for presentation to the outside world. For example, our `Date` class might include methods `getDay()`, `getMonth()`, and `getYear()` to recover the day, month, and year, respectively.

Another category of method tests for the truth or falsity of some condition is called **predicate methods**. Typically they begin with the word `is`, and they return a `boolean` (true/false) result. For example, a `Date` class might include a method `isLeapYear()`, which would return true if the specified year were a leap year, and false otherwise. In could also include methods like `isEqual()`, `isEarlier()`, and `isLater()` to compare two dates chronologically.

Define predicate methods to test for the truth or falsity of conditions associated with any classes you create.

Another very important function of methods is to display the contents of the object in human-readable form. This is accomplished with a special method called `toString()`. The `toString()` method is defined for every Java class, since it is defined in the `Object` class, and every class is a subclass of `Object`. It is used to convert the data stored in an object into a form suitable for printing out. Every class should include a customized `toString()` method to properly format its data for display.

The `toString()` method is automatically called whenever an object is concatenated with a string. For example, in the statement

```
System.out.println( "Date = " + d1);
```

the data in object `d1` is converted into a string and printed on the standard output stream. If `d1` is an object of the `Date` class, and if the `Date` class defines a `toString()` method, then that method will be used to convert the date into a string. The result might be something like

```
Date = 1/5/2002
```

Override the `toString()` method of any classes that you define to create a reasonable display of the class's data.

EXAMPLE 7.1

Creating a `Date` Class: We will illustrate the concepts described in this chapter by creating a `Date` class designed to hold and manipulate dates on the Gregorian calendar.

This class should be able to hold the day, month, and year of a date in instance variables that are protected from outside access. The class must include constructors to create dates, set and get methods to change and retrieve the stored information, predicate methods to recover information about date objects and to allow two `Date` objects to be compared, and a `toString` method to allow the information in a `Date` object to be displayed easily.

SOLUTION

The Date class will need three instance variables, day, month, and year. They will be declared private to protect them from direct manipulation by outside methods. The day variable should have a range of 1–31, corresponding to the days in a month. The month variable should have a range of 1–12, corresponding to the months in a year. The year variable will be greater than or equal to zero.

We will define two constructors for our class. One constructor will have no input parameters and will initialize the date to January 1, 1900. The other constructor will have a day, month, and year as input arguments and will initialize the date to the appropriate values.

We will also define a method setDate() to insert a new date into a Date object, and the three methods getDay(), getMonth(), and getYear() to return the day, month, and year from a given Date object.

The supported predicate methods will include isLeapYear() to test if a year is a leap year. This method will use the leap-year test described in Example 4.3. In addition, we will create the three methods isEqual(), isEarlier(), and isLater() to compare two date objects. Finally, method toString() will format the date as a string in the normal US style: dd/mm/yyyy.

The resulting class is shown in Figure 7.13.

```
/*
   Purpose:
     This class stores and manipulates dates on the
     Gregorian calendar.  It implements constructors,
     set methods, get methods, and predicate methods,
     and overrides the toString method.

     Method list:
        Date()                       Date constructor
        Date(day,month,year)         Date constructor
        setDate(day,month,year)      Set Date
        getDay()                     Get day
        getMonth()                   Get month
        getYear()                    Get year
        isLeapYear()                 Test for leap year
        isEqual()                    Test for equality
        isEarlier()                  Is chronologically earlier
        isLater()                    Is chronologically later
        toString()                   Convert to string for display

   Record of revisions:
      Date           Programmer          Description of change
      ====           ==========          =====================
    05/01/2002    S. J. Chapman        Original code
*/
public class Date {

   // Define instance variables
```

Figure 7.13. The Date class.

```java
private int year;       // Year (0 - xxxx)
private int month;      // Month (1 - 12)
private int day;        // Day (1 - 31)

// Default constructor produces January 1, 1900
public Date() {
   year = 1900;
   month = 1;
   day = 1;
}

// Constructor for specified date
public Date(int day, int month, int year) {
   setDate( day, month, year );
}

// Method to set a date
public void setDate(int day, int month, int year) {
   this.year  = year;
   this.month = month;
   this.day   = day;
}

// Method to get day
public int getDay() {
   return day;
}

// Method to get month
public int getMonth() {
   return month;
}

// Method to get year
public int getYear() {
   return year;
}

// Method to check for leap year
public boolean isLeapYear() {
   boolean leap_year;
   if ( year % 400 == 0 )
      leap_year = true;
   else if ( year % 100 == 0 )
      leap_year = false;
   else if ( year % 4 == 0 )
      leap_year = true;
   else
```

Figure 7.13. (Continued).

```
            leap_year = false;
        return leap_year;
    }


    // Method to check for equality
    public boolean isEqual( Date d ) {
        boolean equal;
        if ( year == d.year && month == d.month && day == d.day )
            equal = true;
        else
            equal = false;
        return equal;
    }


    // Method to check if d is earlier than the
    // value stored in the object.
    public boolean isEarlier( Date d ) {
        boolean earlier;

        // Compare years
        if ( d.year > year )
            earlier = false;
        else if ( d.year < year )
            earlier = true;
        else {

            // Years are equal.  Compare months
            if ( d.month > month )
                earlier = false;
            else if ( d.month < month )
                earlier = true;
            else {

                // Months are equal.  Compare days.
                if ( d.day >= day )
                    earlier = false;
                else
                    earlier = true;
            }
        }
        return earlier;
    }

    // Method to check if d is later than the
    // value stored in the object.
    public boolean isLater( Date d ) {
        boolean later;
```

Figure 7.13. (Continued).

```
         // Compare years
         if ( d.year > year )
            later = true;
         else if ( d.year < year )
            later = false;
         else {

            // Years are equal.  Compare months
            if ( d.month > month )
               later = true;
            else if ( d.month < month )
               later = false;
            else {

               // Months are equal.  Compare days.
               if ( d.day > day )
                  later = true;
               else
                  later = false;
            }
         }
         return later;
      }


      // Method to convert a date to a string.
      public String toString() {

         return (month + "/" + day + "/" + year);
      }
}
```

Figure 7.13.   (Continued).

We must create a test driver class to test the Date class. Such a class is shown in Figure 7.14 . Class TestDate instantiates four Date objects and initializes them using both constructors. It then exercises all of the methods defined in the class [note that the toString() method is implicitly exercised by the System.out.println() statements].

When this program is executed, the results are:

```
D:\book\java\chap7>java TestDate
Date 1 = 1/4/1996
Date 2 = 3/1/1998
Date 3 = 1/3/1996
Date 4 = 1/1/1900
1996 is a leap year.
1998 is not a leap year.
1/3/1996 is not equal to 1/4/1996
1/3/1996 is earlier than 1/4/1996
1/3/1996 is not later than 1/4/1996
```

```
/*
   Purpose:
     This class tests the Date class.

   Record of revisions:
       Date          Programmer              Description of change
       ====          ==========              =====================
     05/01/2002    S. J. Chapman             Original code
*/
public class TestDate {

   // Define the main method to test class Date
   public static void main(String[] args) {

      // Declare variables, and define each variable
      Date d1 = new Date(4,1,1996);    // Date 1
      Date d2 = new Date(1,3,1998);    // Date 2
      Date d3 = new Date();            // Date 3
      Date d4 = new Date();            // Date 4

      // Set d3
      d3.setDate(3,1,1996);

      // Print out dates
      System.out.println ("Date 1 = " + d1);
      System.out.println ("Date 2 = " + d1);
      System.out.println ("Date 3 = " + d2);
      System.out.println ("Date 4 = " + d2);

      // Check isLeapYear
      if ( d1.isLeapYear() )
         System.out.println (d1.getYear() + " is a leap year.");
      else
         System.out.println (d1.getYear() + " is not a leap year.");

      if ( d2.isLeapYear() )
         System.out.println (d2.getYear() + " is a leap year.");
      else
         System.out.println (d2.getYear() + " is not a leap year.");

      // Check isEqual
      if ( d1.isEqual(d3) )
         System.out.println (d3 + " is equal to " + d1);
      else
         System.out.println (d3 + " is not equal to " + d1);

      // Check isEarlier
      if ( d1.isEarlier(d3) )
         System.out.println (d3 + " is earlier than " + d1);
```

Figure 7.14. Class TestDate to test the Date class.

```
        else
            System.out.println (d3 + " is not earlier than " + d1);

        // Check isLater
        if ( d1.isLater(d3) )
            System.out.println (d3 + " is later than " + d1);
        else
            System.out.println (d3 + " is not later than " + d1);


    }
}
```

Figure 7.14. (Continued).

Note that the date strings are being written out in the order month/day/year. From the test results, this class appears to be functioning correctly. ∎

This class works, but it could be improved. For example, no validity checking is performed on the input values in the setDate() method, and the toString() method could be modified to produce dates with explicit month names such as "January 1, 1900". In addition, the U.S. order month/day/year is not used everywhere in the world. It would be possible to customize the toString method to write out date strings in different orders in different parts of the world. We will revisit and improve this class later in the book after we study exceptions.

7.7 MEMBER ACCESS MODIFIERS

There are four types of member access modifiers in Java: public, private, protected, and package. The first three are defined by explicit keywords in an instance variable or method definition, and the last is the default access that results if no access modifier is explicitly selected.

We have already seen the two member access modifiers public and private. A class member that is declared public may be accessed by any method anywhere within a program. A class member that is declared private may be accessed only by methods within the same class as the class member.

Normally the instance variables of a class are declared private and the methods of a class public, so that the methods form an interface with the outside world, hiding the internal behavior of the class from any other parts of the program. This approach has many advantages, since it makes programs more modular. For example, suppose that we have written a program that makes extensive use of Timer objects. If necessary, we could completely redesign the internal behavior of the Timer class, and the program would continue to work properly, as long as we had not changed the parameters or returned values from methods startTimer() and elapsedTime(). This **public**

GOOD PROGRAMMING PRACTICE

The instance variables of a class should normally be declared private, and the class methods should be used to provide a standard interface to the class.

interface isolates the internals of the class from rest of the program, making incremental modifications easier.

There are some exceptions to this general rule. Many classes contain `private` methods that perform specialized calculations in support of the `public` methods of the class. These are called **utility methods**. Since they are not intended to be called directly by users, they are declared with the `private` member access modifier.

If no access modifiers are included in a definition, then the class member has **package access**. The member may be accessed by methods in all classes within the same package (that is, within the same directory) as the class in which the member is defined, but not by methods in other classes. This type of access is sometimes convenient, because the classes in a package are usually related and must work closely together, while the details of their interactions will be hidden from methods outside the package.

Package access is illustrated in Figure 7.15.

```java
// Class to test package access
public class TestPackageAccess {

    // Define the main method to test Class1
    public static void main(String[] args) {

        // Instantiate a AccessTest object
        AccessTest a = new AccessTest();

        // Write out the value of the instance variable
        System.out.println(a.toString());

        // Modify the instance variables of class
        // AccessTest directly
        a.x = 3;
        a.s = "After: ";

        // Write out the value of the instance variable
        System.out.println(a.toString());
    }
}

// Define class AccessTest.  Note that this class has
// package access.
class AccessTest {

    // Instance variables
    int x = 1;
    String s = "Before: ";

    // Method toString()
    public String toString() {
        return (s + x);
    }
}
```

Figure 7.15. A program illustrating package access.

When this program is compiled and executed, the results are:

```
C:\book\java\chap7>javac TestPackageAccess.java
C:\book\java\chap7>java TestPackageAccess
Before: 1
After: 3
```

As we can see, a method in class `TestPackageAccess` modified an instance variable in class `AccessTest` directly.

Package access is inherently dangerous, since the methods of one class may be modifying the members of another class directly. If the class whose members are being modified directly is changed, then that modification may "break" the other classes that are accessing the class members directly. Thus, package access weakens the information hiding and the inherent modifiability of Java classes.

On the other hand, package access is efficient, because the classes' instance variables are being used and set without going through the overhead of `get` and `set` methods. This reduction in overhead allows the whole package to execute faster, while still hiding implementation details from the outside world. If a package contains only a few closely related classes that can be modified and maintained together, then package access can provide an acceptable compromise between speed and safety.

GOOD PROGRAMMING PRACTICE

Package access is inherently dangerous, since it weakens information hiding in Java. Do not use it unless it is absolutely necessary for performance reasons. If it is necessary, restrict the package to a few closely related classes.

The final access modifier is **protected**. Members declared with a `protected` modifier can be accessed by methods in all classes within the same package as the class in which the member is defined, and also by all *subclasses* of the class.

7.8   STANDARD JAVA PACKAGES

Every program that we have written has used classes and methods imported from the Java API. These predefined classes make programming much easier by allowing us to take advantage of other people's work instead of having to "reinvent the wheel" each time we set out to write a program.

The Java API consists of literally hundreds of predefined classes containing thousands of predefined methods. These classes and methods are organized into related groups called **packages**. A package consists of a set of classes and methods that share some related purpose. For example, we could use classes from the `java.io` package to read data into our programs. This package is a set of classes that allow programs to input or output data; we will learn more about it in a later chapter.

A subset of the standard Java API packages as of Java 1.4.x are summarized in Table 7.1.

A Java API class must be **imported** before it can be used in a program. There are two ways to import a Java class. The most common way is to include an **import statement** in the program before the class definition in which the API class will be used. For example, to use the `Arrays` class from the `java.util` package, we would include the line

```
import java.util.Arrays;     // import java.util.Array class
```

TABLE 7.1 The Java API Packages

Java API Package	Explanation
java.applet	*The Java Applet Package* This package contains the Applet class and several interfaces that allow programmers to create applets and control their interactions with a browser.
java.awt	*The Abstract Windowing Toolkit (AWT) Package* This package contains many of the classes and interfaces required to support old-style graphical user interfaces. Portions of this package are also used with the new "Swing" graphical user interfaces.
java.awt.event	*The Java AWT Event Package* This package contains classes and interfaces that support event handling for GUI components.
java.awt.image	*The Java AWT Event Package* This package contains classes and interfaces that enable storing and manipulating images in a program.
java.beans	*The Java Beans Package* This package contains classes and interfaces that enable programmers to create *reusable* software components.
java.io	*The Java Input/Output Package* This package contains classes that enable programs to input and output data.
java.lang	*The Java Language Package* This package contains the basic classes and interfaces required to make Java programs work. It is automatically imported into all Java programs.
java.net	*The Java Networking Package* This package contains classes that enable a program to communicate over a network (the Internet or an intranet).
java.rmi java.rmi.dgc java.rmi.registry java.rmi.server	*The Java Remote Method Invocation Packages* These packages contains classes and interfaces that enable a programmer to create distributed Java programs. A program can use RMI to call methods in other programs, whether they are located on the same computer or on another computer somewhere else on the network.
java.security java.security.acl java.security.interfaces	*The Java Security Packages* These packages contains classes and interfaces that enable a program to encrypt data and to control the access privileges provided to a Java program for security purposes.
java.sql	*The Java Database Connectivity Package* This package contains classes and interfaces that enable a Java program to communicate with a database.
javax.swing	*The Swing Package* This package contains many of the classes and interfaces required to support the new "Swing" graphical user interfaces.
java.text	*The Java Text Package* This package contains classes and interfaces that enable a Java program to manipulate numbers, dates, characters, and strings. This package provides many of Java's internationalization capabilities. For example, date and time strings can be automatically displayed in the proper format for the country in which a Java program is running.

TABLE 7.1 (Continued).

Java API Package	Explanation
java.util	*The Java Utilities Package* This package contains classes and interfaces that perform important utility functions in a program. Examples include date and time manipulations, random-number generation, storing and processing large amounts of data, and certain string manipulations.
java.util.jar	*The Java Utilities Zip Package* This package contains classes and interfaces that allow a Java program to create and read compressed archives called Java Archive (JAR) files. These archives can hold precompiled .class files as well as audio and image information.

at the start of the class in which it is used. It is also possible to import all of the classes and interfaces in an entire package with a statement of the form

```
import java.util.*;        // import entire java.util package
```

The package java.lang contains classes that are fundamental to the operation of all Java programs, and it is automatically imported into every program. No import statement is required for this package.

A detailed description of all of the classes in the Java API can be found in the Java Software Development Kit (SDK) documentation. The SDK may be downloaded for free from http://java.sun.com, and the documentation may be viewed with any Web browser.

7.9 CREATING YOUR OWN PACKAGES

One of the great strengths of Java is the ability to reuse classes written for one project on other projects. Packages are a very useful way to bundle groups of related classes and to make them easy to reuse. If a set of useful classes is created and placed in a package, then you can reuse those classes on other projects by simply importing them into your new programs in the same manner as you import the packages built into the Java API. In fact, we have already been doing this with the chapman.graphics package, which was written for this book.

GOOD PROGRAMMING PRACTICE

Create packages containing groups of related classes to make it easy to reuse those classes in other programs.

It is easy for a programmer to create his or her own packages. Any class that a programmer writes can be included in a package by adding a **package statement** to the file defining the class. For example, the class Class1 shown in Figure 7.16 can be placed in package chapman.testpackage by including a package statement in the file before the beginning of the class definition. This statement indicates that the class defined in this file is a part of the specified package. (Note that the package and import statements are the only two statements in Java that can occur outside of a class definition.)

```
// Class to test creating and using a package
package chapman.testpackage;    // Place in testpackage
public class Class1 {

    // Method mySum
    public int mySum(int a, int b) {
        return a + b;
    }
}
```

Figure 7.16.   A sample class containing a package statement.

When a class containing a `package` statement is compiled, the resulting `.class` file is automatically placed in the directory indicated by the `package` statement. The series of names separated by periods in the package statement is actually the directory hierarchy leading to the directory in which the file will be placed. Thus, the compiled output of this file will be placed in directory `<classroot>\chapman\testpackage` on a PC system or directory `<classroot>/chapman/testpackage` on a Unix or Linux system. The `<classroot>` is the starting directory for the package directory structure on a particular computer, as described in Section 7.9.1.

When a class containing a `package` statement is compiled with the compiler in the Java SDK, the root directory for the package structure `<classroot>` must be specified using the `-d` compiler option. For example, the statement

```
javac -d c:\packages Class1.java
```

specifies that the root directory of the package structure is `c:\packages`. The root directory must already exist when the file is compiled. When this command is executed, the file `Class1.java` will be compiled, and the resulting `.class` file will be placed in directory `c:\packages\chapman\testpackage`. If necessary, the subdirectories will be created to hold the package. Other classes can be added to this package in the same way.

7.9.1 Setting the Class Path

Before a user-defined package can be used, the root directory of the package directory structure `<classroot>` must be inserted into your computer's **class path**. The class path is defined by an environment variable called `CLASSPATH`. When the Java compiler or Java interpreter needs to locate a class in a package, it looks at each directory defined in `CLASSPATH` to see if the directory tree containing the package can be found there.

On a Windows NT 4/2000/XP computer, the class path is set through the System option of the Control Panel.

On a Windows 98/ME PC, the class path can be defined by adding the following line to the `autoexec.bat` file:

```
set CLASSPATH=.;c:\packages
```

If the `CLASSPATH` variable already exists in the file, add a semicolon followed by `c:\packages` to the end of the existing path. You will need to restart your computer before this change takes effect.

On a Unix or Linux machine the class path is set in different ways, depending on the particular shell that you are using. If necessary, see your instructor for help in setting the class path on these computers.

7.9.2 Using User-Defined Packages

Once a package has been created and the class path set, the package can be imported into any class desiring to use the package. For example, the class in Figure 7.17 imports package `testpackage`, and then uses `Class1` from it.

```
// Class to test using a package
import chapman.testpackage.*;
public class TestClass1 {

    // Define the main method to test Class1
    public static void main(String[] args) {

        // Declare variables
        int i = 8, j = 6;

        // Instantiate a Class1 object
        Class1 c = new Class1();

        // Use the object
        System.out.println("i + j = " + c.mySum(i,j));
    }
}
```

Figure 7.17. Importing and using a class from a user-defined package.

This class can be compiled and executed just like any other class. The computer automatically searches the specified class path to locate `testpackage` and import it. When this program is executed, the results are:

```
C:\book\java\chap7>javac TestClass1.java
C:\book\java\chap7>java TestClass1
i + j = 14
```

QUIZ 7-1

This quiz provides a quick check to see if you have understood the concepts introduced in Sections 7.1 through 7.9. If you have trouble with the quiz, reread the section, ask your instructor, or discuss the material with a fellow student. The answers are found in the back of the book.

1. Name the major components of a class and describe their purposes.
2. What types of member access modifiers may be defined in Java, and what access does each type give? What member access modifier should normally be used for instance variables? for methods?
3. What is the difference between class scope and block scope?
4. What happens in a program if a method contains a local variable with the same name as an instance variable in the method's class?
5. What statement(s) do you have to include in a program before you can use classes in Java API packages other than `java.lang`?
6. Explain the difference between `public`, `private`, `protected`, and package access.
7. How do you create a user-defined package? How do you use the package?
8. What is the function of the `CLASSPATH` environment variable?

7.10 FINALIZERS AND GARBAGE COLLECTION

Just before an object is destroyed, it makes a call to a special method called a **finalizer**, which performs any necessary clean-up (releasing resources, and so on) before the object is destroyed. This special method is always named `finalize`. There can be at most one finalizer in a class, and many classes do not need a finalizer at all.

When a class is instantiated with the `new` operator, the class constructor creates a new object. The constructor allocates memory for defined instance variables and objects, and it may acquire other system resources such as open files, network sockets, and so on. These resources are used by the object for as long as it is needed in the program.

When an object is no longer needed, it should be destroyed and its resources returned to the system for re-use. This function is performed automatically in Java by the **garbage collector**. The garbage collector is a low-priority thread[2] within the Java interpreter that normally runs in the background whenever the interpreter is executing. It constantly scans the list of objects created by the program. Any object that no longer has a reference pointing to it is a candidate for garbage collection, *because once all references to an object are gone, the object can no longer be used in any way by the program.* When the garbage collector spots such an object, it makes a call to the object's `finalize` method and then destroys the object, releasing its memory to the system.

A program can force the garbage collector to run at high priority by making an explicit call to the `System.gc()` method. We might want to do this to ensure that garbage collection occurs at a specific time in a program.

The call to the object's `finalize` method is an opportunity for the object to close any files that it might have open and to perform any other required terminal housekeeping. Once the `finalize` method completes, the object is destroyed by the garbage collector.

The `finalize` method is normally declared `protected`, so that it is protected against accidental calls from outside methods. We will illustrate the use of `finalize` methods in Example 7.2 below.

7.11 USING STATIC CLASS MEMBERS

It is possible for both variables and methods in a class to be declared `static`. Such variables and methods have special properties, which are explained in this section.

7.11.1 Static Variables

Each object of a class has its own copy of all of the instance variables defined in the class. If a class defines an instance variable `x`, and two objects `a` and `b` are created from the class, then `a.x` and `b.x` will be two separate variables.

However, it is sometimes useful to have a particular variable in a class shared by all of the objects created from the class. If a variable is declared **static**, then one copy of that variable will be created the first time a class is loaded, and that copy will remain in existence until the program stops running. Any objects instantiated from that class will share the single copy of that variable. Static variables are also known as **class variables**.

This concept is illustrated in Figure 7.18, which shows a class A defining two fields `x` and `y` and a static or class variable `z`. Two objects `a1` and `a2` are instantiated from this class. These two objects contain separate instance variables `x` and `y`, but they share a single copy of static variable `z`.

---

[2]A *thread* or *thread of execution* is a part of a program that can execute in parallel with other parts of the same program. Java supports multithreading as a part of its basic structure, but the discussion of that topic is beyond the scope of this book.

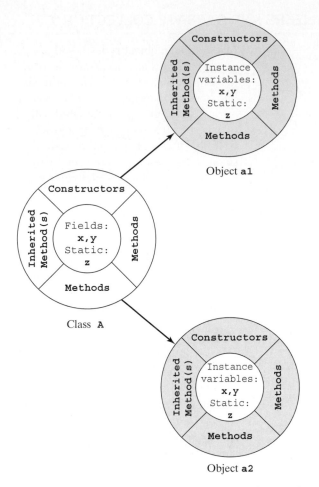

Figure 7.18. Two objects a1 and a2 instantiated from a single class A. These two objects have their own instance variables x and y, but share a single copy of the static variable z.

If an integer or floating-point variable is declared to be `static`, then by default it will be initialized to zero at creation time. A static variable can be initialized to another value by including the value in the variable definition, as shown below.

```
static int count;              // Automatically initialized to 0
static double size = 400.;   // Initialized to 400.
```

Static variables are useful for keeping track of global information, such as the number of objects instantiated from a class or the number of those objects still surviving at any given time. They are also useful for defining single copies of final variables that will be shared among all objects of the class. For example, the speed of light in a vacuum is $c = 2.99792458 \times 10^8$ meters per second. This value could be declared in a class as

```
static final double C = 2.99792458e8;
```

and a single copy of this constant will be created and shared among all of the objects instantiated from the class.

GOOD PROGRAMMING PRACTICE

Use `static` class variables to share a single copy of a variable among all of the objects instantiated from the class.

The *duration* of a `static` variable is different from the duration of an instance variable. Instance variables are created each time an object is instantiated and destroyed when the object is destroyed by the garbage collector. In contrast, `static` variables are created as soon as the class is loaded into memory, and they persist until program execution ends.

Although `static` variables are global in the sense that they are shared among all of the objects instantiated from a class, they still have *class scope*. They are visible outside of the class only by reference to the class in which they are defined.

If a `static` variable is declared `public`, it may be accessed through any object of the class or directly through the class name using the dot operator. For example, suppose that a class `Class1` defines a `public static` variable z, and an object c is instantiated from that class. Then the variable z can be accessed by other objects in the program either by `Class1.z` or by `c.z`.

Note that *the `static` variables in a class can be accessed without first creating an object from that class*. A good example of a `static` variable is out in the `System` class. We have used `System.out` in all of our programs since Chapter 1 without having to first instantiate a `System` object.

7.11.2 Static Methods

Static methods are methods that are declared `static` within a class. These methods can directly access the static variables in the class but *cannot* directly access instance variables. Static methods are also known as **class methods**.

Static methods are commonly used to perform calculations that are independent of any instance data that might be defined in a class. For example, the method `sqrt(x)` in the `Math` class calculates the square root of any value passed to it, and returns the result. This method is independent of any data stored in the `Math` class, so it is declared `static`.

Static methods may be accessed by reference to a class's name without first creating an object from the class. Thus, we are able to use `Math.sqrt(x)` in any program without first instantiating an object from the `Math` class.

Every method in Java must be defined within a class, but some methods such as `sqrt(x)`, `sin(x)` `cos(x)`, are not closely tied to any data within the class. These methods are usually declared `static` so that they can be accessed without having to instantiate an object first.

A very famous static method is `main`, the starting point of any Java application. The `main` method must be static so that it can be executed without first instantiating any object.

GOOD PROGRAMMING PRACTICE

Utility methods that perform functions independent of the instance data within a class may be declared `static` to make them easier to access and use.

EXAMPLE 7.2

Using Static Variables and Finalizers: To illustrate the use of static variables and finalizers, we will create a class containing two static variables. One variable will keep track of the number of times an object is instantiated from the class, and the other will keep track of the number of those objects still in existence. We will make these variables `private` so that no outside methods can tamper with them and will provide `static` get methods to recover their current values when necessary.

In addition, the class will contain a single instance variable, which will contain an integer value and a method to recover that value.

The resulting class is shown in Figure 7.19.

```
/*
   Purpose:
     This class illustrates the use of static variables
     to keep track of the number of objects created
     from the class.

   Record of revisions:
       Date          Programmer            Description of change
       ====          ==========            =====================
     05/02/2002    S. J. Chapman           Original code
*/
public class Widget {

   // Define class variables
   private int value;          // Instance var containing a value
   private static int created; // Total number of objects created
   private static int alive;   // Total number of obs still alive

   // Constructor
   public Widget(int value) {
      this.value = value;
      created++;
      alive++;
   }

   // Method to get number of Widgets created
   public static int getCreated() {
      return created;
   }

   // Method to get number of Widgets still alive
   public static int getAlive() {
      return alive;
   }

   // Method to get value of object
   public int getValue() {
      return value;
   }

   // Finalizer
   protected void finalize() {
      alive—;
      System.out.println("Finalizer running...");
   }
}
```

Figure 7.19. The Widget class.

We must create a test driver class to test the Widget class. Such a class is shown in Figure 7.20.

```
/*
   Purpose:
     This class tests the Widget class.

   Record of revisions:
       Date          Programmer            Description of change
       ====          ==========            =====================
     05/02/2002    S. J. Chapman           Original code
*/
public class TestWidget {

   // Define the main method to test class Widget
   public static void main(String[] args) {

      // Create three new Widgets
      Widget w1 = new Widget(10);    // Widget 1
      Widget w2 = new Widget(20);    // Widget 2
      Widget w3 = new Widget(30);    // Widget 3

      // Check to see how many Widget are created and alive
      System.out.println (Widget.getCreated() + " Widgets created");
      System.out.println (Widget.getAlive() + " Widgets alive");

      // Print values of widgets
      System.out.println ("Widget 1 = " + w1.getValue());
      System.out.println ("Widget 2 = " + w2.getValue());
      System.out.println ("Widget 3 = " + w3.getValue());

      // Nullify references to two Widgets
      w1 = null;
      w2 = null;

      // Check to see how many Widget are created and alive
      System.out.println (Widget.getCreated() + " Widgets created");
      System.out.println (Widget.getAlive() + " Widgets alive");

      // Run the garbage collector
      System.gc();

      // Check to see how many Widget are created and alive
      System.out.println (Widget.getCreated() + " Widgets created");
      System.out.println (Widget.getAlive() + " Widgets alive");
   }
}
```

Figure 7.20.   Test driver for the Widget class.

This class creates three objects of type Widget, initializing them to 10, 20, and 30, respectively. It then calls the static methods Widget.getCreated() and Widget.getAlive() to show how many objects of this type have been created and how many objects are still alive. Next the method calls the method `getValue()` for each object, showing that the instance variables in each object are unique to that object.

Next, the program nullifies the references to objects `w1` and `w2`. Once these references are gone, the objects are inaccessible, and they become candidates for garbage collection. In theory, the two objects could disappear at any time after this point in the program. However, the garbage collector is a low-priority thread, so the objects are not likely to disappear until we explicitly force the garbage collector to run.

When the garbage collector runs, it calls the finalizers for the objects being destroyed before actually destroying them. After starting the garbage collector running, the `main` program continues executing and calls the static methods `Widget.getCreated()` and `Widget.getAlive()` again to show the status of the `Widget` objects.

Note that the garbage collector is running at the *same time* as the `main` program. If the garbage collector has had time to destroy the two objects with nullified references before the `main` program calls `Widget.getAlive()`, the call will show only one object left. However, the timing of the garbage collector will vary from run to run and among versions of the Java SDK.

When this program was executed twice on my computer, the results were:

```
C:\book\java\chap7>java TestWidget
3 Widgets created
3 Widgets alive
Widget 1 = 10
Widget 2 = 20
Widget 3 = 30
3 Widgets created
3 Widgets alive
Finalizer running...
Finalizer running...
3 Widgets created
1 Widgets alive
D:\book\java\chap7>java TestWidget
3 Widgets created
3 Widgets alive
Widget 1 = 10
Widget 2 = 20
Widget 3 = 30
3 Widgets created
3 Widgets alive
3 Widgets created
3 Widgets alive
Finalizer running...
Finalizer running...
```

Note that each object's finalizer ran before the object was destroyed. On the first execution, the garbage collector destroyed the two objects *before* the call to `Widget.getAlive()`. On the second execution, the garbage collector destroyed the two objects *after* the call to `Widget.getAlive()`. Since the garbage collector and the main program are "racing", the number of objects left can vary from run to run. ▪

EXAMPLE 7.3

Extended Math Methods: Class `Math` in package `java.lang` contains a number of common mathematical functions such as `abs()`, `sin()`, `cos()`, `sqrt()`, and so forth. While these functions are useful, the list is limited compared to the elementary functions available in other languages such as Fortran. Write an extended mathematics class ExMath containing static methods implementing the following additional functions:

$$\text{Hyperbolic sine:} \qquad \sinh(x) = \frac{e^x - e^{-x}}{2} \qquad (7.1)$$

$$\text{Hyperbolic cosine:} \quad \cosh(x) = \frac{e^x + e^{-x}}{2} \qquad (7.2)$$

$$\text{Hyperbolic tangent:} \quad \tanh(x) = \frac{e^x - e^{-x}}{e^x + e^{-x}} \qquad (7.3)$$

$$\text{Log to the base 10:} \quad \log_{10}(x) = \frac{\log_e x}{\log_e 10} \qquad (7.4)$$

Insert the class into package chapman.math.

SOLUTION

This class will contain only static methods and the static final variable $\log_e 10$, so that the methods in it can be called without first instantiating an object .

1. **Determine the User Requirements**

   In this case, the user wants us to create a package of utility methods that perform the mathematical calculations specified above. We must write four different methods, implementing the four functions $\sinh(x)$, $\cosh(x)$, $\tanh(x)$, and $\log_{10}(x)$.

   The input to each method will be a single value of type double, and the result will be of type double. Numeric promotion will allow these methods to be used with data of other types.

2. **Analysis and Decomposition**

   There will be a single class, with four methods to calculate the hyperbolic sine, hyperbolic cosine, hyperbolic tangent, and logarithm to the base 10. We will call the class ExMath and make it a subclass of the root class Object.

3. **Detailed Design**

   This class will not have a constructor or a finalizer, since it is never intended to be instantiated. It will have the single final variable LOGE_10, plus the four static methods specified above.

   The pseudocode for the sinh() method is simply implementing Equation (7.1):

   ```
   return ( (Math.exp(x) - Math.exp(-x)) / 2. );
   ```

   The pseudocode for the cosh() method is simply implementing Equation (7.2):

   ```
   return ( (Math.exp(x) + Math.exp(-x)) / 2. );
   ```

   The pseudocode for the tanh() method is simply implementing Equation (7.3):

   ```
   double exp = Math.exp(x);
   double exm = Math.exp(-x);
   return ( (exp - exm) / (exp + exm) );
   ```

   The pseudocode for the log10(x) method is simply implementing Equation (7.4):

   ```
   return ( Math.log(x) / LOGE_10 );
   ```

where LOGE_10 is the constant $\log_e 10$.

4. **Implementation: Convert Algorithms to Java Statements**

The resulting Java methods are shown in Figure 7.21.

```
/*
   Purpose:
     This class defines an extended library of mathematical
     functions beyond those built into the java.lang.Math class.

   Record of revisions:
       Date          Programmer           Description of change
       ====          ==========           =====================
     05/02/2002    S. J. Chapman          Original code
*/

// Specify package for class
package chapman.math;

public class ExMath {

   // Define class variables
   final static private double LOGE_10 = 2.302585092994046;

   // Hyperbolic sine method
   public static double sinh ( double x ) {
      return ( (Math.exp(x) - Math.exp(-x)) / 2. );
   }

   // Hyperbolic cosine method
   public static double cosh ( double x ) {
      return ( (Math.exp(x) + Math.exp(-x)) / 2. );
   }

   // Hyperbolic tangent method
   public static double tanh ( double x ) {
      double exp = Math.exp(x);
      double exm = Math.exp(-x);
      return ( (exp - exm) / (exp + exm) );
   }

   // Logarithm to the base 10
   public static double log10 ( double x ) {
      return ( Math.log(x) / LOGE_10 );
   }
}
```

Figure 7.21. Class ExMath.

5. **Testing**

To test this program, we can manually calculate the values of the hyperbolic sine, hyperbolic cosine, hyperbolic tangent, and logarithm to the base 10 for $x = 1$ and $x = 10$ and compare the results with the output of a test driver program. The results of calculations on a scientific hand calculator are:

x	sinh (x)	cosh (x)	tanh (x)	$\log_{10}(x)$
1	1.175201193	1.543080634	0.7615941559	0.0
10	11013.23287	11013.23292	0.9999999959	1.0

An appropriate test driver program is shown in Figure 7.22. Note that this program must *import* package chapman.math.

```
/*
   Purpose:
     This class tests the ExMath class.

   Record of revisions:
       Date         Programmer           Description of change
       ====         ==========           =====================
    05/02/2002   S. J. Chapman           Original code
*/

import chapman.math.*;    // Get ExMath class

public class TestExMath {

   // Define the main method to test class Date
   public static void main(String[] args) {

      // Call the various methods
      System.out.println("sinh( 1)  = " + ExMath.sinh( 1));
      System.out.println("sinh(10)  = " + ExMath.sinh(10));
      System.out.println("cosh( 1)  = " + ExMath.cosh( 1));
      System.out.println("cosh(10)  = " + ExMath.cosh(10));
      System.out.println("tanh( 1)  = " + ExMath.tanh( 1));
      System.out.println("tanh(10)  = " + ExMath.tanh(10));
      System.out.println("log10( 1) = " + ExMath.log10( 1));
      System.out.println("log10(10) = " + ExMath.log10(10));

   }
}
```

Figure 7.22. Test driver for class ExMath.

When this program is executed, the results are:

```
C:\book\java\chap7>java TestExMath
sinh( 1)  = 1.1752011936438014
sinh(10)  = 11013.232874703397
cosh( 1)  = 1.5430806348152437
cosh(10)  = 11013.232920103328
tanh( 1)  = 0.7615941559557649
tanh(10)  = 0.9999999958776926
log10( 1) = 0.0
log10(10) = 1.0
```

The results of the program agree with our hand calculations to the number of significant digits to which we performed the calculation. ∎

QUIZ 7-2

This quiz provides a quick check to see if you have understood the concepts introduced in Sections 7.10 and 7.11. If you have trouble with the quiz, reread the section, ask your instructor, or discuss the material with a fellow student. The answers are found in the back of the book.

1. What is the garbage collector? How does it operate? When are objects eligible for garbage collection?

2. What are static variables? What are they typically used for?

3. Suppose that you are creating a program with two classes `MyClass` and `YourClass`. A public static variable `count` is declared in class `MyClass`. How can this variable be accessed from class `YourClass`?

4. What are static methods typically used for?

SUMMARY

- An object is a self-contained software component that consists of properties (variables) and methods.

- Objects communicate with each other via messages. An object uses a message to request another object to perform a task for it.

- Classes are the software blueprints from which objects are made. When an object is instantiated from a class, a separate copy of each instance variable is created for the object. All objects derived from a given class share a single copy of each class (`static`) variable.

- All classes reside in a class hierarchy, with the `Object` class at the top of the tree.

- All new classes are derived from (extend) some other class, and each new class inherits the nonprivate variables and methods of its parent class.

- The class on which a new class is based is called the superclass of the new class.

- A new class is known as a subclass of the class on which it is based.

- Groups of related Java classes are usually collected together into special libraries called packages.

- The members of a class are instance variables and methods. Members of a class are accessed using the member access operator—the dot operator.

- Class definitions begin with the keyword `class`. The body of a class definition is included within braces (`{}`).

- An instance variable or method that is declared `public` is visible to any method with access to an object of the class.

- An instance variable or method that is declared `private` is visible only to other members of the class.

- An instance variable or method that is declared `protected` is visible to any method in the same package with access to an object of the class, and also to any method of a subclass of the class.

- An instance variable or method that has no member access modifier is visible to any method in the same package with access to an object of the class.

- A constructor is a special method used to initialize a new object. Constructors may be overloaded to provide multiple ways to initialize a new object.

- A finalizer is a special method used to release resources just before an object is destroyed.

- Within a class's scope, class members may be referenced by their names alone. Outside a class's scope, accessible class members are referenced through a reference to an object plus the dot operator.
- The instance variables in a class are normally declared `private`, and `public` set and get methods are used to control access to them.
- Predicate methods are methods used to test the truth or falsity of some condition relating to an object.
- Java packages are convenient ways to create libraries of reusable software. Classes are placed in packages using the `package` statement and are imported from packages using the `import` statement.
- The `CLASSPATH` environment variable must be set properly before user-defined packages can be imported into programs.
- The `this` reference may be used to reference both methods and instance variables from within an object.
- A static variable is common to all objects created from a given class. Static variables are created when the class is first loaded and remain in existence until the program terminates. Static class variables have class scope.
- A static method cannot access nonstatic class members. Static methods and variables exist independently of objects of a class. Static methods are commonly used for utility operations that are basically independent of objects, such as `Math.sqrt(x)`.

SUMMARY OF GOOD PROGRAMMING PRACTICES

The following guidelines introduced in this chapter will help you to develop good programs:

1. Every instance variable and method definition in a class should be preceded by an explicit member access modifier.
2. The instance variables of a class should normally be declared `private`, and the class methods should be used to provide a standard interface to the class.
3. If the name of a class member is hidden by a local variable name in a method within the same class, use the `this` reference to refer to the class member.
4. Use set methods to check the validity and consistency of input data before it is stored in an object's instance variables.
5. Define predicate methods to test for the truth or falsity of conditions associated with any classes you create.
6. Override the `toString()` method of any classes that you define to create a reasonable display of the class's data.
7. Create packages containing groups of related classes to make it easy to reuse those classes in other programs.
8. Package access is inherently dangerous, since it weakens information hiding in Java. Do not use it unless it is absolutely necessary for performance reasons. If it is necessary, restrict the package to a few closely related classes.
9. Use `static` class variables to share a single copy of a variable among all of the objects instantiated from the class.
10. Utility methods that perform functions independent of the instance data within a class may be declared `static` to make them easier to access and use.

TERMINOLOGY

block scope	instantiated
catch or specify requirement	member access operator
CLASSPATH	method
class hierarchy	object-oriented programming
class members	package access
class methods	package statement
class scope	predicate methods
class variables	private
constructor	programmer-defined types
dot operator	protected
field	public
finalizer	set methods
garbage collector	System.currentTimeMillis()
get methods	static method
immediate superclass	static variable
inheritance	subclass
information hiding	superclass
instance methods	this reference
instance variables	utility method

Exercises

1. List and describe the major components of a class.

2. What is the difference between instance variables and methods and static variables and methods? When should instance variables and methods be used? When should static variables and methods be used?

3. What types of member access modifiers exist in Java? What restriction does each modifier place on access to a class member?

4. **Complex Data Type**   Create a class called Complex to perform arithmetic with complex numbers. The class should have two private instance variables for the real and imaginary parts of the number. In addition, it should have class constructors, a set method to store a complex value, two get methods to recover the real and imaginary parts of the complex number, and methods for addition, subtraction, multiplication, division, and the absolute-value function. The class should override the toString() method to print a complex number as a string of the form $a + bi$, where a is the real part of the number and b the imaginary part.

   If complex numbers c_1 and c_2 are defined as $c_1 = a_1 + b_1 i$ and $c_2 = a_2 + b_2 i$, then the addition, subtraction, multiplication, and division of c_1 and c_2 are defined as:

$$c_1 + c_2 = (a_1 + a_2) + (b_1 + b_2)i \tag{7.5}$$

$$c_1 - c_2 = (a_1 - a_2) + (b_1 - b_2)i \tag{7.6}$$

$$c_1 \times c_2 = (a_1 a_2 - b_1 b_2) + (a_1 b_2 + b_1 a_2)i \tag{7.7}$$

$$\frac{c_1}{c_2} = \frac{a_1 a_2 + b_1 b_2}{a_2^2 + b_2^2} + \frac{b_1 a_2 - a_1 b_2}{a_2^2 + b_2^2}i \tag{7.8}$$

The absolute value of c_1 is defined as

$$|c_1| = \sqrt{a_1^2 + b_1^2} \tag{7.9}$$

Create a test driver program to test your class and confirm that all methods are working properly.

5.   Determine whether the following class is correct or not. If it is in error, specify what is wrong with it. If it is correct, describe what the program does.

```
public class Norm {

    // Define instance data
    private double x;      // x position of point
    private double y;      // y position of point

    // Define constructor
    public void Norm(double x, double y) {
        this.x = x;
        this.y = y;
    }

    public void calcNorm() {
        return Math.sqrt(x*x + y*y);
    }

    public static void main(String s[]) {
        x = 3;
        y = 4;
        System.out.println("The norm is " + Norm.calcNorm() );
    }
}
```

6.   **Extended Math Class**   Expand the extended math class created in this chapter to include the following additional functions:

Inverse hyperbolic sine: $\text{asinh}(x) = \log_e \left[x + \sqrt{x^2 + 1} \right]$ for all x

Inverse hyperbolic cosine: $\text{acosh}(x) = \log_e \left[x + \sqrt{x^2 - 1} \right]$ $x \geq 1$

Inverse hyperbolic tangent: $\text{atanh}(x) = \frac{1}{2} \log_e \left(\frac{1 + x}{1 - x} \right)$ $-1 < x < 1$

Create test driver programs to verify that these functions work properly. The programs should plot the shapes of each function, and you should compare the answers produced by the methods with answers provided by hand calculations.

7.   Enhance the Date class created in this chapter by adding:

1.   A method to calculate the day-of-year for the specified date.
2.   A method to calculate the number of days since January 1, 1900, for the specified date.
3.   A method to calculate the number of days between the date in the current Date object and the date in another Date object.

Also, convert the toString method to generate the date string in the form Month dd, yyyy. Generate a test driver program to test all of the methods in the class.

8. **Three-Dimensional Vectors** The study of the dynamics of objects in motion in three dimensions is an important area of engineering. In the study of dynamics, the position and velocity of objects, forces, torques, and so forth are usually represented by three-component vectors $\mathbf{v} = x\hat{\mathbf{i}} + y\hat{\mathbf{j}} + z\hat{\mathbf{k}}$, where the three components (x, y, z) represent the projection of the vector $\mathbf{v}$ along the x-, y-, and z-axes, respectively, and $\hat{\mathbf{i}}, \hat{\mathbf{j}},$ and $\hat{\mathbf{k}}$ are the unit vectors along the x-, y-, and z-axes (see Figure 7.23). The solutions of many mechanical problems involve manipulating these vectors in specific ways.

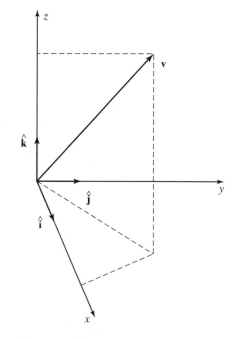

Figure 7.23. A three-dimensional vector.

The most common operations performed on these vectors are:

1. **Addition.** Two vectors are added together by separately adding their x-, y-, and z-components. If $\mathbf{v_1} = x_1\hat{\mathbf{i}} + y_1\hat{\mathbf{j}} + z_1\hat{\mathbf{k}}$ and $\mathbf{v_2} = x_2\hat{\mathbf{i}} + y_2\hat{\mathbf{j}} + z_2\hat{\mathbf{k}}$, then $\mathbf{v_1} + \mathbf{v_2} = (x_1 + x_2)\hat{\mathbf{i}} + (y_1 + y_2)\hat{\mathbf{j}} + (z_1 + z_2)\hat{\mathbf{k}}$.

2. **Subtraction.** Two vectors are subtracted by separately subtracting their x-, y-, and z-components. If $\mathbf{v_1} = x_1\hat{\mathbf{i}} + y_1\hat{\mathbf{j}} + z_1\hat{\mathbf{k}}$ and $\mathbf{v_2} = x_2\hat{\mathbf{i}} + y_2\hat{\mathbf{j}} + z_2\hat{\mathbf{k}}$, then $\mathbf{v_1} - \mathbf{v_2} = (x_1 - x_2)\hat{\mathbf{i}} + (y_1 - y_2)\hat{\mathbf{j}} + (z_1 - z_2)\hat{\mathbf{k}}$.

3. **Multiplication by a Scalar.** A vector is multiplied by a scalar by separately multiplying each component by the scalar. If $\mathbf{v} = x\hat{\mathbf{i}} + y\hat{\mathbf{j}} + z\hat{\mathbf{k}}$, then $a\mathbf{v} = ax\hat{\mathbf{i}} + ay\hat{\mathbf{j}} + az\hat{\mathbf{k}}$.

4. **Division by a Scalar.** A vector is divided by a scalar by separately dividing each component by the scalar. If $\mathbf{v} = x\hat{\mathbf{i}} + y\hat{\mathbf{j}} + z\hat{\mathbf{k}}$, then $\dfrac{\mathbf{v}}{a} = \dfrac{x}{a}\hat{\mathbf{i}} + \dfrac{y}{a}\hat{\mathbf{j}} + \dfrac{z}{a}\hat{\mathbf{k}}$.

5. **The Dot Product.**   The dot product of two vectors is one form of multiplication operation performed on vectors. It produces a scalar that is the sum of the products of the vector's components. If $\mathbf{v_1} = x_1\hat{\mathbf{i}} + y_1\hat{\mathbf{j}} + z_1\hat{\mathbf{k}}$ and $\mathbf{v_2} = x_2\hat{\mathbf{i}} + y_2\hat{\mathbf{j}} + z_2\hat{\mathbf{k}}$, then the dot product of the vectors is $\mathbf{v_1} \cdot \mathbf{v_2} = x_1x_2 + y_1y_2 + z_1z_2$.

6. **The Cross Product.**   The cross product is another multiplication operation that appears frequently between vectors. The cross product of two vectors is another vector whose direction is perpendicular to the plane formed by the two input vectors. If $\mathbf{v_1} = x_1\hat{\mathbf{i}} + y_1\hat{\mathbf{j}} + z_1\hat{\mathbf{k}}$ and $\mathbf{v_2} = x_2\hat{\mathbf{i}} + y_2\hat{\mathbf{j}} + z_2\hat{\mathbf{k}}$, then the cross product of the two vectors is defined as $\mathbf{v_1} \times \mathbf{v_2} = (y_1z_2 - y_2z_1)\hat{\mathbf{i}} + (z_1x_2 - z_2x_1)\hat{\mathbf{j}} + (x_1y_2 - x_2y_1)\hat{\mathbf{k}}$.

Create a class called `Vector3D`, having three components x, y, and z. Define methods to create vectors from three-element arrays, to convert vectors to arrays, and to perform the six vector operations defined above. Define a `toString` method that creates a output string of the form $x\mathbf{i} + y\mathbf{j} + z\mathbf{k}$. Then create a program to test all of the functions of your new class.

9. **Derivative of a Sampled Function**   The *derivative* of a continuous function $f(x)$ is defined by the equation

$$\frac{d}{dx}f(x) = \lim_{\Delta x \to 0} \frac{f(x + \Delta x) - f(x)}{\Delta x} \tag{7.10}$$

In a sampled function, this definition becomes

$$f'(x_i) = \frac{f(x_{i+1}) - f(x_i)}{\Delta x} \tag{7.11}$$

where $\Delta x = x_{i+1} - x_i$. Assume that an array `samples` contains a series of samples of a function taken at a spacing of dx per sample. Create a class `Derivative`, and write a method that will calculate the derivative of this array of samples from Equation (7.11).

To check your method, you should generate a data set whose derivative is known, and compare the result of the method with the known correct answer. A good choice for a test function is $\sin x$. From elementary calculus, we know that

$$\frac{d}{dx}(\sin x) = \cos x$$

Generate an input array containing 100 values of the function $\sin x$, starting at $x = 0$ and using a step size Δx of 0.05. Take the derivative of the vector with your method, and plot the function and its derivative on the same set of axes. Compare the derivative calculated by your method to the known correct answer. How close did your method come to calculating the correct value for the derivative?

10. **Derivative in the Presence of Noise**   We will now explore the effects of input noise on the quality of a numerical derivative. First, generate an input array containing 100 values of the function $\sin x$, starting at $x = 0$ and using a step size Δx of 0.05, just as you did in the previous problem. Next, use method `Math.random()` to generate a small amount of uniform random noise with a maximum amplitude of ± 0.02, and add that random noise to the samples in

your input vector. (See Figure 7.24.) Note that the peak amplitude of the noise is only 2% of the peak amplitude of your signal, since the maximum value of sin x is 1.0. Now take the derivative of the function using the derivative method that you developed in the last problem. Plot the derivative with and without noise on the same set of axes. How close to the theoretical value of the derivative did you come?

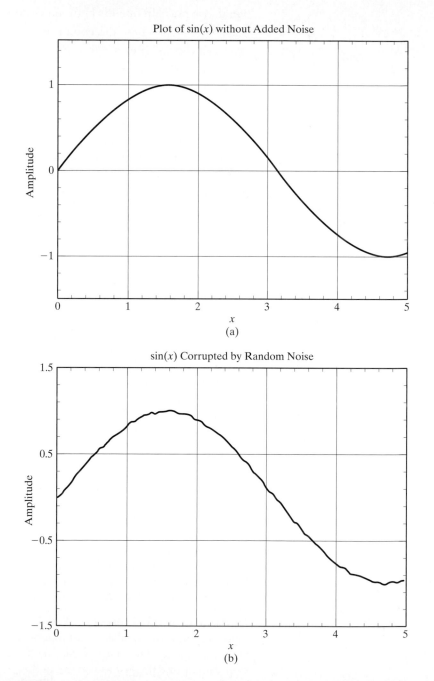

Figure 7.24.   (a) A plot of sin x as a function of x with no noise added to the data. (b) A plot of sin x as a function of x with a 2% peak amplitude uniform random noise added to the data.

11. **Histograms**   A *histogram* is a plot that shows how many times a particular measurement falls within a certain range of values. For example, consider the students in this class. Suppose that there are 30 students in the class and that their scores on the last exam fell within the following ranges:

Range	No. of Students
100–95	3
94–90	6
89–85	9
84–80	7
79–75	4
74–70	2
69–65	1

A plot of the number of students scoring in each range of numbers is a histogram, as shown in Figure 7.25. To create this histogram, we started with a set of data consisting of 30 student grades. We divided the range of possible grades on the test (0 to 100) into 20 bins and then counted how many student scores fell within each bin. Then we plotted the number of grades in each bin. (Since no one scored below 65 on the exam, we didn't bother to plot all of the empty bins between 0 and 64 in Figure 7.25.)

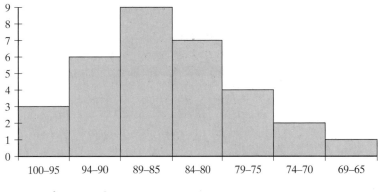

Figure 7.25.   Histogram of Student Scores on Last Test.

Create a `Histogram` class that contains an instance array of bins to accumulate data in. The number of bins and the range that they cover should be specified in the class constructor. (Be sure to include two extra bins in the array for values that fall below and values that fall above the specified range.) The class should include a method `hist` that accepts an array of double values, determines the bin each value falls in, and increments the count in the appropriate bin. It should also include two methods, `getBins()` and `getCount()`, to return arrays containing the centers of each bin and the number of counts in each bin, respectively.

Finally, create a test driver program that reads input data from a user-specified disk file, calculates a histogram from the data using the `Histogram` class, and uses the `JPlot2D` class in package `chapman.graphics` to create a plot of the histogram.

12. Use the random-number method `Math.random()` to generate an array of 20,000 random numbers in the range [0,1). Use the histogram class developed in the previous exercise to divide the range between 0 and 1 into 20 bins and to plot a histogram of the 20,000 random numbers. How uniform was the distribution of the numbers generated by the random number generator?

13. Use the normally distributed random-number method developed in Exercise 9 of Chapter 6 to generate an array of 20,000 random numbers. Use the histogram method developed in the Exercise 11 of this chapter to divide the range between −4 and 4 into 41 bins and to plot a histogram of the 20,000 random numbers. How well does the histogram match the normal probability distribution shown in Figure 6.15?

8

Strings

A **string** is an object containing a group of one or more characters treated as a single unit. For example, in the statement

```
System.out.println("Value = " + value);
```

the term `"Value = "` is a string. The principal importance of strings in our programs is that *they represent information in a form easily readable by humans*, and so they are regularly used to enter information into a program and to display the results of the program.

It is important to understand the difference between a string representing a value and the value itself as it is stored inside a computer. For example, let's compare the integer value `123` and the string `"123"`. The integer value `123` is stored as the binary pattern 01111011 in a memory location inside the computer. In this form the computer can use it directly in its calculations, but it *cannot* be displayed on a computer screen. In contrast, the string `"123"` consists of three Unicode characters encoding the characters 1, 2, and 3, respectively. A computer cannot use the string `"123"` directly in numerical calculations, but humans can easily recognize the number that it represents.

Because humans enter data for computer programs and read the results of the programs, most input and output from programs is in the form of character strings. On the other hand, most internal calculations are performed with the binary representations of numbers. Thus, we must be able to convert from strings to numbers when data is read into a program, and from numbers to strings when data is printed out. The ability to work with strings is vital if we humans are to actually use computers. This chapter teaches us how to manipulate character strings in Java.

There are two types of string objects in Java: `String` and `StringBuffer`. Their fundamental difference between the two classes is that

SECTIONS

OBJECTIVES

- Be able to create `String`s
- Understand `String` methods
- Be able to create `StringBuffer`s
- Understand `StringBuffer` methods
- Be able to use the `StringTokenizer` class
- Be able to utilize command-line arguments

285

the `String` class consists of strings that *never change* once they are created, while the `StringBuffer` class consists of modifiable strings.

Java distinguishes between these two types of strings for efficiency reasons. Java knows that any object of the `String` class can never be changed, once it is created, so the compiler and run-time system can use a single object for all strings containing the same set of characters, thus reducing program size.

8.1 CREATING AND INITIALIZING `Strings`

A reference to a `String` object is created by a statement such as

```
String str1;              // Create a String reference
```

When this statement is executed, reference `str1` is created and set to `null`, since it does not yet point to a `String` object. Attempting to use a null reference in a program will produce a run-time error.

`String` objects may be created and assigned to a `String` reference in several ways. The easiest way is with a `String` **literal**. `String` literals (also known as `String` constants or **anonymous** `String` **objects**) are written as a string of characters between double quotation marks. For example,

```
"This is a test."
```

is a `String` object. A `String` reference can be created and a `String` literal can be assigned to that reference in a single statement:

```
String str1 = "This is a test.";
```

`String` objects can also be created using `String` constructors. `String` constructors can create new strings from other strings, from `StringBuffers`, from arrays of bytes, and from arrays of characters. Some examples of `String` constructors are shown below:

```
String str1 = new String("This is a test.");// From another string
String str2 = new String( buffer );         // From a StringBuffer
String str3 = new String( charArray );      // From a char array
String str4 = new String( byteArray );      // From a byte array
String str5 = new String( );                // New empty string
```

Once it has been created, each `String` object contains a fixed number of characters. The number of characters in any string can always be found using the `length` method. For example, the expression `str1.length()` will return a value of 15 for the string `str1` defined above.

8.2 `String` METHODS

Many methods are available for manipulating strings in Java programs. Some of the more important string methods are summarized in Table 8.1. All of the `String` methods are described in the Java API documentation in class `java.lang.String`.

8.2.1 Substrings

A **substring** is a portion of a string. The method `substring` allows a substring to be extracted from a Java string. There are two forms of this method; the first is

```
s.substring( int st )
```

TABLE 8.1 Selected `String` Methods

Method	Description
char **charAt**(int index)	Returns the character at a specified index in the string.

int **compareTo**(String s)	Compares the string object to another string lexicographically. Returns:
	     0 if string is equal to s
	     <0 if string less than s
	     >0 if string greater than s

String **concat**(String s)	Concatenates the string s to the end of this string.
boolean **endsWith**(String suffix)	Returns true if this string ends with the specified suffix.
boolean **equals**(Object o)	Returns true if o is a `String` and contains exactly the same characters as the string.
boolean **equalsIgnoreCase**(String s)	Returns true if s contains exactly the same characters as the string, disregarding case.
void **getChars**(int i1, int i2, char[] dst, int i3)	Copies the characters in the string from position i1 to position i2 into character array dst, starting at index i3.
int **IndexOf**(char ch)	Returns the index of the *first* location of ch in the string.
int **IndexOf**(char ch, int start)	Returns the index of the *first* location of ch at or after position start in the string.
int **IndexOf**(String s)	Returns the index of the *first* location of substring s in the string.
int **IndexOf**(String s, int start)	Returns the index of the *first* location of substring s at or after position start in the string.
int **LastIndexOf**(char ch)	Returns the index of the *last* location of ch in the string.
int **LastIndexOf**(char ch, int start)	Returns the index of the *last* location of ch at or before position start in the string.
int **LastIndexOf**(String s)	Returns the index of the *last* location of substring s in the string.
int **LastIndexOf**(String s, int start)	Returns the index of the *last* location of substring s at or before position start in the string.
boolean **regionMatches**(int off1, String s, int off2, int len)	This method compares len characters of the string starting at index off1 with len characters of s starting at index off2. If they match, the method returns true. Otherwise, the method returns false.
boolean **regionMatches**(boolean ignoreCase, int off1, with String s, int off2, int len)	This method compares len characters of the string starting at index off1 with len characters of s starting at index off2. If ignoreCase is true and the substrings match, *ignoring case*, the method returns true. If ignoreCase is false and the substrings match *exactly*, the method returns true. Otherwise, the method returns false.
String **replace**(char old, char new)	Returns a new string with every occurrence of character old replaced by character new.
boolean **startsWith**(String p)	Returns true if the beginning of the string exactly matches the string p.
boolean **startsWith**(String p, int off1)	Returns true if the beginning of the substring starting at index off1 exactly matches the string p.
String **substring**(int st)	Returns the substring starting at index st and going to the end of the string.
String **substring**(int st, int en)	Returns the substring starting at index st and going to index en-1.
String **toLowerCase**()	Converts the string to lower case.
String **toUpperCase**()	Converts the string to upper case.
String **trim**()	Removes white space from either end of the string.
static String **valueOf**(boolean b)	Returns the string representation of a boolean argument.
static String **valueOf**(char c)	Returns the string representation of a character argument.
static String **valueOf**(int i)	Returns the string representation of an integer argument.
static String **valueOf**(long l)	Returns the string representation of a long argument.
static String **valueOf**(float f)	Returns the string representation of a float argument.
static String **valueOf**(double d)	Returns the string representation of a double argument.
static String **valueOf**(Object o)	Returns the string representation of an arbitrary Object.

It takes one integer argument that specifies only the starting index of the substring and returns a new string containing the characters from that index to the end of the original string. The second form is

```
s.substring( int st, int en )
```

It takes two integer arguments and specifies both the starting and ending indexes of the substring. If the indexes specified in either case are less than zero or greater than the number of characters in the string, then a `StringIndexOutOfBounds` exception will occur.

The `substring` method regularly confuses novice programmers. As with all of Java, index numbering starts at 0, so a value of 0 in `st` returns the first character of the original string. The second parameter (`en`) specifies the ending index of the substring, *with the last character returned being at index* `en-1`. Thus, a value of 0 in the first argument corresponds to the first character in the string, but a value of 1 in the second argument also corresponds to the first character in the string. For example, suppose that `String s` is defined as:

```
String s = "1234567890";
```

Then the call `s.substring(0,1)` would return the string `"1"`, since the first character of the original string is both the first and last character to return. Similarly, the call `s.substring(1,4)` would return the string `"234"`.

PROGRAMMING PITFALLS

Be careful using the `substring( int st, int en )` method. The parameter `st` specifies the starting index of the substring, while the parameter `en` is *one greater* than the ending index of the substring.

The class shown below illustrates both types of `substring` methods.

```
// Substrings
public class Substring {

    public static void main(String[] args) {
        String s = "abcdefghijABCDEFGHIJabcdefghij";

        // Test substring methods
        System.out.println("String = \"" + s + "\"");
        System.out.println("Substring starting at 18 = "
            + "\"" + s.substring(18) + "\"");

        System.out.println("Substring from 18 to 24  = "
            + "\"" + s.substring(18,24) + "\"");
    }
}
```

When this program is executed, the results are:

```
D:\book\java\chap8>java Substring
String = "abcdefghijABCDEFGHIJabcdefghij"
Substring starting at 18 = "IJabcdefghij"
Substring from 18 to 24  = "IJabcd"
```

8.2.2   Concatenating Strings

Two strings may be **concatenated** (joined end-to-end) using the concat method. The expression

```
s1.concat( s2 )
```

creates a new string by appending the characters in s2 to the end of s1. The original String objects s1 and s2 are not affected. The class shown below illustrates the use of concat.

```
1   // Concatenation
2   public class Concatenate {
3
4      public static void main(String[] args) {
5         String s1 = "abc";
6         String s2 = "def";
7
8         // Test concatenation method
9         System.out.println("Test concatenation:");
10        System.out.println("s1 = " + s1);
11        System.out.println("s2 = " + s2);
12        System.out.println("s1.concat(s2) = "
13             + s1.concat(s2));
14
15        // Watch what happens here!
16        System.out.println("\nBefore assignment:");
17        System.out.println("s1 = " + s1);
18        System.out.println("s2 = " + s2);
19        s1 = s1.concat(s2);
20        System.out.println("\nAfter assignment:");
21        System.out.println("s1 = " + s1);
22        System.out.println("s2 = " + s2);
23     }
24  }
```

When this program is executed, the results are:

```
D:\book\java\chap8>java Concatenate
Test concatenation:
s1 = abc
s2 = def
s1.concat(s2) = abcdef
Before assignment:
s1 = abc
s2 = def
After assignment:
s1 = abcdef
s2 = def
```

Note that the concat method concatenated string s1 with string s2.

The second part of the program illustrates another common source of confusion to novice Java programmers. We stated at the beginning of this chapter that Strings never change once they are created, and yet s1 changes value between lines 17 and 21 in the above program! What is happening here?

The answer is very simple. Remember that s1 and s2 are *references to strings*, not string objects themselves. Lines 5 and 6 of the program create two String objects containing the strings "abc" and "def" and set references s1 and s2 to refer to them. Therefore, lines 17 and 18 print out s1 = "abc" and s2 = "def". The concat method in line 19 creates a *new* String object containing the string "abcdef" and sets the reference s1 to point to the new object. Therefore, line 21 prints out s1 = "abcdef". This process is illustrated in Figure 8.1.

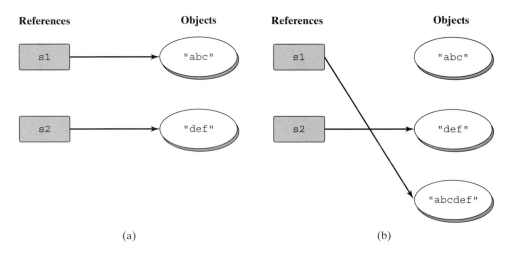

(a)   (b)

Figure 8.1. (a) Initially reference s1 points to the String object containing "abc", and reference s2 points to the String object containing "def". (b) After line 19 is executed, reference s1 points to the String object containing "abcdef", and reference s2 points to the String object containing "def". The object containing "abc" no longer has a reference, and it will be destroyed the next time the garbage collecter runs.

What happened to the original String object pointed to by s1? It is still present, but there is no longer any reference to it. This object can never be used again, and it will be destroyed the next time the garbage collector runs.

8.2.3   Comparing Strings

Two strings may be compared using methods equals, equalsIgnoreCase, compareTo, regionMatches. When two strings are compared, they are compared according to the **lexicographic sequence** of the characters in the strings. This is the sequence in which the characters appear within the character set used by the computer. For example, Appendix A shows the order of the first 127 letters according to the Unicode character set. In this set, the letter 'A' is character 64 and the letter 'a' is 96, so 'A' is lexicographically less than 'a'. *Note that capital letters are not the same as lowercase letters* when they are compared lexicographically.

If the strings being compared are more than one character long, then the comparison starts with the first character in each string. If the two characters are equal, then the comparison moves to the second character in the strings, and so on, until the first difference is found. If there is no difference between the two strings, then they are considered equal.

The method `equals` compares two strings and returns true if they contain identically the same value. For example, if

```
s1 = new String("Hello");
s2 = new String("Hello");
s3 = new String("hello");
```

then the expression `s1.equals( s2 )` will be `true` because the two strings are identically the same, while the expression `s1.equals( s3 )` will be `false` because the two strings differ in the first position.

Note that *comparing two strings with the method equals is not the same as comparing two strings with the == operator.* When the == operator compares two object references, *it checks to see whether the two references point to the same object.* If you are comparing two different objects with the == operator, they will not be equal, even if they have identically the same contents. For example, if `s1` and `s2` are as defined above, the expression

```
s1.equals(s2)
```

will return `true`, because the contents of the two objects are equal, but the expression

```
s1 == s2
```

will return `false`, because `s1` and `s2` are two different objects (see Figure 8.2).

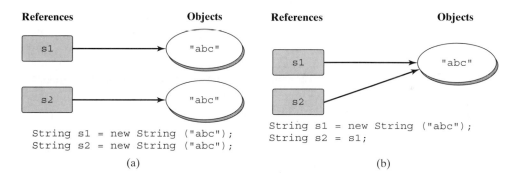

Figure 8.2. The difference between `s1.equals(s2)` and `s1 == s2`. (a) In this case, `s1` and `s2` point to *two different objects* whose contents are equal. Here, `s1.equals(s2)` is true, and `s1 == s2` is false. (b) In this case, `s1` and `s2` point to the same object. Here, `s1.equals(s2)` is true, and `s1 == s2` is also true.

PROGRAMMING PITFALLS

Never attempt to compare two objects for equality with the == operator. This operator checks to see whether two references point to the same object, not to see whether two objects have equal values.

The method `equalsIgnoreCase` is similar to `equals`, except that it ignores the case of letters when comparing the two strings. Thus the expression `s1.equals-IgnoreCase(s3)` will be `true`, because the two strings differ only in the case of the letter `'H'`.

The method s1.compareTo(s2) compares two strings s1 and s2 and returns an integer equal to the *difference in lexicographic position* between the corresponding letters at the first differing location in the strings. This difference will be negative if s1 < s2 and positive if s1 > s2. If the strings are equal, then the method will return a zero. For example, if

```
s1 = new String("Good");
s2 = new String("Help");
s3 = new String("HELP");
s4 = new String("HELP");
```

then the expression s1.compareTo(s2) will be −1, because the letter 'G' appears one character before 'H' in the Unicode character set. Similarly, the expression s2.compareTo(s3) will be 32, because the strings first differ in the second position, and the letter 'e' appears 32 characters after 'E' in the Unicode character set. Finally, the expression s3.compareTo(s4) will be zero, since the strings are equal.

The method regionMatches compares two strings s1 and s2 to determine whether two regions within the strings are equal to each other. There are two forms of this method. The first is

```
s1.regionMatches(i1, s2, i2, len)
```

where i1, i2, and len are all integers. The value i1 is the index in s1 at which to start the comparison, i2 is the index in s2 at which to start the comparison, and len is the number of characters to compare. This method returns true if the two regions match exactly, including case.

The second form of regionMatches is

```
s1.regionMatches(ignoreCase, i1, s2, i2, len)
```

where ignoreCase is a boolean and all other arguments have the same meaning as before. If ignoreCase is true, this method compares the two regions *ignoring case*. Otherwise, it acts exactly like the first form of the method. For example, if

```
s1 = new String("started");
s2 = new String("starting");
s3 = new String("nowStarting");
```

then the method call

```
s1.regionMatches(0, s2, 0, 5)
```

will return a true value, because the first five characters in the two strings are identical (remember that Java indexes start at 0). The method call

```
s1.regionMatches(0, s3, 3, 5)
```

will return a false value, because "start" is not equal to "Start". However, the method call

```
s1.regionMatches(true, 1, s3, 4, 5)
```

will return a true value, because "start" is equal to "Start" ignoring case.

The methods startsWith and endsWith can be used to determine whether or not a string starts with or ends with a particular substring. For example, if

```
s1 = new String("started");
```

then the method call

```
s1.startsWith("st")
```

would return true, because "started" does start with "st". Similarly, the method call

```
s1.endsWith("ed")
```

would return true, because "started" does end with "ed".

All of these comparison methods are illustrated in the Java program shown below.

```java
// Comparisons
public class Compare {

    public static void main(String[] args) {

        String s1, s2, s3, s4;   // Declare references

        // Test equality and inequality
        System.out.println("Test equality:");
        s1 = new String("Hello");
        s2 = new String("Hello");
        s3 = new String("hello");

        System.out.println("s1 = \"" + s1 + "\"");
        System.out.println("s2 = \"" + s2 + "\"");
        System.out.println("s3 = \"" + s3 + "\"");
        System.out.println("s1.equals(s2) = "
            + s1.equals(s2));
        System.out.println("s1.equals(s3) = "
            + s1.equals(s3));
        System.out.println("s1.equalsIgnoreCase(s3) = "
            + s1.equalsIgnoreCase(s3));
        System.out.println("s1 == s2 = "
            + (s1 == s2) );

        // Test comparison
        System.out.println("\nTest compare:");
        s1 = new String("Good");
        s2 = new String("Help");
        s3 = new String("HELP");
        s4 = new String("HELP");

        System.out.println("s1 = \"" + s1 + "\"");
        System.out.println("s2 = \"" + s2 + "\"");
        System.out.println("s3 = \"" + s3 + "\"");
        System.out.println("s4 = \"" + s4 + "\"");
        System.out.println("s1.compareTo(s2) = "
            + s1.compareTo(s2));
        System.out.println("s2.compareTo(s3) = "
            + s2.compareTo(s3));
        System.out.println("s3.compareTo(s4) = "
            + s3.compareTo(s4));

        // Test regionMatches
        System.out.println("\nTest regionMatches:");
        s1 = new String("started");
        s2 = new String("starting");
        s3 = new String("nowStarting");
```

```
            System.out.println("s1 = \"" + s1 + "\"");
            System.out.println("s2 = \"" + s2 + "\"");
            System.out.println("s3 = \"" + s3 + "\"");
            System.out.println("s1.regionMatches(0, s2, 0, 5) = "
                + s1.regionMatches(0, s2, 0, 5));
            System.out.println("s1.regionMatches(0, s3, 3, 5) = "
                + s1.regionMatches(0, s3, 3, 5));
            System.out.println("s1.regionMatches
            (true, 0, s3, 3, 5) = "
                + s1.regionMatches(true, 0, s3, 3, 5));

            // Test startsWith and endsWith
            System.out.println("\nTest startsWith & endsWith:");
            s1 = new String("started");
            s2 = new String("starting");

            System.out.println("s1 = \"" + s1 + "\"");
            System.out.println("s2 = \"" + s2 + "\"");
            System.out.println("s1.startsWith(\"st\") = "
                + s1.startsWith("st"));
            System.out.println("s1.endsWith(\"ed\") = "
                + s1.endsWith("ed"));
            System.out.println("s2.endsWith(\"ed\") = "
                + s2.endsWith("ed"));

        }
    }
```

When this program is executed, the results agree with our previous discussions:

```
D:\book\java\chap8>java Compare
Test equality:
s1 = "Hello"
s2 = "Hello"
s3 = "hello"
s1.equals(s2) = true
s1.equals(s3) = false
s1.equalsIgnoreCase(s3) = true
s1 == s2 = false

Test compare:
s1 = "Good"
s2 = "Help"
s3 = "HELP"
s4 = "HELP"
s1.compareTo(s2) = -1
s2.compareTo(s3) = 32
s3.compareTo(s4) = 0

Test regionMatches:
s1 = "started"
s2 = "starting"
s3 = "nowStarting"
s1.regionMatches(0, s2, 0, 5) = true
```

```
s1.regionMatches(0, s3, 3, 5) = false
s1.regionMatches(true, 0, s3, 3, 5) = true

Test startsWith & endsWith:
s1 = "started"
s2 = "starting"
s1.startsWith("st") = true
s1.endsWith("ed") = true
s2.endsWith("ed") = false
```

8.2.4 Locating Characters and Substrings in a String

A substring can be located inside another string using the `indexOf` and `lastIndexOf` methods. The `indexOf` method takes one of the forms

```
s1.indexOf(String s2);
s1.indexOf(String s2, int start);
s1.indexOf(char c);
s1.indexOf(char c, int start);
```

This method starts at the starting index (or at 0 if the starting index is not specified) and searches string `s1` from *left to right* until it locates an occurrence of the specified substring or character. It returns the index where that substring or character was found, or −1 if it was not found. For example, if

```
s1 = new String("This is a test.");
```

then the expression `s1.indexOf("is")` will return a 2, because the `"is"` in `"This"` starts at index 2. Similarly, the expression `s1.indexOf("is",3)` will return a 5, because this expression begins searching at index 3 in the string, and the first occurrence of `"is"` that it finds will be at index 5. Finally, the expression `s1.indexOf("is",6)` will return a −1, because there is no occurrence of `"is"` after that point in the string.

The `lastIndexOf` method takes one of the forms

```
s1.lastIndexOf(String s2);
s1.lastIndexOf(String s2, int start);
s1.lastIndexOf(char c);
s1.lastIndexOf(char c, int start);
```

This method starts at the starting index (or at the end of the string if the starting index is not specified) and searches string `s1` from *right to left* until it locates an occurrence of the specified substring or character. It returns the index where that substring or character was found, or −1 if it was not found.

The `indexOf` and `lastIndexOf` methods are illustrated in the Java program shown below.

```
// IndexOf
public class Find {

    public static void main(String[] args) {

        // Test indexOf
        System.out.println("Test indexOf:");
        String s1 = new String("This is a test.");
```

```
              System.out.println("s1 = \"" + s1 + "\"");
              System.out.println("s1.indexOf(\"is\") = "
                 + s1.indexOf("is"));
              System.out.println("s1.indexOf(\"is\",3) = "
                 + s1.indexOf("is",3));
              System.out.println("s1.indexOf(\"is\",6) = "
                 + s1.indexOf("is",6));
              System.out.println("s1.indexOf(\'s\') = "
                 + s1.indexOf('s'));

              // Test lastIndexOf
              System.out.println("\nTest lastIndexOf:");
              System.out.println("s1.lastIndexOf(\"is\") = "
                 + s1.lastIndexOf("is"));

           }
        }
```

When this program is executed, the results are:

```
        D:\book\java\chap8>java Find
        Test indexOf:
        s1 = "This is a test."
        s1.indexOf("is") = 2
        s1.indexOf("is",3) = 5
        s1.indexOf("is",6) = -1
        s1.indexOf('s') = 3

        Test lastIndexOf:
        s1.lastIndexOf("is") = 5
```

8.2.5   Miscellaneous String Methods

This section discusses four miscellaneous string methods: replace, toUpperCase, toLowerCase, and trim.

Method replace creates a new string with every occurrence of a specified character in the original string replaced with a different character. The form of this method is

```
        s1.replace(old, new)
```

where s1 is a string, old is the character to replace, and new is the replacement character. For example, if

```
        s1 = "This is a test.";
```

then the expression s1.replace('i','I') will return the string "ThIs Is a test.".

Methods toUpperCase and toLowerCase return strings with all characters shifted to upper case and lower case, respectively. Thus, s1.toUpperCase() will return the string "THIS IS A TEST.", and s1.toLowerCase() will return the string "this is a test.".

Method trim returns a string that is identical to the original string, except that *the leading and trailing white space has been removed*. For example, consider the statements

```
        s1 = "   Hello   ";
        s1.length()
        s2 = s1.trim;
        s2.length()
```

Then string s1 is 11 characters long, and the expression s1.length() will return a value of 11. String s2 will be the same as string s1 with the leading and trailing white space removed, so s2.length() will be 5.

These methods are illustrated in the program below:

```java
// Miscellaneous methods
public class Misc {

    public static void main(String[] args) {

        String s1 = new String("This is a test.");
        String s2;

        System.out.println("Test replace:");
        System.out.println("s1 = \"" + s1 + "\"");
        System.out.println("s1.replace(\'i\',\'I\') = "
            + s1.replace('i','I'));

        System.out.println("\nTest toUpperCase:");
        System.out.println("s1.toUpperCase() = "
            + s1.toUpperCase());

        System.out.println("\nTest toLowerCase:");
        System.out.println("s1.toLowerCase() = "
            + s1.toLowerCase());

        System.out.println("\nTest trim:");
        s1 = new String("   Hello   ");
        s2 = s1.trim();
        System.out.println("s1 = \"" + s1 + "\"");
        System.out.println("s2 = \"" + s2 + "\"");
    }
}
```

When this program is executed, the results are

```
D:\book\java\chap8>java Misc
Test replace:
s1 = "This is a test."
s1.replace('i','I') = ThIs Is a test.

Test toUpperCase:
s1.toUpperCase() = THIS IS A TEST.

Test toLowerCase:
s1.toLowerCase() = this is a test.

Test trim:
s1 = "   Hello   "
s2 = "Hello"
```

8.2.6   The valueOf() Method

Data is stored and used inside a computer in binary format. Before it can be displayed for human use, it must be converted into a String representation. One technique available for this conversion is the String.valueOf method.

The static method `String.valueOf` returns a string representation of the value of its argument, whether the argument is a primitive data type or an object. There are separate versions of this method for each primitive data type and for objects. [The version for objects uses the object's `toString()` method to create a string representation of the object's value.]

Since this is a `static` method, it can be used without first instantiating a `String` object. The following program illustrates the use of the `valueOf()` method, using the `Date` class from Chapter 7 as the example object.

```
// This program tests String.valueOf().  It uses
// class Date from Chapter 7.
public class ValueOf {

    public static void main(String[] args) {

        // Test valueOf
        System.out.println("Test valueOf:");
        int i = 123456;
        float f = 1.2345f;
        double d = Math.PI;
        Object o = new Date(1,1,2000);

        System.out.println("int    = " + String.valueOf(i) );
        System.out.println("float  = " + String.valueOf(f) );
        System.out.println("double = " + String.valueOf(d) );
        System.out.println("object = " + String.valueOf(o) );
    }
}
```

When this program is executed, the results are:

```
C:\book\java\chap8>java ValueOf
Test valueOf:
int    = 123456
float  = 1.2345
double = 3.141592653589793
object = 1/1/2000
```

8.3 THE `StringBuffer` CLASS

The `StringBuffer` class creates objects that contain *modifiable* strings. The contents of a `StringBuffer` may be freely changed, and the size of a `StringBuffer` can grow or shrink during program execution.

A reference to a `StringBuffer` is created by the statement

```
StringBuffer buf1;          // Create a StringBuffer reference
```

When this statement is executed, reference `buf1` is created and set to `null`, since it does not yet point to a `StringBuffer` object. Attempting to use a null reference in a program will produce a run-time exception.

`StringBuffer` objects are created using `StringBuffer` constructors. There are three forms of `StringBuffer` constructors. A constructor with no arguments creates an empty `StringBuffer` object with a capacity of 16 characters. A constructor with an integer argument creates an empty `StringBuffer` object with a capacity specified by the integer. A constructor with a `String` argument creates a `StringBuffer` initialized to the value of the string, with a capacity equal to the number of characters in the string plus 16. Some examples of `StringBuffer` constructors are shown below:

```
StringBuffer buf1, buf2, buf3
buf1 = new StringBuffer();           // 16 char capacity
buf2 = new StringBuffer(50);         // 50 char capacity
buf3 = new StringBuffer("Hello");    // 21 char capacity
```

8.4   **StringBuffer** METHODS

Many methods are available for manipulating `StringBuffers` in Java programs. Some of the more important ones are summarized in Table 8.2. All of the `StringBuffer` methods are described in the Java API documentation in class `java.lang.StringBuffer`.

8.4.1   The Difference between Length and Capacity

Every `StringBuffer` is characterized by two parameters, a **length** and a **capacity**. The **length** of a `StringBuffer` is the number of characters *actually stored* in the `StringBuffer`, while the **capacity** is the number of characters that *can be* stored without allocating additional memory (see Figure 8.3). These two values are independent of each other, except that the capacity of a buffer must always be greater than or equal to the length of the actual characters stored in the buffer. If a method call makes the length of the buffer larger than its current capacity, that capacity is automatically extended so that all of the characters will fit.

The length of a `StringBuffer` object can be determined using the `length` method, and the capacity of a `StringBuffer` object can be determined using the `capacity` method. These methods return the length or capacity of the buffer in units of characters.

The `ensureCapacity` method can be used to force a `StringBuffer` object to have at least a minimum capacity. The form of this method is

```
buf.ensureCapacity(cap)
```

where `cap` is an integer specifying the minimum capacity of the buffer `buf`. Java may choose to allocate more than this capacity, but it guarantees that the buffer will be able to hold at least `cap` characters.

The actual number of characters stored in a buffer can be set using the `length` method. The form of this method is

```
buf.length(len)
```

where `len` is an integer specifying the number of actual characters in the buffer. If `len` is less than the current number of characters in the buffer, the number of characters is truncated to `len`. If `len` is greater than the current number of characters in the buffer, the characters are padded with null characters (the Unicode character `'\u0000'`).

The following program illustrates the use of these methods.

```
// This program tests StringBuffer capacity and length
public class StringBufferCapLen {
```

TABLE 8.2 Selected `StringBuffer` Methods

Method	Description
StringBuffer **append**(Object o)	Appends the string representation of the Object argument to this string buffer.
StringBuffer **append**(String s)	Appends the string to this string buffer.
StringBuffer **append**(Char[] c)	Appends the string representation of the char array c to this string buffer.
StringBuffer **append**(boolean b)	Appends the string representation of the boolean argument to this string buffer.
StringBuffer **append**(char c)	Appends the string representation of the char argument to this string buffer.
StringBuffer **append**(int i)	Appends the string representation of the int argument to this string buffer.
StringBuffer **append**(long l)	Appends the string representation of the long argument to this string buffer.
StringBuffer **append**(float f)	Appends the string representation of the float argument to this string buffer.
StringBuffer **append**(double d)	Appends the string representation of the double argument to this string buffer.
int **capacity**()	Returns the current capacity, which is the number of characters that may be inserted before more memory must be allocated.
char **charAt**(int index)	Returns the character at the specified index.
void **ensureCapacity**(int min)	Ensures that the capacity of the buffer is at least equal to the specified minimum.
StringBuffer **insert**(int n, Object o)	Inserts the string representation of the Object argument at index n in this string buffer.
StringBuffer **insert**(int n, String s)	Inserts the string at index n in this string buffer.
StringBuffer **insert**(int n, Char[] c)	Inserts the string representation of the char array c at index n in this string buffer.
StringBuffer **insert**(int n, boolean b)	Inserts the string representation of the boolean argument at index n in this string buffer.
StringBuffer **insert**(int n, char c)	Inserts the string representation of the char argument at index n in this string buffer.
StringBuffer **insert**(int n, int i)	Inserts the string representation of the int argument at index n in this string buffer.
StringBuffer **insert**(int n, long l)	Inserts the string representation of the long argument at index n in this string buffer.
StringBuffer **insert**(int n, float f)	Inserts the string representation of the float argument at index n in this string buffer.
StringBuffer **insert**(int n, double d)	Inserts the string representation of the double argument at index n in this string buffer.
int **length**()	Returns the number of characters in this string buffer.
StringBuffer **reverse**()	Reverses the sequence of characters in this string buffer.
void **setLength**(int len)	Sets the length (the number of characters) in this buffer. If len is less than the current string buffer length, the string buffer is truncated. If len is greater, then the string buffer is padded with null characters (\u0000).
String **toString**()	Converts the contents of this string buffer into a string.

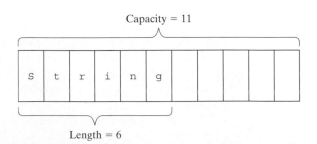

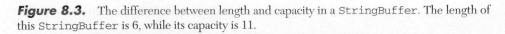

Figure 8.3. The difference between length and capacity in a `StringBuffer`. The length of this `StringBuffer` is 6, while its capacity is 11.

```
public static void main(String[] args) {
    StringBuffer buf;
    buf = new StringBuffer("This is a test string.");

    // Get length and capacity
    System.out.println("Initial conditions:");
    System.out.println("buf       = " + buf );
    System.out.println("Capacity = " + buf.capacity() );
    System.out.println("length   = " + buf.length() );

    // Increase capacity
    System.out.println("\nAfter ensureCapacity:");
    buf.ensureCapacity(75);
    System.out.println("buf       = " + buf );
    System.out.println("Capacity = " + buf.capacity() );
    System.out.println("length   = " + buf.length() );

    // Truncate length
    System.out.println("\nAfter setLength:");
    buf.setLength(10);
    System.out.println("buf       = " + buf );
    System.out.println("Capacity = " + buf.capacity() );
    System.out.println("length   = " + buf.length() );
    }
}
```

When this program is executed, the results are:

```
C:\book\java\chap8>java StringBufferCapLen
Initial conditions:
buf       = This is a test string.
Capacity = 38
length   = 22

After ensureCapacity:
buf       = This is a test string.
Capacity = 78
length   = 22

After setLength:
buf       = This is a
Capacity = 78
length   = 10
```

Note that the initial length of the buffer was 22 characters, and the initial capacity of the buffer was 38 characters (= 22 + 16 extra). After the buf.ensureCapacity(76) method was executed, the new capacity of the buffer was 78. Java ensured that the capacity was at least 76 characters. Finally, after the buf.setLength(10) method was executed, the number of characters in the buffer decreased to 10 while the capacity of the buffer remained at 78.

8.4.2 The append and insert Methods

The most important StringBuffer methods are append and insert. Java allows you insert or append string representations of just about anything (boolean, char, `int`, `long`, `float`, `double`, `String`, or a general `Object`) at any point in a string buffer.

In fact, Java uses the `StringBuffer` append method to implement the `+` and `+=` operators for concatenating strings. A string concatenation expression like

```
String s = "value = " + 1.234;
```

is actually implemented by the Java expression

```
String s = new StringBuffer("value = "). append(1.234).toString();
```

which creates a new `StringBuffer` containing the characters `"value = "`, appends a string representation of the double value 1.234 to it, and then converts the entire `StringBuffer` into a `String`.

The append method appends a character representation of a primitive data type or object to an existing `StringBuffer`. It takes the form

```
buf.append( value );
```

where `value` can be any `boolean`, `char`, `int`, `long`, `float`, `double`, `String`, or a general `Object`.

The insert method inserts a character representation of a primitive data type or object into the middle of an existing `StringBuffer`. It takes the form

```
buf.insert( index, value );
```

where `index` is the index at which to insert the characters, and `value` can be any `boolean`, `char`, `int`, `long`, `float`, `double`, `String`, or a general `Object`.

The following program illustrates the use of these methods. First, it creates a new buffer `buf`, and then it *appends* an `int`, `String`, `double`, `char`, and `Object` to `buf`. The program prints out the resulting string buffer. Next, it resets the length of `buf` to zero, and then *inserts* the same values, starting at index zero each time. The program then prints out the new string buffer. Note that the order of the values is reversed between the two strings, because insert is always adding the new values at position 0 of the `StringBuffer`.

```
// This program tests StringBuffer append and insert.
// It uses class Date from Chapter 7 as an example
// Object.
public class StringBufferInsApp {

    public static void main(String[] args) {

        // Define variables
        StringBuffer buf = new StringBuffer();
        int i = 123456;
        double d = Math.PI;
        Object o = new Date(1,1,2000);

        // Test append
        System.out.println("Test append:");
        buf.append(i);              // int
        buf.append(" ");            // String
        buf.append(d);              // double
        buf.append(' ');            // char
        buf.append(o);              // Object
        System.out.println("buf = " + buf );
```

```
        // Test insert
        System.out.println("\nTest insert:");
        buf.setLength(0);            // Clear buffer
        buf.insert(0,i);             // int
        buf.insert(0," ");           // String
        buf.insert(0,d);             // double
        buf.insert(0,' ');           // char
        buf.insert(0,o);             // Object
        System.out.println("buf = " + buf );
    }
}
```

When this program is executed, the results are:

```
C:\book\java\chap8>java StringBufferInsApp
Test append:
buf = 123456 3.141592653589793 1/1/2000

Test insert:
buf = 1/1/2000 3.141592653589793 123456
```

8.4.3   The reverse Method

One other useful StringBuffer method is reverse. This method reverses the order of the characters stored in a buffer. Its form is

```
buf.reverse();
```

The following program illustrates the use of this method.

```
// This program tests the StringBuffer reverse method.
public class StringBufferReverse {

    public static void main(String[] args) {

        // Define variables
        StringBuffer buf = new StringBuffer("1234567890");

        // Test reverse
        System.out.println("Test reverse:");
        System.out.println("Before: buf = " + buf );
        buf.reverse();
        System.out.println("After:  buf = " + buf );
    }
}
```

When this program is executed, the results are:

```
C:\book\java\chap8>java StringBufferReverse
Test reverse:
Before: buf = 1234567890
After:  buf = 0987654321
```

EXAMPLE 8.1

Comparing `Strings` and `StringBuffers`: Java `Strings` are more efficient for operations such as comparison and matching, while `StringBuffers` are more efficient for operations such as appending or inserting. However, it is possible to do many operations with either `Strings` or `StringBuffers`. For example, we can add a string to the end of another string with the `String concat` method or with the `StringBuffer append` method.

To compare the performance of these two approaches, we will create a new string by concatenating the string `"ab"` 10,000 times with either the `concat` method or the `append` method. Use the `Timer` class to calculate the elapsed time required to concatenate the string using each method.

SOLUTION

The code required to create a string s by concatenating the string `"ab"` 10,000 times using the `concat` method is:

```
String s = new String();
for ( i = 1; i <= 1000; i++ ) {
    s = s.concat("ab");
}
```

The code required to create a string s by concatenating the string `"ab"` 10,000 times using the `append` method is:

```
String s;
StringBuffer buf = new StringBuffer();
for ( i = 1; i <= 1000; i++ ) {
    buf.append("ab");
}
s = buf.toString();
```

A program implementing these two approaches is shown in Figure 8.4.

When this program is executed on a 733-MHz Pentium III-based computer with Java SDK 1.3, the results are:

```
C:\book\java\chap8>java TestConcat
Results with s.concat():
String begins: abababab...
```

```
/*
   Purpose:
     This class tests concatenation using both the
     String method concat and the StringBuffer method
     append.

   Record of revisions:
       Date          Programmer              Description of change
       ====          ==========              =====================
   05/06/2002    S. J. Chapman            Original code
*/
```

Figure 8.4. A program comparing concatenation with `String` objects to appending with `StringBuffer` objects.

```java
public class TestConcat {

   // Define the main method
   public static void main(String[] args) {

      // Definitions of variables
      StringBuffer buf;                    // String buffer
      double elapsedTime;                  // Elapsed time (s)
      String s;                            // String
      Timer t;                             // Timer object

      // Start a Timer
      t = new Timer();

      // Concatenate the data using string
      s = new String();
      for ( int i = 1; i <= 10000; i++ ) {
         s = s.concat("ab");
      }

      // Get elapsed time
      elapsedTime = t.elapsedTime();

      // Display results
      System.out.println("Results with s.concat():");
      System.out.println("String begins: "
                         + s.substring(0,8) + "...");
      System.out.println("String length = " + s.length());
      System.out.println("Time = " + elapsedTime + " s");

      // Reset Timer
      t.resetTimer();

      // Concatenate the data using StringBuffer
      buf = new StringBuffer();
      for ( int i = 1; i <= 10000; i++ ) {
         buf.append("ab");
      }
      s = buf.toString();

      // Get elapsed time
      elapsedTime = t.elapsedTime();

      // Display results
      System.out.println("Results with buf.append():");
      System.out.println("String begins: "
                         + s.substring(0,8) + "...");
      System.out.println("String length = " + s.length());
      System.out.println("Time = " + elapsedTime + " s");
   }
}
```

Figure 8.4.   (Continued).

```
String length = 20000
Time = 2.133 s
Results with buf.append():
String begins: abababab...
String length = 20000
Time = 0.01 s
```

The append method was about 200 times quicker than the concat method! The reason is that every time s.concat() was executed, the program had to create a *new* String object two characters longer than the previous one, and then had to copy the contents of the old object into the new one before adding on the two new characters. This process is very inefficient in both time and memory. Note that it left 9999 String objects in limbo waiting to be destroyed by the garbage collector!

For insert/append operations, StringBuffers are much more efficient than Strings. ∎

8.5   THE **StringTokenizer** CLASS

Java includes a special class called StringTokenizer to break the contents of a string apart into separate units, called **tokens**. A *token* is a connected group of characters separated by from other tokens by **delimiters**, which are usually white-space characters such as blanks, tabs, or newlines. For example, the string "This is a test" contains the four tokens "This", "is", "a", and "test". Class StringTokenizer allows us to chop strings up into such bite-sized pieces for further processing.

Class StringTokenizer has three possible constructors:

```
new StringTokenizer( String s);
new StringTokenizer( String s, String delim);
new StringTokenizer( String s, String delim, boolean returnTokens);
```

where s is the string to split into tokens. If it is included, delim is a string containing all of the characters that mark the boundaries between tokens. By default, the delimiter list is " \t\n\r\f", which is the space character, the tab character, the newline character, the carriage-return character, and the form-feed character. If returnTokens is true, the delimiters between tokens are also returned as tokens. If it is false or if it is not present, the delimiters between tokens are not returned.

The class includes an int method countTokens() to return the number of tokens in the string, a boolean method hasMoreTokens() to indicate that there are still tokens to recover, and a String method nextToken() to recover the next token.

The program shown in Figure 8.5 illustrates the use of the StringTokenizer class.

```
/*
   Purpose:
     This class tests StringTokenizer.

   Record of revisions:
      Date           Programmer              Description of change
      ====           ==========              =====================
   05/08/2002     S. J. Chapman           Original code
*/
import java.util.*;
public class TestStringTokenizer {

   // Define the main method
   public static void main(String[] args) {

      // Definitions of variables
      String s = "Test-case 1, test case 2";
      StringTokenizer st;

      // Create a StringTokenizer with the default options
      st = new StringTokenizer(s);
      System.out.print("Default case:");
      System.out.println("the " + st.countTokens() + " tokens are:");
      while (st.hasMoreTokens()) {
            System.out.println(st.nextToken());
      }

      // Create a StringTokenizer that recognizes "-" and "," as
      // delimiters
      st = new StringTokenizer(s," -,\t\n\r\f");
      System.out.print("\nWith - and ,: ");
      System.out.println("the " + st.countTokens() + " tokens are:");
      while (st.hasMoreTokens()) {
            System.out.println(st.nextToken());
      }
   }
}
```

Figure 8.5. A program illustrating the use of the StringTokenizer class.

When this program is executed, the results are

```
C:\book\java\chap8>java TestStringTokenizer
Default case:the 5 tokens are:
Test-case
1,
test
case
2
```

```
With - and ,: the 6 tokens are:
Test
case
1
test
case
2
```

Use the `StringTokenizer` methods to break strings up into separate tokens for further processing.

8.6   IMPROVING FILE INPUT WITH CLASS `StringTokenizer`

In Chapter 5 we learned how to read files using classes `BufferedReader` and `File-Reader`. We used the `BufferedReader` method `readLine()` to read each line into a `String`, and then converted the string into a `double` or `int` value using methods `Double.parseDouble()` or `Integer.parseInt()`.

While this approach works, it has a key limitation: there must be only *one value per line* in the input file. If there were multiple values on a line, then all of the values on the line would be included in the input string, and the string would produce a `NumberFormat-Exception` in the conversion methods.

Now that we have learned about the `StringTokenizer` class, we can use it to split up multiple values on a single line into separate tokens, and then present the tokens one at a time to the conversion methods `Double.parseDouble()` or `Integer.parseInt()`. The basic approach to reading a file and converting its contents into `double` values is:

1. Read the first line from the file using the `readLine()` method.
2. While the string returned is not `null`, create a `StringTokenizer` object to chop the line up into tokens.
3. Recover the tokens one at a time in a `while` loop, and convert them into `double` values using method `Double.parseDouble()`.
4. When the `StringTokenizer` object is empty, read another line using the `readLine()` method.
5. Repeat Steps 2–4 as long as the returned string is not `null`.

Figure 8.6 shows a class illustrating this algorithm, with the steps outlined above shown in boldface.

```
/*
   Purpose:
     This class reads double values into an array from
     an input file, where there can be any number of
     values on each line.
```

Figure 8.6.   A program allowing the user to read `double` values from an input file, where there can be any number of values on each line.

```
      Record of revisions:
           Date          Programmer           Description of change
           ====          ==========           =====================
       05/11/2002    S. J. Chapman           Original code
*/
import java.io.*;
import java.util.*;
public class TestFileReader1 {

   // Define the main method
   public static void main(String arg[]) throws IOException {

      // Declare variables and arrays
      double a[] = new double[100];        // Input array
      int i = 0;                           // Loop index
      int nvals = 0;                       // Index
      String str1;                         // Input string
      String str2;                         // Current token
      StringTokenizer st;                  // StringTokenizer

      // Create a buffered reader
      BufferedReader in1 = new BufferedReader(
                           new FileReader("infile"));

      // Read the first line
      str1 = in1.readLine();

      // Loop
      while ( str1 != null ) {

         // Create a StringTokenizer to chop up the line
         st = new StringTokenizer( str1 );

         // Get the items from the line one at a time,
         // and convert them to double
         while (st.hasMoreTokens()) {
            str2 = st.nextToken();
            a[nvals++] = Double.parseDouble(str2);
         }

         // Get the next line
         str1 = in1.readLine();
      }

      // We have finished reading, so close the file
      in1.close();

      // Display results
      for ( i = 0; i < nvals; i++ ) {
         System.out.println("a[" + i + "] = " + a[i]);
      }
   }
}
```

Figure 8.6.   (Continued).

To test this program, we will create a file `infile` containing the following data:

```
1.0     -3
-6
3.14159 0 -7.1
0
```

Note that this file has differing numbers of values on different lines. When this program is executed, the results are:

```
D:\book\java\chap8>java TestFileReader1
a[0] = 1.0
a[1] = -3.0
a[2] = -6.0
a[3] = 3.14159
a[4] = 0.0
a[5] = -7.1
a[6] = 0.0
```

As you can see, the program read the input file successfully.

In Chapter 10 we will improve our file reading ability even further. We will learn how to recover from blank lines in the input file, and also how keep a Java program from crashing if it detects bad data in the input file.

GOOD PROGRAMMING PRACTICE

Use class `StringTokenizer` together with classes `BufferedReader` and `FileReader` to allow multiple values to be read from a single line in a disk file.

8.7   STRING ARRAYS AND COMMAND-LINE ARGUMENTS

In Chapter 5 we learned how to use arrays of primitive data types, such as `int` or `double`. It is also possible to create arrays of objects, such as `Strings`. We will now learn how to create an array of `Strings`, but what we learn will also apply to any type of object.

8.7.1   Creating and Using String Arrays

A `String` array is actually *an array of* `String` *references*, each of which can refer to a separate string (see Figure 8.7). A *reference* to a `String` array is declared as follows:

```
String[] s_arr;
```

As in the arrays we studied in Chapter 5, the brackets in the array declaration distinguish a reference to a `String` array from a reference to a `String` itself. A `String` array itself is declared as follows:

```
s_arr = new String[5];
```

This statement creates *an array of five* `String` *references*, which are initially null, since they do not yet refer to actual strings (see Figure 8.8).

Note that the expression `new String[5]` is different from the constructor `new String("abc")`, which we have seen earlier in the chapter. The first expression creates a `String` array, which is an array of references to `String` objects, while the second expression creates an actual `String` object.

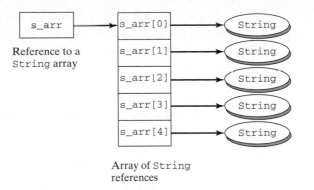

Figure 8.7. A String array is an array of String references, each of which in turn can refer to a String object.

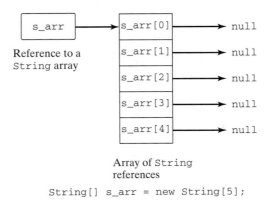

```
String[] s_arr = new String[5];
```

Figure 8.8. When the statement "String[] s_arr = new String[5];" is executed, it creates the reference s_arr, the five-element array of string references s_arr[0], s_arr[1], and so on. Note that these references are initially null.

```
String s_arr = new String[5];
         = new String("My Name");
```

Once a String array has been created, each element of the array can be used exactly like any other String reference anywhere in the program. Example 8.2 will illustrate the use of String arrays and array elements.

8.7.2 Command-Line Arguments

We have unwittingly been using a String array in every one of our programs since the very first HelloWorld application in Chapter 1. In each program, we have defined the main method of a program with the sequence

```
public static void main(String[] args) {
```

Along the way, we have learned the meanings of most of this definition. The keyword public means that the method is visible anywhere in the Java program. The keyword static means that the method can be called directly without first instantiating an object of its class. The keyword void means that the method does not return a value to its caller, and main is the name of the method. So what about the String array args? We have never mentioned it.

String array args is an array containing the arguments typed on the command line after the name of the class to be executed. These arguments are copied into an array of Strings and made available for the program to use. **Command-line arguments** are a convenient way to pass parameters such as file names, options, and so on, to a program as it begins executing. For example, it is possible to pass a file name on the command line and then open the file in the program. We shall see this usage in Example 8.2 below.

A program illustrating the use of command-line arguments is shown in Figure 8.9. This program displays the command-line arguments one at a time using a `for` loop.

```
/*
   Purpose:
     This class tests command-line arguments.

   Record of revisions:
       Date          Programmer           Description of change
       ====          ==========           =====================
    05/11/2002    S. J. Chapman           Original code
*/
public class TestArgs {

   // Define the main method
   public static void main(String[] args) {

      // List arguments
      System.out.println("There are " + args.length
                      + " command-line arguments.");
      System.out.println("The command-line arguments are:");
      for ( int i = 0; i < args.length; i++ )
         System.out.println( args[i] );
   }
}
```

Figure 8.9.   A program illustrating the use of command-line arguments.

When this program is executed, the command-line arguments are broken up into tokens and stored as separate strings in array args. For example,

```
C:\book\java\chap8>java TestArgs Hello! 1 3.14159 "1 2 3"
There are 4 command-line arguments.
The command-line arguments are:
Hello!
1
3.14159
1 2 3
```

Note that all characters within double quotes on the command line are treated as a single string.

GOOD PROGRAMMING PRACTICE

Parameter args in the main method of a program is an array of Strings containing information from the command line that is passed to the program at startup. It can include information such as file names, options, and so forth.

This quiz provides a quick check to see if you have understood the concepts introduced in Sections 8.1 through 8.7. If you have trouble with the quiz, reread the section, ask your instructor, or discuss the material with a fellow student. The answers are found in the back of the book.

1.   What is the difference between a `String` and a `StringBuffer`? When would you want to use a `StringBuffer`?

Determine which of the following Java statements are valid. For each valid statement, specify what will happen in the program. For invalid statements, explain why they are invalid.

2.
```
String s1 = new String("abcdefg");
String s2 = s1.substring(1,8);
```

3.
```
String s1, s2, s3;
s1 = new String("abcdefg");
s2 = new String("123");
s3 = s1.substring(1,3);
s3 = s3.concat(s2);
System.out.println(s3);
```

4.
```
StringBuffer s1, s2, s3;
s1 = new StringBuffer("abcdefg");
s2 = new StringBuffer("123");
s3 = s1.substring(1,3);
s3 = s3.concat(s2);
System.out.println(s3);
```

5.
```
String s1 = new String("Hello");
String s2 = new String("hello");
System.out.println(s1.equals(s2));
System.out.println(s1.equalsIgnoreCase(s2));
```

6.
```
String s1 = new String("Hello");
String s2 = new String("Hello");
System.out.println(s1 == s2);
```

7.   Write the Java code to locate the index of every s in the string `"Sassafras"`, first considering case and then ignoring case.

8.   What is the difference between the length and the capacity of a `StringBuffer`?

9.   What are command-line arguments? How are they accessed?

EXAMPLE 8.2

Alphabetizing Lists of Strings: It is very common to alphabetize lists of names, index entries, and so forth. Create a `SortString` class containing a method `sort` that will sort a collection of `String`s into either ascending or descending alphabetical order, *disregarding case*. Use the selection-sort algorithm that we introduced in Chapter 5 as the basis of the `sort` method. Include an instance variable in the `SortString` class to specify whether the sorting is to be in ascending or descending order.

Also, create a `TestSortString` class containing a `main` method that reads the strings to be sorted from an input file. The name of the input file should be supplied as a command-line argument to the program. In addition, the `main` method should support a command-line switch "-r" to force the sort to be in the reverse direction.

SOLUTION

To solve this problem, we need to create an array of strings to contain the data read from disk, and then actually read the data into the array. Then, the strings in that array must be sorted alphabetically in either ascending or descending order, disregarding case. Unfortunately, Java does not have a string `compareToIgnoreCase` method, so we must perform a case-insensitive comparison in some other way. One approach is to convert both strings to upper case before the comparison, so that the `compareTo` method will provide a result in alphabetical order.

1. **Determine the User Requirements**

In this example, the user wants to have a class that will sort an array of `Strings` into either ascending or descending alphabetical order, disregarding case. We will call the class `SortString` and will use the selection-sort algorithm from Chapter 5 as the basis of the `sort` method. This class must also have a flag to indicate whether it sorts in ascending or descending alphabetical order, and the user has specified that the flag should be an instance variable.

We must also create a class `TestSortString` to test `SortString`. This class must read a set of strings from an input file and store them in a `String` array. It should pass the array to the sort method for alphabetizing and then print out the sorted array. The input file read by class `TestSortString` will be specified as a command-line argument. The class should also support a command-line switch "`-r`" to force the sort to be in the reverse direction.

2. **Analysis and Decomposition**

The inputs to the `main` method in class `TestSortString` will be an input file name plus possibly the "`-r`" switch on the command line. If the "`-r`" switch is specified, it should *precede* the file name according to the Unix convention. The other inputs to the method are a series of strings in the input file specified on the command line, organized one string per line. The output from the `main` method will be the sorted list of strings sent to the standard output stream.

The input to the `sort` method in the `SortString` class will be a `String` array containing the strings to be sorted. The output from the `sort` method will be a reference to the sorted array.

This program will require classes `SortString` and `TestSortString`. Since Class `SortString` can be used to sort data in either forward or reverse order, we will need to create two constructors for the class. The default constructor will not include a sort-order flag, and it will automatically create an object that sorts alphabetically in ascending order. The second constructor will include a `boolean` flag to specify the sort order. If the `boolean` value is true, it will create an object that sorts alphabetically in *descending* order. If the `boolean` value is false, it will create an object that sorts alphabetically in *ascending* order like the default constructor.

The class must also contain method `sort` to do the actual sorting, and a method `comp` to compare two strings in a case-independent manner, taking into account the desired sorting direction.

Class `TestSortString` will contain a single `main` method to read the input strings and store them into a `String` array, create a `SortString` object, sort the strings into the specified order, and write them to the standard output stream.

3. **Detailed Design**

Class `SortString` is the heart of this problem. The pseudocode for the selection-sort algorithm used by method `sort` is the same as that presented in

Chapter 5, and it will not be repeated here. The only change is that the > relational operators will be replaced by a call to method `comp`.

Method `comp` should be private, since it will be called only from within its own class. It must accept two `Strings` s1 and s2 as input parameters. The selection sort attempts to identify the smallest items first and place them at the top of the list. Thus, if the sort order is *ascending*, the method must return a true value if s1 is lexicographically *less than* s2, disregarding case, and false otherwise. If the sort order is *descending*, the method must return a true value if s1 is lexicographically *greater than* s2, disregarding case, and false otherwise. The pseudocode for this method is:

```
if ( !reverse ) {
   // Normal sort order
   if ( (s1.toUpperCase()).compareTo (s2.toUpperCase()) < 0 )
      return true;
   else
      return false;
}
else {
   // Reverse sort order
   if ( (s1.toUpperCase()).compareTo (s2.toUpperCase()) > 0 )
      return true;
   else
      return false;
}
```

The `main` method of the `TestSortString` class must read the arguments, open the input file, create a `String` array, and add each string to the array as it is read. The strings must be read from the input file, and we will not know in advance how many strings there are.

Then the method must create a `SortString` object with the proper sorting direction, and pass the array to it for sorting. Finally, it must print out the sorted strings. The pseudocode for these steps is:

```
(Read file name and open file)

// Create a buffered reader
BufferedReader in = new BufferedReader(
                        new FileReader(fileName));

// Read the data
str = in.readLine();
while ( str != null ) {
   a[nvals++] = str;
   str = in1.readLine();
}

// Close file
in.close();

Create SortString object
Call sort method
Print out sorted strings
```

Before creating a SortString object, main must check to see if there is an "-r" command-line option. The pseudocode for this step is:

```
reverse = false;
if any arguments are present {
    if ( args[0].equals("-r") ) {
        reverse = true;
    }
}
```

4. **Implementation: Convert Algorithms to Java Statements**

Class SortString is shown in Figure 8.10. Note that the comparison operations in the selection-sort method that we studied in Chapter 5 have been replaced by calls to the comp method.

Class TestSortString is shown in Figure 8.11.

```
/*
   Purpose:
     This class sorts a list of strings into ascending
     or descending lexicographic order, depending on
     the value of the reverse instance variable.

   Record of revisions:
      Date          Programmer         Description of change
      ====          ==========         =====================
    05/13/2002    S. J. Chapman        Original code
*/
public class SortString {

   // Define instance variables
   private boolean reverse;    // Reverse order flag

   // Constructors
   public SortString() {
      reverse = false;
   }

   public SortString( boolean reverse ) {
      this.reverse = reverse;
   }
   // comp method.  This method compares two Strings.
   // Note that it converts the strings to uppercase
   // before performing the comparison.
   private boolean comp( String s1, String s2 ) {

      if ( !reverse ) {

         // Normal sort order
         if ( (s1.toUpperCase()).compareTo(s2.toUpperCase()) < 0 )
            return true;
         else
            return false;
      }
```

Figure 8.10. Class SortString.

```
        else {

            // Reverse sort order
            if ( (s1.toUpperCase()).compareTo(s2.toUpperCase()) > 0 )
                return true;
            else
                return false;
        }
    }

    // Define the sort method.  This method sorts the
    // elements of array a.  Here, nvals is the number
    // of Strings in the list.
    public void sort( String[] a, int nvals ) {

        // Declare variables, and define each variable
        int i, j;                   // Loop index
        int iptr;                   // Pointer to smallest value
        String temp;                // Temporary String ref for swapping

        // Sort values
        for ( i = 0; i <= nvals-2; i++ ) {
            // Find the minimum value in a(i) through a(nvals-1)
            iptr = i;
            for ( j = i+1; j <= nvals-1; j++ ) {
                if ( comp(a[j], a[iptr]) )
                    iptr = j;
            }

            // iptr now points to the min value, so swap a(iptr) with
            // a(i) if iptr != i.
            if (i != iptr) {
                temp = a[i];
                a[i] = a[iptr];
                a[iptr] = temp;
            }
        }
    }
}
```

Figure 8.10. (Continued).

```
/*
   Purpose:
      This class reads a collection of strings from
      an input file and stores them in an array.  The input
      file name is specified as a command-line argument
      when the program is started.  It passes the array
      to the sort method of the SortString class to sort
      the strings into ascending or descending lexicographical
```

Figure 8.11. Class TestSortString.

```
        order. Note that this class looks for a command-line
        switch to specify the sorting order. If the "-r" switch
        is present, it must precede the file name.

    Record of revisions:
        Date            Programmer              Description of change
        ====            ==========              =====================
     05/13/2002     S. J. Chapman               Original code
*/
import java.io.*;
public class TestSortString {

    // Define the main method
    public static void main(String[] args) throws IOException {

        // Declare constants
        final int MAX_SIZE = 100;   // Array size

        // Define variables
        String[] a = new String[MAX_SIZE];
                                    // Input array
        String fileName;           // Input file name
        int i;                     // Loop index
        int nvals = 0;             // Number of Strings in file
        boolean reverse;           // Reverse sort switch
        String str;                // Input string

        // Get command-line arguments.  Note that
        // there may be one or two arguments.
        reverse = false;
        if ( args.length == 1 ) {
            fileName = args[0];
        }
        else if ( args.length == 2 ) {
            if ( args[0].equals("-r") ) {
                reverse = true;
            }
            fileName = args[1];
        }
        else {
            System.out.println
                ("Usage: java TestSortString -r fileName");
            return;
        }

        // Create a buffered reader
        BufferedReader in = new BufferedReader(
                            new FileReader(fileName));
```

Figure 8.11. (Continued).

```
     // Read the data
     str = in.readLine();
     while ( str != null ) {
        a[nvals++] = str;
        str = in.readLine();
     }

     // Close file
     in.close();

     // Create the SortString object.
     SortString ss = new SortString ( reverse );

     // Sort the strings
     ss.sort( a, nvals );

     // Print out the resulting strings
     System.out.println("\nThe sorted output is:");
     for ( i = 0; i < nvals; i++ ) {
        System.out.println( a[i] );
     }
   }
}
```

Figure 8.11. (Continued).

5. **Testing**

   To test this program, we will create an input data file containing a series of names. The following information will be placed in a file called `input`:

   ```
   deBrincat, Charles
   Chapman, Stephen
   Johnson, James
   Chapman, Rosa
   Anderson, William
   Johnston, Susan
   Johns, Joe
   ```

   When this program is executed *without* the "`-r`" command-line option, the results are

   ```
   D:\book\java\chap8>java TestSortString input

   The sorted output is:
   Anderson, William
   Chapman, Rosa
   Chapman, Stephen
   deBrincat, Charles
   Johns, Joe
   Johnson, James
   Johnston, Susan
   ```

When this program is executed *with* the "-r" command-line option, the results are

```
D:\book\java\chap8>java TestSortString -r input

The sorted output is:
Johnston, Susan
Johnson, James
Johns, Joe
deBrincat, Charles
Chapman, Stephen
Chapman, Rosa
Anderson, William
```

When this program is executed without command-line parameters, the results are a usage prompt:

```
D:\book\java\chap8>java TestSortString -r input
Usage: java TestSortString -r fileName
```

The program appears to be functioning correctly. Note that "deBrincat" appears in proper order, even though it begins with a lowercase "d". This indicates that we are indeed sorting the strings properly, disregarding case. ∎

SUMMARY

- Strings are objects containing groups of one or more characters. Once they are created, objects of type `String` never change.
- `String` method `length()` returns the number of characters in a `String`.
- `String` method `s1.concat(s2)` returns a new `String` that is the concatenation of strings `s1` and `s2`.
- `String` method `s1.equals(s2)` returns true if the contents of strings `s1` and `s2` are identical.
- `String` method `s1.equalsIgnoreCase(s2)` returns true if the contents of strings `s1` and `s2` are identical, ignoring case.
- The operator `s1 == s2` returns true if references `s1` and `s2` point to *identically the same object* in memory.
- `String` method `s1.compareTo(s2)` returns 0 if `s1` and `s2` are equal, a negative number if `s1` is lexicographically less than `s2`, and a negative number if `s1` is lexicographically greater than `s2`.
- Other common `String` methods are summarized in Table 8.1.
- `StringBuffer` method `length` returns the number of characters currently stored in `StringBuffer`. Method `capacity` returns the number of characters that can be stored in `StringBuffer` without allocating more memory.
- `StringBuffer` method `append` appends the character description of a primitive data type, `String`, or `Object` to the end of a `StringBuffer`.
- `StringBuffer` method `insert` inserts the character description of a primitive data type, `String`, or `Object` at a specified point in a `StringBuffer`.
- Other common `StringBuffer` methods are summarized in Table 8.2.

- Class `StringTokenizer` can be used to chop a character string up into separate blocks called tokens. The delimiters used to separate the tokens can be specified when the `StringTokenizer` is created.
- The `String[]` array `args` in the `main` method can be used to pass command-line arguments to a Java program.

SUMMARY OF GOOD PROGRAMMING PRACTICES

The following guidelines introduced in this chapter will help you to develop good programs:

1. Use the `StringBuffer` insert/append methods instead of the `String` `concat` method for combining strings. The `StringBuffer` methods are much more efficient, and they produce fewer "waste" objects for garbage collection.

2. Use the `StringTokenizer` methods to break strings up into separate tokens for further processing.

3. Use class `StringTokenizer` together with classes `BufferedReader` and `FileReader` to allow multiple values to be read from single line in a disk file.

4. Parameter `args` in the `main` method of a program is an array of `Strings` containing information from the command line that is passed to the program at startup. It can include information such as file names, options, and so forth.

TERMINOLOGY

anonymous `String` object
command-line arguments
concatenate
delimiter
lexicographic sequence
`String` class
`String` literal

`StringBuffer` capacity
`StringBuffer` class
`StringBuffer` length
`StringTokenizer` class
substring
token

Exercises

1. Assume that `s1` and `s2` are `Strings`, and that

        String s = "abcdefghijABCDEFGHIJabcdefghij";

What will be the contents of `s1` and `s2` after the following statements are executed?

a. `s1 = s.substring(10);`
   `s2 = s.substring(10,12);`

b. `s1 = s.substring(1,3);`
   `s2 = s.substring(7,9);`
   `s1 = s1.concat(s2);`

2. Assume the definitions

    ```
    String s1 = "Test1";
    String s2 = "test1";
    String s3 = "Test1";
    String s4 = "Test2";
    String s5 = s1;
    ```

    What will be the results of the following expressions?

    a. `s1.equals(s2);`
    b. `s1.equals(s3);`
    c. `s1.equalsIgnoreCase(s2);`
    d. `s1 == s3;`
    e. `s1 == s5;`
    f. `s1.compareTo(s2);`
    g. `s1.compareTo(s4);`
    h. `s1.regionMatches(1, s2, 1, 3);`
    i. `s1.regionMatches(true, 1, s2, 1, 3);`
    j. `s1.startsWith("Te");`
    k. `s4.endsWith("1");`

3. Assume the definition

    ```
    String s1 = " The first string ";
    ```

    What will be the results of the following expressions?

    a. `s1.indexOf("st");`
    b. `s1.indexOf("st",14);`
    c. `s1.lastIndexOf("st");`
    d. `s1.indexOf('i');`
    e. `s1.replace('s','S');`
    f. `s1.toUpperCase();`
    g. `s1.trim();`

4. Assume the definitions

    ```
    StringBuffer b1 = new StringBuffer("1234567890");
    String s1;
    ```

    What will be the results of the following expressions?

    a. `s1 = new String( b1.append('X') );`
    b. `s1 = new String( b1.insert('X',3) );`

5. Modify the class `TestSortString` of Example 8.2 to check for illegal command-line arguments. If any command-line argument other than "`-r`" or the file name is found, or if the "`-r`" argument is out of order, the program should display the illegal argument(s), provide a list of legal arguments, and shut down.

6. Write a method `caps` that searches for all of the words within a `String` and capitalizes the first letter of each word, while shifting the remainder of the word

to lower case. Use `StringTokenizer` to identify each word, modifying the delimiter list to include punctuation (periods, commas, question marks, and exclamation marks) as well as the default delimiters. Then use `indexOf` to locate the position of that word in the string and replace it by its capitalized equivalent.

7.   **Input Parameter File** A common feature of large programs is an *input parameter file*, in which the user can specify certain values to be used during the execution of the program. In most programs, default values are defined for the input parameters in the file, and *only the input parameters whose defaults need to be modified will be included in the input file*. Furthermore, the values that do appear in the input file may occur in any order. Each parameter in the input file is recognized by a corresponding *keyword* indicating what that parameter is for.

For example, a numerical integration program might include default values for the starting time of the integration, the ending time of the integration, the step size to use, and whether or not to plot the output. These default values could be overridden by lines in the input file. An input parameter file for this program might contain the following items:

```
start = 0.0
stop = 10.0
dt = 0.2
plot off
```

These values could be listed in any order, and some of them could be omitted if the default values were acceptable. In addition, the keywords might appear in upper case, lower case, or mixed case. The program will read this input file a line at a time and update the variables specified by the keyword with the value on the line.

Write a class `TestFile` that tests reading an input parameter file. The class should include the following `private` instance variables, with the defaults as given:

```
private double start = 0.0;
private double stop  = 1.0;
private double dt = 0.1;
private boolean plot = false;
```

The class should also include a `main` method that reads the name of the input parameter file from the command line. It should read the file and call a separate method to interpret each line, displaying the updated parameter values. The separate method should accept a `String` containing a line from the input parameter file, determine the keyword on the line (regardless of case), and update the appropriate private instance variable. It should throw an exception if an unrecognized keyword is found.

Test your program using a variety of input files, containing keywords in various orders, in differing cases, and with invalid keywords added.

8.   **Filters** Filters are programs that read input data from the standard input stream, process it in some fashion, and write it out to the standard output stream. Effectively, they "filter" the input data stream in some specified manner. Write a Java filter that reads lines of data as `Strings` from the input stream, looks for and removes repeated words (tokens) from the lines, and writes the lines out to the standard output stream. The program can use `StringTokenizer` to identify

successive tokens. (Be sure to modify the `StringTokenizer` delimiter list so that it recognizes punctuation marks as a delimiter.) Test your filter on the following data:

```
Paris in the the Spring.
same same, Same same
123 123, 123 456
```

9. **Word Count** Write a program that reads input data from the standard input stream and counts the number of words in the data set. Write the number of words to the standard output device. For these purposes, a word is defined as a set of characters separated by white space. (*Hint:* Use class `StringToke-nizer`.)

10. Write a program that accepts a `String` containing an international telephone number of the form +1−555−555−5555, where the digits before the first dash are the country code, the digits between the first and second dashes are the city code (or area code), and the digits after the second dash are the phone number. Parse the string and print the country code, city code, and phone number separately with appropriate labels. (Note that country codes can have from one to three digits, and that international phone numbers can have from five to eight digits and may or may not have a dash in the middle of the number, so you can't design your program to work with a fixed number of digits.) Test your program with the following phone numbers:

a. +1−800−555−1212

b. +61−3−9527−9527

c. +44−1289−555555

9

Inheritance, Polymorphism, and Interfaces

This chapter explains how inheritance allows Java to treat objects from different subclasses as a single unit by referring to them as objects of their common superclass. It also explains how, when working with a collection of superclass objects, Java is able to automatically apply the proper methods to each object, regardless of the subclass the object came from. This ability is known as **polymorphism**. Finally, it introduces **interfaces** and shows how they reduce duplication in programming effort.

9.1   SUPERCLASSES AND SUBCLASSES

All classes form a part of a class hierarchy. Every class except `Object` is a subclass of some other class, and the class inherits both instance variables and methods from its parent class. The class can add additional instance variables and methods and can also override the behavior of methods inherited from its parent class.

Any class above a specific class in the class hierarchy is known as a *superclass* of that class. The class just above a specific class in the hierarchy is known as the *immediate superclass* of the class. Any class below a specific class in the class hierarchy is known as a *subclass* of that class.

Inheritance is a major advantage of object-oriented programming; once a behavior (method) is defined in a superclass, that behavior is automatically inherited by all subclasses, unless it is explicitly overridden with a modified method. Thus, behaviors need to be coded only *once*, and they can be used by all subclasses. A subclass need only provide methods to implement the *differences* between itself and its parent.

OBJECTIVES

- Understand the concepts of inheritance, superclasses, and subclasses
- Understand polymorphism, and be able to create polymorphic behavior
- Be able to create and use abstract classes
- Be able to create `final` methods and classes, and explain why we would wish to use them
- Be able to use the type-wrapper classes to manipulate primitive data types as objects
- Be able to create and use interfaces
- Understand and be able to use classes that implement the `Collection` and `Iterator` interfaces

9.2 DEFINING SUPERCLASSES AND SUBCLASSES

For example, suppose that we were to create a class `Employee`, describing the characteristics of the employees of a company. This class would contain the name, social security number, address, and so on of the employee, together with pay information. However, most companies have two different types of employees, those on a salary and those paid by the hour. Therefore, we could create two subclasses of `Employee`, `SalariedEmployee` and `HourlyEmployee`, with different methods for calculating monthly pay. Both of these subclasses would inherit all of the common information and methods from `Employee` (name, and so forth) but would override the method used to calculate pay. (See Figure 9.1.)

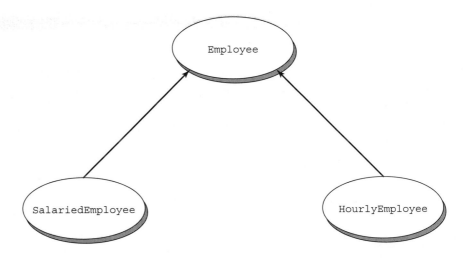

Figure 9.1. A simple inheritance hierarchy. Both `SalariedEmployee` and `HourlyEmployee` inherit from `Employee`, and an object of either of their classes is also an object of the `Employee` class.

Objects of either the `SalariedEmployee` *or* `HourlyEmployee` *classes may be treated as objects of the* `Employee` *class*, and so forth for any additional classes up the inheritance hierarchy. This fact is very important, since objects of the two subclasses can be grouped together and treated as a *single* collection of objects of the superclass `Employee`.

For all practical purposes, any object of class `SalariedEmployee` or `HourlyEmployee` *is* an object of class `Employee`. In object-oriented programming terms, we say that these classes have an "isa" relationship with `Employee`, because an object of either class "is an" object of class `Employee`.

The Java code for the `Employee` class is shown in Figure 9.2. This class includes four instance variables: `firstName`, `lastName`, `ssn`, and `pay`. Notice that these instance variables are declared to have **protected access**, meaning that they can be accessed by the methods of this class and also the methods of any subclass of this class. The class also defines two constructors and seven methods to manipulate the instance variables of the class.

The method `calcPay` in this class returns a zero instead of calculating a valid pay, since the method of calculating the pay will depend on the type of employee, and we don't have that information yet in this class.

```
1    /*
2       Purpose:
3         This class defines an employee record.  It defines
4         basic employee information (first name, last name,
5         and social security number) and provides two
6         constructors and the following methods:
7             setName
8             setSsn
9             getFirstName
10            getLastName
11            getSsn
12            toString
13            calcPay
14
15      Record of revisions:
16          Date           Programmer           Description of change
17          ====           ==========           =====================
18       05/14/2002    S. J. Chapman           Original code
19    */
20
21   public class Employee {
22
23      // Define instance variables
24      protected String firstName;       // First name
25      protected String lastName;        // Last name
26      protected String ssn;             // Social security number
27      protected double pay;             // Monthly pay
28
29      // Constructors
30      public Employee() {
31         firstName = " ";
32         lastName = " ";
33         ssn = "000-00-0000";
34         pay = 0;
35      }
36
37      public Employee(String first, String last, String ssn) {
38         firstName = first;
39         lastName = last;
40         this.ssn = ssn;
41         pay = 0;
42      }
43
44      // Set name
45    public void setName( String first, String last ) {
46         firstName = first;
47         lastName = last;
48      }
49
```

Figure 9.2. The Employee class.

```
50       // Set social security number
51       public void setSsn( String ssn ) {
52           this.ssn = ssn;
53       }
54
55       // Get first name
56       public String getFirstName() {
57           return firstName;
58       }
59
60       // Get last name
61       public String getLastName() {
62           return lastName;
63       }
64
65       // Get social security number
66       public String getSsn() {
67           return ssn;
68       }
69
70       // Convert to string (this method will be
71       // overridden by different subclasses)
72       public String toString() {
73           String s = lastName + ", " + firstName + "    ("
74                   + ssn + ") ";
75           return s;
76       }
77
78       // Method to calculate pay (this method will
79       // be overridden by different subclasses)
80       public double calcPay( double hours ) {
81           pay = 0;
82           return pay;
83       }
84   }
```

Figure 9.2.   (Continued).

The Java code for the SalariedEmployee subclass is shown in Figure 9.3. This class *inherits* the four instance variables, firstName, lastName, ssn, and pay, and adds an additional instance variable salary. Notice that instance variable salary is declared to have private access, because it will not need to be accessed by any subclasses. It also defines a new method setSalary and overrides the methods toString and calcPay from the superclass.

A class is declared as a subclass of another class by including an extends clause in the class definition. In this case, class SalariedEmployee is a subclass of class Employee because of the "extends Employee" clause on Line 13. Therefore, this class inherits all of the nonprivate instance variables and methods from class Employee.

Class SalariedEmployee defines two constructors to build objects of this class. When an object of a subclass is instantiated, *a constructor for its superclass is*

```
1   /*
2      Purpose:
3        This class defines a salaried employee record.
4        It overrides toString and calcPay from class
5        Employee.
6
7      Record of revisions:
8          Date          Programmer           Description of change
9          ====          ==========           =====================
10       05/14/2002    S. J. Chapman         Original code
11  */
12  import java.text.*;
13  public class SalariedEmployee extends Employee {
14
15      // Define instance variables
16      private double salary;            // Monthly salary
17
18      // Constructors
19      public SalariedEmployee() {
20          salary = 0;                 // Implicit call to Employee()
21      }
22
23      public SalariedEmployee( String first, String last,
24                               String ssn, double salary) {
25          // Explicit call to Employee(first, last, ssn)
26          super(first, last, ssn);
27          this.salary = salary;
28          pay = this.salary;
29      }
30
31      // Method setSalary
32      public void setSalary( double salary ) {
33          this.salary = salary;
34          pay = this.salary;
35      }
36
37      // Convert to string
38      public String toString() {
39          DecimalFormat df = new DecimalFormat("$###,###.00")
40          String s = lastName + ", " + firstName + "    ("
41                   + ssn + "): Salary = $"
42                   + df.format(salary);
43          return s;
44      }
```

Figure 9.3. The SalariedEmployee class.

```
45
46      // Method to calculate pay
47      public double calcPay( double hours ) {
48          pay = salary;
49          return pay;
50      }
51  }
```

Figure 9.3. (Continued).

called either implicitly or explicitly before any other initialization is performed. In the constructor on line 19 of class `SalariedEmployee`, the superclass constructor is called implicitly to initialize `firstName`, `lastName`, `ssn`, and `pay` to their default values. (Any implicit call to a superclass constructor is always to the **default constructor**, the one with no input parameters.) In the constructor on line 23 of class `SalariedEmployee`, the superclass constructor is called explicitly to initialize `firstName`, `lastName`, `ssn`, and `pay` to the values provided by the user. The superclass *must* be initialized either implicitly or explicitly before any subclass initialization can occur. Thus the following statements would produce an error:

```
public SalariedEmployee( String first, String last,
                            String ssn, double salary) {
    this.salary = salary;
    pay = this.salary;
    super(first, last, ssn);  // Explicit call to Employee()
}
...
```

GOOD PROGRAMMING PRACTICE

When writing a subclass, call the superclass's constructor either implicitly or explicitly *as the first action in the subclass constructor*. Failure to do so will produce a compile-time error.

Similarly, if a subclass has a finalizer, the *last* statement of the subclass's finalizer should be a call to the superclass's finalizer, so that the superclass can perform clean-up on the resources allocated by the superclass constructor. The form of the subclass's finalize method should be

```
protected void finalize() {
    ...
    super.finalize();
}
```

GOOD PROGRAMMING PRACTICE

When writing a subclass, call the superclass's finalizer explicitly *as the last action in the subclass finalizer*. Failure to do so may result in resources such as files, network sockets, and so on not being released properly.

The Java code for the `HourlyEmployee` subclass is shown in Figure 9.4. This class *inherits* the four instance variables, `firstName`, `lastName`, `ssn`, and `pay`, and adds an additional instance variable `rate`. Notice that instance variable `rate` is declared to have `private` access, because it will not need to be accessed by any subclasses. It also defines a new method `setRate` and overrides the methods `toString` and `calcPay` from the superclass.

```
1   /*
2      Purpose:
3        This class defines an hourly employee record.
4        It overrides toString and calcPay from class
5        Employee.
6
7      Record of revisions:
8          Date        Programmer          Description of change
9          ====        ==========          =====================
10       05/14/2002   S. J. Chapman        Original code
11   */
12   import java.text.*;
13   public class HourlyEmployee extends Employee {
14
15      // Define instance variables
16      private double rate;          // Hourly rate
17
18      // Constructors
19      public HourlyEmployee() {
20         rate = 0;              // Implicit call to Employee()
21         pay = 0;
22      }
23
24      public HourlyEmployee( String first, String last,
25                             String ssn, double rate) {
26         // Explicit call to Employee(first, last, ssn)
27         super(first, last, ssn);
28         this.rate = rate;
29         pay = 0;
30      }
31
32      // Method setRate
33      public void setRate( double rate ) {
34         this.rate = rate;
35      }
36
37      // Convert to string
38      public String toString() {
39         DecimalFormat df = new DecimalFormat("$###,###.00")
40         String s = lastName + ", " + firstName + "    ("
```

Figure 9.4. The `HourlyEmployee` class.

```
41                    + ssn + "): Monthly Pay = $"
42                    + df.format(pay);
43          return s;
44      }
45
46      // Method to calculate pay
47      public double calcPay( double hours ) {
48          pay = hours * rate;
49          return pay;
50      }
51  }
```

Figure 9.4. (Continued).

Class `HourlyEmployee` defines two constructors to build objects of this class and also overrides methods `toString` and `calcPay` to provide appropriate implementations for this subclass.

9.3 THE RELATIONSHIP BETWEEN SUPERCLASS OBJECTS AND SUBCLASS OBJECTS

An object of a subclass inherits all of the nonprivate instance variables and methods of its superclass. In fact, *an object of any subclass may be treated as ("is") an object of its superclass*. This fact implies that we can manipulate objects with either subclass references or superclass references. Figure 9.5 illustrates this point.

```
1   /*
2      Purpose:
3        This class tests access to an objects of class
4        SalariedEmployee and HourlyEmployee using both
5        references to the subclasses and references to
6        the superclass Employee.
7
8      Record of revisions:
9         Date          Programmer           Description of change
10        ====          ==========           =====================
11      05/14/2002    S. J. Chapman          Original code
12   */
13
14  public class TestEmployee {
15
16      // Define the main method to test class Employee
17      public static void main(String[] args) {
18
19          // Create a SalariedEmployee object
20          SalariedEmployee s1 = new SalariedEmployee(
21                  "John","Jones","111-11-1111",3000);
```

Figure 9.5. A program that illustrates the manipulation of objects with superclass references.

```
22
23       // Create an HourlyEmployee object
24       HourlyEmployee h1 = new HourlyEmployee(
25               "Jane","Jones","222-22-2222",12.50);
26
27       // Create an array of Employee objects
28       Employee[] e = new Employee[2];
29       e[0] = s1;
30       e[1] = h1;
31
32       // Calculate pay using subclass references
33       System.out.println("Calculation with subclass refs:");
34       System.out.println("Pay = " + s1.calcPay(160));
35       System.out.println("Pay = " + h1.calcPay(160));
36
37       // Calculate pay using superclass references
38       System.out.println("\nCalculation with superclass refs:");
39       for ( int i = 0; i < e.length; i++ )
40           System.out.println("Pay = " + e[i].calcPay(160));
41
42       // List employee info with superclass refs
43       System.out.println("\nEmployee information:");
44       for ( int i = 0; i < e.length; i++ )
45           System.out.println("Info: " + e[i].toString());
46
47       }
48   }
```

Figure 9.5. (Continued).

This test program creates one `SalariedEmployee` object and one `HourlyEmployee` object and assigns them to references of the same types. Then it creates an array of `Employee` references and assigns references to the two objects to the elements of that array. Normally, it is illegal to assign an object of one type to a reference of another type. However, it is acceptable here because *the objects of the subclasses* `SalariedEmployee` *and* `HourlyEmployee` *are also objects of the superclass* `Employee`.

Once the program assigns the references to the array, it uses both the original references and the array of `Employee` references to access some methods. When this program executes, the results are

```
D:\book\java\chap9>java TestEmployee
Calculation with subclass refs:
Pay = 3000.0
Pay = 2000.0
Calculation with superclass refs:
Pay = 3000.0
Pay = 2000.0
```

```
Employee information:
Info: Jones, John   (111-11-1111): Salary = $3000.00
Info: Jones, Jane   (222-22-2222): Monthly Pay =
   $2000.00
```

Notice that the pay calculated with the subclass references is identical to the pay calculated with the superclass references.

It is possible to freely assign an object of a subclass to a reference of a superclass type, since the object of the subclass is also an object of the superclass. However, the converse is *not* true. An object of a superclass type is *not* an object of its subclass types. Thus, if e is an Employee reference and s is a SalariedEmployee reference, then the statement

```
e = s
```

is perfectly legal, and the SalariedEmployee reference is said to be **upcast** to an Employee reference. In contrast, the statement

```
s = e
```

is illegal and will produce a compile-time error.

It is possible to explicitly **downcast** a superclass type into a subclass type, as shown below:

```
s = (SalariedEmployee) e
```

This statement is legal and will compile correctly. However, the superclass reference e must actually refer to a subclass SalariedEmployee object when the program executes, or Java will throw a **ClassCastException**.

PROGRAMMING PITFALLS

It is illegal to assign a superclass reference to a subclass reference. However, you may *cast* a superclass reference into a subclass reference, as long as the object referred to really is a member of that subclass. If it is not, Java will throw a ClassCastException at run time.

9.4 POLYMORPHISM

Let's look at the program in Figure 9.5 once more. Pay was calculated using superclass references on line 40, and string conversions were performed using superclass references on line 45. Note that the methods calcPay(160) and toString() differed for e[0] and e[1]. The object referred to by e[0] was really a SalariedEmployee, so Java used the SalariedEmployee versions of calcPay(160) and toString() to calculate the appropriate values for it. On the other hand, the object referred to by e[1] was really an HourlyEmployee, so Java used the HourlyEmployee versions of calcPay(160) and toString() to calculate the appropriate values for it. The versions of calcPay(160) and toString() defined in class Employee were never used at all.

Here, we were working with an array of Employee objects, but *this program automatically selected the proper method to apply to each given object based on the subclass that it also belonged to.* This ability to automatically vary methods depending on the subclass that an object belongs to is known as **polymorphism** (meaning "many forms").

Polymorphism is an incredibly powerful feature of object-oriented languages. It makes them very easy to change. For example, suppose that we wrote a program using arrays of Employees to work out a company payroll, and then later the company wanted to add a new type of employee, one paid by the piece. We could define a new subclass called PieceworkEmployee as a subclass of Employee, overriding the calcPay and toString methods appropriately, and create employees of this type. *The rest of the program will not have to be changed*, since the program manipulates arrays of class Employee, and polymorphism allows Java to automatically select the proper version of a method to apply whenever an object belongs to a particular subclass.

GOOD PROGRAMMING PRACTICE

Polymorphism allows multiple objects of different subclasses to be treated as objects of a single superclass, while automatically selecting the proper methods to apply to a particular object based on the subclass that it belongs to.

Note that, for polymorphism to work, the methods to be used must be *defined in the superclass and overridden in the various subclasses*. Polymorphism will *not* work if the method you want to use is defined only in the subclasses. Thus a polymorphic method call like e[1].toString() is legal, because method toString() is defined in class Employee and overridden in subclasses SalariedEmployee and HourlyEmployee. On the other hand, a method call like e[1].setRate() is illegal, because method setRate() is defined only in class HourlyEmployee, and we cannot use an Employee reference to refer to an HourlyEmployee method.

It *is* possible to access a subclass method by casting the superclass reference into a subclass reference, such as

```
((HourlyEmployee) e[1]).setRate(14);
```

However, if e[1] does not really refer to an object of this subclass, the cast will throw a ClassCastException.

GOOD PROGRAMMING PRACTICE

To create polymorphic behavior, declare all polymorphic methods in a common superclass, and then override the behavior of the methods in each subclass that inherits from the superclass.

EXAMPLE 9.1

Polymorphic Behavior: To illustrate polymorphic behavior, let's create a superclass Color and three subclasses Red, Green, and Blue. Class Color should have a single instance variable containing the strength of a particular color on a scale of 0 to 255, plus a constructor and method toString(). Classes Red, Green, and Blue should override the toString() method in the Color class. We will include println statements in each method and constructor to print out a message whenever the method or constructor is executed.

Also, create a test program that creates an array of Color objects of various types and executes the toString() method for each object in the array.

SOLUTION   Class Color is shown in Figure 9.6, and subclass Red is shown in Figure 9.7 (only subclass Red is shown, as subclasses Green and Blue are identical except for their names). Note the println statements in each constructor and method.

```
1   /*
2      Purpose:
3        This class defines the strength of a generic color.
4
5      Record of revisions:
6          Date          Programmer          Description of change
7          ====          ==========          =====================
8        05/15/2002    S. J. Chapman         Original code
9   */
10
11  public class Color {
12
13     // Define instance variables
14     protected int intensity;          // Intensity of color
15
16     // Constructors
17     public Color() {
18        System.out.println("In constructor Color():");
19        intensity = 0;
20     }
21
22     public Color(int intensity) {
23        System.out.println("In constructor Color(int intensity):");
24        this.intensity = intensity;
25     }
26
27     // Convert to string
28     public String toString() {
29        System.out.println("In Color.toString():");
30        String s = "Color: intensity = " + intensity;
31        return s;
32     }
33  }
```

Figure 9.6. Class Color.

```
1   /*
2      Purpose:
3        This class defines the color Red.
4
5      Record of revisions:
6          Date          Programmer          Description of change
7          ====          ==========          =====================
8        05/15/2002    S. J. Chapman         Original code
9   */
```

Figure 9.7. Class Red.

```
10
11   public class Red extends Color {
12
13       // Constructors
14       public Red() {
15           System.out.println("In constructor Red():");
16       }
17
18       public Red(int intensity) {
19           super(intensity);
20           System.out.println("In constructor Red(int intensity):");
21       }
22
23       // Convert to string
24       public String toString() {
25           System.out.println("In Red.toString():");
26           String s = "Red: intensity = " + intensity;
27           return s;
28       }
29   }
```

Figure 9.7.   (Continued).

The class TestColor is shown in Figure 9.8. It defines an array of Color references and creates Red, Green, and Blue objects with them. Note that two of the new
objects are created with specific intensity values, while one of them uses the default constructor. After creating the objects, the program prints out their contents in a for loop
using the toString() method.

```
1    /*
2       Purpose:
3          This class tests class Color and its subclasses.
4
5       Record of revisions:
6          Date            Programmer              Description of change
7          ====            ==========              =====================
8       05/15/2002    S. J. Chapman             Original code
9    */
10
11   public class TestColor {
12
13       public static void main(String[] args) {
14
15           // Create an array of Colors
16           Color c[] = new Color[3];
17           c[0] = new Red(120);
```

Figure 9.8.   Class TestColor.

```
18          c[1] = new Green(255);
19          c[2] = new Blue();
20
21          // Display color values
22          System.out.println("\nColor values:");
23          for ( int i = 0; i < c.length; i++ )
24              System.out.println("Color = " + c[i]);
25      }
26  }
```

Figure 9.8. (Continued).

When this program is executed, the results are

```
D:\book\java\chap9>java TestColor
In constructor Color(int intensity):
In constructor Red(int intensity):
In constructor Color(int intensity):
In constructor Green(int intensity):
In constructor Color():
In constructor Blue():

Color values:
In Red.toString():
Color = Red: intensity = 120
In Green.toString():
Color = Green: intensity = 255
In Blue.toString():
Color = Blue: intensity = 0
```

Note that when each Red, Green, and Blue object was created, the constructor for that object called the constructor for the superclass Color as its first action. Also, when the toString() method was invoked with a Color reference, the toString() method in class Color was *not* used. Instead, in the toString() method the appropriate subclass was invoked polymorphically.

9.5   ABSTRACT CLASSES

Look at the Employee class again. Note that we defined methods calcPay and toString in that class, but *neither method is ever used*. Since we only ever instantiate members of the subclasses SalariedEmployee and HourlyEmployee, these methods are *always* overridden polymorphically by the corresponding methods in the two subclasses. If these methods are never going to be used, why did we bother to write them at all? The answer is that in order for polymorphism to work, the polymorphic methods must be declared both in the parent class and in all of the subclasses.

However, the *bodies* of the polymorphic methods in the parent class will never be used if no objects are ever instantiated from that class, so Java allows us to declare the headers only without writing the body of the methods. Such methods are called **abstract methods**, and classes containing abstract methods are known as **abstract classes** (as opposed to ordinary classes, which are called **concrete classes**).

Abstract methods are declared using the abstract keyword in the method header, with no method body. For example, an abstract method calcPay would be declared as

```
public abstract double calcPay( double hours );
```

Any class containing an abstract method, or failing to override an abstract method inherited from its superclass, is an abstract class. Abstract classes must also be declared with the abstract keyword. For example, if class Employee contained any abstract methods, it would be declared as

public abstract class Employee {

An abstract version of the Employee class is shown in Figure 9.9.

```
1   /*
2      Purpose:
3        This class defines an employee record.  It defines
4        basic employee information (first name, last name,
5        and social security number) and provides two
6        constructors and the following methods:
7            setName
8            setSsn
9            getFirstName
10           getLastName
11           getSsn
12           toString
13           calcPay
14
15     Record of revisions:
16         Date         Programmer             Description of change
17         ====         ==========             =====================
18      05/16/2002   S. J. Chapman           Original code
19   */
20
21   public abstract class Employee {
22
23      // Define instance variables
24      protected String firstName;       // First name
25      protected String lastName;        // Last name
26      protected String ssn;             // Social security number
27      protected double pay;             // Monthly pay
28
29      // Constructors
30      public Employee() {
31         firstName = " ";
32         lastName = " ";
33         ssn = "000-00-0000";
34         pay = 0;
35      }
36
37      public Employee(String first, String last, String ssn) {
38         firstName = first;
39         lastName = last;
40         this.ssn = ssn;
41         pay = 0;
42      }
```

Figure 9.9. An abstract Employee class.

```
43
44      // Set name
45    public void setName( String first, String last ) {
46        firstName = first;
47        lastName = last;
48    }
49
50      // Set social security number
51    public void setSsn( String ssn ) {
52        this.ssn = ssn;
53    }
54
55      // Get first name
56    public String getFirstName() {
57        return firstName;
58    }
59
60      // Get last name
61    public String getLastName() {
62        return lastName;
63    }
64
65      // Get social security number
66    public String getSsn() {
67        return ssn;
68    }
69
70      // Convert to string (this method will be
71      // overridden by different subclasses)
72    public abstract String toString();
73
74      // Method to calculate pay (this method will
75      // be overridden by different subclasses)
76    public abstract double calcPay( double hours );
77  }
```

Figure 9.9. (Continued).

Abstract classes define the list of methods that will be available to subclasses of the class, and can provide partial implementations of those methods. For example, the abstract class Employee in Figure 9.9 provides implementations of setName and setSsn that will be inherited by the subclasses of Employee, but does *not* provide implementations of calcPay and toString.

Any subclasses of an abstract class *must* override all abstract methods of the superclass, or they will be abstract themselves. Thus classes SalariedEmployee and HourlyEmployee must override methods calcPay and toString, or they will be abstract themselves.

Unlike concrete classes, *no objects may be instantiated from an abstract class*. Since an abstract class does not provide a complete definition of the behavior of an object, no object may be created from it. The class serves as a template for concrete subclasses, and objects may be instantiated from those concrete subclasses. An abstract class defines the types of polymorphic behaviors that can be used with subclasses of the class but does *not* define the details of those behaviors.

Objects may not be instantiated from an abstract class.

Abstract classes often appear at the top of an object-oriented programming class hierarchy, defining the broad types of actions possible with objects of all subclasses of the class. Concrete classes appear at lower levels in a hierarchy, providing implementations details for each subclass.

Use abstract classes to define broad types of behaviors at the top of an object-oriented programming class hierarchy, and use concrete classes to provide implementation details in the subclasses of the abstract classes.

In summary, to create polymorphic behavior in a program:

1.   Create a parent class containing all methods that will be needed to solve the problem.   The methods that will change in different subclasses can be declared `abstract`, if desired, and we will not have to define a method body for them in the superclass. Note that this makes the superclass `abstract`—no objects may be instantiated directly from it.

2.   Define subclasses for each type of object to be manipulated.   The subclasses must implement a specific method for each abstract method in the superclass definition.

3.   Create objects of the various subclasses, and refer to them using superclass references.   When a method call appears with a superclass reference, Java automatically executes the method in the object's actual subclass.

The trick to getting polymorphism right is to determine what behaviors objects of the superclass must exhibit, and to make sure that there is a method to represent every behavior in the superclass definition.

9.6   FINAL METHODS AND CLASSES

We saw in Chapter 2 that variables can be declared `final` to indicate that they cannot be modified, once they are declared and initialized. Effectively, `final` variables become named constants.

It is also possible to define **final methods** and **final classes**. A method that is declared `final` cannot be overridden in a subclass, so it can never exhibit polymorphic behavior. Since a `final` method's definition will never change, Java can perform compiler optimizations on the code to speed up execution. This can be especially useful for "utility methods" that are executed many times, since the optimizations can speed up the overall execution of the program.

Methods that are declared `static` or `private` are automatically `final`, since they can never be overridden in a subclass.

A class that is declared `final` cannot be a superclass, since no portion of the class may be overridden. All methods in a `final` class are automatically `final`, and the Java compiler is free to optimize them just like any other `final` method.

Many of the classes in the Java API are declared `final` to ensure that their behavior cannot be overridden. This practice helps to ensure that the Java API behaves in a consistent fashion at all times.

9.7   THE TYPE-WRAPPER CLASSES FOR PRIMITIVE TYPES

The discussions of classes in Chapters 7 and 9 describe how Java manipulates objects. Many Java classes are designed to polymorphically manipulate objects of type `Object`, which means that they can manipulate any object in Java, since ultimately all classes inherit from `Object`.

The odd men out in this whole structure are the primitive data types: `byte`, `short`, `int`, `long`, `char`, `float`, `double`, and `boolean`. They alone do not inherit from class `Object`, and so cannot be manipulated by many Java classes.

To get around this problem, Java defines a **type-wrapper class** for each primitive data type. These classes are called `Byte`, `Short`, `Integer`, `Character`, `Long`, `Float`, `Double`, and `Boolean`. Each class contains a single instance variable of the primitive type indicated by its name, along with methods to manipulate that variable. These classes enable a program to manipulate variables of primitive data types as objects of class `Object`, and so combine them with other objects in a program.

All of the numeric classes inherit from the abstract class `Number`, which defines basic methods that can be applied polymorphically to all of the numeric subclasses. This class structure is shown in Figure 9.10.

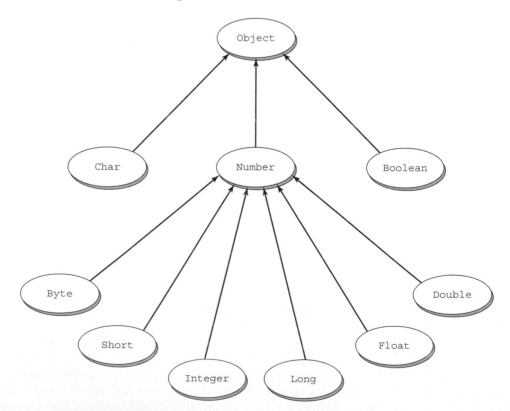

Figure 9.10.   The class hierarchy of the type-wrapper classes.

The type-wrapper classes are all `final` classes, and many of the methods in the type-wrapper classes are declared `static`. They are commonly used to process primitive data types. For example, we began in Chapter 2 using methods from type-wrapper classes to convert a string `str` containing the character representation of a number into a value itself. In the statement

```
v1 = Double.parseDouble(str);
```

the static method `parseDouble(str)` converts the character representation in string `str` into a `double` value.

If you need to manipulate primitive data types in your program, refer to the SDK documentation for the type-wrapper classes. They may fill your need without your having to write your own custom classes.

EXAMPLE 9.2

Abstract Classes and Polymorphic Behavior: To illustrate the concepts of abstract classes and polymorphic behaviors, let's consider generic two-dimensional shapes. There are many types of shapes, including circles, triangles, squares, rectangles, pentagons, and so forth. All of these shapes have certain characteristics in common, since they are closed two-dimensional shapes having an enclosed area and a perimeter of finite length.

Create a generic shape class having methods to determine the area and perimeter of a shape, and then create an appropriate class hierarchy for the following specific shapes: circles, equilateral triangles, squares, rectangles, and regular pentagons. The shape class should also include a static variable to keep track of the number of shapes which have been instantiated at any time. Then, illustrate polymorphic behavior by creating shapes of each type and determining their area and perimeter, using references to the generic shape class.

SOLUTION

To solve this problem, we should create a general `Shape` class and a series of subclasses below it. The `Shape` class should be abstract, since we will never directly instantiate any objects of that class, and since the methods to determine area and perimeter will be different for each subclass.

The listed shapes fall into a logical hierarchy based on their relationships. Circles, equilateral triangles, rectangles, and pentagons are all specific types of shapes, so they should be subclasses of our general `Shape` class. A square is a special kind of rectangle, so it should be a subclass of the `Rectangle` class. These relationships are shown in Figure 9.11.

A circle can be completely specified by it radius r, and the area A and perimeter (circumference) P of a circle can be calculated from the equations:

$$A = \pi r^2 \tag{9.1}$$
$$P = 2\pi r \tag{9.2}$$

An equilateral triangle can be completely specified by the length of one side s, and the area A and perimeter P of the equilateral triangle can be calculated from the equations:

$$A = \frac{\sqrt{3}}{4} s^2 \tag{9.3}$$
$$P = 3s \tag{9.4}$$

A rectangle can be completely specified by its length l and its width w, and the area A and perimeter P of the rectangle can be calculated from the equations:

$$A = lw \tag{9.5}$$
$$P = 2(l + w) \tag{9.6}$$

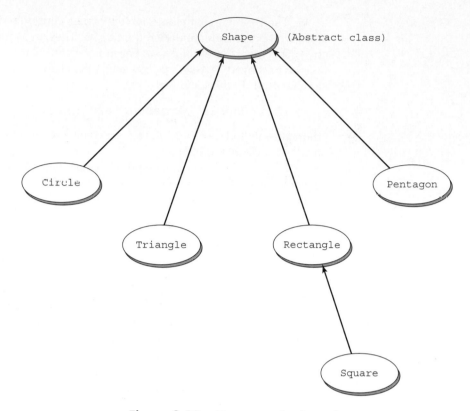

Figure 9.11. The Shape class hierarchy.

A square is a special rectangle whose length is equal to its width, so it can be completely specified by setting the length and width of a rectangle to the same size s. The area A and perimeter P of the square can then be calculated from the Equations (9.5) and (9.6).

A regular pentagon can be completely specified by the length of one side s, and the area A and perimeter P of the pentagon can be calculated from the equations:

$$A = \frac{5}{4}s^2 \cot\frac{\pi}{5} \qquad (9.7)$$
$$P = 5s \qquad (9.8)$$

where cot is the cotangent, which is the reciprocal of the tangent.

1. **Determine the User Requirements**

   Define and implement a generic class Shape with methods to calculate the area and perimeter of a specified shape. Define and implement appropriate subclasses for circles, equilateral triangles, rectangles, squares, and regular pentagons, with the area and perimeter calculations appropriate for each shape. The Shape class should also have a static variable to contain a count of the number of objects currently instantiated from the class and its subclasses.

2. **Analysis and Decomposition**

   Each class will need constructors capable of creating the appropriate objects. For circles, the constructor will need the radius r. For equilateral triangles, the constructor will need the length of a side s. For rectangles, the constructor will need the length l and width w. For squares, the constructor will need the length of a side s. For regular pentagons, the constructor will need the length of a side s.

Each of these classes will contain `area`, `perimeter`, and `toString` methods, returning the area, perimeter, and a string representation of the shape, respectively.

The classes required for this problem are `Shape`, `Circle`, `Triangle`, `Rectangle`, `Square`, and `Pentagon`. `Shape` is an abstract superclass representing a closed, two-dimensional object with a finite area and perimeter. `Circle`, `Triangle`, `Rectangle`, and `Pentagon` are special kinds of shapes, so they should be subclasses of `Shape`. `Square` is a special kind of rectangle, so it should be a subclass of `Rectangle`. The methods in each class will be the class constructor, `area`, `perimeter`, `toString`, and `finalize`. In addition, the `Shape` class itself must have a static method to return the number of shapes that have been created.

Note that `Shape` will be an `abstract` class, since we will not implement the methods `area` and `perimeter` in that class.

3. **Detailed Design**

The constructor of the `Shape` class must increment the `static` shape counter, but it does not have to do anything else. The constructors of the individual subclasses will initialize objects of the specified types and call the superclass constructor to increment the shape counter.

The finalizer of the `Shape` class must decrement the `static` shape counter, but it does not have to do anything else. The finalizers of the individual subclasses will call the superclass finalizer to decrement the shape counter.

The pseudocode for the `area()` method in the `Circle` class is:

```
return ( Math.PI * r*r );
```

The pseudocode for the `perimeter()` method in the `Circle` class is:

```
return ( 2. * Math.PI * r );
```

The pseudocode for the `area()` method in the `Triangle` class is:

```
return ( Math.sqrt(3.)/4. * s*s );
```

The pseudocode for the `perimeter()` method in the `Triangle` class is:

```
return ( 3. * s );
```

The pseudocode for the `area()` method in the `Rectangle` class is:

```
return ( l * w );
```

The pseudocode for the `perimeter()` method in the `Rectangle` class is:

```
return ( 2. * (l + w) );
```

The pseudocode for the `area()` and `perimeter()` methods in the `Square` class is the same as for the `Rectangle` class. These methods may be directly inherited from the `Rectangle` class.

The pseudocode for the `area()` method in the `Pentagon` class is:

```
return ( 1.25 * s*s / Math.tan( Math.PI / 5. ) );
```

The pseudocode for the `perimeter()` method in the `Pentagon` class is:

```
return ( 5. * s );
```

4. **Implementation: Convert Algorithms to Java Statements**

The abstract class Shape is shown in Figure 9.12. Note that this class defines abstract methods area() and perimeter(), so that all subclasses will be required to implement these methods, and they may be used polymorphically with objects of type Shape. The method toString() does not appear in this class, but it is present because it is inherited from class Object. Thus, toString() will also exhibit polymorphic behavior.

The class also provides a concrete implementation of method getCounter(), so this method will be inherited by all subclasses.

```
/*
   Purpose:
     This abstract class defines a generic shape, and
     abstract methods to calculate the area and
     perimeter of the shape.  It also includes a
     shape counter.

   Record of revisions:
       Date          Programmer           Description of change
       ====          ==========           =====================
     05/18/2002    S. J. Chapman          Original code
*/
public abstract class Shape {
   // Define instance variables
   private static int counter;     // Shape counter

   // Constructor
   public Shape() {
      counter++;
   }

   // Calculate area
   public abstract double area( );

   // Calculate perimeter
   public abstract double perimeter( );

   // Get number of shapes
   public int getCount() {
      return counter;
   }

   // Finalizer
   protected void finalize() {
      counter--;
   }
}
```

Figure 9.12. Abstract class Shape.

The class `Circle` is shown in Figure 9.13. This class defines an instance variable r for the radius of the circle and provides concrete implementations of `area()`, `perimeter()`, and `toString()`.

```
/*
   Purpose:
     This class defines the shape Circle, with
     methods to calculate the area and perimeter
     of the shape.

   Record of revisions:
       Date          Programmer          Description of change
       ====          ==========          =====================
     05/18/2002   S. J. Chapman          Original code
*/
public class Circle extends Shape {
   // Define instance variables
   private double r;          // Radius of circle

   // Constructor
   public Circle(double r) {
      super();
      this.r = r;
   }

   // Calculate area
   public double area( ) {
      return ( Math.PI * r*r );
   }
   // Calculate perimeter
   public double perimeter( ) {
      return ( 2 * Math.PI * r );
   }

   // Convert to string
   public String toString() {
      return ("Circle of radius " + r);
   }
   // Finalizer
   protected void finalize() {
      super.finalize();
   }
}
```

Figure 9.13. Class `Circle`.

The class `Triangle` is shown in Figure 9.14. This class defines an instance variable s for the length of the side of the triangle and provides concrete implementations of `area()`, `perimeter()`, and `toString()`.

```
/*
   Purpose:
     This class defines the shape Triangle, with
     methods to calculate the area and perimeter
     of the shape.

   Record of revisions:
       Date          Programmer          Description of change
       ====          ==========          =====================
     05/18/2002    S. J. Chapman         Original code
*/
public class Triangle extends Shape {
   // Define instance variables
   private double s;        // Length of side

   // Constructor
   public Triangle(double s) {
      super();
      this.s = s;
   }

   // Calculate area
   public double area( ) {
      return ( Math.sqrt(3.)/4 * s*s );
   }

   // Calculate perimeter
   public double perimeter( ) {
      return ( 3. * s );
   }

   // Convert to string
   public String toString() {
      return ("Equilateral triangle of side " + s);
   }

   // Finalizer
   protected void finalize() {
      super.finalize();
   }
}
```

Figure 9.14. Class Triangle.

The class Rectangle is shown in Figure 9.15. This class defines instance variables l and w for the length and width of the rectangle and provides concrete implementations of area(), perimeter(), and toString(). Note that the instance variables l and w are declared protected instead of private, because they must be inherited by subclass Square.

```
/*
   Purpose:
     This class defines the shape Rectangle, with
     methods to calculate the area and perimeter
     of the shape.

   Record of revisions:
       Date         Programmer           Description of change
       ====         ==========           =====================
     05/18/2002    S. J. Chapman         Original code
*/

public class Rectangle extends Shape {
   // Define instance variables
   protected double l;        // Length of rectangle
   protected double w;        // Width of rectangle

   // Constructor
   public Rectangle(double l, double w) {
      super();
      this.l = l;
      this.w = w;
   }

   // Calculate area
   public double area( ) {
      return ( l * w );
   }
   // Calculate perimeter
   public double perimeter( ) {
      return ( 2. * (l + w) );
   }

   // Convert to string
   public String toString() {
      return ("Rectangle of length " + l + " and width " + w);
   }
   // Finalizer
   protected void finalize() {
      super.finalize();
   }
}
```

Figure 9.15. Class Rectangle.

The class Square is shown in Figure 9.16. Since a square is just a rectangle with its length equal to its width, this class *inherits* its instance variables l and w from class Rectangle, as well as concrete implementations of area() and perimeter(). The class overrides method toString().

The class Pentagon is shown in Figure 9.17. This class defines an instance variable s for the length of the side of the pentagon and provides concrete implementations of area(), perimeter(), and toString().

```
/*
   Purpose:
     This class defines the shape Square, with
     methods to calculate the area and perimeter
     of the shape.

   Record of revisions:
       Date            Programmer              Description of change
       ====            ==========              =====================
     05/18/2002     S. J. Chapman            Original code
*/
public class Square extends Rectangle {
   // All instance variables are inherited from Rectangle

   // Constructor
   public Square(double s) {
      super(s,s);
   }

   // Convert to string
   public String toString() {
      return ("Square of side " + l);
   }

   // Finalizer
   protected void finalize() {
      super.finalize();
   }
}
```

Figure 9.16. Class Square.

```
/*
   Purpose:
     This class defines the shape Pentagon, with
     methods to calculate the area and perimeter
     of the shape.

   Record of revisions:
       Date            Programmer              Description of change
       ====            ==========              =====================
     05/18/2002     S. J. Chapman            Original code
*/
public class Pentagon extends Shape {
   // Define instance variables
   private double s;          // Length of side

   // Constructor
   public Pentagon(double s) {
```

Figure 9.17. Class Pentagon.

```
        super();
        this.s = s;
    }

    // Calculate area
    public double area( ) {
        return ( 1.25 * s*s / Math.tan( Math.PI / 5. ) );
    }

    // Calculate perimeter
    public double perimeter( ) {
        return ( 5. * s );
    }

    // Convert to string
    public String toString() {
        return ("Pentagon of side " + s);
    }

    // Finalizer
    protected void finalize() {
        super.finalize();
    }
}
```

Figure 9.17.   (Continued).

5.   **Testing**
      To test this program, we will calculate the area and perimeter of several shapes
      by hand and compare the results with those produced by a test driver program.

Shape	Area	Perimeter
Circle of radius 2:	$A = \pi r^2 = 12.5664$	$P = 2\pi r = 12.5664$
Triangle of side 2:	$A = \dfrac{\sqrt{3}}{4}s^2 = 1.7321$	$P = 3s = 6$
Rectangle of length 2 and width 1:	$A = lw = 2$	$P = 2(l + w) = 6$
Square of side 2:	$A = lw = 2 \times 2 = 4$	$P = 2(l + w) = 8$
Pentagon of side 2:	$A = \dfrac{5}{4}s^2 \cot\dfrac{\pi}{5} = 6.8819$	$P = 5s = 10$

An appropriate test driver program is shown in Figure 9.18. Note
that this program creates an array of references of type `Shape[]` and then
creates objects of various subclasses, assigning them to elements of the
array. It then uses method `getCount()` to report the number of `Shape`
objects created, and uses the methods `toString()`, `area()`, and
`perimeter()` on each object in array s.

```
/*
    Purpose:
      This class tests class Shape and its subclasses.

    Record of revisions:
         Date           Programmer          Description of change
         ====           ==========          =====================
     05/18/2002    S. J. Chapman           Original code
*/
public class TestShape {

    // Define the main method to test class Shape
    public static void main(String[] args) {

        // Create an array of Shapes
        Shape[] s = new Shape[5];

        // Create objects
        s[0] = new Circle(2);
        s[1] = new Triangle(2);
        s[2] = new Rectangle(2,1);
        s[3] = new Square(2);
        s[4] = new Pentagon(2);

        // Print out number of shapes created
        System.out.println(s[0].getCount() + " shapes created.");

        // Print out information about the shapes
        for (int i = 0; i < s.length; i++ ) {
            System.out.println("\n" + s[i].toString());
            System.out.println("Area      = " + s[i].area());
            System.out.println("Perimeter = " + s[i].perimeter());
        }
    }
}
```

Figure 9.18. Program to test class Shape and its subclasses.

When this program is executed, the results are:

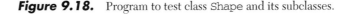

```
D:\book\java\chap9>java TestShape
5 shapes created.
Circle of radius 2.0
Area      = 12.566370614359172
Perimeter = 12.566370614359172

Equilateral triangle of side 2.0
Area      = 1.7320508075688772
Perimeter = 6.0

Rectangle of length 2.0 and width 1.0
Area      = 2.0
Perimeter = 6.0

Square of side 2.0
Area      = 4.0
Perimeter = 8.0
```

```
Pentagon of side 2.0
Area      = 6.881909602355868
Perimeter = 10.0
```

The results of the program agree with our hand calculations to the number of significant digits to which we performed the calculation. Note that the program called the correct polymorphic version of each method. Also, note that each time an object of any subclass was created, the total count of Shapes increased by one. This happened because each subclass constructor called its superclass constructor, and the Shape constructor increased the total count of shapes. ■

9.8   INTERFACES

An **interface** is a special kind of block containing method signatures (and possibly constants) only. Interfaces define the signatures of a set of methods, without the method bodies that would implement their functionality. Method declarations in an interface are essentially the same as method declarations in abstract classes.

Interfaces have no direct inherited relationship with any particular class—they are defined independently. An example interface is shown in Figure 9.19.

```
/*
   Purpose:
     This interface defines the relationship between
     two objects, according to the "natural order"
     of the objects.

   Record of revisions:
       Date          Programmer            Description of change
       ====          ==========            =====================
     05/18/2002    S. J. Chapman          Original code
*/
public interface Relation {

   // Returns true if a > b
   public boolean isGreater( Object a, Object b );

   // Returns true if a < b
   public boolean isLess( Object a, Object b );

   // Returns true if a == b
   public boolean isEqual( Object a, Object b );
}
```

Figure 9.19.   An example of an interface. Interface Relation defines the method signature of three methods that can be used to compare two objects.

9.8.1   Implementing Interfaces

Any class may choose to **implement** an interface by adding an implements clause to its class definition. If a class chooses to implement an interface, then it guarantees that it will provide an implementation for *every* method in the interface, and the methods will have the same sequence of calling arguments as shown in the interface definition. If these conditions are not met, the Java compiler will generate an error.

A class that implements an interface has an "isa" relationship with that interface, just as a subclass has an "isa" relationship with its superclass. Just as an object of a subclass can be treated as an object of its superclass type, an object of a class that implements an interface can be treated as an object of the interface type, and can be used by any method that uses objects of the interface type (see Figure 9.20).

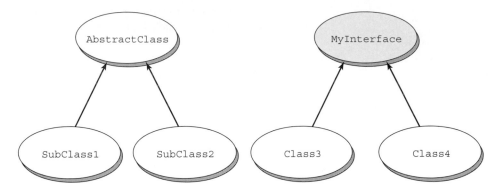

Figure 9.20. Classes that implement an interface bear the same relationship to the interface as the subclasses of an abstract class bear to their parent class. Just as an object of SubClass1 is an ("isa") object of AbstractClass, so an object of Class3 is an ("isa") object of MyInterface.

What is the big deal about interfaces? Interfaces define a standard and public way of specifying the behavior of classes. They allow classes, regardless of their locations in the class hierarchy, to implement common behaviors. For example, suppose that we were to create 10 different classes of different types, and we would like to be able to sort objects of each of these classes into ascending order. Without an interface, we would have to implement a sort method for each class separately, requiring us to write the same basic code 10 times! On the other hand, if each of the 10 classes implements the Relation interface defined in Figure 9-19, we can write a *single* method to sort objects of the Relation type, and that method will work for *any* of the classes implementing the Relation interface.

Note that interfaces exhibit **polymorphism**, since a program may call an interface method, and the proper version of that method will be executed depending on the type of object passed to the interface method in the call.

GOOD PROGRAMMING PRACTICE

Use interfaces to create the same standard method definitions in many different classes. Once a set of standard method definitions is created, you can write a *single* method to manipulate (sort, search, and so on) all of the classes that implement the interface.

If a class implements an interface, *it must implement all of the methods specified in the interface*, since the methods calling that interface will rely on the existence of those methods.

A sample class Line that implements the interface Relation is shown in Figure 9.21. This class defines a line segment by its two endpoints (x_1,y_1) and (x_2,y_2), and provides a method length() to calculate the length of the line segment. This class implements interface Relation, so it must define methods isGreater(), isLess(), and isEqual() *with exactly the same calling sequence as in the interface*. Note that this interface requires Objects to be passed to the methods. Inside the methods, these Objects are cast to Lines, so that the length() method can be used to compare them, and the appropriate boolean value is returned to the calling method.

```
/*
   Purpose:
     This class defines a line segment in terms of
     two (x,y) endpoints.  It provides a method
     to calculate the length of the line segment,
     and implements interface Relation so that
     the lines can be sorted by length.
   Record of revisions:
       Date          Programmer            Description of change
       ====          ==========            =====================
     05/19/2002    S. J. Chapman           Original code
*/
public class Line implements Relation {
   // Instance variables
   private double x1;        // First x-value
   private double x2;        // Second x-value
   private double y1;        // First y-value
   private double y2;        // Second y-value

   // Constructor
   public Line(double x1, double y1, double x2, double y2) {
      this.x1 = x1;
      this.x2 = x2;
      this.y1 = y1;
      this.y2 = y2;
   }

   // Calculate length
   public double length( ) {
      return Math.sqrt( (x2-x1)*(x2-x1) + (y2-y1)*(y2-y1) );
   }

   // Returns true if a > b
   public boolean isGreater( Object a, Object b ) {
      return ((Line)a).length() > ((Line)b).length();
   }

   // Returns true if a < b
   public boolean isLess( Object a, Object b ) {
      return ((Line)a).length() < ((Line)b).length();
   }

   // Returns true if a == b
   public boolean isEqual( Object a, Object b ) {
      return ((Line)a).length() == ((Line)b).length();
   }

   // toString()
   public String toString( ) {
      String s;
      s = "Line from (" + x1 + "," + y1 + ") to ("
        + x2 + "," + y2 + "): Length = " + length();
      return s;
   }
}
```

Figure 9.21. Class Line, which implements interface Relation.

9.8.2   Calling Interface Methods

A static method that uses the `Relation` interface to sort objects is shown in Figure 9.22. This method accepts any array of class `Object` and sorts the array using the methods defined in the `Relation` interface. Note that *in order to sort the objects using the methods*

```
/*
   Purpose:
     This class contains a static method to sort objects using
     the selection-sort algorithm.  It supports any class that
     implements the Relation interface.  Note that this is not
     a particularly efficient sorting technique--it is used here
     only because it is easy to understand.
   Record of revisions:
       Date          Programmer              Description of change
       ====          ==========              =====================
     05/19/2002    S. J. Chapman             Original code
*/
public class SortObj {

   // Define the sort method
   public static Object[] sort ( Object[] o ) {

      // Declare variables, and define each variable
      int i, j;              // Loop index
      int iptr;              // Pointer to "smallest" value
      Object temp;           // Temporary variable for swapping

      // Sort values
      for ( i = 0; i < o.length-1; i++ ) {

         // Find the minimum value in o[i] through o[nvals-1]
         iptr = i;
         for ( j = i+1; j < o.length; j++ ) {
            if ( ((Relation)o[0]).isLess(
                       (Relation) o[j], (Relation) o[iptr] ))
               iptr = j;
         }

         // iptr now points to the min value, so swap o[iptr] with
         // o[i] if iptr != i.
         if (i != iptr) {
            temp = o[i];
            o[i] = o[iptr];
            o[iptr] = temp;
         }
      }
      // Return sorted objects
      return o;
   }
}
```

Figure 9.22.   A method to sort objects that implement interface `Relation` into ascending order using the selection sort.

in the Relation *interface, the objects must be cast into type* Relation *when the methods are invoked.* An example of this manipulation is

((Relation) o[0]).isLess((Relation) o[j], (Relation) o[iptr])

The expression (Relation) o[j] casts the object reference o[j] into a Relation type, which can be used with the method isLess() defined in the interface. If the object o[j] is of a class that does not support the Relation interface, this expression will cause a run-time exception.

     This method will sort arrays of any class that implements the Relation interface, so we need to write only one sort method to work with many different classes.

     A test driver program that creates Line objects and sorts them using the SortObj.sort() method is shown in Figure 9.23. This method creates an array of Object references and assigns five new Line objects to that array. It then sorts the array into ascending order of length using method SortObj.sort().

```
/*
   Purpose:
     This class tests class Line and the Relation
     interface.

   Record of revisions:
       Date            Programmer             Description of change
       ====            ==========             =====================
     05/19/2002     S. J. Chapman          Original code
*/
public class TestLine {

   // Define the main method
   public static void main(String[] args) {

      // Create an array of Objects
      Object o[] = new Line[5];

      // Create objects
      o[0] = new Line(0,0,2,1);
      o[1] = new Line(0,0,1,-1);
      o[2] = new Line(-1,1,1,1);
      o[3] = new Line(2,0,0,0);
      o[4] = new Line(0,2,-2,0);

      // Sort the objects in ascending order
      SortObj.sort( o );

      // Print out information about the Lines
      for (int i = 0; i < o.length; i++ ) {
         System.out.println(o[i].toString());
      }
   }
}
```

Figure 9.23. A test driver program for classes Line and SortObj.

When this program is executed, the results are:

```
D:\book\java\chap9>java TestLine
Line from (0.0,0.0) to (1.0,-1.0): Length = 1.4142135623730951
Line from (-1.0,1.0) to (1.0,1.0): Length = 2.0
Line from (2.0,0.0) to (0.0,0.0): Length = 2.0
Line from (0.0,0.0) to (2.0,1.0): Length = 2.23606797749979
Line from (0.0,2.0) to (-2.0,0.0): Length = 2.8284271247461903
```

9.8.3   Using Interfaces to Define Constants

An interface may contain constants only, with no method definitions. An example of such an interface is shown in Figure 9.24. An interface like this defines constants that can be used in many class definitions. Any class that implements this interface can use these constants anywhere within the class definition.

```
public interface Constants {
    public static final double PI = 3.14159265358979;
    public static final double E = 2.71828182845905;
}
```

Figure 9.24.   An interface containing only constants.

9.8.4   The Significance of Interfaces

A class that implements an interface is almost identical in behavior to a subclass of an abstract class that defines the same abstract methods. If this is so, why bother to define interfaces at all? Why not just use abstract classes for everything?

The basic reason for interfaces is that *a class can inherit only from one immediate parent class, but it can implement many different interfaces.* Interfaces permit a single class to implement many different types of standard behaviors, and so make the class more flexible and easier to use.

QUIZ 9-1

This quiz provides a quick check to see if you have understood the concepts introduced in Sections 9.1 through 9.8. If you have trouble with the quiz, reread the section, ask your instructor, or discuss the material with a fellow student. The answers are found in the back of the book.

1.   What is inheritance?
2.   What is polymorphism?
3.   What are abstract classes and abstract methods? Why would you wish to use abstract classes and methods in your programs?
4.   What are the advantages of declaring methods or classes to be final? What are the disadvantages?
5.   What is an interface? How do interfaces save programming effort?

9.9   THE `Collection` AND `Iterator` INTERFACES

The `Collection` and `Iterator` interfaces are new features introduced in Java SDK 1.2. They can serve as good examples of how interfaces are used in Java. The `Collection` interface defines a standard set of methods to access all the different types of collections implemented by Java, while the `Iterator` interface defines a standard way of stepping through the collection on an element-by-element basis.

A "collection" in data structure terms is a group of data elements. Some types of collections that are supported by Java include:

- `List`—a collection containing an ordered sequence of elements
- `Set`—a collection containing a mathematical set of elements, with no duplication
- `Map`—a collection that maps keys into values

`List`, `Set`, and `Map` are subinterfaces of the `Collection` interface. Similarly, `List-Iterator` is a subinterface of the `Iterator` interface. We now consider the `List` and `ListIterator` interfaces in more detail. Information about the `Set` and `Map` interfaces may be found in the Java API documentation.

Examples of `Lists` implemented by Java include `Vectors` and `LinkedLists`. The **vector** class defines a list of objects that can be accessed in random order by an index [see Figure 9.25(a)]. It is like an array of references to objects, except that the size of a vector can grow and shrink, while the size of an array is fixed.

In contrast, a **linked list** is a list of objects, each containing a data element plus a reference to the next object in the list [see Figure 9.25(b)]. It is easy to add and remove elements in a linked list, but the data in the list can only be accessed sequentially. For example, suppose that a user wanted to use the 25th element on a linked list. The program would have to start at the reference to the beginning of the linked list, then follow the references through elements 1, 2, 3, ..., 24, before finding the required information.

Linked lists and vectors have very different properties. It is easy to add and remove data from the ends of a linked list, but random access to the data in the linked list is very difficult, since the program has to perform a linear search from the beginning or the end of the list to find a particular element. On the other hand, it is hard to add or delete elements from a vector, since the remaining elements must be physically moved each time something is added or deleted. However, it is very easy to randomly access elements in a vector in any order. Thus, lists that will have frequent additions and deletions and that are always searched sequentially might be best implemented as linked lists, while lists whose values will be accessed randomly might be best implemented as vectors.

Even though these types of lists are very different, they both implement the `List` and `ListIterator` interfaces, so *the two types of lists can be used in exactly the same way* by other methods in a program. The details of the list implementation are hidden from the user. This fact is very significant, because a program can be written using one form of list, and then the list can be replaced by a different form with *no other change* in the program. We might want to make such a switch while optimizing the execution speed of a program.

The following example illustrates the use of linked lists and vectors through the `List` interface.

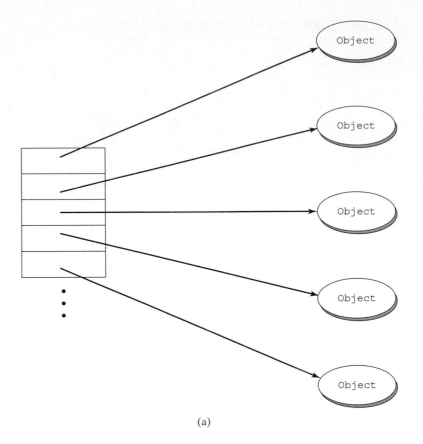

(a)

Figure 9.25. (a) A Vector consists of an array of references, each element of which points to a specific object. Vectors are very efficient for random access, since locating a specific array element is very quick. However, it takes a long time to add elements to the middle of a vector, because all of the higher values in the array of references must be shifted upward when a new value is inserted.

EXAMPLE 9.3

Using Linked Lists and Vectors: To illustrate the use of interfaces in Java, create a LinkedList and a Vector (both are types of lists), store 10,000 Double objects in each list, and then access the objects both in sequential order using ListIterator interface methods and in random order using the List interface methods. Compare the time required to perform each operation for each type of list.

SOLUTION

To solve this problem, we will create a LinkedList and a Vector, using a reference of type Object to refer to each of them. We will then add elements to the lists using List interface methods, access the elements sequentially using ListIterator interface methods, and access the elements randomly using List interface methods. We will use the Timer class developed in Chapter 7 to time each operation.

Some selected List interface methods are shown in Table 9.1, and some selected ListIterator methods are shown in Table 9.2. A complete list of List and ListIterator methods may be found in the Java API Documentation. We will use the add method in the List interface to add elements to each list, the next method in the ListIterator interface to recover elements in sequential order, and the get method on the List interface to recover elements in random order.

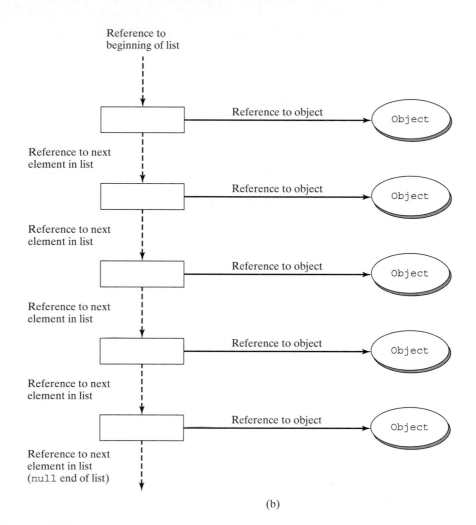

Reference to
beginning of list

Reference to object

Object

Reference to next
element in list

Reference to object

Object

Reference to next
element in list

Reference to object

Object

Reference to next
element in list

Reference to object

Object

Reference to next
element in list

Reference to object

Object

Reference to next
element in list
(null end of list)

(b)

Figure 9.25.   (b) A LinkedList is a series of objects, each containing two references. One reference points to the next item in the linked list (the dashed line), and the other points to the object stored at that location in the list (the solid line). It is very efficient to add a new element in the middle of a linked list, because only the reference values in the new element and in the element just before it need to be changed. However, it is very inefficient to access elements randomly, since locating an element requires a sequential search from the top of the list.

We will use the new operator to create each list:

```
o = new LinkedList();
```

or

```
o = new Vector();
```

where o is a reference to an arbitrary Object.

Next, we will use the add method from the List interface to add elements to each list. In order to do this, we must cast the object reference o into a List:

```
((List)o).add(new Double(temp));
```

Similarly, we will use the get method from the List interface to get the elements from the list in random order.

```
d = ((List)o).get(index);
```

TABLE 9.1 Selected List Interface Methods

Method	Description
boolean **add** (Object o)	Appends the specified element to the end of this List.
void **add** (int index, Object element)	Inserts the specified element at the specified position in this List. Shifts the element currently at that position and any subsequent elements to the right (adds one to their indices).
Object **get** (int index)	Returns the element at the specified position in this List.
ListIterator **listIterator** ()	Returns a ListIterator of the elements in this List (in proper sequence). This object can be used to walk through the list sequentially, using the methods in the ListIterator interface.
Object **remove** (int index)	Removes the element at the specified position in this List. Shifts any subsequent elements to the left (subtracts one from their indices). Returns the element that was removed from the List.
Object **set** (int index, Object element)	Replaces the element at the specified position in this List with the specified element.
int **size** ()	Returns the number of elements in this List.

TABLE 9.2 Selected ListIterator Interface Methods

Method	Description
boolean **hasNext** ()	Returns true if this ListIterator has more elements when traversing the List in the forward direction.
boolean **hasPrevious** ()	Returns true if this ListIterator has more elements when traversing the List in the reverse direction.
public Object **next** ()	Returns the next element in the List. This method may be called repeatedly to iterate through the List, or intermixed with calls to previous to go back and forth.
public Object **previous** ()	Returns the previous element in the List.

Finally, we will use the next method from the ListIterator interface to step through the elements in sequential order.

```
d = it.next();
```

The resulting program is shown in Figure 9.26. This program creates a new List and adds 10,000 Double objects to it, using the add method. It then creates a ListIterator and uses it to step through the list sequentially. Finally, it uses the get method to recover 10,000 randomly ordered values from the list. It calculates the elapsed time required in each case.

```
/*
   Purpose:
      This class tests classes Vector and LinkedList, using
      interfaces List and ListIterator to access each class.
      Note that the code to build the lists and access the
      lists is completely identical in each case, because we
      are using the common interface List and ListIterator.

   Record of revisions:
       Date          Programmer              Description of change
       ====          ==========              =====================
     05/19/2002    S. J. Chapman             Original code
*/
import java.util.*;
public class TestList {

   // Define the main method
   public static void main(String[] args) {

      // Define variables
      Object d;                     // Temp Double object
      int index;                    // Index
      ListIterator it;              // ListIterator
      double temp;                  // Scratch variable

      // Instantiate timer
      Timer t = new Timer();

      //*********************************************
      //   This portion of the code creates a new
      //   vector of Double values, stores 10,000
      //   elements in it, and accesses the elements
      //   10,000 times in random order.
      //*********************************************
      Object o = new Vector();
      System.out.println("Vector:");

      // Reset timer
      t.resetTimer();

      // Add random values in successive locations
      for (int i = 0; i < 10000; i++) {
         temp = 1000 * Math.random();
         ((List)o).add(new Double(temp));
      }
      // Get elapsed time to add elements
      System.out.println( "Time to add elements = " +
                       t.elapsedTime() );
```

Figure 9.26.   A program to create and manipulate linked lists and vectors using the `List` and
`ListIterator` interfaces.

```
        // Reset timer
        t.resetTimer();

        // Access elements in sequential order
        it = ((List)o).listIterator();
        for (int i = 0; i < 10000; i++) {
            d = it.next();
            temp = ((Double) d).doubleValue();
        }

        // Get elapsed time to access elements
        System.out.println(
            "Time to get sequential elements = " +
            t.elapsedTime() );

        // Reset timer
        t.resetTimer();

        // Access elements in random order
        for (int i = 0; i < 10000; i++) {
            index = (int) (1000 * Math.random());
            if ( index == 1000 ) index = 0;
            d = ((List)o).get(index);
            temp = ((Double) d).doubleValue();
        }

        // Get elapsed time to access elements
        System.out.println(
            "Time to get random elements = " +
            t.elapsedTime() );

        //**********************************************
        //  This portion of the code creates a new
        //  LinkedList of Double values, stores 10,000
        //  elements in it, and accesses the elements
        //  10,000 times in random order.
        //**********************************************
        o = new LinkedList();
        System.out.println("Linked list:");

        // Reset timer
        t.resetTimer();

        // Add random values in successive location
        for (int i = 0; i < 10000; i++) {
            temp = 1000 * Math.random();
            ((List)o).add(new Double(temp));
        }

        // Get elapsed time to add elements
        System.out.println( "Time to add elements = " +
                            t.elapsedTime() );
```

Figure 9.26.   (Continued).

```
    // Reset timer
    t.resetTimer();

    // Access elements in sequential order
    it = ((List)o).listIterator();
    for (int i = 0; i < 10000; i++) {
        d = it.next();
        temp = ((Double) d).doubleValue();
    }

    // Get elapsed time to access elements
    System.out.println(
        "Time to get sequential elements = " +
        t.elapsedTime() );

    // Reset timer
    t.resetTimer();

    // Access elements in random order
    for (int i = 0; i < 10000; i++) {
        index = (int) (1000 * Math.random());
        if ( index == 1000 ) index = 0;
        d = ((List)o).get(index);
        temp = ((Double) d).doubleValue();
    }

    // Get elapsed time to access elements
    System.out.println(
        "Time to get random elements = " +
        t.elapsedTime() );
    }
}
```

Figure 9.26.   (Continued).

When this program is executed, the results are:

```
D:\book\java\chap9>java TestList
Vector:
Time to add elements = 0.461
Time to get sequential elements = 0.1
Time to get random elements = 0.25
Linked list:
Time to add elements = 1.122
Time to get sequential elements = 0.05
Time to get random elements = 7.08
```

The results of the program agree with our previous discussion about the nature of linked lists and vectors. Vectors are faster for random access, while linked lists are faster for sequential access.   ■

The most important point of this example is that *both linked lists and vectors can be accessed using identically the same statements*, because they both support the List and ListIterator interfaces. This design allows us to change the type of list we are using in a program after the program has been written, with almost no impact on the rest of the code.

SUMMARY

- Through inheritance, a new subclass inherits the instance variables and methods of its previously defined superclass. The subclass only needs to provide instance variables and methods to implement the *differences* between itself and its parent.

- An object of a subclass may be treated as an object of its corresponding superclass. Thus an object of a subclass may be freely assigned to a superclass reference.

- An *object* of a superclass type may not be assigned to a reference of a subclass type. However, a *reference* of a superclass type may be cast into a reference of a subclass type. If the object pointed to by the reference is really of this subclass, this operation will work. Otherwise, it will throw a `ClassCast-Exception`.

- A subclass's constructor must make an explicit or implicit call to its superclass's constructor as the *first* action in the subclass constructor.

- A subclass's finalizer must make an explicit call to its superclass's finalizer as the *last* action in the subclass finalizer.

- Polymorphism is the ability to automatically vary methods depending on the subclass that an object belongs to.

- To create polymorphic behavior, define all polymorphic methods in the common superclass, and override the behavior of the methods in each subclass that inherits from the superclass.

- An abstract method is a method whose heading is declared without an associated body. It defines the calling sequence of the method, but not how it will be implemented. An abstract method is declared by prefixing the method definition with the keyword `abstract`.

- An abstract class is a class containing one or more abstract methods.

- Each subclass of an abstract class must provide an implementation of all abstract methods, or the subclass will remain abstract.

- Methods and classes can be declared `final` to indicate that they cannot be overridden in a subclass. Final methods are usually more efficient than ordinary methods, because the Java compiler can perform extra optimizations on them.

- All of the methods in a `final` class are implicitly `final`.

- Java provides type-wrapper classes for primitive data types so that they may be used with data structures that work only with objects (for example, `LinkedList` or `Vector`).

- An interface is a special kind of block containing method signatures (and possibly constants) only.

- Any class may choose to implement an interface by adding an `implements` clause to its class definition. If a class implements an interface, it should provide an implementation for each method in the interface, and the methods will have the same signature as shown in the interface definition.

- To use an interface method, a calling method must cast an object's reference into the interface type. If the object's class does not support the interface type, this will cause a run-time exception.

- Interfaces are used by Java to provide a standard means of accessing various data structures while hiding the implementation details of the structures.

SUMMARY OF GOOD PROGRAMMING PRACTICES

The following guidelines introduced in this chapter will help you to develop good programs:

1. When writing a subclass, call the superclass's constructor either implicitly or explicitly *as the first action in the subclass constructor*. Failure to do so will produce a compile-time error.

2. When writing a subclass, call the superclass's finalizer explicitly *as the last action in the subclass finalizer*. Failure to do so may result in resources such as files, network sockets, and so on not being released properly.

3. Polymorphism allows multiple objects of different subclasses to be treated as objects of a single superclass, while automatically selecting the proper methods to apply to a particular object based on the subclass that it belongs to.

4. To create polymorphic behavior, define all polymorphic methods in a common superclass, then override the behavior of the methods in each subclass that inherits from the superclass.

5. Use abstract classes to define broad types of behaviors at the top of an object-oriented programming class hierarchy, and use concrete classes to provide implementation details in the subclasses of the abstract classes.

6. You may declare commonly used methods that do not need to be inherited to be `final`. This practice allows the Java compiler to optimize the method calls and speed up program execution. Note that `static` methods are automatically final.

7. Use interfaces to create the same standard method definitions in many different classes. Once a set of standard method definitions is created, you can write a *single* method to manipulate (sort, search, and so forth) all of the classes that implement the interface.

TERMINOLOGY

abstract class
abstract method
`Collection` interface
concrete class
downcast
`implements` clause
interface
`Iterator` interface
`LinkedList` class

`List` interface
`ListIterator` interface
linked list
polymorphism
`protected` access
type-wrapper class
upcast
`Vector` class

Exercises

1. Create a new class called `SalaryPlusEmployee` as a subclass of the `Employee` class created in this chapter. A salary-plus employee will receive a fixed salary for his/her normal work week, plus bonus overtime pay at an hourly rate for any hours exceeding 42 in any given week. Override all of the necessary methods for this subclass. Then modify class `TestEmployee` to demonstrate the proper operation of all three subclasses of `Employee`.

2. Modify `Employee` and its subclasses to implement the `Relation` interface to compare employee social security numbers. Then, use the pre-existing method `SortObj.sort()` to sort an array of employees by ascending order of social security numbers.

3. Modify the `Shape` class and its subclasses to implement the `Relation` interface. The `Relation` interface methods should compare the areas of individual shapes. Then, write a test program that creates a series of shapes and sorts them into ascending order of size, using the `SortObj.sort()` method.

4. Replace the abstract class `Shape` by an interface called `Shape`, and make all of the former subclasses of `Shape` implement the new interface. Create a test program that calls the interface methods with `Circles`, `Triangles`, and so on, to show that the interface calls the proper version of each method for each object.

5. **General Polygons**   Create a class called `Point`, containing two instance variables `x` and `y`, representing the (x, y) location of a point on a cartesian plane. Then, define a class `Polygon` as a subclass of `Shape` developed in Example 9.2. The polygon should be specified by an ordered series of (x, y) points denoting the ends of each line segment forming the polygon. For example, a triangle is specified by three (x, y) points, a quadrilateral is specified by three (x, y) points, and so forth.

   The constructor for this class should accept the number of points used to specify a particular polygon, and should allocate an array of `Point` objects to hold the (x, y) information. The class should implement set and get methods to allow the locations of each point to be set and retrieved, as well as area and perimeter calculations.

   The area of a general polygon may be found from the equation

$$A = \tfrac{1}{2}(x_1 y_2 + x_2 y_3 + \cdots + x_{n-1} y_n$$
$$+ x_n y_1 - y_1 x_2 - y_2 x_3 - \cdots - y_{n-1} x_n - y_n x_1)$$

   where x_i and y_i are (x, y) values of the ith point. The perimeter of the general polygon will be the sum of the lengths of each line segment, where the length of segment i is found from the equation:

$$\text{length} = \sqrt{(x_{i+1} - x_i)^2 + (y_{i+1} - y_i)^2}$$

   The class should also implement the `Relation` interface to compare polygons by their enclosed areas.

   Once this class is created, write a test program that creates an array of `Shapes` of various sorts, including general polygons, and sorts the shapes into ascending order of area.

6. Write a method to test the relative performance of a linked list and a vector when objects are inserted in the middle of the list. First, create a vector and a linked list with 10 items in each. Next add 10,000 new elements, one at a time, at position 5 in each type of list. Use the `Collections` interface methods to insert the elements in each list, and use `Timer` objects to measure the time required to add the elements to each type of list. How does the time required to insert 10,000 elements into the middle of a `Vector` compare to the time required to insert 10,000 elements into the middle of a `LinkedList`?

7.   A disadvantage of linked lists is that they can only be searched sequentially from the beginning of the list, so any random or reverse access to the items in the list is very slow. This problem can be partially overcome be creating a *doubly linked list*, in which each list element in the list has references both to the element following it and to the element preceding it. A doubly linked list can be searched either from front to back or from back to front with equal ease. Create a class that implements a doubly linked list, and demonstrate that it is equally fast at front-to-back and back-to-front accesses.

8.   Create an abstract class called Vec, which includes instance variables x and y, and abstract methods to add and subtract two vectors. Create two subclasses, Vec2D and Vec3D, that implement these methods for two-dimensional and three-dimensional vectors, respectively. Class Vec3D must also define the additional instance variable z. Write a test program to demonstrate that the proper methods are called polymorphically when Vec references are passed to the addition and subtraction methods.

9.   Create an interface called Vec, which defines methods to add and subtract two vectors. Create two classes, Vec2D and Vec3D, that implement this interface for two-dimensional and three-dimensional vectors, respectively. Class Vec2D must define instance variables x and y. Class Vec3D must define instance variables x, y, and z. Write a test program to demonstrate that the proper methods are called polymorphically when the interface methods are called.

10

Exceptions and Enhanced File I/O

Exceptions are the technique used by Java to handle unusual conditions (such as missing files or improperly formatted numbers) that interrupt the normal operation of the program. When something unusual (or exceptional—hence the name *exception*) happens during the execution of a program, the program must have some way to process and recover from the error. For example, if the user supplies an invalid file name to the program, the program should recognize that an error has occurred, and recover from the error gracefully. In the case of an invalid file name, the program should prompt the user to supply a correct file name. If the error is an invalid number, then the program should prompt the user to re-enter the number correctly.

In this chapter we will learn about how Java handles and recovers from these types of errors. Then we will use our knowledge to improve the ability of our programs to read data from disk files and from the standard input stream. The I/O operations serve as an excellent example of how exceptions are used in Java programming.

10.1 EXCEPTIONS AND EXCEPTION HANDLING

Java differs from most other computer languages in the way it handles errors. For example, suppose that we would like to open a disk file in a program and read data from it. In Fortran or C, if the disk file does not exist, the `open` statement will return a value in a status variable indicating that the file could not be found. The program must check that status variable and deal with the error at that point.

By contrast, when Java finds an error like this, it creates or "throws" a special Java object called an **exception**. The exception can be handled or "caught," which allows the program to correct the error that caused the problem, or else to shut down gracefully. An exception can be caught by the method in which it occurred, or by any method in the calling

SECTIONS

10.1 Exceptions and Exception Handling
10.2 Enhanced I/O Operations

OBJECTIVES

- Understand what an exception is.
- Know how to create exceptions.
- Know how to handle exceptions using a `try/catch` structure.
- Understand how exceptions help to create robust file I/O operations.

chain all the way back to the `main` method that started the program. Thus Java's error-handling mechanism is much more general than that in other languages. In this chapter we learn how to generate (throw) and handle (catch) exceptions.

10.1.1 What Is an Exception?

Just what is an exception? It is an event that interrupts the normal processing flow of a program. This event is usually an error of some sort. For example, an attempt to divide an integer value by zero will produce a run-time exception called `ArithmeticException`. Also, an attempt to open and read from a nonexistent file will produce a `FileNotFoundException`. There are many other examples of exceptions throughout the Java API.

Whenever a Java method cannot complete its normal processing, it **throws an exception**, which means that it creates a exception and passes it back to the calling method. Like everything else in Java, an exception is an object. Exceptions are objects of the `Exception` class or of some subclass of the `Exception` class. If an exception is **thrown** by a method and not **caught** by an exception handler, the program generating the exception will abort.

Exceptions are intended primarily as a way to handle errors that must be dealt with in a different scope (at a different level of the program) from the one that detected the error. For example, the Java API includes many standard classes that can be utilized by a programmer when he or she is writing a new program. If an error occurs in a method in one of the Java API classes, *the error must be dealt with by the programmer* in his/her own code, since there is no way the original writers of the Java API could possibly guess what the programmer would want to do about the error. The method in the Java API throws an exception, which may be caught and handled in the programmer's code (see Figure 10.1).

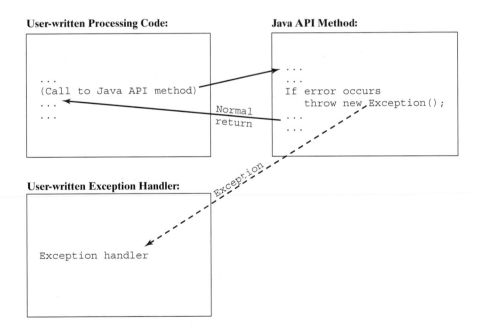

Figure 10.1. When a program calls a method in the Java API, the API method usually executes to completion, and program flow returns to the next statement following the one where the API method was called. This normal program flow is represented by the solid arrows in the diagram. If an error occurs in the API method, it throws an exception, which must be caught by a user-written exception handler. This abnormal program flow is shown by the dashed arrow. Note that the exception handler does *not* have to be in the method that made the API call.

There are two fundamental types of exceptions in Java, **run-time exceptions** and **checked exceptions**. Run-time exceptions are those that occur within the Java run-time system, including arithmetic exceptions (such as `int` division by 0), pointer exceptions (such as trying to access an object through a null reference), and indexing exceptions (such as attempting to access an array element through an index that is too large or too small). These sorts of exceptions can occur *anywhere* in a program, so Java does not force a programmer to list every possible run-time exception that can occur in every method.

All other exceptions in a Java program are known as **checked exceptions**, because the compiler checks that these exceptions are either caught or explicitly ignored by any method in which the exception could possibly occur. If an exception is to be ignored by a method, the method must explicitly "throw" the exception in the method declaration, so that a method higher up the calling tree can have a chance to "catch" it.

Every Java method has a **catch or specify requirement** for any checked exceptions that can be thrown *within the scope of that method*. This means that the exception must be explicitly caught and handled by the method, or else the method must explicitly declare that it throws the method. The words "within the scope of the method" imply that the method must either catch or throw exceptions that were thrown by the method itself or by any other method directly or indirectly called by the method.

GOOD PROGRAMMING PRACTICE

Use exceptions to trap and correct errors in Java programs, especially if the errors occur in lower-level general-purpose classes that manipulate files or data.

10.1.2 Creating an Exception

An exception is an object of the `Exception` class or one of its subclasses. The `Exception` class includes two constructors of the forms shown below:

```
public Exception()
public Exception( String s )
```

The first form creates a new `Exception` object with no arguments. The second form creates a new object and specifies an error message string that will be stored in the object. The `Exception` class includes two important methods that are useful in building exception handlers and debugging programs. Method `getMessage()` returns the error message stored in the `Exception` object so that it can be displayed. Method `printStackTrace()` prints a listing of the sequence of method calls that led up to the exception, which can help to identify the cause of the error. We will see examples of both of these methods later in the chapter.

TABLE 10.1 Exception Methods

Method	Description
`public String getMessage()`	Returns the error message embedded in the Exception object.
`public void printStackTrace()`	Prints the name of this exception and its stack trace to the standard error stream.

The Java language includes a hierarchy of exception classes organized under the general `Exception` class. There are many direct subclasses of `Exception`, and most of them have further subclasses, with each subclass representing a specific type of exception. Figure 10.2 shows a portion of the `Exception` class hierarchy. The root of the

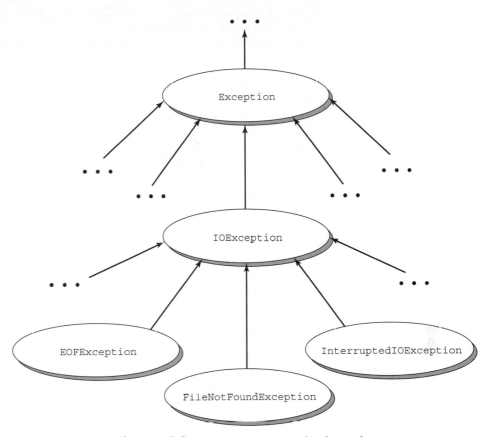

Figure 10.2. Partial Exception class hierarchy.

hierarchy is class Exception, which could represent any type of exception in a program. One subclass of Exception is IOException, which is the type of exception produced by input/output failures. Subclasses of IOException include EOFException, FileNotFoundException, and so forth. These subclasses are specific types of I/O exceptions. Notice that each subclass in the exception hierarchy is more specific than the superclass above it. A complete list of the predefined exception classes can be found in the Java SDK documentation.

Any Java method can throw any of the predefined exception classes. You may find that one of the predefined exceptions will be a good description of a problem that you encounter, in which case you can throw that exception in your code.

If none of the predefined exceptions meet your needs exactly, then you can create your own exception class as a subclass of any existing class in the exception hierarchy. For example, let's reconsider the Date class that we created in Chapter 7. What would happen in that class if a user passed an invalid date to a Date object using the setDate method? At the moment, nothing would happen, since the values passed to setDate are stored without validity checking. It would be better if we checked for the validity of the date, and threw an exception if an invalid date was passed to the method. We can create a special subclass of Exception called InvalidDateException for this purpose.

A possible InvalidDateException class is defined in Figure 10.3. Note that the expression "InvalidDateException extends Exception" means that our new class is a direct subclass of class Exception. This new class contains a single constructor, which initializes the class. The super method is a call to the constructor of the superclass Exception. It specifies the error string that will be available for display whenever this exception occurs.

```
// InvalidDateException
public class InvalidDateException extends Exception {
    // Define a constructor for this class
    public InvalidDateException() {
        super("Invalid date: please try again...");
    }
}
```

Figure 10.3. Class `InvalidDateException`.

10.1.3 Throwing an Exception

Now that we have created an `InvalidDateException`, how would the method `setDate` throw the exception? This can be done by including a **throw statement** at any desired point within the method. The `throw` statement must consist of the keyword `throw` followed by an object of the `Exception` class or one of its subclasses. The location of the `throw` statement is known as the **throw point**.

A version of the `setDate` method that throws an `InvalidDateException` is shown in Figure 10.4. This method checks to see whether the year, month, and day

```
// Method to set a date
public void setDate(int day, int month, int year)
                    throws InvalidDateException {
    int maxDays = 0;   // Max days in a month

    // Determine if year is valid
    if ( year < 0 )
        throw new InvalidDateException();
    else
        this.year  = year;

    // Determine if month is valid
    if ( month < 1 || month > 12 )
        throw new InvalidDateException();
    else
        this.month = month;

    // Determine if day is valid.  This
    // depends on the month.
    switch ( month ) {
        case 1:  case 3:  case 5:  case 7:
        case 8:  case 10: case 12:
            maxDays = 31;
            break;
        case 4: case 6: case 9: case 11:
            maxDays = 30;
            break;
        case 2:
            if ( isLeapYear() )
                maxDays = 29;
            else
```

Figure 10.4. A version of method `setDate` that throws an `InvalidDateException`.

```
                    maxDays = 28;
        }
        if ( day < 1 || day > maxDays )
            throw new InvalidDateException();
        else
            this.day = day;
    }
```

Figure 10.4. (Continued).

specified in the call are valid. If they are, it saves the information in the Date object. If not, it creates a new object of the InvalidDateException class and throws that object.

A complete version of the Date class that contains methods capable of throwing an InvalidDateException is shown in Figure 10.5. Note that the constructor

```
/*
   Purpose:
     This class stores and manipulates dates on the
     Gregorian calendar.  It implements constructors,
     set methods, get methods, and predicate methods,
     and overrides the toString method.

     Method list:
         Date()                      Date constructor
         Date(day,month,year)        Date constructor
         setDate(day,month,year)     Set Date
         getDay()                    Get day
         getMonth()                  Get month
         getYear()                   Get year
         isLeapYear()                Test for leap year
         isEqual()                   Test for equality
         isEarlier()                 Is chronologically earlier
         isLater()                   Is chronologically later
         toString()                  Convert to string for display

   Record of revisions:
       Date          Programmer        Description of change
       ====          ==========        =====================
     05/01/2002    S. J. Chapman       Original code
  1. 05/18/2002    S. J. Chapman       Modified to throw
                                          InvalidDateException
*/
public class Date {

   // Define instance variables
   private int year;        // Year (0 - xxxx)
   private int month;       // Month (1 - 12)
```

Figure 10.5. An improved Date class that contains methods to check for invalid dates and throw an InvalidDateException when an invalid input is supplied.

```
   private int day;           // Day (1 - 31)

// Default date is January 1, 1900
public Date() {
   year = 1900;
   month = 1;
   day = 1;
}

// Constructor for specified date
public Date(int day, int month, int year)
                  throws InvalidDateException {
   setDate( day, month, year );
}

// Method to set a date
public void setDate(int day, int month, int year)
                  throws InvalidDateException {
   int maxDays = 0;    // Max days in a month

   // Determine if year is valid
   if ( year < 0 )
      throw new InvalidDateException();
   else
      this.year  = year;

   // Determine if month is valid
   if ( month < 1 || month > 12 )
      throw new InvalidDateException();
   else
      this.month = month;

   // Determine if day is valid.  This
   // depends on the month.
   switch ( month ) {
      case 1:  case 3:  case 5:  case 7:
      case 8:  case 10: case 12:
         maxDays = 31;
         break;
      case 4: case 6: case 9: case 11:
         maxDays = 30;
         break;
      case 2:
         if ( isLeapYear() )
            maxDays = 29;
         else
            maxDays = 28;
   }
   if ( day < 1 || day > maxDays )
      throw new InvalidDateException();
   else
      this.day = day;
}
```

Figure 10.5. (Continued).

```
// Method to get day
public int getDay() {
   return day;
}

// Method to get month
public int getMonth() {
   return month;
}

// Method to get year
public int getYear() {
   return year;
}

// Method to check for leap year
public boolean isLeapYear() {
   boolean leap_year;
   if ( year % 400 == 0 )
      leap_year = true;
   else if ( year % 100 == 0 )
      leap_year = false;
   else if ( year % 4 == 0 )
      leap_year = true;
   else
      leap_year = false;
   return leap_year;
}

// Method to check for equality
public boolean isEqual( Date d ) {
   boolean equal;
   if ( year == d.year && month == d.month &&
        day == d.day )
      equal = true;
   else
      equal = false;
   return equal;
}

// Method to check if d is earlier than the
// value stored in the object.
public boolean isEarlier( Date d ) {
   boolean earlier;

   // Compare years
   if ( d.year > year )
      earlier = false;
   else if ( d.year < year )
      earlier = true;
   else {
```

Figure 10.5. (Continued).

```
               // Years are equal.  Compare months
               if ( d.month > month )
                  earlier = false;
               else if ( d.month < month )
                  earlier = true;
               else {

                  // Months are equal.  Compare days.
                  if ( d.day >= day )
                     earlier = false;
                  else
                     earlier = true;
               }
            }
         return earlier;
      }

      // Method to check if d is later than the
      // value stored in the object.
      public boolean isLater( Date d ) {
         boolean later;

         // Compare years
         if ( d.year > year )
            later = true;
         else if ( d.year < year )
            later = false;
         else {

            // Years are equal.  Compare months
            if ( d.month > month )
               later = true;
            else if ( d.month < month )
               later = false;
            else {

               // Months are equal.  Compare days.
               if ( d.day > day )
                  later = true;
               else
                  later = false;
            }
         }
         return later;
      }
      // Method to convert a date to a string.
      public String toString() {
         return (month + "/" + day + "/" + year);

      }
   }
```

Figure 10.5. (Continued).

`Date(day,month,year)` throws an `InvalidDateException`, because it calls method `setDate`, which throws that exception.

10.1.4 Handling Exceptions

Any exception that is thrown by a method must be either caught or rethrown by every method above that method in the calling tree. The Java compiler enforces this requirement. However, it does *not* force some method to catch and handle the exception—it is possible for every method all the way back to `main` to simply rethrow the exception.

If an exception is *not* caught by some method in the user's program, then the exception will cause the program to abort. For example, the program shown in Figure 10.6 attempts to create a new `Date` object with an invalid date.

```
/*
   Purpose:
     This class attempts to create a Date object with an
     invalid date.

   Record of revisions:
       Date           Programmer            Description of change
       ====           ==========            =====================
     05/19/2002   S. J. Chapman             Original code
*/
public class BadDate {

   // Define the main method
   public static void main(String[] args)
             throws InvalidDateException {

      // Create a new Date object
      Date d = new Date(29,2,1998);

      // Print out date
      System.out.println ("Date = " + d);

   }
}
```

Figure 10.6. A program that attempts to create a new `Date` object with an invalid date.

```
D:\book\java\chap10>java BadDate
InvalidDateException: Invalid date: please try again...
        at Date.setDate(Date.java:84)
        at Date.<init>(Date.java:45)
        at BadDate.main(BadDate.java:18)
```

It is possible for a method to **catch** an exception and handle the error that caused the problem. This is done with a **try/catch structure**. The form of a `try/catch` structure is

```
                    try {
                       ...
                    }
                    catch(exception1) {
                       ...
                    }
                    catch(exception2) {
                       ...
                    }
                    ...
                    finally {
                       ...
                    }
```

where the `try` block contains a set of statements to be executed, and the `catch` block(s) contain the **exception handlers**, which are sets of statements to be executed if the specified exceptions occur while the statements in the `try` block are being executed. There can be more than one `catch` block, with each one catching a different type of exception. In addition there can be a single `finally` block. The code in this block will be executed regardless of whether or not an exception occurs. It is typically used to release resources allocated by the `try` block so that they may be returned to the system.

Figure 10.7 illustrates the use of `try/catch` blocks for exception handling. This class contains two `try/catch` blocks surrounding statements that attempt to create new `Date` objects. The first new `Date` object is invalid, while the second one is valid.

```
/*
   Purpose:
     This class attempts to create a Date object with an
     invalid date, and catches the error in an exception
     handler.

   Record of revisions:
       Date          Programmer          Description of change
       ====          ==========          =====================
     05/19/2002    S. J. Chapman         Original code
*/
public class CatchBadDate {

   // Define the main method
   public static void main(String[] args) {

       // Try to create an invalid date
       System.out.println("\nFirst try/catch block:");
       try {

           // Create a new Date object
           Date d1 = new Date(29,2,1998);

           // Print out date
           System.out.println ("Date = " + d1);
       }

       catch (InvalidDateException e) {

           // Tell user
           System.err.println("The exception is:\n   " +
```

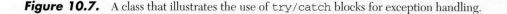

Figure 10.7. A class that illustrates the use of try/catch blocks for exception handling.

```
                                    e.getMessage());
        System.err.println("\nThe stack trace is:");
        e.printStackTrace();
    }
    finally {
        System.out.println("Finally always executes...");
    }

    // Try to create a valid date
    System.out.println("\nSecond try/catch block:");
    try {

        // Create a new Date object
        Date d2 = new Date(29,2,1996);

        // Print out date
        System.out.println ("Date = " + d2);
    }

    catch (InvalidDateException e) {

        // Tell user
        System.err.println("The exception is:\n  " +
                              e.getMessage());
        System.err.println("\nThe stack trace is:");
        e.printStackTrace();
    }
    finally {
        System.out.println("Finally always executes...");
    }
    }
}
```

Figure 10.7. (Continued).

When this program is executed, the first attempt to create a new Date object produces an InvalidDateException, which is caught by the catch block. This block prints out information about the exception using the getMessage() and printStackTrace() methods, and then allows execution to continue. Next, the finally block is executed whether an error occurs or not.

The second attempt to create a new Date object is valid, so the code in the try block is executed completely, and the catch block is skipped. Again, the finally block is executed whether an error occurs or not.

When this program is executed, the results are:

```
D:\book\java\chap10>java CatchBadDate

First try/catch block:
The exception is:
   Invalid date: please try again...
The stack trace is:
InvalidDateException: Invalid date: please try again...
        at Date.setDate(Date.java:84)
        at Date.<init>(Date.java:45)
        at CatchBadDate.main(CatchBadDate.java:22)
```

```
Finally always executes...

Second try/catch block:
Date = 2/29/1996
Finally always executes...
```

Use `try`/`catch` structures to trap and handle exceptions without causing the program producing the exception to abort.

10.1.5 The Exceptions Hierarchy and Inheritance

All exceptions inherit either directly or indirectly from the superclass `Exception`. Exception types form a tree or hierarchy, with the upper levels being very general and the lower levels more specific.

Because all exceptions inherit from the superclass `Exception`, every exception, regardless of subclass, is also an `Exception` and will respond to a `catch` block set to catch objects of type `Exception`. Thus the following `try`/`catch` structure would catch every possible exception that could occur, regardless of its specific class:

```
try {
    ...
}
catch ( Exception e ) {
    System.err.println("An exception occurred!);
    System.err.println("The stack trace is:");
    e.printStackTrace();

}
```

If this single `catch` block can catch every possible exception, then why do we bother to create an elaborate structure of different exceptions? The answer is that the lower the level of an exception, the more detail we have about what went wrong in the program. For example, if we set up a `catch` block that traps a `FileNotFoundException`, we would know very specifically that a specified file was not found during an I/O operation. If, instead, we set up a `catch` block that traps an `IOException`, the block would also trap the `FileNotFoundException`, but the code would know only that a general I/O error occurred, not specifically that a file was not found. The lower the level at which we trap the exception, the more specific our correction of the problem can be.

Try to catch exceptions at the lowest exception subclass possible, in order to have as much information as possible about what went wrong.

On the other hand, it can be very tedious to trap every possible error. To reduce the effort required, it may be convenient to trap exceptions at some higher level. For example, in some programs, it might be convenient to trap all I/O exceptions with a `catch` (`IOException e`) block. A compromise is often made between creating a long list of low-level `catch` blocks with very specific information and creating a single `catch` block to trap all exceptions. This trade-off must be made on a case-by-case method.

It is usual to have the most important exceptions for a specific application explicitly listed in their own `catch` blocks, with all other possible exceptions handled by a single higher-level `catch` block. For example, if we were opening a file, there might be a specific `catch` block for the `FileNotFoundException`, and an additional `catch` block for `IOException`. The second `catch` block will handle all exceptions that are not `FileNotFoundExceptions`. If this design is used, the more general `catch` block must occur *after* the specific catch blocks in a `try/catch` structure. The following `try/catch` structure specifically tests for a `FileNotFoundException` and processes it separately, then catches any other I/O exceptions in a generic `catch` block.

```
try {
   ...
}
catch ( FileNotFoundException e ) {
   ...
}
catch ( IOException e ) {
   ...
```

10.1.6 Nested `try/catch` Structures

Exceptions can occur at any level in a program, and `try/catch` blocks can occur at any level as well. Thus the `main` method of a program may include a `try/catch` block covering a major part of the program, while a lower-level method within the scope of that `try` block may include another `try/catch` block associated with opening a file for the program. In this case, the two `try/catch` blocks are effectively *nested* inside each other.

If an exception occurs inside a set of nested `try/catch` blocks, it is presented to the *innermost* set of `catch` blocks first. Those blocks will catch the exception if it is of a type that they are set to trap. If not, the exception is presented to the next innermost set of `catch` blocks. Those blocks will catch the exception if it is of a type that they are set to trap. This process repeats until the outermost set of `catch` blocks are reached. If they cannot process the exception, then the program will abort.

It is possible for an exception to be caught and handled on more than one level. An inner `catch` block can catch the exception and perform partial processing on it, then rethrow it so that a higher-level `catch` block can finish the processing. This behavior is illustrated in the sample program in Figure 10.8.

```
/*
  Purpose:
    This class illustrates the way that exceptions can
    be caught and re-thrown at multiple levels.

  Record of revisions:
     Date          Programmer            Description of change
     ====          ==========            =====================
   05/19/2002    S. J. Chapman          Original code
```

Figure 10.8. A program illustrating nested try/catch structures, with the inner structure partially processing and rethrowing an exception.

```
*/
public class CatchException {

    // Define the main method
    public static void main(String[] args) {

        try {
            throwsException();
        }

        catch (Exception e) {

            // Tell user
            System.err.println("\nException caught in main.");
            System.err.println("The stack trace is:");
            e.printStackTrace();
        }
    }

    public static void throwsException() throws Exception {
        // Throw an exception and catch it
        try {
            System.out.println("In method throwsException...");
            throw new Exception("New exception!");
        }

        catch (Exception e) {

            // Tell user
            System.err.println("Exception caught in throwsException.");
            System.err.println("The stack trace is:");
            e.printStackTrace();

            // Re-throw the exception for further processing
            throw e;
        }
    }
}
```

Figure 10.8.   (Continued).

The program in Figure 10.8 contains two methods, method `main` and method `throwsException`. Method `main` calls method `throwsException` within a `try/catch` structure, and method `throwsException` throws an exception within a `try/catch` structure of its own. Since the innermost `try/catch` structure has a `catch` block for this type of exception, it is processed there first. Since that `catch` block re-throws the exception, it is also processed by the `catch` block in the outer structure.

When this program executes, the results are:

```
D:\book\java\chap10>java CatchException
In method throwsException...
Exception caught in throwsException.
The stack trace is:
java.lang.Exception: New exception!
        at CatchException.throwsException
           (CatchException.java:35)
        at CatchException.main(CatchException.java:17)
```

```
        Exception caught in main.
        The stack trace is:
        java.lang.Exception: New exception!
                at CatchException.throwsException
                    (CatchException.java:35)
                at CatchException.main(CatchException.java:17)
```

EXAMPLE 10.1

Using a `try/catch` structure to trap input errors: One possible way to use a `try/catch` structure to trap input errors is to place the entire structure inside a `do/while` loop, with the `try` and `catch` blocks setting the control boolean for the loop. If this is done properly, the loop will repeat until a valid set of input data is entered.

To illustrate this point, we will create a program that prompts the user to enter a date and creates a new object of the `Date` class. This will be done inside a `do/while` loop and a `try/catch` structure, so that we can trap `InvalidDateExceptions` if they are generated, and prompt the user to try again.

SOLUTION

This program must have an outer `do/while` loop whose loop continuation condition is set to `false` only when a valid date is entered. This is accomplished by setting the boolean as the last statement in the `try` block. This statement will be executed only if a valid date has been set into the `Date` object. Otherwise, an `InvalidDateException` will occur, the `catch` block will print out an error message, and the loop will run again.

As we have done since Chapter 2, this program will read input values using the `BufferedReader` method `readLine()`. This method can throw an `IOException`, so we have always declared the method containing the call to `readLine()` with the clause "`throws  IOException`". No more! This time the program will include a `catch` clause to handle `IOExceptions` when they occur. (See Figure 10.9.)

```
/*
    Purpose:
      This class prompts a user to enter a date, and
      reads the date from the standard input stream.
      If the user enters an invalid date, it tries again.

    Record of revisions:
        Date         Programmer          Description of change
        ====         ==========          =====================
     05/19/2002   S. J. Chapman         Original code
*/
import java.io.*;
public class GetDate {

   // Define the main method
   public static void main(String[] args) {

      // Declare variables
      int day, month, year;    // Day, month, and year
      Date d = new Date();     // New Date object
```

Figure 10.9.   A program that uses a `try/catch` structure to trap and correct input errors.

```java
    String str;                // Input string
    boolean valid = false;     // Valid date flag

    // Create a buffered reader
    BufferedReader in1 = new BufferedReader(
                         new InputStreamReader(System.in));

    // while loop to get date
    do {

        // Get information to create a date object
        try {

            // Get day
            System.out.print("Enter day (dd):    ");
            str = in1.readLine();
            day = Integer.parseInt(str);

            // Get month
            System.out.print("Enter month (mm):  ");
            str = in1.readLine();
            month = Integer.parseInt(str);

            // Get year
            System.out.print("Enter year (yyyy): ");
            str = in1.readLine();
            year = Integer.parseInt(str);

            // Set Date into object
            d.setDate(day,month,year);

            // Set valid flag
            valid = true;
        }

        catch ( InvalidDateException e ) {
            System.err.println("Invalid date entered—try again!\n");
            valid = false;
        }

        catch ( IOException e ) {
            System.err.println("Unspecified I/O error—try again!\n");
            valid = false;
        }

    } while ( !valid );
    // Display final date
    System.out.println("\nThe date is: " + d);
    }
}
```

Figure 10.9. (Continued).

When this program executes, the results are:

```
D:\book\java\chap10>java GetDate
Enter day (dd):    30
Enter month (mm):  13
Enter year (yyyy): 1998
Invalid date entered—try again!
Enter day (dd):    29
Enter month (mm):  2
Enter year (yyyy): 1998
Invalid date entered—try again!
Enter day (dd):    29
Enter month (mm):  2
Enter year (yyyy): 1996
The date is: 2/29/1996
```

Note that the program keeps prompting the user until a valid date is entered. ■

10.1.7 Invalid Results That Do Not Produce Exceptions

One major part of the Java language does *not* throw an exception when an error occurs: the floating-point math library. Java uses IEEE Standard 754 floating-point arithmetic, which defines its own way of handling errors. Java treats floating-point math errors in the manner specified by the standard, and not with exceptions.

The IEEE Standard 754 defines two special bit patterns to handle errors: NaN and Infinity. NaN stands for "Not a Number," and it is produced whenever a mathematical operation cannot produce a real result. For example, the result of the method call Math.sqrt (−1) is NaN, since $\sqrt{-1}$ has no valid real answer. Infinity is produced as the result of a floating-point division by zero. If either error occurs, the program continues to run without generating an exception, but with the NaN or Infinity as the result of the calculations.

Java provides methods to detect NaN and Infinity results in floating-point variables. The static Java methods Double.isNan(d) or Double.isInfinite(d) return a true result if the value of the double variable d is a NaN or Infinite, respectively. Similarly, methods Float.isNan(f) or Float.isInfinite(f) return a true result if the value of the float variable f is a NaN or Infinite.

Interestingly, Java treats integer arithmetic differently than floating-point arithmetic. Integer arithmetic *does* produce exceptions. For example, integer division by zero produces an ArithmeticException. A program to illustrate floating-point and integer error handling is shown in Figure 10.10.

```
/*
   Purpose:
     This class illustrates the use of isNaN and isInf
     to check for floating-point math errors, and also
     the exception thrown for integer math errors.

   Record of revisions:
      Date          Programmer           Description of change
      ====          ==========           =====================
    05/19/2002    S. J. Chapman          Original code
```

Figure 10.10. A program to illustrate floating-point and integer error handling in Java.

```
*/
import java.io.*;
public class MathError {

   // Define the main method
   public static void main(String[] args)  throws IOException {

      double a, b, c;
      int i,j, k;

      // Create a buffered reader
      BufferedReader in1 = new BufferedReader(
                          new InputStreamReader(System.in));

      // Get input for square root
      System.out.print("Enter value for sqrt: ");
      a = Double.parseDouble( in1.readLine() );
      b = Math.sqrt(a);
      if ( Double.isNaN(b) )
         System.out.println("Error!  Result = " + b);
      else
         System.out.println("sqrt("+a+") = " + b);

      // Get input for floating-point division
      System.out.println("\nFloating-point division:");
      System.out.print("Enter numerator:    ");
      a = Double.parseDouble( in1.readLine() );
      System.out.print("Enter denominator: ");
      b = Double.parseDouble( in1.readLine() );
      c = a / b;
      if ( Double.isInfinite(c) )
         System.out.println
              ("Division by 0!  Result = " + c);
      else
         System.out.println("a/b = " + c);

      // Get input for integer division
      System.out.println("\nInteger division:");
      System.out.print("Enter numerator:    ");
      i = Integer.parseInt( in1.readLine() );
      System.out.print("Enter denominator: ");
      j = Integer.parseInt( in1.readLine() );
      k = i / j;
      System.out.println("i/j = " + k);
   }
}
```

Figure 10.10. (Continued).

When this program is executed, the results are:

```
D:\book\java\chap10>java MathError
Enter value for sqrt: -1
Error!  Result = NaN
```

```
Floating-point division:
Enter numerator:    5
Enter denominator: 0
Division by 0!  Result = Infinity

Integer division:
Enter numerator:    5
Enter denominator: 0
Exception in thread "main"
   java.lang.ArithmeticException: / by zero
         at MathError.main(MathError.java:53)
```

Note that the floating-point math errors did not create an exception. Instead, program execution continued normally. The integer math error did produce an exception, which would cause the program to abort if no try/catch structure handled it. Also, note that ArithmeticException is a run-time exception, so it did not have to be declared in a throws clause.

QUIZ 10-1

This quiz provides a quick check to see if you have understood the concepts introduced in Section 10.1. If you have trouble with the quiz, reread the section, ask your instructor, or discuss the material with a fellow student. The answers are found in the back of the book.

1.   What is an exception?

2.   What is the difference between a run-time exception and a checked exception?

3.   What is meant by Java's catch or specify requirement?

4.   How can a programmer design a Java program to recover from an exception instead of crashing when one occurs?

5.   What methods are available with an Exception object? How are they used in a typical Java program that handles exceptions?

10.2   ENHANCED I/O OPERATIONS

Now that we have studied exceptions, it is possible to create more robust Java input and output operations. We have been reading data from the standard input stream since Chapter 2, using a BufferedReader to get data a line at a time, and various conversion methods to translate the corresponding lines into int, double, and so on, data. While this technique has worked, it is rather fragile. For example, if a user enters an incorrect string that can't be converted into the specified data type, the program will crash with a run-time exception.

The program in Figure 10.11 illustrates this problem. It retrieves an entire line of data from the standard input stream and translates the string into an int value. If a user mistypes the input characters, this program will crash with a run-time NumberFormatException.

```
// This program shows the result of invalid input data on the
// standard input stream.
import java.io.*;
public class TestReadError {
```

Figure 10.11.   This Java program will crash if the user enters a character string that cannot be translated into an int value.

```
    // Define the main method
    public static void main(String[] args) throws IOException {

        int v1;              // Test value
        String str;          // Input string

        // Create a buffered reader
        BufferedReader in1 = new BufferedReader(
                            new InputStreamReader(System.in));

        // Prompt for a double value
        System.out.print("Enter an int value: ");
        str = in1.readLine();
        v1 = Integer.parseInt(str);
        System.out.println("Value = " + v1 );
    }
}
```

Figure 10.11. (Continued).

When this program is executed and the user types in an incorrect string, the results are

```
D:\book\java\chap10>java TestReadError
Enter an int value: 5t6
Exception in thread "main"
   java.lang.NumberFormatException: 5t6
           at java.lang.Integer.parseInt(Integer.java:423)
           at java.lang.Integer.parseInt(Integer.java:463)
           at TestReadError.main(TestReadError.java:19)
```

Similarly, the techniques that we have developed for reading data from disk files have been fragile. We could only read data that was organized with one value per line. Having either two values on a line or no values on a line caused the program to crash. The read technique was improved with the introduction of the StringTokenizer class in Chapter 8, but we can make it even better now.

10.2.1 Reading Data from the Standard Input Stream

We will now create a class called StdIn that reads data from the standard input stream in a more robust fashion. The class must be able to read double, int, boolean, or String values from the standard input stream and must be able to recover from errors. To be robust, this class needs to include the following features:

1. Use StringTokenizer to separate out the first token from a line, so that if a user types two or more items on a line, it won't cause the program to crash. The nextToken() method of class StringTokenizer throws a run-time exception called NoSuchElementException if there are no more tokens available on the line, so we must handle that exception by including the call to nextToken() within a try/catch structure, and including a catch clause for that exception.

2. Use a try/catch structure to handle IOExceptions, if they should occur. IOExceptions can be generated by a call to the BufferedReader method readLine(). If an IOException occurs, the program should tell the user about the problem and return a zero or false value to the caller. This is true because IOExceptions on the standard input stream usually mean

that there is a serious problem, or that there is no more data to read if the standard input stream has been redirected to a file. In either case, the only reasonable recovery is to tell the user about the problem and to go on from there.

3.   Use a try/catch structure to handle NumberFormatExceptions, if they should occur. A NumberFormatException can occur whenever we are attempting to read a double or int value, if the user accidentally types an incorrect number. This is a recoverable error, so the user should be told what is wrong and be allowed to re-enter the number correctly.

The constructor for this class must create a BufferedReader on the standard input stream, so that the methods in the class can extract data a line at a time from it. The class must also contain an instance variable to refer to the BufferedReader object. That instance variable will be available to all of the methods in the class, so that any method will be able to read a line of data.

The method to read a double value from the standard input stream will be called readDouble(). This method must read a line of data from the standard input stream and feed the line to a StringTokenizer object. Then, the StringTokenizer method nextToken() can be used to extract the characters to be converted into a double value. These characters will be presented to the method Double.parseDouble(str) to actually convert the characters into a double value.

To make this code robust, the readLine(), nextToken(), and parseDouble methods must all occur within a try/catch structure. This structure must catch NumberFormatException, NoSuchElementException, and IOException. If one of the first two exceptions occur, then the program must tell the user and allow him or her to re-enter the number. If the third exception occurs, the program must tell the user, supply a default value, and return to the calling method. The try/catch structure itself will lie within a while loop, which will repeat until an acceptable value has been retrieved.

```
// Read a double value from the standard input stream
public double readDouble() {

   // Declare local variables
   boolean inputOk = false;       // Input OK flag
   double d = 0.0;                // Value to return
   StringTokenizer st;            // StringTokenizer

   // Loop until we get the required value
   while ( !inputOk ) {
      try {
         st = new StringTokenizer( br.readLine() );
         d = Double.parseDouble(st.nextToken());
         inputOk = true;
      }
      catch ( NumberFormatException e ) {
         System.out.println("Invalid format for double-try again:");
      }
      catch ( NoSuchElementException e ) {
         System.out.println("Blank line-try again:");
      }
      catch ( IOException e ) {
         System.out.println("IO Exception: 0.0 returned");
```

```
              d = 0.0;
              inputOk = true;
          }
      }
      return d;
  }
```

The other methods in this class will be similar, except that there can be no possibility of a `NumberFormatException` when reading `boolean` values; any string that is not "true" is interpreted as false, regardless of its contents. The completed class is shown in Figure 10.12.

A program to test class `StdIn` is shown in Figure 10.13. Note that the `main` method in this class does not have to throw any exceptions—they are all caught and handled within class `StdIn`!

```
/*
  Purpose:
    This class reads data from the standard input stream,
    converting it to int, double, boolean, or String values,
    as appropriate.  It traps exceptions and recovers from
    errors.
  Record of revisions:
      Date         Programmer           Description of change
      ====         ==========           =====================
    05/24/2002   S. J. Chapman          Original code
*/
import java.io.*;
import java.util.*;
public class StdIn {
  // Declare instance variables
  BufferedReader br;                    // Reference to BufferedReader

  // Constructor
  public StdIn() {
     br = new BufferedReader(new InputStreamReader(System.in));
  }
  // Read a double value from the standard input stream
  public double readDouble() {
     // Declare local variables
     boolean inputOk = false;          // Input OK flag
     double d = 0.0;                    // Value to return
     StringTokenizer st;               // StringTokenizer
     // Loop until we get the required value
     while ( !inputOk ) {
        try {
           st = new StringTokenizer( br.readLine() );
           d = Double.parseDouble(st.nextToken());
```

Figure 10.12. Class `StdIn`.

```java
            inputOk = true;
        }
        catch ( NumberFormatException e ) {
            System.out.print("Invalid format for double-try again: ");
        }
        catch ( NoSuchElementException e ) {
            System.out.print("Blank line-try again: ");
        }
        catch ( IOException e ) {
            System.out.print("IO Exception: 0.0 returned");
            d = 0.0;
            inputOk = true;
        }
    }
    return d;
}

// Read an int value from the standard input stream
public int readInt() {

    // Declare local variables
    boolean inputOk = false;      // Input OK flag
    int i = 0;                    // Value to return
    StringTokenizer st;           // StringTokenizer

    // Loop until we get the required value
    while ( !inputOk ) {
        try {
            st = new StringTokenizer( br.readLine() );
            i = Integer.parseInt(st.nextToken());
            inputOk = true;
        }
        catch ( NumberFormatException e ) {
            System.out.print("Invalid format for int-try again: ");
        }
        catch ( NoSuchElementException e ) {
            System.out.print("Blank line-try again: ");
        }
        catch ( IOException e ) {
            System.out.print("IO Exception: 0 returned");
            i = 0;
            inputOk = true;
        }
    }
    return i;
}

// Read a boolean value from the standard input stream
public boolean readBoolean() {

    // Declare local variables
    boolean inputOk = false;      // Input OK flag
```

Figure 10.12. (Continued).

```java
        boolean b = false;          // Value to return
        StringTokenizer st;         // StringTokenizer

        // Loop until we get the required value
        while ( !inputOk ) {
            try {
                st = new StringTokenizer( br.readLine() );
                b = new Boolean(st.nextToken()).booleanValue();
                inputOk = true;
            }
            catch ( NoSuchElementException e ) {
                System.out.print("Blank line-try again: ");
            }
            catch ( IOException e ) {
                System.out.print("IO Exception: false returned");
                b = false;
                inputOk = true;
            }
        }
        return b;
    }
    // Read a line from the standard input stream
    public String readLine() {
        try {
            return br.readLine();
        }
        catch ( IOException e ) {
            System.out.print("IO Exception: null String returned");
            return "";
        }
    }
}
```

Figure 10.12. (Continued).

```java
/*
   Purpose:
     This class tests class StdIn.

   Record of revisions:
       Date          Programmer            Description of change
       ====          ==========            =====================
    05/24/2002    S. J. Chapman            Original code
*/
public class TestStdIn {

    // Define the main method
    public static void main(String[] args) {
        double a;
```

Figure 10.13. A program to test class StdIn.

```
        int b;
        boolean c;
        String d;

        // Create a StdIn object
        StdIn in = new StdIn();

        // Get a double value
        System.out.print("Enter a double value: ");
        a = in.readDouble();
        System.out.println("Value = " + a);

        // Get an int value
        System.out.print("Enter an int value: ");
        b = in.readInt();
        System.out.println("Value = " + b);

        // Get an int value
        System.out.print("Enter a boolean value: ");
        c = in.readBoolean();
        System.out.println("Value = " + c);

        // Get an String value
        System.out.print("Enter a String value: ");
        d = in.readLine();
        System.out.println("Value = " + d);
    }
}
```

Figure 10.13.   (Continued).

When this program is executed and the user types in incorrect strings, the results are as follows:

```
D:\book\java\chap10>java TestStdIn
Enter a double value: -3m2
Invalid format for double-try again: <cr>
Blank line-try again: -3.2e5
Value = -320000.0
Enter an int value: -3.2e5
Invalid format for int-try again: -3
Value = -3
Enter a boolean value: <cr>
Blank line-try again: junk
Value = false
Enter a String value: This is a test!
Value = This is a test!
```

Here, <cr> represents pressing the Enter key without entering a string. Note that the methods in this class gracefully recover from most errors, giving users an opportunity to correct their typing errors without crashing the program.

We will re-use this improved class in future programs that must read data from the standard input stream.

10.2.2 Reading Data from the Disk Files

It is also possible to make reading data from disk files more robust. We learned in Chapter 8 how to use StringTokenizer to allow us to read multiple values from a single line, but the technique shown there still has numerous weaknesses. For example, it would crash the program if there were blank lines in the input file, or if there were invalid values in the input file.

Figure 10.14 shows a class that reads double or int values from an input file and will not crash if the file is not present, if one or more lines are blank, or if some of the data in the file is formatted incorrectly. This class reads data from the file one line at a time and

```
/*
    Purpose:
      This class demonstrates how to read data from a disk file,
      converting it to double or int values.  It traps exceptions
      and allows the user to recover from errors, when possible.

    Record of revisions:
        Date          Programmer            Description of change
        ====          ==========            =====================
      05/24/2002    S. J. Chapman           Original code
*/
import java.io.*;
import java.util.*;
public class ReadFile {
    // Declare instance variables
    BufferedReader br;                  // Reference to BufferedReader
    StringTokenizer st;                 // Reference to StringTokenizer

    // Constructor
    public ReadFile(String fileName) throws FileNotFoundException,
                                    IOException {

        // Local variables
        boolean inputOk = false;       // Input OK flag

        // Open buffered reader
        br = new BufferedReader(new FileReader(fileName));

        // Get the first line of valid data in a StringTokenizer
        while ( !inputOk ) {
            try {
                st = new StringTokenizer( br.readLine() );
                inputOk = true;
            }
            catch ( NoSuchElementException e ) {
                // Blank line, so skip it and try again
                inputOk = false;
            }
            catch ( IOException e ) {
                // We can't do anything about this, so re-throw it
                throw e;
            }
        }
    }
```

Figure 10.14. Class ReadFile.

```java
// Read a double value from the file
public double readDouble() throws IOException {

    // Local variables
    double d = 0;                  // Double value
    boolean inputOk = false;       // Input OK flag
    String str;                    // Input string

    // Get a double value
    while ( !inputOk ) {
        try {
            if (st.hasMoreTokens()) {

                // Get the next value from the current line
                d = Double.parseDouble(st.nextToken());
                inputOk = true;
            }
            else {

                // Get a new line and try again
                str = br.readLine();
                if ( str != null ) {
                    st = new StringTokenizer(str);
                    inputOk = false;
                }
                else {

                    // At EOF, so throw EOF exception
                    throw new EOFException();
                }
            }
        }
        catch ( NoSuchElementException e ) {

            // Blank line, so skip it and try again
            inputOk = false;
        }
    }
    return d;
}

// Read an int value from the file
public int readInt() throws IOException {

    // Local variables
    int i = 0;                     // int value
    boolean inputOk = false;       // Input OK flag
    String str;                    // Input string
```

Figure 10.14.   (Continued).

```
        // Get a double value
        while ( !inputOk ) {
            try {
                if (st.hasMoreTokens()) {

                    // Get the next value from the current line
                    i = Integer.parseInt(st.nextToken());
                    inputOk = true;
                }
                else {

                    // Get a new line and try again
                    str = br.readLine();
                    if ( str != null ) {
                        st = new StringTokenizer(str);
                        inputOk = false;
                    }
                    else {

                        // At EOF, so throw EOF exception
                        throw new EOFException();
                    }
                }
            }
            catch ( NoSuchElementException e ) {

                // Blank line, so skip it and try again
                inputOk = false;
            }
        }
        return i;
    }
    // Method to close the file
    public void close() throws IOException {
        br.close();
    }
}
```

Figure 10.14. (Continued).

creates StringTokenizer objects for each line. The StringTokenizer then parcels out the data one token at a time, and the token is converted into the proper type using the Double.parseDouble or Integer.parseInt methods.

Note that this class opens the file, reads values, and converts them within try/catch structures, which allow the program to recover from any errors that may occur. Also, this class creates and throws an EOFException when the end of the input file is reached. [The end of the input file is reached when the input string returned by readLine() is null.]

A program that tests class ReadFile is shown in Figure 10.15. It gets an input file name from a user and attempts to create a ReadFile object on that file within a try/catch structure. If there is a problem with the file, it is caught by the catch clause(s), and the user can provide a corrected file name. Similarly, the actual calls to read data occur within a try/catch structure to handle the end of the file and improperly formatted data.

```
/*
   Purpose:
     This class tests class ReadFile.

   Record of revisions:
       Date          Programmer           Description of change
       ====          ==========           =====================
     05/24/2002    S. J. Chapman          Original code
*/
import java.io.*;
public class TestReadFile {

   // Define the main method
   public static void main(String[] args) {

      // Local variables
      int count;                        // Count of input values
      boolean done = false;             // Read done flag
      boolean fileOk = false;           // File OK flag
      String fileName;                  // Input file name
      ReadFile rf = null;               // ReadFile object reference
      double v;                         // Input value

      // Create a StdIn object
      StdIn in = new StdIn();

      // Prompt user for the name of the file to read
      while ( !fileOk ) {
         System.out.print("Enter input file name: ");
         fileName = in.readLine();

         // Open the file, protecting against errors
         try {
            rf = new ReadFile(fileName);
            fileOk = true;
         }
         catch ( FileNotFoundException e ) {

            // Tell user about the error
            System.out.println("File " + fileName + " not found!"
                               + " Please try again." );
         }
         catch ( IOException e ) {

            // Tell user about the error
            System.out.println("File " + fileName + " error!"
                               + " Please try again." );
         }
      }

      // Now get all of the values from the file.  We will
      // display the values and tell the user if any invalid
      // values are found.
```

Figure 10.15. A program to test class ReadFile.

```
        done = false;
        count = 0;
        if (rf != null) {
            while ( !done ) {
                // Read and display a value
                try {

                    // Get and display value
                    v = rf.readDouble();
                    count++;
                    System.out.println("Value " + count + " = " + v);
                }
                catch ( NumberFormatException e ) {

                    // Tell user about bad value
                    count++;
                    System.out.println("Value " + count + " = invalid");
                }
                catch ( EOFException e ) {

                    // We are done, so get out!
                    System.out.println("End of file reached!");
                    done = true;
                }
                catch ( IOException e ) {

                    // We are done, so get out!
                    System.out.println("Unknown IO error: " + e.getMessage());
                    done = true;
                }
            }

            // Close the input file
            try {
                System.out.println("Closing file");
                rf.close();
            }
            catch ( IOException e ) {
            }
        }
        System.out.println("Done");
    }
}
```

Figure 10.15. (Continued).

To test this program, we will create a file named `input`, whose contents are

```
11   -5.3    6
2.2  1.2e-7  xx
6
```

When this program is executed, the results are as follows:

```
D:\book\java\chap10>java TestReadFile
Enter input file name: badname
```

```
File badname not found! Please try again.
Enter input file name: input
Value 1 = 11.0
Value 2 = -5.3
Value 3 = 6.0
Value 4 = 2.2
Value 5 = 1.2E-7
Value 6 = invalid
Value 7 = 6.0
End of file reached!
Closing file
Done
```

Note that the program trapped the invalid input file name and allowed the user to change it to the proper name. Also, the program identified the invalid token without causing the program to crash.

Use `try`/`catch` structures with file I/O operations to trap and correct exceptions, instead of allowing a program to crash when an error occurs.

You will be asked to design a robust file output class in an end-of-chapter exercise.

SUMMARY

- Exceptions are objects created when an error occurs during normal processing. They are typically used when the error occurs in a different scope from that where the malfunction was detected.

- Exception handling should be used to process exceptions from software components such as libraries of classes that are likely to be widely used, since the writer of the classes cannot anticipate what the final user would like to do about each exception.

- When a Java method encounters an error that it cannot handle, it creates and throws an exception.

- There are two types of exceptions—run-time exceptions and checked exceptions.

- Programmers must catch or specifically throw any checked exception that may be produced with the scope of a method.

- Exceptions can be caught and handled by enclosing code within a `try`/`catch` structure.

- The catch block `catch (Exception e)` will catch all exceptions, since the `Exception` class is at the top of the exception class hierarchy.

- Exception handlers are searched in order from innermost to outermost for an handler capable of dealing with the exception type. The first handler capable of dealing with the exception is executed.

- A `catch` block may rethrow an exception to an outer `try`/`catch` structure.

- The `finally` block is always executed in a `try`/`catch` structure. It may be used to release allocated resources.

SUMMARY OF GOOD PROGRAMMING PRACTICES

The following guidelines introduced in this chapter will help you to develop good programs:

1. Use exceptions to trap and correct errors in Java programs, especially if the errors occur in lower-level general-purpose classes that manipulate files or data.

2. Use `try`/`catch` structures to trap and handle exceptions without causing the program producing the exception to abort.

3. Try to catch exceptions at the lowest exception subclass possible, in order to have as much information as possible about what went wrong.

4. Use `try`/`catch` structures with file I/O operations to trap and correct exceptions, instead of allowing a program to crash when an error occurs.

TERMINOLOGY

catch or specify requirement	one-dimensional array
checked exception	run-time exception
exception	throw an exception
`Exception` class	`throw` statement
exception handling	throw point
`finally` clause	`try`/`catch` structure

Exercises

1. What is an exception? What is the difference between a run-time exception and a checked exception?

2. Why are exceptions especially useful for dealing with errors within Java API methods?

3. If no exceptions are thrown within a `try` block, where does execution continue after the `try` block is finished? If an exception is thrown within a `try` block and caught in a `catch` block, where does execution continue after the `catch` block is finished?

4. Write a class that creates a 15-element array a and initializes its elements to the values 1 through 15. Include a method in the class that attempts to take the square root of *16* elements in the array. What exception occurs when this happens? Is this a run-time exception or a checked exception? Write a `try`/`catch` structure that traps it.

5. What sort of exception occurs if a modulo operation is evaluated with zero as the second operand (for example, `4 % 0`)?

6. Write a program that reads two `int` values and calculates and displays the sum, difference, product, quotient, and modulus of the numbers. Include a `try`/`catch` structure to trap and report any possible run-time exceptions.

7. Create a class `WriteFile` (analogous to the `ReadFile` in this chapter) that writes data to an output file, trapping any exceptions that may occur.

8. When class `ReadFile` encounters an invalid value in an input file, it throws a run-time `NumberFormatException`. Assume that, instead of returning a `NumberFormatException`, a user would like the class to return a `NaN` for invalid `double` values or a zero for invalid `int` values and just keep on processing. Write and test a modified class that treats invalid values in this fashion.

11

Multidimensional Arrays

This chapter introduces multidimensional arrays and provides examples of how to use them to solve scientific and engineering problems.

11.1 TWO-DIMENSIONAL ARRAYS

The arrays that we have worked with so far in this book are **one-dimensional arrays**. They can be visualized as a series of values laid out in a column, with a single subscript used to select the individual array elements [Figure 11.1(a)]. Such arrays are useful to describe data that is a function of one independent variable, such as a series of temperature measurements made at fixed intervals of time.

Some types of data are functions of more than one independent variable. For example, we might wish to measure the temperature at five different locations at four different times. In this case, our 20 measurements could logically be grouped into five different columns of four measurements each, with a separate column for each location [Figure 11.1(b)]. Java does not directly support two-dimensional arrays like this, but *Java arrays can be created with any type of data, including primitive data types, references to objects, or references to other arrays*. Therefore, we can declare an array, each of whose elements is a reference to another array, and the result is effectively a two-dimensional array (see Figure 11.2).

The elements of two-dimensional arrays are addressed with two subscripts, and any particular element in the array is selected by simultaneously choosing values for both of them. For example, Figure 11.3(a) shows a set of four generators whose power output has been measured at six different times. Figure 11.3(b) shows an array consisting of the six different power measurements for each of the four different generators. In this example, each row specifies a generator

OBJECTIVES

- Be able to create and use multidimensional arrays.

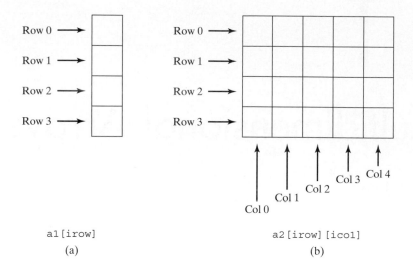

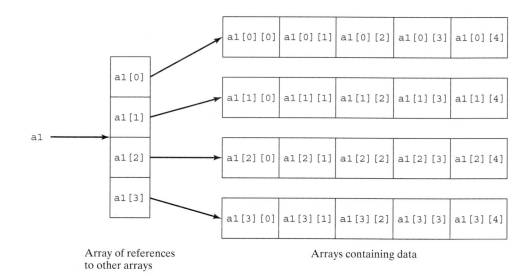

Figure 11.1. Representations of (a) one- and (b) two-dimensional arrays.

Figure 11.2. It is possible to create an array of references to other arrays.

number, and each column specifies a measurement time. The array element containing the power supplied by generator 2 at time 3 would be power[2][3]; its value is 41.1 MW.

11.1.1 Declaring Two-Dimensional Arrays

Java implements two-dimensional arrays by creating *a one-dimensional array, each of whose elements is itself an array*. To declare a two-dimensional array, we must first declare a reference to *an array of arrays*, and afterward create the individual arrays associated with each element of that array. The declaration of a reference to an array of arrays looks similar to the examples seen earlier, except that there are *two* brackets after the array name. For example, a reference to an array of double arrays is created by the statement

```
double[][] x;  // Create a reference to an array of arrays
```

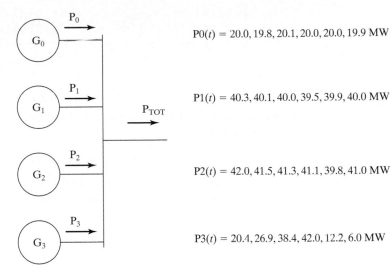

$P0(t) = 20.0, 19.8, 20.1, 20.0, 20.0, 19.9$ MW

$P1(t) = 40.3, 40.1, 40.0, 39.5, 39.9, 40.0$ MW

$P2(t) = 42.0, 41.5, 41.3, 41.1, 39.8, 41.0$ MW

$P3(t) = 20.4, 26.9, 38.4, 42.0, 12.2, 6.0$ MW

(a)

	T0	T1	T2	T3	T4	T5
Gen 0	20.0	19.8	20.1	20.0	20.0	19.9
Gen 1	40.3	40.1	40.0	39.5	39.9	40.0
Gen 2	42.0	41.5	41.3	41.1	39.8	41.0
Gen 3	20.4	26.9	38.4	42.0	12.2	6.0

(b)

Figure 11.3. (a) A power generating station consisting of four different generators. The power output of each generator is measured at six different times. (b) A two-dimensional matrix of power measurements.

When this statement is executed, the array reference x is created. However, the value of the reference is initially **null**, since it doesn't "point to" an array object yet. Attempting to use a null reference in a program will produce a run-time exception.

Once the reference is created, we can create arrays to assign to the reference using the **new** operator. For example, the following statement creates an array of three new five-element arrays and sets the reference x to refer to that array:

```
x = new double[3][5];   // Create array objects
```

The new operator is followed by the data type of the array object to be created and square brackets containing the number of elements to be allocated at each level. When the elements are allocated, they are automatically initialized to zero.

Note that *since a two-dimensional array is really an array of arrays, each subarray can be declared independently.* The subarrays may have different lengths, but they must all have the same type. For example, the following statements create an integer array with two rows, with row 0 containing five columns and row 1 containing three columns.

```
int[][] a;              // Declare reference
a = new int[2][];       // Create row of array references
a[0] = new int[5];      // Create columns for row 0
a[0] = new int[3];      // Create columns for row 1
```

11.1.2 Initializing Two-Dimensional Arrays

A two-dimensional array may be initialized using *nested* array initializers. For example, the statement

```
int[][] b = { {1,2,3}, {4,5,6} };
```

declares a reference to a two-dimensional array b and initializes the array with two rows, each containing three columns. The values are grouped by row in braces, so the row-0 elements b[0][0], b[0][1], and b[0][2] contain 1, 2, and 3, while the row-1 elements b[1][0], b[1][1], and b[1][2] contain 4, 5, and 6. The resulting data structure is shown in Figure 11.4(a).

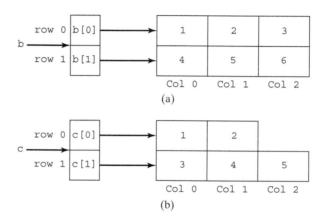

Figure 11.4. (a) A two-dimensional array with two rows and three columns per row. (b) A two-dimensional array with an uneven number of columns per row. This array has two rows; row 0 has two columns and row 1 has three columns.

Two-dimensional arrays can also be initialized with an uneven number of columns. For example, the statement

```
int[][] c = { {1,2}, {3,4,5} };
```

declares a reference to a two-dimensional array c with two rows. Row 0 contains two columns, while row 1 contains three columns. Here, c[0][0] and c[0][1] contain 1 and 2, while c[1][0], c[1][1], and c[1][2] contain 3, 4, and 5. Note that there is no element c[0][2] for this array. The resulting data structure is shown in Figure 11.4(b).

11.1.3 Initializing Two-Dimensional Arrays From a File

It is also possible to initialize a two-dimensional array by reading in data from a disk file. For example, a programmer might wish to initialize a 3 × 5 array v1 by reading the following data from a file input3:

```
2.34   14.31   5.02   5.01   -9.92
8.62   -1.01   2.01   3.55   -1.01
6.11   12.21   3.16   3.09   -7.89
```

This data can be read using the `ReadFile` class, using a pair of nested `for` loops to assign the proper value to each array element. A sample program that initializes array `v1` from a disk file is shown in Figure 11.5.

```java
// Reading 2-D arrays from a file
import java.io.*;
import java.text.DecimalFormat;
public class Read2DArray {

    // Define the main method
    public static void main(String arg[]) throws IOException {

        // Declare variables and arrays
        double[][] v1 = new double[3][5]; // Input array
        int i = 0, j = 0;                  // Loop index

        // Open file
        ReadFile rf = new ReadFile("input3");

        // Read input data from the file
        for ( i = 0; i < 3; i++ ) {
            for ( j = 0; j < 5; j++ ) {
                v1[i][j] = rf.readDouble();
            }
        }

         // Close file
         rf.close();

        // Display the data that we read in
        DecimalFormat df1  = new DecimalFormat("####.0000");
        for ( i = 0; i < 3; i++ ) {
            for ( j = 0; j < 5; j++ ) {
                System.out.print(df1.format(v1[i][j]) + "   ");
            }
            System.out.println();
        }
    }
}
```

Figure 11.5. Example program illustrating the initialization of two-dimensional arrays from a disk file.

When the program is executed with this data set, the results are

```
D:\book\java\chap5>java Read2DArray
    2.3400     14.3100      5.0200      5.0100     -9.9200
    8.6200     -1.0100      2.0100      3.5500     -1.0100
    6.1100     12.2100      3.1600      3.0900     -7.8900
```

11.1.4 Example Problem

EXAMPLE 11.1

Electric Power Generation: Figure 11.3(b) shows a series of electrical output power measurements at six different times for four different generators at the Acme Electric

Power generating station. Write a program to read these values from an input file and to calculate the average power supplied by each generator over the measurement period and the total power supplied by all of the generators at each time in the measurement period. Allow the user to specify the input file name, and trap any errors in opening the file. Also, be sure to trap any bad values in the file and tell the user about them.

SOLUTION

1. **Determine the User Requirements**

The user requires a program that will calculate the average power supplied by each generator in the station over the measurement period and calculate the total instantaneous power supplied by the generating station at each time within that period. Write those values out on the standard output device.

The input to this program is a set of 24 real data values in an input file, representing the power supplied by each of the four generators at each of six different times. The data in the input file must be organized so that the six values associated with generator G_0 appear on the first line, followed by the six values associated with generator G_1, and so on.

The outputs from this program are the average power supplied by each generator in the station over the measurement period, and the total instantaneous power supplied by the generating station at each time within the measurement period.

The user also wants the program to detect and report I/O errors. Where possible, the user should be allowed a chance to correct mistakes.

2. **Analysis and Decomposition**

There will be a single class, and only the main method within that class. We will call the class `Generator` and make it a subclass of the root class `Object`.

3. **Detailed Design**

The `main` method can be broken down into five major steps:

```
Get the input file name
Read the input data into an array
Calculate the total instantaneous output power
   at each time
Calculate the average output power of each
   generator
Write the output values
```

When the program reads the input file name and opens the input file, it should do so within a `try`/`catch` structure that allows the user to correct invalid file names without crashing the program. The detailed pseudocode for this step is

```
while ( !fileOk ) {
   Get file name from user
   // Open the file, protecting against errors
   try {
      Open file
      fileOk = true;
   }
```

```
      catch ( FileNotFoundException e ) {
         Tell user about bad file, go back to try again
      }
      catch ( IOException e ) {
         Tell user about bad file, go back to try again
      }
   }
```

The next step is to read in the input data. We should also do this within a `try/catch` loop to catch errors. However, if there are errors in the input file, the best we can do is to tell the user what is wrong and quit. There is no way to average the power data if the input values are not correct. The detailed pseudocode for this step is

```
try {
   // Read input data from the standard input stream
   for ( igen = 0; igen < MAX_GEN; igen++ ) {
      for ( itime = 0; itime < MAX_TIME; itime++ ) {
         power[igen][itime] = rf.readDouble();
      }
   }
}
catch ( NumberFormatException e ) {
   Tell user about bad value, and quit
}
catch ( EOFException e ) {
   Tell user about EOF, and quit
}
catch ( IOException e ) {
   Tell user about I/O error, and quit
}
```

The third step is to calculate the instantaneous power for each time. The detailed pseudocode for this step is

```
// Calculate the instantaneous output power of the station
for ( igen = 0; igen < MAX_GEN; igen++ ) {
   for ( itime = 0; itime < MAX_TIME; itime++ ) {
      powerSum[itime] = power[igen][itime] + powerSum[itime];
   }
}
```

The fourth step is to calculate the average power for each generator. The detailed pseudocode for this step is:

```
// Calculate the average output power of each generator
for ( igen = 0; igen < MAX_GEN; igen++ ) {
   for ( itime = 0; itime < MAX_TIME; itime++ ) {
      powerAve[igen] = power[igen][itime] + powerAve[igen];
   }
   powerAve[igen] = powerAve[igen] / MAX_TIME;
}
```

The fifth step is display the results. The detailed pseudocode for this step is

```
for ( itime = 0; itime < MAX_TIME; itime++ ) {
   Display power at each time
}
for ( igen = 0; igen < MAX_GEN; igen++ ) {
   Display average power for each generator
}
```

4. **Implementation: Convert Algorithms to Java Statements**
    The resulting Java program is shown in Figure 11.6.

```
/*

   Purpose:
     To calculate total instantaneous power supplied by a generating
     station at each instant of time, and to calculate the average
     power supplied by each generator over the period of measurement.

   Record of revisions:
       Date          Programmer             Description of change
       ====          ==========             =====================
     05/29/2002    S. J. Chapman            Original code
*/
import java.io.*;
import java.text.DecimalFormat;
public class Generator {

   // Define the main method
   public static void main(String[] args) {

      // Declare constants
      final int MAX_GEN = 4;      // Max number of generators
      final int MAX_TIME = 6;     // Max number of times

      // Declare variables, and define each variable
      String fileName;            // Input file name
      boolean fileOk = false;     // File OK flag
      int igen;                   // Loop index: generators
      int itime;                  // Loop index: time
      double[][] power = new double[MAX_GEN][MAX_TIME];
                                  // Power of each generator at each time
      double[] powerAve = new double[MAX_GEN];
                                  // Ave power of each gen over all times
      double[] powerSum = new double[MAX_TIME];
                                  // Total power of station at each time
      ReadFile rf = null;         // ReadFile object reference

      // Create StdIn object
      StdIn in = new StdIn();
```

Figure 11.6. Program to calculate the instantaneous power produced by a generating station, and the average power produced by each generator within the station.

```
      // Prompt user for the name of the file to read
      while ( !fileOk ) {
         System.out.print("Enter input file name: ");
         fileName = in.readLine();

         // Open the file, protecting against errors
         try {
            rf = new ReadFile(fileName);
            fileOk = true;
         }
         catch ( FileNotFoundException e ) {

            // Tell user about the error
            System.out.println("File " + fileName + " not found!"
                               + " Please try again." );
         }
         catch ( IOException e ) {

            // Tell user about the error
            System.out.println("File " + fileName + " error!"
                               + " Please try again." );
         }
      }

      // Now get the input values from the file.
      if (rf != null) {

         try {

            // Read input data from the standard input stream
            for ( igen = 0; igen < MAX_GEN; igen++ ) {
               for ( itime = 0; itime < MAX_TIME; itime++ ) {
                  power[igen][itime] = rf.readDouble();
               }
            }
         }
         catch ( NumberFormatException e ) {

            // Tell user about bad value
            System.out.println("Bad value in input file: "
                               + e.getMessage() );
            System.exit(0);
         }
         catch ( EOFException e ) {
            // EOF too soon
            System.out.println("EOF before all data read!");
            System.exit(0);
         }
         catch ( IOException e ) {
            // We are done, so get out!
            System.out.println("Unknown IO error: " + e.getMessage());
            System.exit(0);
```

Figure 11.6. (Continued).

```
        }
    }
    // Close input file
    try {
        rf.close();
    }
    catch ( IOException e ) {
    }
    // Calculate the instantaneous output power of the station
    for ( igen = 0; igen < MAX_GEN; igen++ ) {
        for ( itime = 0; itime < MAX_TIME; itime++ ) {
            powerSum[itime] = power[igen][itime] + powerSum[itime];
        }
    }

    // Calculate the average output power of each generator
    for ( igen = 0; igen < MAX_GEN; igen++ ) {
        for ( itime = 0; itime < MAX_TIME; itime++ ) {
            powerAve[igen] = power[igen][itime] + powerAve[igen];
        }
        powerAve[igen] = powerAve[igen] / MAX_TIME;
    }

    // Tell user.
    DecimalFormat df1 = new DecimalFormat("####.00");
    for ( itime = 0; itime < MAX_TIME; itime++ ) {
        System.out.println("Power at time " + itime + " = "
                        + df1.format(powerSum[itime]) + " MW");
    }
    for ( igen = 0; igen < MAX_GEN; igen++ ) {
        System.out.println("Ave power of Gen " + igen + " = "
                        + df1.format(powerAve[igen]) + " MW");
    }
    }
}
```

Figure 11.6. (Continued).

5. **Testing**

To test this program, we will place the data from Figure 11.3(b) into a file called `gendat`. The contents of file `gendat` are shown below:

```
20.0    19.8    20.1    20.0    20.0    19.9
40.3    40.1    40.0    39.5    39.9    40.0
42.0    41.5    41.3    41.1    39.8    41.0
20.4    26.9    38.4    42.0    12.2     6.0
```

Note that each row of the file corresponds to a specific generator, and each column corresponds to a specific time. Next, we will calculate the answers by hand for one generator and one time, and compare the results with those from the program. At time 3, the total instantaneous power being supplied by all of the generators is

$$P_{\text{TOT}} = 20.1 \text{ MW} + 40.0 \text{ MW} + 41.3 \text{ MW} + 38.4 \text{ MW} = 139.8 \text{ MW}$$

The average power for Generator 1 is

$$P_{\text{G1,AVE}} = \frac{(20.1 + 19.8 + 20.1 + 20.0 + 20.0 + 19.9)}{6} = 19.98 \text{ MW}$$

The output from the program is

```
D:\book\java\chap10>java Generator
Enter file name: gendat
Power at time 0 = 122.70 MW
Power at time 1 = 128.30 MW
Power at time 2 = 139.80 MW
Power at time 3 - 142.60 MW
Power at time 4 = 111.90 MW
Power at time 5 = 106.90 MW
Ave power of Gen 0 = 19.97 MW
Ave power of Gen 1 = 39.97 MW
Ave power of Gen 2 = 41.12 MW
Ave power of Gen 3 = 24.32 MW
```

so the numbers match, and the program appears to be working correctly. ■

11.2 MULTIDIMENSIONAL ARRAYS

It is possible to declare and manipulate arrays with more than two dimensions in Java. This is done as a direct extension of the way Java implements two-dimensional arrays, by simply adding additional subscripts and additional layers of subarrays. For example, a new three-dimensional `double` array could be declared and initialized to zero with the following statements:

```
double[][][] x = new double[3][5][7];
```

Array x would have a total of 105 elements ($= 3 \times 5 \times 7$), with the first index having the range 0–2, the second having the range 0–4, and the third having the range 0–6.

A three-dimensional array can also be initialized to nonzero values using an array initializer. For example, a $2 \times 2 \times 2$ array `arr3` could be declared and initialized with the statement shown in Figure 11.7. Note that there are three levels of braces in this array initializer, which initialize the three indices of the array.

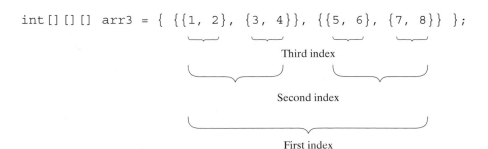

Figure 11.7. A three-dimensional array can be initialized with a nested set of three braces in an array initializer. The outermost braces set the values for the first dimension, the middle braces set the values for the second dimension, and the innermost braces set the values for the third dimension.

Figure 11.8 shows a simple program illustrating the initialization and use of a three-dimensional array.

```
// Initialize and write out a 3D array
public class Test3DArray {

    // Define the main method
    public static void main(String[] args) {
        int[][][] arr3 = { {{1, 2}, {3, 4}}, {{5, 6}, {7, 8}} };
        for (int i = 0; i < 2; i++) {
            for (int j = 0; j < 2; j++) {
                for (int k = 0; k < 2; k++) {
                    System.out.println("arr3[" + i + "][" + j + "][" + k
                                  + "] = " + arr3[i][j][k]);
                }
            }
        }
    }
}
```

Figure 11.8. Program illustrating the initialization and use of a three-dimensional array.

When this program is executed, the results are

```
D:\book\java\chap10>java Test3DArray
arr3[0][0][0] = 1
arr3[0][0][1] = 2
arr3[0][1][0] = 3
arr3[0][1][1] = 4
arr3[1][0][0] = 5
arr3[1][0][1] = 6
arr3[1][1][0] = 7
arr3[1][1][1] = 8
```

Note that the innermost array index is the one that changes most rapidly.

QUIZ 11-1

This quiz provides a quick check to see if you have understood the concepts introduced in Sections 11.1 and 11.2. If you have trouble with the quiz, reread the sections, ask your instructor, or discuss the material with a fellow student. The answers are found in the back of the book.

For Questions 1 and 2, determine the number of elements in the array specified by the declaration statements and the valid subscript range(s) for each array.

1.  ```
    double[][] z = new double[5][7];
    ```

2.  ```
    double[][] z;
    z = new double[3];
    z[0] = new double[2];
    z[1] = new double[4];
    z[2] = new double[3];
    ```

3.   `double[][][] y = new double[4][4][2];`

Determine which of the following Java statements are valid. If they are invalid, explain why they are invalid.

4.   `double a[][] = { {1, 3, 2}, {-1, 2} };`

5.   `int c[][];`
        `c = new double[3][3];`

6.   `double x[];`
        `x = new double[3][3];`

Assume that a three-dimensional array is declared and initialized as follows:

```
int[][][] a = { {{1, 2, 3}, {4, 5, 6}},
                {{7, 8, 9},{10,11,12}} };
```

Determine which of the following array elements are valid and which are invalid. If an array element is valid, give its value.

7.   `a[2][1][0];`

8.   `a[0][1][2];`

9.   `a[1][1][1];`

SUMMARY

- Two-dimensional arrays are those whose elements have two subscripts instead of one. An element within the array is addressed by supplying values for both subscripts.
- Two-dimensional arrays are implemented in Java as arrays of arrays.
- Java also supports arrays with higher dimensions. Java arrays with any number of dimensions can be created and used.

TERMINOLOGY

one-dimensional array
two-dimensional array

Exercises

1.   Modify class `Read2DArray` in Figure 11.5 to trap any exceptions that may occur when it is used.

2.   Determine the shape and size of the arrays specified by the following declaration statements, and the valid subscript range for each dimension of each array. How many elements are there in each of the arrays?
   a.   `float[] data = new float[6][6];`
   b.   `double data1;`
        `data1[][] = new double[3];`
        `data1[0] = new double[3];`
        `data1[1] = new double[2];`
        `data1[2] = new double[4];`
   c.   `int[][][] data2 = new int[3][4][5]`
   d.   `float[][] data3 = new double[5][7];`

3.   Determine whether or not the following Java program fragment is valid. If it is, specify what will happen in the program. If not, explain why not.

```
int[] b = new int[6][4];
int temp;
...
for ( i = 0; i < 6; i++ ) {
    for ( j = 0; j < 4; j++ ) {
        temp    = b(i,j);
        b(i,j) = b(j,i);
        b(j,i) = temp;
    }
}
```

4. Write a program that can read in a two-dimensional array from a user-specified file and calculate the sums of all the data in each row and each column in the array. The size of the array to read in will be specified by two numbers on the first line in the input file, and the elements in each row of the array will be found on a single line of the input file. An example of an input data file containing a 2-row × 4-column array is shown below:

```
    2           4
-24.0      -1121.        812.1       11.1
 35.6       8.1E3       135.23      -17.3
```

Write out the results in the form:

```
Sum of row  1 =
Sum of row  2 =
    ...
Sum of col  1 =
    ...
```

5. Test the program that you wrote in Exercise 11.4 by running it on the following array:

$$\text{array} = \begin{bmatrix} 33. & -12. & 16. & 0.5 & -1.9 \\ -6. & -14. & 3.5 & 11. & 2.1 \\ 4.4 & 1.1 & -7.1 & 9.3 & -16.1 \\ 0.3 & 6.2 & -9.9 & -12. & 6.8 \end{bmatrix}$$

6. Write a set of Java statements that would search a three-dimensional array `arr` and limit the maximum value of any array element to be less than or equal to 1000. If any element exceeds 1000, its value should be set to 1000. Assume that array `arr` has dimensions $1000 \times 10 \times 30$.

7. **Average Annual Temperature** As a part of a meteorological experiment, average annual temperature measurements were collected at 36 locations specified by latitude and longitude as shown in the chart below.

	90.0° W long	90.5° W long	91.0° W long	91.5° W long	92.0° W long	92.5° W long
30.0° N lat	68.2	72.1	72.5	74.1	74.4	74.2
30.5° N lat	69.4	71.1	71.9	73.1	73.6	73.7
31.0° N lat	68.9	70.5	70.9	71.5	72.8	73.0
31.5° N lat	68.6	69.9	70.4	70.8	71.5	72.2
32.0° N lat	68.1	69.3	69.8	70.2	70.9	71.2
32.5° N lat	68.3	68.8	69.6	70.0	70.5	70.9

Write a Java program that calculates the average annual temperature along each latitude included in the experiment, and the average annual temperature along each longitude included in the experiment. Finally, calculate the average annual temperature for all of the locations in the experiment.

8. **Matrix Multiplication** Matrix multiplication is only defined for two matrices in which *the number of columns in the first matrix is equal to the number of rows in the second matrix*. If matrix A is an $N \times L$ matrix, and matrix B is an $L \times M$ matrix, then the product $C = A \times B$ is an $N \times M$ matrix whose elements are given by the equation

$$c_{ik} = \sum_{j=1}^{L} a_{ij} b_{jk}$$

For example, if matrices A and B are 2×2 matrices

$$A = \begin{bmatrix} 3.0 & -1.0 \\ 1.0 & 2.0 \end{bmatrix} \quad \text{and} \quad B = \begin{bmatrix} 1.0 & 4.0 \\ 2.0 & -3.0 \end{bmatrix}$$

then the elements of matrix C will be

$$c_{11} = a_{11}b_{11} + a_{12}b_{21} = (3.0)(1.0) + (-1.0)(2.0) = 1.0$$
$$c_{12} = a_{11}b_{12} + a_{12}b_{22} = (3.0)(4.0) + (-1.0)(-3.0) = 15.0$$
$$c_{21} = a_{21}b_{11} + a_{22}b_{21} = (1.0)(1.0) + (2.0)(2.0) = 5.0$$
$$c_{22} = a_{21}b_{12} + a_{22}b_{22} = (1.0)(4.0) + (2.0)(-3.0) = -2.0$$

Write a program that can read two matrices of arbitrary size from two input disk files, multiply them if they are of compatible sizes, and write the result to a third user-specified file. If the matrices are of incompatible sizes, an appropriate error message should be printed. The number of rows and columns in each matrix will be specified by two integers on the first line in each file, and the elements in each row of the matrix will be found on a single line of the input file (this format is the same as that in Exercise 10.11). Use arrays to hold both the input matrices and the resulting output matrix. Verify your program by creating two input data files containing matrices of the compatible sizes, calculating the resulting values, and checking the answers by hand. Also, verify the proper behavior of the program if it is given two matrices are of incompatible sizes.

9. Use the program produced in Exercise 11.8 to calculate $C = A \times B$, where

$$A = \begin{bmatrix} 1.0 & -5.0 & 4.0 & 2.0 \\ -6.0 & -4.0 & 2.0 & 2.0 \end{bmatrix} \quad \text{and} \quad B = \begin{bmatrix} 1.0 & -2.0 & -1.0 \\ 2.0 & 3.0 & 4.0 \\ 0.0 & -1.0 & 2.0 \\ 0.0 & -3.0 & 1.0 \end{bmatrix}$$

How many rows and how many columns are present in the resulting matrix C?

10. **Relative Maxima** A point in a two-dimensional array is said to be a *relative maximum* if it is higher than any of the 8 points surrounding it. For example,

the element at position (2, 2) in the array shown below is a relative maximum, since it is larger than any of the surrounding points.

$$\begin{bmatrix} 11 & 7 & -2 \\ -7 & 14 & 3 \\ 2 & -3 & 5 \end{bmatrix}$$

Write a program to read a matrix a from a file attached to the standard input stream and to scan for all relative maxima within the matrix. The first line in the file should contain the number of rows and the number of columns in the matrix, and then the next lines should contain the values in the matrix, with all of the values in a given row on a single line of the input disk file. The program should consider only interior points within the matrix, since any point along an edge of the matrix cannot be completely surrounded by points lower than itself. Test your program by finding all of the relative maxima in the following matrix, which can be found in file findpeak:

$$A = \begin{bmatrix} 2. & -1. & -2. & 1. & 3. & -5. & 2. & 1. \\ -2. & 0. & -2.5 & 5. & -2. & 2. & 1. & 0. \\ -3. & -3. & -3. & 3. & 0. & 0. & -1. & -2. \\ -4.5 & -4. & -7. & 6. & 1. & -3. & 0. & 5. \\ -3.5 & -3. & -5. & 0. & 4. & 17. & 11. & 5. \\ -9. & -6. & -5. & -3. & 1. & 2. & 0. & 0.5 \\ -7. & -4. & -5. & -3. & 2. & 4. & 3. & -1. \\ -6. & -5. & -5. & -2. & 0. & 1. & 2. & 5. \end{bmatrix}$$

11. **Temperature Distribution on a Metallic Plate**   Under steady-state conditions, the temperature at any point on the surface of a metallic plate will be the average of the temperatures of all points surrounding it. This fact can be used in an iterative procedure to calculate the temperature distribution at all points on the plate.

Figure 11.9 shows a square plate divided into 100 squares or nodes by a grid. The temperatures of the nodes form a two-dimensional array T. The temperature in all nodes at the edges of the plate is constrained to be 20° C by a cooling system, and the temperature of the node (2, 7) is fixed at 100° C by exposure to boiling water.

A new estimate of the temperature $T_{i,j}$ in any given node can be calculated from the average of the temperatures in all segments surrounding it:

$$T_{ij,\text{new}} = \frac{1}{4}(T_{i+1,j} + T_{i-1,j} + T_{i,j+1} + T_{i,j-1}) \tag{11.1}$$

To determine the temperature distribution on the surface of a plate, an initial assumption must be made about the temperatures in each node. Then Equation (11.1) is applied to each node whose temperature is not fixed to calculate a new estimate of the temperature in that node. These updated temperature estimates are used to calculate newer estimates, and the process is repeated until the new temperature estimates in each node differ from the old ones by only a small amount. At that point, a steady-state solution has been found.

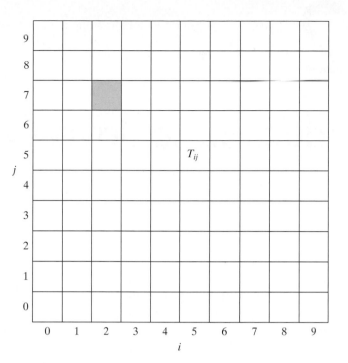

Figure 11.9.   A metallic plate divided into 100 small segments.

Write a program to calculate the steady-state temperature distribution throughout the plate, making an initial assumption that all interior segments are at a temperature of 50° C. Remember that all outside segments are fixed at a temperature of 20° C and segment (2, 7) is fixed at a temperature of 100° C. The program should apply Equation (11.1) iteratively until the maximum temperature change between iterations in any node is less than 0.01 degree. What will the steady-state temperature of segment (4, 4) be?

12

Introduction to Java Graphics

We now begin our discussion of one of Java's most interesting and important features—its built-in device- and platform-independent graphics. Java's graphics system has evolved rapidly from Java SDK 1.0 through SDK 1.1 to SDK 1.2 (now renamed Java 2), expanding dramatically in terms of power, flexibility, and capability. (It has been more stable since then.) This growth has been accomplished while maintaining backward compatibility with earlier versions of the graphics system, which has unfortunately resulted in a complex mishmash of old and new graphics classes and interfaces.

In this book, we will restrict ourselves to a small fraction of Java's graphics classes and methods, concentrating on only the most recent and capable techniques, which use the Java 2D geometry package and the Swing graphical user interface (GUI). The Java 2D geometry package is an improved set of classes for creating high-quality 2D graphics. It is the principal topic of this chapter. The Swing GUI is a new, more efficient, and more flexible graphical user interface system that is the preferred way to create GUIs in Java 2. It will be discussed in detail beginning in the next chapter.

Note that if you are modifying older pre-existing programs, you will need to consult other texts or the on-line SDK documentation for the details of how the earlier GUI and graphics systems worked.

Java's graphics system can be found in the Abstract Windowing Toolkit (AWT) package, the Swing package, and in several subordinate packages, the most important of which are summarized in Table 12.1.

In this chapter we will learn about the basic graphics concepts of a **container** and a **component**, and then concentrate on learning how to draw graphical elements on the computer screen. In the next two chapters we will expand on this beginning by learning how to create a graphical user interface (GUI), complete with buttons, sliders, text boxes, and so on, that can respond to input from the keyboard or the mouse.

SECTIONS

OBJECTIVES

- To understand how to create and display Java graphics.
- To be able to draw lines, rectangles, rounded rectangles, ellipses, and arcs.
- To be able to control the line style and color used to draw objects.
- To be able to fill objects with selected colors.
- To be able to create objects of arbitrary shape with `GeneralPath` objects.
- To be able to display text in various fonts.
- To understand and be able to use affine transforms to shift, rotate, and skew graphics objects.

TABLE 12.1 Selected Java AWT Packages

Java API Package	Explanation
java.awt	*The Abstract Windowing Toolkit (AWT) Package*
	This package contains the classes and interfaces required to create Graphical User Interfaces. The term "abstract" is applied to this package because it can create GUI windows on any type of computer, regardless of the underlying operating system type.
java.awt.datatransfer	*The Java Data Transfer Package*
	This package contains classes and interfaces that allow a program to transfer data between a Java program and a computer's clipboard (a temporary storage area used for cut-and-paste operations).
java.awt.dnd	*The Java Drag and Drop Package*
	This package provides interfaces and classes for supporting drag-and-drop operations.
java.awt.event	*The Java AWT Event Package*
	This package contains classes and interfaces that support event handling for GUI components.
java.awt.font	*The Java AWT Font Package*
	This package contains classes and interfaces relating to fonts.
java.awt.geom	*The Java AWT Geometry Package*
	This package provides the Java 2D classes for defining and performing operations on objects related to two-dimensional geometry.
java.awt.image	*The Java AWT Image Package*
	This package contains classes and interfaces that enable storing and manipulating images in a program.
java.awt.peer	*The Java AWT Peer Package*
	This package contains interfaces that allow Java's GUI components to interact with their platform-specific versions (for example, a button is actually implemented differently on a Macintosh than it is on a Windows or an X-Windows machine). This package should never be used directly by Java programmers.
java.awt.print	*The Java AWT Printing Package*
	This package contains classes and interfaces that support a general-purpose printing API.
javax.swing	*The Swing Package*
	This package contains many of the classes and interfaces required to support the newer Swing graphical user interface.

12.1 CONTAINERS AND COMPONENTS

Two of the most important graphics objects are components and containers. A **component** is a visual object containing text or graphics, which can respond to keyboard or mouse inputs. All Swing components are subclasses of the abstract class `javax.swing.JComponent`. Examples of components include buttons, labels, text boxes, check boxes, and lists. A completely blank component is known as a **canvas** (like an artist's canvas). A canvas can be used as a drawing area for text or graphics.[1] All components inherit a common set of methods, the most important of which is **paintComponent**. The paintComponent method causes a component to be drawn or redrawn whenever it is called. This method is called automatically whenever a component is made visible, or in response to such actions as dragging or resizing with a mouse.

A **container** is a graphical object that can hold components or other containers. The most important type of container is a **frame**, which is an area of the computer screen surrounded by borders and a title bar. Frames are implemented by class java.swing.JFrame. The inheritance hierarchy of these classes is shown in Figure 12.1.

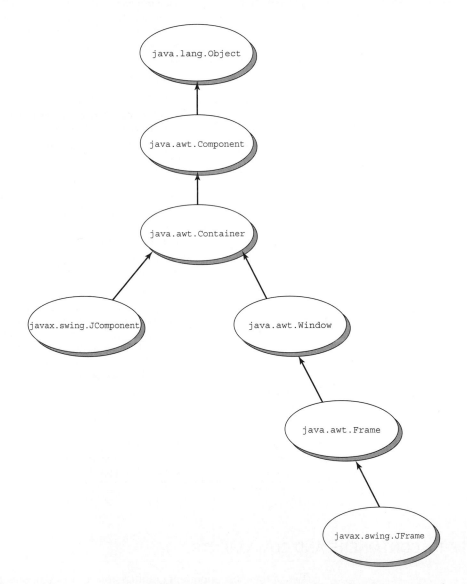

Figure 12.1. A portion of the graphics class inheritance hierarchy, showing the classes JComponent and JFrame.

---

[1]There is a standard Canvas class in the older Java AWT GUI, but there is no equivalent JCanvas class in the Swing GUI. In the Swing GUI, subclasses of java.swing.JComponent are used as a canvas.

12.1.1 Creating and Displaying a Frame and a Component

The basic steps required to display graphics in Java are:

1. Create the component or components to display.
2. Create a frame to hold the component(s), and place the component(s) into the frame.
3. Create a "listener" object to detect and respond to mouse clicks, and assign the listener to the frame.

In this chapter the only container we will use is `JFrame`, and the only components we will use are direct subclasses of `JComponent`. Additional components will be introduced in Chapters 13 and 14. The "listener" object will monitor the mouse and will respond if a click occurs while the cursor is pointing at the frame. The listener is very important, because without it we could never close a frame, once it was created.

Figures 12.2 and 12.3 show a simple program that displays the basic skeleton required to create Java graphics. The first step in this process is to create a component to

```
1    // This class produces a simple blank component by extending
2    // javax.swing.JComponent.
3    import java.awt.*;
4    import javax.swing.*;
5    public class JCanvas extends JComponent {
6
7        public JCanvas() {
8            setDoubleBuffered( true );
9        }
10
11       public void paintComponent( Graphics g ) {
12
13           Dimension size = getSize();
14           g.setColor(getBackground());
15           g.fillRect(0, 0, size.width, size.height);
16       }
17   }
```

Figure 12.2. A class that creates a blank yellow component.

```
1    import java.awt.*;
2    import java.awt.event.*;
3    import javax.swing.*;
4    public class TestJCanvas {
5
6        // This method illustrates how to create graphics in Java.
7        // It creates a new JFrame, attaches a JCanvas component to
8        // it, and makes the frame and canvas visible on the screen.
9        public static void main(String s[]) {
```

Figure 12.3. A program that creates a frame, places a blank component within it, and displays the result. This is the basic core structure required to display Java graphics.

```
10
11          // Create a Window Listener to handle "close" events
12          MyWindowListener l = new MyWindowListener();
13
14          // Create a blank yellow JCanvas
15          JCanvas c = new JCanvas();
16          c.setBackground( Color.yellow );
17
18          // Create a frame and place the canvas in the center
19          // of the frame.
20          JFrame f = new JFrame("Test JCanvas ...");
21          f.addWindowListener(l);
22          f.getContentPane().add(c, BorderLayout.CENTER);
23          f.pack();
24          f.setSize(400,400);
25          f.show();
26      }
27 }


 1
 2  class MyWindowListener extends WindowAdapter {
 3
 4      // This method implements a simple listener that detects
 5      // the "window closing event" and stops the program.
 6      public void windowClosing(WindowEvent e) {
 7          System.exit(0);
 8      };
 9  }
```

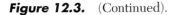

Figure 12.3. (Continued).

display. Figure 12.2 shows a class called JCanvas that creates a simple blank component. This class extends JComponent, overrides the method paintComponent to fill the component with a background color, and does nothing else.

The default constructor for this class is found in lines 7–9 of the figure. Line 8 sets the component to use *double buffering*, which means that the component has memory for two complete sets of graphical images. Graphical images are drawn in one memory buffer while the other buffer is being displayed. When all of the graphics have been drawn on the component, the buffers are switched, causing the displayed image to update instantly. Double buffering prevents the computer display from flickering as a component is updated, and it should always be used.

Method paintComponent is found on lines 11–16. It gets the current size and background color of the component, using methods inherited from superclasses of this component, and draws a rectangle of that color to fill the component. We will discuss these methods in detail later in the chapter.

The next step in creating Java graphics is to create a frame and place the component into it. The program shown in Figure 12.3 creates a new yellow JCanvas, creates a new JFrame, places the component within the frame, and displays the frame on the computer's display. It also includes a listener to respond to mouse clicks.

Lines 15 and 16 of this program create a new JCanvas component. The background color of the canvas is set to yellow. Line 20 creates a new JFrame and sets its title bar to display the words "`Test JCanvas ...`". Line 22 adds the `JCanvas` to the center of the frame, and the statement "`f.pack()`" on line 23 causes the component to fill the entire frame. The statement "`f.setSize(400,400)`" sets the size of the frame to display in pixels, with the first number being the length and the second the width of the frame. Finally, the statement "`f.show()`" makes the frame visible and brings it to the front of any other windows being displayed on your computer.

Line 12 creates a `MyWindowListener` object, whose job is to listen for mouse clicks within the frame and to perform an action if such a mouse click occurs. The definition of the `MyWindowListener` class appears at the bottom of the figure. Such "listener classes" will be discussed in Chapter 13. In this case, the class listens for a mouse click in the "close window" box of the frame, closing the frame when the click is detected. Line 21 adds this listener to the `JFrame`, so that it will monitor mouse clicks that happen within the frame.

When this program is executed, the result is a frame with a blank yellow canvas, as shown in Figure 12.4. Note that a mouse click in the "close window" box will close the frame, because the listener executes the statement "`System.exit(0)`" when the mouse click occurs.

Figure 12.4. The output of program `TestJCanvas`. It consists of a (400 × 400)-pixel frame containing a blank yellow canvas. (The yellow color does not show up in this black-and-white text.)

GOOD PROGRAMMING PRACTICE

To display Java graphics:
1. Create a component or components to display.
2. Create a `JFrame` to hold the component(s), and place the component(s) into the frame.
3. Create a "listener" object to detect and respond to mouse clicks, and assign the listener to the `JFrame`.

12.1.2 How to Display Graphics on a Component

Every Swing component is a subclass of JComponent. This class has a special **paintComponent method** associated with it. When this method is called, the component issues graphics commands to draw or redraw itself. Class JComponent is an abstract class, and method paintComponent is an abstract method within that class. Therefore, every component *must* override the paintComponent method inherited from JComponent.

The way to create useful graphics is to create a *subclass* of JComponent and to override the paintComponent method in the subclass to display the data that you are interested in.

The paintComponent method always has the calling sequence

```
paintComponent ( Graphics g );
```

where g is a reference to the java.awt.Graphics object used to draw lines, figures, text, and so on. To use the modern Java graphics features, this Graphics object must be immediately downcast to a java.awt.Graphics2D object, and then all of the tools in the java.awt.geom package can be applied to draw graphics on the screen.[2]

A sample class that extends JComponent and draws a single line on a white background is shown in Figure 12.5, together with the resulting output. Note that this

```
import java.awt.*;
import java.awt.event.*;
import java.awt.geom.*;
import javax.swing.*;
public class DrawLine extends JComponent {

   // Constructor
   public DrawLine() {
      setDoubleBuffered( true );
   }

   // This method extends JComponent and draws a line on the
   // component.
   public void paintComponent ( Graphics g ) {

      // Cast the graphics object to Graph2D
      Graphics2D g2 = (Graphics2D) g;

      // Set background color
      Dimension size = getSize();
      g2.setColor( Color.white );
      g2.fill(new Rectangle2D.Double(0,0,size.width,size.height));

      // Draw line
      g2.setColor( Color.black );
```

Figure 12.5. Class DrawLine extends JComponent and draws a single line on a white background.

---

[2] This rather silly business of forcing every paintComponent method to accept a Graphics object and immediately casting it to a Graphics2D object is for backward compatibility with earlier versions of Java. The first Java SDK had rather primitive graphics that supported only Graphics objects—if the paintComponent methods were changed to pass the new Graphics2D objects as parameters, all of those older programs would no longer work.

```
        Line2D line = new Line2D.Double (10., 10., 360., 360.);
        g2.draw(line);
    }

    public static void main(String s[]) {

        // Create a Window Listener to handle "close" events
        MyWindowListener l = new MyWindowListener();

        // Create a DrawLine object
        DrawLine c = new DrawLine();

        // Create a frame and place the object in the center
        // of the frame.
        JFrame f = new JFrame("Test Line ...");
        f.addWindowListener(l);
        f.getContentPane().add(c, BorderLayout.CENTER);
        f.pack();
        f.setSize(400,400);
        f.show();
    }
}
```

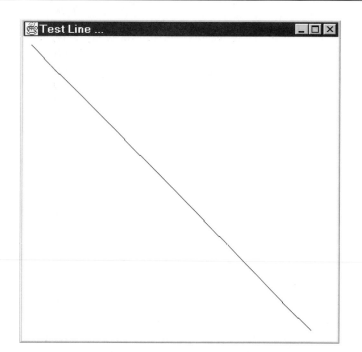

Figure 12.5. (Continued).

class immediately casts the Graphics reference to a Graphics2D reference and uses that reference to draw the line on the screen. Also note that the class imports package java.awt.geom. All of Java's 2D drawing tools are in this package, so you must always import it into your graphics programs.

12.1.3 The Graphics Coordinate System

Java employs a coordinate system whose origin is in the upper left-hand corner of the screen, with positive x-values to the right and positive y-values down (see Figure 12.6). By default, the units of the coordinate system are **pixels**, 72 to an inch. However, we shall see later that this mapping can be changed.

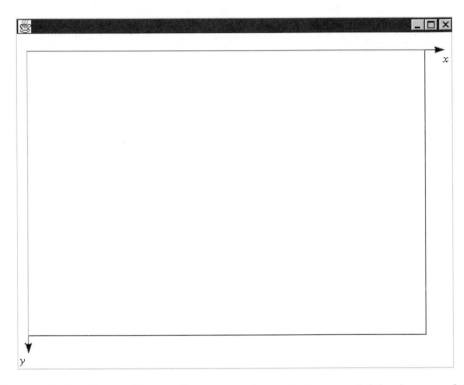

Figure 12.6. The graphics coordinate system begins in the upper left-hand corner of the display device, with the x-axis extending horizontally and the y-axis extending downward.

In class `DrawLine`, we drew a line from (10, 10) to (360, 360). The resulting line extended from the upper left-hand corner of the component (10, 10) to the lower right-hand corner of the component (360, 360).

12.2 DRAWING LINES

In this section we will learn how to draw lines on a graphics device. In the process of doing so, we will learn about controlling line color, line width, and line style, all of which will apply to other shapes as well. Finally, we will learn how to eliminate jagged edges from lines using Java's antialiasing technology.

12.2.1 Drawing Simple Lines

The basic class used to draw a line in Java is **java.awt.geom.Line2D**. This is an abstract class with two concrete subclasses: Line2D.Double and Line2D.Float. The only difference between these subclasses is that one expects double input parameters and the other expects float input parameters.

The most common constructors for a Line2D object have the form

```
Line2D.Double(double x1, double y1, double x2, double y2)
Line2D.Float( float x1, float y1, float x2, float y2 )
```

where the line is defined from point (x_1, y_1) to point (x_2, y_2) on the display. Once a line object is created, the actual line can be drawn by calling the Graphics2D draw method with a reference to the line object. For example, the following statements create a line going from (10, 10) to (360, 360), and draw the line on the current graphics object, as we saw above.

```
Line2D line = new Line2D.Double (10., 10., 360., 360.);
g2.draw(line);
```

12.2.2 Controlling Line Color, Width, and Style

The color, width, and style of any line (or any other Java2D object) may be easily controlled. The color is set by a call to the Graphics2D method **setColor**. The form of this method call is

```
g2.setColor(color)
```

where color is any object of class java.awt.Color. This class includes many predefined color constants (see Table 12.2). (To create your own custom colors, use the methods in class java.awt.Color. They are described in the Java SDK on-line documentation.)

TABLE 12.2 Predefined Java Colors

Color.black	Color.magenta
Color.blue	Color.orange
Color.cyan	Color.pink
Color.darkGray	Color.red
Color.green	Color.white
Color.lightGray	Color.yellow

The width, style, and ends of a line are controlled by a special class called **java.awt.BasicStroke**. This class defines four basic attributes of lines

- Line width in pixels
- The shape of line end caps
- The shape of decorations where two line segments meet
- The style of the line (solid, dashed, dotted, and so on.)

The two most common constructors for a BasicStroke object have the form:

```
BasicStroke(float width);
BasicStroke(float width, int cap, int join, float miterlimit,
            float[] dash, float dash_phase);
```

The meanings of these parameters are listed in Table 12.3.

TABLE 12.3 BasicStroke Parameters

Parameter	Description
width	A float value representing the width of the line in pixels.
cap	An int value representing the type of caps to draw on the ends of the lines. Possible choices are CAP_BUTT, CAP_SQUARE (default), and CAP_ROUND.
join	An int value representing the connection to be made between line segments. Possible choices are JOIN_BEVEL, JOIN_MITER (default), and JOIN_ROUND.
dash	A float array representing the dashing pattern in pixels. Even-numbered ([0], [2], ...) elements in the array represent the lengths of visible segments, in pixels, and odd-numbered ([1], [3], ...) elements in the array represent the lengths of transparent segments, in pixels.
dash phase	A float value containing the offset in pixels at which to start the dash pattern.

The program in Figure 12.7 illustrates the use of these features to control the way a line is displayed. This program creates and displays two lines. The first is red, solid, and 2 pixels wide, while the second is blue, dashed, and 4 pixels wide.

```java
import java.awt.*;
import java.awt.event.*;
import java.awt.geom.*;
import javax.swing.*;
public class DrawLine2 extends JComponent {

   // Constructor
   public DrawLine2() {
      setDoubleBuffered( true );
   }

   // This method draws two lines with color and styles.
   public void paintComponent ( Graphics g ) {
      BasicStroke bs;                       // Ref to BasicStroke
      Line2D line;                          // Ref to line
      float[] solid = {12.0f,0.0f};         // Solid line style
      float[] dashed = {12.0f,12.0f};       // Dashed line style

      // Cast the graphics object to Graph2D
      Graphics2D g2 = (Graphics2D) g;

      // Set background color
      Dimension size = getSize();
      g2.setColor( Color.white );
      g2.fill(new Rectangle2D.Double(0,0,size.width,size.height));

      // Set the Color and BasicStroke
      g2.setColor(Color.red);
      bs = new BasicStroke( 2.0f, BasicStroke.CAP_SQUARE,
                     BasicStroke.JOIN_MITER, 1.0f,
                     solid, 0.0f );
      g2.setStroke(bs);
```

Figure 12.7. Class DrawLine2.

```
        // Draw line
        line = new Line2D.Double (10., 10., 360., 360.);
        g2.draw(line);

        // Set the Color and BasicStroke
        g2.setColor(Color.blue);
        bs = new BasicStroke( 4.0f, BasicStroke.CAP_SQUARE,
                              BasicStroke.JOIN_MITER, 1.0f,
                              dashed, 0.0f );
        g2.setStroke(bs);

        // Draw line
        line = new Line2D.Double (10., 300., 360., 10.);
        g2.draw(line);
    }
    public static void main(String s[]) {

        // Create a Window Listener to handle "close" events
        MyWindowListener l = new MyWindowListener();

        // Create a DrawLine2 object
        DrawLine2 c = new DrawLine2();

        // Create a frame and place the object in the center
        // of the frame
        JFrame f = new JFrame("DrawLine2 ...");
        f.addWindowListener(l);
        f.getContentPane().add(c, BorderLayout.CENTER);
        f.pack();
        f.setSize(400,400);
        f.show();
    }
}
```

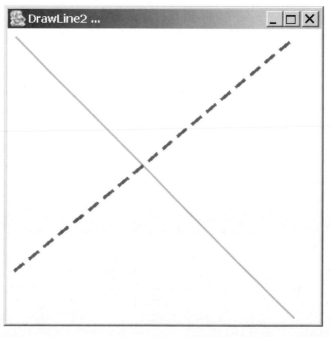

Figure 12.7. (Continued).

12.2.3 Eliminating Jagged Edges from Lines

If you look closely at the lines drawn in Figure 12.7, you may notice that the edges of the lines have a slightly jagged appearance. The reason is that the component on which the lines are drawn has only a finite number of pixels, and each pixel is either fully on or off. When a line jumps over by one pixel, the jump can leave a rough edge.

Java graphics includes a special technology know as **antialiasing** to eliminate these rough edges. When it is turned on, it allows pixels at the edges of the line to be partially on or off, causing the edge of the line to appear smooth to a human observer. This technology is controlled by a `Graphics2D` method called `setRenderingHints`. The command to turn on antialiasing is

```
// Set rendering hints to improve display quality
g2.setRenderingHint(RenderingHints.KEY_ANTIALIASING,
                    RenderingHints.VALUE_ANTIALIAS_ON);
```

When this command is included in the `paintComponent` method of class `DrawLine2`, the results are as shown Figure 12.8. Note how much smoother and cleaner the lines appear to be in that figure.

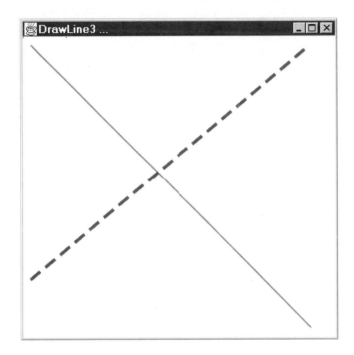

Figure 12.8. The output of program `DrawLine2` with antialiasing turned on. Note how much smoother the edges of the lines are here compared to Figure 12.7.

GOOD PROGRAMMING PRACTICE

To draw lines in Java:

1. Select a line color using the Graphics2D `setColor` method.
2. Select a line width and line style using a `BasicStroke` object, and associate that basic stroke with the line using the Graphics2D `setBasicStroke` method.
3. Set the endpoints of the line using a `Line2D.Double` or `Line2D.float` method, and draw the line with a call to the Graphics2D `draw` method.

Eliminate jagged edges from your lines by turning on antialiasing with the `Graphics2D` method `setRenderingHints`.

EXAMPLE 12.1

Plotting the Function sin θ: The `Line2D` class can be used to plot curves of arbitrary shape by breaking each curve into small, straight line segments and plotting each segment separately. To illustrate this operation, we will create a plot of the function sin θ over the range $0 \leq \theta \leq 2\pi$. The plotted curve should be a solid blue line 4 pixels wide. Use antialiasing to smooth the edges of the curve.

SOLUTION

To create an overall sinusoidal shape, we will divide this curve into 40 line segments and plot each segment separately. The code required to generate the 41 points bounding the 40 line segments is:

```
double theta[] = new double[41];
double sin[] = new double[41];
delta = 2 * Math.PI / 40;
for ( i = 0; i < theta.length; i++ ) {
    theta[i] = delta * i;
    sin[i] = Math.sin(theta[i]);
}
```

Once we have the ends of the line segments, it is necessary to plot them in the space provided. If we assume that the space available for the plot is about 380 × 380 pixels, then the range of possible values of θ must be mapped into 380 horizontal pixels, and the range of possible values of sin θ must be mapped into 380 vertical pixels. The range of θ is $0 \leq \theta \leq 2\pi$, so a suitable mapping function would be

$$xpos = \left(\frac{380}{2\pi}\right)\theta = \left(\frac{190}{\pi}\right)\theta \tag{12.1}$$

Similarly, the range of possible value of sin θ is $-1 \leq \sin\theta \leq 1$, so the 380 vertical pixels must be mapped to that range. The y-axis mapping is trickier, though, because y-values *increase downward*. To make the plot come out right, we must make -1 map to pixel 380, and $+1$ map to pixel 0. A suitable mapping function would be

$$ypos = 180 - 180\sin\theta \tag{12.2}$$

The code required to apply these mappings to the function is:

```
for ( i = 0; i < theta.length; i++ ) {
    theta[i] = (190/Math.PI) * theta[i];
    sin[i] = 180 - 180 * sin[i];
}
```

Finally, the code required to plot the 40 line segments is:

```
for ( i = 0; i < theta.length-1; i++ ) {
    line = new Line2D.Double (theta[i], sin[i],
                              theta[i+1], sin[i+1]);
    g2.draw(line);
}
```

The paintComponent method required to generate this curve is shown in Figure 12.9. The rest of the program is not shown, because it is essentially the same as the previous two programs.

```java
// This method plots one cycle of a sine wave.
public void paintComponent ( Graphics g ) {

   BasicStroke bs;                      // Ref to BasicStroke
   double delta;                        // Step between points
   int i;                               // Loop index
   Line2D line;                         // Ref to line
   double sin[] = new double[41];       // sin(theta)
   float[] solid = {12.0f,0.0f};        // Solid line style
   double theta[] = new double[41];     // Angles in radians

   // Cast the graphics object to Graph2D
   Graphics2D g2 = (Graphics2D) g;

   // Set rendering hints to improve display quality
   g2.setRenderingHint(RenderingHints.KEY_ANTIALIASING,
                       RenderingHints.VALUE_ANTIALIAS_ON);

      // Set background color
      Dimension size = getSize();
      g2.setColor( Color.white );
      g2.fill(new Rectangle2D.Double(0,0,size.width,size.height));

   // Set the Color and BasicStroke
   g2.setColor(Color.blue);
   bs = new BasicStroke( 4.0f, BasicStroke.CAP_SQUARE,
                         BasicStroke.JOIN_MITER, 1.0f,
                         solid, 0.0f );
   g2.setStroke(bs);

   // Calculate points on curve
   delta = 2 * Math.PI / 40;
   for ( i = 0; i < theta.length; i++ ) {
      theta[i] = delta * i;
      sin[i] = Math.sin(theta[i]);
   }

   // Translate curve position to pixels
   for ( i = 0; i < theta.length; i++ ) {
      theta[i] = (190/Math.PI) * theta[i];
      sin[i] = 180 - 180 * sin[i];
   }

   // Plot curve
   for ( i = 0; i < theta.length-1; i++ ) {
      line = new Line2D.Double (theta[i], sin[i],
                                theta[i+1], sin[i+1]);
      g2.draw(line);
   }
}
```

Figure 12.9. The paintComponent method from a program to plot the function $\sin \theta$ for $0 \leq \theta \leq 2\pi$.

When this program is executed, the results are as shown in Figure 12.10.

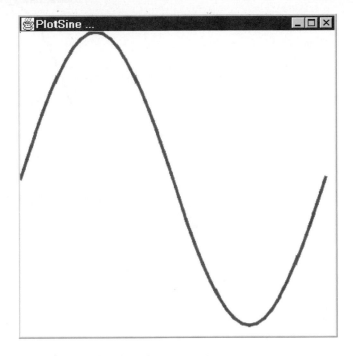

Figure 12.10. The output of program PlotSine.

■

EXAMPLE 12.2

Automatic Scaling of Plots: The program in Example 12.1 contains a serious flaw. Note that we designed the plot to occupy a space of 380×380 pixels. What would happen to this plot if we changed the size of the frame it was plotted in? For example, suppose that we used the mouse to make the frame larger or smaller. What would we see? If the frame is made smaller, then only a portion of the curve will be displayed. If the frame is made larger, then the curve will only occupy a portion of the available space. These problems are illustrated in Figure 12.11.

What we need is a way to determine the size of the canvas that we are plotting on, so that the plot can automatically rescale whenever the size changes. Fortunately, every Java Component includes a method **getSize()** to recover the size of the Component. Since JComponent is a subclass of Component, it automatically inherits the getSize() method.

The method getSize() is used as follows:

```
Dimension size = getSize();
```

This method returns a Dimension object, which has two public instance variables, height and width. Thus the component's height in pixels will be size.height and its width of in pixels will be size.width.

We can use this information to create a paintComponent method that automatically resizes whenever its container is resized by changing the mappings to be

$$xpos = \left(\frac{\texttt{size.width}}{2\pi} \right)\theta \qquad (12.3)$$

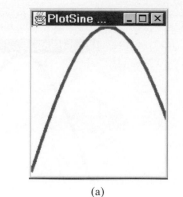

(a)

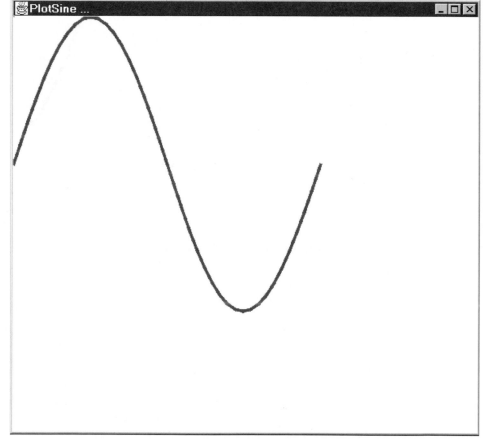

(b)

Figure 12.11. When the frame containing the sinusoidal plot is resized, the plot does not change size to match: (a) small frame, (b) large frame.

and

$$ypos = \frac{\texttt{size.height}}{2} - \frac{\texttt{size.height}}{2} \sin \theta \tag{12.4}$$

The `paintComponent` method with automatic resizing is shown in Figure 12.12.

```
// This method plots one cycle of a sine wave.
public void paintComponent ( Graphics g ) {

   BasicStroke bs;                      // Ref to BasicStroke
   double delta;                        // Step between points
   int i;                               // Loop index
   Line2D line;                         // Ref to line
   double sin[] = new double[41];       // sin(theta)
   float[] solid = {12.0f,0.0f};        // Solid line style
   double theta[] = new double[41];     // Angles in radians

   // Cast the graphics object to Graph2D
   Graphics2D g2 = (Graphics2D) g;

   // Set rendering hints to improve display quality
   g2.setRenderingHint(RenderingHints.KEY_ANTIALIASING,
                      RenderingHints.VALUE_ANTIALIAS_ON);

   // Get plot size
   Dimension size = getSize();

   // Set background color
   g2.setColor( Color.white );
      g2.fill(new
              Rectangle2D.Double(0,0,size.width,size.height));

   // Set the Color and BasicStroke
   g2.setColor(Color.blue);
   bs = new BasicStroke( 4.0f, BasicStroke.CAP_SQUARE,
                        BasicStroke.JOIN_MITER, 1.0f,
                        solid, 0.0f );
   g2.setStroke(bs);

   // Calculate points on curve
   delta = 2 * Math.PI / 40;
   for ( i = 0; i < theta.length; i++ ) {
      theta[i] = delta * i;
      sin[i] = Math.sin(theta[i]);
   }

   // Translate curve position to pixels
   for ( i = 0; i < theta.length; i++ ) {
      theta[i] = (size.width/(2*Math.PI)) * theta[i];
      sin[i] = size.height/2 - size.height/2 * sin[i];
   }
   // Plot curve
   for ( i = 0; i < theta.length-1; i++ ) {
      line = new Line2D.Double (theta[i], sin[i],
                                theta[i+1], sin[i+1]);
      g2.draw(line);
   }
}
```

Figure 12.12.   The paintComponent method to plot sin θ with automatic resizing.

Execute this program and resize its frame with a mouse. Notice how the plot changes size to take advantage of the available space.

This plot program is still not perfect. Note that the curve is clipped a bit at the top and the bottom of the plot. You should rewrite it again to make the curve scale properly, while still leaving a small amount of space around each of the edges.

12.3 DRAWING OTHER SHAPES

The java.awt.geom package includes classes to draw several other shapes, including rectangles, rounded rectangles, ellipses, arcs, and quadratic and cubic curves. All of these shapes function in a manner basically similar to the Line2D class that we saw in the previous section. They all use the same techniques to set color, line width, and line style, so we already know most of what we need to know to use them.

12.3.1 Rectangles

The basic class used to draw a rectangle is **java.awt.geom.Rectangle2D**. This is an abstract class with two concrete subclasses: Rectangle2D.Double and Rectangle2D.Float. The only difference between these two classes is that one expects double input parameters and the other expects float input parameters.

The most common constructors for a Rectangle2D object have the form

```
Rectangle2D.Double( double x, double y, double w, double h )
Rectangle2D.Float( float x, float y, float w, float h )
```

where the upper left-hand corner of the rectangle is a point (x, y), and the rectangle is w pixels wide and h pixels high. For example, the following statements create a rectangle starting at position (30, 40) that is 200 pixels wide and 150 pixels high and draw it on the current graphics device:

```
Rectangle2D rect = new Rectangle2D.Double (30., 40., 200., 150.);
g2.draw(rect);
```

Unlike a line, a rectangle is a closed shape that has an interior and a border. The method g2.draw(rect) draws the *border* of the rectangle but leaves the interior empty. It is also possible to fill the interior of a rectangle with the Graphics2D method fill. For example, the following statements create a 200 × 150 rectangle object, fill its interior with yellow, and draw a black border around it.

```
bs = new BasicStroke( 3.0f, BasicStroke.CAP_SQUARE,
                      BasicStroke.JOIN_MITER, 1.0f,
                      solid, 0.0f );
g2.setStroke(bs);

Rectangle2D rect = new Rectangle2D.Double (30., 40., 200., 150.);
g2.setColor(Color.yellow);
g2.fill(rect);
g2.setColor(Color.black);
g2.draw(rect);
```

The resulting shape is shown in Figure 12.13.

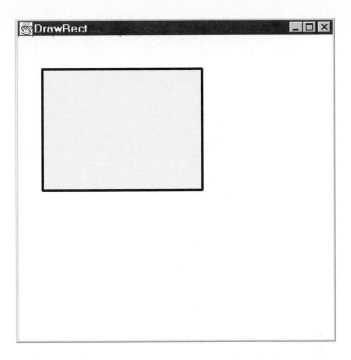

Figure 12.13. A yellow rectangle with a black border.

12.3.2 Rounded Rectangles

The class used to draw a rectangle with rounded corners is **java.awt.geom.RoundRectangle2D**. This is an abstract class with two concrete subclasses: RoundRectangle2D.Double and RoundRectangle2D.Float. The only difference between these two classes is that one expects `double` input parameters and the other expects `float` input parameters.

The simplest constructor for a RoundRectangle2D object has the form

```
RoundRectangle2D.Double( double x, double y, double w,
                         double h, double arcw,
                         double arch )
RoundRectangle2D.Float( float x, float y, float w,
                        float h, float arcw,
                        float arch )
```

where the upper left-hand corner of the rectangle is a point (x, y), and the rectangle is w pixels wide and h pixels high. The values *arcw* and *arch* specify the width and height, respectively, of the arcs that round off the corners of the rectangle. For example, the following statements create a rounded rectangle starting at position (30, 40) that is 200 pixels wide and 150 pixels high with 40-pixel-wide arcs at the corners:

```
RoundRectangle2D rect
rect = new RoundRectangle2D.Double
        (30.,40.,200.,150.,40.,40.);
g2.draw(rect);
```

Similarly, the following statements create a 200×150 rounded rectangle object with 40-pixel arcs in both height and width, fill its interior with pink, and draw a dashed black border around it.

```
bs = new BasicStroke( 3.0f, BasicStroke.CAP_SQUARE,
                      BasicStroke.JOIN_MITER, 1.0f,
                      dashed, 0.0f );
g2.setStroke(bs);
RoundRectangle2D rect = new RoundRectangle2D.Double
                  (30., 40., 200., 150., 40., 40.);
g2.setColor(Color.pink);
g2.fill(rect);
g2.setColor(Color.black);
g2.draw(rect);
```

The resulting shape is shown in Figure 12.14.

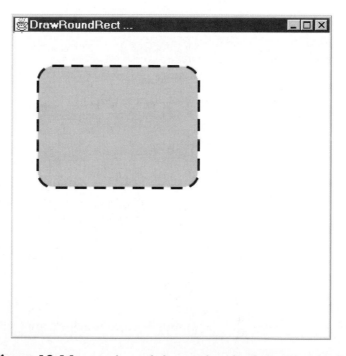

Figure 12.14. A pink rounded rectangle with a dashed black border.

GOOD PROGRAMMING PRACTICE

Use the RoundRectangle2D classes to create rectangles with rounded edges.

12.3.3 Ellipses

The class used to draw circles and ellipses is `java.awt.geom.Ellipse2D`. This is an abstract class with two concrete subclasses: `Ellipse2D.Double` and `Ellipse2D.Float`. The only difference between these two classes is that one expects `double` input parameters and the other expects `float` input parameters.

The constructor for an `Ellipse2D` object has the form

```
Ellipse2D.Double( double x, double y, double w, double h);
Ellipse2D.Float( float x, float y, float w, float h);
```

where the upper left-hand corner of the rectangular box in which the ellipse is drawn is point (x, y), and the ellipse is w pixels wide and h pixels high. Note that if w and h are equal, this class draws a circle. For example, the following statements create an ellipse starting at position (30, 40) that is 200 pixels wide and 150 pixels high.

```
Ellipse2D ell
ell = new Ellipse2D.Double (30.,40.,200.,150.);
g2.draw(ell);
```

Similarly, the following statements create a 200 × 150 ellipse object and fill its interior with black.

```
Ellipse2D rect = new Ellipse2D.Double (30., 40., 200., 150.);
g2.setColor(Color.black);
g2.fill(rect);
```

The resulting shape is shown in Figure 12.15.

Figure 12.15. An ellipse.

12.3.4 Arcs

An *arc* is a portion of an ellipse. An arc is drawn from a *starting angle* and covers an *extent*, both of which are given in degrees. The starting angle is the angle at which the arc begins, and the extent is the number of degrees covered by the arc. For this purpose, angles are defined as they are on a cartesian coordinate plane, positive counterclockwise from the positive x-axis (see Figure 12.16). Arcs with a positive extent sweep clockwise from the starting angle, while arcs with a negative extent sweep counterclockwise from the starting angle.

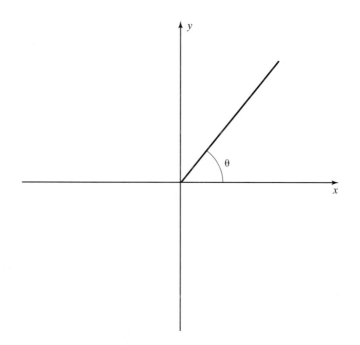

Figure 12.16. Arc starting angles are measured from the positive x-axis and are considered to be positive counterclockwise. Arc extents are positive if they are counterclockwise and negative if clockwise.

The class used to draw arcs is **Arc2D**. This is an abstract class with two concrete subclasses: `Arc2D.Double` and `Arc2D.Float`. The only difference between these two classes is that one expects `double` input parameters and the other expects `float` input parameters. The constructors for `Arc2D` objects have the form

```
Arc2D.Double( double x, double y, double w, double h,
              double start, double extent, int type );
Arc2D.Float( float x, float y, float w, float h,
             float start, float extent, int type );
```

where the upper left-hand corner of the rectangular box in which the arc is drawn is point (x, y), and the arc is w pixels wide and h pixels high. The starting angle of the arc is *start* radians, measured counterclockwise from the positive x-axis, and the extent of the arc is *extent* radians. Finally, *type* is the closure type for the arc. There are three possible closure types: Arc2D.OPEN, Arc2D.CHORD, and Arc2D.PIE. The Arc2D.OPEN type leaves the end of the arc open, while the Arc2D.CHORD type connects the ends with a straight line, and the Arc2D.PIE type connects the end with a pie slice.

For example, the following statements create an ellipse starting at position (30, 40) that is 200 pixels wide and 150 pixels high. The starting angle is 0°, and the extent is 90°. The closure type for this arc is Arc2D.OPEN.

```
Arc2D arc = new Arc2D.Double (30.,40.,200.,150.,
                           0., 90., Arc2D.OPEN);

    g2.draw(arc);
```

It is also possible to fill an arc with the fill method.

Figure 12.17 show the paintComponent method of a program that illustrates more of the arc options. This method creates four arcs with various combinations of starting angles, extents, fills, and closures.

```
// This method draws several arcs with different options.
public void paintComponent ( Graphics g ) {
   BasicStroke bs;                   // Ref to BasicStroke
   Arc2D arc;                        // Ref to arc
   float[] solid = {12.0f,0.0f};     // Solid line style

   // Cast the graphics object to Graph2D
   Graphics2D g2 = (Graphics2D) g;

   // Set rendering hints to improve display quality
   g2.setRenderingHint(RenderingHints.KEY_ANTIALIASING,
                  RenderingHints.VALUE_ANTIALIAS_ON);

   // Set background color
   Dimension size = getSize();
   g2.setColor( Color.white );
      g2.fill(new Rectangle2D.Double(0,0,size.width,size.height));

   // Set the basic stroke
   bs = new BasicStroke( 3.0f, BasicStroke.CAP_SQUARE,
                  BasicStroke.JOIN_MITER, 1.0f,
                  solid, 0.0f );
   g2.setStroke(bs);

   // Define arc1
   arc = new Arc2D.Double (20., 40., 100., 150.,
                0., 60., Arc2D.PIE);
   g2.setColor(Color.yellow);
   g2.fill(arc);
   g2.setColor(Color.black);
   g2.draw(arc);

   // Define arc2
   arc = new Arc2D.Double (10., 200., 100., 100.,
                90., 180., Arc2D.CHORD);
```

Figure 12.17. A paintComponent method to draw four arcs.

```
    g2.setColor(Color.black);
    g2.draw(arc);
    // Define arc3
    arc = new Arc2D.Double (220., 10., 80., 200.,
                    0., 120., Arc2D.OPEN);
    g2.setColor(Color.lightGray);
    g2.fill(arc);
    g2.setColor(Color.black);
    g2.draw(arc);
    // Define arc4
    arc = new Arc2D.Double (220., 220., 100., 100.,
                    -30., -300., Arc2D.PIE);
    g2.setColor(Color.orange);
    g2.fill(arc);
}
```

Figure 12.17. (Continued).

The resulting arcs are shown in Figure 12.18.

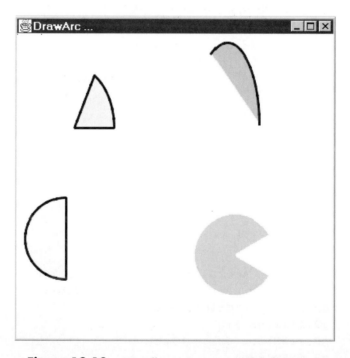

Figure 12.18. Miscellaneous arcs created with Arc2D.

GOOD PROGRAMMING PRACTICE

Use the Arc2D classes to create elliptical and circular arcs.

The angles in class `Arc2D` are given in *degrees*, while the angles in almost every other Java class are given in *radians*. Be careful not to confuse the angle units when using `Arc2D`.

12.3.5 General Paths

In addition to the specific shapes described above, Java includes a **java.awt.geom.GeneralPath** class to allow the construction of completely arbitrary shapes. This class is much more complex than the shapes we have examined so far, but it is very powerful and deserves careful attention.

The most common constructor for a `GeneralPath` object has the form:

```
GeneralPath();
```

Once a `GeneralPath` object has been created, a user can add as many points to the object as he or she wishes, and the points may optionally be connected by straight lines or curves. Table 12.4 contains a summary of the more important methods associated with this class.

TABLE 12.4 `GeneralPath` Methods

Method	Description
`closePath()`	Closes the current subpath by drawing a straight line from the current point back to the last `moveTo` position.
`curveTo(float x1, float y1, float x2, float y2, float x3, float y3);`	Adds a point to the path by drawing a Bezier curve from the current point through (x_1, y_1) and (x_2, y_2) to (x_3, y_3).
`lineTo(float x, float y);`	Adds a point to the path by drawing a straight line from the current coordinates to the newly specified coordinates.
`moveTo(float x, float y);`	Adds a point to the path by moving to the specified coordinates *without drawing a line*.
`quadTo(float x1, float y1, float x2, float y2);`	Adds a point to the path by drawing a quadratic curve from the current point through (x_1, y_1) to (x_2, y_2).
`setWindingRule(int rule);`	Sets a winding rule to determine the interior regions of the path. The options are WIND_NON_ZERO (default) or WIND_EVEN_ODD.

As a simple example, suppose that we want to construct an equilateral triangle. The statements required to construct and plot an equilateral triangle with vertices at (100, 300), (300, 300), and (200, 127) are:

```
GeneralPath p = new GeneralPath();
p.moveTo(100.0f,300.0f);
p.lineTo(300.0f,300.0f);
p.lineTo(200.0f,127.0f);
p.closePath();
g2.setColor( Color.lightGray );
g2.fill(p);
g2.setColor( Color.blue );
g2.draw(p);
```

The resulting shape is shown in Figure 12.19. Note that GeneralPath methods work with float parameters, not double. Be sure to cast any double values to float before using them to construct a GeneralPath.

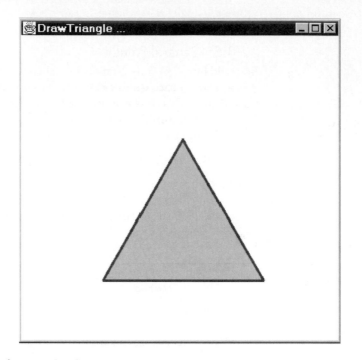

Figure 12.19. An equilateral triangle created with a GeneralPath.

It is possible for a single GeneralPath to create multiple overlapping closed paths by using multiple moveTo methods. For example, the following statements produce two overlapping equilateral triangles.

```
GeneralPath p = new GeneralPath();

// First triangle
p.moveTo( 50.0f,300.0f);
p.lineTo(250.0f,300.0f);
p.lineTo(150.0f,127.0f);
p.closePath();

// Second triangle
p.moveTo(150.0f,250.0f);
p.lineTo(350.0f,250.0f);
p.lineTo(250.0f, 77.0f);
p.closePath();

g2.setColor( Color.lightGray );
g2.fill(p);
g2.setColor( Color.black );
g2.draw(p);
```

The resulting overlapping triangles are shown in Figure 12.20.

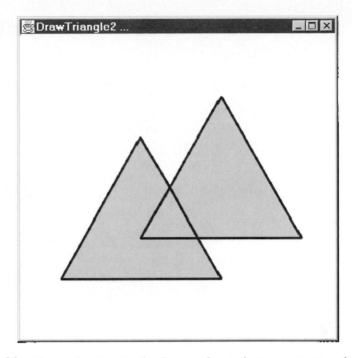

Figure 12.20.   Two overlapping triangles drawn with a single GeneralPath and the default winding rule.

The triangles in Figure 12.20 are filled with a light gray color, including the region common to both triangles. There might actually be some confusion about the overlapping region—did we intend that region to be inside both shapes, or did we intend to draw two nonoverlapping shapes with the "common" region outside of both? To resolve this ambiguity, Java provides two "winding rules" to determine the interior regions to fill. The default winding rule is GeneralPath.WIND_NON_ZERO. It treats overlapping regions as inside the shapes, and so it fills them as we saw in Figure 12.20. If the winding rule is set to GeneralPath.WIND_EVEN_ODD with the setWindingRule method, the overlapping area will be treated as outside the shapes. Figure 12.21 shows the result when the winding rule is WIND_EVEN_ODD.

GOOD PROGRAMMING PRACTICE

Use class GeneralPath to create arbitrarily complex graphics shapes.

GOOD PROGRAMMING PRACTICE

If a GeneralPath object includes two or more overlapping shapes, specify a winding rule to determine how to treat the overlapping regions. The default winding rule treats overlapping regions as interior to the shape, while the WIND_EVEN_ODD rule treats overlapping regions as exterior to the shape.

Figure 12.21. Two overlapping triangles drawn with a single `GeneralPath` and winding rule `WIND_EVEN_ODD`.

EXAMPLE 12.3

Creating Stars: To test the general shape class, create a five-pointed star and plot it three times: once as a line drawing only, once with a fill using the `WIND_NON_ZERO` winding rule, and once with a fill using the `WIND_EVEN_ODD` winding rule.

SOLUTION

A five-pointed star has five vertices located at the vertices of a regular pentagon [see Figure 12.22(a)]. The star is created by drawing straight lines that connect *every other vertex* until the lines close on themselves. The vertices can be calculated from the knowledge that a pentagram has five equal sides, and the outside angles of each vertex are spaced 72° apart.

The location of each vertex can be found from the equations

$$x_1 = (length)\cos\theta \tag{12.5}$$

$$y_1 = (length)\sin\theta \tag{12.6}$$

where *length* is the length of a side. If θ increases by 72° at each step around the circle, we can find each of the vertices in succession. Since we know one vertex is straight up, we can start at θ = 90° and work around the circle. Therefore the Java code to calculate the vertices of a pentagon centered on the origin would be:

```
double[] x = new double[5];
double[] y = new double[5];
...
theta  = 90 * Math.PI/180;
delta  = 72 * Math.PI/180;
for ( i = 0; i < x.length; i++ ) {
   x[i] = length * Math.cos(theta);
   y[i] = length * Math.sin(theta);
   theta += delta;
}
```

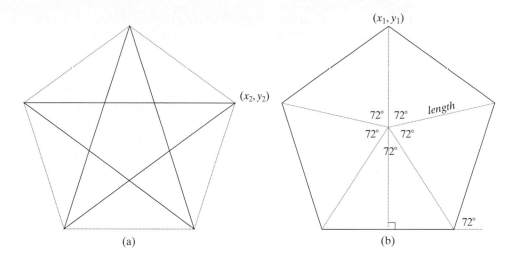

Figure 12.22. (a) A five-pointed star is formed by drawing lines between every other vertex of a regular pentagon. (b) The vertices are at equal distances from the origin and spaced 72° apart.

Now we know where the vertices of the pentagon are when it is centered on the origin, but the display is *not* centered on the origin, so we must translate the vertices to the center of the display, and also reverse the y-values to account for the fact that the y-axis is positive downward. The Java code for this step is:

```
// Get plot size
Dimension size = getSize();

// Shift the reference position to the center of
// the display.  The center of the display is
// size.width/2 and size.height/2.
for ( i = 0; i < x.length; i++ ) {
   x[i] = size.width/2 + x[i];
   y[i] = size.height/2 - y[i];
}
```

At this point we can draw the star by placing line segments between every other vertex with a `GeneralPath` object.

```
GeneralPath p = new GeneralPath();
p.moveTo((float) x[0],(float) y[0]);
p.lineTo((float) x[2],(float) y[2]);
p.lineTo((float) x[4],(float) y[4]);
p.lineTo((float) x[1],(float) y[1]);
p.lineTo((float) x[3],(float) y[3]);
p.closePath();
```

We will actually draw three stars, offset from each other so that they do not overlap, leaving one in outline only and filling the other two. The `paintComponent` method from the program to draw the three stars is shown in Figure 12.23.

The display produced when this program is executed is shown in Figure 12.24.

```java
// This method draws three stars.
public void paintComponent ( Graphics g ) {

    BasicStroke bs;                     // Ref to BasicStroke
    double delta;                       // Delta angle (radians)
    int i;                              // Loop index
    double length = 80;                 // Length of a side of pentagon
    GeneralPath p;                      // Ref to GeneralPath
    float[] solid = {12.0f,0.0f};       // Solid line style
    double theta;                       // Angle (radians)
    double[] x = new double[5];         // Vertices of reference pentagon
    double[] y = new double[5];         // Vertices of reference pentagon
    double[] x1 = new double[5];        // Vertices of shifted pentagon
    double[] y1 = new double[5];        // Vertices of shifted pentagon

    // Cast the graphics object to Graph2D
    Graphics2D g2 = (Graphics2D) g;

    // Get plot size
    Dimension size = getSize();

    // Set rendering hints to improve display quality
    g2.setRenderingHint(RenderingHints.KEY_ANTIALIASING,
                        RenderingHints.VALUE_ANTIALIAS_ON);

    // Set background color
    g2.setColor( Color.white );
    g2.fill(new Rectangle2D.Double(0,0,size.width,size.height));

    // Set the basic stroke
    bs = new BasicStroke( 3.0f, BasicStroke.CAP_SQUARE,
                          BasicStroke.JOIN_MITER, 1.0f,
                          solid, 0.0f );
    g2.setStroke(bs);

    // Calculate the locations of the vertices of the
    // pentagon surrounding the star.
    theta  = 90 * Math.PI/180;
    delta  = 72 * Math.PI/180;
    for ( i = 0; i < x.length; i++ ) {
        x[i] = length * Math.cos(theta);
        y[i] = length * Math.sin(theta);
        theta += delta;
    }

    // Shift the reference position to the center of
    // the display.  The center of the display is
    // size.width/2 and size.height/2.
    for ( i = 0; i < x.length; i++ ) {
        x[i] = size.width/2 + x[i];
        y[i] = size.height/2 - y[i];
    }
```

Figure 12.23. The paintComponent method to draw three stars using GeneralPath objects.

```
      // Create a star in the top center and draw
      // lines only
      for ( i = 0; i < x.length; i++ ) {
         x1[i] = x[i];
         y1[i] = y[i] - size.height/4;
      }
      p = new GeneralPath();
      p.moveTo((float) x1[0],(float) y1[0]);
      p.lineTo((float) x1[2],(float) y1[2]);
      p.lineTo((float) x1[4],(float) y1[4]);
      p.lineTo((float) x1[1],(float) y1[1]);
      p.lineTo((float) x1[3],(float) y1[3]);
      p.closePath();

      // Set color and draw
      g2.setColor(Color.black);
      g2.draw(p);

      // Create a star in the lower left and draw
      // with the default winding rule
      for ( i = 0; i < x.length; i++ ) {
         x1[i] = x[i] - size.width/4;
         y1[i] = y[i] + size.height/4;
      }
      p = new GeneralPath();
      p.moveTo((float) x1[0],(float) y1[0]);
      p.lineTo((float) x1[2],(float) y1[2]);
      p.lineTo((float) x1[4],(float) y1[4]);
      p.lineTo((float) x1[1],(float) y1[1]);
      p.lineTo((float) x1[3],(float) y1[3]);
      p.setWindingRule(GeneralPath.WIND_NON_ZERO);
      p.closePath();

      // Set color and draw
      g2.setColor(Color.yellow);
      g2.fill(p);
      g2.setColor(Color.black);
      g2.draw(p);

      // Create a star in the lower right and draw
      // with the WIND_EVEN_ODD winding rule
      for ( i = 0; i < x.length; i++ ) {
         x1[i] = x[i] + size.width/4;
         y1[i] = y[i] + size.height/4;
      }
      p = new GeneralPath();
      p.moveTo((float) x1[0],(float) y1[0]);
      p.lineTo((float) x1[2],(float) y1[2]);
      p.lineTo((float) x1[4],(float) y1[4]);
      p.lineTo((float) x1[1],(float) y1[1]);
```

Figure 12.23. (Continued).

```
      p.lineTo((float) x1[3],(float) y1[3]);
      p.setWindingRule(GeneralPath.WIND_EVEN_ODD);
      p.closePath();

      // Set color and draw
      g2.setColor(Color.green);
      g2.fill(p);
      g2.setColor(Color.black);
      g2.draw(p);
   }

   public static void main(String ε[]) {
      // Create a Window Listener to handle "close" events
      MyWindowListener l = new MyWindowListener();

      // Create a DrawStar object
      DrawStar c = new DrawStar();

      // Create a frame and place the object in the center
      // of the frame.
      JFrame f = new JFrame("DrawStar ...");
      f.addWindowListener(l);
      f.getContentPane().add(c, BorderLayout.CENTER);
      f.pack();
      f.setSize(400,400);
      f.show();
   }
```

Figure 12.23. (Continued).

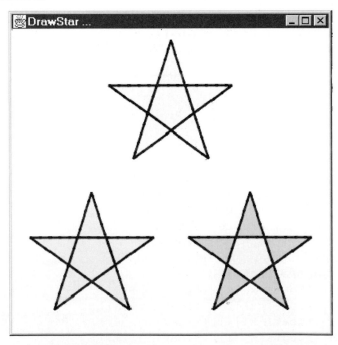

Figure 12.24. The output of program DrawStar.

12.4   DISPLAYING TEXT

Text may be displayed on a graphics device using the `Graphics2D` method **drawString**. The most common forms of this method are

```
drawString(String s, int x, int y);
drawString(String s, float x, float y);
```

where s is the string to display, and (x, y) is the *lower left-hand corner* of region where the `String` will be displayed. When this method is executed, the characters in s will be displayed on the screen in the current color, using the current `Font`.

The `paintComponent` method from an example program that displays a `String` is shown in Figure 12.25, together with the result produced on the display.

```
// This method displays a string on the graphics device.
public void paintComponent ( Graphics g ) {

    // Cast the graphics object to Graph2D
    Graphics2D g2 = (Graphics2D) g;

    // Set rendering hints to improve display quality
    g2.setRenderingHint(RenderingHints.KEY_ANTIALIASING,
                        RenderingHints.VALUE_ANTIALIAS_ON);

    // Set background color
    Dimension size = getSize();
    g2.setColor( Color.white );
    g2.fill(new Rectangle2D.Double(0,0,size.width,size.height));

    // Display string
    g2.setColor( Color.black );
    g2.drawString("This is a test!",20,40);
}
```

Figure 12.25. Method demonstrating how to write a `String` to a graphics device.

Note that if you specify a y-value of 0, no text will be visible, since 0 corresponds to the *top* of the display area, and it also marks the *bottom* of the region where the `String` will be displayed! This is a common mistake made by novice Java programmers.

PROGRAMMING PITFALLS

Do not to display text at an (x, y) position with a y-value of 0. It will be displayed above the top of the display window, and so will be invisible!

12.4.1 Selecting and Controlling Fonts

The font used to display text on a graphics device can be controlled by defining a **java.awt.Font** object and then specifying that object to be the current font. A Font object is declared with a constructor of the form

```
Font( String s, int style, int size );
```

where s is the name of the font to use, style is the style of the font (plain, italic, bold, or bold italic), and size is the point size of the font. There may be many fonts available on a system, but Java guarantees that the fonts shown in Table 12.5 will *always* be available on every Java implementation.

TABLE 12.5   Standard Font Names

Font Name	Description
Serif	This is the standard serif font for a particular system. Examples are Times and Times New Roman.
SansSerif	This is the standard sans-serif font for a particular system. Examples are Helvetica and Arial.
Monospaced	This is the standard monospaced font for a particular system. Examples are Courier and Courier New.
Dialog	This is the standard font for dialog boxes on a particular system.
DialogInput	This is the standard font for dialog inputs on a particular system.

The font style may be specified by one or more of the constants Font.PLAIN, Font.BOLD, and Font.ITALIC. Note that it is possible to use the BOLD and ITALIC styles at the same time by simply adding the two constants together. The font size can be any integer point size. For example, the statement shown below creates a 14-point bold italic monospaced font.

```
Font font1 = new Font( "Monospaced", Font.BOLD+Font.ITALIC, 14);
```

Once a font has been created, it can be set to be the current font with the Graphics2D method setFont. The form of this method is

```
g2.setFont( font1 );
```

After this method is executed, any subsequent text will be displayed in the specified font.

The program in Figure 12.26 illustrates various combinations of font names, styles, and sizes.

A summary of useful methods in the java.awt.Font class can be found in Table 12.6.

TABLE 12.6   Methods in the java.awt.Font Class

Font Name	Description
public int getStyle()	Returns an integer value containing the current font style
public int getSize()	Returns an integer value containing the current font size
public String getName()	Returns the current font name as a String
public String getFamily()	Returns the current font family as a String
isBold()	Returns true if the font is bold
isItalic()	Returns true if the font is bold
isPlain()	Returns true if the font is bold

```
// This method tests various fonts
public void paintComponent ( Graphics g ) {

    // Cast the graphics object to Graph2D
    Graphics2D g2 = (Graphics2D) g;

    // Set rendering hints to improve display quality
    g2.setRenderingHint(RenderingHints.KEY_ANTIALIASING,
                        RenderingHints.VALUE_ANTIALIAS_ON);

    // Set background color
    Dimension size = getSize();
    g2.setColor( Color.white );
    g2.fill(new Rectangle2D.Double(0,0,size.width,size.height));

    // Define several fonts...
    Font f1 = new Font("Serif",Font.PLAIN,12);
    Font f2 = new Font("SansSerif",Font.ITALIC,16);
    Font f3 = new Font("Monospaced",Font.BOLD,14);
    Font f4 = new Font("Serif",Font.BOLD+Font.ITALIC,20);

    // Display fonts
    g2.setColor( Color.black );
    g2.setFont(f1);
    g2.drawString("12-point plain Serif",20,40);
    g2.setFont(f2);
    g2.drawString("16-point italic SansSerif",20,80);
    g2.setFont(f3);
    g2.drawString("14-point bold Monospaced",20,120);
    g2.setFont(f4);
    g2.drawString("20-point bold italic Serif",20,160);
}
```

Figure 12.26. Method displaying various fonts.

12.4.2 Getting Information about Fonts

It is sometimes necessary to get precise information about a font that is being used in an application. For example, we may need to place two or more lines of text under each other at a comfortable spacing. How can we tell precisely how tall and long a particular line is, so that we can place other information above, below, or to the side of it? Java contains a special class called **java.awt.FontMetrics** to provide this information about any specified font.

Several types of metrics are associated with a font. They include the font's *height, ascent* (the amount a normal character rises above the baseline), *descent* (the amount a character dips below the baseline), and *leading* (the amount above the ascent line occupied by especially tall characters). These quantities are illustrated in Figure 12.27.

Figure 12.27. Font metrics.

A new FontMetrics object can be declared with a constructor of the form:

```
FontMetrics fm = new FontMetrics( Font f );
```

In addition, a FontMetrics object for the current font can be created using the getFontMetrics() method of the Graphics2D class:

```
FontMetrics fm = g2.getFontMetrics();
```

Once the object has been created by one of these techniques, information about the font can be retrieved with any of the methods in Table 12.7.

TABLE 12.7 Methods in the FontMetrics Class

Method Name	Description
public int getAscent()	Returns the ascent of a font in pixels
public int getDescent()	Returns the descent of a font in pixels
public int getHeight()	Returns the height of a font in pixels
public int getLeading()	Returns the leading of a font in pixels

The paintComponent method in Figure 12.28 illustrates the use of these methods to recover information about the current font.

```
// This method illustrates the use of FontMetrics
public void paintComponent ( Graphics g ) {

   // Cast the graphics object to Graph2D
   Graphics2D g2 = (Graphics2D) g;
```

Figure 12.28. Method displaying font metrics.

```
        // Define a font...
        Font f1 = new Font("Serif",Font.PLAIN,14);

        // Set font
        g2.setFont(f1);

        // Get information about the font
        FontMetrics fm = g2.getFontMetrics();

        // Get information about the current font
        System.out.println("Font metrics:");
        System.out.println("Font height  = " + fm.getHeight());
        System.out.println("Font ascent  = " + fm.getAscent());
        System.out.println("Font descent = " + fm.getDescent());
        System.out.println("Font leading = " + fm.getLeading());
    }
```

Figure 12.28.   (Continued).

When this program is executed, the results are:

```
D:\book\java\chap12>java ShowFontMetrics
Font metrics:
Font height  = 20
Font ascent  = 15
Font descent = 4
Font leading = 1
```

Thus the spacing between successive lines of this font must be greater than 20 pixels.

EXAMPLE 12.4

Displaying Multiple Lines of Text: Write a program that will display three lines of text, leaving the proper vertical spacing between lines. Calculate the proper spacing using the FontMetrics methods.

SOLUTION

The program in Figure 12.28 displays the required data. Note that it uses the height returned from the getHeight() method to set the spacing between successive lines. The display produced when this program is executed is also shown in Figure 12.29.

```
import java.awt.*;
import java.awt.event.*;
import java.awt.geom.*;
import javax.swing.*;
public class DisplayStrings extends JComponent {

    // Constructor
    public DisplayStrings() {
        setDoubleBuffered( true );
    }

    // This method illustrates the use of FontMetrics
    // to automatically set the proper spacing between
```

Figure 12.29.   A program to display three lines of text with proper spacing.

```java
    // lines.
    public void paintComponent ( Graphics g ) {

        // Cast the graphics object to Graph2D
        Graphics2D g2 = (Graphics2D) g;

        // Set rendering hints to improve display quality
        g2.setRenderingHint(RenderingHints.KEY_ANTIALIASING,
                            RenderingHints.VALUE_ANTIALIAS_ON);

        // Set background color
        Dimension size = getSize();
        g2.setColor( Color.white );
        g2.fill(new Rectangle2D.Double(0,0,size.width,size.height));

        // Define a font...
        Font f1 = new Font("Serif",Font.BOLD,16);

        // Set font
        g2.setFont(f1);

        // Get font height
        int height = g2.getFontMetrics().getHeight();

        // Display the text
        g2.setColor( Color.black );
        g2.drawString("This is line 1.",20,  height+20);
        g2.drawString("This is line 2.",20,2*height+20);
        g2.drawString("This is line 3.",20,3*height+20);
    }

    public static void main(String s[]) {

        // Create a Window Listener to handle "close" events
        MyWindowListener l = new MyWindowListener();

        // Create a DisplayStrings object
        DisplayStrings c = new DisplayStrings();

        // Create a frame and place the object in the center
        // of the frame.
        JFrame f = new JFrame("DisplayStrings ...");
        f.addWindowListener(l);
        f.getContentPane().add(c, BorderLayout.CENTER);
        f.pack();
        f.setSize(300,200);
        f.show();
    }
}
```

Figure 12.29. (Continued).

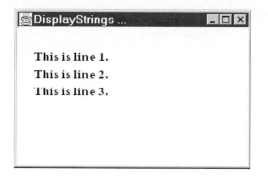

Figure 12.29. (Continued).

12.5 THE AFFINE TRANSFORM

An **affine transform** is a user-specified combination of translations, scalings, rotations, and shears that is automatically applied to any Graphics2D object whenever it is rendered on a graphics device. (The term *affine transform* refers to a transformation that converts an input shape into an output shape while preserving parallel lines.) The types of transformations that may be applied include

1. **Translations**—Moving from one place to another within the display window without changing the shape of the object.

2. **Scalings**—Making the object larger or smaller.

3. **Rotations**—Rotating the object about a user-specified axis.

4. **Shears**—Causing one side of the object to be displaced relative to the other side, so that it appears "slanted."

Any combination of these transformations may be applied in any desired order.

When a new Graphics2D object is created, an affine transform is automatically associated with the object. The default affine transform is a 1:1 mapping, meaning that any shape or text created by a Java 2D class is displayed without modification on the graphics device. However, a programmer can modify this mapping at any time while displaying text or graphics on the device.

A new **java.awt.geom.AffineTransform** object can be created with a constructor of the form:

```
AffineTransform at = new AffineTransform();
```

Once the object has been created, the methods in Table 12.8 can be used to add translations, scalings, rotations, and shears to the data that will be displayed on a graphics device. *Note that the effects of each method call will be added to the effects of all previous calls*, so it possible to build very complex behaviors with these methods. Finally, after all transformations have been added, the affine transform object must be associated with a specific Graphics2D object, using the Graphics2D method setTransform.

```
g2.setTransform(at);
```

The program in Figure 12.30 illustrates how to use the affine transform. It writes out the string "Hello, World!" eight times, rotating the string by 45° ($\pi/4$) each time the text is printed out. Note that the effect of the calls to rotate is cumulative, so the text rotates by a total of 360°.

TABLE 12.8 Selected Methods in the `AffineTransform` Class

Method Name	Description
`public void rotate(double theta)`	Rotates data by theta radians. A positive angle corresponds to a *clockwise* rotation.
`public void rotate(double theta,` `        double x, double y)`	Rotates data by theta radians about point (x, y). A positive angle corresponds to a *clockwise* rotation.
`public void scale(double sx,` `        double sy)`	Scales (multiplies) x- and y-axes by the specified amounts.
`public void shear(double shx,` `        double shy)`	Shears x- and y-axes by the specified amounts. The equations applied are $x' = x + (\mathrm{shx})y$ and $y' = y + (\mathrm{shy})x$.
`public void translate(double tx,` `        double ty)`	Moves data a distance tx in the x-direction and ty in the y-direction.

```
// This method tests an affine transform by displaying
// rotated text.
public void paintComponent ( Graphics g ) {

    AffineTransform at;              // Ref to affine transform
    int i;                           // Loop index

    // Cast the graphics object to Graph2D
    Graphics2D g2 = (Graphics2D) g;

    // Get plot size
    Dimension size = getSize();

    // Set rendering hints to improve display quality
    g2.setRenderingHint(RenderingHints.KEY_ANTIALIASING,
                        RenderingHints.VALUE_ANTIALIAS_ON);

    // Set background color
    g2.setColor( Color.white );
    g2.fill(new Rectangle2D.Double(0,0,size.width,size.height));

    // Get the affine transform
    at = new AffineTransform();

    // Define and set font
    Font f1 = new Font("Serif",Font.BOLD,18);
    g2.setFont(f1);

    //
    Color colorArray[] = new Color[10];
    colorArray[0] = Color.blue;
    colorArray[1] = Color.green;
    colorArray[2] = Color.magenta;
    colorArray[3] = Color.black;
    colorArray[4] = Color.blue;
    colorArray[5] = Color.green;
    colorArray[6] = Color.magenta;
    colorArray[7] = Color.black;
```

Figure 12.30. A program to test the affine transform by rotating a text string.

```
     for ( i = 0;   i < 8; i++){
        at.rotate(Math.PI/4, 180, 200);
        g2.setTransform(at);
        g2.setColor(colorArray[i]);
        g2.drawString("Hello, World!", 200, 200);
        }
  }

public static void main(String s[]) {

    // Create a Window Listener to handle "close" events
    MyWindowListener l = new MyWindowListener();

    // Create a TestAffineTransform object
    TestAffineTransform c = new TestAffineTransform();

    // Create a frame and place the object in the center
    // of the frame.
    JFrame f = new JFrame("TestAffineTransform ...");
    f.addWindowListener(l);
    f.getContentPane().add(c, BorderLayout.CENTER);
    f.pack();
    f.setSize(400,400);
    f.show();
  }
```

Figure 12.30.   (Continued).

EXAMPLE 12.5

Applying the Affine Transform: Illustrate the use of the affine transform by displaying a single `Rectangle2D` object in four different ways on a single canvas:

1.   Display the original rectangle in the upper left-hand quadrant of the canvas.
2.   Display the rectangle rotated by 45° in the upper right-hand quadrant of the canvas.
3.   Display the rectangle at one-half size and rotated by 90° in the lower left-hand quadrant of the canvas.
4.   Display the rectangle with a 30° horizontal shear in the lower right-hand quadrant of the canvas.

SOLUTION

To display the rectangle four times as specified, we must first create a `Rectangle2D.double` object. For simplicity, we will create the object centered at the origin $(0, 0)$, and then translate it to the desired quadrant with an affine transform each time it is displayed.

```
// Define rectangle centered about (0,0)
rect = new Rectangle2D.Double (-75., -40., 150., 80.);
```

The display in the upper left-hand corner is very simple, since all we have to do is to shift the center of the shape from the origin to the middle of that quadrant. The affine transform to perform this shift is

```
at = new AffineTransform();
at.translate(100.,120.);
g2.setTransform(at);
```

The display in the upper right-hand corner is more complex, since we must both shift the rectangle and rotate it by 45°. Remember that rotation angles are specified in *radians*, with a positive number corresponding to a clockwise rotation. Therefore, the affine transform to perform the shift to the upper right-hand quadrant and the 45° rotation is

```
at = new AffineTransform();
at.translate(300.,120.);
at.rotate(Math.PI/4);
g2.setTransform(at);
```

The display in the lower left-hand corner requires us to shift the rectangle to that corner, rotate it by 90° $(\pi/2)$, and reduce it to half size. Therefore, the affine transform to create this display is

```
at = new AffineTransform();
at.translate(100.,280.);
at.rotate(Math.PI/2);
at.scale(0.5,0.5);
g2.setTransform(at);
```

The display in the lower right-hand corner requires us to shift the rectangle to that corner and apply a 30° shear. The shear angle can be determined from basic trigonometry. Figure 12.31 shows the relationship between the shear value specified in the transform and the resulting shear angle. By simple trigonometry,

$$\tan \theta = \frac{\Delta x}{y} = \frac{(\text{shx})y}{y} = \text{shx} \tag{12.7}$$

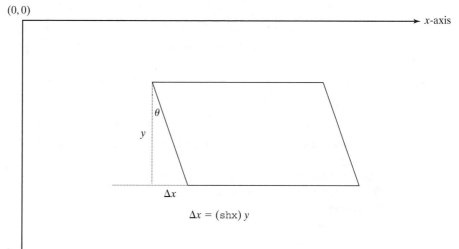

Figure 12.31.   The relationship between the sheer angle θ and the `sheer` method parameter `shx`.

so an angle of 30° would require a value of `shx` = 0.577. Therefore, the affine transform to create this display is

```
at = new AffineTransform();
at.translate(280.,280.);
at.shear(0.577,0.);
g2.setTransform(at);
```

The final `paintComponent` method is shown in Figure 12.32, together with the resulting graphics output.

```
// This method tests the affine transform.
public void paintComponent ( Graphics g ) {

   AffineTransform at;              // Ref to AffineTransform
   BasicStroke bs;                  // Ref to BasicStroke
   Rectangle2D rect;                // Ref to rectangle
   float[] solid = {12.0f,0.0f};    // Solid line style

   // Cast the graphics object to Graph2D
   Graphics2D g2 = (Graphics2D) g;
```

Figure 12.32.   A program that displays the same rectangular shape in four different locations with varying scales, rotations, and shears.

```
// Set rendering hints to improve display quality
g2.setRenderingHint(RenderingHints.KEY_ANTIALIASING,
                    RenderingHints.VALUE_ANTIALIAS_ON);

// Set background color
Dimension size = getSize();
g2.setColor( Color.white );
g2.fill(new Rectangle2D.Double(0,0,size.width,size.height));

// Set the basic stroke
bs = new BasicStroke( 3.0f, BasicStroke.CAP_SQUARE,
                      BasicStroke.JOIN_MITER, 1.0f,
                      solid, 0.0f );
g2.setStroke(bs);

// Define rectangle centered about (0,0)
rect = new Rectangle2D.Double (-75., -40., 150., 80.);

// Now translate the rectangle to the upper left-hand
// quadrant
at = new AffineTransform();
at.translate(100.,120.);
g2.setTransform(at);
g2.setColor(Color.red);
g2.fill(rect);
g2.setColor(Color.black);
g2.draw(rect);

// Now rotate the rectangle 45 deg and translate it
// to the upper right-hand quadrant
at = new AffineTransform();
at.translate(300.,120.);
at.rotate(Math.PI/4);
g2.setTransform(at);
g2.setColor(Color.red);
g2.fill(rect);
g2.setColor(Color.black);
g2.draw(rect);

// Now display at half size, rotated 90 deg in the
// lower left-hand quadrant
at = new AffineTransform();
at.translate(100.,280.);
at.rotate(Math.PI/2);
at.scale(0.5,0.5);
g2.setTransform(at);
g2.setColor(Color.red);
g2.fill(rect);
g2.setColor(Color.black);
g2.draw(rect);
```

Figure 12.32. (Continued).

```
    // Now apply a 30 deg horizontal sheer and display
    // in the lower right-hand quadrant
    at = new AffineTransform();
    at.translate(280.,280.);
    at.shear(0.577,0.);
    g2.setTransform(at);
    g2.setColor(Color.red);
    g2.fill(rect);
    g2.setColor(Color.black);
    g2.draw(rect);
}
```

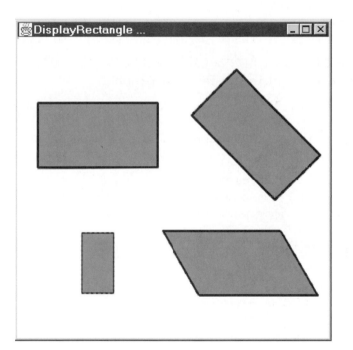

Figure 12.32.   (Continued).

12.6   XOR MODE

When two overlapping objects are drawn on a graphics device, the second object will normally cover up the underlying object in the region of overlap, making it impossible to determine the exact shape of the first object in the region that is covered up. However, it is sometimes useful to see the full outlines of both shapes, even if they overlap. For those circumstances, Java includes a special paint mode known as XOR (exclusive OR) mode.

In XOR mode, the outlines of both objects are visible, and the region of overlap is painted in a special color to make it obvious. XOR mode is set by the `Graphics2D` method `setXORmode`. The calling sequence for this method is

```
    g2.setXORMode ( Color c );
```

where g2 is a `Graphics2D` device and c is a `Color` object. When overlapping objects are drawn in the *same* color, then the XOR mode color is used to draw the overlapping region.

The `paintComponent` method in Figure 12.33 illustrates the use of XOR mode to display overlapping regions of both objects. Note that the XOR color is used only when both overlapping objects have the same color.

```
// This method tests XOR mode.
public void paintComponent ( Graphics g ) {

    AffineTransform at;                 // Ref to AffineTransform
    BasicStroke bs;                     // Ref to BasicStroke
    Ellipse2D ell1, ell2;               // Ref to ellipse
    float[] solid = {12.0f,0.0f};       // Solid line style

    // Cast the graphics object to Graph2D
    Graphics2D g2 = (Graphics2D) g;

    // Set rendering hints to improve display quality
    g2.setRenderingHint(RenderingHints.KEY_ANTIALIASING,
                        RenderingHints.VALUE_ANTIALIAS_ON);

    // Set background color
    Dimension size = getSize();
    g2.setColor( Color.white );
    g2.fill(new Rectangle2D.Double(0,0,size.width,size.height));

    // Define two ellipses and plot them in normal mode
    ell1 = new Ellipse2D.Double (30., 30., 150., 80.);
    ell2 = new Ellipse2D.Double (130., 30., 150., 80.);
    g2.setColor(Color.green);
    g2.fill(ell1);
    g2.setColor(Color.orange);
    g2.fill(ell2);

    // Define two ellipses with different colors and
    // plot them in XOR mode
    ell1 = new Ellipse2D.Double (70., 140., 150., 80.);
    ell2 = new Ellipse2D.Double (170., 140., 150., 80.);
    g2.setXORMode(Color.white);
    g2.setColor(Color.green);
    g2.fill(ell1);
    g2.setColor(Color.orange);
    g2.fill(ell2);

    // Define two ellipses with the same color and
    // plot them in XOR mode
```

Figure 12.33.   A program that tests the XOR paint mode.

```
    ell1 = new Ellipse2D.Double (110., 250., 150., 80.);
    ell2 = new Ellipse2D.Double (210., 250., 150., 80.);
    g2.setXORMode(Color.white);
    g2.setColor(Color.green);
    g2.fill(ell1);
    g2.setColor(Color.green);
    g2.fill(ell2);
}
```

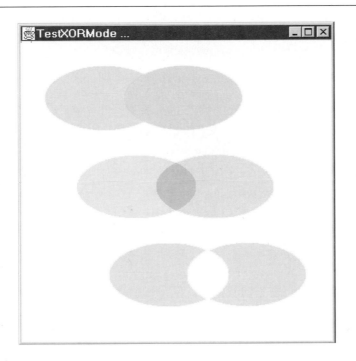

Figure 12.33. (Continued).

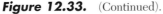

GOOD PROGRAMMING PRACTICE

Use the `Graphics2D` method `setXORMode` to make the overlapping regions of objects visible.

12.7 DESIGNING EFFECTIVE GRAPHICS FOR PRINTING

The `BasicStroke` class allows a programmer to customize the color and line style of Java 2D objects such as lines, rectangles, and other shapes. This flexibility allows a programmer to display multiple types of data on a single plot, while keeping the data items distinct from each other.

When a novice programmer first starts creating graphics with this flexibility, there is a tendency to rely heavily on color to distinguish the many lines on the graph. Unfortunately, color is usually not preserved when a graph is printed, so a display that is very effective on the computer screen may appear confusing when printed on a monochrome printer.

As a programmer, you should always consider both the display on a screen and the printed-out version of the display when designing your graphics. Use combinations of color, line style, and line width to distinguish your lines, so that they will still appear different when printed on a monochrome printer.

GOOD PROGRAMMING PRACTICE

Use combinations of color, line style, and line width to distinguish your lines, so that they will still appear different when printed on a monochrome printer.

QUIZ 12-1

This quiz provides a quick check to see if you have understood the concepts introduced in Sections 12.1 through 12.6. If you have trouble with the quiz, reread the section, ask your instructor, or discuss the material with a fellow student. The answers are found in the back of the book.

1.   What is a container? Which type of container are we using in this chapter?
2.   What is a component? Which type of component(s) are we using in this chapter?
3.   What steps are required to display graphics in Java?
4.   What coordinate systems is used to display graphics in Java? Where is the point (0, 0) in this system?
5.   What class does the method `getSize()` belong to? How is it used?
6.   What class controls the style of lines and borders in Java?
7.   How is text displayed on a Java graphics device? What classes are used to set and get information about the font being used?
8.   What is an affine transform? How is it used?

12.8   PUTTING IT ALL TOGETHER: BUILDING A PLOTTING CLASS

In this section, we will combine what we have learned about plotting lines and text strings, plus affine transforms, to create a class capable of creating two-dimensional plots.

EXAMPLE 12.6

Creating a Plotting Class: At the time that we introduced the class `chapman.graphics.Jplot2D` in Chapter 5, we said that you would learn how to create a plotting class of your own later in the book. We now have all of the tools required to create a plotting class.

Create a class that plots a line specified by a series of (x, y) points, where the x-values and the y-values are supplied to two double arrays. The plot should be placed within a rectangular box, with a plot title and labels for the x- and y-axes. The class should have a constructor, and it should include methods to allow the user to (1) set the data to display, (2) set the line color, (3) set the plot title, (4) set the plot x-axis label, and (5) set the plot y-axis label.

SOLUTION

To create this class, we must define instance variables, a constructor, some set several methods, and a `paintComponent` method.

1.   **Defining the Instance Variables**
     The instance variables required by this class must hold the x and y arrays to plot, the line color to use, and strings containing the title, x-axis label, and

y-axis label. In addition, we must define validity flags to indicate when we have valid arrays and strings, because we can't display the data items before they are defined. If the program attempted to display data using a null reference, it would abort with a run-time exception. We, will arbitrarily choose black as the default color for the lines. The required instance variables are shown below:

```
// Line data
private double[] x; // Array of x-values to plot
private double[] y; // Array of y-values to plot
boolean validLine;   // True if there is data to plot
private Color lineColor = Color.black; // Line color

// Title data
private String title;    // Title of plot
boolean validTitle;      // True if title present

// Axis labels
private String xLabel;   // X-axis label
private String yLabel;   // Y-axis label
boolean validXLabel;     // True if X label present
boolean validYLabel;     // True if Y label present
```

2.   **Create the Constructor**
The constructor required for this class is very simple. It must turn on double buffering and must initialize all validity flags to `false`, since no data or strings have been defined yet. The constructor is shown below:

```
public PlotXY() {
   setDoubleBuffered( true );
   validLine = false;
   validTitle = false;
   validXLabel = false;
   validYLabel = false;
}
```

3.   **Create the "set" Methods**
The methods to set the data to display, the line color, the title, and the axis labels are all similar. In each case, the input data is stored in the appropriate instance variable, and the corresponding validity flag is set to true. The methods are shown below:

```
// Method to set display data
public void setXY(double[] x, double[] y) {
   this.x = x;
   this.y = y;
   validLine = true;
}

// Method to set line color
public void setColor(Color lineColor) {
   this.lineColor = lineColor;
}
```

```
// Method to set title
public void setTitle(String title) {
   this.title = title;
   validTitle = true;
}

// Method to set X-axis label
public void setXLabel(String xLabel) {
   this.xLabel = xLabel;
   validXLabel = true;
}

// Method to set Y-axis label
public void setYLabel(String yLabel) {
   this.yLabel = yLabel;
   validYLabel = true;
}
```

4. **Create the** `paintComponent` **Method**

Now comes the hard part—creating the `paintComponent` method to draw the actual plot on the face of the component. We need to draw a rectangular box on the component, and then plot the data within the box. The box must be sufficiently smaller than the size of the component to allow room for the title and axis labels to be added along its edges.

The size of a component can always be determined using the `getSize()` method of the component. This method returns a `Dimension` object, which has two public instance variables, `height` and `width`. The component's height *in pixels* will be `size.height`, and its width *in pixels* will be `size.width`.

The size of a component in pixels is very inconvenient to work with, since it can change whenever the user resizes the frame displaying the component. It is easier to define a *normalized* scale for plotting, with both the width and height varying from 0 to 1 (see Figure 12.34). The plot itself will be placed in a smaller area, with margins on each side to hold the title, axis labels, and so forth.

The normalized margins of the plot can be arbitrarily selected, and for now we will set them as follows:

```
final double xLeftMargin = 0.125;
final double xRightMargin = 0.045;
final double yTopMargin = 0.075;
final double yBottomMargin = 0.075;
```

Note that we are declaring these values as `final`, since they should never change. Also, note that we are leaving extra room on the left margin for the *y*-axis label. With these definitions, the size and endpoints of the normalized plotting area become:

```
normalWidth  = 1.0 - xLeftMargin - xRightMargin;
normalHeight = 1.0 - yTopMargin - yBottomMargin;
normalStartX = xLeftMargin;
normalStartY = yTopMargin;
normalEndX   = normalStartX + normalWidth;
normalEndY   = normalStartY + normalHeight;
```

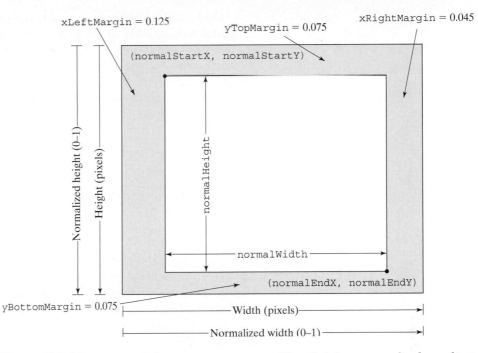

Figure 12.34. Layout of the `PlotYX` component. We will define a normalized coordinate system going from 0 to 1 in width and height. The plotting area will be smaller than the component, with margins on each side large enough to hold the title and labels.

The box around the plotting area can be drawn with four lines, connecting the points (x_{start}, y_{start}), (x_{end}, y_{start}), (x_{end}, y_{end}), and (x_{start}, y_{end}). The Java statements to draw this box are shown below. The normalized starting and ending positions are being translated back into pixels by multiplying the x-values by the component width in pixels and the y-values by the height in pixels.

```java
line = new Line2D.Double(size.width  * normalStartX,
                         size.height * normalStartY,
                         size.width  * normalEndX,
                         size.height * normalStartY);

g2.draw(line);
line = new Line2D.Double(size.width  * normalEndX,
                         size.height * normalStartY,
                         size.width  * normalEndX,
                         size.height * normalEndY);
g2.draw(line);
line = new Line2D.Double(size.width  * normalEndX,
                         size.height * normalEndY,
                         size.width  * normalStartX,
                         size.height * normalEndY);
g2.draw(line);
line = new Line2D.Double(size.width  * normalStartX,
                         size.height * normalEndY,
                         size.width  * normalStartX,
                         size.height * normalStartY);
g2.draw(line);
```

How can the plot be mapped onto the plotting area inside this box? If the plot is to occupy the entire plotting area, then the *minimum* x-value in the plot should be at the left margin of the plotting area (`normalStartX`), the *maximum* x-value should be at the right margin of the plotting area (`normalEndX`), and the normalized range of possible x-values should be `normalWidth`. The multiplier required make the full range of x-values fit into the plotting space is

$$x_{\text{scale}} = \frac{\texttt{normalWidth}}{x_{\max} - x_{\min}} \tag{12.8}$$

and the equation to map the x-values into the plot is

$$x_{\textit{normalized}} = (x - x_{\min}) \times x_{\text{scale}} + \texttt{normalStartY} \tag{12.9}$$

Similarly, if the plot is to occupy the entire plotting area, then the *minimum* y-value in the plot should be at the bottom margin of the plotting area (`normalEndY`), the *maximum* y-value should be at the top margin of the plotting area (`normalStartY`), and the normalized range of possible y-values should be `normalHeight`. (Note that this is inverted, because Java places the zero point for the y-axis at the *top* of the plot.) The multiplier required make the full range of y-values fit into the plotting space is

$$y_{\text{scale}} = \frac{\texttt{normalHeight}}{y_{\max} - y_{\min}} \tag{12.10}$$

and the equation to map the y-values into the plot is

$$y_{\text{normalized}} = -(y - y_{\min}) \times y_{\text{scale}} + \texttt{normalStartY} \tag{12.11}$$

The negative sign in Equation (12.11) takes into account the fact that the zero point is at the top of the plot.

The final x- and y-positions in pixels can be found from the normalized values by multiplying the normalized x- and y-values by the component width and height, respectively.

$$x_{\text{pixel}} = x_{\text{normalized}} \times \text{width in pixels} \tag{12.12}$$

$$y_{\text{pixel}} = y_{\text{normalized}} \times \text{height in pixels} \tag{12.13}$$

Once the position of each point is known in pixels, the line can be plotted by creating `Line2D` objects between consecutive (x, y) pairs of points, and plotting the line segments.

5. **Adding Text to the Plot**

After the plot has been created, we need to add the title, the x-axis label, and the y-axis label. These labels are created by defining a font to display the labels in, setting that font to be used by the graphics object, and then calling the `drawString` method. For example, the plot title could be created as follows:

```
font = new Font("Helvetica", Font.BOLD, 14);
g2.setFont(font);
g2.drawString(title,...);
```

How do we know where to plot the title string? Recall that the location of the text in a `drawString` method is specified by an (x, y) value in the *lower left-hand corner* of the string.

To locate the text properly, we will have to know how wide and how tall each string is, so that we can calculate the (x, y) location to place the string. Fortunately, the `FontMetrics` class can calculate this information. If a font for the title string is defined as shown above, then the programmer can create a `FontMetrics` object with the following statement

```
fm = g2.getFontMetrics();
```

The length of the string in pixels can be found from the function `fm.stringWidth(title)`, and the height of the string in pixels can be found from the function `fm.getHeight()`. Once these widths and heights are known, they can be converted to normalized values by dividing by the total component size in pixels.

```
normalStringWidth = (double) fm.stringWidth(title) / size.width;
normalStringHeight = (double) fm.getHeight() / size.height;
```

With this information, it is possible to calculate the normalized (x, y) value in the lower left-hand corner of the title string. The title string needs to be centered in the top margin over the plotting region, so the starting x position will be the beginning of the plotting area plus half of the plot width, minus half of the string width. The title string needs to be in the middle of the top margin, so the starting y position will be half of the top margin plus half of the string height.

```
normalStringXPos = normalStartX + normalWidth/2 - normalStringWidth/2;
normalStringYPos = normalStartY/2 + normalStringHeight/2;
```

Once we have this information, the title can be drawn in its proper position with the following statement.

```
g2.drawString(title,
            (int) Math.round(size.width  * normalStringXPos),
            (int) Math.round(size.height * normalStringYPos));
```

The x-axis label works the same way, except that it is centered under the plotting region in the middle of the bottom margin.

The y-axis label is trickier, however. It needs to be centered in the left margin and rotated counterclockwise by 90°. This can be done by means of an affine transform. The transform will translate the string in the x direction until it will be centered in the left margin after rotation, and translate the string in the y direction until it will be centered vertically after rotation. Then, the string is rotated by $-\pi/2$ radians. This transform is applied to the graphics object before the text is drawn, and the text is drawn translated and rotated.

The final plotting class is shown in Figure 12.35.

6. **Testing the Class**

A program to text class `PlotXY` is shown in Figure 12.36. This program calculates the function $y(x) = x^2 - 2x + 1$ from -3 to 3 in steps of 0.1, and

```
/*
    Purpose:
      To create a 2D plot of two variables stored in 2 double
      arrays, including a title and axis labels.

    Record of revisions:
        Date          Programmer           Description of change
        ====          ==========           =====================
     11/02/2002    S. J. Chapman           Original code
*/
import java.awt.*;
import java.awt.event.*;
import java.awt.geom.*;
import javax.swing.*;
public class PlotXY extends JComponent {
   //**********************************************************
   // Declare instance variables
   //**********************************************************
   // Line data
   private double[] x;          // Array of x-values to plot
   private double[] y;          // Array of y-values to plot
   boolean validLine;           // True if there is data to plot
   private Color lineColor = Color.black; // Line color

   // Title data
   private String title;        // Title of plot
   boolean validTitle;          // True if title present

   // Axis labels
   private String xLabel;       // X-axis label
   private String yLabel;       // Y-axis label
   boolean validXLabel;         // True if X label present
   boolean validYLabel;         // True if Y label present

   //**********************************************************
   // Constructor
   //**********************************************************
   public PlotXY() {
      setDoubleBuffered( true );
      validLine = false;
      validTitle = false;
      validXLabel = false;
      validYLabel = false;
   }

   //**********************************************************
   // Set methods
   //**********************************************************
   // Method to set display data
```

Figure 12.35. Class PlotXY.

```
public void setXY(double[] x, double[] y) {
   this.x = x;
   this.y = y;
   validLine = true;
}

// Method to set line color
public void setColor(Color lineColor) {
   this.lineColor = lineColor;
}

// Method to set title
public void setTitle(String title) {
   this.title = title;
   validTitle = true;
}

// Method to set X-axis label
public void setXLabel(String xLabel) {
   this.xLabel = xLabel;
   validXLabel = true;
}

// Method to set Y-axis label
public void setYLabel(String yLabel) {
   this.yLabel = yLabel;
   validYLabel = true;
}

//************************************************************
// This method creates the plot to display
//************************************************************
public void paintComponent ( Graphics g ) {

   BasicStroke bs;                   // Ref to BasicStroke
   FontMetrics fm;                   // Ref to FontMetrics
   Font font;                        // Ref to font
   int i;                            // Loop index
   Line2D line;                      // Ref to line
   double normalHeight;              // Normalized height of plot area
   double normalWidth;               // Normalized width of plot area
   double normalStartX;              // Normalized x (upper left corner)
   double normalStartY;              // Normalized y (upper left corner)
   double normalStringHeight;        // Normalized string height
   double normalStringWidth;         // Normalized string width
   double normalStringXPos;          // Normalized string x pos
   double normalStringYPos;          // Normalized string y pos
   double normalEndX;                // Normalized x (lower right corner)
   double normalEndY;                // Normalized y (lower right corner)
```

Figure 12.35.   (Continued).

```
      int plotHeight;                    // Plot height (pixels)
      int plotWidth;                     // Plot width (pixels)
      int plotStartX;                    // Plot starting position (pixels)
      int plotStartY;                    // Plot starting position (pixels)
      float[] solid = {12.0f,0.0f};      // Solid line style
      int stringHeight;                  // String height in pixels
      int stringWidth;                   // String width in pixels
      double x1;                         // Starting x-value of segment
      double x2;                         // Ending x-value of segment
      double xMax;                       // Max x-value to plot
      double xMin;                       // Min x-value to plot
      double xScale;                     // Multiplier to make plot fit
      double y1;                         // Starting y-value of segment
      double y2;                         // Ending y-value of segment
      double yMax;                       // Max y-value to plot
      double yMin;                       // Min y-value to plot
      double yScale;                     // Multiplier to make plot fit

   // Declare normalized margins of plot area, assuming that
   // width and height are normalized to 1.0.
   final double xLeftMargin = 0.125;
   final double xRightMargin = 0.045;
   final double yTopMargin = 0.075;
   final double yBottomMargin = 0.075;

   // Cast the graphics object to Graph2D
   Graphics2D g2 = (Graphics2D) g;

   // Set rendering hints to improve display quality
   g2.setRenderingHint(RenderingHints.KEY_ANTIALIASING,
                   RenderingHints.VALUE_ANTIALIAS_ON);

   // Get plot size
   Dimension size = getSize();

   // Set background color
   g2.setColor( Color.white );
   g2.fill(new Rectangle2D.Double(0,0,size.width,size.height));

   // Calculate the size and location of the "plot" area
   // in normalized units (0-1).
   normalWidth  = 1.0 - xLeftMargin - xRightMargin;
   normalHeight = 1.0 - yTopMargin - yBottomMargin;
   normalStartX = xLeftMargin;
   normalStartY = yTopMargin;
   normalEndX   = normalStartX + normalWidth;
   normalEndY   = normalStartY + normalHeight;

   // Calculate the size and location of the "plot" area
   // in pixels (needed to place the text).
```

Figure 12.35. (Continued).

```
plotWidth  = (int) Math.round(size.width * normalWidth);
plotHeight = (int) Math.round(size.height * normalHeight);
plotStartX = (int) Math.round(size.width * normalStartX);
plotStartY = (int) Math.round(size.height * normalStartY);

// Set the stroke for the bounding box around the
// plot—a thin solid black line.
g2.setColor(Color.black);
bs = new BasicStroke( 1.0f,
                      BasicStroke.CAP_SQUARE,
                      BasicStroke.JOIN_MITER,
                      6.0f, solid, 0.0f );
g2.setStroke(bs);

// Draw the bounding box, converting normalized
// positions back to pixels.
line = new Line2D.Double( size.width  * normalStartX,
                          size.height * normalStartY,
                          size.width  * normalEndX,
                          size.height * normalStartY);
g2.draw(line);
line = new Line2D.Double( size.width  * normalEndX,
                          size.height * normalStartY,
                          size.width  * normalEndX,
                          size.height * normalEndY);
g2.draw(line);
line = new Line2D.Double( size.width  * normalEndX,
                          size.height * normalEndY,
                          size.width  * normalStartX,
                          size.height * normalEndY);
g2.draw(line);
line = new Line2D.Double( size.width  * normalStartX,
                          size.height * normalEndY,
                          size.width  * normalStartX,
                          size.height * normalStartY);
g2.draw(line);

// Now calculate the limits of the data to display
xMax = x[0];
xMin = x[0];
for (i = 0; i < x.length; i++ ) {
   xMax = Math.max( xMax, x[i] );
   xMin = Math.min( xMin, x[i] );
}
yMax = y[0];
yMin = y[0];
for (i = 0; i < x.length; i++ ) {
   yMax = Math.max( yMax, y[i] );
```

Figure 12.35.   (Continued).

```
         yMin = Math.min( yMin, y[i] );
   }

   // Calculate a scale so that this plot will fill the
   // available plotting area.  If the min and max values
   // are the same, set the scale to 1 so that the scale
   // won't be infinite.
   if ( Math.abs( xMax - xMin ) > 0 )
      xScale = normalWidth / ( xMax - xMin );
   else
      xScale = 1;

   if ( Math.abs( yMax - yMin ) > 0 )
      yScale = normalHeight / ( yMax - yMin );
   else
      yScale = 1;

   // Set the Color and BasicStroke for the line to plot
   g2.setColor(Color.blue);
   bs = new BasicStroke( 4.0f, BasicStroke.CAP_SQUARE,
                         BasicStroke.JOIN_MITER, 1.0f,
                         solid, 0.0f );
   g2.setStroke(bs);

   // Plot the line
   if ( validLine ) {
      for ( i = 0; i < x.length-1; i++ ) {

         // Get line segment in normalized coordinates
         x1 =  (x[i] - xMin) * xScale + normalStartX;
         x2 =  (x[i+1] - xMin) * xScale + normalStartX;
         y1 = -(y[i] - yMax) * yScale + normalStartY;
         y2 = -(y[i+1] - yMax) * yScale + normalStartY;

         // Convert to pixels and plot
         line = new Line2D.Double (  size.width * x1,
                                     size.height * y1,
                                     size.width * x2,
                                     size.height * y2);

         g2.draw(line);
      }
   }
   //*********************************************************
   // Add title and labels
   //*********************************************************
   g2.setColor(Color.black);

   // Draw title
   if ( validTitle ) {
      font = new Font("Helvetica", Font.BOLD, 14);
      g2.setFont(font);
```

Figure 12.35. (Continued).

```
            fm = g2.getFontMetrics();
            normalStringWidth = (double) fm.stringWidth(title) / size.width;
            normalStringHeight = (double) fm.getHeight() / size.height;
            normalStringXPos = normalStartX + normalWidth/2
                            - normalStringWidth/2;
            normalStringYPos = normalStartY/2 + normalStringHeight/2;
            g2.drawString(title,
                        (int) Math.round(size.width  * normalStringXPos),
                        (int) Math.round(size.height * normalStringYPos));
        }

        // Draw x label
        if ( validXLabel ) {
            font = new Font("Helvetica", Font.PLAIN, 14);
            g2.setFont(font);
            fm = g2.getFontMetrics();
            normalStringWidth = (double) fm.stringWidth(xLabel) / size.width;
            normalStringHeight = (double) fm.getHeight() / size.height;
            normalStringXPos = normalStartX + normalWidth/2
                            - normalStringWidth/2;
            normalStringYPos = normalEndY + yBottomMargin/2
                            + normalStringHeight/2;
            g2.drawString(xLabel,
                        (int) Math.round(size.width  * normalStringXPos),
                        (int) Math.round(size.height * normalStringYPos));
        }

        // Draw y label
        if ( validYLabel ) {
            font = new Font("Helvetica", Font.PLAIN, 14);
            g2.setFont(font);
            fm = g2.getFontMetrics();
            normalStringWidth = (double) fm.stringWidth(yLabel) / size.height;
            normalStringHeight = (double) fm.getHeight() / size.width;
            normalStringXPos = normalStartX/2 - normalStringHeight/2;
            normalStringYPos = normalStartY + normalHeight/2
                            + normalStringWidth;

            // Translate and rotate
            AffineTransform at = new AffineTransform();
            at.translate(size.width  * normalStringXPos,
                        size.height * normalStringYPos);
            at.rotate(-Math.PI/2);
            g2.setTransform(at);

            g2.drawString(yLabel,
                        (int) Math.round(size.width  * normalStringWidth),
                        (int) Math.round(size.height * normalStringHeight));
        }
    }
}
```

Figure 12.35. (Continued).

```
/*
    Purpose:
       To test the 2D plotting class PlotXY.  This class creates
       a frame and places a PlotXY component within the frame.
       It then plots the function "y = x^2 - 2*x" + 1 from -3.0
       to 3.0 in steps of 0.1.

    Record of revisions:
        Date          Programmer            Description of change
        ====          ==========            =====================
     11/02/2002    S. J. Chapman            Original code
*/
import java.awt.*;
import java.awt.event.*;
import java.awt.geom.*;
import javax.swing.*;
public class TestPlotXY extends JComponent {

   public static void main(String s[]) {

       // Define arrays to hold the two curves to plot
       double[] x = new double[61];
       double[] y = new double[61];

       // Create a Window Listener to handle "close" events
       MyWindowListener l = new MyWindowListener();

       // Create data to display
       for ( int i = 0; i < x.length; i++ ) {
          x[i] = 0.1 * (i - 30);
          y[i] = x[i]*x[i] - 2. * x[i] + 1;
       }

       // Create a PlotXY object
       PlotXY p = new PlotXY();
       p.setXY(x,y);
       p.setColor(Color.blue);
       p.setTitle("Plot of x^2 - 2*x + 1");
       p.setXLabel("x axis");
       p.setYLabel("y axis");

       // Create a frame and place the object in the center
       // of the frame.
       JFrame f = new JFrame("Test PlotXY ...");
       f.addWindowListener(l);
       f.getContentPane().add(p, BorderLayout.CENTER);
       f.pack();
       f.setSize(400,400);
       f.show();
   }
}
```

Figure 12.36. Program to test class PlotXY.

plots the resulting curve with a blue line. It also sets a title and x- and y-axis labels. When this program is executed, the results are as shown in Figure 12.37. ∎

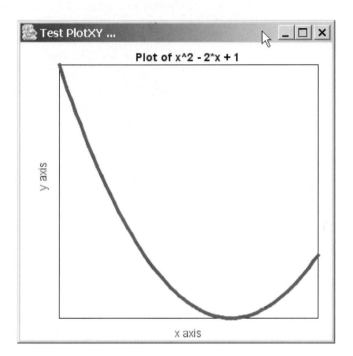

Figure 12.37. The output from program `TestPlotXY`.

This program has produced a working two-dimensional linear plot with labels. However, many enhancements are still missing, such as axis scales, grids, and so on. You will be asked to enhance this class further in several end-of-chapter exercises.

SUMMARY

- The `java.awt` and `java.awt.geom` packages contain the classes necessary to work with graphics. The `javax.swing` package contains the classes necessary to create Swing GUIs.

- A component is a visual object containing text or graphics, which can respond to keyboard or mouse inputs. In the Swing GUI, components are implemented as subclasses of class `JComponent`.

- A container is a graphical object that can hold components or other containers.

- A frame is a container with borders and a title bar. In the Swing GUI, frames are implemented by class `JFrame`.

- Every subclass of `JComponent` includes a `paintComponent` method, which is called whenever the object is to be displayed on a graphics device. Every `paintComponent` method has a single parameter, which is an object of the `java.awt.Graphics` class.

- Every `paintComponent` method should immediately downcast the `Graphics` object to a `Graphics2D` object, so that the "2D" classes can be used with it.
- The `Graphics2D` methods `draw` and `fill` are used to draw and fill the interior of an object on a graphics device.
- The abstract class `Line2D` is used to draw lines on a graphics device. There are two concrete subclasses of this class: `Line2D.Double` and `Line2D.Float`.
- The abstract class `Rectangle2D` is used to draw rectangles on a Java graphics device. There are two concrete subclasses of this class: `Rectangle2D.Double` and `Rectangle2D.Float`.
- The abstract class `RoundRectangle2D` is used to draw rectangles with rounded corners on a Java graphics device. There are two concrete subclasses of this class: `RoundRectangle2D.Double` and `RoundRectangle2D.Float`.
- The abstract class `Ellipse2D` is used to draw circles and ellipses on a Java graphics device. There are two concrete subclasses of this class: `Ellipse2D.Double` and `Ellipse2D.Float`.
- The abstract class `Arc2D` is used to draw arcs on a Java graphics device. There are two concrete subclasses of this class: `Arc2D.Double` and `Arc2D.Float`.
- The class `GeneralPath` is used to create arbitrary shapes on a Java graphics device. It includes `moveTo`, `lineTo`, `curveTo`, and `quadTo` methods, which allow a user to connect arbitrary points with straight lines, quadratic curves, or Bezier curves.
- The width, style, and ends of a "2D" line or border are controlled by an object of the `BasicStroke` class.
- The color of an object displayed on a graphics device may be controlled with the `Graphics2D` method `setColor`. This method has a single parameter, which is an object of the `java.awt.Color` class.
- Antialiasing may be used to eliminate jagged edges from objects displayed on a Java graphics device. Antialiasing is controlled with the `Graphics2D` method `setRenderingHints`.
- Text may be displayed on a graphics device with the `Graphics2D` method `drawString`. The font used to display the text is set with the `Graphics2D` method `setFont`.
- Class `Font` is used to specify the characteristics of a particular font.
- Class `Metrics` is used get information about the characteristics of a particular font.
- Class `AffineTransform` is used to translate, scale, rotate, or shear objects before they are displayed on a Java graphics device. It is applied to a graphics device by calling the `Graphics2D` method `setTransform` before calling the methods `draw` or `drawString`.
- Normally, when two objects overlap on a graphics device, the later object covers up the earlier one. The `Graphics2D` method `setXORMode` can be used to modify this behavior so that both objects are visible.
- A summary of the `Graphics2D` methods discussed in the chapter is presented in Table 12.9.

TABLE 12.9   Summary of `Graphics2D` Methods Discussed in Chapter 12

Parameter	Description
`draw (Shape s);`	Draws the outline of a `Shape` object, such as `Rectangle2D`, `Arc2D`, etc.
`drawString (String s, float x, float y)` `drawString (String s, int x, int y)`	Draws the specified text at location (x, y), using the current color and font.
`fill (Shape s);`	Fills the interior of a `Shape` object, such as `Rectangle2D`, `Arc2D`, etc.
`getFontMetrics();`	Returns a `FontMetrics` object containing the current font metrics.
`setColor(Color c)`	Sets the color with which to draw objects on this graphics device.
`setFont(Font f)`	Sets the specified font as the current font to use when rendering text on this graphics device.
`setRenderingHint (String hintKey,` `Object hintValue)`	Sets the preferences for the rendering algorithms. Used to specify the use of antialiasing algorithms.
`setStroke (BasicStroke b)`	Sets the basic stroke to use when drawing the outlines of objects.
`setTransform (AffineTransform at)`	Sets the affine transform to apply to objects drawn on this graphics device.
`setXORMode (Color c)`	Sets the paintComponent mode to XOR mode, so that if shapes overlap, both of their outlines are visible.

SUMMARY OF GOOD PROGRAMMING PRACTICES

The following guidelines introduced in this chapter will help you to develop good programs:

1. To display Java graphics, (1) create a component to display; (2) create a `JFrame` to hold the component, and place the component into the frame; and (3) create a "listener" object to detect and respond to mouse clicks, and assign the listener to the `JFrame`.

2. To create Java graphics, write a class that extends class `JComponent` and overrides the `paintComponent` method to produce the desired output.

3. To draw lines in Java: (1) select a line color using the Graphics2D `setColor` method; (2) select a line width and line style using a `BasicStroke` object; (3) set the endpoints of the line using a `Line2D.Double` or `Line2D.float` method, and draw the line with a call to the Graphics2D `draw` method.

4. Eliminate jagged edges from your lines by turning on antialiasing with the `Graphics2D` method `setRenderingHints`.

5. Use the `Rectangle2D` classes to create rectangles.

6. Use the `RoundRectangle2D` classes to create rectangles with rounded edges.

7. Use the `Ellipse2D` classes to create circles and ellipses.

8. Use the `Arc2D` classes to create elliptical and circular arcs.

9. Use class `GeneralPath` to create arbitrarily complex graphics shapes.

10. If a `GeneralPath` object includes two or more overlapping shapes, specify a winding rule to determine how to treat the overlapping regions. The default winding rule treats overlapping regions as interior to the shape, while the `WIND_EVEN_ODD` rule treats overlapping regions as exterior to the shape.

11. Use `AffineTransforms` to translate, scale, rotate, or shear your `Graphics2D` shapes and text.

12. Use the `Graphics2D` method `setXORMode` to make the overlapping regions of objects visible.

13. Use combinations of color, line style, and line width to distinguish your lines, so that they will still appear different when printed on a monochrome printer.

TERMINOLOGY

affine transform
`chapman.graphics.JComponent` class
component
container
draw method
`drawString` method
`fill` method
`java.awt.BasicStroke` class
`java.awt.Container` class
`java.awt.Font` class
`java.awt.FontMetrics` class
`java.awt.geom.AffineTransform` class
`java.awt.geom.Arc2D` class
`java.awt.geom.Ellipse2D` class

`java.awt.geom.GeneralPath` class
`java.awt.geom.Line2D` class
`java.awt.geom.Rectangle2D` class
`java.awt.geom.RoundRectangle2D` class
`java.awt.Graphics2D` class
`javax.swing.JComponent` class
`javax.swing.JFrame` class
`paintComponent` method
`setColor` method
`setRenderingHints` method
`setStroke` method
`setTransform` method
`setXORMode` method
XOR paint mode

Exercises

1. Explain the steps required to generate graphics in Java.

2. Write a program that draws a series of five concentric circles. The radii of the circles should differ by 20 pixels, with the innermost circle having a 20-pixel radius and the outer circle a 100-pixel radius. Fill each circle with a different color.

3. Modify the program of Exercise 2 so that each circle is surrounded by a 2-pixel-wide black border. Be sure to use antialiasing to make the borders smooth.

4. Create a program that plots the function e^x over the range $-1 \le x \le 1$. Use a solid 4-pixel-wide blue line to plot the curve, and use solid 1-pixel-wide black curves for the x- and y-axes.

5. Modify the program created in Exercise 3 so that it automatically rescales whenever the frame containing it is resized.

6. Write a program that creates and plots a red dashed spiral using a `GeneralPath` object. A spiral can be specified by two values, r and θ, where r is the distance from the origin to a point and θ is the angle counterclockwise from the positive x-axis to the point. In these terms, the spiral will be specified by the equation

$$r = \frac{\theta}{2\pi} \qquad \text{for } 0 \le \theta \le 6\pi$$

7.   Create a plot of $\cos x$ versus x for $-2\pi \le x \le 2\pi$. Use a solid 6-pixel-wide line for the plot. Add a thin black box around the plot, and create a title and x- and y-axis labels. Note that you will need to use an affine transform to rotate the text for the y-axis label.

8.   Modify the plot in Exercise 7 to add thin dotted grid lines in both the horizontal and vertical directions.

9.   Modify the plot in Exercise 7 to resize properly whenever the frame containing the plot is resized.

10.   Create a program that displays samples of all the standard Java fonts on your computer.

11.   What is the height of a line of 24-point `SansSerif` text? What class and method did you use to obtain this information?

12.   Create a program that plots four ellipses of random size and shape. Each ellipse should be a distinct color.

13.   Modify the previous program to use the XOR paint mode. How does the output of the program change?

14.   Write a program that creates a bar plot, using `Rectangle2D` objects to create each bar.

15.   Write a program that displays a line of text, and then displays the same text upside down.

16.   Create a new class `Triangle2D` to create triangles. This class should include a constructor of the form

```
Triangle2D( double x, double y, double w, double h);
```

where (x, y) is the upper left-hand corner of the box in which the triangle fits, w is the width of the triangle, and h is the height of the triangle. The class should use a `GeneralPath` object to actually draw the triangle. Create a test program that draws triangles in several sizes, colors, and shears, using `Triangle2D` objects and affine transforms.

17.   Class `PlotXY` in Example 12.6 creates two-dimensional plots, but it has a number of deficiencies. For example, the class does not display the limits of the data values on the x- and y-axes. Modify this class so that the largest and smallest values on each axis are displayed.

18.   Enhance class `PlotXY` from Exercise 17 so that it can display tic marks and gridlines over the plotting area. Use 2-pixel-wide solid lines for the tic marks and 1-pixel-wide dotted lines for the gridlines. Make the use of gridlines optional by defining a boolean instance variable `useGridLines` and providing a set method to turn the gridlines on and off. (The tic marks should be displayed, regardless of the value of this variable.) Also, display the x-value of each vertical gridline/tic mark, and the y-value of each horizontal gridline/tic mark.

19.   Enhance class `PlotXY` from Exercise 18 so that a user can select the linestyle to apply to the line. Support solid, dashed, dotted, and dash-dot line styles. Define an instance variable to hold the current line style, and a set method to allow the user to set it. Also, declare public constants for each line style, so that the user can specify a line style as `PlotXY.SOLID`, `PlotXY.DASHED`, and so forth.

20.   The `PlotXY` class will work correctly only if the x and y arrays are of the same length. Create a new exception called `MismatchedArrayLengthException`, and modify method `setXY` to throw this exception if the lengths of arrays x and y differ.

21.   Create a class called `PlotSemilogY` that displays the x-axis in linear units and the y-axis in logarithmic units. Test your class by plotting the function $y(x) = e^{0.25x}$ from -4 to 4 using both class `PlotXY` and class `PlotSemilogY`. What does the function look like on each plot?

13

Basic Graphical User Interfaces

A graphical user interface (GUI) is a pictorial interface to a program. A good GUI can make programs easier to use by providing them with a consistent appearance and with intuitive controls such as push buttons, sliders, pull-down lists, and menus. The GUI should behave in an understandable and predictable manner, so that a user knows what to expect when he or she performs an action. For example, when a mouse click occurs on a push button, the GUI should initiate the action described on the label of the button.

The Java API contains two different graphical user interfaces. The "Old GUI" is generally known as the Abstract Windowing Toolkit (AWT) GUI; it was introduced with Java SDK 1.0. The "New GUI" is known as the Swing GUI; it became a part of the standard Java SDK with the release of Java 2. The Swing GUI consists of additional classes built on top of the older AWT classes. It is faster and more flexible than the AWT GUI and is recommended for all new program development. This book teaches the Swing GUI only—if you must work with older programs containing the AWT GUI, please refer to the Java 2 SDK on-line documentation.

This chapter contains an introduction to the basic elements of the Swing GUIs. It does *not* contain a complete description of GUI features, but it does provide us with the basics required to create functional GUIs for our programs. Additional features of GUIs are covered in Chapter 14.

13.1 HOW A GRAPHICAL USER INTERFACE WORKS

A graphical user interface provides the user with a familiar environment in which to work. It contains push buttons, drop-down lists, menus, text fields, and so forth, all of which are already familiar to the user, so that he or she can concentrate on the purpose of the application instead of the mechanics involved

OBJECTIVES

- Understand the operation of graphical user interfaces.
- Be able to build basic graphical user interfaces.
- Understand the role events and event handlers play in GUI operation.
- Understand `ActionEvents` and the `ActionListener` interface.
- Be able to create and manipulate labels, buttons, check boxes, radio buttons, text fields, password fields, combo boxes, and panels.
- Understand and be able to use layout managers.

in doing things. However, GUIs are harder for the programmer, because a GUI-based program must be prepared for mouse clicks (or possibly keyboard input) for any GUI element at any time. Such inputs are known as **events**, and a program that responds to events is said to be *event driven*.

The four principal elements required to create a Java Graphical User Interface are:

1. **Components**. Each item on a Java Graphical User Interface (push buttons, labels, text fields, and so on) is a **component**, meaning that the item inherits from the JComponent class introduced in Chapter 12. Regardless of their function, components all share a common set of methods, because the methods are defined in the superclass JComponent.

2. **Container**. The components of a GUI must be arranged within a **container**, which is a class ultimately derived from class Container. In this chapter, we will work with two types of containers: **JPanel** and **JFrame**. A JPanel is a very simple container to which components can be attached. It lays out the components left to right and top to bottom. A JFrame is a more complex container with borders and a title bar.

3. **Layout Manager**. When the components of a GUI are added to a container, a **layout manager** controls the location at which they will be placed within the container. Java provides six standard layout managers, each of which lays out components in a different fashion. A layout manager is automatically associated with each container when it is created, but the programmer can freely change the layout manager, if desired.

4. **Event Handlers**. Finally, there must be some way to perform an action if a user clicks a mouse on a button or types information on a keyboard. A mouse click or a key press creates an **event**, which is an object, like everything else in Java. Events are handled by creating **listener classes**, which listen for a specific type of event, and execute a specific method (called an **event handler**) if the event occurs. Listener classes implement **listener interfaces**, which specify the names of the event-handler methods required to handle specific types of events. The standard listener interfaces can be found in package **java.awt.event**.

A subset of the basic GUI elements are summarized in Table 13.1. We will study examples of these elements in the next two chapters, and then build working GUIs from them. Figure 13.1 shows the inheritance hierarchy for some of the component, container, and layout classes in the java.awt and javax.swing packages.

13.2 CREATING AND DISPLAYING A GRAPHICAL USER INTERFACE

The basic steps required to create a Java GUI are:

1. Create a container class to hold the GUI components. In this chapter we will use subclasses of JPanel as the basic container.

2. Select a layout manager for the container, if the default layout manager is not acceptable.

3. Create components and add them to the container.

4. Create "listener" objects to detect and respond to the events expected by each GUI component, and register the listeners with appropriate components.

5. Create a JFrame object, and place the completed container in the center of **content pane** associated with the frame. [The content pane is the location where GUI objects are attached to a JFrame or JApplet container. The method getContentPane() returns a reference to a container's content pane.]

Figure 13.2 shows a program that creates a simple GUI with a single button and a single label field. The label field contains the number of times that the button has been

TABLE 13.1 Some Basic GUI Elements

Element	Description
Components	
JButton	A graphical object that implements a push button. It triggers an event when clicked with a mouse.
JCheckBox	A graphical object that is either selected or not selected. This element creates check boxes.
JComboBox	A drop-down list of items, one of which may be selected. Single-clicking an item selects it, while double-clicking an item generates an action event.
JDialog	Creates a dialog window to display messages, warnings, and so on, to the user.
JLabel	An area to display a label (text and/or images that a user cannot change).
JList	An area where a list of items is displayed. Single-clicking an item selects it, while double-clicking an item generates an action event.
JTable	An area where a table of items is displayed.
JPasswordField	Displays a text field that can be used to enter passwords. Asterisks are printed out in the field as characters are entered.
JRadioButton	A graphical object that implements a radio button: a set of buttons, only one of which can be selected at a time.
JTextField	An area (surrounded by a box) where a program can display text data and a user can optionally enter text data.
Containers	
Box	A simple container with no borders or title bar that uses the BoxLayout manager.
JDialog	A simple container for warning, error, and information messages.
JFrame	A container with borders and a title bar.
JPanel	A simple container with no borders or title bar that uses the FlowLayout manager.
Layout Managers	
BorderLayout	A layout manager that lays out elements in a central region and four surrounding borders. This is the default layout manager for a JFrame.
BoxLayout	A layout manager that allows multiple components to be laid out either vertically or horizontally, without wrapping. This is the default layout manager for a Box.
CardLayout	A layout manager that stacks components like a deck of cards, only the top one of which is visible.
FlowLayout	A layout manager that lays out elements left-to-right and top-to-bottom within a container. This is the default layout manager for a JPanel.
GridBagLayout	A layout manager that lays out elements in a flexible grid, where the size of each element can vary.
GridLayout	A layout manager that lays out elements in a rigid grid.
Menu Components	
JMenu	A class to create menus.
JMenuBar	A container for menus. This is the bar running across the top of a container, and containing one or more menus.
JMenuItem	A single item within a menu.
JCheckBoxMenuItem	A single item within a menu that has a toggled on/off state.
JPopUpMenu	A menu that can be accessed by right-clicking the mouse.

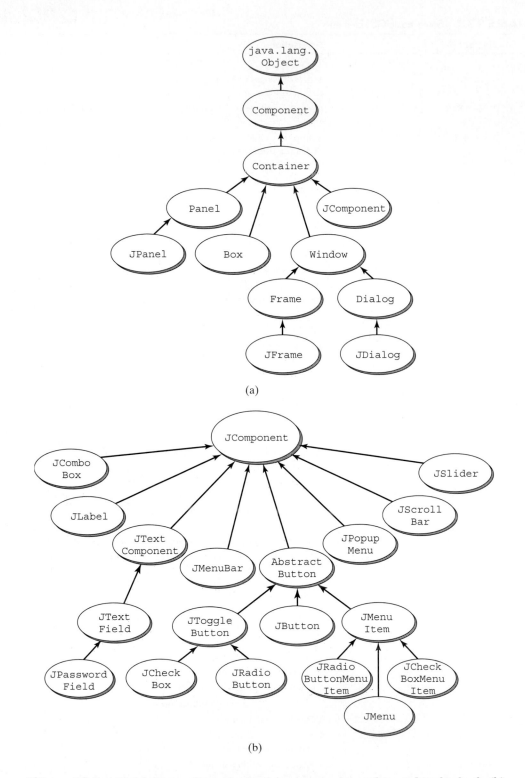

Figure 13.1. (a) Inheritance hierarchy for the container classes discussed in this book. (b) Inheritance hierarchy for the component classes discussed in this book. (Box and all classes with names starting with J are in package javax.swing. The other classes are in package java.awt.)

```
1    // A first GUI.  This class creates a label and
2    // a button.  The count in the label is incremented
3    // each time the button is pressed.
4    import java.awt.*;
5    import java.awt.event.*;
6    import javax.swing.*;
7    public class FirstGUI extends JPanel {
8
9       // Instance variables
10      private int count = 0;        // Number of pushes
11      private JButton pushButton;  // Push button
12      private JLabel label;         // Label
13
14      // Initialization method
15      public void init() {
16
17         // Set the layout manager
18         setLayout( new BorderLayout() );
19
20         // Create a label to hold push count
21         label = new JLabel("Push Count: 0");
22         add( label, BorderLayout.NORTH );
23         label.setHorizontalAlignment( label.CENTER );
24
25         // Create a button
26         pushButton = new JButton("Test Button");
27         pushButton.addActionListener( new ButtonHandler(this) );
28         add( pushButton, BorderLayout.SOUTH );
29      }
30
31      // Method to update push count
32      public void updateLabel() {
33         label.setText( "Push Count: " + (++count) );
34      }
35   }
36
37      // Main method to create frame
38      public static void main(String s[]) {
39
40         // Create a frame to hold the application
41         JFrame fr = new JFrame("FirstGUI ...");
42         fr.setSize(200,100);
43
44         // Create a Window Listener to handle "close" events
45         WindowHandler l = new WindowHandler();
46         fr.addWindowListener(l);
```

Figure 13.2. A program that creates a container, sets a layout manager for the container, adds components and listeners for the components, and places the whole container within a JFrame. This is the basic core structure required to create Java GUIs.

```
47
48        // Create and initialize a FirstGUI object
49        FirstGUI fg = new FirstGUI();
50        fg.init();
51
52        // Add the object to the center of the frame
53        fr.getContentPane().add(fg, BorderLayout.CENTER);
54
55        // Display the frame
56        fr.setVisible( true );
57     }
58
59   class ButtonHandler implements ActionListener {
60      private FirstGUI fg;
61
62      // Constructor
63      public ButtonHandler ( FirstGUI fg1 ) {
64         fg = fg1;
65      }
66
67      // Execute when an event occurs
68      public void actionPerformed( ActionEvent e ) {
69         fg.updateLabel();
70      }
```

Figure 13.2. (Continued).

pressed since the program started. Note that class FirstGUI extends JPanel, and this class serves as the container for our GUI components (step 1 above).

This program contains two classes: class FirstGUI to create and display the GUI, and class ButtonHandler to respond to mouse clicks on the button.

Class FirstGUI contains three methods: init(), updateLabel(), and main. Method init() initializes the GUI.[1] It specifies which layout manager to use with the container (line 18), creates the JButton and JLabel components (lines 21 and 26), and adds them to the container (lines 22 and 28). In addition, it creates a "listener" object of class ButtonHandler to listen for and handle events generated by mouse clicks, and assigns that object to monitor mouse clicks on the button (line 27).

Method updateLabel() (lines 32–34) is the method that should be called every time that a button click occurs. It updates the label with the number of button clicks that have occurred.

The main method creates a new JFrame (line 41), creates and initializes a FirstGUI object (lines 49–50), places the FirstGUI object in the center of the frame (line 53), and makes the frame visible (line 56).

Class ButtonHandler is a "listener" class designed to listen for and handle mouse clicks on the button. It implements the ActionListener interface, which guarantees that the class will have a method called actionPerformed. If an object of this class is

---

[1]It is customary (but not required) to use the name init() for the method that sets up a GUI in a Java application. It *is* required to use the name init() for the method that sets up a GUI in a Java applet.

associated (*registered*) with a GUI button, then *the* `actionPerformed` *method in the object will be called every time a user clicks on the button with the mouse.* An object of this class is registered to handle events from the button in class `FirstGUI` (line 27); whenever this button is clicked, the `ButtonHandler` method `actionPerformed` is called. Since that method calls the `FirstGUI` method `updateLabel()`, each mouse click causes the count displayed by the label to increase by one.

When this program is executed, the `main` method creates a new `JFrame`, creates and initializes a `FirstGUI` object, places the object in the center of the content pane associated with the frame, and makes the frame visible. The `FirstGUI` object creates a label and a button, as well as a `ButtonHandler` to listen for button clicks. At this point, program execution stops, and it will resume *only* if an external event such as a mouse click occurs. If a mouse click occurs on the button, Java automatically calls method `actionPerformed`, because the `ButtonHandler` object was set to listen for mouse clicks on the button. This method calls method `updateLabel()`, which increases the button-click count and updates the display.

13.3   EVENTS AND EVENT HANDLING

An **event** is an object that is created by some external action, such as a mouse click, key press, and so on. When an event such as a mouse click occurs, *Java automatically sends that event to the GUI object that was clicked on*. For example, if a mouse click occurs over a button, Java sends the event to the GUI object that created that button.

When the mouse-click event is received, the button checks to see if an object has *registered* with it to receive mouse events, and it forwards the event to the `actionPerformed` method of that object. The `actionPerformed` method is known as an **event handler**, because it performs whatever steps are required to process the event. In many cases, this event handler makes a call to a **callback method** in the object that created the GUI, since such methods can update instance variables within the object directly.

This process is illustrated in Figure 13.3 for the `FirstGUI` program. When a mouse click occurs on the button, an event is created and sent to the `JButton` object. Since the `ButtonHandler` object is registered to handle mouse clicks on the button, the `JButton` object calls the `actionPerformed` method of the `ButtonHandler` object. This method makes a callback to `FirstGUI` method `updateLabel`, which actually performs the required work (updating the instance variable `count` and the label text).

This basic procedure works for all types of Java events, but the name of the event-handling method will differ for different types of events.

13.4   SELECTED GRAPHICAL USER INTERFACE COMPONENTS

This section summarizes the basic characteristics of some common graphical user interface components. It describes how to create and use each component, as well as the types of events each component can generate. The components discussed are

- Labels
- Push buttons
- Text fields and password fields
- Combo boxes (drop-down lists)
- Check boxes
- Radio buttons
- Blank components (canvases)

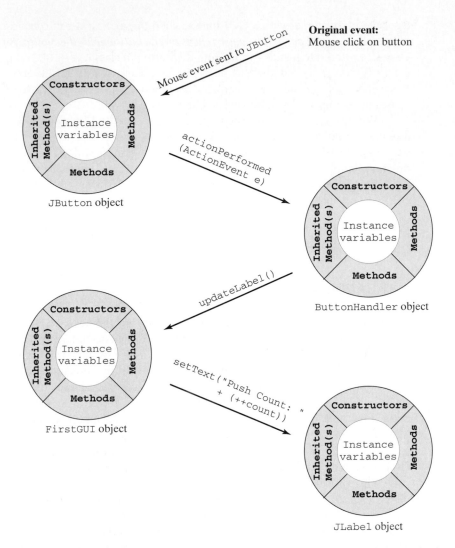

Figure 13.3. Event handling in program FirstGUI. When a user clicks on the button with the mouse, an event is sent to the JButton object. The JButton object calls the actionPerformed method of the ButtonHandler object, because that object is registered to handle the button's mouse click events. The actionPerformed method calls the update method of the FirstGUI object, which in turn calls the setText method of the JLabel object to change the push count.

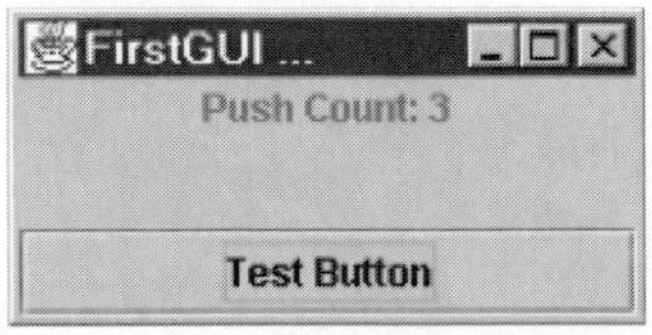

Figure 13.4. The display produced by program FirstGUI after three button clicks.

13.4.1 Labels

A **label** is an object that displays a single line of *read-only text and/or an image*. A JLabel object can display either text, or an image, or both. You can specify how the text and image are aligned in the display area by setting the vertical and horizontal alignment, and you can specify whether the text is placed left, right, above, or below the image. By default, text-only labels are left aligned, and image-only labels are horizontally centered. If both text and image are present, text is to the right of the image by default.

A label is created with the JLabel class using one of the following constructors:

```
public JLabel();
public JLabel(String s);
public JLabel(String s, int horizontalAlignment);
public JLabel(Icon image);
public JLabel(Icon image, int horizontalAlignment);
public JLabel(String s, Icon image, int horizontalAlignment);
```

In these constructors, s is a string containing the text to display on the label, image is the image to display on the label, and horizontalAlignment is the alignment of the text and image within the label. Possible alignment values are JLabel.LEFT, JLabel.RIGHT, and JLabel.CENTER. Note that the first constructor creates a label containing neither text nor an image.

Some of the methods in class JLabel are described in Table 13.2. Note that JLabels do not generate any events, so no listener interfaces or classes are associated with them.

TABLE 13.2 JLabel Methods

Method	Description
public Icon getIcon()	Returns the image from a JLabel.
public String getText()	Returns the text from a JLabel.
public void setIcon(Icon image)	Sets the JLabel image.
public void setText(String s)	Sets the JLabel text.
public void setHorizontalAlignment(int alignment)	Sets the horizontal alignment of the JLabel text and image. Legal values are LEFT, CENTER, and RIGHT.
public void setHorizontalTextPosition(int textPosition)	Sets the position of the text relative to the image. Legal values are LEFT, CENTER, and RIGHT.
public void setVerticalAlignment(int alignment)	Sets the vertical alignment of the JLabel text and images. Legal values are TOP, CENTER, and BOTTOM.
public void setVerticalTextPosition(int textPosition)	Sets the position of the text relative to the image. Legal values are TOP, CENTER, and BOTTOM.

The program shown in Figure 13.5 shows how to create labels with and without images. The first label consists of an image followed by text, left justified in its field. The second label consists of text followed by an image, right justified in its field. The third label consists of text only, centered in its field. Note that the images may be stored in GIF or JPEG files, which can be read by creating an ImageIcon object.

```java
// Test labels.  This program creates a GUI containing
// three labels, with and without images.
import java.awt.*;
import java.awt.event.*;
import javax.swing.*;
public class TestLabel extends JPanel {
    // Instance variables
    private JLabel l1, l2, l3;  // Labels

    // Initialization method
    public void init() {
        // Set the layout manager
        setLayout( new BorderLayout() );

        // Get the images to display
        ImageIcon right = new ImageIcon("BlueRightArrow.gif");
        ImageIcon left = new ImageIcon("BlueLeftArrow.gif");

        // Create a label with icon and text
        l1 = new JLabel("Label 1", right, JLabel.LEFT);
        add( l1, BorderLayout.NORTH );

        // Create a label with text and icon
        l2 = new JLabel("Label 2", left, JLabel.RIGHT);
        add( l2, BorderLayout.CENTER );
        l2.setHorizontalTextPosition( JLabel.LEFT );

        // Create a label with text only
        l3 = new JLabel("Label 3 (Text only)", JLabel.CENTER);
        add( l3, BorderLayout.SOUTH );
    }

    // Main method to create frame
    public static void main(String s[]) {
        // Create a frame to hold the application
        JFrame fr = new JFrame("TestLabel ...");
        fr.setSize(200,100);

        // Create a Window Listener to handle "close" events
        MyWindowListener l = new MyWindowListener();
        fr.addWindowListener(l);

        // Create and initialize a TestLabel object
        TestLabel tl = new TestLabel();
        tl.init();

        // Add the object to the center of the frame
        fr.getContentPane().add(tl, BorderLayout.CENTER);

        // Display the frame
        fr.setVisible( true );
    }
}
```

Figure 13.5. A program illustrating the use of labels, with and without images.

When this program is executed, the results are as shown in Figure 13.6.

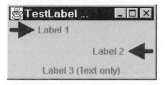

Figure 13.6. The display produced by program `TestLabel`.

13.4.2 Push Buttons and Associated Events

A **push button** is a component that a user can click on to trigger a specific action. Push buttons are created by the **JButton** class. Each JButton has a label and/or icon printed on its face to identify its purpose. A GUI can have many buttons, but each button label should be unique, so that a user can tell them apart.

Swing buttons are very flexible. Each button may be labeled with text, an image, or both, and the location of the text and image on the button can be controlled. Buttons may be enabled and disabled during program execution; when a button is disabled, it is grayed out and cannot be pressed. The icon displayed by a button can be automatically changed whenever it is pressed or disabled. In addition, **keyboard shortcuts** (mnemonic keys) can be defined to allow a user to activate the button via the keyboard. Finally, Java buttons support **tool tips**, which are messages that are displayed in a pop-up window whenever the cursor rests over the top of the button. Tool tips are used to explain the functions of the buttons to the program's user.

A push button is created with one of the following constructors:

```
public JButton();
public JButton(String s);
public JButton(Icon image);
public JButton(String s, Icon image);
```

These constructors create new buttons with a text label, an image, or both. Note that the first constructor creates a button containing neither text nor an image. Some of the methods in class Button are described in Table 13.3.

Events Associated with Buttons

When the mouse button is *both pressed and released* while the cursor is over a button, the button generates an ActionEvent and sends that event to any objects that have been registered with it as listeners. An **ActionEvent** is a special kind of event that means that the usual action associated with the component has occurred. For example, buttons are meant to be clicked on, so an ActionEvent from a button means that the button has been clicked on. (ActionEvents from other components will have different meanings.)

ActionEvents include several methods that allow a program to recover information about the triggering event. The most important of these methods are listed in Table 13.4.

The `ActionListener` Interface

ActionEvents are processed by classes that implement the **ActionListener interface**, which defines the single event-handling method **actionPerformed**. When an ActionListener object is registered with a button using the JButton method add-ActionListener, the ActionListener method actionPerformed will be automatically called whenever a click occurs on that button. (See Table 13.5.)

TABLE 13.3 JButton Methods

Method	Description
public void addActionListener(ActionListener l)	Adds the specified action listener to receive action events from this button.
public Icon getIcon()	Returns the image from a JButton.
public String getLabel()	Returns the label of this button.
public void setActionCommand(String s)	Set the action command string generated by this button when it is pressed.
public void setDisabledIcon(Icon icon)	Sets the icon to display when the button is disabled.
public void setEnabled(boolean b)	Enables or disables this button.
public void setHorizontalAlignment(int alignment)	Sets the horizontal alignment of the text and images. Legal values are LEFT, CENTER, and RIGHT.
public void setHorizontalTextPosition(int textPosition)	Sets the position of the text relative to the images. Legal values are LEFT, CENTER, and RIGHT.
public void setLabel(String s)	Sets the label of this button to the specified String.
public void setIcon(Icon icon)	Sets the default icon for this button.
public void setMnemonic(char mnemonic)	Set the keyboard character combination used to activate the button from the keyboard.
public void setPressedIcon(Icon icon)	Sets the icon to display when the button is pressed.
public void setToolTipText(String text)	Sets the tool tip text to display when the cursor rests over the button.
public void setVerticalAlignment(int alignment)	Sets the vertical alignment of the text and images. Legal values are TOP, CENTER, and BOTTOM.
public void setVerticalTextPosition(int textPosition)	Sets the position of the text relative to the images. Legal values are TOP, CENTER, and BOTTOM.

TABLE 13.4 ActionEvent Methods

Method	Description
public String getActionCommand()	Returns the command string associated with this action. By default, this method returns the *text printed on the button*.
public int getModifiers()	Returns the modifier keys held down during this action event. Possible modifiers are ALT_MASK, CTRL_MASK, META_MASK, and SHIFT_MASK.
public String paramString()	Returns a parameter string identifying this action event. This method is useful for event logging and for debugging.

TABLE 13.5 ActionListener Interface Method

Method	Description
void actionPerformed(ActionEvent e)	Method invoked when an ActionEvent occurs.

The program shown in Figure 13.7 illustrates the use of push buttons. It defines three buttons, with text and images on each. The left button enables the center button when it is clicked, and the right button disables the center button when clicked. If the center button is enabled, each click on the button will increment the displayed count by one. Note that disabled buttons are "grayed out," and mouse clicks on them are ignored.

```java
// This program tests push buttons.
import java.awt.*;
import java.awt.event.*;
import javax.swing.*;
public class TestPushButtons extends JPanel
                   implements ActionListener {

   // Instance variables
   private int c = 0;              // Count
   private JButton b1, b2, b3;     // Buttons

   // Initialization method
   public void init() {

      // Set the layout manager
      setLayout( new FlowLayout() );

      // Get the images to display
      ImageIcon right = new ImageIcon("RightArrow.gif");
      ImageIcon left = new ImageIcon("LeftArrow.gif");
      ImageIcon green = new ImageIcon("green-ball.gif");
      ImageIcon red = new ImageIcon("red-ball.gif");
      ImageIcon yellow = new ImageIcon("yellow-ball.gif");

      // Create buttons
      b1 = new JButton("Enable",right);
      b1.addActionListener( this );
      b1.setMnemonic('e');
      b1.setToolTipText("Enable middle button");
      add(b1);

      String s = "Count = " + c;
      b2 = new JButton(s,green);
      b2.addActionListener( this );
      b2.setMnemonic('c');
      b2.setEnabled(false);
      b2.setToolTipText("Press to increment count");
      b2.setPressedIcon(yellow);
      b2.setDisabledIcon(red);
      add(b2);

      b3 = new JButton("Disable",left);
      b3.addActionListener( this );
      b3.setMnemonic('d');
      b3.setEnabled(false);
```

Figure 13.7. A program to test the operation of push buttons.

```
      b3.setToolTipText("Disable middle button");
      add(b3);
   }

   // Event handler to handle button pushes
   public void actionPerformed(ActionEvent e) {
      String button = e.getActionCommand();

      if (button.equals("Enable")) {
         b1.setEnabled(false);
         b2.setEnabled(true);
         b3.setEnabled(true);
      }
      else if (button.substring(0,5).equals("Count")) {
         b2.setText("Count = " + (++c));
      }
      else if (button.equals("Disable")) {
         b1.setEnabled(true);
         b2.setEnabled(false);
         b3.setEnabled(false);
      }
   }

   // Main method to create frame
   public static void main(String s[]) {

      // Create a frame to hold the application
      JFrame fr = new JFrame("TestPushButtons ...");
      fr.setSize(400,80);

      // Create a Window Listener to handle "close" events
      MyWindowListener l = new MyWindowListener();
      fr.addWindowListener(l);
      // Create and initialize a TestPushButtons object
      TestPushButtons ob = new TestPushButtons();
      ob.init();

      // Add the object to the center of the frame
      fr.getContentPane().add(ob, BorderLayout.CENTER);

      // Display the frame
      fr.setVisible( true );
   }
}
```

Figure 13.7.   (Continued).

Each button has a keyboard shortcut (mnemonic) assigned to it, so the key combination ALT+e will press the left button, ALT+c the center button, and ALT+d the right button.

This application also illustrates the display of multiple images, depending on the state of a button. When the middle button is disabled, it displays a red ball. When enabled, it displays a green ball. Finally, when the button is clicked, the ball turns yellow.

This program also shows how a class can handle its own events. Note that the TestPushButtons class implements the ActionListener interface, and this class is registered with each button using the method `addActionListener(this)`. When an enabled button is clicked, it sends an `ActionEvent` to the `actionPerformed` method of the `TestPushButtons` class. This method checks to see which button generated the event, using the string returned by the `ActionEvent` method `getActionCommand()` to distinguish among them. Note that for buttons the default string returned by `getActionCommand()` is the text on the label of the button. As long as this text is different for every button, we can use that label to tell which button was pressed.

When the left button is pressed, the `actionPerformed` method is called automatically, and the result of `e.getActionCommand()` will be "Enable". When the right button is pressed, the `actionPerformed` method is called automatically, and the result of `e.getActionCommand()` will be "Disable". When the center button is pressed, the `actionPerformed` method is called automatically, and the first five letters returned by `e.getActionCommand()` will be "Count". An `if` structure can test the value of string `button` and perform the proper action, depending on which button was pressed.

Figure 13.8(a) shows the initial state of the program, with the center button disabled. Figure 13.8(b) shows the program after the center button has been enabled and pressed twice.

(a)

(b)

Figure 13.8.   (a) The display produced by program `TestPushButtons` when it is first started. (b) The display produced by the program after one button click on the left button and two clicks on the center button.

GOOD PROGRAMMING PRACTICE

Buttons generate `ActionEvents` when pressed. To handle button events, use a class that implements the `ActionListener` interface and contains an `actionPerformed` method. Register an object from this class with each button, and code the `actionPerformed` method to do whatever is required when the button is pressed.

GOOD PROGRAMMING PRACTICE

One `ActionListener` object can monitor many buttons, using the result of the `getActionCommand` method to determine the button that created a particular event.

13.4.3 Text Fields and Password Fields

A text field is a single-line area in which text can be entered by a user from the keyboard. When a user types information into a JTextField and presses the ENTER key, an ActionEvent is generated. If an ActionListener has been registered with the text field, then the event will be handled by the actionPerformed method, and the data typed by the user is available for use in the program. A JTextField may also be used to display read-only text that a user cannot modify. A JPasswordField field is identical to a text field, except that asterisks are displayed instead of the characters that are typed on the keyboard.

A text field or password field is created with one of the following constructors:

```
public JTextField();
public JTextField(int cols);
public JTextField(String s);
public JTextField(String s, int cols);
public JPasswordField();
public JPasswordField(int columns);
public JPasswordField(String s);
public JPasswordField(String s, int cols);
```

The first form of constructor creates a new blank JTextField or JPasswordField, while the second form of constructor creates a new blank JTextField or JPasswordField large enough to contain cols characters. The third form of the constructor creates a new JTextField or JPasswordField initialized with the specified string, and the fourth form of the constructor creates a new JTextField or JPasswordField large enough to contain columns characters and initialized with the specified string. Some of the methods in these classes are described in Table 13.6.

TABLE 13.6 JTextField and JPasswordField Methods

Method	Description
public String getText()	Gets the text currently displayed in this component.
public String getSelectedText()	Gets the selected text from the text currently displayed in this component.
public void setActionCommand(String s)	Sets the action command string generated by this text field when it is pressed.
public void setEditable(boolean b)	Sets the editability status of the field. If true, a user can change the data in the field. If false, the user cannot change the data in the field.
public void setText(String t)	Displays the text in string t.
public void setToolTipText(String text)	Sets the tool-tip text to display when the cursor rests over the text field.

An ActionEvent object is created whenever a user presses ENTER on the keyboard after typing data into a text field. The getActionCommand() method of the ActionEvent object will return a string containing the data that was typed in, unless method setActionCommand is used to specify another string. As before, this event may be handled by the actionEvent method of an ActionListener.

The program shown in Figure 13.9 illustrates the use of editable and read-only text fields, plus a password field. The first text field in this program is an ordinary text field, in which the data that a user types is visible. The second field is a JPasswordField, in which the data that a user types is replaced by asterisks. The third text field TextField

```
// This program tests text fields.
import java.awt.*;
import java.awt.event.*;
import javax.swing.*;
public class TestTextField extends JPanel {

    // Instance variables
    private JLabel l1, l2, l3;          // Labels
    private JTextField t1, t3;          // Text Fields
    private JPasswordField t2;          // Password Field
    private TextFieldHandler handler;   // ActionEvent handler

    // Initialization method
    public void init() {

        // Set background color
        setBackground( Color.lightGray );

        // Set the layout manager
        setLayout( new FlowLayout() );

        // Create ActionEvent handler
        handler = new TextFieldHandler( this );

        // Create first Text Field
        l1 = new JLabel("Visible text here:",JLabel.RIGHT);
        add( l1 );
        t1 = new JTextField("Enter Text Here",25);
        t1.addActionListener( handler );
        add( t1 );

        // Create Password Field
        l2 = new JLabel("Hidden text here:",JLabel.RIGHT);
        add( l2 );
        t2 = new JPasswordField("Enter Text Here",25);
        t2.addActionListener( handler );
        add( t2 );

        // Create third Text Field
        l3 = new JLabel("Results:",JLabel.RIGHT);
        add( l3 );
        t3 = new JTextField(25);
        t3.setEditable( false );
        add( t3 );
    }

    // Method to update t3
    public void updateT3( String s ) {
        t3.setText( s );
    }

    // Main method to create frame
    public static void main(String s[]) {
```

Figure 13.9. A program to test JTextField and JPasswordField objects.

```
            // Create a frame to hold the application
            JFrame fr = new JFrame("TestTextField ...");
            fr.setSize(400,130);

            (rest of main is the same as previous examples...)
        }
    }

class TextFieldHandler implements ActionListener {
    private TestTextField ttf;

    // Constructor
    public TextFieldHandler ( TestTextField t ) {
        ttf = t;
    }

    // Execute when an event occurs
    public void actionPerformed( ActionEvent e ) {
        ttf.updateT3(e.getActionCommand());
    }
}
```

Figure 13.9. (Continued).

is a "read-only" text field. It is used to display the data returned by the event handler after a user presses the ENTER key on one of the other text fields.

When information is typed in Text Field 1 and the ENTER key is pressed, an `ActionEvent` is generated and handled by the `actionPerformed` method. This method makes a callback to method `updateT3` to display the typed information in the read-only field.

When this program is executed, the results after information is typed into Text Field 1 are shown in Figure 13.10(a), and the results after information is typed into Text Field 2 are shown in Figure 13.10(b).

Figure 13.10. Results when information is typed in the the text and password fields.

Use `JTextFields` to accept single lines of input data from a user, or to display single lines of read-only data to the user.

Use `JPasswordFields` to accept input data from a user that you do not wish to have echoed to the screen, such as passwords.

EXAMPLE 13.1

Temperature Conversion: Write a program that converts temperature from degrees Fahrenheit to degrees Celsius and vice versa, using a GUI to accept data and display results.

SOLUTION

To create this program, we will need a label and text field for the temperature in degrees Fahrenheit and another label and text field for the temperature in degrees Celsius. We will also need a method to convert degrees Fahrenheit to degrees Celsius, and a method to convert degrees Celsius to degrees Fahrenheit. Finally, we will need two event handlers to accept text entry in the two text fields.

The `init()` method for this program must create two labels and two text fields to hold the temperature in degrees Celsius and degrees Fahrenheit. In addition, it must create `ActionListener` objects for both text fields. The code for these steps is

```
// Create ActionEvent handlers
cHnd = new DegCHandler( this );
fHnd = new DegFHandler( this );

// Create degrees Celsius field
l1 = new JLabel("deg C:", JLabel.RIGHT);
add( l1 );
t1 = new JTextField("0.0",15);
t1.addActionListener( cHnd );
add( t1 );

// Create degrees Fahrenheit field
l2 = new JLabel("deg F:", JLabel.RIGHT);
add( l2 );
t2 = new JTextField("32.0",15);
t2.addActionListener( fHnd );
add( t2 );
```

Method `toC` will convert temperature from degrees Fahrenheit to degrees Celsius. It must implement the equation

$$\deg C = \frac{5}{9}(\deg F - 32) \tag{13.1}$$

and must update the text fields with this information. The pseudocode for these steps is

```
DecimalFormat df = new DecimalFormat("###.0");
degC ← (5. / 9.) * (degF - 32);
t1.setText( df.format(degC) );
t2.setText( df.format(degF) );
```

Note that we are using the `DecimalFormat` class to format the temperatures for display. Method `toF` will convert temperature from degrees Celsius to degrees Fahrenheit. It must implement the equation

$$\deg F = \frac{9}{5}\deg C + 32 \qquad (13.2)$$

and must update the text fields with this information. The pseudocode for these steps is

```
DecimalFormat df = new DecimalFormat("###.0");
degF ← (9. / 5.) * degC + 32;
t1.setText( df.format(degC) );
t2.setText( df.format(degF) );
```

The `ActionListeners` must listen for inputs in a text field, convert the input `String` into a `double` value, and call the appropriate `toC` or `toF` method. For example, the `actionPerformed` method that monitors the degrees Celsius text field would be:

```
public void actionPerformed( ActionEvent e ) {
    String input = e.getActionCommand();
    double degC = new Double(input).doubleValue();
    tc.toF( degC );
}
```

The final program is shown in Figure 13.11.

```
/*
   Purpose:
     This GUI-based program converts temperature in
     degrees Fahrenheit to degrees Celsius, and vice versa.

   Record of revisions:
      Date          Programmer           Description of change
      ====          ==========           =====================
    07/06/2002    S. J. Chapman          Original code
*/
import java.awt.*;
import java.awt.event.*;
import javax.swing.*;
import java.text.DecimalFormat;
public class TempConversion extends JPanel {

   // Instance variables
   private JLabel l1, l2;        // Labels
   private JTextField t1, t2;    // Text Fields
   private DegCHandler cHnd;     // ActionEvent handler
   private DegFHandler fHnd;     // ActionEvent handler

   // Initialization method
   public void init() {
```

Figure 13.11. A GUI-based temperature-conversion program.

```
      // Set the layout manager
      setLayout( new FlowLayout() );

      // Create ActionEvent handlers
      cHnd = new DegCHandler( this );
      fHnd = new DegFHandler( this );

      // Create degrees Celsius field
      l1 = new JLabel("deg C:", JLabel.RIGHT);
      add( l1 );
      t1 = new JTextField("0.0",15);
      t1.addActionListener( cHnd );
      add( t1 );

      // Create degrees Fahrenheit field
      l2 = new JLabel("deg F:", JLabel.RIGHT);
      add( l2 );
      t2 = new JTextField("32.0",15);
      t2.addActionListener( fHnd );
      add( t2 );
   }

   // Method to convert deg F to deg C
   // and display result
   public void toC( double degF ) {
      DecimalFormat df = new DecimalFormat("###.0");
      double degC = (5. / 9.) * (degF - 32);
      t1.setText( df.format(degC) );
      t2.setText( df.format(degF) );
   }

   // Method to convert deg C to deg F
   // and display result
   public void toF( double degC ) {
      DecimalFormat df = new DecimalFormat("###.0");
      double degF = (9. / 5.) * degC + 32;
      t1.setText( df.format(degC) );
      t2.setText( df.format(degF) );
   }

   // Main method to create frame
   public static void main(String s[]) {

      // Create a frame to hold the application
      JFrame fr = new JFrame("TempConversion ...");
      fr.setSize(250,100);

      // Create a Window Listener to handle "close" events
      MyWindowListener l = new MyWindowListener();
      fr.addWindowListener(l);

      // Create and initialize a TempConversion object
      TempConversion tf = new TempConversion();
```

Figure 13.11. (Continued).

```
        tf.init();

        // Add the object to the center of the frame
        fr.getContentPane().add(tf, BorderLayout.CENTER);

        // Display the frame
        fr.setVisible( true );
    }
}

class DegCHandler implements ActionListener {
    private TempConversion tc;

    // Constructor
    public DegCHandler( TempConversion t ) { tc = t; }

    // Execute when an event occurs
    public void actionPerformed( ActionEvent e ) {
        String input = e.getActionCommand();
        double degC = Double.parseDouble(input);
        tc.toF( degC );
    }
}

class DegFHandler implements ActionListener {
    private TempConversion tc;

    // Constructor
    public DegFHandler( TempConversion t ) { tc = t; }

    // Execute when an event occurs
    public void actionPerformed( ActionEvent e ) {
        String input = e.getActionCommand();
        double degF = Double.parseDouble(input);
        tc.toC( degF );
    }
}
```

Figure 13.11. (Continued).

When this program is executed, the results are as shown in Figure 13.12. Try this program for yourself with several different temperature values. ∎

13.4.4 Combo Boxes

A **combo box** is a field in which a user can either type an entry or select an entry from a *drop-down list* of choices. If desired, the combo box can be restricted so that only choices in the drop-down list may be selected. The selected choice is displayed in the combo box field after a selection has been made.

Combo boxes are implemented by the JComboBox class. A JComboBox is created with the following constructors:

```
public JComboBox();
public JComboBox( Object[] );
public JComboBox( Vector );
```

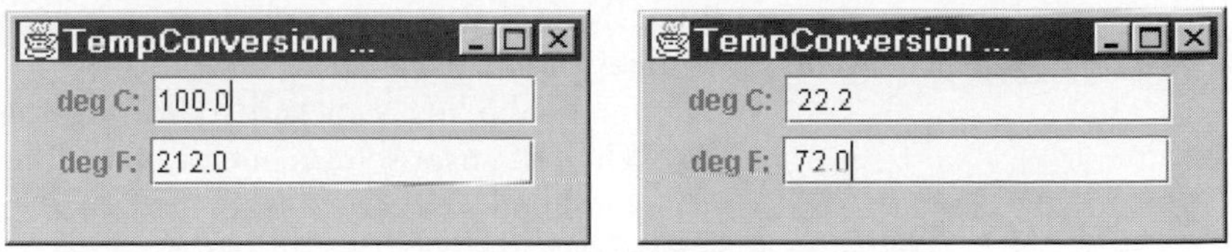

(a) (b)

Figure 13.12. (a) Result when the user enters 100° C. (b) Result when the user enters 72° F.

The first constructor creates an empty combo box. The second constructor builds a new combo box with the array of objects (such as `Strings`) used to initialize the choices in the box. The last constructor builds a new combo box with a `Vector` of objects (such as `Strings`) used to initialize the choices in the box. Some of the methods in class `JComboBox` are described in Table 13.7.

TABLE 13.7 Selected JComboBox Methods

Method	Description
`public void addActionListener(` `        ActionListener l)`	Adds the specified listener to receive ActionEvents from this JComboBox list. These events happen when selection is complete.
`public void addItem(Object o)`	Adds an item to the JComboBox list.
`public Object getItemAt(int index)`	Returns the JComboBox item at location index.
`public int getItemCount()`	Returns the number of items in this JComboBox list.
`public int getSelectedIndex()`	Returns the index of the selected JComboBox item.
`public Object getSelectedItem()`	Returns the selected JComboBox item.
`public boolean isEditable()`	Returns the editable state of the JComboBox.
`public void insertItemAt(Object o, int i)`	Inserts an item at position i in the JComboBox list.
`public void removeItem(Object o)`	Removes the specified JComboBox item.
`public void removeItemAt(int index)`	Removes the JComboBox item at location index.
`public void setEditable(boolean b)`	If true, user can type in the combo box (default is false).
`public void setToolTipText(String text)`	Sets the tool-tip text to display when the cursor rests over the text field.

Class `JComboBox` implements the `ActionListener` interface, which means that it generates `ActionEvents`. When an item is accepted in a `JComboBox` field, the `JComboBox` generates an `ActionEvent` and sends that event to any objects that have been registered with it as listeners.

The program in Figure 13.13 shows how to create a `JComboBox` and to implement choices based on selections in that field. This class creates a combo box and a read-only text field. The user selects a font name from the choice list (Serif, SansSerif, Monospaced, or Dialog), and the sample text is displayed with appropriate formatting in the text field. (Note that this example uses an *uneditable* combo box, because only the valid font names supplied should be selectable.)

When the combo box is clicked, a drop-down list appears with the four possible font names. When the user selects one of these font names by clicking on it, an `ActionEvent` is created and the `actionPerformed` method is called. This method in turn calls `updateFont()` to display the new font. Method `updateFont()` gets the new font name from the choice list using the `getSelectedItem()` method, which returns an `Object` reference. This reference is downcast to a `String`, and that font name is used to create a new font with that name and the original font style (`PLAIN`, `BOLD`, etc.) and size. Finally, the `JTextField` is repainted to display the new font.

When this program is executed, the results are as shown in Figure 13.14.

```
// This program tests combo boxes.
import java.awt.*;
import java.awt.event.*;
import javax.swing.*;
public class TestComboBox extends JPanel {

   // Instance variables
   private JComboBox c1;             // Combo box
   private JTextField t1;            // TextField
   private ComboHandler handler;     // ActionEvent handler

   // Initialization method
   public void init() {

      // Set background color
      setBackground( Color.lightGray );

      // Set the layout manager
      setLayout( new FlowLayout() );

      // Create ActionEvent handler
      handler = new ComboHandler( this );

      // Create the JComboBox
      String[] s = {"Serif","SansSerif","Monospaced",
                    "Dialog"};
      c1 = new JComboBox(s);
      c1.addActionListener( handler );
      add( c1 );

      // Create the text field with default font
      Font font = new Font(c1.getItemAt(0).toString(),
                           Font.PLAIN, 14);
      t1 = new JTextField("Test string",30);
      t1.setEditable( false );
```

Figure 13.13. A program showing how different fonts can be selected with a `JComboBox`.

```
        t1.setFont( font );
        add( t1 );
    }

    // Method to update font
    public void updateFont() {
        int valBold, valItalic;

        // Get current font info
        int fontStyle   = t1.getFont().getStyle();
        int fontSize    = t1.getFont().getSize();

        // Get new font name
        String fontName = (String) c1.getSelectedItem();

        // Set new font
        t1.setFont( new Font(fontName, fontStyle, fontSize) );

        // Repaint the JTextField
        t1.repaint();
    }

    // Main method to create frame
    public static void main(String s[]) {

        // Create a frame to hold the application
        JFrame fr = new JFrame("TestComboBox ...");
        fr.setSize(400,100);

        (rest of main is the same as previous examples...)
    }
}

class ComboHandler implements ActionListener {
    private TestComboBox tcb;

    // Constructor
    public ComboHandler( TestComboBox t ) { tcb = t; }

    // Execute when an event occurs
    public void actionPerformed( ActionEvent e ) {

        // State has changed, so call updateFont
        tcb.updateFont();
    }
}
```

Figure 13.13. (Continued).

(a)

(b)

(c)

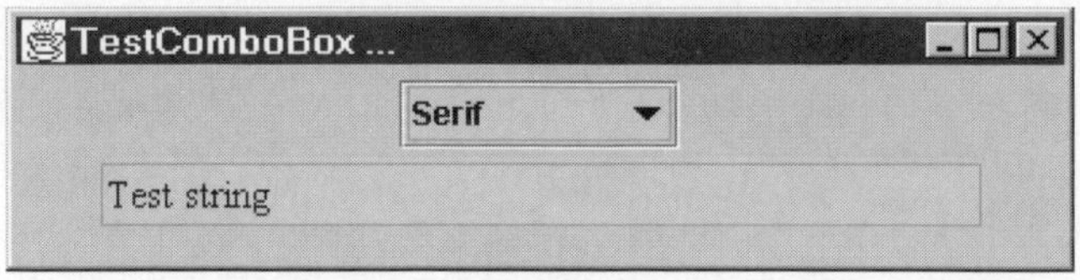

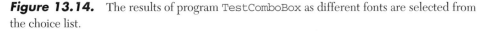

Figure 13.14. The results of program `TestComboBox` as different fonts are selected from the choice list.

GOOD PROGRAMMING PRACTICE

Use `JComboBoxes` to make a single selection from a list of mutually exclusive choices.

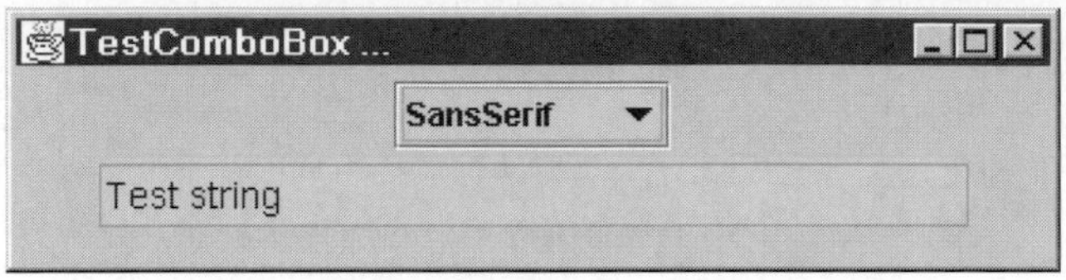

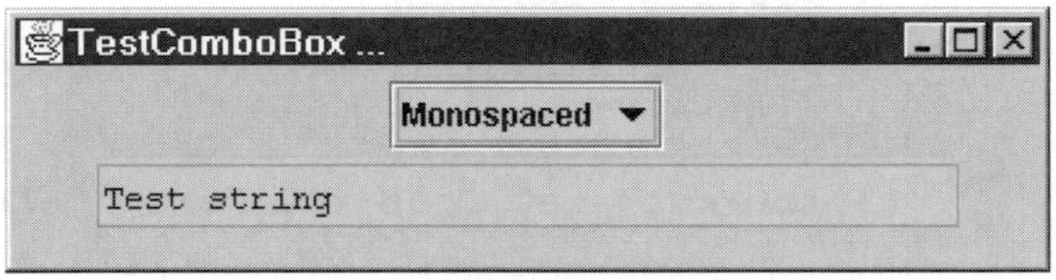

13.4.5 Check Boxes and Radio Buttons

A **check box** is a type of button that toggles between two possible states: ON/OFF or TRUE/FALSE. When the check box is ON, a small check mark appears in it, and when the check box is OFF, the mark is removed. Each time the mouse clicks on a check box, the check box toggles to the opposite state. Check boxes look like small square boxes with check marks in them, but they are in fact fully fledged buttons with all of the features that we learned about when studying push buttons. For example, it is possible to include both text and images on a check box, and it is possible to define keyboard shortcuts for them. Check boxes are implemented by the **`JCheckBox`** class.

A `JCheckBox` is created with the constructors:

```
public JCheckBox( String s );
public JCheckBox( String s, boolean state );
public JCheckBox( Icon Image );
public JCheckBox( Icon image, boolean state );
public JCheckBox( String s, Icon image );
public JCheckBox( String s, Icon image, boolean state );
```

In these constructors, s is the text label for the check box, image is the image to display on the check box, and state is the initial ON/OFF state of the check box. If state is absent from a constructor, then the new check box defaults to off. Some of the methods in class JCheckBox are described in Table 13.8.

TABLE 13.8   Selected JCheckBox and JRadioButton Methods

Method	Description
public Icon getIcon()	Returns the image from a JCheckBox.
public String getLabel()	Returns the label from the JCheckBox.
public boolean isSelected()	Returns the state of the JCheckBox (TRUE or FALSE).
public void setLabel(String s)	Sets a new label into the JCheckBox.
public void setActionCommand(String s)	Set the action command string generated by this button when it is pressed.
public void setDisabledIcon(Icon icon)	Sets the icon to display when the button is disabled.
public void setEnabled(boolean b)	Enables or disables this button.
public void setHorizontalAlignment(int alignment)	Sets the horizontal alignment of the text and images. Legal values are LEFT, CENTER, and RIGHT.
public void setHorizontalTextPosition(int textPosition)	Sets the position of the text relative to the images. Legal values are LEFT, CENTER, and RIGHT.
public void setLabel(String s)	Sets the label of this button to the specified String.
public void setIcon(Icon icon)	Sets the default icon for this button.
public void setMnemonic(char mnemonic)	Set the keyboard character combination used to activate the button from the keyboard.
public void setPressedIcon(Icon icon)	Sets the icon to display when the button is pressed.
public void setSelected(boolean b)	Sets a new state into the JCheckBox.
public void setToolTipText(String text)	Sets the tool-tip text to display when the cursor rests over the check box or button.
public void setVerticalAlignment(int alignment)	Sets the vertical alignment of the text and images. Legal values are TOP, CENTER, and BOTTOM.
public void setVerticalTextPosition(int textPosition)	Sets the position of the text relative to the images. Legal values are TOP, CENTER, and BOTTOM.

Class JCheckBox implements the ActionListener interface, which means that it generates ActionEvents. When a Checkbox is clicked, the Checkbox generates an ActionEvent and sends that event to any objects that have been registered with it as listeners.

The program in Figure 13.15 shows how to create JCheckBoxes, and to implement choices based on the state of the JCheckBoxes. This class expands on the previous program by adding two check boxes to select bold and/or italic font types for display.

When a check box is clicked (or activated by the proper keyboard combination), an ActionEvent is created and the actionPerformed method in class Action Handler is called. This method in turn calls updateFont() to display the new font. Method updateFont() gets the status of the Bold and Italic check boxes, using the isSelected() method, and creates a new font with that style.

```
// This program tests check boxes.
import java.awt.*;
import java.awt.event.*;
import javax.swing.*;
public class TestCheckBox extends JPanel {

    // Instance variables
    private JCheckBox cb1, cb2;      // Check boxes
    private JComboBox c1;            // Combo box
    private JTextField t1;           // TextField
    private ActionHandler h1;        // ActionEvent handler

    // Initialization method
    public void init() {

        // Set the layout manager
        setLayout( new FlowLayout() );

        // Create ActionEvent handler
        h1 = new ActionHandler( this );

        // Create the JComboBox for font names
        String[] s = {"Serif","SansSerif","Monospaced",
                      "Dialog"};
        c1 = new JComboBox(s);
        c1.addActionListener( h1 );
        add( c1 );

        // Create the text field with default font
        Font font = new Font( c1.getItemAt(0).toString(),
                              Font.PLAIN, 14);
        t1 = new JTextField("Test string",20);
        t1.setEditable( false );
        t1.setFont( font );
        add( t1 );

        // Create check boxes for bold and italic
        cb1 = new JCheckBox("Bold");
        cb1.addActionListener( h1 );
        cb1.setMnemonic('b');
        add( cb1 );
        cb2 = new JCheckBox("Italic");
        cb2.addActionListener( h1 );
        cb2.setMnemonic('i');
        add( cb2 );
    }

    // Method to update font
    public void updateFont() {
        int valBold, valItalic;
```

Figure 13.15. A program using JCheckBoxes to select bold and italic font styles.

```
        // Get current font info
        int fontStyle   = t1.getFont().getStyle();
        int fontSize    = t1.getFont().getSize();

        // Get new font name
        String fontName = (String) c1.getSelectedItem();

        // Get new font style
        valBold   = cb1.isSelected() ? Font.BOLD    : Font.PLAIN;
        valItalic = cb2.isSelected() ? Font.ITALIC : Font.PLAIN;
        fontStyle = valBold + valItalic;

        // Set new font
        t1.setFont( new Font(fontName, fontStyle, fontSize) );

        // Repaint the JTextField
        t1.repaint();
    }

    // Main method to create frame
    public static void main(String s[]) {

        // Create a frame to hold the application
        JFrame fr = new JFrame("TestCheckBox ...");
        fr.setSize(380,100);

        (rest of main is the same as previous examples...)
    }
}
class ActionHandler implements ActionListener {
    private TestCheckBox tcb;

    // Constructor
    public ActionHandler( TestCheckBox t ) { tcb = t; }

    // Execute when an event occurs
    public void actionPerformed( ActionEvent e ) {

        // State has changed, so call updateFont
        tcb.updateFont();
    }
}
```

Figure 13.15.   (Continued).

When this program is executed, the results are as shown in Figure 13.16.

GOOD PROGRAMMING PRACTICE

Use JCheckBoxes to select the state of items represented by boolean variables, which can be only true or false.

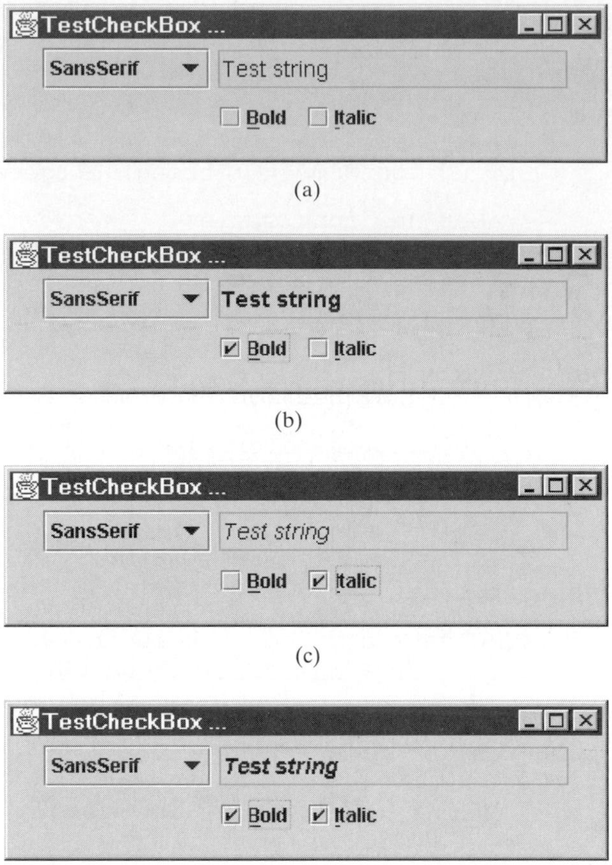

(a)

(b)

(c)

(d)

Figure 13.16.   The results of program TestCheckBox as different combinations of the Bold and Italic check boxes are turned on.

Radio buttons are a group of checkboxes in which *at most one checkbox can be on at a time*. Radio buttons look like small circles with a dot inside the selected one, but otherwise have the same characteristics as any button. Radio buttons are implemented by the **JRadioButton** class.

A JRadioButton is created with the constructors:

```
    public JRadioButton( String s );
    public JRadioButton( String s, boolean state );
 public JRadioButton( Icon Image );
 public JRadioButton( Icon image, boolean state );
 public JRadioButton( String s, Icon image );
 public JRadioButton( String s, Icon image, boolean state );
```

In these constructors, s is the text label for the radio button, image is the image to display on the radio button, and state is the initial ON/OFF state of the radio button. If state is absent from a constructor, then the new radio button defaults to OFF. The methods in class JRadioButton are the same as those in class JCheckBox and are described in Table 13.8.

A group of radio buttons is made mutually exclusive (only one can be on at a time) by being placed in a **ButtonGroup**. The ButtonGroup ensures that when one of the JRadioButtons is turned ON, the others are all OFF.

A `ButtonGroup` is created with the constructor:

```
public ButtonGroup();
```

Some of the methods in class `ButtonGroup` are described in Table 13.9.

TABLE 13.9   Selected `ButtonGroup` Methods

Method	Description
public void add(AbstractButton b)	Add a button to the `ButtonGroup`.
public void remove(AbstractButton b)	Remove a button from the `ButtonGroup`.

The program in Figure 13.17 shows how to create a set of radio buttons using `JRadioButtons` in a `ButtonGroup`. This class modifies the previous program by using four radio buttons instead of two check boxes to select bold and/or italic font types for display.

```java
// This program tests radio buttons.
import java.awt.*;
import java.awt.event.*;
import javax.swing.*;
public class TestRadioButton extends JPanel {

    // Instance variables
    private ButtonGroup bg;                    // ButtonGroup
    private JRadioButton b1, b2, b3, b4; // Check boxes
    private JComboBox c1;                      // Combo box
    private JTextField t1;                     // TextField
    private ActionHandler h1;                  // ActionEvent handler

    // Initialization method
    public void init() {

        // Set the layout manager
        setLayout( new FlowLayout() );

        // Create ActionEvent handler
        h1 = new ActionHandler( this );

        // Create the JComboBox for font names
        String[] s = {"Serif","SansSerif","Monospaced",
                      "Dialog"};
        c1 = new JComboBox(s);
        c1.addActionListener( h1 );
        add( c1 );

        // Create the text field with default font
        Font font = new Font( c1.getItemAt(0).toString(),
                              Font.PLAIN, 14);
        t1 = new JTextField("Test string",20);
        t1.setEditable( false );
        t1.setFont( font );
```

Figure 13.17.   A program using radio buttons to select font styles.

```
        add( t1 );

        // Create radio buttons
        b1 = new JRadioButton("Plain", true );
        b1.addActionListener( h1 );
        add( b1 );
        b2 = new JRadioButton("Bold", false );
        b2.addActionListener( h1 );
        add( b2 );
        b3 = new JRadioButton("Italic", false );
        b3.addActionListener( h1 );
        add( b3 );
        b4 = new JRadioButton("Bold Italic", false );
        b4.addActionListener( h1 );
        add( b4 );

        // Create button group, and add radio buttons
        bg = new ButtonGroup();
        bg.add( b1 );
        bg.add( b2 );
        bg.add( b3 );
        bg.add( b4 );
    }

    // Method to update font
    public void updateFont() {
        int valBold, valItalic;

        // Get current font info
        int fontStyle  = t1.getFont().getStyle();
        int fontSize   = t1.getFont().getSize();

        // Get new font name
        String fontName = (String) c1.getSelectedItem();

        // Get new font style
        if ( b1.isSelected() )
           fontStyle = Font.PLAIN;
        else if ( b2.isSelected() )
           fontStyle = Font.BOLD;
        else if ( b3.isSelected() )
           fontStyle = Font.ITALIC;
        else if ( b4.isSelected() )
           fontStyle = Font.BOLD + Font.ITALIC;

        // Set new font
        t1.setFont( new Font(fontName, fontStyle, fontSize) );

        // Repaint the JTextField
        t1.repaint();
    }

    // Main method to create frame
```

Figure 13.17. (Continued).

```
   public static void main(String s[]) {

      // Create a frame to hold the application
      JFrame fr = new JFrame("TestRadioButton ...");
      fr.setSize(380,100);

      (rest of main is the same as previous examples...)
   }
}
class ActionHandler implements ActionListener {
   private TestRadioButton tcb;

   // Constructor
   public ActionHandler( TestRadioButton t ) { tcb = t; }

   // Execute when an event occurs
   public void actionPerformed( ActionEvent e ) {

      // State has changed, so call updateFont
      tcb.updateFont();
   }
```

Figure 13.17.   (Continued).

When a radio button is clicked, an `ActionEvent` is created and the `action`
`Performed` method in class `ActionHandler` is called. This method in turn calls
`updateFont()` to display the new font. Method `updateFont()` determines which
radio button is selected, using the `isSelected()` method, and creates a new font
with that style. Note that the `ButtonGroup` ensures that only one of the radio buttons
will be selected at a time.

When this program is executed, the results are as shown in Figure 13.18.

GOOD PROGRAMMING PRACTICE

Use `JRadioButtons` to select the state of a set of items represented by boolean variables, only one of which can
be `true` at any time.

13.4.6 Blank Components (Canvases)

As we learned in Chapter 12, a **canvas** is a blank component that can be used for drawing. The older AWT GUI had a special class called `Canvas` for this purpose, but the
Swing GUI does not have a corresponding blank class. Instead, a user can create a subclass of `JComponent` to draw on.

A blank component can be created using a subclass of `JComponent`. To create
custom graphics, a program should create a subclass of `JComponent` and override the
`paintComponent` method in that subclass. To redraw the component after a change
has occurred, a programmer should call the component's `repaint()` method. Some
common methods associated with `JComponent` are given in Table 13.10.

Blank components can be used to add graphics to a graphical user interface. They
can be added to the GUI just like any other component. For example, the program in
Figure 13.19 creates a blank component that displays an ellipse and adds it to a `JPanel`
that also includes labels and text fields. The program changes the size of the ellipse

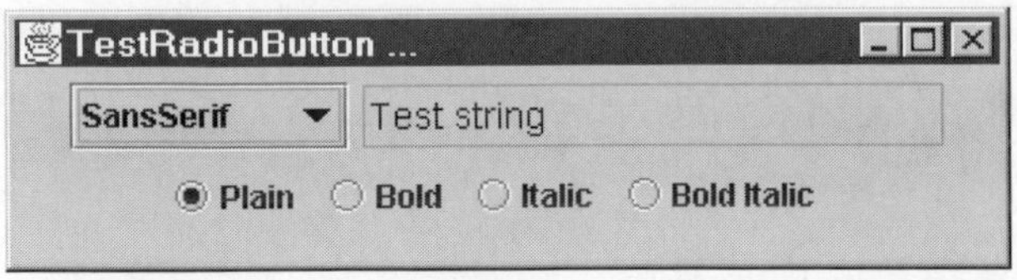

(a)

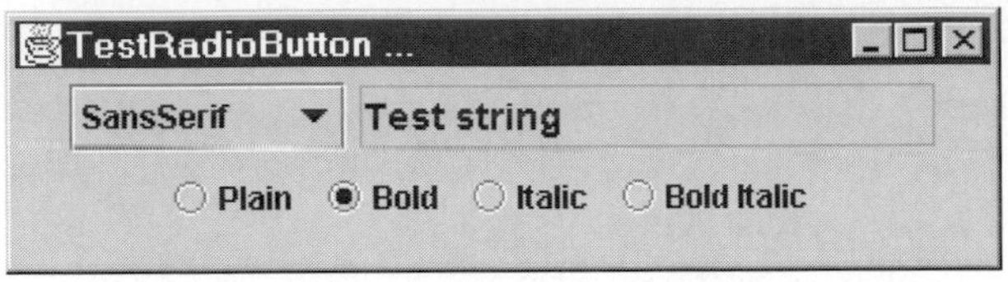

(b)

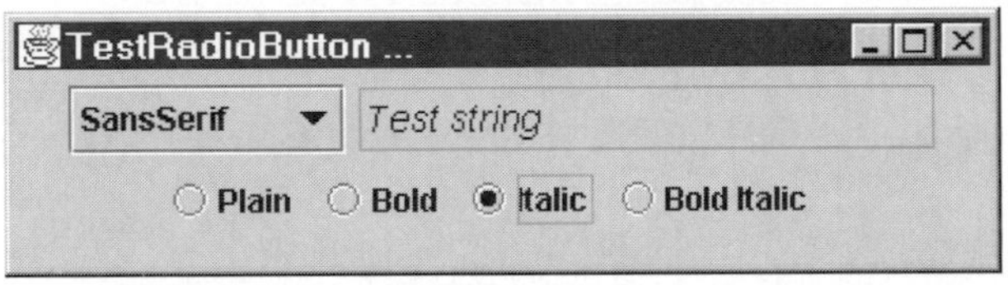

(c)

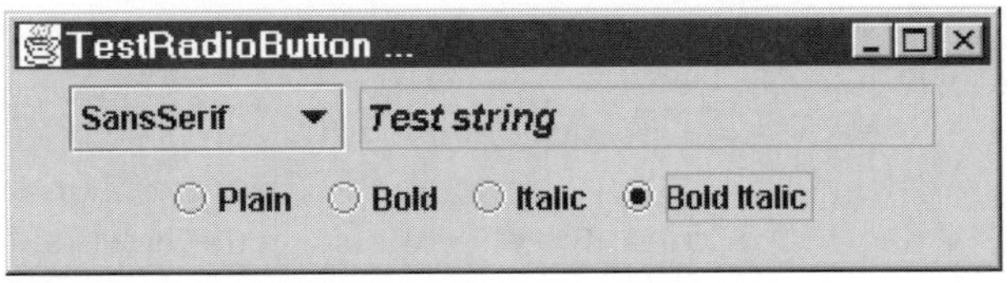

(d)

Figure 13.18. The results of program `TestRadioButton` as different radio buttons are turned on.

based on values input into the text fields. Note that the program calls the `redraw()` method to redraw the ellipse whenever its size has changed.

When a user types a height or width into the appropriate text field, an `ActionEvent` is created, and the corresponding event handler is called. This event handler gets the `String` typed by the user with the `getActionCommand()` method,

TABLE 13.10 Selected `JComponent` Methods

Method	Description
`setMinimumSize(Dimension d)`	Sets the minimum size of the component in pixels. The dimension object used to set the size is created with the constructor: `new Dimension(int width, int height);`
`setMaximumSize(Dimension d)`	Sets the maximum size of the component in pixels. The dimension object used to set the size is created with the constructor: `new Dimension(int width, int height);`
`public void paintComponent( Graphics g)`	Paints text and graphics on the component.
`public void repaint()`	Repaints text and graphics on the component.
`setPreferredSize(Dimension d)`	Sets the preferred size of the component in pixels. The dimension object used to set the size is created with the constructor: `new Dimension(int width, int height);`

```
// This class tests drawing and redrawing a blank
// component as part of a GUI.
import java.awt.*;
import java.awt.event.*;
import java.awt.geom.*;
import javax.swing.*;
public class TestGraphics extends JPanel {

    // Instance variables
    private DrawEllipse dr;           // DrawEllipse object
    private JLabel l1, l2;            // Labels
    private JTextField t1, t2;        // TextFields
    private HeightHandler h1;         // ActionEvent handler
    private WidthHandler h2;          // ActionEvent handler
    private double height = 100;      // Height
    private double width = 150;       // Width

    // Initialization method
    public void init() {

        // Set background color
        setBackground( Color.lightGray );

        // Set the layout manager
        setLayout( new FlowLayout() );

        // Create height and width handlers
        h1 = new HeightHandler( this );
        h2 = new WidthHandler( this );

        // Create drawing area
        dr = new DrawEllipse( width, height );
        dr.setPreferredSize(new Dimension(400,300));
        add ( dr );

        // Create height JTextField
        l1 = new JLabel("Height:");
        add( l1 );
        l1.setHorizontalAlignment( JLabel.RIGHT );
        t1 = new JTextField("100",10);
        t1.addActionListener( h1 );
        add( t1 );

        // Create width JTextField
        l2 = new JLabel("Width:");
        add( l2 );
        l2.setHorizontalAlignment( JLabel.RIGHT );
```

Figure 13.19. A program that uses a blank component to add graphics to a GUI.

```
        t2 = new JTextField("150",10);
        t2.addActionListener( h2 );
        add( t2 );
    }

    // Method to update height
    public void updateHeight( double height ) {
        this.height = height;
        dr.setHeight(height);
        dr.repaint();
    }

    // Method to update width
    public void updateWidth( double width ) {
        this.width = width;
        dr.setWidth(width);
        dr.repaint();
    }

    // Main method to create frame
    public static void main(String s[]) {

        // Create a frame to hold the application
        JFrame fr = new JFrame("TestGraphics ...");
        fr.setSize(400,370);

        // Create a Window Listener to handle "close" events
        MyWindowListener l = new MyWindowListener();
        fr.addWindowListener(l);

        // Create and initialize a TestGraphics object
        TestGraphics tc = new TestGraphics();
        tc.init();

        // Add the object to the center of the frame
        fr.getContentPane().add(tc, BorderLayout.CENTER);

        // Display the frame
        fr.setVisible( true );
    }
}

class HeightHandler implements ActionListener {
    private TestGraphics tc;

    // Constructor
    public HeightHandler( TestGraphics t ) { tc = t; }
```

Figure 13.19. (Continued).

```java
      // Execute when an event occurs
   public void actionPerformed( ActionEvent e ) {
      double height =
          new Double(e.getActionCommand()).doubleValue();
      tc.updateHeight(height);
   }
}

class WidthHandler implements ActionListener {
   private TestGraphics tc;
   // Constructor
   public WidthHandler( TestGraphics t ) { tc = t; }

   // Execute when an event occurs
   public void actionPerformed( ActionEvent e ) {
      double width =
          new Double(e.getActionCommand()).doubleValue();
      tc.updateWidth(width);
   }
}

// This class extends JComponent and draws an ellipse
class DrawEllipse extends JComponent {

   // Instance variables
   private double height;        // Ellipse height
   private double width;         // Ellipse width

   // Constructor
   public DrawEllipse( double width, double height ) {
      this.height = height;
      this.width = width;
   }

   public void paintComponent( Graphics g ) {

      BasicStroke bs;                      // Ref to BasicStroke
      Ellipse2D ell;                       // Ref to Ellipse

      // Cast the graphics object to Graph2D
      Graphics2D g2 = (Graphics2D) g;

      // Set background color
      Dimension size = getSize();
      g2.setColor( Color.white );
      g2.fill(new Rectangle2D.Double(0,0,size.width,size.height));

      // Set rendering hints to improve display quality
      g2.setRenderingHint(RenderingHints.KEY_ANTIALIASING,
                          RenderingHints.VALUE_ANTIALIAS_ON);
```

Figure 13.19. (Continued).

```
        // Define Ellipse
        ell = new Ellipse2D.Double (30., 40., width, height);
        g2.setColor(Color.yellow);
        g2.fill(ell);
        g2.setColor(Color.black);
        g2.draw(ell);
    }
    public void setHeight ( double height ) {
        this.height = height;
    }
    public void setWidth ( double width ) {
        this.width = width;
    }
```

Figure 13.19. (Continued).

and converts the `String` into a `double` value. The event handler calls the method `updateHeight` or `updateWidth`, which in turn sets the height or width of the ellipse. A typical output from this program is shown in Figure 13.20.

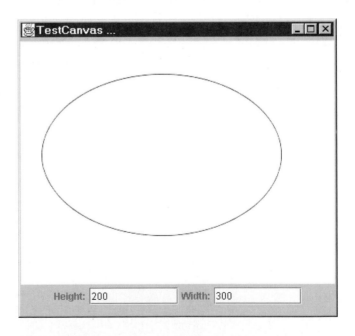

Figure 13.20. Output from the program `TestGraphics`.

GOOD PROGRAMMING PRACTICE

Use subclasses of `JComponent` to add graphical displays to a GUI.

13.5 LAYOUT MANAGERS

A **layout manager** is a helper class that is designed to automatically arrange GUI components within a container for presentation purposes. The layout managers allow a user to add components to a container without worrying about the specifics of how to place them within the container. They are especially useful for cross-platform applications, because the size of a particular component may vary slightly from platform to platform, and the layout manager will automatically adjust the spacing of components to accommodate these differences.

The six standard layout managers in Java are summarized in Table 13.11. Only the `BorderLayout`, `BoxLayout`, `FlowLayout`, and `GridLayout` managers will be described in this book. Refer to the Java 2 SDK documentation for information about the `CardLayout` and `GridBagLayout` managers.

TABLE 13.11 Standard Layout Managers

Element	Description
BorderLayout	A layout manager that lays out elements in a central region and four surrounding borders. This is the default layout manager for a JFrame.
BoxLayout	A layout manager that lays out elements in a row horizontally or vertically. Unlike FlowLayout, the elements in a BoxLayout do not wrap around. This is the default layout manager for a Box.
CardLayout	A layout manager that stacks components like a deck of cards, only the top one of which is visible.
FlowLayout	A layout manager that lays out elements left-to-right and top-to-bottom within a container. This is the default layout manager for a JPanel.
GridBagLayout	A layout manager that lays out elements in a flexible grid, where the size of each element can vary.
GridLayout	A layout manager that lays out elements in a rigid grid.

13.5.1 `BorderLayout` Layout Manager

The `BorderLayout` layout manager arranges components in five regions, known as *North*, *South*, *East*, *West*, and *Center* (with North being the top of the container). A `BorderLayout` is created with one of the following constructors:

```
public BorderLayout();
public BorderLayout(int horizontalGap, int verticalGap);
```

The first constructor creates a `BorderLayout` with no pixel gaps between components, while the second constructor creates a `BorderLayout` with the programmer-specified gaps between components.

After a layout object has been created, it is associated with a container by the container's **setLayout** method. For example, the statement required to create a new `BorderLayout` object and to associate it with the current container is:

```
setLayout( new BorderLayout() );
```

Objects should be added to a `BorderLayout` using the `add` method qualified by one of the constants NORTH, SOUTH, EAST, WEST, or CENTER. For example, the following statements produce a GUI containing five buttons, one in each region:

```
setLayout(new BorderLayout());
add(new Button("North"), BorderLayout.NORTH);
```

```
          add(new Button("South"), BorderLayout.SOUTH);
          add(new Button("East"), BorderLayout.EAST);
          add(new Button("West"), BorderLayout.WEST);
          add(new Button ("Center"), BorderLayout.CENTER)
```
and these statements will produce the GUI shown in Figure 13.21.

Figure 13.21. A typical `BorderLayout`.

In a `BorderLayout`, the component in the center expands to use up all remaining space in the container. `BorderLayout` is the default layout manager for `JFrame`, and all of our frames have used it. Examine the `main` method in any of the programs in this chapter. Note that the `JPanels` that we have created were added to the `CENTER` section of the `Frame`, and none of the other sections were used. Since the center section of a `BorderLayout` expands to use all available space, the `JPanels` have completely filled their frames.

Programs `FirstGUI` in Figure 13.2 and `TestLabel` in Figure 13.5 also illustrate the use of the `BorderLayout` layout manager.

13.5.2 `FlowLayout` Layout Manager

The `FlowLayout` layout manager arranges components in order from left to right and top to bottom across a container. Components are added to a line until there is no more room, and then they are added to the next line. The components that do fit into a line are displayed centered horizontally on the line. A `FlowLayout` is created with one of the following constructors:

```
public FlowLayout();
public FlowLayout(int align);
public FlowLayout(int align, int horizontalGap, int verticalGap);
```

The first constructor creates a `FlowLayout` with no pixel gaps between components and with the components centered on each line, while the second constructor creates a `FlowLayout` with no pixel gaps between components and with the specified alignment. Possible alignments are `LEFT`, `RIGHT`, and `CENTER`. The third constructor allows the programmer to specify both the alignment on each line and the horizontal and vertical gap between components.

Objects should be added to a `FlowLayout` using the `add` method. For example, the following statements produce a GUI containing five buttons, centered on each line, with a 5-pixel gap between buttons:

```
          setLayout(new FlowLayout(FlowLayout.CENTER,5,0));
          add(new JButton("Button 1"));
          add(new JButton("Button 2"));
          add(new JButton("Long Button 3"));
          add(new JButton("B4"));
          add(new JButton("Button 5"));
```
and these statements will produce the GUI shown in Figure 13.22.

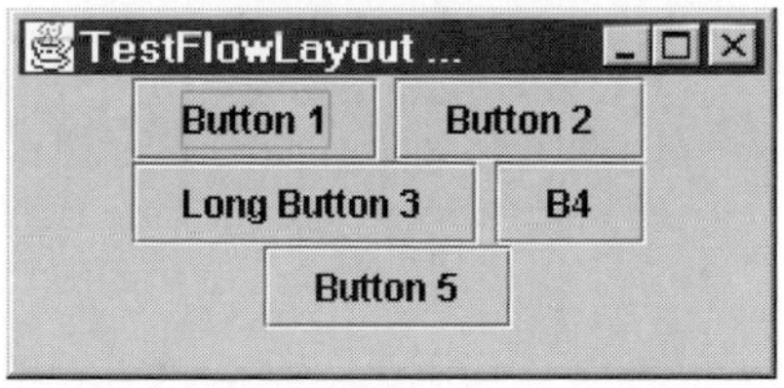

Figure 13.22. A typical FlowLayout.

Most of the programs in the chapter have used `FlowLayout` to lay out the components on their panels. `FlowLayout` is the default layout manager for `JPanel` and for applets (class `JApplet`).

13.5.3 GridLayout Layout Manager

The `GridLayout` layout manager arranges components in a rigid rectangular grid structure. The container is divided into equal-sized rectangles, and one component is placed in each rectangle. A `GridLayout` is created with one of the following constructors:

```
public GridLayout(int rows, int cols);
public GridLayout(int rows, int cols, int horizGap, int vertGap);
```

The first constructor creates a `GridLayout` with `rows` rows and `cols` columns, and no pixel gaps between components. The second constructor creates a `GridLayout` with `rows` rows and `cols` columns, and with the specified horizontal and vertical gaps between components.

Objects are be added to a `GridLayout` using the `add` method. For example, the following statements produce a GUI containing six buttons in a 3×2 grid.

```
setLayout(new GridLayout(3,2));
add(new JButton("1"));
add(new JButton("2"));
add(new JButton("3"));
add(new JButton("4"));
add(new JButton("5"));
add(new JButton("6"));
```

and these statements will produce the GUI shown in Figure 13.23.

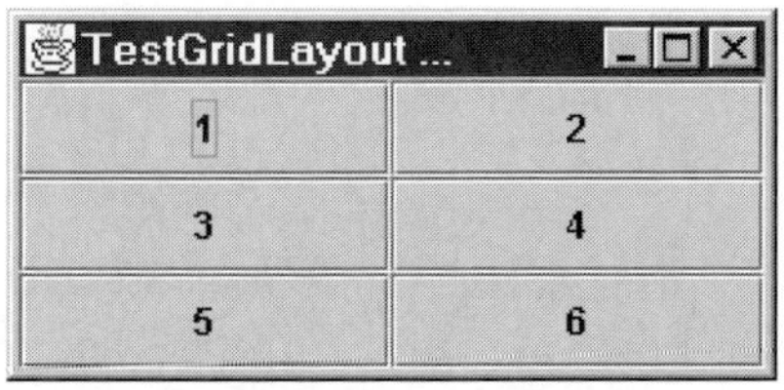

Figure 13.23. A typical GridLayout.

13.5.4 BoxLayout Layout Manager

The `BoxLayout` layout manager arranges components within a container in a single row or a single column. It is more flexible than the other layout managers that we have discussed, since the spacing and alignment of each element on each row or column can be individually controlled. Containers using BoxLayout layout managers can be nested inside each other to produce arbitrarily complex structures that do not change shape when the size of a component or container is changed.

A BoxLayout is created with the following constructor:

```
public BoxLayout(Container c, int direction);
```

The first parameter in the constructor specifies the container that the layout manager will control, and the second parameter specifies the axis along which the components will be laid out (legal values are BoxLayout.X_AXIS and BoxLayout.Y_AXIS).

Objects are added to a BoxLayout using the add method. For example, the following statements produce a GUI containing three buttons arranged vertically.

```
// Create a new panel
JPanel p = new JPanel();

// Set the layout manager
p.setLayout(new BoxLayout(p, BoxLayout.Y_AXIS));

// Add buttons
p.add( new JButton("Button 1") );
p.add( new JButton("Button 2") );
p.add( new JButton("Button 3") );

// Add the new panel to the existing container
add(p);
```

These statements will produce the GUI shown in Figure 13.24.

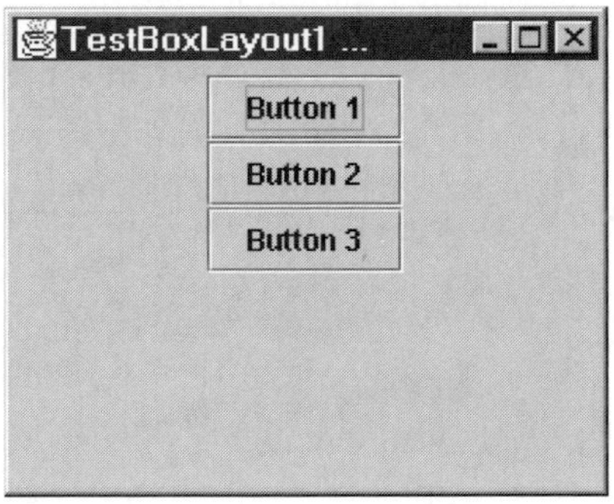

Figure 13.24. A typical vertical BoxLayout.

The flexibility of the BoxLayout manager is enhanced by two additional constraints that can be added to the layout process: rigid areas and glue regions. **Rigid areas** are fixed horizontal and/or vertical spacings between components that can be individually specified between any two adjacent components. **Glue regions** are regions that expand or contract to absorb any extra space present when a container changes size. Rigid areas and glue regions are created using the methods in Table 13.12.

To illustrate the use of these components, we will create a new GUI that lays out the same three buttons vertically as before, but places a fixed 20-pixel vertical spacing between Button 1 and Button 2, and a fixed 5-pixel spacing between Button 2 and Button 3. The code for this example is

TABLE 13.12 Methods to Control Spacing in a BoxLayout

Method	Description
Box.createRigidArea(Dimension d)	Creates a rigid spacing in pixels between two components in a BoxLayout. The Dimension object specifies the vertical and horizontal spacing between the two components.
Box.createHorizontalGlue()	Creates a "virtual component" that uses up all the extra horizontal space in a container.
Box.createVerticalGlue()	Creates a "virtual component" that uses up all the extra vertical space in a container.

```
// Create a new panel
JPanel p = new JPanel();

// Set the layout manager
p.setLayout(new BoxLayout(p, BoxLayout.Y_AXIS));

// Add buttons
p.add( new JButton("Button 1") );
p.add( Box.createRigidArea(new Dimension(0,20)) );
p.add( new JButton("Button 2") );
p.add( Box.createRigidArea(new Dimension(0,5)) );
p.add( new JButton("Button 3") );

// Add the new panel to the existing container
add(p);
```

and these statements will produce the GUI shown in Figure 13.25.

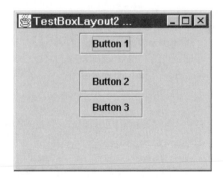

Figure 13.25. A BoxLayout illustrating the use of rigid areas to control spacing between components.

13.5.5 Combining Layout Managers to Produce a Result

Using a standard layout manager, it is often difficult to create exactly the GUI that we want, and this fact can be very frustrating. However, it is sometimes possible to *combine* layout managers to achieve a desired appearance. Only one layout manager can be used with a given container at any time, but one container can be placed inside another container, and the two containers can have different layout managers.

To understand how multiple layout managers can be better than a single one, let's reconsider the temperature-conversion program of Example 13.1. That program used a FlowLayout, which means that the components of the program were laid out horizontally until the end of a line and then started over on the next line. Unfortunately,

530 Chapter 13 Basic Graphical User Interfaces

such a design will fail if a user resizes the application, or if the size of the components differs significantly from platform to platform. Figure 13.26 illustrates this problem, showing how the appearance of the application changes as the program frame is resized.

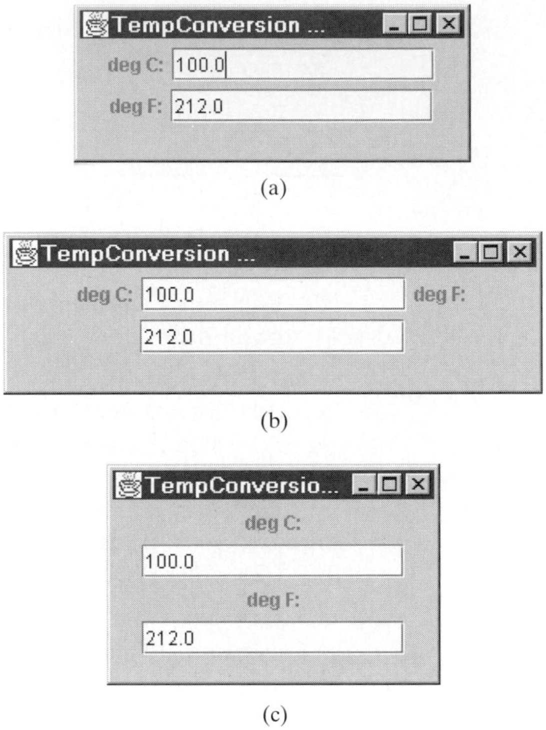

(a)

(b)

(c)

Figure 13.26. (a) The TempConversion program laid out with the default width and height. (b) The program after the frame width has been increased. (c) The program after the frame width has been decreased.

Instead of using a FlowLayout with a single container, we can create the same interface using three containers and BoxLayouts. The first container (pHoriz) will use a horizontal BoxLayout, and the other two containers (pVertL and pVertR) will be placed inside the first one and use vertical BoxLayouts. The labels will be placed in container pVertL, and the text fields will be placed in container pVertR. The horizontal space between these two containers will be set by adding a rigid area to the top-level container. The code to build this structure is shown below:

```
// Create a new high-level panel
JPanel pHoriz = new JPanel();
pHoriz.setLayout(new BoxLayout(pHoriz, BoxLayout.X_AXIS));
add( pHoriz );

// Create two subordinate panels
JPanel pVertL = new JPanel();
JPanel pVertR = new JPanel();
pVertL.setLayout(new BoxLayout(pVertL, BoxLayout.Y_AXIS));
pVertR.setLayout(new BoxLayout(pVertR, BoxLayout.Y_AXIS));
```

```
// Add to pHoriz with a horizontal space between panels
pHoriz.add( pVertL );
pHoriz.add( Box.createRigidArea(new Dimension(20,0)) );
pHoriz.add( pVertR );
// Create degrees Celsius field
l1 = new JLabel("deg C:", JLabel.RIGHT);
pVertL.add( l1 );
t1 = new JTextField("0.0",15);
t1.addActionListener( cHnd );
pVertR.add( t1 );

// Create degrees Fahrenheit field
l2 = new JLabel("deg F:", JLabel.RIGHT);
pVertL.add( l2 );
t2 = new JTextField("32.0",15);
t2.addActionListener( fHnd );
pVertR.add( t2 );
```

Figure 13.27 shows the behavior of this program as the frame containing the GUI is resized. This time, the GUI preserves its shape despite changes in frame size.

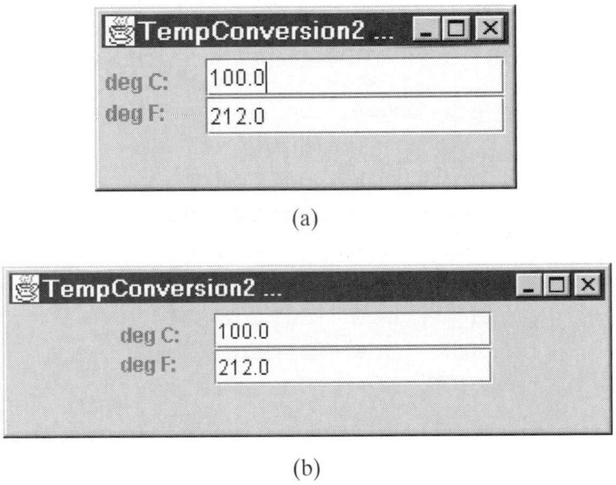

(a)

(b)

Figure 13.27.   (a) The `TempConversion2` program laid out with the default width and height. (b) The program after the frame width has been increased. Note that the relative positions of the labels and text fields have been preserved.

EXAMPLE 13.2

Creating a Calculator GUI: Write a program that creates the graphical user interface for a calculator.

SOLUTION

A calculator GUI should have a display window for results all across the top, with a rectangular grid of buttons below it. We cannot create such a display with a `Border Layout` manager, `FlowLayout` manager, a `GridLayout` manager, or a `BoxLayout` manager by itself, but we *can* create it if we can combine a `BorderLayout` manager with a `GridLayout` manager.

The code shown in Figure 13.28 creates two containers, both `JPanels`. The outer container uses the `BorderLayout` manager, and the inner container uses the

```java
// Create a GUI for a calculator.
import java.awt.*;
import java.awt.event.*;
import javax.swing.*;
public class CalculatorGUI extends JPanel {

    // Initialization method
    public void init() {

        // Set the layout manager
        setLayout( new BorderLayout() );

        // Add the result field to the panel
        JTextField t1 = new JTextField(10);
        t1.setEditable( false );
        t1.setBackground( Color.white );
        add( t1, BorderLayout.NORTH );

        // Create another Panel for the keypad, and place it
        // in the high-level panel
        JPanel p2 = new JPanel();
        p2.setLayout( new GridLayout(4,5) );
        add( p2, BorderLayout.CENTER );

        // Add keys to the panel
        p2.add( new JButton("7") );
        p2.add( new JButton("8") );
        p2.add( new JButton("9") );
        p2.add( new JButton("/") );
        p2.add( new JButton("sqrt") );
        p2.add( new JButton("4") );
        p2.add( new JButton("5") );
        p2.add( new JButton("6") );
        p2.add( new JButton("*") );
        p2.add( new JButton("%") );
        p2.add( new JButton("1") );
        p2.add( new JButton("2") );
        p2.add( new JButton("3") );
        p2.add( new JButton("-") );
        p2.add( new JButton("1/x") );
        p2.add( new JButton("0") );
        p2.add( new JButton("+/-") );
        p2.add( new JButton(".") );
        p2.add( new JButton("+") );
        p2.add( new JButton("=") );
    }
```

Figure 13.28. Creating a calculator GUI by combining two different containers with different layout managers.

`GridLayout` manager. The inner container `p2` uses the `GridLayout` manager to lay out a keypad, and then the entire inner container is placed in the center region of the outer container. The results window is placed in the `NORTH` region of the outer container. The resulting GUI is shown in Figure 13.29.

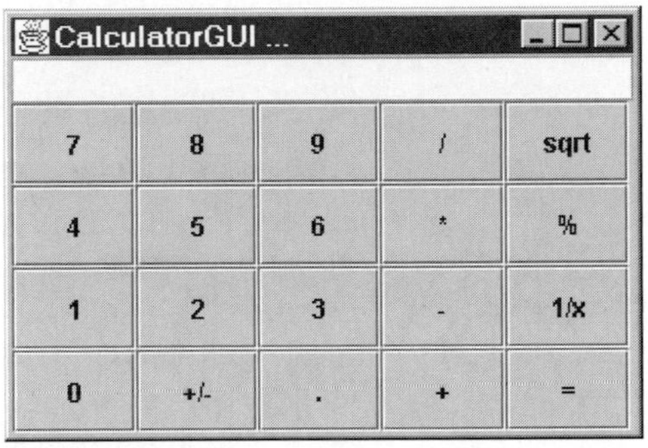

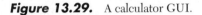

Figure 13.29. A calculator GUI.

■

QUIZ 13.1

This quiz provides a quick check to see if you have understood the concepts introduced in Sections 13.1 through 13.5. If you have trouble with the quiz, reread the section, ask your instructor, or discuss the material with a fellow student. The answers are found in the back of the book.

1. What is a container? Which type of containers(s) are we using in this chapter?
2. What is a component? Which type of components are we using in this chapter?
3. What is a layout manager? What does it do?
4. Why would you wish to use more than one layout manager in a single program?
5. What is an event handler? How are events handled in Java?
6. What listener interface(s) were introduced in this chapter? What does each one do, and which components produce it?

13.6 PUTTING IT ALL TOGETHER

We will now put together the material that we have discussed in the last two chapters to produce a sample application with a working GUI.

EXAMPLE 13.3

Plotting Data: Create a program that plots sin x, cos x, or both, depending on the values of two check boxes. The curves should be plotted for the range $0 \leq x \leq 2\pi$. Use `BoxLayout` so that the locations of the components will be preserved when the application changes size.

SOLUTION

We can plot the data using `chapman.graphics.JPlot2D`, which is a Swing component just like any other component. This program will require one `JPlot2D` object and two check boxes, as well as an `ActionListener` to monitor the state of the check boxes.

1. **Determine the User Requirements**

   The user requirements is to create a GUI-based program that plots sin x, cos x, or both depending on the values of two check boxes. Ensure that the layout of the components does not change as the window is resized.

   The inputs to this program are the status of the two check boxes "Plot sine" and "Plot cosine". The output from the program is a plot of the sine and/or cosine, depending on the status of the check boxes.

2. **Analysis and Decomposition**

   This program requires two classes to function properly. The principal class (called `PlotSinCos`) must contain three separate methods: (1) a method `init()` to generate the GUI display, (2) a method `display()` to display the desired curve(s), and (3) a `main` method to start up the application when it is used in that mode. The second required class is a `ActionListener` class to respond to events from the two check boxes.

3. **Detailed Design**

   The `init()` method of the `PlotSinCos` class must create the GUI. It must lay out the graphical elements. We would like to arrange the GUI so that the plot appears on top of the display, and the two check boxes appear side-by-side below it. One way to achieve this design is with nested panels using `BoxLayouts`, as shown in Figure 13.30. The top-level panel `pVert` will use a vertical `BoxLayout`, and the `JPlot2D` object and a horizontal panel `pHoriz` will be added to it. Then, the two check boxes can be added to the horizontal panel.

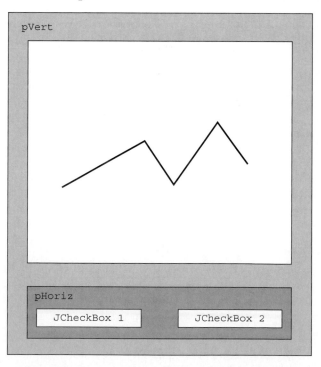

Figure 13.30. The structure of containers and layout managers required to create the GUI for the `PlotSinCos` program.

The code required to create this GUI is shown below.

```
// Create event handler
hSinCos = new CheckBoxHandler(this);

// Create a new high-level panel
JPanel pVert = new JPanel();
pVert.setLayout(new BoxLayout(pVert, BoxLay out.Y_AXIS));
add( pVert );

// Add a blank plot
pl = new JPlot2D();
pl.setPreferredSize(new Dimension(400,400));
pVert.add( pl );

// Create a subordinate panel for the bottom
JPanel pHoriz = new JPanel();
pHoriz.setLayout(new BoxLayout(pHoriz, BoxLayout.X_AXIS));
pVert.add( pHoriz );

// Create the "Add sine" check box
b1 = new JCheckBox("Add sine");
b1.addActionListener( hSinCos );
pHoriz.add( b1 );
pHoriz.add( Box.createRigidArea(new Dimension(40,0)) );

// Create the "Add cosine" check box
b2 = new JCheckBox("Add cosine");
b2.addActionListener( hSinCos );
pHoriz.add( b2 );
```

Method `init()` must also create the data to plot when a plot is requested. The code required for this step is

```
for ( int i = 0; i < x.length; i++ ) {
    x[i]  = (i+1) * 2 * Math.PI / 40;
    y1[i] = Math.sin(x[i]);
    y2[i] = Math.cos(x[i]);
}
```

Method `display()` must display the requested curves. To do this, it must first remove any existing curves on the plot with the `JPlot2D` method `removeAll()`, and then add the requested curves back into the plot. The method can check the state of each check box using the `isSelected()` method. This code is shown in the complete program below.

Method `actionListener()` in the `CheckBoxHandler` class is very simple. It must listen for any change in either check box, and call method `display()` when one occurs. Method `display()` does all the hard work, including determining which boxes are checked.

Finally, method `main()` is essentially identical to the ones shown earlier in this chapter.

4. **Implementation: Convert Algorithms to Java Statements**

The resulting Java program is shown in Figure 13.31.

5. **Testing**

To test this program, we will execute it both as an application and as an applet, and observe the results. Figure 13.32 shows the appearance of the program at

```
/*
   Purpose:
     This program plots sin x and/or cos x for 0 <= x <= PI
     depending on the state of two check boxes.

   Record of revisions:
       Date          Programmer            Description of change
       ====          ==========            =====================
     07/08/2002    S. J. Chapman           Original code
*/
import java.awt.*;
import java.awt.event.*;
import javax.swing.*;
import chapman.graphics.JPlot2D;
public class PlotSinCos extends JPanel {

   // Instance variables
   private ActionListener hSinCos;      // ActionListener
   private JCheckBox b1, b2;            // Check boxes
   private JPlot2D pl;                  // Plot
   double[] x, y1, y2;                  // Data to plot

   // Initialization method
   public void init() {

      // Create event handler
      hSinCos = new CheckBoxHandler(this);

      // Create a new high-level panel
      JPanel pVert = new JPanel();
      pVert.setLayout(new BoxLayout(pVert, BoxLayout.Y_AXIS));
      add( pVert );

      // Add a blank plot
      pl = new JPlot2D();
      pl.setPreferredSize(new Dimension(400,400));
      pVert.add( pl );

      // Create a subordinate panel for the bottom
      JPanel pHoriz = new JPanel();
      pHoriz.setLayout(new BoxLayout(pHoriz, BoxLayout.X_AXIS));
      pVert.add( pHoriz );

      // Create the "Add sine" check box
      b1 = new JCheckBox("Add sine");
      b1.addActionListener( hSinCos );
      pHoriz.add( b1 );
      pHoriz.add( Box.createRigidArea(new Dimension(40,0)) );

      // Create the "Add cosine" check box
      b2 = new JCheckBox("Add cosine");
      b2.addActionListener( hSinCos );
      pHoriz.add( b2 );
```

Figure 13.31. The PlotSinCos application.

```java
      // Define arrays to hold the two curves to plot
      x  = new double[41];
      y1 = new double[41];
      y2 = new double[41];

      // Calculate a sine and a cosine wave
      for ( int i = 0; i < x.length; i++ ) {
         x[i]  = (i+1) * 2 * Math.PI / 40;
         y1[i] = Math.sin(x[i]);
         y2[i] = Math.cos(x[i]);
      }
   }

   // Method to display sine and cosine plots
   public void display() {

      // Remove old curves
      pl.removeAll();

      // Add sine curve
      if ( b1.isSelected() ) {
         pl.addCurve(x, y1);
         pl.setLineColor( Color.blue );
         pl.setLineWidth( 2.0f );
         pl.setLineStyle( JPlot2D.LINESTYLE_SOLID );
      }

      // Add cosine curve
      if ( b2.isSelected() ) {
         pl.addCurve(x, y2);
         pl.setLineColor( Color.red );
         pl.setLineWidth( 2.0f );
         pl.setLineStyle( JPlot2D.LINESTYLE_LONGDASH );
      }

      // Turn on grid
      pl.setGridState( JPlot2D.GRID_ON );

      // Repaint plot
      pl.repaint();
   }

   // Main method to create frame
   public static void main(String s[]) {

      // Create a frame to hold the application
      JFrame fr = new JFrame("PlotSinCos ...");
      fr.setSize(400,460);

      // Create a Window Listener to handle "close" events
      MyWindowListener l = new MyWindowListener();
      fr.addWindowListener(l);

      // Create and initialize a PlotSinCos object
```

Figure 13.31. (Continued).

```
        PlotSinCos ps = new PlotSinCos();
        ps.init();

        // Add the object to the center of the frame
        fr.getContentPane().add(ps, BorderLayout.CENTER);

        // Display the frame
        fr.setVisible( true );
    }
}

//*******************************************
//   Event handler
//*******************************************

class CheckBoxHandler implements ActionListener {
    private PlotSinCos ps;

    // Constructor
    public CheckBoxHandler( PlotSinCos ps1 ) {ps = ps1;}

    // Execute when an event occurs
    public void actionPerformed( ActionEvent e ) {
        String input = e.getActionCommand();

        if ( input.equals("Add sine") )
            ps.display();

        else if ( input.equals("Add cosine") )
            ps.display();
    }
}
```

Figure 13.31. (Continued).

the time when both checkboxes are ticked. Execute the program yourself to verify that it functions properly. Also, resize the application and see if the GUI components preserve their relative locations. ∎

SUMMARY

- The principal elements required to create a Java GUI are components, a container to hold them, a layout manager, and event handlers.
- The JLabel class creates a GUI component that displays read-only text.
- The JButton class creates a GUI component that implements push buttons. This class generates an ActionEvent containing the button label when a button is clicked.
- The JTextField class creates a GUI component that allows a user to display and edit text. This class generates an ActionEvent containing the field's text when the ENTER key is pressed.
- The JPasswordField class is identical to the JTextField class, except that asterisks are displayed in the field instead of the typed text.
- The JComboBox class creates a drop-down list of choices, allowing the user to select one of them by clicking with the mouse. It may optionally be set to allow the user to type text directly into the combo box. This class generates an ActionEvent when a selection is made.

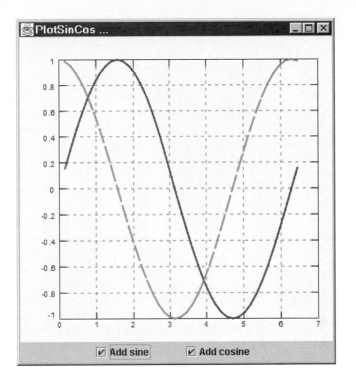

Figure 13.32. The GUI created by program `PlotSinCos`.

- The `JCheckBox` class creates a check box, which is a type of button that is either on or off. This class generates an `ActionEvent` when a state change occurs.
- The `JRadioButton` class creates a radio button, which is a type of check box designed to be grouped into sets. A `ButtonGroup` object is used to group together all the radio buttons which form a set. Only *one* button within a set of radio buttons may be on at any given time.
- A canvas is a blank component that can be used to display custom graphics. It can be created by subclassing `JComponent`.
- A layout manager is a helper class that is designed to automatically arrange GUI components within a container for presentation purposes. There are six standard layout managers: `BorderLayout`, `CardLayout`, `FlowLayout`, `BoxLayout`, `GridLayout`, and `GridBagLayout`.

SUMMARY OF GOOD PROGRAMMING PRACTICES

The following guidelines introduced in this chapter will help you to develop good programs:

1. To handle button events, use a class that implements the `ActionListener` interface and contains an `actionPerformed` method. Register an object from this class with each button, and code the `actionPerformed` method to do whatever is required when the button is pressed.

2. One `ActionListener` object can monitor many buttons, using the result of the `getActionCommand` method to determine the button that created a particular event.

3. Use `JTextFields` to accept single lines of input data from a user, or to display single lines of read-only data to the user.

4. Use `JPasswordFields` to accept input data from a user that you do not wish to have echoed to the screen, such as passwords.

5. Use `JComboBoxes` fields to make a single selection from a list of mutually exclusive choices.

6. Use `JCheckBoxes` to select the state of items represented by boolean variables, which can only be `true` or `false`.

7. Use `JRadioButtons` to select the state of a set of items represented by boolean variables, only one of which can be `true` at any time.

8. Use subclasses of `JComponent` to add graphical displays to a GUI.

TERMINOLOGY

`ActionEvent` class	`java.awt.event` package
`ActionListener` interface	`JButton` class
`actionPerformed` method	`JCheckBox` class
`BorderLayout` class	`JComboBox` class
`BoxLayout` class	`JFrame` class
`ButtonGroup` class	`JLabel` class
callback method	`JPanel` class
`CardLayout` class	`JPasswordField` class
check box	`JRadioButton` class
component	`JTextField` class
container	keyboard shortcut
event handler	layout manager
`FlowLayout` class	radio button
`GridBagLayout` class	`setLayout` method
`GridLayout` class	tool tips

Exercises

1. Explain the steps required to create a GUI in Java.

2. Modify the temperature conversion GUI of Example 13.1 to add a "thermometer." The thermometer should be a canvas with a drawing of a thermometer shape and a fluid level corresponding to the current temperature in degrees Celsius. The range of the thermometer should be 0°–100° C.

3. Convert the calculator GUI of Figure 13.29 into a fully functional calculator.

4. Create a GUI that uses a `JComboBox` to select the background color displayed by the GUI.

5. Write a class that displays a circle of random size and color, and calculates and displays its radius, diameter, area, and circumference. Use a blank component to draw the circle, and use read-only `JTextFields` to display the information about the circle. Include a button that can be clicked to cause the program to generate a new randomly selected circle. (*Note:* In determining the size of the circle, assume that there are 72 pixels per inch.)

6. Write a GUI program that plots the equation $y(x) = ax^2 + bx + c$. The program should use class `PlotXY` from Chapter 12 for the plot, and should have GUI elements to read the values of a, b, c, and the minimum and maximum x to plot. (*Note:* If you enhanced class `PlotXY` in Exercises 12.17 through 12.20, use the enhanced version of the class in this exercise.)

7. Modify the plot program of Example 13.3 to display zero, one, or two sinusoids of the form

$$y(t) = A \cos (2\pi ft + \theta) \qquad (13.3)$$

where A is the amplitude of the sinusoid, f is the frequency of the sinusoid in Hz, and θ is the phase of the sinusoid in degrees. This change should be accomplished by creating frequency, amplitude, and phase text fields for each of the sinusoids, as well as the check boxes to indicate whether each one will be displayed. Finally, you must create text fields to specify the minimum and maximum times to plot.

8. Modify the plot program of Example 13.3 to display up to four sinusoids of the form given in Equation (13.3). To do this, you should create a GUI element that allows the user to select the number of sinusoids to use in the input. The range of this input value should be 0–4. The GUI should have a combo box to specify the current sinusoid, plus a single set of frequency, amplitude, and phase text fields that refer to whichever sinusoid is currently selected.

9. Create three GUIs that place five buttons into a `JPanel` using the `BorderLayout`, `FlowLayout`, `GridLayout`, and `BoxLayout` layout managers. What do the resulting GUIs look like?

10. Create a GUI that displays a user-selected image. The GUI should contain a combo box (drop-down list) to select the desired image, and a label display the image. The Chapter 12 files available at the book's Web site include GIF files containing pictures of a dog, a cat, a cow, a pig, and a rabbit. The user should be able to select one of these pictures in the drop-down list, and the appropriate picture should be displayed.

11. Modify the GUI created in Exercise 10 to use a set of five radio buttons to select the image to display. The radio buttons should be lined up along the left-hand side of the GUI, with the image on the right-hand side of the GUI. What sort of layout manager(s) are required to create this GUI?

12. Write an application that draws 10 randomly sized shapes in randomly selected colors. The type of shape to draw (square, circle, ellipse, and so on) should be selectable through a `JComboBox`, and the display should be redrawn whenever the user presses a "Go" button on the GUI.

13. **Least-Squares Fit** Write a GUI-based application that reads a series of (x, y) values from a disk file, performs a linear least-squares fit on the values, and displays both the points and the least-squares fit line using class `JPlot2D`. The least-squares fit algorithm is described in Exercise 16 of Chapter 6, and the method developed there can be used with this application.

The GUI elements in the program should include a `JTextField` for the input file name, a `JButton` to read the file, two read-only `JTextFields` for the slope and intercept of the fitted line, and class `JPlot2D` to display the input points and the fitted results.

How many containers and which layout managers are required to create this GUI?

14

Additional GUI Components

This chapter continues the study of graphical user interfaces. First we will learn about some additional GUI components, plus how to create menus and dialog boxes for our applications. Then we will learn more about mouse events and event handling, including the use of adapter classes. The final topic is pluggable look and feel, which allows us to create a Java application that looks like a native application on any computer that it runs on.

14.1 ADDITIONAL GRAPHICAL USER INTERFACE COMPONENTS

The Swing GUI has an extremely rich set of graphical user interface components, more than can possibly be covered in this brief text. This section introduces two additional GUI components. It describes how to create and manipulate the components, as well as the types of events they can generate. The additional components discussed in this section are:

- Lists
- Tables

All of the components that we studied in Chapter 13 implemented the `ActionListener` interface and generated `ActionEvents`, so event handling was essentially the same in all cases. The components that we are introducing now implement different interfaces and generate different types of events, so the event handling for these components will be slightly different from what we learned about in Chapter 13.

14.1.1 Lists

A list is a class that displays a list of `Objects` (usually `Strings`) in a box and allows the user to select one or more of the items. Depending on the list initialization options, a

OBJECTIVES

- Be able to create and manipulate lists, tables, menus, and dialog boxes.
- Understand events, event interfaces, and adapter classes.
- Understand pluggable look and feel.

user can select one or many items from the list. Lists are implemented by the **JList** class, which also provides methods to determine which items are selected at any given time.

JList objects can operate in three possible modes: *single selection mode*, *single interval selection mode*, or *multiple interval selection mode*. Single selection mode is the default. In this mode, clicking on an object in the list automatically deselects the previously selected object in the list. Single interval selection mode allows a user to select a starting and ending object; all of those in between will be selected automatically. The user selects the first object in the interval by clicking on it, and selects the last object in the interval by clicking on it while holding down the space bar. Multiple interval selection mode allows a user to select any number of items from the list in any order. The user selects the first object by clicking on it, then selects each other object of interest by clicking on it while holding down the CTRL key.

A JList is created with one of the following constructors:

```
public JList();
public JList(Object[] o);
public JList(Vector v);
```

The first constructor creates an empty list. The second and third constructors create new lists containing either the elements in the Object array or the elements of the Vector. Selected methods from class JList are described in Table 14.1.

TABLE 14.1 Selected JList Methods

Method	Description
void addListSelectionListener (ListSelectionListener)	Adds the specified listener to receive ListSelectionEvents from this JList.
public void clearSelection()	Clears all item selections.
public int getMaxSelectionIndex()	Gets the index of the last selected value.
public int getMinSelectionIndex()	Gets the index of the first selected value.
public int getSelectedIndex()	Gets the first selected index.
public int[] getSelectedIndices()	Gets all selected indices.
public Object getSelectedValue()	Gets the first selected value.
public Object[] getSelectedValues()	Gets all of the selected values.
public int getSelectionMode()	Gets the selection mode for this JLIST. Legal values are SINGLE_SELECTION, SINGLE_INTERVAL_SELECTION, or MULTIPLE_INTERVAL_SELECTION.
public boolean isSelectedIndex(int i)	Returns true if the specified index is selected.
public boolean isSelectionEmpty()	Returns true if no selection has been made.
public void setPreferredSize(Dimension d)	Sets the preferred size of the list in pixels.
public void setSelectedIndex(int i)	Sets the selected index.
public void setSelectedIndices(int[] i)	Sets all of the selected indices.
public void setSelectedInterval(int i1, int i2)	Selects the specified interval from the list.
public void setSelectedValue(Object o, boolean scroll)	Selects the specified value from the list. If the boolean is true, the list will scroll to make the selection visible.
public void setSelectionMode(int m)	Sets the selection mode for this JList. Legal values are the constants SINGLE_SELECTION, SINGLE_INTERVAL_SELECTION, or MULTIPLE_INTERVAL_SELECTION. These constants are found in class ListSelectionModel.

By itself, a `JList` has no ability to scroll, so if the list of objects to be displayed is longer than the space available to display them, the objects that don't fit on the screen will not be visible or selectable. To make a list scrollable, you must wrap a **JScrollPane** around it. First create the `JList`, then create the `JScrollPane` with the `JList` as an argument of the constructor. Finally, the `JScrollPane` may be added to the container.

```
JList list = new JList(Object[] o);
JScrollPane scrollPane = new JScrollPane(list);
add( scrollPane );
```

The following code fragment illustrates how to create both nonscrollable and scrollable lists. The results of this program are shown in Figure 14.1.

```
// Partial list of states
String[] states = { "Alabama", "Alaska",
    "Arizona", "Arkansas", "California", "Colorado",
    "Connecticut", "Delaware", "Florida", "Georgia"};

// Create a non scrollable JList
JList l1 = new JList(states);
l1.setPreferredSize(new Dimension(200,100));
add( l1 );

// Add space between the two lists
add( Box.createRigidArea(new Dimension(15,0)) );

// Create a scrollable JList
JList l2 = new JList(states);
JScrollPane scrollPane = new JScrollPane(l2);
scrollPane.setPreferredSize(new Dimension(200,100));
add( scrollPane );
```

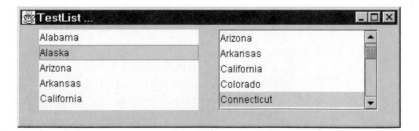

Figure 14.1. Sample `JList`s with and without scrollbars. Note that for the `JList` on the left, none of the states below California may be selected.

Lists often vary in size in different runs of a program, and sometimes they may grow to be very large. To ensure that you will always be able to access all parts of your lists, you should always use scrollable lists on all of your programs.

Use class `JList` to create lists of objects for display and selection in a GUI.

Always use scrollable `JLists` in all of your programs to ensure that a user can see all of the values in the list.

Events Associated with *JLists*

Class `JList` generates `ListSelectionEvents`. A `ListSelectionEvent` is produced each time that a user selects or deselects any item in the list. `ListSelectionEvents` include several methods that allow a program to recover information about the triggering event. The most important of these methods are listed in Table 14.2.

TABLE 14.2 `ListSelectionEvent` Methods

Method	Description
`public int getFirstIndex()`	Returns the index of the first item whose selection may have changed.
`public int getLastIndex()`	Returns the index of the last item whose selection may have changed.
`public Object getSource()`	Returns the `Object` from which this event originated.
`public boolean getValueIsAdjusting()`	Returns true if this event is one of a rapid series of events. This flag lets a program ignore the events until the last one in the series, and process only the final result.
`public String paramString()`	Returns a parameter string identifying this event. This method is useful for event logging and for debugging.

The *ListSelectionListener* Interface

`ListSelectionEvents` are processed by classes that implement the **ListSelectionListener interface**, which is defined in package `javax.swing.event`. This interface defines the single event-handling method **valueChanged**. When a `ListSelectionListener` object is registered with a `JLIST` using the method `addListSelectionListener`, the method `valueChanged` will be called automatically whenever a selection or deselection occurs in the list. (See Table 14.3.)

TABLE 14.3 `ListSelectionListener` Interface Method

Method	Description
`public void valueChanged(` `        ListSelectionEvent e)`	Method invoked when a `ListSelectionEvent` occurs.

EXAMPLE 14.1

Using Lists: Create a program that contains a list of all the states in the United States. The program should allow for single selection, single interval selection, and multiple interval selection. It should display the total 1980 population of all selected states in a text field.

SOLUTION

This program will require a `JList` to hold the state names, a `JComboBox` to select the list selection mode, a `JTextField` to display the total population, and a `JLabel` to label the results display. It will also be necessary to create listeners for the `JList` and `JComboBox` events.

1. **Determine the User Requirements**

    The user's requirement is to create a GUI-based program that will display all U.S. states in a list, and sum the total population of all selected states. The program must be capable of supporting the selection of single states, ranges of states, or several states selected in random order. Use the 1980 census figures for the population of the states.

    The inputs to this program are the names of the states and their population in 1980, plus a combo box specifying the selection mode of the list. These inputs will be hard-coded into arrays in the program. The output from the program is the sum of the population of all selected states.

2. **Analysis and Decomposition**

    This program requires three classes to function properly. The principal class (called `TestList1`) must contain separate methods (1) to generate the GUI display, (2) to update the selection mode when the user changes it, and (3) to add up and display the total population in all selected states.

    In addition, the program must contain two event-handling classes to handle the events generated by the `JList` and `JComboBox` input GUI elements. The `JList` will require a `ListSelectionListener` and the `JComboBox` will require an `ActionListener`.

3. **Detailed Design**

    The `init()` method of the `TestList1` class must create the GUI. It must lay out four graphical elements, consisting of one list, one combo box, one label, and one read-only text field. The elements should be organized with the list on top, the combo box below it, and the label and text field side by side below the combo box.

    This type of layout requires a total of two nested containers to create. The highest-level panel (`pV1`) uses a vertically oriented `BoxLayout`. That panel contains the list, the combo box, and a panel with a horizontally oriented `BoxLayout`. The label and the text field can be placed in the horizontally oriented panel, with a space between them (see Figure 14.2). The code to create this structure is shown below:

```
// Create a top-level vertical panel
JPanel pV = new JPanel();
pV.setLayout(new BoxLayout(pV, BoxLayout.Y_AXIS));
add( pV );

(Create and add scrollable list)
(Create and add combo box)

// Create a horizontal panel
JPanel pH = new JPanel();
```

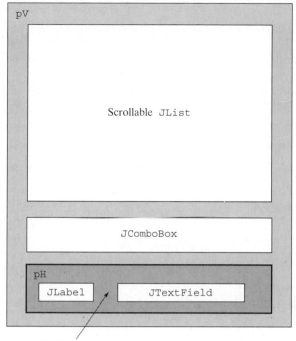

Figure 14.2. The structure of containers and layout managers required to create the GUI for the TestList1 program.

```
pH.setLayout(new BoxLayout(pH, BoxLayout.X_AXIS));
        pV.add( pH );

        (Create and add JLabel to horizontal panel)
        (Create and add JTextField to horizontal panel)
```

The code to create the four graphical elements is shown in Figure 14.3.

Method updateMode() must update the JList selection mode whenever the user changes it. This code must get the index of the selected selection mode and use method setSelectionMode to turn enable that mode. The code for this method is

```
int[] vals={ListSelectionModel.SINGLE_SELECTION,
        ListSelectionModel. SINGLE_INTERVAL_SELECTION,
        ListSelectionModel. MULTIPLE_INTERVAL_SELECTION };
list.setSelectionMode( vals[c1.getSelectedIndex()] );
```

Method updatePopulation() must update add up the population for each state that is selected. The code for this method is

```
int sum = 0;
for (int i = 0; i < states.length; i++ ) {
    if (list.isSelectedIndex(i)) {
        sum += pop[i];
    }
}
```

The two event handlers should detect events on the JComboBox and the JList and call the methods updateMode() and updatePopulation(). Note that the ListSelectionListener should not respond if a series of rapid changes are occurring—it should respond only to the final result, when things settle down. This is done by updating the GUI only when the method getValueIsAdjusting() returns false.

```
if ( ! e.getValueIsAdjusting() ) {
    tl.updatePopulation();
}
```

4. **Implementation: Convert Algorithms to Java Statements**

The resulting Java program is shown in Figure 14.3.

```
/*
   Purpose:
     This program sums the total 1980 population of all
     selected states and displays the results in a GUI.

   Record of revisions:
       Date          Programmer            Description of change
       ====          ==========            =====================
     08/01/2002    S. J. Chapman           Original code
*/
import java.awt.*;
import java.awt.event.*;
import javax.swing.*;
import javax.swing.event.*;
public class TestList1 extends JPanel {

   // Instance variables
   JComboBox c1;                // Selection mode combo box
   JLabel l1;                   // Label for total
   JList list;                  // List of states
   JScrollPane scrollPane;      // Scrollpane for list
   JTextField t1;               // Text field to display total
   ListHandler h1;              // List handler
   ComboHandler h2;             // Combo box handler

   // List of states
   String[] states = { "Alabama", "Alaska",
      "Arizona", "Arkansas", "California", "Colorado",
      "Connecticut", "Delaware", "District of Columbia",
      "Florida", "Georgia", "Hawaii", "Idaho", "Illinois",
      "Indiana", "Iowa", "Kansas", "Kentucky", "Louisiana",
      "Maine", "Maryland", "Massachusetts", "Michigan",
      "Minnesota", "Mississippi", "Missouri", "Montana",
      "Nebraska", "Nevada", "New Hampshire", "New Jersey",
      "New Mexico", "New York", "North Carolina",
      "North Dakota", "Ohio", "Oklahoma", "Oregon",
      "Pennsylvania", "Rhode Island", "South Carolina",
```

Figure 14.3. GUI-based program to calculate the total 1980 population of all selected states.

```
      "South Dakota", "Tennessee", "Texas", "Utah",
      "Vermont", "Virginia", "Washington", "West Virginia",
      "Wisconsin", "Wyoming" };
   // 1980 population
   int[] pop = {3893888,    401851,   2718425,   2286435, 23667565,
                2889735,   3107576,    594317,    638432,  9746342,
                5463105,    964691,    944038, 11426596,   5490260,
                2913808,   2364236,   3660257,   4206312,  1125027,
                4216975,   5737037,   9262078,   4075970,  2520638,
                4916759,    786690,   1569825,    800493,   920610,
                7364823,   1302981, 17558072,   5881813,   652717,
               10797624,   3025290,   2633149, 11863895,   947154,
                3121833,    690768,   4591120, 14229288,  1461037,
                 511456,   5346818,   4132180,   1950279,  4705521,
                 469557 };

   // Initialization method
   public void init() {

      // Create event handlers
      h1 = new ListHandler( this );
      h2 = new ComboHandler( this );

      // Create a top-level vertical panel
      JPanel pV = new JPanel();
      pV.setLayout(new BoxLayout(pV, BoxLayout.Y_AXIS));
      add( pV );

      // Create a scrollable JList
      list = new JList(states);
      list.addListSelectionListener( h1 );
      scrollPane = new JScrollPane(list);
      scrollPane.setPreferredSize(new Dimension(200,100));
      pV.add( scrollPane );

      // Add space
      pV.add( Box.createRigidArea(new Dimension(0,10)) );

      // Create a Combo Box specifying the mode of the list
      String[] s = {"Single Selection","Single Interval Selection",
                    "Multiple Interval Selection"};
      c1 = new JComboBox(s);
      c1.addActionListener( h2 );
      pV.add( c1 );

      // Add space
      pV.add( Box.createRigidArea(new Dimension(0,10)) );

      // Create a horizontal panel
      JPanel pH = new JPanel();
      pH.setLayout(new BoxLayout(pH, BoxLayout.X_AXIS));
      pV.add( pH );
```

Figure 14.3.   (Continued).

```java
        // Add a text field for the results
        l1 = new JLabel("Total");
        pH.add( l1 );
        pH.add( Box.createRigidArea(new Dimension(5,0)) );
        t1 = new JTextField(10);
        t1.setEditable( false );
        pH.add( t1 );
    }

    // Method to set selection mode
    public void updateMode() {

        int[] vals={ListSelectionModel.SINGLE_SELECTION,
                    ListSelectionModel.SINGLE_INTERVAL_SELECTION,
                    ListSelectionModel.MULTIPLE_INTERVAL_SELECTION };
        list.setSelectionMode( vals[c1.getSelectedIndex()] );
        updatePopulation();
    }

    // Method to add up all selected states
    public void updatePopulation() {
        int sum = 0;
        for (int i = 0; i < states.length; i++ ) {
            if (list.isSelectedIndex(i)) {
                sum += pop[i];
            }
        }
        t1.setText("" + sum );
        t1.repaint();
    }

    // Main method to create frame
    (not shown to save space)
class ComboHandler implements ActionListener {
    private TestList1 tl;

    // Constructor
    public ComboHandler( TestList1 t ) { tl = t; }

    // Execute when an event occurs
    public void actionPerformed( ActionEvent e ) {

        // List mode has changed
        tl.updateMode();
    }
}
class ListHandler implements ListSelectionListener {
    private TestList1 tl;

    // Constructor
    public ListHandler( TestList1 t ) { tl = t; }

    // Execute when an event occurs
```

Figure 14.3. (Continued).

```
public void valueChanged( ListSelectionEvent e ) {

    // Update after value stabilizes
    if ( ! e.getValueIsAdjusting() ) {
       tl.updatePopulation();
    }
  }
}
```

Figure 14.3. (Continued).

5. **Testing**

To test this program, we will execute it and examine the results. Figure 14.4 shows typical results for single selection mode, single interval mode, and multiple interval mode. Execute this program for yourself and experiment with the operation of the list. ■

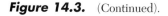

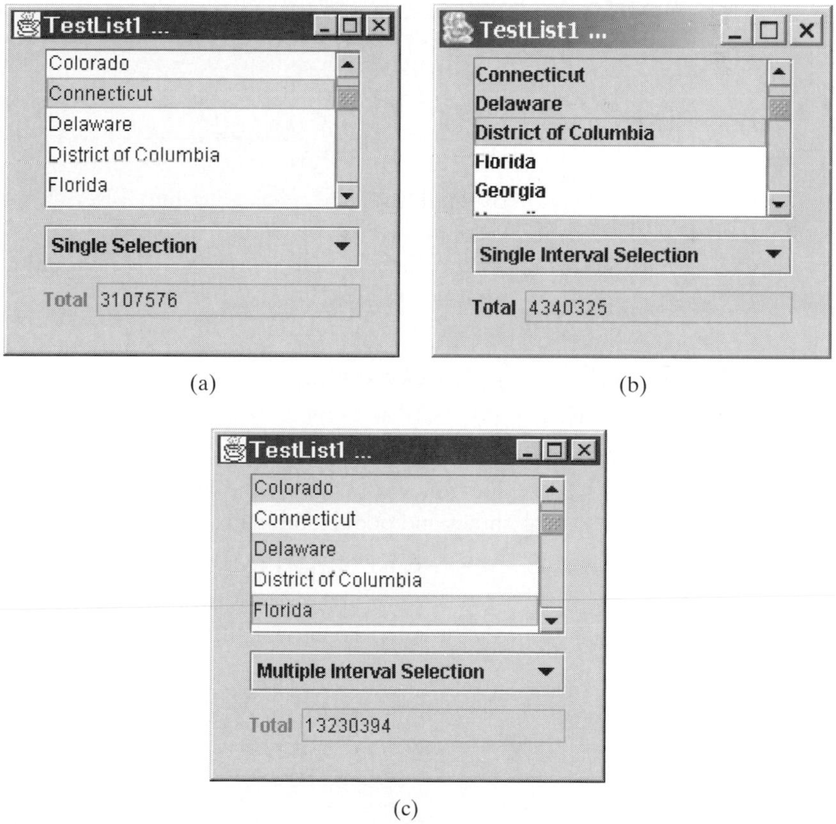

(a)   (b)

(c)

Figure 14.4. (a) Example results for single selection mode. (b) Example results for single interval selection mode. (c) Example results for multiple interval selection mode.

14.1.2 Tables

A table is a class that displays a table of Objects. The class can be customized to allow the objects in different columns to be displayed in different formats and to allow the values in the table to be dynamically edited by the user. These details may be found in the Java 2 SDK documentation. In this text, we will restrict ourselves to using a table as a way to display data only, not to modify it. Be aware that tables have many more capabilities than are demonstrated here.

A Java table is implemented by class **JTable**. Some of the simpler constructors for this class are shown below:

```
public JTable();
public JTable(Object[][] data, Object[] headings);
public JTable(Vector data, Vector headings);
```

The first constructor creates an empty list. The second and third constructors create new tables containing either the elements in the Object 2D array data or the elements of the Vector data. The array headings or the vector headings contains the column headings for each column of the table. Selected methods from class JTable are described in Table 14.2.

TABLE 14.2 Selected JTable Methods

Method	Description
public void setPreferredScrollableViewportSize(Dimension d)	Sets the preferred size when viewed through a JScrollPane.
public void setPreferredSize(Dimension d)	Sets the preferred size of the list in pixels.

By itself, a JTable has no ability to scroll, so if the list of objects to be displayed is longer than the space available to display them, the objects that don't fit on the screen will not be visible. To make a list scrollable, you must wrap a **JScrollPane** around it.

First create the JTable, then create the JScrollPane with the JTable as an argument of the constructor. Finally, the JScrollPane may be added to the container.

```
JTable table = new JTable(data, columnNames);
JScrollPane scrollPane = new JScrollPane(table);
add( scrollPane );
```

The following code fragment illustrates how to create a scrollable table containing state names and population figures. The results of this program are shown in Figure 14.4.

```
// Initialization method.  This method creates a
// table of 1980 population by state.
public void init() {

// Convert population figures into objects
String[] popString = new String[ pop.length ];
for ( int i = 0; i < pop.length; i++ ) {
    popString[i] = Fmt.sprintf("%10d", pop[i]);
}

// Create the two-dimensional array of objects
// to pass to the table
Object[][] data = new Object[states.length][2];
for ( int i = 0; i < states.length; i++ ) {
    data[i][0] = states[i];
    data[i][1] = popString[i];
}
```

```
                    // Create column headers
                    String[] headers = { "State", "1980 Population" };

                    // Create a scrollable JTable
                    table = new JTable(data,headers);
                    scrollPane = new JScrollPane(table);
                    scrollPane.setPreferredSize(new Dimension(250,200));
                    add( scrollPane );
                }
```

Tables can be greatly enhanced by modifying the `TableModel` used to represent the data displayed in the table. For example, a custom `TableModel` would allow the table in Figure 14.5 to display the population numbers right-aligned. Refer to the `JTable` and `TableModel` descriptions in the Java 2 SDK for details about creating custom table models.

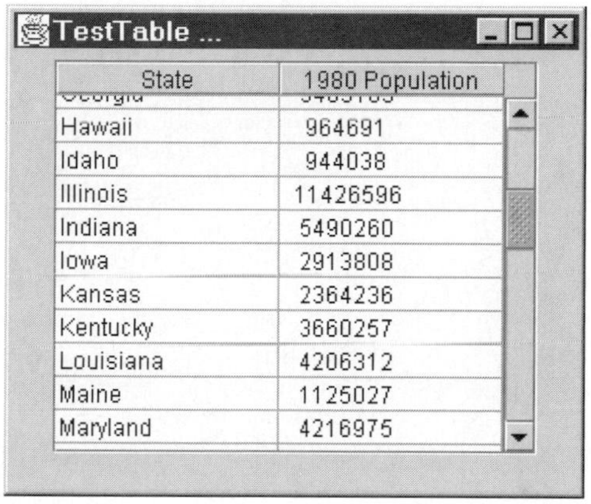

Figure 14.5. A simple table showing 1980 population by state.

GOOD PROGRAMMING PRACTICE

Use `JTable`s to display tabular data.

14.2   MENUS

Menus can be added to Java GUIs. In general, a menu allows a user to select actions without additional components appearing on the GUI display. Menus are useful for selecting less commonly used options without cluttering up the GUI with a lot of extra buttons.

There are two type of menus, pull-down and pop-up. Pull-down menus are attached to a bar at the top of a container, and they open downward whenever a user clicks on the menu. Pop-up menus are those that "pop up" over a component when a user right-clicks the mouse over that component.

The items in a Java menu are just specially shaped buttons that become visible when you click on a menu bar. Because they are buttons, we already know most of what we need to know to use them. Like all buttons, they generate `ActionEvents` when a mouse clicks on them. Also, it is possible to define a keyboard accelerator for a menu item.

There are three types of menu items, corresponding to the three types of buttons:

- **Menu items**—these behave just like push buttons
- **Check box menu items**—these behave just like check boxes
- **Radio button menu items**—these behave just like radio buttons

14.2.1 Menu Components

Menus are composed of five basic components: `JMenuBars`, `JMenus`, `JMenuItems`, `JCheckBoxMenuItems`, and `JRadioButtonMenuItems` (see Figures 14.6 and 14.7). A **menu bar** is the bar across the top of the frame to which the menus are attached. A

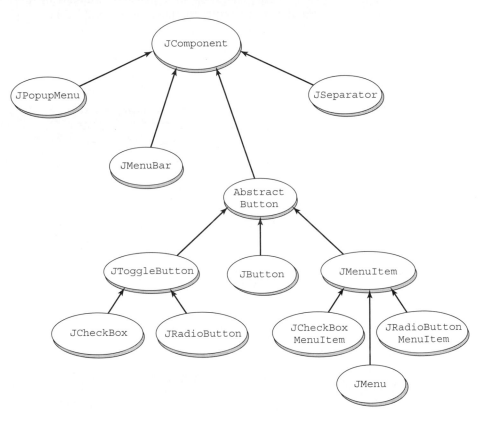

Figure 14.6.   The inheritance hierarchy of Swing menu components. Note that menu items inherit from `AbstractButton`, so they are effectively buttons that appear when the menu bar is clicked.

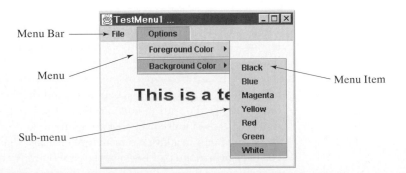

Figure 14.7.   A Java GUI with menus, showing a menu bar, menus, submenus, and menu items.

menu is an individual list of items that is pulled down from the menu bar when the user clicks on the menu name. A **menu item** is an object inside a menu that, when selected, causes an action to be performed. (Note that a menu item can be a **sub-menu**, which contains menu items of its own.) Finally, **check-box menu items** and **radio-button menu items** function like check boxes and radio buttons, respectively.

A menu bar is created with class `JMenuBar`. The default constructor is

```
public JMenuBar();
```

This constructor creates a blank menu bar across the top of a compatible container (a `JFrame`, `JApplet`, `JDialog`, `JRootPane`, or `JInternalFrame`). The menu bar is attached to the container using the container's `setJMenuBar` method. Selected methods from class `JMenuBar` are described in Table 14.3.

TABLE 14.3   Selected `JMenuBar` Methods

Method	Description
`public void add(JMenu m)`	Adds a `JMenu` to the `JMenuBar`.
`public JMenu getHelpMenu()`	Gets the help menu on the menu bar.
`public JMenu getMenu(int i)`	Gets the specified menu.
`public int getMenuCount()`	Gets the number of menus on the menu bar.
`public void setHelpMenu(JMenu m)`	Sets the help menu on this menu bar to be the specified menu.

A `JMenu` is created with the constructor

```
public JMenu(String label);
```

This constructor creates a new empty menu with the name `label`. The menu is attached to the menu bar using the menu bar's `add` method. Selected methods from class `JMenu` are described in Table 14.4.

TABLE 14.4   Selected `JMenu` Methods

Method	Description
`public JMenuItem add(JMenuItem mi)`	Adds the specified menu item to this menu. (*Note:* This could be another menu.)
`public void addSeparator()`	Adds a separator line to the menu at the current position.
`public JMenuItem getItem(int index)`	Gets the item located at the specified index of this menu.
`public int getItemCount()`	Gets the number of items in this menu.
`public void insert(JMenuItem mi,int pos)`	Inserts the specified menu item at the given position.
`public String paramString()`	Gets the parameter string representing the state of this menu.
`public void remove(Component c)`	Removes the specified component from this menu.

A `JMenuItem` works like a push button—it generates an `ActionEvent` when a mouse click occurs on it. It is created with one of the following constructors:

```
public JMenuItem(String label);
public JMenuItem(Icon image);
public JMenuItem(String label, Icon image);
public JMenuItem(String label, int mnemonic);
```

The first constructor creates a new menu item with a text label. The second constructor creates a new menu item with an image label. The third constructor creates a new menu item with both text and an image on the label. The final constructor creates a new menu item with a text label, and also creates a keyboard shortcut for the menu item. The menu item is attached to a menu using the menu's `add` method. The most important methods for `JMenuItem` are the same as those for `JButton`, which are given in Table 13.3.

A `JCheckBoxMenuItem` works like a `JCheckBox`—it has two states (ON/OFF or TRUE/FALSE), and the state is toggled whenever a mouse click occurs on it. Note that this component generates an `ActionEvent` when a mouse click occurs on it, just as a `JCheckBox` does. It is created with one of the following constructors:

```
public JCheckBoxMenuItem( String s );
public JCheckBoxMenuItem( String s, boolean state );
public JCheckBoxMenuItem( Icon Image );
public JCheckBoxMenuItem( Icon image, boolean state );
public JCheckBoxMenuItem( String s, Icon image );
public JCheckBoxMenuItem( String s, Icon image, boolean state );
```

In these constructors, `s` is the text label for the check-box menu item, `image` is the image to display on the check-box menu item, and `state` is the initial ON/OFF state of the check-box menu item. If `state` is absent from a constructor, then the new check-box menu item defaults to OFF. The methods in class `JCheckBoxMenuItem` are essentially identical to those in `JCheckBox`, which are described in Table 13.8.

A `JRadioButtonMenuItem` works like a `JRadioButton`. Each radio-button menu item has two states (ON/OFF or TRUE/FALSE), and many radio buttons are grouped together into a `ButtonGroup`. Only one of the radio-button menu items in a `ButtonGroup` may be ON at any given time. If one is turned ON, the others are automatically turned OFF. Note that this component generates an `ActionEvent` when a mouse click occurs on it, just as a `JRadioButton` does. It is created with one of the following constructors:

```
public JRadioButtonMenuItem( String s );
public JRadioButtonMenuItem( String s, boolean state );
public JRadioButtonMenuItem( Icon Image );
public JRadioButtonMenuItem( Icon image, boolean state );
public JRadioButtonMenuItem( String s, Icon image );
public JRadioButtonMenuItem( String s, Icon image, boolean state );
```

In these constructors, `s` is the text label for the radio-button menu item, `image` is the image to display on the radio-button menu item, and `state` is the initial ON/OFF state of the radio-button menu item. If `state` is absent from a constructor, then the new radio button defaults to OFF. The methods in class `JRadioButtonMenuItem` are the same as those in class `JRadioButton`, which are described in Table 13.8.

14.2.2 Events Associated With Menu Components

All menu item classes generate `ActionEvents`, just as buttons do. An `ActionEvent` is produced each time a user makes a mouse click on a menu item. This event can be handled by a class that implements the ActionListener interface. When the menu item is selected, the actionPerformed method of the listener class is called.

Figure 14.8 shows a simple application with menus. This application displays a test string and allows the user to change its foreground and background colors using menu selections.

```java
// This program tests menus.
import java.awt.*;
import java.awt.geom.*;
import java.awt.event.*;
import javax.swing.*;
public class TestMenu1 extends JPanel {

    // Instance variables
    private String colorNames[] = {"Black", "Blue",
        "Magenta", "Yellow", "Red", "Green", "White"};
    private Color colorValues[] = {Color.black,
        Color.blue, Color.magenta, Color.yellow,
        Color.red, Color.green, Color.white};

    private ActionListener hBg, hFg, hEnable, hExit;
                                    // Action listeners
    private JMenuBar bar;          // Menu bar
    private JMenu fileMenu;        // File menu
    private JMenu optionsMenu;     // Options menu
    private JMenu fgColorMenu;     // Foreground Color menu
    private JMenu bgColorMenu;     // Background Color menu
    private JCheckBoxMenuItem enable; // Enable Options menu
    private JMenuItem exit;        // Exit "menu" item
    private JMenuItem fgColors[]; // Foreground colors menu items
    private JMenuItem bgColors[]; // Background colors menu items

    // Initialization method
    public void init() {

        // Create event handlers
        hBg     = new BgColorHandler( this );
        hFg     = new FgColorHandler( this );
        hEnable = new EnableHandler( this );
        hExit   = new ExitHandler();

        // Set foreground color
        setForeground( Color.black );

        // Set background color
        setBackground( Color.white );

        // Create menu bar
        bar = new JMenuBar();
```

Figure 14.8. A simple application that supports menus.

```
      // Create "File" menu
      fileMenu = new JMenu("File");
      fileMenu.setMnemonic('f');

      // Create and add "Enable Options" checkbox menu item
      enable = new JCheckBoxMenuItem("Enable Options", true);
      enable.addActionListener(hEnable);
      fileMenu.add( enable );

      // Create and add "Exit" menu item
      exit = new JMenuItem( "Exit" );
      exit.addActionListener(hExit);
      exit.setMnemonic('x');
      fileMenu.add ( exit );

      // Create "Options" menu
      optionsMenu = new JMenu("Options");
      fileMenu.setMnemonic('o');

      // Create color sub menus and add to Options menu
      fgColorMenu = new JMenu("Foreground Color");
      bgColorMenu = new JMenu("Background Color");
      optionsMenu.add ( fgColorMenu );
      optionsMenu.addSeparator();
      optionsMenu.add ( bgColorMenu );

      // Create foreground colors list
      fgColors = new JMenuItem[ colorNames.length ];
      for ( int i = 0; i < colorNames.length; i++ ) {
         fgColors[i] = new JMenuItem( colorNames[i] );
         fgColorMenu.add ( fgColors[i] );
         fgColors[i].addActionListener(hFg);
      }

      // Create background colors list
      bgColors = new JMenuItem[ colorNames.length ];
      for ( int i = 0; i < colorNames.length; i++ ) {
         bgColors[i] = new JMenuItem( colorNames[i] );
         bgColorMenu.add ( bgColors[i] );
         bgColors[i].addActionListener(hBg);
      }

      // Add the menus to the menu bar
      bar.add ( fileMenu );
      bar.add ( optionsMenu );
   }
   // Update foreground color
   public void updateFgColor( String color ) {

      for ( int i = 0; i < colorNames.length; i++ ) {
         if ( color.equals( colorNames[i]) ) {
            setForeground ( colorValues[i] );
         }
      }
```

Figure 14.8. (Continued).

```
        repaint();
    }
    // Update background color
    public void updateBgColor( String color ) {
        for ( int i = 0; i < colorNames.length; i++ ) {
            if ( color.equals( colorNames[i]) ) {
                setBackground ( colorValues[i] );
            }
        }
        repaint();
    }
    // Update options menu state
    public void updateOptionsMenuState() {
        if (enable.isSelected() )
            optionsMenu.setEnabled(true);
        else
            optionsMenu.setEnabled(false);
    }
    public void paintComponent ( Graphics g ) {
        // Cast the graphics object to Graph2D
        Graphics2D g2 = (Graphics2D) g;

        // Set rendering hints to improve display quality
        g2.setRenderingHint(RenderingHints.KEY_ANTIALIASING,
                            RenderingHints.VALUE_ANTIALIAS_ON);

        // Set background color
        Dimension size = getSize();
        g2.setColor( getBackground() );
        g2.fill(new Rectangle2D.Double(0,0,size.width,size.height));

        // Define a font ...
        Font f = new Font("SansSerif",Font.BOLD,24);

        // Display fonts
        g2.setFont(f);
        g2.setColor( getForeground() );
        g2.drawString("This is a test!",50,90);
    }
    // Main method to create frame
    public static void main(String s[]) {
        // Create a frame to hold the application
        JFrame fr = new JFrame("TestMenu1 ...");
        fr.setSize(300,220);

        // Create a Window Listener to handle "close" events
        MyWindowListener l = new MyWindowListener();
        fr.addWindowListener(l);
```

Figure 14.8.   (Continued).

```java
        // Create and initialize a TestMenu1 object
        TestMenu1 tm = new TestMenu1();
        tm.init();

        // Add the menu bar to the frame
        fr.setJMenuBar( tm.bar );

        // Add the object to the center of the frame
        fr.getContentPane().add(tm, BorderLayout.CENTER);

        // Display the frame
        fr.setVisible( true );
    }
}
class FgColorHandler implements ActionListener {
    private TestMenu1 tm1;

    // Constructor
    public FgColorHandler( TestMenu1 t ) {tm1 = t;}

    // Execute when an event occurs
    public void actionPerformed( ActionEvent e ) {
        tm1.updateFgColor(e.getActionCommand());
    }
}
class BgColorHandler implements ActionListener {
    private TestMenu1 tm1;

    // Constructor
    public BgColorHandler( TestMenu1 t ) {tm1 = t;}

    // Execute when an event occurs
    public void actionPerformed( ActionEvent e ) {
        tm1.updateBgColor(e.getActionCommand());
    }
}
class EnableHandler implements ActionListener {
    private TestMenu1 tm1;

    // Constructor
    public EnableHandler( TestMenu1 t ) {tm1 = t;}

    // Execute when an event occurs
    public void actionPerformed( ActionEvent e ) {
      tm1.updateOptionsMenuState();
    }
}
class ExitHandler implements ActionListener {
    // Execute when an event occurs
    public void actionPerformed( ActionEvent e ) {
        System.exit(0);
    }
}
```

Figure 14.8. (Continued).

This application has two menus on a menu bar, a "File" menu and an "Options" menu. The "File" menu contains two menu items labeled "Enable Options" and "Exit". The "Enable Options" menu item is a `JCheckBoxMenuItem` that controls whether or not the "Options" menu is enabled. When it is selected, the program generates an `ActionEvent` which is handled by the `actionPerformed` method of `EnableHandler`, which calls `updateOptionsMenuState()` to update the "Options" menu state. When the "Exit" menu item is selected, the program generates an `ActionEvent` which is handled by the `ExitHandler`, and the `ExitHandler` shuts down the program.

The "Options" menu contains two submenus, one for the foreground color and one for the background color. If one of these menu items is selected, the corresponding submenu is displayed, and the user can select a color. When a color is selected, the generates an `ActionEvent`, which is handled by the `actionPerformed` method of `fgColorHandler` or `bgColorHandler`, and the corresponding handler updates the display colors.

Note that this program demonstrates the use of keyboard shortcuts as well as the ability to enable and disable menus.

When this program is executed, it produces the GUI shown in Figure 14.9. Execute the program and try changing the foreground and background colors with the menu selections.

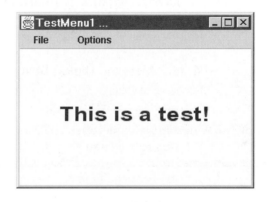

Figure 14.9. The GUI produced by the `TestMenu1` application.

GOOD PROGRAMMING PRACTICE

Use menus to display less frequently used options such as opening and saving files. This keeps infrequently used options from using up space in the GUI.

14.3   DIALOG BOXES

A **dialog box** is a special type of container that is used to get information from a user or to provide error or warning messages. It is a separate window similar to a frame but is much easier to use. Dialog boxes are normally popped up for some specific purpose, then made invisible or destroyed immediately after they are used.

Dialog boxes may be **modal** or nonmodal. A modal dialog box does not allow any other window in the application to be accessed until it is dismissed, while a nonmodal dialog box does not block access to other windows. We will discuss only modal dialog boxes. They are typically used for warning and error messages that need urgent attention and cannot be ignored.

Dialogs may be created with the `JDialog` class, but Java predefines several easy-to-use dialog box types as `static` methods in the `JOptionPane` class. These are very easy to use, so generally you should use them instead of working with `JDialog` directly. (In fact, we have been using these `JOptionPane` dialog boxes since Chapter 3 for GUI-based input and output.) There are several different standard dialog boxes which can be used to display messages or ask for information. The standard types of dialogs include:

- **showMessageDialog**—This dialog displays a modal dialog box with one button, which is labeled "OK". You can easily specify the message, icon, and title that the dialog displays.
- **showConfirmDialog**—This dialog displays a modal dialog box with two buttons, labeled "Yes" and "No", or three buttons labeled "Yes", "No", and "Cancel".
- **showInputDialog**—This dialog displays a modal dialog box that gets a string from the user. An input dialog displays either a text field for the user to type into or a fixed set of options in an uneditable combo box.
- **showOptionDialog**—This dialog displays a modal dialog box with the specified buttons, icons, message, title, and so on. You can use this method to change the text that appears on the buttons of standard dialogs and to perform many other kinds of customization. It is the most flexible dialog box option.

Only the first three types of dialog boxes are discussed here, since they are usually sufficient for simple programs. The details of all types of dialog boxes may be found in the description of class `JOptionPane` in the Java 2 SDK documentation.

14.3.1 Message Dialog Boxes

Message dialog boxes are used to display a message only. The `static` methods used to create a message dialog box are

```
void JOptionPane.showMessageDialog(Component parentComponent,
        Object message, String title, int messageType);
void JOptionPane.showMessageDialog(Component parentComponent,
        Object message, String title, int messageType, Icon icon);
```

The parameters in these methods are defined in Table 14.5.

TABLE 14.5 Parameters for showxxxxDialogs

Method	Description
`Component parentComponent`	Determines the frame in which the dialog will be displayed. If null, a default frame will be created.
`Object message`	The message to display (usually a `String`).
`String title`	The title string for the dialog box.
`int messageType`	The type of message to be displayed: `ERROR_MESSAGE`, `INFORMATION_MESSAGE`, `WARNING_MESSAGE`, `QUESTION_MESSAGE`, or `PLAIN_MESSAGE`. (All constants are defined in class `JOptionPane`.)
`int optionType`	The type of options to be offered to user: `YES_NO_OPTION`, or `YES_NO_CANCEL_OPTION`.
`Icon icon`	An icon to display in the dialog box. If not present, appropriate default icons are displayed for error, information, warning, and question message boxes.
`Object[] selectionValues`	An array of possible choices.
`Object initialSelectionValue`	The default choice in the input box.

The program shown in Figure 14.10 creates example message dialog boxes. The results are shown in Figure 14.11. (Note that the Question Message Box is rather stupid. It asks a question but does not allow the user to reply. I cannot figure out any use for this particular option.)

```
// This program tests message dialog boxes.
import javax.swing.JOptionPane;
public class TestMessageDialog {

   // Main method to create frame
   public static void main(String s[]) {

      // Create error message.
      JOptionPane.showMessageDialog(null,
            "This is an error message!", "Error",
            JOptionPane.ERROR_MESSAGE);

      // Create warning message.
      JOptionPane.showMessageDialog(null,
            "This is a warning message!", "Warning",
            JOptionPane.WARNING_MESSAGE);

      // Create information message.
      JOptionPane.showMessageDialog(null,
            "This is an information message!", "Information",
            JOptionPane.INFORMATION_MESSAGE);

      // Create question message.
      JOptionPane.showMessageDialog(null,
            "Are you sure?", "Question",
            JOptionPane.QUESTION_MESSAGE);

      // Create plain message.
      JOptionPane.showMessageDialog(null,
            "This is a plain message.", "Plain",
            JOptionPane.PLAIN_MESSAGE);

      System.exit(0);
   }
}
```

Figure 14.10. A program to test message dialog boxes.

14.3.2 Confirm Dialog Boxes

Confirm dialog boxes allow a user to confirm or reject an action. The `static` methods used to create an input dialog box are

```
String JOptionPane.showConfirmDialog(Component parentComponent,
            Object message, String title, int optionType);
int JOptionPane.showConfirmDialog(Component parentComponent,
            Object message, String title, int optionType,
            int messageType);
```

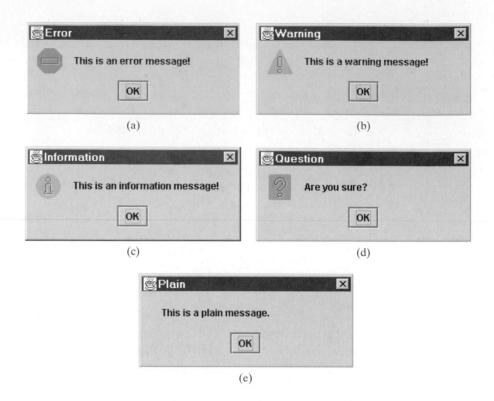

Figure 14.11. (a) Error dialog box. (b) Warning dialog box. (c) Information dialog box. (d) Question dialog box. (e) Plain dialog box.

```
int JOptionPane.showConfirmDialog(Component parentComponent,
               Object message, String title, int optionType,
               int messageType, Icon icon);
```

The parameters in these methods are defined in Table 14.5. These methods return an int to the calling method, which will have one of the following values: YES_OPTION, NO_OPTION, CANCEL_OPTION, or CLOSED_OPTION. The YES_OPTION is returned if the user clicks the "Yes" button, and so forth. The CLOSED_OPTION is returned if the user closes the dialog box without making a selection; it should usually be treated as a "Cancel" or "No".

The program shown in Figure 14.12 creates example confirmation dialog boxes. The results are shown in Figure 14.13.

```
// This program tests confirm dialog boxes.
import javax.swing.JOptionPane;
public class TestConfirmDialog {

    // Main method to create frame
    public static void main(String s[]) {

        int res;          // Result

        // Create YES/NO message
        res = JOptionPane.showConfirmDialog(null,
```

Figure 14.12. A program to test confirmation dialog boxes.

```
                        "Are you sure you want to delete this file?",
                        "Confirm File Delete",
                        JOptionPane.YES_NO_OPTION,
                        JOptionPane.QUESTION_MESSAGE);

        // What happened?
        if ( res == JOptionPane.YES_OPTION )
            System.out.println("Result = YES");
        else if ( res == JOptionPane.NO_OPTION )
            System.out.println("Result = NO");
        else if ( res == JOptionPane.CANCEL_OPTION )
            System.out.println("Result = Cancel");
        else if ( res == JOptionPane.CLOSED_OPTION )
            System.out.println("Result = Closed Window");
        else
            System.out.println("Unknown Result = " + res);

        // Create YES/NO/CANCEL message
        res = JOptionPane.showConfirmDialog(null,
                "Overwrite the existing file?",
                "Warning",
                JOptionPane.YES_NO_CANCEL_OPTION,
                JOptionPane.WARNING_MESSAGE);

        // What happened?
        if ( res == JOptionPane.YES_OPTION )
            System.out.println("Result = YES");
        else if ( res == JOptionPane.NO_OPTION )
            System.out.println("Result = NO");
        else if ( res == JOptionPane.CANCEL_OPTION )
            System.out.println("Result = Cancel");
        else if ( res == JOptionPane.CLOSED_OPTION )
            System.out.println("Result = Closed Window");
        else
            System.out.println("Unknown Result = " + res);

        System.exit(0);
    }
}
```

Figure 14.12.   (Continued).

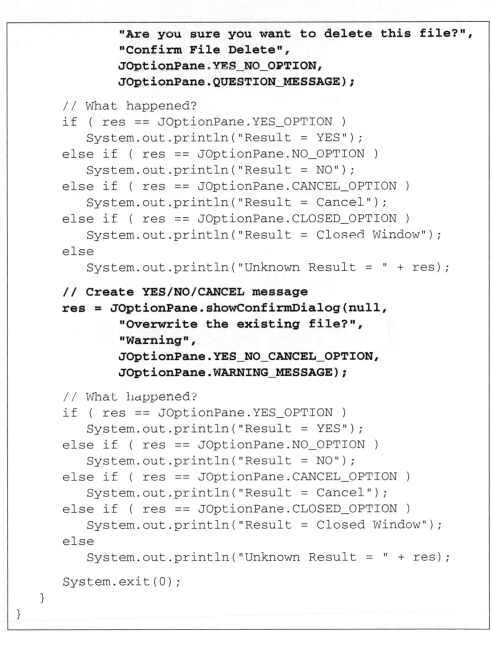

Figure 14.13.   (a) Yes/No confirmation dialog box. (b) Yes/No/Cancel confirmation dialog box.

14.3.3 Input Dialog Boxes

Input dialog boxes allow a user to input values into a text field or to select an option from a combo box. The `static` methods used to create an input dialog box are

```
String JOptionPane.showInputDialog(Object message);
String JOptionPane.showInputDialog(Component parentComponent,
               Object message);
String JOptionPane.showInputDialog(Component parentComponent,
               Object message, String title, int messageType);
Object JOptionPane.showInputDialog(Component parentComponent,
               Object message, String title, int messageType,
               Icon icon, Object[] selectionValues,
               Object initialSelectionValue );
```

The parameters in these methods are defined in Table 14.5. The first three methods return a `String`, and the last one returns an `Object`. We have been using the version of this dialog box that returns a `String` since Chapter 3. The use of additional versions of these methods will be demonstrated in end-of-chapter Exercise 14.2.

GOOD PROGRAMMING PRACTICE

Use dialog boxes to display error and warning messages to the user, to confirm irrevocable actions such as overwriting files, and to get input values from a user.

14.4 INTERFACES AND ADAPTER CLASSES

In Chapters 13 and 14, we learned that the Java event model is based on specifically defined interfaces. For each type of event, Java includes an interface that *defines the names and parameters* of the methods that will be called to handle that event. For example, a `JButton` creates an `ActionEvent` when it is clicked, and the `ActionEvent` is handled by a class that implements the `ActionListener` interface, which must contain an `actionPerformed` method. Similarly, a `JList` creates a `ListSelectionEvent` when it is clicked, and the `ListSelectionEvent` is handled by a class that implements the `ListSelectionListener` interface, which must contain a `valueChanged` method.

There are many types of events and corresponding interfaces in Java, and a very brief summary of some them can be found in Table 14.6. This table lists the two high-level events that we have used so far, plus mouse and window events. The inheritance hierarchy of these interfaces and events is shown in Figures 14.14 and 14.15, respectively.

Note that some interfaces include many different methods to represent different actions that can be performed on an object. A very important example is the `WindowEvent`, which can be created by objects of the `Window` class and its subclasses, including `JFrame`. Note that there are separate methods for all of the different actions that can be performed with a window, including activating, deactivating, opening, closing, iconifying, and deiconifying.

Complex interfaces such as the `WindowListener` interface present a problem for a programmer, because *if a class implements an interface, it must implement every method in the interface*, even if the programmer has no intention of ever using some of the methods. For example, suppose a programmer needs to use the `windowClosing` method of the `WindowListener` interface to ensure that a program shuts down properly. In order to do so, he or she must actually implement all seven methods in the interface, even though six of them will do nothing! An example of such a listener class is shown in Figure 14.16.

TABLE 14.6 Selected Java Events and Interfaces

Event	Interface	Method(s)	Description
ActionEvent	ActionListener	actionPerformed	Indicates that a high-level event has been performed, such as a button click.
ListSelectionEvent	ListSelectionListener	valueChanged	Indicates that a selection has been made from a list.
MouseEvent	MouseListener	mousePressed mouseClicked mouseReleased mouseEntered mouseExited	Indicates that the specific mouse selection actions have occurred.
MouseEvent	MouseMotionListener	mouseDragged mouseMoved	Indicates that the specific mouse motion actions have occurred.
WindowEvent	WindowListener	windowActivated windowClosed windowClosing windowDeactivated windowDeiconified windowIconified windowOpened	Indicates that the specific window actions have occurred. This interface is implemented by JFrame.

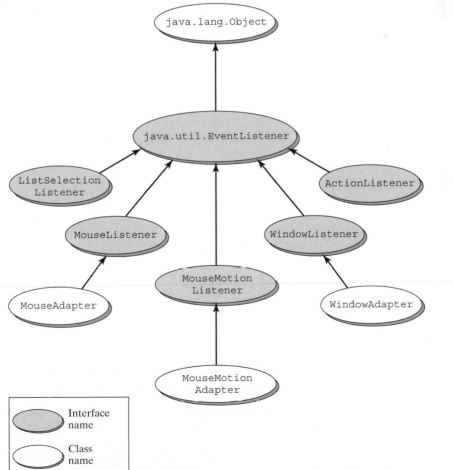

Figure 14.14. Inheritance hierarchy for selected event interfaces and adapter classes. The ListSelectionInterface is found in package javax.swing.event; all others are found in package java.awt.event.

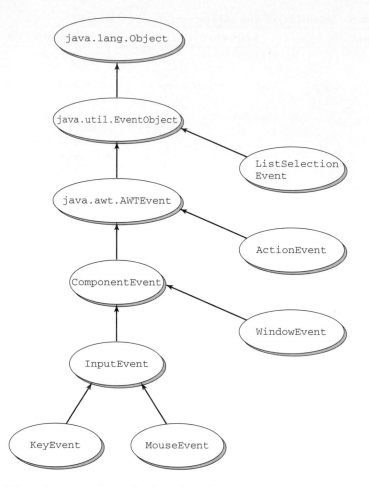

Figure 14.15. Inheritance hierarchy for selected events. The ListSelectionEvent is found in package javax.swing.event; the others are found in package java.awt.event.

```
import java.awt.event.*;
public class WindowHandler implements WindowListener {
   // This method implements a simple listener that detects
   // the "window closing event" and stops the program.
   public void windowClosing(WindowEvent e) {
      System.exit(0);
   };
   // Methods that do nothing, but must be here to
   // implement the interface.
   public void windowActivated(WindowEvent e) {};
   public void windowClosed(WindowEvent e) {};
   public void windowDeactivated(WindowEvent e) {};
   public void windowDeiconified(WindowEvent e) {};
   public void windowIconified(WindowEvent e) {};
   public void windowOpened(WindowEvent e) {};
}
```

Figure 14.16. A class that implements the WindowListener interface, showing that every method in the interface must be implemented, even if they will not be used.

Java includes special **adapter classes** to avoid the wasted effort involved in writing useless methods like the ones in Figure 14.16. An adapter class implements all of the methods in an interface, *with each method doing absolutely nothing*. We can write a new class that extends an adapter class, overriding *only* the methods that we wish to implement, and the adapter class will take care of all the "useless" interface method declarations.

For example, the adapter class that implements the `WindowListener` interface is called `WindowAdapter`. If we create our `WindowHandler` class as a subclass of `WindowAdapter`, only the methods that we wish to change have to be implemented in the class (see Figure 14.17). All of the other required methods will be inherited from `WindowAdapter`. Figure 14.18 illustrates such a class.

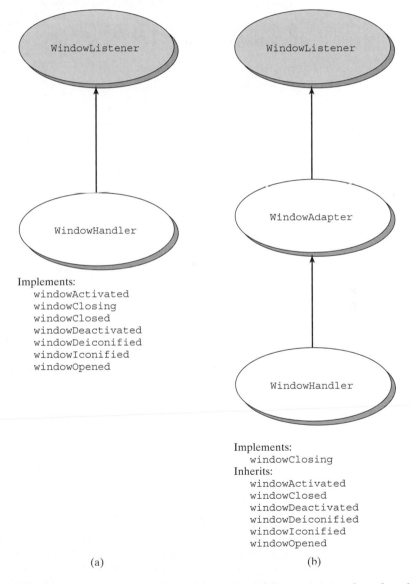

(a) (b)

Figure 14.17. (a) An event-handling class that implements an interface directly must implement every method in the interface. (b) An event-handling class that extends an adapter class has to override only the methods whose behavior must be changed.

```
import java.awt.event.*;
public class WindowHandler extends WindowAdapter {

    // This method implements a simple listener that detects
    // the "window closing event" and stops the program.
    public void windowClosing(WindowEvent e) {
        System.exit(0);
    };
}
```

Figure 14.18. A class that implements the WindowListener interface by extending WindowAdapter. Only the method that we wish to use has to be included in the class, since all of the "useless" methods in the interface are inherited from WindowAdapter.

GOOD PROGRAMMING PRACTICE

Extend adapter classes to create event-handling classes. If you extend existing adapter classes, you will not have to add empty methods to your event handlers.

14.5 POP-UP MENUS

Pop-up menus are menus that "pop up" on the screen when a user right-clicks the mouse over a component. Pop-up menus can be attached to any component in a GUI, and different pop-up menus can be created for each GUI component.

A pop-up menu is created by class JPopupMenu, which is very similar to class JMenu in its function and methods. The constructors are

```
public JPopupMenu();
public JPopupMenu(String label);
```

The first constructor creates a pop-up menu without a title, while the second creates a pop-up menu with the title label as a title. Some of the methods in JPopupMenu are described in Table 14.7.

TABLE 14.7 Selected JPopupMenu Methods

Method	Description
public JMenuItem add(JMenuItem mi)	Adds the specified menu item to this menu. (*Note:* This could be another menu.)
public void addSeparator()	Adds a separator line to the menu at the current position.
public JMenuItem getItem(int index)	Gets the item located at the specified index of this menu.
public int getItemCount()	Gets the number of items in this menu.
public void insert(Component component, int index)	Inserts the specified component into the menu at a given position in the menu.
public String paramString()	Gets the parameter string representing the state of this menu.
public void remove(Component comp)	Removes the specified component from this pop-up menu.
public void setPopupSize(Dimension d)	Sets the pop-up window size.
public void setPopupSize(int width, int height)	Sets the pop-up window size.
public void show(Component invoker, int x, int y)	Display the pop-up menu at the position (x, y) in the coordinate space of the specified component.

Since pop-up menus are triggered by mouse events, we must write a mouse handler in order to use a pop-up menu. This handler must implement the `MouseListener` interface described in the previous section and must receive `MouseEvents`. `MouseEvents` include several methods that allow a program to recover information about the triggering event, including whether or not the event was a pop-up trigger. The most important of these methods are listed in Table 14.7.

TABLE 14.7 MouseEvent Methods

Method	Description
`public int getClickCount()`	Returns the number of mouse clicks associated with this event.
`public Component getComponent()`	Returns the originator of this event.
`public int getX()`	Returns the horizontal position of the mouse click in pixels, relative to the source component.
`public int getY()`	Returns the vertical position of the mouse click in pixels, relative to the source component.
`public boolean isPopupTrigger()`	Returns a true if this event is a pop-up menu trigger.
`public String paramString()`	Returns a `String` describing this event.

The program in Figure 14.19 shows how to create a pop-up menu and attach it to a component. This program creates a `JLabel` and adds a pop-up menu to it to set the color of the text being displayed. The pop-up menu is created and then added to the `JLabel` that it is supposed to trigger on. Note that a mouse event handler must also be added to that component, so that a pop-up event can be detected. The mouse event handler is called `MouseHandler`. It extends `MouseAdapter`, so we have to implement only the `MouseListener` methods that we need to detect pop-up events.

```
// Test pop-up menus.  This program changes the
// color of a JLabel based a pop-up menu.
import java.awt.*;
import java.awt.event.*;
import javax.swing.*;
public class TestPopupMenu extends JPanel
                    implements ActionListener {

   // Instance variables
   private JLabel l1;                     // Labels
   private JMenuItem mi1, mi2, mi3;  // Menu items
   private JPopupMenu popup;              // Pop-up menu
   private MouseHandler h1;               // Pop-up listener

   // Initialization method
   public void init() {
```

Figure 14.19. A class that demonstrates the use of popup menus.

```
        // Create a label with icon and text
        l1 = new JLabel("Label 1", JLabel.LEFT);
        l1.setFont(new Font("SansSerif",Font.BOLD,20));
        l1.setForeground( Color.black );
        add( l1, BorderLayout.CENTER );

        // Create a pop-up menu and add to label
        popup = new JPopupMenu();
        l1.add( popup );

        // Create a pop-up handler
        h1 = new MouseHandler(popup);
        l1.addMouseListener( h1 );

        // Create three menu items specifying colors
        mi1 = new JMenuItem("Black");
        mi1.addActionListener(this);
        popup.add( mi1 );
        mi2 = new JMenuItem("Blue");
        mi2.addActionListener(this);
        popup.add( mi2 );
        mi3 = new JMenuItem("Red");
        mi3.addActionListener(this);
        popup.add( mi3 );
    }

    public void actionPerformed( ActionEvent e) {

        if ( e.getActionCommand().equals("Black") )
            l1.setForeground( Color.black );
        else if ( e.getActionCommand().equals("Blue") )
            l1.setForeground( Color.blue );
        if ( e.getActionCommand().equals("Red") )
            l1.setForeground( Color.red );
    }
    (main method not shown to save space)
}

class MouseHandler extends MouseAdapter {

    private JPopupMenu popup;
    public MouseHandler(JPopupMenu p) { popup = p; }

    public void mousePressed(MouseEvent e) {
        if (e.isPopupTrigger())
            popup.show(e.getComponent(), e.getX(), e.getY());
    }

    public void mouseReleased(MouseEvent e) {
        if (e.isPopupTrigger())
            popup.show(e.getComponent(), e.getX(), e.getY());
    }
}
```

Figure 14.19. (Continued).

Figure 14.20 shows the program running with the pop-up menu visible.

Figure 14.20.   The TestPopupMenu program in operation.

14.6   PLUGGABLE LOOK AND FEEL

One of the special features of the Swing GUI is support for Pluggable Look and Feel. The "**Look and Feel**" of a program is a combination of the appearance of the windows and the way that the program responds to mouse clicks, keyboard inputs, and so on. The idea of a "pluggable" Look and Feel is that a Java program can be written just once, and its appearance can be adjusted with a single method call to match the appearance of programs on the computer on which it is executed.

Java programs can appear as if they were Unix programs (the Motif Look and Feel), or as if they were windows programs (the Windows Look and Feel). Alternately, they can be written to look identical across all platforms (the Java Look and Feel).

All programs that we have seen so far have used the Java Look and Feel, which is the default for Swing GUI components. This Look and Feel has the advantage of being exactly the same across all platforms, but it makes Java programs appear different from native programs on any particular computer. A programmer can choose to write programs that automatically adopt the Look and Feel of whatever computer they are running on, making them appear to be native programs.

The Look and Feel settings of a program are controlled by class UIManager in the javax.swing package. Selected UIManager methods are shown in Table 14.8, and the standard Look and Feels in the Java Development Kit are shown in Table 14.9.

TABLE 14.8   Selected UIManager Methods

Method	Description
public static String getCrossPlatformLookAndFeelClassName()	Returns a String containing the name of the cross-platform look and feel (the Java Look and Feel).
public static UIManager.LookAndFeelInfo[] getInstalledLookAndFeels()	Returns an array containing all of the Looks and Feels available on a particular computer.
public static String getSystemLookAndFeelClassName()	Returns a String containing the standard Look and Feel for the system that the program is executing on.
public static void setLookAndFeel(String name)	Sets the specified Look and Feel for use by this program. The name is the class name of the desired Look and Feel class.

TABLE 14.9 Standard Look and Feels

Class	Description
`javax.swing.plaf.metal.MetalLookAndFeel`	The cross-platform (Java) Look and Feel
`com.sun.java.swing.plaf.motif.MotifLookAndFeel`	Unix (Motif) Look and Feel
`com.sun.java.swing.plaf.windows.WindowsLookAndFeel`	Windows Look and Feel

To specify the Java Look and Feel for a program, a programmer would include the following lines in the `init()` method for the program:

```
try {
    UIManager.setLookAndFeel(
      UIManager.getCrossPlatformLookAndFeelClassName());
}
catch (Exception e) {
    System.err.println("Couldn't use the cross-platform "
                            + "look and feel: " + e);
}
```

Note that these statement should be included in a `try/catch` structure in case the Java Look and Feel is not available on some computer running the program.

To specify that the local computer's Look and Feel should be used for a program, a programmer would include the following lines in the `init()` method for the program:

```
try {
    UIManager.setLookAndFeel(
        UIManager.getSystemLookAndFeelClassName());
}
catch (Exception e) {
    System.err.println("Couldn't use the "
                            + "look and feel: " + e);
```

Figure 14.21 illustrates the effect of setting the Look and Feel on the appearance of a program. It displays the `PlotSinCos` program of the last chapter with two different Look and Feels.

EXAMPLE 14.2

Displaying a Histogram: Create a GUI-based program that reads in a numeric data set from a file and displays a histogram of the data. The program should include a "File" menu with options to open a data set and to exit the program. It should use dialogs to get the name of the file to read, and also to inform the user if the file does not exist. Finally, it should automatically set the program's Look and Feel to match the system on which the program is executing.

SOLUTION

This program will require a menu containing two menu items, "Open" and "Exit". In addition, it will require an object of class `chapman.graphics.JHist` to create and display the histogram. Documentation for class `JHist` is available on line in standard Java 2 SDK format.

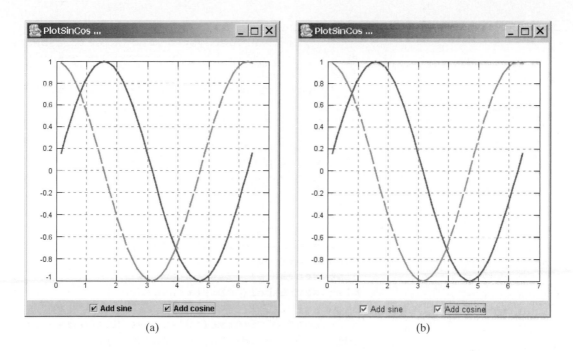

(a)　　　　　　　　　　　　　　(b)

Figure 14.21. Program `PlotSinCos` with two different Look and Feel settings: (a) Java Look and Feel. (b) Windows Look and Feel.

1. **Determine the User Requirements**

   The user's requirement is to create a GUI-based program that reads in a numeric data set from a file and displays a histogram of the data. The program should have a Look and Feel that matches the system on which it is executing.

   The inputs to this program are the name of the file containing the data set, and the data in the file. The data in the file must be in numeric format. The output from the program is a plot of the histogram of the data.

2. **Analysis and Decomposition**

   This program requires three classes to function properly. The principal class (called `Histogram`) must contain three separate methods: (1) a method `init()` to generate the GUI display, (2) a method to read a file when the user clicks on the "Open" menu item, and (3) a `main` method to start up the application.

   In addition, the program must contain two event-handling classes to handle the events generated by the `Open` and `Exit` menu items.

3. **Detailed Design**

   The `init()` method of the `Histogram` class must create the GUI. It must set the desired Look and Feel, create the menu, and lay out the graphical elements. Since there is only one graphical element occupying the entire display, it is logical to use a `BorderLayout` and place the element in the center region. To create the menu, we will need one `JMenuBar`, one `JMenu`, and two `JMenuItems`. We should also add keyboard accelerators to the menu items and a tool tip to the graphical element to help the user. The code required to create the single `JHist` object and the menu is shown below:

   ```
   // Set local system look and feel
   try {
   ```

```
      UIManager.setLookAndFeel(
        UIManager.getSystemLookAndFeelClassName());
}
catch (Exception e) {
   System.err.println("Couldn't use the "
                  + "look and feel: " + e);
}

// Set layout manager
setLayout( new BorderLayout() );

// Create event handlers
hExit   = new ExitHandler();
hOpen   = new OpenHandler(this);

// Create and add histogram object
hist = new JHist(21);
hist.setTitle( "Histogram" );
hist.setXLabel( "Distribution" );
hist.setYLabel( "Count" );
hist.setToolTipText("Displays Histogram");
add( hist, BorderLayout.CENTER );

// Create menu bar
bar = new JMenuBar();

// Create "File" menu
fileMenu = new JMenu("File");
fileMenu.setMnemonic('f');

// Create and add "Open" menu item
open = new JMenuItem( "Open" );
open.addActionListener(hOpen);
open.setMnemonic('o');
fileMenu.add ( open );

// Add separator
fileMenu.addSeparator();

// Create and add "Exit" menu item
exit = new JMenuItem( "Exit" );
exit.addActionListener(hExit);
exit.setMnemonic('x');
fileMenu.add ( exit );

// Add the menu to the menu bar
bar.add ( fileMenu );
```

Method openFile() must prompt the user for a file name and open the file. If the file exists, it should read in the data, send the data to the JHist object, and paint the new histogram. The method will use an input dialog box to get the file name, and will open the file with the class ReadFile that we created in Chapter 10. If the file does not exist, it will pop up an error dialog box to tell the user. Note that we are using a try/catch structure to trap exceptions in ReadFile. The code required for this step is:

```
// Get name of file to open
fileName = JOptionPane.showInputDialog(null,
        "Enter file to open", "Open Dialog",
        JOptionPane.PLAIN_MESSAGE);

// Open the file, protecting against errors
// with a try/catch structure.
data = new Vector();
try {
   // Open the file
   ReadFile in = new ReadFile(fileName);

   (read in data here)
}
catch ( FileNotFoundException e ) {

   String s = "File " + fileName + " not found!";
   JOptionPane.showMessageDialog(null, s,
        "I/O Error", JOptionPane.ERROR_MESSAGE);
}
catch ( IOException e ) {

   String s = "I/O exception in " + fileName;
   JOptionPane.showMessageDialog(null, s,
        "I/O Error", JOptionPane.ERROR_MESSAGE);
}
```

If the file *does* exist, we will have to read in an unknown number of data values from it, so we must store the values in a data structure that can grow to accommodate any number of elements. A Vector (see Section 9.9) is a good choice, since it can hold any number of objects. Note that Vectors hold Objects, so we will have to convert the numeric values to Double objects to store them in the Vector. Also, the method in.readDouble() must be placed within a try/catch structure to trap I/O exceptions. The code to read the values and store them in a Vector is:

```
// Read all the numbers from the file into
// a Vector, protecting against invalid values.
try {
   while (true) {
      data.add(new Double(in.readDouble()));
   }
}
catch ( NumberFormatException e ) {

   // Tell user about bad value
   JOptionPane.showMessageDialog(null, "Value invalid",
       "I/O Error", JOptionPane.ERROR_MESSAGE);
   System.out.println("Value invalid");
}
catch ( EOFException e ) {
```

```
                    // The EOFException means that we have reached the
                    // end of the file, so get out of the while loop!
          }
```

Once all of the data has been read, it must be stored in a `double` array to send to the histogram object. The data can be fetched an element at a time from the `Vector` using the `get` method, as shown below:

```
          data1 = new double[ data.size() ];
          for (int i = 0; i< data1.length; i++ ) {
             Object o = data.get(i);
             data1[i] = ((Double)o).doubleValue();
          }
```

Finally, the data will be sent to the histogram object:

```
          hist.setData( data1 );
          hist.repaint();
```

The two event handlers should detect events on the "Open" and "Exit" menu items. The "File" event handler should call the method `openFile()`, while the "Exit" event handler should shut down the program.

4. **Implementation: Convert Algorithms to Java Statements**

The resulting Java program is shown in Figure 14.22.

5. **Testing**

To test this program, we will execute it twice, once with a 2000-value data set in file `x.dat` and once with an invalid file name `y.dat`. When the program

```
/*
   Purpose:
     This GUI-based program reads in a data set from a
     user-specified file and creates a histogram of the
     data.

   Record of revisions:
       Date          Programmer             Description of change
       ====          ==========             =====================
     08/03/2002    S. J. Chapman            Original code
*/
import java.awt.*;
import java.awt.geom.*;
import java.awt.event.*;
import java.io.*;
import javax.swing.*;
import java.util.*;
import chapman.graphics.JHist;
public class Histogram extends JPanel {

   // Instance variables
   private ActionListener hOpen, hExit;
                              // Action listeners
```

Figure 14.22. A GUI-based program to create and plot a histogram of a data set.

```
private JMenuBar bar;          // Menu bar
private JMenu fileMenu;        // File menu
private JMenuItem open;        // Load "menu" item
private JMenuItem exit;        // Exit "menu" item
Vector data;                   // Input data
double[] data1;                // Data as an array
String fileName;               // File to open
JHist hist;                    // Histogram

//*********************************************

//  init() method

//*********************************************
// Initialization method
public void init() {

   // Set local system look and feel
   try {
       UIManager.setLookAndFeel(
          UIManager.getSystemLookAndFeelClassName());
   }
   catch (Exception e) {
      System.err.println("Couldn't use the "
                   + "look and feel: " + e);
   }

   // Set layout manager
   setLayout( new BorderLayout() );

   // Create event handlers
   hExit   = new ExitHandler();
   hOpen   = new OpenHandler(this);

   // Create and add histogram object
   hist = new JHist(21);
   hist.setTitle( "Histogram" );
   hist.setXLabel( "Distribution" );
   hist.setYLabel( "Count" );
   hist.setToolTipText("Displays Histogram");
   add( hist, BorderLayout.CENTER );

   // Create menu bar
   bar = new JMenuBar();

   // Create "File" menu
   fileMenu = new JMenu("File");
   fileMenu.setMnemonic('f');

   // Create and add "Open" menu item
   open = new JMenuItem( "Open" );
```

Figure 14.22. (Continued).

```
      open.addActionListener(hOpen);
      open.setMnemonic('o');
      fileMenu.add ( open );

      // Add separator
      fileMenu.addSeparator();

      // Create and add "Exit" menu item
      exit = new JMenuItem( "Exit" );
      exit.addActionListener(hExit);
      exit.setMnemonic('x');
      fileMenu.add ( exit );

      // Add the menu to the menu bar
      bar.add ( fileMenu );
   }

//*********************************************
//  Method to read data from a file
//*********************************************
public void openFile() {

   // Get name of file to open
   fileName = JOptionPane.showInputDialog(null,
               "Enter file to open", "Open Dialog",
               JOptionPane.PLAIN_MESSAGE);
   // Open the file, protecting against errors
   // with a try/catch structure.
   data = new Vector();
   try {
      // Open the file
      ReadFile in = new ReadFile(fileName);

      // Read all the numbers from the file into
      // a Vector, protecting against invalid
      // values
      try {
         while (true) {
            data.add(new Double(in.readDouble()));
         }
      }
      catch ( NumberFormatException e ) {

         // Tell user about bad value
         JOptionPane.showMessageDialog(null, "Value invalid",
             "I/O Error", JOptionPane.ERROR_MESSAGE);
         System.out.println("Value invalid");
      }
      catch ( EOFException e ) {
```

Figure 14.22. (Continued).

```
                // The EOFException means that we have reached the
                // end of the file, so get out of the while loop!
            }

            // Convert to a double[] for use in processing
            System.out.println(data.size());
            data1 = new double[ data.size() ];
            for (int i = 0; I< data1.length; i++ ) {
                Object o = data.get(i);
                data1[i] = ((Double)o).doubleValue();
            }

            // Throw away the objects for recycling
            data = null;

            // Close file
            in.close();

            // Modify the title to reflect the number
            // of data values
            hist.setTitle("Histogram (N = " + data1.length + ")");

            // Set the new data into the histogram
            hist.setData( data1 );
            hist.repaint();
        }
        catch ( FileNotFoundException e ) {

            String s = "File " + fileName + " not found!";
            JOptionPane.showMessageDialog(null, s,
                    "I/O Error", JOptionPane.ERROR_MESSAGE);
        }
        catch ( IOException e ) {

            String s = "I/O exception in " + fileName;
            JOptionPane.showMessageDialog(null, s,
                    "I/O Error", JOptionPane.ERROR_MESSAGE);
        }
    }

    //*********************************************
    //  main method
    //*********************************************

    // Main method to create frame
    public static void main(String s[]) {

        // Create a frame to hold the application
        JFrame fr = new JFrame("Histogram ...");
        fr.setSize(400,400);
```

Figure 14.22. (Continued).

```
        // Create a Window Listener to handle "close" events
        MyWindowListener l = new MyWindowListener();
        fr.addWindowListener(l);

        // Create and initialize a Histogram object
        Histogram tm = new Histogram();
        tm.init();

        // Add the menu bar to the frame
        fr.setJMenuBar( tm.bar );

        // Add the object to the center of the frame
        fr.getContentPane().add(tm, BorderLayout.CENTER);

        // Display the frame
        fr.setVisible( true );
    }
}

//***********************************************
//   Event handlers
//***********************************************
class OpenHandler implements ActionListener {
    private Histogram h1;

    // Constructor
    public OpenHandler( Histogram h ) {h1 = h;}

    // Execute when an event occurs
    public void actionPerformed( ActionEvent e ) {
      h1.openFile();
    }
}

class ExitHandler implements ActionListener {

    // Execute when an event occurs
    public void actionPerformed( ActionEvent e ) {
       System.exit(0);
    }
}
```

Figure 14.22. (Continued).

executes with the valid file name, the histogram shown in Figure 14.23(a) will be created. When the program executes with an invalid file name, the error message shown in Figure 14.23(b) will be displayed. Note that this program uses the Windows Look and Feel, since it was executed on a PC.

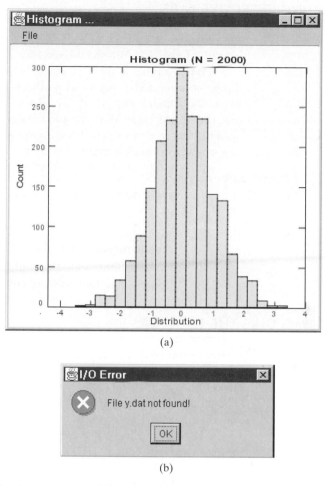

(a)

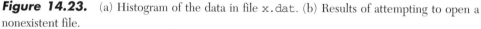

(b)

Figure 14.23. (a) Histogram of the data in file x.dat. (b) Results of attempting to open a nonexistent file.

QUIZ 14-1

This quiz provides a quick check to see if you have understood the concepts introduced in Sections 14.1 through 14.6. If you have trouble with the quiz, reread the section, ask your instructor, or discuss the material with a fellow student. The answers are found in the back of the book.

1. What is a JList? What type of events does a JList generate?
2. Why should a JList be placed inside a JScrollPane?
3. What is necessary in order to add menus to an application or applet? What types of containers support menus?
4. What are dialog boxes? Write the statements required to create a dialog box asking a user whether or not to replace a file.
5. List the listener interfaces introduced in this chapter and in Chapter 13. What does each one do, and which components produce it?
6. What are adapter classes? Why are they useful?
7. How does a pop-up menu differ from an ordinary one?
8. How can you set up a Java application so that it looks the same across all types of computers? How can you set up a Java application so that it looks like a native application on each type of computer that it executes on?

14.7 CREATING EFFECTIVE GUIS

The purpose of a GUI is to make it easy for a user to execute a program or to get some sort of information. You should never forget this simple fact.

When a programmer first learns how to create GUIs, there is a tendency to create flashy, complicated displays that positively get in the way of program usage, just because he or she knows how to do it. We all see examples of such trashy design every time we use the World Wide Web. People create Web sites with animations, flashing objects, sounds, and so on that convey no information, take a long time to download, and get in the way of information transfer. Don't fall into this trap!

In general, you should follow a few simple guidelines in creating a GUI:

1. Place the information that a user will most want in a prominent location on the GUI. Don't bury it in menus or in lower-level displays.

2. Keep the GUI as uncluttered as possible. Relegate infrequently used options to menus, where they will not be in the way.

3. Do not clutter a GUI up with useless animations, images, and the like, just because you think they are cute.

14.8 BUILDING GUIS THE EASY WAY

So far in this book, the design of a GUI-based program has been rather complex and tedious, requiring us to specify one or more layout managers and then to carefully lay out the components of the GUI. We have also had to manually create any required listener classes. Getting the component layout and sizes right has dominated the effort involved in creating a GUI-based program.

Fortunately, there is a *much* easier way. Many companies sell Java Integrated Development Environments (IDEs), which combine visual design forms for laying out GUI-based applications with editors and symbolic debuggers. The IDEs are available from Sun, IBM, Borland, and others, and they enormously simplify the design and building of a GUI application. Even more significantly, almost all vendors offer some versions of their IDEs for free—simply go to their Web sites and download the application.

These environments make it possible to design a GUI-based application by selecting GUI components from a pallet and dropping them onto a container such as a `JPanel`. You can resize the components and drag the components around until they are just where you want them without a layout manager. Once the positions and sizes are just right, the IDE can automatically apply a layout manager to keep the components in place as the GUI is resized. When everything is correct, the IDE will automatically generate the skeletons of all the required classes and methods, including listener classes, to build the GUI. The programmer can just go to each class and add the unique behaviors required for his or her application.

Figure 14.24 illustrates the process of laying out a new GUI-based application with a typical IDE, Borland JBuilder 8 Personal. The programmer selects components, menu items, and so forth from the pallet displayed across the top of the design area, and then drops the components onto the container. The components can be moved around and resized with the mouse, and the properties of each component can be set in the Property Editor appearing on the right of the design area. When the layout is complete, the IDE will allow the user to apply a layout manager to keep the components in place. It will then generate the skeletons of all required classes and methods, which the programmer edits to complete the application.

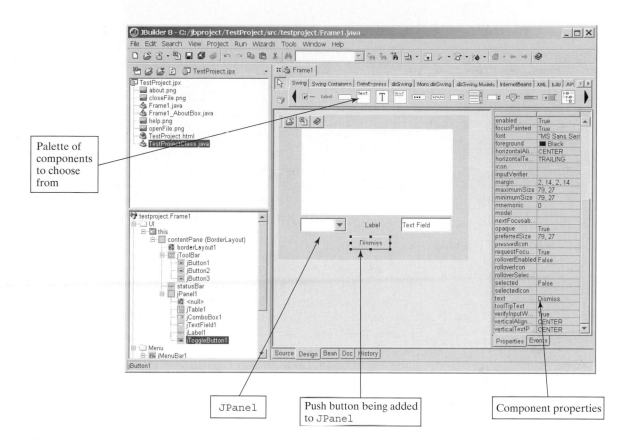

Palette of
components
to choose
from

JPanel

Push button being added
to JPanel

Component properties

Figure 14.24. Laying out a GUI-based application using Borland JBuilder 8 Personal. The programmer clicks on a component in the palette, then places the component on the container.

This book has not taught you how to use IDEs, because they differ from vendor to vendor. However, I highly recommend that you get one of them and learn how to use it. You will be much more productive.

GOOD PROGRAMMING PRACTICE

Acquire and learn to use one of the Integrated Development Environments available for creating Java programs.

SUMMARY

- The JList class creates a GUI component that implements single- or multiple-selection lists. JLists function in three modes: single selection mode, single interval selection mode, or multiple interval selection mode.
- A JList can be made scrollable by placing it inside a JScrollPane.
- JLists generate ListSelectionEvents, which are handled by classes implementing the ListSelectionListener interface.
- The JTable class creates a GUI component that displays a table of objects.
- Pull-down menus can be added to containers of type JFrame, JApplet, JDialog, JRootPane, or JInternalFrame..
- Pop-up menus can be added to any Java component.

- Menus are composed of five basic components: `JMenuBar`, `JMenu`, `JMenuItems`, `JCheckBoxMenuItem`, and `JRadioButtonMenuItem`.
- A **menu bar** is the bar across the top of the frame to which the menus are attached.
- A **menu** is an individual list of items that is pulled down from the menu bar when the user clicks on the menu name.
- A **menu item** is a string inside a menu that, when selected, causes an action to be performed.
- All types of menu items generate `ActionEvents`, which are handled by `ActionListeners`.
- A dialog box is a special type of container that is used to get information from a user or to provide error or warning messages. They may be modal or non-modal, but all examples in this text are modal. The standard types of dialog boxes are `showMessageDialog`, `showConfirmDialog`, `showInputDialog`, and `showOptionDialog`.
- The Look and Feel of a Java program can be set to be the same across all platforms, or the program can be made to match the Look and Feel of the computer on which it is executing. The Look and Feel of a program is controlled by class `UIManager`.

SUMMARY OF GOOD PROGRAMMING PRACTICES

The following guidelines introduced in this chapter will help you to develop good programs:

1. Use class `JList` to create lists of objects for display and selection in a GUI.
2. Always use scrollable `JLists` in all of your programs to ensure that a user can see all the values in the list.
3. Use `JTables` to display tabular data.
4. Use menus to display less frequently used options such as opening and saving files. This keeps them from using up space in the GUI.
5. Use dialog boxes to display error and warning messages to the user, to confirm irrevocable actions such as overwriting files, and to get input values from a user.
6. Extend adapter classes to create event-handling classes. If you extend existing adapter classes, you will not have to add empty methods to your event handlers.
7. Acquire and learn to use one of the Integrated Development Environments available for creating Java programs.

TERMINOLOGY

adapter classes	`JScrollPane` class
check-box menu item	`JTable` class
dialog box	`ListSelectionEvent` class
IDE	`ListSelectionListener`
interface	Look and Feel
`JCheckBoxMenuItem` class	menu
`JList` class	menu bar
`JMenu` class	menu item
`JMenuBar` class	modal dialog box
`JMenuItem` class	radio-button menu item
`JRadioButtonMenuItem` class	submenu
`JOptionPane` class	`valueChanged` method

Exercises

1. Add a set of menus to the plot sine/cosine program of Example 13.3. There should be two menus: "File" and "Options." The "File" menus should include "Load," "Save," and "Exit" menu items, with the "Load" and "Save" menu items loading and saving the program parameters from run to run. The "Options" menu should allow the user to select line color, line style, and so on, independently for the two curves.

2. Create a program that tests the `showInputDialog` methods described in Section 14.3.3.

3. Create a program with a blank component (canvas). The program should monitor mouse clicks and draw 30-pixel-wide circle with a 2-pixel-wide solid border around the center of each mouse click. Note that you will need a `MouseListener` to determine the location of the clicks. Include a menu on the program. The menu should allow the user to erase the component and start over, and should also allow the user to change the color of the circles.

4. Modify the program of Exercise 3 to include a pop-up menu. It should allow the user to erase the component.

5. Write a program that determines which Look and Feels are installed on your computer. Uses the `UIManager` method `getInstalledLookAndFeels` to get the list, and use method `gctSystemLookAndFeelClassName()` to determine the default Look and Feel for your system.

6. Modify the plot sine/cosine program of Example 13.3 by adding a menu that allows the user to select the Look and Feel of the program while it is running.

7. In Chapter 5 we learned how to calculate the mean, median, and standard deviation of a data set. Modify the `Histogram` program of Example 14.2 to show the mean, median, and standard deviation of the displayed data set in non-editable text fields below the plot of the histogram. Create methods based on the algorithms in Chapter 5 to calculate the values to display. Include appropriate labels for each text field. Note that you will need cascaded layout managers to create an appropriate GUI for this program.

8. Modify the least-squares fit program of Exercise 13 of Chapter 13 to include a "File" menu with "Open" and "Exit" menu items. Add a file open dialog box, and include appropriate error messages. Also, add a scrollable `JTable` to display the actual (x, y) points being plotted.

15

Applets

The chapter contains a study of applets, explaining the differences between applets and applications and showing how to create a single program that can run as either an application or an applet.

15.1 INTRODUCTION TO APPLETS

An **applet** is a special type of Java program that is designed to work within a World Wide Web browser, such as Mozilla, Microsoft Internet Explorer, or Netscape Navigator. Applets are usually quite small and are designed to be downloaded, executed, and discarded whenever the browser points to a site containing the Java applet.

    Applets are quite restricted compared to Java applications. For security reasons, applets are not allowed access to the computer on which they are executing, so an applet cannot read or write disk files, for example. These restrictions make them less useful than applications for many data-analysis purposes.

    Applets are most commonly used for creating eye-catching graphics and animations on Web pages.

15.2 THE `JApplet` CLASS

An *applet* is any class that extends class `javax.swing.JApplet`. Class **`javax.swing.JApplet`** is a container into which components can be placed (see Figure 15.1). It is very similar to `JFrame`, in that the components must be added to a content pane retrieved by the `getContentPane()` method. In addition, class

OBJECTIVES

- Be able to create applets, including the HTML files that execute them.
- Understand applet parameters and how to apply them.
- Be able to create applets that can also run as applications.
- Understand how to create Java Archive Files, and how to add and extract files from the JAR files.
- Be able to execute Java applications and applets from within a JAR file.

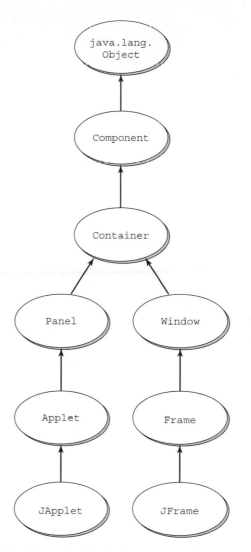

Figure 15.1. Partial class hierarchy of Container classes. Note that JApplet is a subclass of Container, so it can be used as a container for components.

JApplet implements a set of methods that form the interface between the applet and the Web browser. These methods are summarized in Table 15.1.

Every applet has five key methods: init, start, stop, destroy, and paintComponent. Method init() is called by the browser when the applet is first loaded in memory. This method should allocate resources and create the GUI required for the applet. Method start() is called when the applet should start running. This call can be used to start animations, and so on, when the applet becomes visible. Method stop() is called when the applet should stop running—for example, when its window is covered or when it is iconized. This call is also made just before an applet is destroyed. Method destroy() is the final call to the applet before it is destroyed. The applet should release all resources at the time of this call. Finally, method paintComponent is called whenever the applet must be drawn or redrawn.

Class JApplet implements all five of these methods as simple calls that do nothing. A practical applet will override as many of them as it needs to, in order to perform its function. Simple applets that respond only to user events will need to override only the init() and possibly the paintComponent methods.

TABLE 15.1 Selected `JApplet` Methods

Method	Description
`public boolean isActive();`	Determines whether this applet is active.
`public void init();`	Method called by the browser to inform this applet that it has been loaded into the system.
`public void start();`	Method called by the browser to inform this applet that it should start execution. This call will always follow a call to `init()`.
`public void stop();`	Method called by the browser to inform this applet that it should stop execution.
`public void destroy();`	Method called by the browser to inform this applet that it is being destroyed, and it should deallocate any resources that it holds. This call will always follow a call to `stop()`.
`public String getAppletInfo();`	Returns information about this applet. This can be a version number, copyright, and so on.
`public String getParameter(String name);`	Returns the value of the named parameter in the HTML tag.
`public String[] [] getParameterInfo();`	Returns information about the parameters that are understood by this applet.
`public void paintComponent(Graphics g);`	Method to paint the applet.
`public void repaint();`	Repaints the applet.
`public void showStatus(String msg);`	Displays the argument string in the applet's "status window."

15.3 CREATING AND DISPLAYING AN APPLET

The basic steps required to create and run a Java applet are:

1. Create a container class to hold the GUI components. This class will always be a subclass of `JApplet`.

2. Select a layout manager for the container, if the default layout manager (`FlowLayout`) is not acceptable.

3. Create components and add them to *the content pane* of the `JApplet` container.

4. Create "listener" objects to detect and respond to the events expected by each GUI component, and assign the listeners to appropriate components.

5. Create an HTML text file to specify to the browser which Java applet should be loaded and executed.

These steps are very similar to th]e one required to create a Java application, except that we use `JApplet` instead of `JPanel` as the container class, and we create an HTML file instead of a `JFrame` to execute the program. Note that all components must be added to the `JApplet`'s content pane, just as with `JFrame`.

Figure 15.2 shows an applet that creates a simple GUI with a single button and a single label field. The label field contains the number of times that the button has been pressed since the program started. This applet is identical to the `FirstGUI` application in Figure 13.2, except that it has been converted to run as an applet. Note that class `FirstApplet` extends `JApplet`, and this class serves as the container for our GUI components (step 1 above).

This applet contains two classes: class `FirstApplet` to create and display the GUI, and class `ButtonHandler` to respond to mouse clicks on the button.

Class `FirstApplet` contains two methods: `init()` and `updateLabel()`. Method `init()` overrides the `init()` in class `JApplet`, and it initializes the GUI. It will be called by the browser when the applet is just starting. This class specifies which layout manager to use with the container (line 18), creates the `JLabel` and `JButton`

```
1   // A first Applet.  This class creates a label and
2   // a button.  The count in the label is incremented
3   // each time the button is pressed.
4   import java.awt.*;
5   import java.awt.event.*;
6   import javax.swing.*;
7   public class FirstApplet extends JApplet {
8
9       // Instance variables
10      private int count = 0;        // Number of pushes
11      private JButton pushButton;   // Push button
12      private JLabel label;         // Label
13
14      // Initialization method
15      public void init() {
16
17          // Set the layout manager
18          getContentPane().setLayout( new BorderLayout() );
19
20          // Create a label to hold push count
21          label = new JLabel("Push Count: 0");
22          getContentPane().add( label, BorderLayout.NORTH );
23          label.setHorizontalAlignment( label.CENTER );
24
25          // Create a button
26          pushButton = new JButton("Test Button");
27          pushButton.addActionListener( new ButtonHandler(this) );
28          getContentPane().add( pushButton, BorderLayout.SOUTH );
29      }
30
31      // Method to update push count
32      public void updateLabel() {
33          label.setText( "Push Count: " + (++count) );
34      }
35  }
36
37  class ButtonHandler implements ActionListener {
38      private FirstApplet fa;
39
40      // Constructor
41      public ButtonHandler ( FirstApplet fa1 ) {
42          fa = fa1;
43      }
44
45      // Execute when an event occurs
46      public void actionPerformed( ActionEvent e ) {
47          fa.updateLabel();
48      }
49  }
```

Figure 15.2.   An applet that creates a container, sets a layout manager for the container, and adds components and listeners for the components. This is the basic core structure required to create Java applets.

components (lines 21 and 26), and adds them to the container (lines 22 and 28). In addition, it creates a "listener" object of class `ButtonHandler` to listen for and handle events generated by mouse clicks, and assigns that object to monitor mouse clicks on the button (line 27).

Method `updateLabel()` (lines 32–34) is the method that should be called by the event handler every time a button click occurs. It updates the label with the number of button clicks that have occurred. Class `ButtonHandler` is a "listener" class identical to those we discussed in Chapter 13. Its `actionPerformed` method calls method `updateLabel()` whenever a click occurs on the button.

To execute this applet in a Web browser, we must also create an HTML (Hyper-Text Markup Language) document to tell the browser to load and execute the applet. An example HTML document is shown in Figure 15.3. An HTML document consists of a series of **tags** marking the beginning and ending of various items. For example, the beginning of HTML document is marked by an `<html>` tag, and the end by the `</html>` tag. Similarly, the beginning of an applet description is marked by an `<applet>` tag, and the end is by the `</applet>` tag. The series of values after the applet tag are known as *attributes*. The three required attributes specify the name of the class file to execute and the size of the applet in units of pixels.

```
1 <html>
2 <applet code="FirstApplet.class" width=200 height=100>
3 </applet>
4 </html>
```

Figure 15.3. HTML file required to execute the `FirstApplet` applet.

The applet is executed by loading the corresponding HTML document into a Java-enabled Web browser, such as Mozilla, Microsoft Internet Explorer, or Netscape Navigator. In addition, an applet can be tested with a special program called `appletviewer`, which is supplied in the Java SDK. The applet can be executed with the following command, and the results are as shown in Figure 15.4.

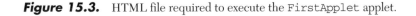

The applet can be executed with the following command, and the results are as shown in Figure 15.4.

D:\book\java\chap14>**appletviewer FirstApplet.html**

Figure 15.4. The display produced by applet `FirstApplet`.

Note that the GUI produced by this applet is identical to the one produced by the `FirstGUI` application, except that the applet includes a status line at the bottom of the window (the status line says "Applet started.").

15.4   DISPLAYING STATUS INFORMATION

The Applet Viewer and all browsers that support Java include a **status line** at the bottom of the display, where an applet can display useful information. For example, the status line in Figure 15.4 displays the message "Applet started". This field may be used to display information with the showStatus message.

The status line is very useful for programmers in the process of debugging an applet, but you should not count on it to supply information to the ultimate user. Many different messages are written to a browser's status line, and they replace any previous messages on the line. As a result, the messages that you send to the status line might be visible for only a fraction of a second before they are replaced by another message.

The applet shown in Figure 15.5 creates a GUI containing two buttons. When a button is pushed, it displays the number of times it has been pushed on the status line of the applet.

```java
// This program sends messages to the status line
import java.awt.*;
import java.awt.event.*;
import javax.swing.*;
public class TestStatusLine extends JApplet
                    implements ActionListener {

   // Instance variables
   private int c1 = 0, c2 = 0;      // Counters
   private JButton b1, b2;          // Buttons

   // Initialization method
   public void init() {

      // Set the layout manager
      getContentPane().setLayout( new FlowLayout() );

      // Create buttons
      b1 = new JButton("Button 1");
      b1.addActionListener( this );
      getContentPane().add( b1 );

      b2 = new JButton("Button 2");
      b2.addActionListener( this );
      getContentPane().add( b2 );
   }

   // Method to handle button pushes
   public void actionPerformed(ActionEvent e) {
      String button = e.getActionCommand();

      if (button.equals("Button 1"))
         showStatus("Button 1 pressed: count = " + (++c1));
      else if (button.equals("Button 2"))
         showStatus("Button 2 pressed: count = " + (++c2));
   }
}
```

Figure 15.5.   An applet that displays information on the status line whenever a user clicks a button.

To execute this applet, we must also create an HTML file to load it into the browser. The required file will be identical to the one shown in Figure 15.3, except that the class name to load is `TestStatusLine.class`. When this applet is executed with the Applet Viewer, the results are as shown in Figure 15.6.

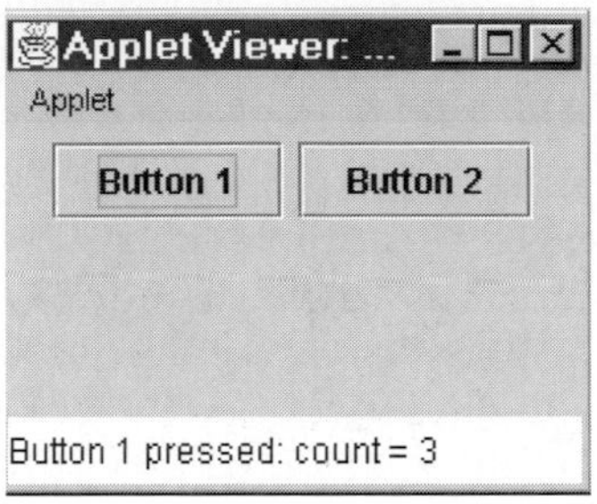

Figure 15.6.   The display produced by applet `TestStatusLine`.

15.5   APPLET PARAMETERS

Many applets are designed to accept input information from a user when the applet is started. These "startup parameters" are embedded in the HTML file that starts the applet. When the applet starts up, it can read the parameters from the HTML file and customise its operation based on their values. This is analogous to the command-line parameters that can be passed to an application when it starts up.

Parameters consist of (keyword, value) pairs, marked by a `PARAM` tag, that are embedded between the `<APPLET>` and `</APPLET>` tags in the HTML file. They take the form

```
<PARAM NAME="xxx" VALUE="yyy">
```

Any text string can serve as a keyword or a value. Each name and each value *must be a text string*. If you need to pass a number to the applet, then it must be passed as a string and converted into a number within the program.

A typical HTML file containing parameters is shown in Figure 15.7.

```
1   <html>
2   <applet code="TestApplet.class" width=200 height=100>
3   <PARAM NAME="buttonText" VALUE="Click Me">
4   <PARAM NAME="color" VALUE="GREEN">
5   </applet>
6   </html>
```

Figure 15.7.   An HTML file invoking an applet with two parameters.

An applet can retrieve parameters from the HTML file using the applet method `getParameter(name)`, where `name` is a `String` containing the keyword for the particular parameter. If the parameter is present in the HTML file, then the method will return a string containing the corresponding value. If the parameter is *not* present, then the method will return a null value. The applet can test the returned value and apply the parameter only if the returned value is not null.

Figure 15.8 shows an applet called `TestApplet` that reads and uses the `color` and `buttonText` parameters. This program is similar to `FirstApplet`, except that it

```
// An applet that demonstrates reading and using
// HTML parameters.
import java.awt.*;
import java.awt.event.*;
import javax.swing.*;
public class TestApplet extends JApplet {

    // Color constants
    private String colorNames[] = {"Black", "Blue",
        "Magenta", "Yellow", "Red", "Green", "White"};
    private Color colorValues[] = {Color.black,
        Color.blue, Color.magenta, Color.yellow,
        Color.red, Color.green, Color.white};

    // Instance variables
    String buttonText;              // Button text
    String color;                   // Background color
    private int count = 0;          // Number of pushes
    private JButton pushButton;     // Push button
    private JLabel label;           // Label

    // Initialization method
    public void init() {

        // Get parameters from HTML file
        buttonText = getParameter("buttonText");
        color = getParameter("color");

        // Set the layout manager
        getContentPane().setLayout( new BorderLayout() );

        // Select the background color
        for ( int i = 0; i < colorNames.length; i++ ) {
            if ( color.equals( colorNames[i]) ) {
                getContentPane().setBackground ( colorValues[i] );
            }
        }
        // Create a label to hold push count
        label = new JLabel("Push Count: 0");
        getContentPane().add( label, BorderLayout.NORTH );
        label.setHorizontalAlignment( label.CENTER );

        // Create a button
        if (buttonText != null)
            pushButton = new JButton(buttonText);
        else
            pushButton = new JButton("Test Button");
        pushButton.addActionListener( new ButtonHandler(this) );
        getContentPane().add( pushButton, BorderLayout.SOUTH );
    }

    // Method to update push count
```

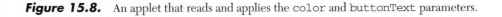

Figure 15.8. An applet that reads and applies the color and buttonText parameters.

```
    public void updateLabel() {
        label.setText( "Push Count: " + (++count) );
    }
}

class ButtonHandler implements ActionListener {
    private TestApplet ta;

    // Constructor
    public ButtonHandler ( TestApplet ta1 ) {
        ta = ta1;
    }

    // Execute when an event occurs
    public void actionPerformed( ActionEvent e ) {
        ta.updateLabel();
    }
}
```

Figure 15.8. (Continued).

uses the `color` parameter to specify the background color of the container and the `buttonText` parameter to specify the text to display on the pushbutton.

When this applet is executed using the HTML file shown in Figure 15.7, the resulting GUI is as shown in Figure 15.9.

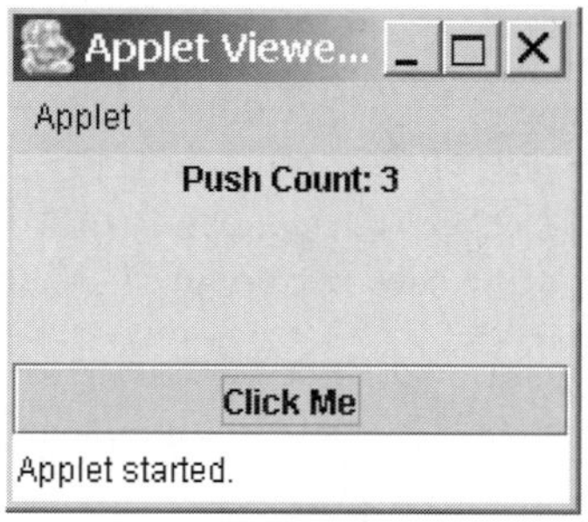

Figure 15.9. The display produced by applet `TestApplet`.

GOOD PROGRAMMING PRACTICE

Use HTML parameters to allow users to customize your applets at execution time.

15.6 USING PACKAGES WITHIN APPLETS

Because applets are designed to be transferred through the internet from a server to a browser, there must be a special convention to tell the applet where to find the classes that the applet needs to execute. This convention is illustrated in Figure 15.10.

If an applet uses a class that is *not* built into a package, then that class must be present in the *same directory* as the HTML file used to start the applet [see Figure 15.10(a)]. This could be a local directory on your computer or a directory on a server on the other

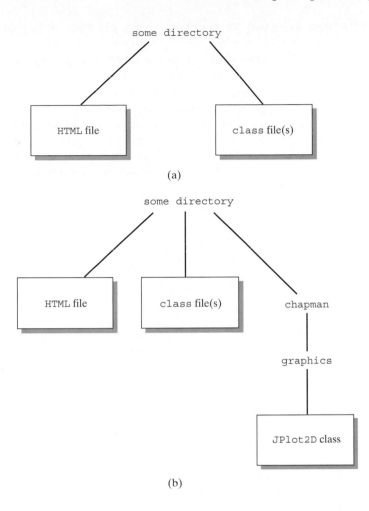

Figure 15.10. (a) The classes required by an applet that *are not* included in a package must appear in the same directory as the HTML file. (b) The classes required by an applet that *are* included in a package must appear in an appropriate subdirectory of the directory containing the HTML file. Class chapman.graphics.JPlot2D is shown in this figure.

side of the world—it doesn't matter as long as the class files and the HTML file are in the same directory. When the HTML file is loaded into the browser, all of the required classes will be transferred over the network to the browser, so that they can be executed on the local computer. Note that applets should be small, because they are transferred over the network each time that they are used.

If an applet uses a class that appears in a package that is not a part of standard Java, then *the package must appear in the appropriate subdirectory* of the directory containing the HTML file. For example, suppose that an applet uses the class JPlot2D from package chapman.graphics. When a browser executes this applet, it will look for the JPlot2D class in subdirectory chapman\graphics under the directory containing the HTML file [see Figure 15.10(b)]. This structure is always the same whether the directory containing the HTML file is local to your computer or located on a remote server across the network. Unlike Java applications, applets ignore the CLASSPATH environment variable. They look only in subdirectories of the directory containing the HTML file to locate the classes in packages.

15.7   CREATING AN APPLET THAT IS ALSO AN APPLICATION

It is possible to design a single Java program to run as either an applet or an application. We can create such a dual-purpose program by first creating a working applet and then adding a `main` method to it. The `main` method will be designed to create a `JFrame`, place the applet into the frame, and execute the applet's `init()` and `start()` methods. The window listener associated with the frame will be designed to execute the applet's `stop()` and `destroy()` methods when the program is closed down.

A typical dual-purpose application/applet is shown in Figure 15.11. This is a version of the plot sine/cosine application from Chapter 13. When this program is executed

```
/*
   Purpose:
     This program plots sin x and/or cos x for 0 <= x <= PI
     depending on the state of two check boxes.

   Record of revisions:
       Date          Programmer          Description of change
       ====          ==========          =====================
     07/08/2002     S. J. Chapman        Original code
  1. 08/02/2002     S. J. Chapman        Modified for applet
*/
import java.awt.*;
import java.awt.event.*;
import javax.swing.*;
import chapman.graphics.JPlot2D;
public class PlotSinCosApplet extends JApplet {

   // Instance variables
   private ActionListener hSinCos;       // ActionListener
   private JCheckBox b1, b2;             // Check boxes
   private JPlot2D p1;                   // Plot
   double[] x, y1, y2;                   // Data to plot

   // Initialization method
   public void init() {

      // Create event handler
      hSinCos = new CheckBoxHandler(this);

      // Create a new high-level panel
      JPanel pVert = new JPanel();
      pVert.setLayout(new BoxLayout(pVert, BoxLayout.Y_AXIS));
      getContentPane().add( pVert );

      // Add a blank plot
      p1 = new JPlot2D();
      p1.setPreferredSize(new Dimension(400,400));
      pVert.add( p1 );

      // Create a subordinate panel for the bottom
      JPanel pHoriz = new JPanel();
      pHoriz.setLayout(new BoxLayout(pHoriz, BoxLayout.X_AXIS));
      pVert.add( pHoriz );
```

Figure 15.11.   A dual-purpose application/applet version of the `PlotSinCos` application from Chapter 13.

```
      // Create the "Add sine" check box
      b1 = new JCheckBox("Add sine");
      b1.addActionListener( hSinCos );
      pHoriz.add( b1 );
      pHoriz.add( Box.createRigidArea(new Dimension(40,0)) );

      // Create the "Add cosine" check box
      b2 = new JCheckBox("Add cosine");
      b2.addActionListener( hSinCos );
      pHoriz.add( b2 );

      // Define arrays to hold the two curves to plot
      x  = new double[41];
      y1 = new double[41];
      y2 = new double[41];

      // Calculate a sine and a cosine wave
      for ( int i = 0; i < x.length; i++ ) {
         x[i]  = (i+1) * 2 * Math.PI / 40;
         y1[i] = Math.sin(x[i]);
         y2[i] = Math.cos(x[i]);
      }
   }

   // Method to display sine and cosine plots
   public void display() {
      // Remove old curves
      pl.removeAll();

      // Add sine curve
      if ( b1.isSelected() ) {
         pl.addCurve(x, y1);
         pl.setLineColor( Color.blue );
         pl.setLineWidth( 2.0f );
         pl.setLineStyle( JPlot2D.LINESTYLE_SOLID );
      }

      // Add cosine curve
      if ( b2.isSelected() ) {
         pl.addCurve(x, y2);
         pl.setLineColor( Color.red );
         pl.setLineWidth( 2.0f );
         pl.setLineStyle( JPlot2D.LINESTYLE_LONGDASH );
      }

      // Turn on grid
      pl.setGridState( JPlot2D.GRID_ON );

      // Repaint plot
      pl.repaint();
   }

   // Main method to create frame
   public static void main(String s[]) {
      // Create a frame to hold the application
      JFrame fr = new JFrame("PlotSinCos ...");
```

Figure 15.11. (Continued).

```
      fr.setSize(400,460);

      // Create and initialize a PlotSinCosApplet object
      PlotSinCosApplet ps = new PlotSinCosApplet();
      ps.init();
      ps.start();

      // Create a Window Listener to handle "close" events
      AppletWindowHandler l = new AppletWindowHandler(ps);
      fr.addWindowListener(l);

      // Add the object to the center of the frame
      fr.getContentPane().add(ps, BorderLayout.CENTER);

      // Display the frame
      fr.setVisible( true );
   }
}
//**********************************************
//   Event handler
//**********************************************

class CheckBoxHandler implements ActionListener {
   private PlotSinCosApplet ps;

   // Constructor
   public CheckBoxHandler( PlotSinCosApplet ps1 ) {ps = ps1;}

   // Execute when an event occurs
   public void actionPerformed( ActionEvent e ) {
      String input = e.getActionCommand();

      if ( input.equals("Add sine") )
         ps.display();

      else if ( input.equals("Add cosine") )
         ps.display();
   }
}
//**********************************************
//   Window handler
//**********************************************

class AppletWindowHandler extends WindowAdapter {
   JApplet ap;

   // Constructor
   public AppletWindowHandler ( JApplet a ) { ap = a; }

   // This method implements a listener that detects
   // the "window closing event," shuts down the applet,
   // and stops the program.
   public void windowClosing(WindowEvent e) {
      ap.stop();
      ap.destroy();
      System.exit(0);
   };
}
```

Figure 15.11. (Continued).

as an applet, the main method is ignored and it runs as a conventional applet. When the program is executed as an application, the main method creates a JFrame, places the applet into the frame, and runs the applet's init() and start() methods. Note that the AppletWindowHandler executes the applet's stop() and destroy() methods when the frame is closed. Figure 15.12 shows the HTML file that is required to execute this program as an applet.

```
1   <html>
2   <applet code="PlotSinCosApplet.class" width=400 height=460>
3   </applet>
4   </html>
```

Figure 15.12. HTML file required to execute PlotSinCosApplet as an applet.

Figure 15.13 shows the GUI created by this program when it is executed as an application and as an applet. Note that the program behaves identically in either case.

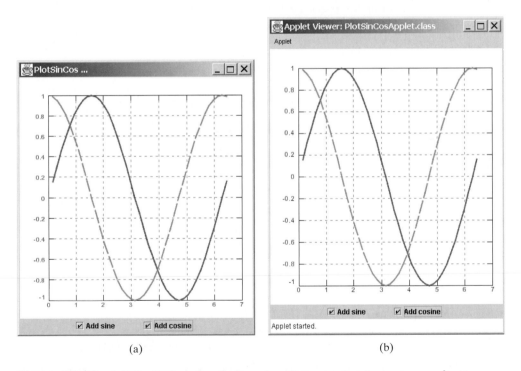

(a)   (b)

Figure 15.13. (a) The GUI produced when PlotSinCosApplet is run as an application. (b) The GUI produced when PlotSinCosApplet is run as an applet.

Finally, note that this program uses the JPlot2D class from package chapman.graphics. In order for this program to work successfully as an applet, the file JPlot2D.class must be found in the subdirectory chapman\graphics below the directory containing the file PlotSinCosApplet.html.

> **GOOD PROGRAMMING PRACTICE**
>
> Whenever possible, design your programs to be dual-purpose applications/applets.

15.8 JAVA ARCHIVE (JAR) FILES AND APPLETS

When a Java applet stored on one computer is executed by a second computer over a network, the browser running the applet must download all of the applet's classes and all the required data files from the first computer. This means that the browser will have to request and transfer each file individually from the source computer to the destination computer over the network. This process can take a long time. The delay happens for two reasons. First, each file to be transferred causes the browser to establish a separate link between the source computer and the destination computer. Each such link can take a second or so to establish. Second, the data-transfer rate of network connections is usually much slower than that of the local computer's disk. If files are large, it will take a long time to transfer them over the net. Because of this limit, applets should be relatively small programs.

Executing an applet over the network is slow because of the delays associated with transferring the applet's classes and supporting files between computers. If the user has a modem, the transfer will be at 54 kilobits per second or slower. Even if the user has a cable modem or Ethernet connection, the transfer rate will be much slower than that from a local disk. If there were some way to speed up this transfer, the whole Java applet would run faster.

A good way to speed up the data transfer is to compress the applet's classes and data before transmission, so that they require fewer bytes, and to place all of the compressed classes and data into a single file. Java accomplishes this task with a special compressed file format known as a **Java Archive File** (JAR file for short).

A JAR file is a special type of file that stores other files in a compressed format. It is exactly the same as a Windows ZIP file, but the default file extent is `*.jar` instead of `*.zip`. A user can add files to the archive, extract files from the archive, or view the files in the archive using the `jar` command.

JAR files can be used as a compact way to archive Java programs, but they can serve other functions as well. JAR files are a convenient way to save a complete Java application or applet into a single file for distribution to end users. Users can execute the Java programs directly from within the archive, without having to unpack them first.

15.8.1 Adding, Viewing, and Extracting Files from a JAR File

The basic commands required to work with Java Archive files are summarized in Table 15.2. The command to create a JAR file is

```
jar cf jar-file-name input-file(s)
```

Here, the letters `cf` mean that we want to **c**reate a new **f**ile whose name is *jar-file-name* and place the *input-file(s)* into the new archive. There can be more than one item in the input file list, and each item can include wildcard (*) characters, if desired. For example, suppose that a directory contains the following files:

```
C:\book\chap15\PlotSinCosApplet>dir
 Volume in drive C is SYSTEM
 Volume Serial Number is 7384-615E

 Directory of C:\book\chap15\PlotSinCosApplet
```

```
16/08/2002  03:48p    <DIR>          .
16/08/2002  03:48p    <DIR>          ..
16/08/2002  03:48p    <DIR>          chapman
16/08/2002  03:07p           526  AppletWindowHandler.class
16/08/2002  03:07p           687  CheckBoxHandler.class
16/08/2002  03:07p         2,933  PlotSinCosApplet.class
16/08/2002  03:05p            89  PlotSinCosApplet.html
16/08/2002  03:01p         4,639  PlotSinCosApplet.java
                5 File(s)     8,874 bytes
                3 Dir(s)     696,451,072 bytes free
```

A new JAR file named `PlotSinCos.jar` can be created, and the entire contents of this directory (including the contents of all subdirectories) can be added it, using the following command:

```
jar cf PlotSinCos.jar *
```

The contents of this file can be examined using the "`tf`" option.

```
C:\book\chap15\PlotSinCosApplet>jar tf PlotSinCos.jar
META-INF/
META-INF/MANIFEST.MF
AppletWindowHandler.class
chapman/
chapman/graphics/
chapman/graphics/InvalidPlotValueException.class
chapman/graphics/JPlot2D.class
chapman/math/
chapman/math/Array.class
chapman/math/Complex.class
chapman/math/InvalidArraySizeException.class
chapman/math/Math1.class
chapman/math/SigProc.class
chapman/math/Statistics.class
CheckBoxHandler.class
PlotSinCosApplet.class
PlotSinCosApplet.html
PlotSinCosApplet.java
```

Note that the contents of the current directory and the contents of all subdirectories have been added to the file. In addition, the `jar` tool has created a new directory called `META-INF` within the archive, and added a new file called `MANIFEST.MF` within it. This is a special file that Java uses to hold information about files within the archive.

All of the files stored within a Java Archive can be extracted to a directory using the following command:

```
jar xf jar-file-name
```

Here, the letters `xf` mean that we want to e**x**tract the contents of the named **f**ile. The contents will be restored to the current directory, or to subdirectories of the current directory, preserving the relative pathnames stored in the file. Selected files can also be restored from a Java Archive using the command

```
jar xf jar-file-name archived_file(s)
```

There can be more than one item in the archived file list, and each item can include wildcard (°) characters, if desired. In this case, only files with the specified file names will be extracted.

TABLE 15.2 Java Archive Commands

Operation	Command
Create a JAR file.	jar cf *jar-file-name input-file(s)*
Add files to an existing JAR file.	jar uf *jar-file-name input-file(s)*
View the contents of a JAR file.	jar tf *jar-file-name*
Extract the contents of a JAR file.	jar xf *jar-file-name*

Run an applet packaged as a JAR file.	`<applet code=`*AppletClassName.class*
	`            archive="`*JarFileName.jar*`"`
	`            width=`*width*`, height=`*height*`>`
	
	`</applet>`

Run an application packaged as a JAR file.	java -cp *app.jar MainClass*

15.8.2 Executing an Applet from Within a JAR File

An applet can be executed directly within a JAR file. To do this, we must modify the HTML file, adding an "archive" tag to specify the name of the JAR file containing the applet to execute. Figure 15.14 shows this modified HTML file.

```
1  <html>
2  <applet code="PlotSinCosApplet.class" archive="PlotSinCos.jar"
3          width=400 height=460>
4  </applet>
5  </html>
```

Figure 15.14. HTML file required to execute the PlotSinCosApplet as an applet within JAR file PlotSinCos.jar.

If this HTML file and the JAR file are placed in the same directory, then a browser that reads this HTML file will execute the applet directly from the JAR file. The JAR file contains all of the required classes and data files necessary to run the applet, so only the JAR file will have to be transferred across the network to the computer running the browser. Since this file is also compressed, the file transfer will be much faster, and the application will start much sooner.

GOOD PROGRAMMING PRACTICE

Place your applets within JAR files, along with all required resources and supporting classes. The applet will transfer transfer more rapidly over the network and will start up more quickly.

15.8.3 Executing an Application from Within a JAR File

An application can also be executed directly from within a JAR file. To do this, we must use the Java run-time's −cp option to specify that the interpreter should search the JAR file for classes to execute. The modified command is[1]

```
D:\book\chap15>java -cp PlotSinCos.jar PlotSinCosApplet
```

---

[1] There is also another way to execute an application within a JAR file: java −jar *app.jar*. This command works only if the manifest file within the JAR file contains special information to tell the Java interpreter which class within the archive to execute first. See the Java SDK documentation for a description of this option.

QUIZ 15-1

This quiz provides a quick check to see if you have understood the concepts introduced in Sections 15.1 through 15.8. If you have trouble with the quiz, reread the section, ask your instructor, or discuss the material with a fellow student. The answers are found in the back of the book.

1. What is an applet? How does it differ from an application?

2. What are the five key methods in an applet? What do they do?

3. How can a user pass parameters to an applet when it is started? How does the applet read the parameters supplied by the user?

4. How can you write a single program that can run as either an applet or an application?

5. What is an applet? How does it differ from an application?

6. What is a Java Archive file? How can a JAR file be used to simplify the distribution of Java applets and applications?

7. What are the advantages of saving a complete applet within a JAR file, instead of leaving the applet's classes and resources in separate files?

SUMMARY

- An applet is a special type of Java program that is designed to work within a World Wide Web browser.

- Applets are usually quite small and are designed to be downloaded, executed, and discarded whenever the browser points to a site containing the Java applet.

- For security reasons, applets are not allowed access to the computer on which they are executing.

- An applet is created by extending class `javax.swing.JApplet`.

- An applet is executed within a browser by loading an html page containing an `<applet>` tag referring to the applet.

- Information may be displayed on the browser's status line using the applet's `showStatus` method.

- Applets can be designed to read parameters passed in the HTML file that starts the application running. A parameter in the HTML file is marked by a PARAM tag. It takes the form `<PARAM NAME="xxx" VALUE="yyy">`, located between the `<APPLET>` and `</APPLET>` tags.

- Parameter values can be recovered using the applet method `getParameter(name)`.

- If an applet uses a class that appears in a package, then the package must appear in a subdirectory of the directory containing the HTML file.

- We can create such a dual-purpose application/applet by first creating a working applet and then adding a `main` method to the applet.

- A JAR file is a special type of file that stores Java classes in a compressed format. Java applications and applets can be executed directly within the JAR file without first extracting them.

- JAR files are compressed, so they can be transferred more quickly across a network than the corresponding uncompressed files.

SUMMARY OF GOOD PROGRAMMING PRACTICES

The following guidelines introduced in this chapter will help you to develop good programs:

1. Use HTML parameters to allow users to customize your applets at execution time.

2. Whenever possible, design your programs to be dual-purpose applications/applets.

3. Place your applets within JAR files, along with all required resources and supporting classes. The applet will transfer more rapidly over the network and will start up more quickly.

TERMINOLOGY

applet
<applet> tag
destroy() method
init() method
JApplet class

JAR file
showStatus() method
start() method
stop() method

Exercises

1. Modify the temperature-conversion program from Example 13.1 to run as either an application or an applet. Demonstrate its operation in both modes.

2. Modify the temperature-conversion program from Exercise 1 so that it reads an HTML parameter for the number of decimal places to use in the display of temperature values.

3. Place the temperature-conversion program from Exercise 1 into a JAR file, and demonstrate execution both as an application and as an applet from the JAR file.

4. Create an elapsed-time-measurement applet. The applet should contain two read-only text fields displaying the applet status and elapsed time, plus three buttons, labeled "Start", "Elapsed Time", and "Stop". When the "Start" button is pressed, the timer should start running, the status field should be set to display "Running", and the timer field should display zero elapsed time. When the "Elapsed Time" button is pressed, the timer field should display the elapsed time since the "Start" button was last pressed. When the "Stop" button is pressed, the the status field should display "Stopped", and the timer field should display the elapsed time between the pressing of the "Start" button and the pressing of the "Stop" button.

5. Convert the elapsed-time applet of Exercise 4 into a dual application/applet.

6. Create a calculator applet that can perform addition, subtraction, multiplication, and division. Use the GUI created in Example 13.2 as a starting point, and implement the methods required to make the calculator functional.

7. Package all of the classes from the calculator applet in a single JAR file, and compare the size of the JAR file to the size of the individual classes. How much space was saved by placing the classes in the JAR file?

16

Input and Output

The Java input/output (I/O) system is very complex, both because of the wide variety of things it tries to do and because there are actually *two* layers of I/O systems created at different times. Java contains both an original I/O system released with the Java SDK version 1.0, and a newer system of convenience classes overlaid on top of it in Java SDK 1.1. The two systems intertwine, which doesn't make life any easier.

In other languages, such as Fortran and C, there are simple integrated statements for reading and writing data to files. For example, in Fortran the statement

```
WRITE (10,*) a, b, c
```

would write character representations of the values of a, b, and c to the file associated with unit 10. In these languages, any number of variables can be included in an input or output statement, and they may be of different types.

The Java I/O system does not do anything simply. Instead, it consists of many classes containing *components* of an I/O system, and it is the programmer's responsibility to string the components together in the proper order to accomplish whatever type of I/O operation is desired. The result is so messy that programmers almost always build and use **convenience classes** for each type of I/O operation that they wish to perform. Each convenience class contains all of the lower-level Java I/O classes arranged in the proper order for one specific type of I/O operation. The classes StdIn and ReadFile that we created in Chapter 10 are examples of such convenience classes.

SECTIONS

OBJECTIVES

- Understand the structure of the Java I/O system.
- Be able to read Strings from a formatted sequential file or the standard input stream.
- Be able to read numeric data from a formatted sequential file or the standard input stream.
- Be able to write to a formatted sequential file.
- Be able to perform unformatted input and output to sequential files.
- Be able to read and write objects to sequential files.
- Understand the java.io.Serializable interface.
- Be able to perform unformatted input and output to random access files.
- Be able to get information about a file or directory using the File class.

Among the reasons for the Java I/O system's complexity are the following:

1. **Many different types of sources and sinks.** A **source** is a device that data can be read from, and a **sink** is a device that data can be written to. Java can read data from and write data to files, arrays of bytes, `Strings`, pipes (connections between two programs or threads), and other sources such as Internet connections.

2. **Two different types of file access.** For historical reasons going back to the earliest computers, the data in most files are read sequentially in order from the beginning of the file to the end. This **sequential access** was the standard, because many early I/O devices such as tapes and card readers could only be read sequentially. However, today's disks are **random-access** devices; the data on a disk can be read in any arbitrary order. Random access is very useful for databases and other applications where any particular piece of information could be requested at any time. Java supports both sequential access and random access to files, using different classes in each case.

3. **Two different types of storage formats.** Java supports two different types of data-storage formats, **formatted** and **unformatted**. A **formatted file** contains information written out as character strings, so that it is easy for a human to see and understand. For example, the statement `System.out.println("pi = " + Math.PI);` produces formatted output. It prints out a visible character string to the standard output stream, which is usually connected to our computer screen.

By contrast, an **unformatted file** contains data stored as raw bit patterns. Java can read and write these bit patterns in a platform-independent way, but they mean nothing to a human examining the file. Unformatted files pack data into less space than formatted files. Java supports both formatted and unformatted data storage, using different classes for each.

4. **Two different I/O systems.** The original Java SDK 1.0 contained an I/O system that was based on transferring *bytes* of data to and from sources and sinks. Unfortunately, all of Java's characters and strings are based on Unicode, which uses 16 bits to represent a character of data. Transferring characters is the most common operation in the I/O system, and it was awkward under Java SDK 1.0. To alleviate this problem, Java SDK 1.1 introduced a new set of convenience classes for formatted I/O based on transferring characters instead of bytes.

Unfortunately, the new character-based I/O system is *not* a complete replacement for the older byte-based I/O system. Many parts of Java were not converted to work with the character-based classes, including the standard input, output, and error streams, the data-compression classes (zip file creator and users), and the direct-access I/O classes. In addition, unformatted I/O is supported only through the older byte-based I/O system. As a result, we now have the original byte-based family of classes, the new character-based family of convenience classes, and a set of bridges between them.

It is not possible for a programmer to work only with the old classes, because parts of them have been declared **deprecated**, meaning that they are candidates for deletion in future versions of the language. It is not possible for a programmer to work only with the new classes, because the new classes are not complete by themselves. Instead, the programmer must work with a complex mishmash of 50 or so classes and try to pick his or her own way through the mess.

5. **A variety of "filter" or "modifier" classes.** In addition to the basic I/O functions, Java includes a series of classes that filter or modify the input and output data streams. These classes improve the efficiency of I/O operations or provide other services such as counting line numbers, dividing data into tokens, and so on. Naturally, some of these classes come in pairs, one to work with the old I/O system and one to work with the new I/O system.

This chapter will introduce only the basics of the Java I/O system. We will learn how to do only the most important types of I/O operations, and ignore the rest.

16.1 THE STRUCTURE OF THE JAVA I/O SYSTEM

The Java I/O system can be divided into a series of categories based on the method of access, the direction of data transfer (input or output), the types of devices used, whether the data is transferred as bytes or characters, and whether the data is formatted or unformatted.

The first division in the Java I/O System is based on the method of access: sequential or random (see Figure 16.1).[1] Random access is supported for files only, and

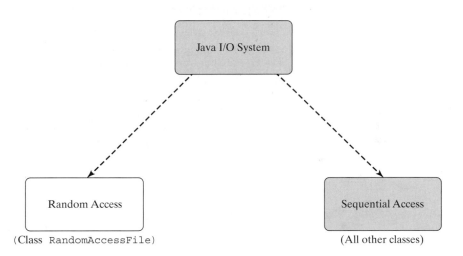

Figure 16.1. The Java I/O System may be divided by access method into random access and sequential access. Random access is implemented only for files using class `RandomAccessFile`. All other classes implement sequential access.

for unformatted I/O only, by class `RandomAccessFile`. This class supports both reading and writing random-access files. All other I/O classes support sequential access.

GOOD PROGRAMMING PRACTICE

Use class `RandomAccessFile` to read and write data in random access files.

Sequential access may be subdivided by the *direction of data flow*—input or output. Except for random-access files, Java I/O classes support data input only or data output only. Unlike many other languages, it is not possible to open a sequential Java file for read/write access. Instead, the file must be written completely, closed, and then opened separately for reading. Figure 16.2 shows this dichotomy between reading and writing.

---

[1]Note that the dashed arrows in these figures indicate a logical relationship, and the solid arrows indicate data flow. Neither type of arrow has anything to do with inheritance or the class hierarchy of Java classes.

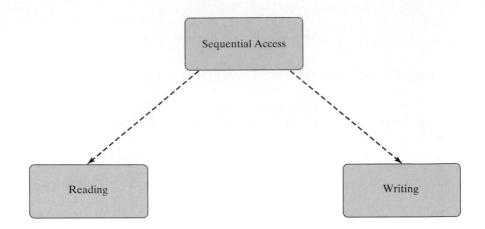

Figure 16.2.   Sequential I/O is subdivided into classes for reading and classes for writing. There is no such thing as read/write access for sequential files in Java.

16.2   SEQUENTIAL DATA INPUT

There are two ways to read a sequential data stream—as a byte stream and as a character stream. The byte-stream approach goes back to Java SDK 1.0, and classes that implement this approach usually have the words "InputStream" in their names. The character-stream approach was introduced in Java SDK 1.1, and classes that implement this approach usually have the word "Reader" in their names (see Figure 16.3). Each of these approaches can be further subdivided by the type of the data source being read from: byte or char arrays, Strings, files, or pipes.

There is also a "bridge class" InputStreamReader that converts a byte-based InputStream into a character-based Reader. This class is necessary because certain parts of Java work only with byte streams. For example, the standard input device is implemented as a byte stream, and the classes that read zip files are implemented as byte streams. This "bridge class" allows byte data to be converted to character data for use with the Reader classes.

We mentioned earlier that Java supports formatted and unformatted data-storage formats. The *unformatted* data-storage format consists of data stored as raw bit patterns. Java reads these bit patterns in a platform-independent way through class DataInputStream, which can be connected to any of the "InputStream" sources. This class provides methods such as readInt(), readDouble(), and so on to read unformatted data from an InputStream and convert it into the appropriate data type. The *formatted* data-storage format consists of data stored as sequences of human-readable characters. Java converts these into Strings through class BufferedReader, which can be connected to any of the "Reader" sources. This class provides methods such as readLine() to read an entire line of characters and place them into a String.

There is also a special type of unformatted data storage designed to save or transfer entire objects as a whole, with all of their internal data intact. Java reads objects stored in this special format using an ObjectInputStream, which can be connected to any of the "InputStream" sources. This class implements method readObject(), as well as the methods readInt() and readDouble(), to handle primitive data types.

There are also two **buffering classes**, one to support InputStreams and one to support Readers. These classes greatly improve system performance when reading from files. The normal input classes request data from the disk *a few bytes at a time*, so they cause many delays while the computer reads from the disk. The buffer classes

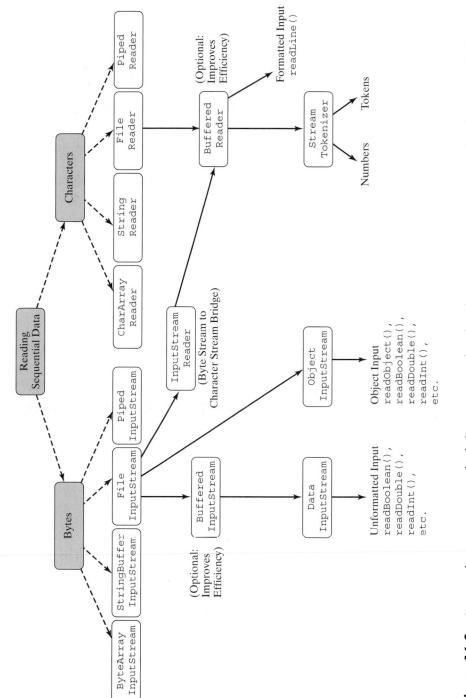

Figure 16.3. Sequential input streams are divided into two types, byte-based InputStreams and character-based Readers. Both InputStreams and Readers can read from arrays, Strings, files, or pipes. This picture illustrates the possible data flows from an input file for both unformatted and formatted data. The dotted lines indicate logical relationships, and the solid black lines indicate the possible directions of data flows.

speed up operations by reading a large amount of data from the disk, holding it in memory, and parceling it out a few bytes at a time as it is needed. You should *always* use the `BufferedInputStream` class when reading from a `FileInputStream`, and the `BufferedReader` class when reading from a `FileReader` or from an `InputStreamReader` whose original data source was a `FileInputStream`.

Finally, there is a class `StreamTokenizer` that will accept a line of character data from a `Reader` and break it up into individual tokens. Numeric tokens are automatically translated into `double` numbers, and character tokens are automatically translated into `Strings`.

Figure 16.3 shows the overall sequential input data architecture. From it, we can see that:

1.   *Unformatted data* is read through any of the `InputStream` sources and is converted into usable data values by methods in class `DataInputStream`. If the source is a `FileInputStream`, then the data should be routed through a `BufferedInputStream` to improve performance.

2.   *Unformatted data* in the special "object" format is read through any of the `InputStream` sources and is converted into usable data values by methods in class `ObjectInputStream`. No buffering is required in this case, because the `ObjectInputStream` reads data in large chunks anyway.

3.   *Formatted data* is read through any of the `Reader` sources and is converted into usable data values by methods in classes `BufferedReader` and/or `StreamTokenizer`. If the source is a `FileReader`, or an `InputStreamReader` whose original data source was a `FileInputStream`, then the data should be routed through a `BufferedReader` to improve performance.

GOOD PROGRAMMING PRACTICE

Read unformatted data using the "`InputStream`" sources and convert it to a useful form using the `DataInputStream` class.

GOOD PROGRAMMING PRACTICE

Read formatted data using the "`Reader`" sources and convert it to a useful form using the `BufferedReader` class. If you are reading from the standard input stream, convert the data into a `Reader` using the `InputStreamReader` class before sending it to the `BufferedReader` class.

GOOD PROGRAMMING PRACTICE

Always use the `BufferedInputStream` or `BufferedReader` classes to improve efficiency when reading data from a file.

16.3   SEQUENTIAL DATA OUTPUT

There are two ways to write sequential data streams—as a byte stream and as a character stream. The byte-stream approach goes back to Java SDK 1.0, and classes that implement this approach usually have the words "`OutputStream`" in their names. The character-stream approach was introduced in Java SDK 1.1, and classes that implement this approach usually have the word "`Writer`" in their names (see Figure 16.4). Each of

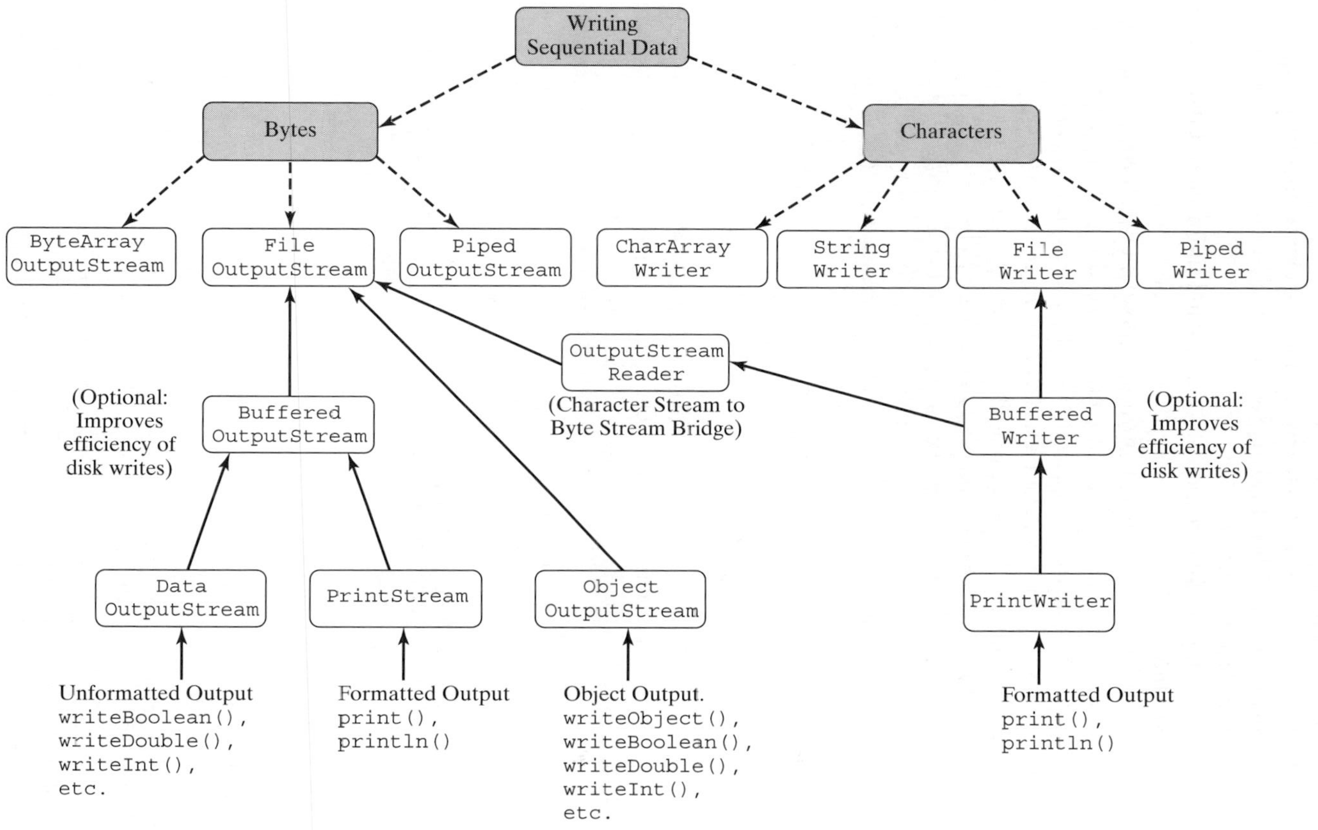

Figure 16.4. Sequential output streams are divided into two types, byte-based `OutputStreams` and character-based `Writers`. `OutputStreams` can write to byte arrays, files, or pipes, and `Writers` can write to character arrays, `Strings`, files, or pipes. This picture illustrates the possible data flows to an output file for both unformatted and formatted data. The dotted lines indicate logical relationships, and the solid black lines indicate the possible directions of data flows.

these approaches can be further subdivided by the type of the data sink being written to: `byte` arrays, files, or pipes for the `OutputStream` classes, and `char` arrays, `Strings`, files or pipes for the `Writer` classes.

There is also a "bridge class" `OutputStreamWriter` that converts a character-based `Writer` into a byte-based `OutputStream`. This class is necessary because certain parts of Java work only with byte streams. For example, the standard output device is implemented as a byte stream, and the classes that write zip files are implemented as byte streams. This "bridge class" allows character data to be converted to byte data for use with the `OutputStream` classes.

Java can write both formatted and unformatted data-storage formats. The *unformatted* data-storage format consists of data stored as raw bit patterns. Java writes these bit patterns in a platform-independent way through class `DataOutputStream`, which can be connected to any of the "`OutputStream`" sinks. This class provides methods such as `writeInt()`, `writeDouble()`, and so on to write unformatted data to an `OutputStream`. The *formatted* data-storage format consists of data stored as sequences of human-readable characters. Java writes formatted data through classes `PrintStream` and `PrintWriter`. These two classes each provide methods `print()` and `println()` to output formatted data to `OutputStreams` or `Writers`. Note that `PrintWriter` is the preferred class of the two, except for debugging purposes or for formatted data written to the standard output or standard error devices.

Finally, entire objects can be written to any sink in a platform-independent way using class `ObjectOutputStream`. This class implements method `writeObject()` as well as methods such as `writeInt()`, `writeDouble()`, and so on to handle primitive data types.

There are also two **buffering classes**, one to support `OutputStreams` and one to support `Writers`. These classes greatly improve system performance when writing to files. The normal output classes write data to the disk *a few bytes at a time*, so they cause many delays while the computer writes to the disk. The buffer classes speed up operations by saving up a large amount of data in memory, then writing it all at once to the disk. You should *always* use the `BufferedOuputStream` class when writing to a `FileOutputStream`, and the `BufferedWriter` class when writing to a `FileWriter` or to an `OutputStreamWriter` whose final destination is a `FileOutputStream`.

Figure 16.4 shows the overall sequential output data architecture. From it, we can see that

1. *Unformatted data* is created by methods in `DataOutputStream` and is written through any of the `OutputStream` sinks. If the destination is a `FileOutputStream`, then the data should be routed through a `BufferedOutputStream` to improve performance.
2. *Unformatted data* in the special "object" format is written through any of the `OutputStream` sinks using class `ObjectOutputStream`.
3. *Formatted data* is created by methods in `PrintStream` or in `PrintWriter`. The `PrintStream` data is written through any of the `OutputStream` sinks. The `PrintWriter` data is written through any of the `Writer` sinks. The `PrintWriter` methods are preferred over the `PrintStream` methods, except when working with the standard output and standard error devices. If the destination is a `FileOutputStream` or a `FileWriter`, then the data should be routed through a `Buffered-OutputStream` or a `BufferedWriter` to improve performance.

Create unformatted output data with methods in the `DataOutputStream` class and write it out using the "`OutputStream`" sinks.

Create formatted output data using the `print()` and `println()` methods found in the `PrintStream` and `PrintWriter` classes and write it out using the `OutputStream` and `OutputWriter` sinks, respectively. Use the `PrintWriter` methods, except when working with the standard output or standard error devices.

Always use the `BufferedOutputStream` or `BufferedWrite` classes to improve efficiency when writing data to a file.

16.4 FORMATTED INPUT AND OUTPUT

As we saw in the previous sections, the preferred way to read character data is with the `readLine()` method of `BufferedReader`, and the preferred way to write character data is with the `print()` and `println()` methods of `PrintWriter`. We will now show how to read and write data files using these methods.

16.4.1 Reading `String`s from a Formatted Sequential File

The class that allows us to open and read formatted character data from a file is `FileReader`. This class has three different forms of constructors, which contain different ways to specify the file to open and read data from:

```
FileReader(String fileName);
FileReader(File file);
FileReader(FileDescriptor fd);
```

The first constructor is the most common form, the one we used in Chapter 10. It specifies the file to open by its file name. The second form specifies the file by an object of the `File` class, and the third form specifies the object by a predefined file descriptor.

When a `FileReader` object is created, the corresponding file is automatically opened and prepared for reading. If the file cannot be opened, `FileReader` will throw a `FileNotFoundException`.

For efficiency reasons, the output of a `FileReader` should always be sent to a `BufferedReader`, as shown in Figure 16.3. (In Java terms, we say that the `FileReader` is *wrapped* in a `BufferedReader`, because the file data goes through the `BufferedReader` before it is used.) This is typically accomplished as follows:

```
BufferedReader br = new BufferedReader(
                        new FileReader( fileName ));
```

Once a `BufferedReader` has been created, each line of data in the file can be read with the `readLine()` method. When no more data is available in the file, the `readline()` method will return a `null` reference.

After the data has been read from a file, the file should be explicitly closed with a call to the `close()` method. This should be done as soon as possible to release the file resources for possible reuse by this program or other programs. Note that once a file is closed, any attempt to read data from it will produce an `IOException`.

GOOD PROGRAMMING PRACTICE

Always close any files you use just as soon as you are finished with them. This action releases the file resources for possible use elsewhere within the computer.

EXAMPLE 16.1

Reading Lines of Data as `Strings` from a Formatted Sequential Input File:
Write a program that reads and displays `Strings` a line at a time from a user-specified input file.

SOLUTION

An example program that reads lines from a user-specified file and displays them is shown in Figure 16.5. The name of the file to read is passed as a command-line argument to the program. This program creates a new `FileReader` object and wraps it in a `BufferedReader` object for efficiency. It uses the `readLine()` method of the `BufferedReader` object to read the file one line at a time and display the results on the standard output device. Note that the `BufferedReader` is created within a `try/catch` structure to trap `FileNotFound` and `IOExceptions`, if they occur.

```java
// Read a formatted file
import java.io.*;
public class ReadFormattedFile {

    public static void main(String[] args) {

        // Define variables
        String s;          // String reference

        // Trap exceptions if they occur
        try {

            // Create BufferedReader
            BufferedReader in =
                new BufferedReader(
                    new FileReader(args[0]));

            // Read file and display data
            while( (s = in.readLine()) != null) {
                System.out.println(s);
            }

            // Close file
            in.close();
        }

        // Catch FileNotFoundException
```

Figure 16.5. A sample program that reads a formatted file and returns the data a line at a time as a `String`.

```
        catch (FileNotFoundException e) {
            System.out.println("File not found: " + args[0]);
        }

        // Catch other IOExceptions
        catch (IOException e) {
            System.out.println("IOException: the stack trace is:");
            e.printStackTrace();
        }
    }
}
```

Figure 16.5. (Continued).

To test this program, we will execute it twice. The first time we will pass the program the name of an existing file, and the second time we will pass the program the name of a nonexistent file. When this program is executed with an existing file input.txt, the results are

```
D:\book\java\chap16>java ReadFormattedFile input.txt
This is line 1 of the test file.
This is line 2 of the test file.
This is the last line of the test file.
```

When this program is executed with a nonexistent file input2.txt, the results are

```
D:\book\java\chap16>java ReadFormattedFile input2.txt
File not found: input2.txt
```

The program appears to be working correctly in both cases.

GOOD PROGRAMMING PRACTICE

To read Strings from a formatted sequential input file, create a FileReader (wrapped in a BufferedReader for efficiency) and use the readLine() method of the BufferedReader to read the data a line at a time.

16.4.2 Reading Numeric Data from a Formatted Sequential File

If the output from a BufferedReader is sent to an object of the StreamTokenizer class, the data in a formatted sequential file can be separated into discrete tokens,[2] and the tokens that represent numbers can be automatically translated into double values by this class.

The StreamTokenizer class includes three public instance variables and a number of constants, which are summarized in Table 16.1.

The class includes many methods, of which the most important is nextToken(). Each time that nextToken() is called, the method gets the next token from the Reader. Then, it decides whether the token is a word, a quoted string, or a number. If

[2]Remember from Chapter 10 that *tokens* are sequences of characters separated from other sequences of characters by white space.

TABLE 16.1 StreamTokenizer Instance Variables

Instance Variable	Description
double **nval**	If the current token is a number, this variable contains the value of the number.
String **sval**	If the current token is a word token (if it has alphabetic characters in it), this variable contains the characters in the token.
int **ttype**	After a call to the nextToken() method, this field contains the type of the token just read. For a quoted string token, its value is the quote character (34). Otherwise, its value is TT_WORD if the token is a word, TT_NUMBER if the token is a number, and TT_EOF if we are at the end of the file.
int **TT_EOF**	A constant indicating that we are at the end of the input file.
int **TT_NUMBER**	A constant indicating that the current token is a number.
int **TT_WORD**	A constant indicating that the current token is a word.

it is a word, the method sets ttype to TT_WORD and returns the word in sval. If it is a quoted string, the method sets ttype to the quote character and returns the string in sval. If it is a number, the method sets ttype to TT_NUMBER and returns the value in nval. If the token is a single character, then its value is returned directly in ttype.

This class is very flexible, with the ability to recognize quoted strings and escape characters such as \t and \n. However, it has two very important limitations. It does not recognize the + character as numeric, so a number like +12.3 will be interpreted as single character token followed by the number 12.3. Also, it doesn't recognize the exponent letter e in expressions such as 6.02e23, so such tokens will not be translated correctly.

EXAMPLE 16.2

Reading Tokens from a Formatted Sequential Input File: Write a program that reads individual tokens from a formatted sequential input file and converts the tokens representing numbers into double values.

SOLUTION

This program must create a FileReader wrapped in a BufferedReader wrapped in a StreamTokenizer, so that the output of the FileReader goes to the BufferedReader and the output of the buffered reader goes to the StreamTokenizer. Then, the method nextToken() can be used to recover and translate successive tokens from the file.

An example program using StreamTokenizer is shown in Figure 16.6.

To test this program, we will create a file token.txt containing the following lines.

```
This is a test.
"This is a test."
123.45
4.2e6 +6
```

When this program is executed, the results are:

```
D:\book\java\chap16>java TestStreamTokenizer tokens.txt
String: value = This
String: value = is
String: value = a
String: value = test.
Quote:  value = This is a test.
Number: value = 123.45
Number: value = 4.2
String: value = e6
Character: value = 43
Number: value = 6.0
```

```java
// Test the operation of StreamTokenizer
import java.io.*;
public class TestStreamTokenizer {

    public static void main(String[] args) {

        // Define variables
        String s;          // String reference

        // Trap exceptions if they occur
        try {

            // Create StreamTokenizer
            BufferedReader in =
                new BufferedReader(
                    new FileReader(args[0]));
            StreamTokenizer st =
                new StreamTokenizer(in);

            // Get and display tokens
            st.nextToken();
            while( st.ttype != st.TT_EOF ) {
                if ( st.ttype == st.TT_NUMBER )
                    System.out.println("Number: value = " + st.nval);
                else if ( st.ttype == st.TT_WORD )
                    System.out.println("String: value = " + st.sval);
                else if ( st.ttype == 34 )
                    System.out.println("Quote:  value = " + st.sval);
                else
                    System.out.println("Character: value = " + st.ttype);
                st.nextToken();
            }

            // Close file
            in.close();
        }

        // Catch FileNotFoundException
        catch (FileNotFoundException e) {
            System.out.println("File not found: " + args[0]);
        }

        // Catch other IOExceptions
        catch (IOException e) {
            System.out.println("IOException: the stack trace is:");
            e.printStackTrace();
        }
    }
}
```

Figure 16.6. Program to test StreamTokenizer.

For the most part, this program interpreted the data correctly. It made two errors, in that it failed to recognize 4.2e6 as a number and it failed to recognize the + sign as a part of the number +6. With these limitations in mind, StreamTokenizer can be used to read Strings and numbers from a Reader.

We can get around the numeric-conversion problems noted above by using StringTokenizer instead of StreamTokenizer and passing the resulting strings to method Double.parseDouble(). This is the approach that we used in class ReadFile in Chapter 10. Method Double.parseDouble() is smart enough to recognize the + sign and the e as components of floating-point numbers. ∎

16.4.3 Reading Formatted Data from the Standard Input Stream

The standard input device on a computer is automatically opened and connected to object System.in whenever a Java program starts running. Unfortunately, System.in is an InputStream instead of a Reader. To read formatted data, we need to send the data from System.in to an InputStreamReader so that it can be translated into character data. For efficiency reasons, the InputStreamReader should always be wrapped in a BufferedReader, as shown in Figure 16.3. This is typically accomplished as follows:

```
BufferedReader br = new BufferedReader(
                        new InputStreamReader (System.in));
```

Once a BufferedReader has been created, a program can read lines of data from the standard input stream with the readLine() method. When no more data is available, the readline() method will return a null reference.

If individual tokens are desired, then the BufferedReader can be wrapped in a StreamTokenizer, as we saw in Section 16.4.2, and the data from the standard input stream can be converted directly into tokens and numeric values. Alternatively, it can be wrapped in a StringTokenizer, as we saw in Chapter 10 in class StdIn.

EXAMPLE 16.3

Reading Lines of Data as Strings from the Standard Input Stream: Write a program that reads and displays Strings a line at a time from the standard input stream.

SOLUTION

This program must create an InputStreamReader wrapped in a BufferedReader, so that the readLine() method of the BufferedReader can be used to read lines of data from the standard input stream.

The program shown in Figure 16.7 reads lines from the standard input stream and displays them. This program reads lines of data from the standard input stream until either there is no more data to read or there is an "x" in the first character of a line.

The program has two terminating conditions because of the nature of the standard input stream. If the standard input stream is redirected to come from a file, readLine() will return a null when there is no more data in the file, and the program will terminate. However, if the standard input stream comes from the keyboard, it will never be "empty" and readLine() will never return a null. The separate test to terminate the loop when an "x" is the first character in a line handles this case.

To test this program, we will execute it twice. The first time we will redirect the standard input stream to come from file input.txt. The second time we will enter data directly from the keyboard. When this program is executed with the standard input stream redirected to come from file input.txt, the results are

```
D:\book\java\chap16>java ReadFormattedStdin < input.txt
Line = This is line 1 of the test file.
Line = This is line 2 of the test file.
Line = This is the last line of the test file.
```

```java
// Read formatted data from the standard input stream
import java.io.*;
public class ReadFormattedStdin {

    public static void main(String[] args) {

        // Define variables
        String s;          // String reference
        String s1;         // First character in s

        // Trap exceptions if they occur
        try {

            // Create BufferedReader
            BufferedReader in =
                new BufferedReader(
                    new InputStreamReader(System.in));

            // Read file and display data.  Allow the
            // process to terminate if either the
            // input stream runs out of data or if an
            // "x" appears as the first character in
            // a line.
            s = in.readLine();
            while( s != null ) {
                s1 = s.substring(0,1);
                if ( s1.compareTo("x") == 0 ) break;
                System.out.println("Line = " + s);
                s = in.readLine();
            }
        }

        // Catch IOExceptions
        catch (IOException e) {
            System.out.println("IOException: the stack trace is:");
            e.printStackTrace();
        }
    }
}
```

Figure 16.7.   A sample program that reads formatted data from the standard input stream and returns the data a line at a time as a String.

When this program is executed with data read directly from the keyboard, the results are

```
D:\book\java\chap16>java ReadFormattedStdin
Line 1
Line = Line 1
Line 2
Line = Line 2
x
```

The program appears to work correctly in both cases.

16.4.4 Formatted Output to a Sequential File

The class that allows us to open and write formatted character data to a file is `FileWriter`. This class has four different forms of constructors, which are four different ways to specify the file to open and write data to:

```
FileWriter(String fileName);
FileWriter(String fileName, boolean append);
FileWriter(File file);
FileWriter(FileDescriptor fd);
```

The first, third, and fourth constructors specify the file to open by file name, `File` object, and file descriptor, respectively. When the file is opened with one of these constructors, any previously existing file is automatically deleted. The second constructor includes a boolean parameter `append`. If `append` is true, any previously existing file is opened and the new data is appended to the file. If `append` is false, any previously existing file is deleted.

When a `FileWriter` object is created, the corresponding file is automatically opened and prepared for writing. If the file cannot be opened, `FileWriter` will throw an `IOException`.

For efficiency reasons, a `FileWriter` should always be wrapped in a `BufferedWriter`, which should be wrapped in a `PrintWriter`, as shown in Figure 16.4. This is typically accomplished as follows:

```
PrintWriter out =
    new PrintWriter(
        new BufferedWriter(
            new FileWriter( fileName )));
```

Once a `PrintWriter` has been created, data can be written to the file with the `print()` and `println()` methods.

After the data has been written to a file, the file should be explicitly closed with a call to the `close()` method. This should be done as soon as possible to release the file resources for possible reuse by this program or other programs. Note that, once a file is closed, any attempt to write data from it will produce an `IOException`.

EXAMPLE 16.4

Writing Data to a Formatted Sequential File: Create a program that writes output data to a formatted sequential output file.

SOLUTION

An example program that writes lines to a user-specified file is shown in Figure 16.8. The name of the file to write and an append flag are passed as a command-line arguments to the program. This program creates a new `PrintWriter` object, with the data being transferred from a `PrintWriter` to a `BufferedWriter` to a `FileWriter`, as shown in Figure 16.4. If the append flag is false or absent, it deletes any previously existing file. If the append flag is true, it opens any previously existing file and adds the new data to the end of it.

The program uses the `PrintWriter` object to write data one line at a time to the file. Note that the `PrintWriter` is created within a `try/catch` structure to trap `IOExceptions`, if they occur.

To test this program, we will execute it twice. The first time we will pass the program a file name without the append flag, and the second time we will pass the program the same file name with an append flag. When this program is executed with the file name `output.txt`, the results are

```
// Write a formatted file
import java.io.*;
import java.text.DecimalFormat;
public class WriteFormattedFile {

    public static void main(String[] args) {

        // Define variables
        boolean append;  // Append flag
        String s;        // String reference

        // Trap exceptions if they occur
        try {

            // Get the append flag, if present
            append = false;
            if ( args.length >= 2 ) {
                if ( args[1].equalsIgnoreCase("true") )
                    append = true;
            }

            // Create PrintWriter
            PrintWriter out =
                new PrintWriter(
                    new BufferedWriter(
                        new FileWriter(args[0],append)));

            // Write data to file
            DecimalFormat df = new DecimalFormat("###.000000");
            out.println("This is line 1.");
            out.println("This is line 2.");
            out.println("This is line 3.");
            out.println("pi = " + df.format(Math.PI));

            // Close file
            out.close();
        }

        // Catch IOExceptions
        catch (IOException e) {
            System.out.println("IOException: the stack trace is:");
            e.printStackTrace();
        }
    }
}
```

Figure 16.8. A sample program that writes data to a formatted file.

```
D:\book\java\chap16>java WriteFormattedFile output.txt

D:\book\java\chap16>type output.txt
This is line 1.
This is line 2.
This is line 3.
pi = 3.141593
```

The contents of the file are the four lines that we expected. When this program is executed with the file name `output.txt` and the append flag, the results are

```
D:\book\java\chap16>java WriteFormattedFile output.txt true
```

```
D:\book\java\chap16>type output.txt
This is line 1.
This is line 2.
This is line 3.
pi = 3.141593
This is line 1.
This is line 2.
This is line 3.
pi = 3.141593
```

This time the output data was appended to the previously existing file. The program appears to work correctly in both cases.

This example also shows that we can use the formatting capabilities of the `DecimalFormat` class with output files. The `DecimalFormat` method `format` produces a `String`, and that `String` can be sent to the output file with the `println` method just like any other `String`. ∎

16.5 UNFORMATTED INPUT AND OUTPUT

As we mentioned in the Section 16.2, the preferred way to read unformatted data is with the `readInt()`, `readDouble()`, and so on, methods of `DataInputStream`, and the preferred way to write unformatted data is with the `writeInt()`, `writeDouble()`, and so on, methods of `DataOutputStream`. We will now show how to read and write data files using these methods.

16.5.1 Unformatted Input from a Sequential File

The class that allows us to read unformatted data from a sequential file in a machine-independent way is `DataInputStream`. As shown in Figure 16.3, unformatted input data flows from a `FileInputStream` object to a `BufferedInputStream` object, and from there to the `DataInputStream` object. The constructor of the `DataInputStream` class is

```
DataInputStream(InputStream in);
```

This constructor creates an object that reads data from `in` and translates it into the appropriate `int`, `double`, and so forth.

For efficiency reasons, a `FileInputStream` should always be wrapped in a `BufferedInputStream` before it is wrapped in a `DataInputStream`, as shown in Figure 16.3. This is typically accomplished as follows:

```
DataInputStream in = new DataInputStream(
                new BufferedInputStream(
                    new FileInputStream( fileName )));
```

Once a `DataInputStream` has been created, each value can be read with the `readInt()`, `readDouble()`, and so on methods. When no more data available is in the file, the read methods will throw an `EOFException`.

The methods in class `DataInputStream` are part of the `DataInput` interface, which is implemented by `DataInputStream`. Some of these methods are summarized in Table 16.2. All of them are listed in the Java SDK documentation.

TABLE 16.2 Selected `DataInput` Methods

Method	Description
`boolean readBoolean()`	Reads one input byte and returns `true` if that byte is nonzero, and `false` if that byte is zero.
`byte readByte()`	Reads and returns one byte.
`char readChar()`	Reads and returns one `char` value.
`double readDouble()`	Reads and returns one `double` value.
`float readFloat()`	Reads and returns one `float` value.
`int readInt()`	Reads and returns one `int` value.
`short readShort()`	Reads and returns one `short` value.
`String readUTF()`	Reads and returns a string coded in UTF format.

After the data has been read from a file, the file should be explicitly closed with a call to the `close()` method. This should be done as soon as possible in order to release the file resources for possible reuse by this program or other programs. Note that once a file is closed, any attempt to read data from it will produce an `IOException`.

16.5.2 Unformatted Output to a Sequential File

The class that allows us to write unformatted data to a sequential file in a machine-independent way is `DataOutputStream`. As shown in Figure 16.4, unformatted output data flows from a `DataOutputStream` object to a `BufferedOutputStream` object, and from there to the `FileOutputStream` object. The constructor of the `DataOutputStream` class is

```
DataOutputStream(OutputStream out);
```

This constructor creates an object that writes unformatted `ints`, `doubles`, and so on in a device-independent way to the output file.

For efficiency reasons, a `FileOutputStream` should always be wrapped in a `BufferedOutputStream` before it is wrapped in a `DataOutputStream`, as shown in Figure 16.4. This is typically accomplished as follows:

```
DataOutputStream out = new DataOutputStream(
                new BufferedOutputStream(
                    new FileOutputStream( fileName )));
```

Once a `DataOutputStream` has been created, each value can be written to the file with calls to methods `writeInt()`, `writeDouble()`, and so on.

After the data has been written to a file, the file should be explicitly closed with a call to the `close()` method. This should be done as soon as possible in order to release the file resources for possible reuse by this program or other programs. Note that once a file is closed, any attempt to write data to it will produce an `IOException`.

The methods in class `DataOutputStream` are part of the `DataOutput` interface, which is implemented by `DataOutputStream`. Some of these methods are summarized in Table 16.3. All of them are listed in the Java SDK documentation.

TABLE 16.3 Selected `DataOutput` Methods

Method	Description
void writeBoolean(boolean v)	Writes a `boolean` value to the output stream.
void writeByte(int v)	Writes the 8 low-order bits of the argument v to the output stream.
void writeChar(int v)	Writes a `char` value, which is comprised of 2 bytes, to the output stream.
void writeDouble(double v)	Writes a `double` value, which is comprised of 8 bytes, to the output stream.
void writeFloat(float v)	Writes a `float` value, which is comprised of 4 bytes, to the output stream.
void writeInt(int v)	Writes an `int` value, which is comprised of 4 bytes, to the output stream.
void writeLong(long v)	Writes a `long` value, which is comprised of 8 bytes, to the output stream.
short writeShort(short v)	Writes a `short` value, which is comprised of 2 bytes, to the output stream.
void writeUTF(String s)	Writes a string coded in UTF format.

EXAMPLE 16.5

Writing and Reading Data with Unformatted Sequential Files: Create a program that writes unformatted output data to a sequential output file and closes the file. The program should then open the file and read the data back in to confirm that it was written correctly.

SOLUTION

The example program shown in Figure 16.9 opens a file for output, writes unformatted data to it, and closes the file. Then it opens the file for reading, reads the same data back out, and closes the file again. This program illustrates the proper way to perform unformatted input and output to sequential files.

```java
// Unformatted I/O
import java.io.*;
import java.text.DecimalFormat;
public class TestUnformattedIO {

    public static void main(String[] args) {

        // Define variables
        double a1[] = {5., 10., 15., 20.};
        double a2[] = new double[4];
        int i1[] = {1, -10};
        int i2[] = new int[2];

        // Trap exceptions if they occur
        try {
```

Figure 16.9. A sample program illustrating unformatted input and output.

```
            // Create DataOutputStream
            DataOutputStream out = new DataOutputStream(
                                new BufferedOutputStream(
                                    new FileOutputStream ("unf.dat")));

            // Write data to file
            for ( int i = 0; i < a1.length; i++ )
                out.writeDouble( a1[i] );
            for ( int i = 0; i < i1.length; i++ )
                out.writeInt( i1[i] );

            // Close file
            out.close();

            // Create DataInputStream
            DataInputStream in = new DataInputStream(
                                new BufferedInputStream(
                                    new FileInputStream("unf.dat")));

            // Read data from file
            for ( int i = 0; i < a2.length; i++ )
                a2[i] = in.readDouble();
            for ( int i = 0; i < i2.length; i++ )
                i2[i] = in.readInt();

            // Close file
            in.close();

            // Compare the data written to the data read back
            System.out.println("Printing old and new values:");
            DecimalFormat df1 = new DecimalFormat("###.0000");
            for ( int i = 0; i < a1.length; i++ ) {
                System.out.println( "Old = " + df1.format(a1[i]) );
                System.out.println( "New = " + df1.format(a2[i]) );
            }
            DecimalFormat df2 = new DecimalFormat("###");
            for ( int i = 0; i < i1.length; i++ ) {
                System.out.println(  "Old = " + df2.format(i1[i]) );
                System.out.println(  "New = " + df2.format(i2[i]) );
            }
        }

        // Catch IOExceptions
        catch (IOException e) {
            System.out.println("IOException: the stack trace is:");
            e.printStackTrace();
        }
    }
}
```

Figure 16.9.   (Continued).

When this program is executed, the results are

```
C:\book\java\chap16>java TestUnformattedIO
Printing old and new values:
Old =   5.0000
New =   5.0000
Old =  10.0000
New =  10.0000
Old =  15.0000
New =  15.0000
Old =  20.0000
New =  20.0000
Old = 1
New = 1
Old = -10
New = -10
```

The contents of the data read from the file are identical to the contents of the data written to the file.

EXAMPLE 16.6

Comparing Formatted and Unformatted Sequential Files: To compare the operation of formatted and unformatted sequential-access files, we will create two files containing 20,000 `double` values. One file should be formatted and the other unformatted. Compare the time that it takes to write the two files, and the sizes of the two files. Then read the two files into arrays, and compare the time that it takes to read the two files. Finally, look at the sizes of the formatted and unformatted files on disk. How do formatted and unformatted files compare in terms of speed and size?

Use method `System.random()` to generate the 20,000 double values to be written out in each file, and use the `Timer` class from Chapter 7 to measure the elapsed time of file reads and writes.

SOLUTION

A program to write the two files and then read them is shown in Figure 16.10. Note that this program calculates the elapsed time for both writes and reads.

```
/*
   Purpose:
      To compare the time required to read and write
      formatted and unformatted files, and the sizes
      of those files.

   Record of revisions:
      Date          Programmer          Description of change
      ====          ==========          =====================
   8/19/2002     S. J. Chapman          Original code
*/
import java.io.*;
public class CompareFormat {
```

Figure 16.10. Program to compare the execution times and file sizes for formatted and unformatted sequential access files.

```java
public static void main(String[] args)
                throws IOException {

    // Define variables
    double a1[] = new double[20000]; // Original array
    double a2[] = new double[20000]; // Array from unformatted file
    double a3[] = new double[20000]; // Array from formatted file
    int i;                           // Loop index
    double readTimeFmt;              // Read time for fmt file
    double readTimeUnf;              // Read time for unf file
    Timer t = new Timer();           // Timer object
    double writeTimeFmt;             // Write time for fmt file
    double writeTimeUnf;             // Write time for unf file

    //********************************************************
    // Create a data set to save
    //********************************************************
    for ( i = 0; i < a1.length; i++ )
        a1[i] = Math.random();

    //********************************************************
    // Write unformatted file
    //********************************************************
    t.resetTimer();

    // Create unformatted file
    DataOutputStream out1 = new DataOutputStream(
                        new BufferedOutputStream(
                            new FileOutputStream(
                                "unformat.dat")));

    // Write data
    for ( i = 0; i < a1.length; i++ )
        out1.writeDouble( a1[i] );

    // Close file
    out1.close();

    // Get elapsed time
    writeTimeUnf = t.elapsedTime();

    //********************************************************
    // Write formatted file
    //********************************************************
    // Start timer
    t.resetTimer();

    // Create formatted file
    PrintWriter out2 =
        new PrintWriter(
            new BufferedWriter(
                new FileWriter("format.dat")));
```

Figure 16.10. (Continued).

```
          // Write data
          for ( i = 0; i < a1.length; i++ )
             out2.println( a1[i] );

          // Close file
          out2.close();

          // Get elapsed time
          writeTimeFmt = t.elapsedTime();

          //*********************************************************
          // Read unformatted file
          //*********************************************************
          t.resetTimer();

          // Open unformatted file
          DataInputStream in1 = new DataInputStream(
                                  new BufferedInputStream(
                                     new FileInputStream(
                                        "unformat.dat")));

          // Read data
          for ( i = 0; i < a1.length; i++ )
             a2[i] = in1.readDouble();

          // Close file
          in1.close();

          // Get elapsed time
          readTimeUnf = t.elapsedTime();

          //*********************************************************
          // Read formatted file
          //*********************************************************
          t.resetTimer();

          // Open formatted file
             BufferedReader in2 =
                new BufferedReader(
                   new FileReader("format.dat"));
             StreamTokenizer st =
                new StreamTokenizer(in2);

          // Read data
          for ( i = 0; i < a1.length; i++ ) {
             st.nextToken();
             while( st.ttype != st.TT_NUMBER )
                st.nextToken();
             a3[i] = st.nval;
          }
          // Close file
          in2.close();
```

Figure 16.10.   (Continued).

```
      // Get elapsed time
      readTimeFmt = t.elapsedTime();

      //*********************************************************
      // Display results
      //*********************************************************
      System.out.println("Unformatted write time = "
                         + writeTimeUnf);
      System.out.println("Formatted write time   = "
                         + writeTimeFmt);
      System.out.println("Unformatted read time  = "
                         + readTimeUnf);
      System.out.println("Formatted read time    = "
                         + readTimeFmt);
      System.out.println("a1[19999] = " + a1[19999]);
      System.out.println("a2[19999] = " + a2[19999]);
      System.out.println("a3[19999] = " + a3[19999]);
   }
}
```

Figure 16.10.   (Continued).

When the program is executed, the results are

```
D:\book\java\chap16>java CompareFormat
Unformatted write time = 0.701
Formatted write time   = 8.983
Unformatted read time  = 0.862
Formatted read time    = 3.965
a1[19999] = 0.605629588261877
a2[19999] = 0.605629588261877
a3[19999] = 0.605629588261877
```

The formatted writes and reads took *much* longer than the unformatted ones. If we compare the sizes of the resulting files, we see that the formatted file is also much larger than the unformatted file.

```
D:\book\java\chap16>dir *.dat
 Volume in drive D is DRIVE D
 Volume Serial Number is 1091-0CC3

 Directory of D:\book\java\chap16

05/11/98  05:42p                405,426 format.dat
05/11/98  05:42p                160,000 unformat.dat
              2 File(s)         565,426 bytes
                           251,916,800 bytes free
```

Unformatted sequential-access files are both smaller and faster than formatted files, so they are the preferred way to store information when it will be read back in by a Java program. However, unformatted files cannot be examined by people, and they cannot be easily read in by programs written in other computer languages. If you need to type input that will be read by a Java program, or if you need to examine the results of a program, or if you need to exchange data with non-Java programs, then you should use formatted I/O. Otherwise you should use unformatted I/O. ∎

GOOD PROGRAMMING PRACTICE

Unformatted sequential access files are both smaller and faster than formatted files, so they are the preferred way to store information when it will be read back in by a Java program. Use unformatted files to store and exchange data, unless a human needs to examine it, or it is to be exchanged with non-Java programs.

16.6 OBJECT INPUT AND OUTPUT

As we saw in the Section 16.2, Java includes two classes `ObjectOutputStream` and `ObjectInputStream` to allow us to write and read entire objects as a unit. These classes convert the data (the instance variables) inside an object into a serial stream of bytes, which can be written to a file, a pipe, or any other Java sink. The stream of data includes the identity of each instance variable as well as its value, so that the object can be reconstructed properly when it is read back in.

Class `ObjectOutputStream` contains method `writeObject()`, which is responsible for converting the data in the object into a serial stream of bytes, and class `ObjectInputStream` contains method `readObject()`, which is responsible for converting the serial stream of bytes back into an object of the appropriate type. Note that these classes save and restore only *instance variables*, not static variables or methods. Static variables are excluded because they do not belong to any single object, and methods are excluded because they will already be compiled into the receiving program. Also, instance variables labelled `transient` (and containing scratch or temporary data) will not be converted and restored.

Only objects that implement the `java.io.Serializable` interface can be saved and restored using object streams. The definition of the `java.io.Serializable` interface is very simple, since it includes no methods or fields. It simply serves as a marker for a class that can be converted into a serial stream of bytes. This is mostly a security measure: if a class does not implement `java.io.Serializable`, then it is protected from being written out and being examined or modified.

Why would we want to read objects from and write objects to a data stream? There are two good reasons:

1. If the objects are written to a data file, they can be made *persistent* between executions of a program. Before a program shuts down, it can write out the state of all its objects. When it is restarted, the program can read the objects back in, and it can start up right where it left off the previous time.

2. If the objects are written to a pipe, then they can passed from program to program. The two programs could be running on opposite sides of the world, but if they are connected by a network, they can exchange data, including objects.

GOOD PROGRAMMING PRACTICE

Use `ObjectOutputStreams` and `ObjectInputStreams` to save objects to a file for later reuse, and to exchange objects between programs running on different computers.

16.6.1 Writing Objects to a File

The class that allows us to write objects to a sequential file in a machine-independent way is `ObjectOutputStream`. As shown in Figure 16.4, unformatted output data flows from an `ObjectOutputStream` object to the `FileOutputStream` object. The constructor of the `ObjectOutputStream` class is

```
ObjectOutputStream(OutputStream out);
```

This constructor creates an object that can write any object implementing the `Serializable` interface to the output file. This class also implements the `DataOutput` interface, so it can also write primitive data types such as `ints`, `doubles`, and so on to the output file. An `ObjectOutputStream` may be created as follows:

```
ObjectOutputStream out = new ObjectOutputStream(
                             new FileOutputStream(
                                 fileName ));
```

Once an `ObjectOutputStream` has been created, each object can be written to the file using calls to the `writeObject()` method, and primitive data types can be written to the file with calls to methods `writeInt()`, `writeDouble()`, and so on.

After the data has been written to a file, the file should be explicitly closed with a call to the `close()` method. This should be done as soon as possible in order to release the file resources for possible reuse by this program or other programs. Note that once a file is closed, any attempt to write data to will produce an `IOException`.

The most important methods in class `ObjectOutputStream` are summarized in Table 16.4. All of them are listed in the Java SDK documentation.

TABLE 16.4 Selected `ObjectOutputStream` Methods

Method	Description
`void writeObject(Object o)`	Writes an serializable object to the output stream. If the object is not serializable, the method throws a `NotSerializableException`, which is a subclass of `IOException`.
`void writeBoolean(boolean v)`	Writes a `boolean` value to the output stream.
`void writeByte(int v)`	Writes the 8 low-order bits of the argument v to the output stream.
`void writeChar(int v)`	Writes a `char` value, which is comprised of 2 bytes, to the output stream.
`void writeDouble(double v)`	Writes a `double` value, which is comprised of 8 bytes, to the output stream.
`void writeFloat(float v)`	Writes a `float` value, which is comprised of 4 bytes, to the output stream.
`void writeInt(int v)`	Writes an `int` value, which is comprised of 4 bytes, to the output stream.
`void writeLong(long v)`	Writes a `long` value, which is comprised of 8 bytes, to the output stream.
`short writeShort(short v)`	Writes a `short` value, which is comprised of 2 bytes, to the output stream.
`void writeUTF(String s)`	Writes a string coded in UTF format.

The code shown in Figure 16.11 illustrates writing objects and primitive data types to a file using an `ObjectOutputStream`. It writes an `int` value, a `String`, and a `java.util.Date` object to the file.

```
// Write objects to a file
import java.io.*;
import java.util.Date;
public class TestWriteObject {

    public static void main (String[] args) throws IOException {

        // Open file and create object output stream
        ObjectOutputStream oos = new ObjectOutputStream(
                        new FileOutputStream("object_data"));

        // Write a primitive value, a String, and a Date object
        oos.writeInt(12345);
        oos.writeObject("Today");
        oos.writeObject(new Date());

        // Close file
        oos.close();
    }
}
```

Figure 16.11. A sample program illustrating writing objects to a file.

16.6.2 Reading Objects From a File

The class that allows us to read objects from a sequential file in a machine-independent way is `ObjectInputStream`. As shown in Figure 16.3, unformatted output data flows from `FileInputStream` object to the `ObjectInputStream` object. The constructor of the `ObjectOutputStream` class is

> `ObjectInputStream(InputStream in);`

This constructor creates an object that can read object data from the input data stream and reconstruct the original object. This class also implements the `DataInput` interface, so it can also read primitive data types such as `int`s, `double`s, and so on from the input file. Note that the objects and primitive data types *must be read in in exactly the same order* in which they were written out.

An `ObjectInputStream` may be created as follows:

> `ObjectInputStream out = new ObjectInputStream(`
> `                new FileInputStream`
> `                    ( fileName ));`

Once an `ObjectInputStream` has been created, each object can be read from the file using calls to the `readObject()` method, and primitive data types can be read from the file with calls to methods `readInt()`, `readDouble()`, and so on. When no more data is available in the file, the read methods will throw an `EOFException`.

The most important methods in class `ObjectInputStream` are summarized in Table 16.5. All of them are listed in the Java SDK documentation.

The code shown in Figure 16.12 illustrates reading objects and primitive data types from a file using an `ObjectInputStream`. It reads an `int` value, a `String`, and a `java.util.Date` object from the file created by the program in the previous section. Note that method `readObject()` returns references to *objects*, which must be downcast to the proper data type before the objects are used.

TABLE 16.5 Selected `ObjectOutputStream` Methods

Method	Description
`Object readObject()`	Reads an object from the output stream. If the object is not found, this method throws a `ClassNotFoundException`.
`boolean readBoolean()`	Reads 1 input byte and returns true if that byte is nonzero, and `false` if that byte is zero.
`byte readByte()`	Reads and returns 1 byte.
`char readChar()`	Reads and returns 1 `char` value.
`double readDouble()`	Reads and returns 1 `double` value.
`float readFloat()`	Reads and returns 1 `float` value.
`int readInt()`	Reads and returns 1 `int` value.
`short readShort()`	Reads and returns 1 `short` value.
`String readUTF()`	Reads and returns a string coded in UTF format.

```java
// Read objects to a file
import java.io.*;
import java.util.Date;
public class TestReadObject {

    public static void main (String[] args)
                throws IOException, ClassNotFoundException {

        // Define variables
        Date d;            // Date reference
        int i;             // Integer
        String s;          // String reference

        // Open file and create object output stream
        ObjectInputStream ois = new ObjectInputStream(
                        new FileInputStream("object_data"));

        // Read a primitive value, a String, and a Date object
        i = ois.readInt();
        s = (String) ois.readObject();
        d = (Date) ois.readObject();

        // Display results
        System.out.println("i      = " + i);
        System.out.println("String = " + s);
        System.out.println("Date   = " + d);

        // Close file
        ois.close();
    }
}
```

Figure 16.12. A sample program illustrating reading objects from a file.

When this program is executed, the results are as shown below. Note that the program correctly recovered the objects saved to the file.

```
D:\book\java\chap16>java TestReadObject
i      = 12345
String = Today
Date   = Tue Nov 19 02:52:20 GMT 2002
```

16.7 RANDOM-ACCESS FILES

Random-access files differ from sequential-access files in that the records in a random-access file can be accessed in *any* order. Random-access files are implemented by class `RandomAccessFile`, and the `seek()` method of that class can be used to move around among the records of the file.

Interestingly, the records in a random-access file do not have to be of any specific length—we just have to be able to determine how big a record is and where it is placed in the file.

Class `RandomAccessFile` handles both input and output to random-access files. It implements the `DataInput` and `DataOutput` interfaces, so the methods in Tables 15.2 and 15.3 can be used to read or write data in these files. `RandomAccessFile` supports the additional methods shown in Table 16.6.

TABLE 16.6 Additional Methods in `RandomAccessFile`

Method	Description
void close()	Closes this random-access file.
long getFilePointer()	Returns the current offset into this file, in bytes.
long length()	Returns the length of this file, in bytes.
void seek(long pos)	Sets the file-pointer offset in bytes, measured from the beginning of this file, at which the next read or write occurs. The offset may be set beyond the end of the file. Setting the offset beyond the end of the file does not change the file length. The file length will change only by writing after the offset has been set beyond the end of the file.
void setLength(long len)	Sets a new length in bytes for the file. If len is shorter than the current file length, the file is truncated and the file pointer points to the end of the file. If len is longer than the current file length, the file is extended, but the contents of the extended part of the file are undefined.

The constructor for this class takes the forms

```
RandomAccessFile(String fileName, String mode)
RandomAccessFile(File file, String mode)
```

The first constructor is the most common form. It specifies the file to open by its file name. The second form specifies the file by an object of the `File` class. In either case, the constructor takes a `mode` string to specify whether the file is to be opened for reading only, or for reading and writing. The possible forms of this string are `'r'` and `'rw'`.

Once a file is opened, it is possible to move around freely within the file using `seek()`, and to read or write data at the specified location. However, any attempt to read data beyond the end of a file will produce an `EOFException`.

EXAMPLE 16.7

Writing and Reading Data with Unformatted Random-Access Files: Create a program that writes 10 double values in sequence to a random-access file and then directly modifies the value in record 4. Then, show that the program can read back the data either sequentially or in random order.

SOLUTION

The example program shown in Figure 16.13 illustrates the use of random file access. It opens a random-access file for reading and writing, writes 10 double values to it, and then closes the file. Then it illustrates random writing by reopening the file for reading and writing, going directly to record 4, and modifying the data in that record. (The program knows where record 4 is, because each record is 8 bytes long, and the first record starts at byte 0.) Finally, it opens the file for reading only, reads the 10 records in order, and then jumps back and rereads record 6.

```
/*
   Purpose:
     To test reading and writing to random access files.

   Record of revisions:
       Date         Programmer           Description of change
       ====         ==========           =====================
     8/20/2002    S. J. Chapman          Original code
*/
import java.io.*;
public class TestRandomAccess {

   public static void main(String[] args)
                   throws IOException {

     // Define variables
     int i;                            // Loop index
     RandomAccessFile r;               // File reference

     //********************************************************
     // Save data in a RandomAccessFile and close the file
     //********************************************************
     r = new RandomAccessFile("random.dat","rw");
     for ( i = 0; i < 10; i++ )
        r.writeDouble( i * Math.PI );
     r.close();

     //********************************************************
     // Re-open the file and change the fourth record.  Note
     // that each double is 8 bytes long.
     //********************************************************
     r = new RandomAccessFile("random.dat","rw");
     r.seek ( 3*8 );
     r.writeDouble( 1.0 );
     r.close();

     //********************************************************
```

Figure 16.13. Program to test random-access files.

```
      // Open and read data from the file in sequential order
      //****************************************************
      r = new RandomAccessFile("random.dat","r");
      System.out.println("The data in the file is:");
      for ( i = 0; i < 10; i++ )
         System.out.println(r.readDouble());

      //****************************************************
      // Recover the data from the sixth record
      //****************************************************
      r.seek( 5*8 );
      System.out.println("Record 6 = " + r.readDouble());
      r.close();
   }
}
```

Figure 16.13. (Continued).

When this program is executed, the results are

```
D:\book\java\chap16>java TestRandomAccess
The data in the file is:
0.0
3.141592653589793
6.283185307179586
1.0
12.566370614359172
15.707963267948966
18.84955592153876
21.991148575128552
25.132741228718345
28.274333882308138
Record 6 = 15.707963267948966
```

This program correctly modified the fourth record and correctly reread the sixth record, so method seek() is working correctly. ∎

16.8 GETTING INFORMATION ABOUT FILES: THE `File` CLASS

The File class can be used to recover information about files and directories. This class includes methods to get directory listings, to make directories, to create temporary files, to delete files, to determine whether a specified file exists, and to perform similar utility functions. Note that a File object can be created to represent *either a file or a directory*.

A File constructor takes one of the following forms:

```
File (String path);
File (String path, String name);
File (File dir, String name);
```

where path is the path to a particular directory (without the terminating separator), name is a file name, and dir is a file object representing a parent directory. Some of the methods in class File are listed in Table 16.7. Descriptions of all of the methods in File can be found in the Java API documentation.

TABLE 16.7   Selected Methods in File

Method	Description
boolean canRead()	Tests whether an application can read a particular file.
boolean canWrite()	Tests whether an application can write to particular file.
File createTempFile(String p)	Creates a temporary file in the system temporary directory, using string p as the base of the file name.
boolean delete()	Delete the file specified by this object.
boolean exists()	Tests whether the file specified by this object exists.
String getCanonicalPath()	Returns the path to this file object.
String getName()	Get the name of this file object.
boolean isDirectory()	Tests whether this object is a directory.
boolean isFile()	Tests whether this object is a file.
long lastModified()	Returns date of last modification.
long length()	Returns length of file in bytes.
String list()	Returns the list of files in the current directory.
boolean mkdir()	Makes the directory specified by this object.
boolean mkdirs()	Makes the directory specified by this object, including any required parent directories.
boolean renameTo(File n)	Renames the file to the name specified in n.

Figure 16.14 contains an example that uses the File class to recover a list of the files in a specific directory. Note the double backslashes used in the path name. Since a single backslash (\) is a escape character, a backslash must be represented by (\\).

```java
// Get a directory listing
import java.io.*;
public class GetDirList {

    public static void main(String[] args) {

        // Define variables
        String path = "d:\\book\\java\\chap16";
        String s[];

        // Create a new File object representing a directory
        File f = new File(path);

        // Get a directory listing
        s = f.list();

        // Tell user.
        System.out.println("Directory " + path + " contains:");

        for (int i = 0; i < s.length; i++ )
            System.out.println(s[i]);
    }
}
```

Figure 16.14.   Program to get a directory listing using a File object.

When this program is executed, the results are

```
D:\book\java\chap16>java GetDirList
Directory d:\book\java\chap16 contains:
capt16.doc
chap16.doc
CompareFormat.class
CompareFormat.java
fig16-1.drw
fig16-2.drw
fig16-3.drw
fig16-4.drw
format.dat
GetDirList.class
GetDirList.java
input.txt
output.txt
random.dat
ReadFormattedFile.class
ReadFormattedFile.java
ReadFormattedStdin.class
ReadFormattedStdin.java
test
test1
TestRandomAccess.class
TestRandomAccess.java
TestStreamTokenizer.class
TestStreamTokenizer.java
TestUnformattedIO.class
TestUnformattedIO.java
Timer.class
Timer.java
tokens.txt
unf.dat
unformat.dat
WriteFormattedFile.class
WriteFormattedFile.java
```

QUIZ 16-1

This quiz provides a quick check to see if you have understood the concepts introduced in Sections 16.1 through 16.8. If you have trouble with the quiz, reread the section, ask your instructor, or discuss the material with a fellow student. The answers are found in the back of the book.

1. What is the difference between an `OutputStream` and a `Writer`? What is the difference between an `InputStream` and a `Reader`?

2. What is the difference between sequential access and random access? How do you implement random access in Java?

3. What classes would you use to read character data from a formatted sequential file?

4. What classes would you use to read numeric data from a formatted sequential file?

5.   What classes would you use to write data to a formatted sequential file?

6.   What classes would you use to read unformatted data from a sequential file?

7.   What classes would you use to write unformatted data to a sequential file?

8.   What classes would you use to read objects from a sequential file?

9.   What classes would you use to write objects to a sequential file?

10. What types of objects may be read and written to a data stream? What types of objects may *not* be read and written to a data stream?

11. What classes would you use to read and write data to a random-access file?

SUMMARY

- The Java I/O system consists of many different classes, each performing a small part of the job. It is the programmer's responsibility to string these classes together in useful ways to solve a particular problem.

- There are actually two layers of Java I/O systems. Java version 1.0 had a byte-based I/O system, and Java version 1.1 introduced an additional character-based set of convenience classes to better handle Unicode characters.

- In general, all unformatted and direct-access I/O should be done using the original byte-based I/O system. These classes implement the `DataInput` and `DataOutput` interfaces.

- Serializable objects can be read and written to data streams using `ObjectOutputStream` and `ObjectInputStream`. If these streams wrap files, the objects will be stored on disk for later reuse.

- Formatted I/O to files should be done using the character-based `Reader` and `Writer` classes.

- Formatted input from the standard input streams should use the bridge class `InputStreamReader` to convert it into character-based data.

- The `StreamTokenizer` class may be used to break formatted input streams up into discrete tokens, and to convert numeric tokens into their corresponding `double` values.

- Class `File` can be used to perform general-purpose file manipulations such as getting directory listings, getting information about files, creating temporary files, and so forth.

SUMMARY OF GOOD PROGRAMMING PRACTICES

The following guidelines introduced in this chapter will help you to develop good programs:

1.   Use class `RandomAccessFile` to read and write data in random access files.

2.   Read unformatted data using the "`InputStream`" sources, and convert the data to a useful form using the `DataInputStream` class.

3.   Read formatted data using the "`Reader`" sources, and convert the data to a useful form using the `BufferedReader` class. If you are reading from the standard input stream, convert the data into a `Reader` using the `InputStreamReader` class before sending it to the `BufferedReader` class.

4. Always use the `BufferedInputStream` or `BufferedReader` classes to improve efficiency when reading data from a file.

5. Create unformatted output data with methods in the `DataOutputStream` class, and write it out using the "OutputStream" sinks.

6. Create formatted output data using the `print()` and `println()` methods found in the `PrintStream` and `PrintWriter` classes, and write it out using the `OutputStream` and `OutputWriter` sinks, respectively. Use the `PrintWriter` methods, except when working with the standard output or standard error devices.

7. Always use the `BufferedOutputStream` or `BufferedWrites` classes to improve efficiency when writing data to a file.

8. Always close any files you use just as soon as you are finished with them. This action releases the file resources for possible use elsewhere within the computer.

9. Use `ObjectOutputStreams` and `ObjectInputStreams` to save objects to a file for later reuse, and to exchange objects between programs running on different computers.

10. Unformatted sequential-access files are both smaller and faster than formatted files, so they are the preferred way to store information when it will be read back in by a Java program. Use unformatted files to store and exchange data, unless a human needs to examine it, or it is to be exchanged with nonJava programs.

TERMINOLOGY

`BufferedInputStream` class	`InputStreamReader` class
`BufferedReader` class	`ObjectInputStream` class
buffering class	`ObjectOutputStream` class
convenience class	random access
`DataInputStream` class	`RandomAccessFile` class
`DataOutputStream` class	`readObject()` method
deprecated	sequential access
`FileInputStream` class	serializable
`FileOutputStream` class	sink
`FileReader` class	source
`FileWriter` class	`StreamTokenizer` class
filter class	unformatted file
formatted file	`writeObject()` method

Exercises

1. Write a program to read a series of `Strings` from a formatted sequential input file, sort them into ascending order, and write them to a formatted sequential output file. You may assume that each string appears on a separate line in the input file. Pass the input and output file names to your program as command-line arguments.

2. Write a GUI program to read a series of `Strings` from a formatted sequential input file and display them in a `List`. The GUI should include a `TextField` for the input file name and a "Read File" `Button`. You may assume that each string appears on a separate line in the input file.

3.   Create a GUI-based program that (1) reads a series of Strings from a formatted sequential input file, (2) displays them in a List, (3) allows the user to modify the order of the strings, and (4) writes them to an output file. The program should include TextFields for the input and output file names, as well as "Read File" and "Write File" Buttons. The program should allow the user to modify the order of the strings by highlighting a particular item and moving it up or down in the list by clicking on "Up" or "Down" buttons. (You may assume that each string appears on a separate line in the input file.)

4.   Write a program to read a series of double values from a formatted sequential input file, sort them into ascending order, and write them to a formatted sequential output file. Pass the input and output file names to your program as command-line arguments.

5.   Modify the program in Exercise 4 to read from the standard input stream instead of an input file.

6.   We mentioned in this chapter that the StreamTokenizer class has limitations, in that it fails to properly translate numbers beginning with a "+" or numbers in exponential format. Can you suggest a way to create an input class that will properly handle all forms of numeric inputs? (*Hint:* Consider using the StringTokenizer class and the Double type wrapper class.) Write such a class and test it using the following input data (this data can be found in file input1.txt):

```
10.0  -12.1  +14.4
32.e6  -1.6e-19 +6.02e23
```

7.   **File Copy While Trimming Trailing Blanks**   Write a program that reads an input file name and an output file name from the command line and then copies the input file to the output file, trimming trailing blanks off the end of each line before writing it out. If no file names are present on the command line, the program should prompt the user for the input file name and the output file name. After the copy process is completed, the program should ask the user whether or not to delete the original file. If requested, the program should delete the input file using the delete() method in class File.

8.   Modify the program of Exercise 7 so that it checks for the existence of the specified output file, and if it already exists, prompts the user before overwriting it.

9.   Modify the program of Exercise 7 so that it supports an optional "−a" flag to cause the output data to be appended to the output file, if it already exists.

10.   Create a class Student, containing instance variables for first name, middle initial, last name, and student ID number. The first three fields are Strings and the last field is an int. The class should also contain a static variable number, which is equal to the number of student objects created. The class should include methods for getting and changing the various fields, plus one or more constructors to create new Student objects.

    Then, create a program that accepts student information for an arbitrary number of students from the user and saves the student database to a user-specified file using an ObjectOutputStream. The program should save first the number of students, using method writeInt(), and then the individual student objects, using method writeObject().

Finally, create another program to read the database back from the file, using an `ObjectInputStream`, and display it to verify that the data had been stored correctly.

11. **Word Count** Write a program that reads a formatted sequential data set from an input file specified on the command line and counts the number of words in the data set. Write the number of words to the standard output device. For these purposes, a word is defined as a set of characters separated by white space. (*Hint:* Use class `StringTokenizer`.)

12. **Histogram Program** Modify the histogram program of Example 14.2 so that the input dialog box offers the user a choice of all the files in the current directory ending with the extent ".`dat`". Use the `File` class to create this list, and use the proper form of input dialog box to display the list.

13. Write a GUI-based program that plots the equation $y(x) = ax^2 + bx + c$. The program should use class `PlotXY` for the plot, and should have GUI elements to read the values of a, b, c, and the minimum and maximum x to plot. These values should be instance variables of the class. (Use the enhanced version of class `PlotXY` if you have created it in the Chapter 12 end-of-chapter exercises.)

Design this program so that the instance variables are always saved when the program exits and are automatically restored to their previous values when the program restarts.

14. The program in Exercise 5 of Chapter 13 displays a circle in a specified color and displays information about the circle in text fields. Modify the program to preserve the information about the circle being displayed between invocations of the program. Do this by making the class serializable, writing the object to a file before exiting, and reading the object from the file when starting up again. Be sure that the program starts up properly whether or not there is a file on disk to initialize the object.

Appendix A
ASCII Character Set

The ASCII character set is a subset of the Unicode character set. It contains the first 127 characters of the Unicode character set, which are the ones most commonly used in Java programs. The full details of the Unicode character set can be found by consulting the World Wide Web site http://unicode.org.

The table shown below includes the first 127 characters, with the first two digits of the character number defined by the row, and the third digit defined by the column. Thus, the letter 'R' is on row 8 and column 2, so it is character 82 in the ASCII (and Unicode) character set.

	0	1	2	3	4	5	6	7	8	9
0	nul	soh	stx	etx	eot	enq	ack	bel	bs	ht
1	nl	vt	ff	cr	so	si	dle	dc1	dc2	dc3
2	dc4	nak	syn	etb	can	em	sub	esc	fs	gs
3	rs	us	sp	!	"	#	$	%	&	'
4	(	)	°	+	,	−	.	/	0	1
5	2	3	4	5	6	7	8	9	:	;
6	<	=	>	?	@	A	B	C	D	E
7	F	G	H	I	J	K	L	M	N	O
8	P	Q	R	S	T	U	V	W	X	Y
9	Z	[	\	]	^	_	`	a	b	c
10	d	e	f	g	h	I	j	k	l	m
11	n	o	p	q	r	s	t	u	v	w
12	x	y	z	{	|	}	~	del		

Appendix B
Operator Precedence Chart

The Java operators are shown in decreasing order of precedence from top of bottom, with the operators in each section having equal precedence.

Operator	Type	Associativity
`()`	parenthese	left to right
`[]`	array subscript	
`.`	member selection	right to left
`++`	unary preincrement	
`++`	unary postincrement	
`--`	unary predecrement	
`--`	unary postdecrement	
`+`	unary plus	
`-`	unary minus	
`!`	unary logical negation	
`~`	unary bitwise complement	
`(type)`	unary cast	
`*`	multiplication	left to right
`/`	division	
`%`	modulus	
`+`	addition	left to right
`-`	subtraction	
`<<`	bitwise left shift	left to right
`>>`	bitwise right shift with sign extension	
`>>>`	bitwise right shift with zero extension	
`<`	relational less than	left to right
`<=`	relational less than or equal to	
`>`	relational greater than	
`>`	relational greater than or equal to	
`instanceOf`	type comparison	
`==`	relational is equal to	left to right
`!=`	relational is not equal to	
`&`	bitwise AND	left to right

Operator	Type	Associativity
^	bitwise inclusive OR boolean logical inclusive OR	left to right
|	bitwise exclusive OR boolean logical exclusive OR	left to right
&&	logical AND	left to right
||	logical OR	left to right
?:	ternary conditional	right to left
= += −= *= /= %= &= ^= |=	assignment addition assignment subtraction assignment multiplication assignment division assignment modulus assignment bitwise AND assignment bitwise exclusive OR assignment bitwise inclusive OR assignment	right to left
<<= >>= >>>=	bitwise left shift assignment bitwise right shift with sign extension assignment bitwise right shift with zero extension assignment	

Appendix C

Answers to Quizzes

QUIZ 1-1

1. a. 11011_2

    b. 1011_2

    c 100011_2

    d 1111111_2

2. a 14_{10}

    b. 14_{10}

    c. 85_{10}

3. a. $E5AD_{16}$ or 162655_8

    b. $3BD_{16}$ or 1675_8

    c. $973F_{16}$ or 113477_8

4. $131_{10} = 10000011_2$, so the fourth bit is zero

5. smallest integer value $= -2^{15} = -32,768$; largest integer value $= 2^{15} - 1 = 32,767$

6. A four-byte `float` variable can store larger numbers than a four byte integer, but only by giving up significant digits of precision. Since 8 bits are devoted to the exponent of the number, the remaining 16 bits can represent only 6-7 significant digits of precision.

QUIZ 2-1

1. Valid `double` constant
2. Invalid—commas not allowed
3. Valid `double` constant
4. Valid `char` constant
5. Invalid—to create a `char` constant containing a single quote, use the backslash escape character: ' \ "
6. Valid `double` constant

7. Valid `String` constant
8. Valid `boolean` constant
9. Same value
10. Same value
11. Different value
12. Valid name—would be a variable or a method name
13. Valid name—would be a class name
14. Invalid—name may not begin with a number
15. Invalid—true is a reserved keyword
16. Valid name—would be a constant (or final variable)
17. Valid
18. Invalid—`MAX_COUNT` is a `short`, and 100000 is an `int`. An explicit cast is required to convert `int` to `short`. In addition, 100000 is too large a number to be represented in a `short`.
19. Invalid—can't assign a `String` to a `char`.
20. These statements are illegal. They try to assign a new value to the constant (final variable) k.

QUIZ 2-2

1. The order of evaluation is:
   1. Expressions in parentheses, working from the innermost parentheses out
   2. Multiplications, divisions, and mod, working from left to right
   3. Additions and subtractions, working from left to right

2. a. Legal—result is 12
   b. Legal—result is 42
   c. Legal—result is 2
   d. Legal—result is 2.25
   e. Legal—result is 2.3333333
   f. Legal—result is 1

3. a. Legal—result is 7
   b. Legal—result is −21
   c. Legal—result is 7
   d. Legal—result is 9

4. These statements are legal: `x = 16; y = 3; result = 17.5`.
5. These statements are illegal. The expression evaluates to a `double` 17.5, but the variable result is an `int`. This assignment is a narrowing conversion, which is illegal unless an explicit cast is used.

QUIZ 2-3

1. `rEq = r1 + r2 + r3 + r4;`
2. `rEq = 1 / (1/r1 + 1/r2 + 1/r3 + 1/r4);`
3. `t = 2 * Math.PI * Math.sqrt( l / g );`
4. `v = vm * Math.exp( -alpha*t ) * Math.cos( omega*t );`

5. $d = \dfrac{1}{2}at^2 + v_0t + d_0$

6. $f = \dfrac{1}{2\pi\sqrt{LC}}$

7. $E = \dfrac{1}{2}Li^2$

8. a. Illegal—mismatched parentheses.

   b. Illegal—explicit cast needed to convert `double` to `int`.

   c. Illegal—explicit cast needed to convert `double` to `int`. [*Note:* This one is tricky. Because the cast operator `(int)` is evaluated before division, `a` is converted to an `int`. Since `a / b` is a `double` divided by an `int`, the result is a `double`, and it illegal to assign the `double` value to `k`.]

   d. Legal—`b = 3.666667`

   e. This is legal, but the calculation includes a floating-point division by zero; the result is `infinite`.

9. The results are: `a = 2.0, b = 3.0, c = 4.666666666666667, i = 5, j = 0, k = 2`.

10.
```
import java.io.*;
public class CalcHypotenuse {

    // Define the main method
    public static void main(String[] args) throws IOException {

        double a, b, c;
        String str;

        // Create a buffered reader
        BufferedReader in1 = new BufferedReader(
                        new InputStreamReader(System.in));

        // Prompt for the hypotenuse
        System.out.print("Enter the length of side 1: ");
        str = in1.readLine();
        a = Double.parseDouble(str);

        // Prompt for the angle
        System.out.print("Enter the length of side 2: ");
        str = in1.readLine();
        b = Double.parseDouble(str);

        // Calculate hypotenuse
        c = Math.sqrt( a*a + b*b );

        // Write results
        System.out.println("Hypotenuse = " + c);
    }
}
```

QUIZ 3-1

1. a. false

   b. Illegal—can't use the not (`!`) operator with a `double` value

   c. true

     d. true

     e. true

     f. false

2.
```
if ( x >= 0 ) {
    sqrtX = Math.sqrt(x);
}
else {
    System.out.println("Error: x < 0");
    sqrtX = 0;
}
```

3.
```
if ( Math.abs(denominator) < 1.0E-30 )
    System.out.println("Divide by 0 error.");
else {
    fun = numerator / denominator;
    System.out.println("fun = " +fun)
}
```

4.
```
if ( distance <= 100. )
    cost = 0.50 * distance;
else if ( distance <= 300. )
    cost = 50. + 0.30 * (distance - 100);
else
    cost - 110. + 0.20 * (distance - 300);
```

5. These statement will compile correctly, but they will not do what the programmer intended. Since there is no "`else`" in front of the second `if` statement, the second `if` statement will be executed regardless of the result of the first `if` statement. Thus if `volts = 130`, both `"WARNING: High voltage on line."` and `"Line voltage is within tolerances."` will be printed out.

6. Since `i < j`, the expression `j / i` will be executed, and the result will be `k = 1.6666666666666667`.

7. These statements are incorrect—a colon is required after the keyword `default`.

8. These statement will compile correctly, but they will not do what the programmer intended. If the `temperature` is 150, these statements will print out `"Human body temperature exceeded."` instead of `"Boiling point of water exceeded."`, because the `if` structure executes the first `true` condition and skips the rest. To get proper behavior, the order of these tests should be reversed.

QUIZ 4-1

1. 4 times

2. This is an infinite loop. The values of `j` are 7, 6, 5, 4, 3, 2, 1, 0, −1, ... Since the loop terminates when `j > 10`, the loop will never terminate. (*Advanced comment*: Actually, since integer arithmetic wraps around, the most negative possible integer minus one is equal to the most positive possible integer. After `j` decrements to the number −2,147,483,648, the next number will be a positive 2,147,483,647. This number is greater than 10, so the loop will terminate. However, it will have executed, 2,147,483,655 times before then!)

3. 1 time

4. 9 times

5. 7 times

6. 9 times

7. infinite loop (but see note on 2 above)

8. `ires` = 10, and the loop executes 10 times
9. `ires` = 55, and the loop executes 10 times
10. `ires` = 15, and the loop executes 5 times
11. `ires` = 15, and the loop executes 5 times
12. `ires` = 15, and the loop executes 5 times
13. `ires` = 18, and the loop executes 6 times
14. `ires` = 3, and the loop executes 3 times
15. `ires` = 25; the outer loop executes 5 times and the inner loop executes 25 times
16. `ires` = 15; the outer loop executes 5 times and the inner loop executes 15 times
17. `ires` = 2; the outer loop executes 1 time and the inner loop executes 3 times
18. `ires` = 10; the outer loop executes 5 times and the inner loop executes 15 times
19. Invalid. Variable `i` is used to control both loops.
20. Invalid. These statements will compile and execute, but they will produce an infinite loop. The semicolon after the `while` statement terminates the while loop without changing the value of x, so x will never be less than or equal to 0.
21. Invalid. The `i--` modifies the value of the loop variable, producing an infinite loop. This loop will not compile.

QUIZ 5-1

1. An array is a special object containing (1) a group of contiguous memory locations that all have the same name and same type, and (2) a separate instance variable containing an integer constant equal to the number of elements in the array. An element of an array is addressed by the arra name followed by an integer subscript in square brackets (`[ ]`). The components of the array are the elements of the array plus the constant containing the length of the array.

2. A reference is a "handle" or "pointer" to an object that permits Java to locate the object in memory when it is needed.

3. An array object is created with the `new` operator. For example:

```
double[] x = new double[5];
```

creates a new five-element `double` array.

4. An array can be initialized by assignment statements, or by the use of an initializer when the array is created. For example,

```
int a[] = {1, 2, 3, 4, 5};
```

creates a new five-element `int` array, and initializes the values of the array elements to 1, 2, 3, 4, and 5.

5. A 100-element array would be addressed with the subscripts 0 to 99. Any other subscripts would produce an `ArrayIndexOutOfBoundsException`.

6. If only one array reference points to an array, and that reference is re-assigned to point to a different array, then the original array can never be accessed again by the program. It is "lost".

7. Valid. These statements create a new 10-element `double` array.

8. Invalid. A `double` reference cannot refer to an `int` array.

9. Invalid. An initializer can only be used in an array declaration, not in an assignment statement.

10. Invalid. Can't use `[]` when assigning array references.

11. Valid. These statements assign reference `aaa` to point to the same array as reference `bbb`.

12. Valid. These statements will print out the second through fifth elements in the array. They will *not* print the first element, since the subscript for the first element is 0, and the loop begins at 1.
13. Valid. These statements will print out the first through fifth elements in the array *in reverse order*.

QUIZ 6-1

1. Incorrect. The `int` array is the first parameter in `method1`, but the second parameter in the call to `method1`.
2. Incorrect—`method2` is declared void but returns a value.
3. Correct. The `main` method calls `method3` with array `x`, and `method3` sums the values in the elements of array `x`, and divides that result by the number of elements in the array. The `main` method the prints out this result, which will be −0.5.

QUIZ 6-2

1. The duration of a variable is the time during which it exists. The types of duration in Java are automatic duration and static duration.
2. The duration of a local variable within a Java method is the time during which the method is being executed. When the method execution ends, the variable is destroyed.
3. A recursive method is a method that either directly or indirectly calls itself.
4. When a method containing `double` parameters is called with `int` arguments, the int aruguments are automatically coerced into `double` values and passed to the method. When a method containing `int` parameters is called with `double` arguments, this is a compile-time error, since narrowing conversions are illegal unless the user explicitly performs a cast.
5. Method overloading is the process of defining several methods with the same name but different sets of parameters (based on the number, types, and order of the parameters). When an overloaded method is called, the Java compiler selects the proper method by examining the number, type, and order of the calling arguments.
6. This program is incorrect. Variable `i` is redefined within the `while` loop, which is illegal.
7. This program is incorrect. The two overloaded methods `m1` have the same signature, and so cannot be distinguished from each other.

QUIZ 7-1

1. The major components of a class are fields, constructors, methods, and finalizers. Fields define the instance variables that will be created when an object is instantiated from a class. Constructors are special methods that specify how to initialize the instance variables in an object when it is created. Methods implement the behaviors of a class. A finalizer is a special method that is called just before an object is destroyed to release any resources allocated to the object.
2. The types of member access modifiers are `public`, `private`, `protected`, and package. Private access is normally used for instance variables, and public access is normally used for methods.
3. A variable with class scope is visible anywhere within the class in which it is defined, while a variable with block scope is only visible within the block in which it is defined.

4. If a method contains a local variable with the same name as an instance variable in the method's class, the instance variable will be "hidden", and so will not be directly accessible from the method. However, the method can still access the instance variable using the `this` reference.

5. To use classes in packages other than `java.lang`, you must include an `import` statement for each package at the beginning of the source file. Note that the `import` statements must appear *before* the class definition.

6. A variable or method declared with `PUBLIC` access may be accessed from any class anywhere within a program. A variable or method declared with `PRIVATE` access may only be accessed from within the class in which it is defined. A variable or method declared with package access may be accessed from within the class in which it is defined, or from any class within the same package. A variable or method declared with `PROTECTED` access may be accessed from within the class in which it is defined, from any class within the same package, or from any subclass of the class in which it is defined.

7. To create a user-defined package, include a `package` statement in the source file of each class to go into the package, and compile each class with the "`-d`" option to specify the location of the package directory structure. Include an `import` statement in each class using the package, and be sure to set the `CLASSPATH` environment variable so that the package can be found by the Java compiler.

8. The `CLASSPATH` environment variable tells the Java compiler and the Java runtime system where to look for packages being imported.

QUIZ 7-2

1. The garbage collector is a low-priority thread that searches for and destroys objects that are no longer needed. It runs automatically in the background while a Java program is executing. A Java object is eligible for garbage collection when no reference to the object exists, because the object can no longer be used once there are no longer any references to it.

2. Static variables are variables that are *shared* by all objects created from the class in which the variables are defined. These variables are automatically created as soon as a class is loaded into memory, and they remain in existence until the program stops executing. Static variables are useful for keeping track of global information such as the number of objects instantiated from a class, or the number of those objects still surviving at any given time. They are also useful for defining single copies of final variables that will be shared among all objects of the class.

3. The variable can be accessed using the name of the class followed by a dot, and followed by the variable name: `MyClass.count`.

4. Static methods are commonly used to perform calculations that are independent of any instance data that might be defined in a class. The methods in class `java.lang.Math` (sin, cos, sqrt, etc.) are good examples of static methods.

QUIZ 8-1

1. The fundamental difference between `Strings` and `StringBuffers` is that the `String` class consists of strings that *never change* once they are created, while the `StringBuffer` class consists of modifiable strings. The `StringBuffers` should be used whenever you are working with strings that must be modified (for example, where you wish to insert or delete characters).

2. Invalid. These statements will compile successfully, but the will produce an `StringIndexOutOfBoundsException` at runtime, since s1 is not eight characters long.

3. Valid. The statement "`s3 = s1.substring(1,3);`" selects the characters at indices 1 and 2 of s1, which is the string `"bc"`. The following statement concatenates the characters `"123"` to it, so the final result is `"bc123"`.

4.   Invalid. You can't use the substring and concat methods with object of class StringBuffer, only with objects of class String.

5.   Valid. The equals test will be false, because the two Strings are not identical. However, the equals-IgnoreCase test will be true.

6.   Valid. The result is false, since the two references point to physically different objects, even though the contents of the objects are identical.

7.   There are many ways to do this. One possible class is shown below, but it is *not* the only correct answer.

```
 1 public class Finds {
 2
 3     public static void main(String[] args) {
 4
 5         String s1 = new String("Sassafras");
 6         System.out.println("Locations of 's':");
 7
 8         int loc = 0;
 9         while ( true ) {
10             loc = s1.indexOf("s",loc);
11             if ( loc >= 0 )
12                 System.out.println("s at position " + loc++);
13             if ( loc >= s1.length() )
14                 break;
15         }
16     }
17 }
```

When this program is executed, the results are:

```
C:\book\java\app_c>java Finds
Locations of 's':
s at position 2
s at position 3
s at position 8
```

To convert this program to find both uppercase and lowercase letters, add the line "s1 = s1.toLower-Case()" after line 5 above.

8.   The length of a StringBuffer is the number of characters *actually stored* in the StringBuffer, while the capacity is the number of characters that *can be* stored without allocating additional memory.

9.   Command line arguments are the arguments typed on the command line after the name of a Java program. The are passed to the main method in String array args.

QUIZ 9-1

1.   Inheritance is the process by which the non-private instance variables and methods of a class are automatically defined in all subclasses of that class unless they are explicitly overridden in the subclass. Once a behavior (method) is defined in a superclass, that behavior is automatically inherited by all subclasses unless it is explicitly overridden with a modified method. Thus behaviors only need to be coded *once*, and they can be used by all subclasses. A subclass need only provide methods to implement the *differences* between itself and its parent.

2.   Polymorphism is the ability to automatically select the proper version of a method to apply to objects of different subclasses when the objects are addressed using superclass references. In order for polymorphism to

work, the method must be defined in the superclass, and that definition must be overridden with the appropriate methods in each subclass.

3. Abstract methods are method declarations that do not have code bodies attached to them. Abstract methods may be used in a parent class to declare a method that will be overridden in all of the subclasses of the class. If the method is going to be overridden in all subclasses, why bother to write code for it at all? Abstract classes are classes containing one or more abstract methods.

4. The principal advantage of declaring a class to be `final` is that the Java compiler can optimize the class for faster execution. Also, since the class cannot be overridden, its behavior will be the same on every Java virtual machine executing the class. The principal disadvantage of a final class is that it cannot serve as a superclass for further subclasses.

5. An interface is a special kind of block containing method signatures (and possibly constants) only. Interfaces define the signatures of a set of methods, without the method bodies that would implement their functionality. Interfaces have no direct inherited relationship with any particular class—they are defined independently. Therefore, methods that are designed to work with a particular interface can be re-used with any class that implements that interface. For example, a `sort` method that works with the `Comparable` interface can sort objects of any class implementing the interface—only one `sort` method is required to sort many different types of objects.

QUIZ 10-1

1. An exception is an event that interrupts the normal processing flow of a program. This event is usually an error of some sort.

2. Runtime exceptions are those exceptions that occur within the Java runtime system, including arithmetic exceptions, pointer exceptions, and indexing exceptions. These sorts of exceptions can occur *anywhere* in a program, so Java does not force a programmer to list every possible runtime exception that can occur in every method. All other exceptions in a Java program are known as checked exceptions, because the compiler checks that these exceptions are either caught or explicitly ignored by any method in which the exception could possibly occur.

3. The Java compiler explicitly checks to see that all checked exceptions are either caught or explicitly ignored by any method in which the exception could possibly occur. If an exception is to be ignored by a method, the method must explicitly "throw" the exception in it's method declaration, so that a method higher up the calling tree can have a chance to "catch" it. This is known as the "catch or specify" requirement.

4. A programmer can design a program to recover from an exception instead of crashing by including the line that could cause the exception within a `try` / `catch` structure, and including the exception to be caught in one of the `catch` clauses. If the exception occurs, control will transfer to the `catch` clause, where the program can place code to recover from the exception.

5. An exception object has two important methods: `getMessage()` and `printStackTrace()`. The first method returns the message embedded in the exception as a string, and the second method prints out the stack trace to the line which caused the exception to occur.

QUIZ 11-1

1. This array contains 35 elements, addressed by the subscripts `[0][0]` to `[4][6]`.

2. This array contains 9 elements, addressed by the subscripts `[0][0]`, `[0][1]`, `[1][0]`, `[1][1]`, `[1][2]`, `[1][3]`, `[2][0]`, `[2][1]`, and `[3][2]`.

3. This array contains 32 elements, addressed by the subscripts `[0][0][0]` to `[3][3][1]`.

4. Valid.

5. Invalid—an `int` array reference cannot refer to a `double` array.

6. Invalid—a one-dimensional reference cannot refer to a two-dimensional array.

7. Invalid, since the first subscript of `a[2][1][0]` can only take on the values 0 or 1.

8. Valid. `a[0][1][2]` = 6.

9. Valid. `a[1][1][1]` = 11.

QUIZ 12-1

1. A `Container` is a graphical object that can hold `Components` or other `Containers`. The type of container used in this chapter is a `JFrame`.

2. A `Component` is a visual object containing text or graphics, which can respond to keyboard or mouse inputs. The type of component used in this chapter is a `JCanvas`.

3. The basic steps required to display graphics in Java are:
   1. Create the component or components to display.
   2. Create a frame to hold the component(s), and place the component(s) into the frame(s).
   3. Create a "listener" object to detect and respond to mouse clicks, and assign the listener to the frame.

4. Java employs a coordinate system whose origin (0,0) is in the upper left hand corner of the screen, with positive *x* values to the right and positive *y* values down. The units of the coordinate system are pixels, with 72 pixels to an inch.

5. Method `getSize()` belongs to class `java.awt.Component`. Since this class is a superclass of any component or container, all components and containers include this method. The method is used to return the width and height of a particular component or container in pixels. This information can be used by the component to re-scale itself whenever the size of the window in which it is drawn changes.

6. The style of lines and borders is controlled by class `BasicStroke`.

7. Text is displayed on a graphics device using the `Graphics2D` method `drawstring`. The font in which the text is displayed is specified by creating a new `Font` object, and using the `Graphics2D` method `setFont` to specify the use of that font. Information about a font can be recovered with the `FontMetrics` class.

8. An affine transform is a user-specified combination of translations, scalings, rotations, and shears that is automatically applied to any `Graphics2D` object whenever it is rendered on a graphics device. The term *affine transform* refers to a transformation that converts an input shape into an output shape while preserving parallel lines. It is used by creating a new `AffineTransform`, specifying the desired translations, rotations, etc., and using the `Graphics2D` method `setAffineTransform` to specify the use of that transform.

QUIZ 13-1

1. A `Container` is a graphical object that can hold `Components` or other `Containers`. We are using `JPanels` and `JFrames` in this chapter.

2. A `Component` is a visual object containing text or graphics, which can respond to keyboard or mouse inputs. The types of components used in this chapter are: `JButton`, `JCheckbox`, `JComboBox`, `JComponent`, `JLabel`, `JPasswordField`, `JRadioButton`, and `JTextField`.

3. A layout manager controls the location at which components will be placed within a container.

4. Cascaded layout managers permit a program to construct layouts that are more complex than can be accomplished with a single layout manager.

5.   An event handler is a special method within a listener class that is called whenever a specific type of event occurs in a GUI component. The listener must first be registered with the GUI component.

6.   The listener interface introduced in this chapter is the `ActionListener` interface. The `ActionListener` interface handles action events, which can be produced by all the components that we studied in this chapter, except for `JLabels`.

QUIZ 14-1

1.   A `JList` is a list of objects. Depending on the options selected, a user may select one item, one continuous interval of items, or many continuous intervals of items. A list can be made scrollable by placing it inside a `JScrollPane`. Lists generate `ListSelectionEvents` when an item is selected or de-selected.

2.   A `JList` should be placed inside a `JScrollPane` to allow the list to scroll so that all parts of the list will be visible. Even small lists should be placed in scroll panes, because the number of items in the list might grow.

3.   Menus may be added to an application or an applet by creating a `JMenuBar` and adding it to the top-level container of the application or applet. `JMenus` can then be added to the `JMenuBar`, and `JMenuItems` can be added to the `JMenus`. Menus can be added to `JFrame`, `JApplet`, `JDialog`, `JRootPane`, or `JInternalFrame`.

4.   Dialog boxes are special windows that pop up with a warning or a question. They are modal, meaning that no other part of the application can be accessed until the dialog box is dismissed. A dialog asking a user whether or not to replace an existing file can be created by the statement:

```
res = JOptionPane.showConfirmDialog(null,
        "Replace the existing file?",
        "Warning",
        JOptionPane.YES_NO_OPTION,
        JOptionPane.WARNING_MESSAGE);
```

5.   The listener interface introduced in Chapter 13 is the `ActionListener` interface. The `ActionListener` interface handles action events, which can be produced by classes `JButton`, `JCheckbox`, `JComboBox`, `JComponent`, `JPasswordField`, `JRadioButton`, and `JTextField`. The listener interfaces introduced in this chapter are the `ListSelectionListener`, `MouseListener`, `MouseMotionListener`, and `WindowListener` interfaces. The `ListSelectionListener` interface is produced by class `JList`. The `WindowListener` interface handles window events, such as opening, closing, iconifying, etc., which can be produced by class `JFrame`. The mouse interfaces are low-level interfaces whose events are normally converted into higher-level events before we use them. However, the `MouseListner` is used directly to detect popup events.

6.   An adapter class is a class that implements all of the methods in an interface, *with each method doing nothing*. A programmer can write a new class that extends an adapter class, overriding only the methods that he or she wishes to implement, and the adapter class will take care of all the "useless" interface method declarations.

7.   Popup menus differ from ordinary menus in that they can be attached to any type of component, while ordinary menus can only be attached to `JFrame`, `JApplet`, `JDialog`, `JRootPane`, or `JInternalFrame`. Also, popup menus are triggered by a right-click on the mouse, while ordinary menus are triggered by a regular mouse on the menu bar.

8.   You can make an application appear the same across all type of computers by specifying that the application use the Java Look and Feel, which is guaranteed to be present in all implementations of Java. You can make a program look like a native application on each type of computer by detecting the standard look and feel for a particular computer and setting the application to use that. The code to do this automatic detection is

```
try {
    UIManager.setLookAndFeel(
        UIManager.getSystemLookAndFeelClassName());
}
catch (Exception e) {
    System.err.println("Couldn't use the "
                        + "look and feel: " + e);
}
```

QUIZ 15-1

1. An applet is a special type of Java program that is designed to work within a World Wide Web browser. Applets are usually quite small, and are designed to be downloaded, executed, and discarded whenever the browser points to a site containing the Java applet. They are restricted compared to applications, since they are usually not allowed access to the computer's resources (files, etc.) for security reasons.

2. Every applet has five key methods: `init`, `start`, `stop`, `destroy`, and `paintComponent`. Method `init()` is called by the browser when the applet is first loaded in memory. This method should allocate resources and create the GUI required for the applet. Method `start()` is called when the applet should start running. This call can be used to start animations, etc. when the applet becomes visible. Method `stop()` is called when the applet should stop running, for example when its window is covered or when it is iconized. This call is also make just before an applet is destroyed. Method `destroy()` is the final call to the applet before it is destroyed. The applet should release all resources at the time of this call. Finally, method `paintComponent` is called whenever the applet must be drawn or re-drawn.

3. A user can pass parameters to an applet when it is started by embedding them in the HTML file that starts the applet. The parameters should be in the form of "keyword, value" pairs placed inside a `PARAM` tag. The form of a keyword, value pair is:

    ```
    <PARAM NAME="xxx" VALUE="yyy">
    ```

4. This can be done by making the base class of the Java program extend `JApplet`, and then calling `init()` and `start()` in the program's `main` method. Methods `stop()` and `destroy()` should be called when the program is shutting down, for example when a window close event is detected.

5. A Java Archive (JAR) file is a collection of Java classes and resources stored in a single file in a compressed format. The file uses standard Windows Zip compression algorithms. A JAR file can simplify the distribution of Java applets, because all of the classes and data necessary to run the applet can be placed in the single file, which can be transmitted across the network with one request.

6. Saving a complete applet and its resources in a JAR file greatly speeds up starting the applet, because only one request is required to fetch it from a remote computer, and also because the compressed file is smaller. A Java application or applet can be executed directly in the JAR file, without first decompressing and extracting it.

QUIZ 16-1

1. `OutputStreams` output data a byte at a time, while `Writers` output data a character at a time. Similarly, `InputStreams` read data a byte at a time, while `Readers` read data a character at a time.

2. Sequential access involves reading the data in a file in order from the beginning of the file to the end of the file. Random access allows any part of the data in a file to be read in any order. Random access is implemented with class `RandomAccessFile`.

3. To read character data from a formatted sequential file, use a `FileReader` wrapped by a `Buffered-Reader`. The `readLine()` method of the `BufferedReader` reads the data a line at a time.

4. To read numeric data from a formatted sequential file, use a `FileReader` wrapped by a `Buffered-Reader` wrapped by a `StreamTokenizer`. The character strings produced by the `BufferedReader` are converted into tokens by the `StreamTokenizer`, and then translated into numeric values. Alternatively, you can substitute a `StringTokenizer` for the `StreamTokenizer`, and send the tokens to methods `Double.parseDouble()` and `Integer.parseInt()` to translate the tokens into numeric values.

5. To write data to a formatted sequential file, use a `FileWriter` wrapped by a `BufferedWriter`, wrapped by a `PrintWriter`. The `print()` and `println()` methods of the `PrintWriter` format the data into character strings for writing to the file.

6. To read numeric data from an unformatted sequential file, use a `FileInputStream` wrapped by a `BufferedInputStream` wrapped by a `DataInputStream`. The `DataInputStream` contains methods to read the unformatted data.

7. To write numeric data to an unformatted sequential file, use a `FileOutputStream` wrapped by a `BufferedOutputStream` wrapped by a `DataOutputStream`. The `DataOutputStream` contains methods to write the unformatted data.

8. To read objects from an unformatted sequential file, use a `FileInputStream` wrapped by an `Object-InputStream`. The `ObjectInputStream` contains method `readObject()` to read the objects from the file.

9. To write objects to an unformatted sequential file, use a `FileOutputStream` wrapped by a `Object-OutputStream`. The `ObjectOutputStream` contains method `writeObject()` to write the object to the file.

10. Objects must have been declared to be `Serializable` can be written to and read from data streams. If the object is not `Serializable`, then it cannot be saved in this fashion.

11. All random access I/O is performed with class `RandomAccessFile`.

Index